Vani

English-English Dictionary

Vani

English-English Dictionary

Editor

Dr. Brajmohan
Dr. Shivnarayan Chaturvedi

VANI PRAKASHAN

VANI PRAKASHAN

4695, 21-A, Daryaganj, New Delhi 110 002, India

Phone : +91 11 23273167 **Fax :** +91 11 23275710

Branch

Ashok Rajpath, Patna 800 004, Bihar

Coffee House Campus, Mahatma Gandhi Marg, Allahabad 211 001, Uttar Pradesh

Mahatma Gandhi International Hindi University, Wardha 442 001, Maharashtra

Sultania Road, Motiya Park, Bhopal 462 001, Madhya Pradesh

www.vaniprakashan.in
marketing@vaniprakashan.in
sales@vaniprakashan.in

VANI ENGLISH-ENGLISH DICTIONARY
Edited by Dr. Brajmohan & Dr. Shivnarayan Chaturvedi

ISBN : 978-93-88434-97-3
Dictionary

First Edition 2019

Price : ₹ 995

Printed at M.S. Printers, Delhi-110 093 (India)

Vani Prakashan's signature motif is created by Artist Maqbool Fida Husain

A the first letter of the English alphabet.

Aardvark *n.* South-African quadruped.

Aardwolf *n.* the earth-wolf of South Africa.

Aaronic (-al) *adjs.* pertaining to the Jewish high priest.

Aaron's beard *n.* a species of plants grown in hanging pots.

Ab *n.* the fifth month of the Jewish civil year, a Latin prefix which signifies 'from'.

Abaca *n.* plantain, Manilla hemp.

Aback *adv.* towards the back; backwards; behind.

Abaction *n.* the stealing of a number of cattle at once.

Abactor *n.* cattle-thief.

Abacus *n.* a calculating frame with balls of different colours.

Abandon *n.* hell, bottomless pit or its angel.

Abaft *adv.* & *prep.* on the hinder part of a ship, behind.

Abalienate *v.t.* to transfer the title of a property to someone.

Abalone *n.* a shell known as sea-car from which mother of pearl is obtained.

Abandon *v.t.* full surrender of a thing or place, to give up entirely.

Abandonee *n.* an under-writer to whom salvage of wreck is abandoned.

Abase *v.t.* to lower, to humiliate, to degrade.

Abash *v.t.* to put to shame, to put to confusion, to make ashamed.

Abate *v.t.* & *i.* to make or grow less; to deduct; to become less intense.

Abatis, Abattis *ns.* defence made of felled trees.

Abattoir *n.* a place where animals used for food are slaughtered.

Abb *n.* woof or weft of yarn.

Abbacy *n.* office of an abbot.

Abbatial *adj.* pertaining to an abbot or an abbey.

Abbe *n.* French clergy.

Abbess *n.* female head of nunnery; a woman who is the head of a convent.

Abbey *n.* body of monks or nuns; a monastery; a place of worship.

Abbot *n.* head of an abbey.

Abbreviation *n.* shortening.

Abdicant *adj.* renouncer.

Abdicate *v.t.* & *i.* to give up voluntarily; renounce a throne.

Abdicant *adj.* renouncer.

Abdicator *n.* renouncer; one who renounces formally.

Abdomen *n.* the belly; hinder part of the human body.

Abdominous *adj.* pot-bellied; corpulent.

Abduct *v.t.* carry away wrongfully; to kidnap.

Abductor *n.* one guilty of abduction.

Abeam *adv.* at right angles to the line of a vessel's keel.

Abecedarian *adj.* & *n.* one who is learning the alphabet, a novice.

Abed *adv.* in bed; on a bed; to bed.

Aberrant *adj.* straying from moral standard; not normal or acceptable.

Abet *v.t.* to instigate; to assist (an offence).

Abettor *n.* one who abets or incites.

Abeyance *n.* state of temporary suspension (*prep.* '*in*' is used before this word.)

Abhor *v.t.* to regard with repugnance; to detest; to dislike; to hate; to scorn.

Abide *v.t.* & *i.* to remain, to continue; to dwell or stay (used with '*by*'), to remain faithful to.

Abiding *adj.* permanent; continuing.

Ability *n.* the state of being able, legally or financially.

Abiogenesis *n.* spontaneous generation.

Abject *adj.* sunk to a low condition; mean; despicable; base; de-grade.

Abjuration *n.* renunciation on oath.

Abjure *v.t.* to renounce under an oath; to recant; to repudiate.

Ablative *adj.* & *n.* of fifth case ending (in Sanskrit).

Ablaze *adv.* on fire, glittering, excited.

Able *adj.* talented; skilful; having adequate power; competent.

Abloom *adv.* & *adj.* blooming; in blossom.

Ablution *n.* ceremonial or ordinary personal washing.

Ably *adv.* with ability; capably.

Abnegate *v.t.* to deny.

Abnodate *v.t.* to cut off the knots (as of trees & etc.).

Abnormal *adj.* unusual; irregular; not according to rule.

Aboard *adv.* & *prep.* on board; on or into a ship, train, aeroplane, bus etc.

Abode *n.* place of residence; dwelling place.

Aboil *adv.* & *adj.* boiling.

Abolish *v.t.* to do away with; put an end to; to annul.

Abolition *adj.* the act of abolishing, repeal.

Abominable *adj.* hateful; revolting.

Aboriginal *n.* earliest inhabitant; primitive native.

Aborigines *n. pl.* primitive inhabitants.

Abort *v.i.* to miscarry in giving birth.

Abortive *adj.* born before time or prematurely; fruitless.

Abound *v.i.* to be abundance; be plentiful; be infested with.

About *adv.* around from outside or centre; on every side; not far away.

Above *adv.* higher up; overhead; in heaven.

Abrade *v.t.* to scrape off; to injure by rubbing.

Abrasion *n.* act of rubbing off; a scratch produced by rubbing.

Abreast *adv.* side by side and equally advanced; not behind.

Abridge *v.t.* to shorten; to curtail; to epitomize; to condense.

Abroad *adv.* widely, in different directions, out of doors, in another country.

Abrogate *v.t.* to repeal; to cancel by authority; to abolish.

Abrupt *adj.* beginning; ending suddenly; unexpected; steep.

Abscess *n.* collection of puss in cavity of the body.

Abscind *v.t.* to cut off; to separate.

Abscond *v.t.* go away secretly; fly from the law.

Absconder *n.* one who disappears from public view.

Abseil *v.i.* to descend a steep slope or rock face attached to a double rope that is fixed at a higher point.

Absence *n.* not being present; lack; want; being away from.

Absent *adj.* not present; missing; inattentive, keep onself away.

Absinth(e) *n.* worm-wood.

Absolute *adj.* free from relation of restriction; unlimited; independent.

Absolutism *n.* the principles of absolute government.

Absolve *v.t.* to set free, as from obligation; to acquit; to pardon.

Absonant *adj.* absurd; unreasonable.

Absorb *v.t.* to drink in; suck up; to swallow up; to engage wholly.

Absorbent *adj.* tending to suck in.

Absorption *n.* act of absorbing, entire occupation of mind.

Abstain *v.t.* to keep oneself back; to refrain from.

Abstemious *adj.* moderate in food and drink.

Abstention *n.* refraining; holding back or away; abstinance.

Abstergent *adj.* serving to cleanse.

Abstersive *adj.* able to cleanse.

Abstinence *n.* keep away or refraining from some indulgence.

Abstract *adj.* not practical; not concrete; general; theoretical; ideal.

Abstracted *adj.* essenced; withdrawn in thought; absent-minded.

Abstraction *n.* the act of taking away, absence of mind.

Abstruse *adj.* difficult to understand; obscures; mystical; profound.

Absurd *adj.* opposed to reason; unreasonable; silly.

Abundance *n.* plenty; profusion; affluence.

Abuse *v.t.* to make bad use of; to rebuke; to revile.

Abusive *adj.* full of abuse; insulting; vituperative.

Abut *v.t.* & *i.* to join at a boundary, to meet.

Abuzz *adv*. full of buzzing sound.

Abysmal *adj*. extreme; profound; bottomless; immeasurable.

Abyss, abysm *ns*. bottomless chasm depth; an abyss.

Abyssinian *n*. native of Abyssinia.

Acacia *n*. genus of tree yielding gum; gum arabic.

Academian *n*. a member of an academy.

Academy *n*. school of arts and science; society of learned men; *esp*. an intermediate between school and a college; *i.e*. I.A and F.A.

Accelerate *v.t*. & *i*. to make quick, to become swift, to put on pace.

Accent *n*. modulation or stres on voice; mark used for this.

Accentuate *v.t*. to emphasize; to mark with an accent.

Accept *v.t*. & *i*. to agree to, to consent, to believe, to regard with favour, (with of), to receive, to agree to meet a bill.

Access *n*. near approach, means of approaching, admittance, advance, passage, growth, attack (of illness).

Accessary *n*. contributor; helper in an act. *adj*. extra.

Accessible *adj*. easy to access; that may be approached.

Accession *n*. the act of addition; attainment of office; succession to a throne.

Accessory *adj*. helping; extra; additional. *n*. helper in an act.

Accident *n*. happening or coming by chance without design or cause; unexpected event, mishap.

Acclaim *v.t*. to applaud loudly; to shout; to hail; to welcome or approve enthusiastically.

Acclamation *n*. loud and eager assent.

Acclimatize, Acclimate *v.t*. habituate or immune to new climate.

Acclivity *n*. an upward slope.

Acclivous *n*. sloping upwards.

Accolade *n*. award; music.

Accommodate *v.t*. to make suitable, to correspond, to supply, to sette difference between, to adapt.

Accompaniment *n*. something that attends another; accompanying thing.

Accompany *v.t*. to go with; to play subordinate musical part.

Accomplice *n*. an associate in wrong or crime; abettor.

Accomplish *v.t*. to finish entirely, to fulfil.

Accord *v.i*. & *t*. to be in harmony with; to grant; to agree.

According *adv*. agreeing, in accordance with.

Accordion *n*. portable musical instrument with bellows, and metal reeds, keys.

Accost *v.t*. go up to and speak to (in courtesy at meeting); to approach and speak to.

Accouchement *n.* delivery in childbed.

Accoucheur *n.* guide in a delivery; a man who assists women in childbirth.

Account *v.t.* & *i.* to estimate; to value; to consider; to esteem.

Accountant *n.* one who keeps account.

Accoutre *v.t.* to equip; to furnish.

Accredit *v.t.* to place credit in (someone's responsibility); to authorize.

Accrete *v.t.* & *i.* to grow together, to get attached; grown into one with something else.

Accretion *n.* growth or increase (in property, limbs or stems) by organic enlargement.

Accretive *adj.* increasing by growth.

Accrue *v.t.* to increase (by way of interest, etc.).

Accubation *n.* reclining.

Accumbent *adj.* reclining against anything.

Accumulate *v.t.* & *i.* to file up; to amass; to collect (wealth); to heap up (of dust, etc.)

Accumulative *adj.* given to hoarding; arising from collection; acquisitive.

Accumulator *n.* what accumulate, a storage battery.

Accuracy *n.* exactness; correctness; preciseness.

Accurately *adv.* exactly; with strict correctness.

Accurse *v.t.* to call down curses on.

Accursed, Accurst *adjs.* annoying; detestable; laying under a curse.

Accusable *adj.* that may be accused.

Accusation *n.* a charge of offence or crime.

Accusative *n.* accusing, the objective case.

Accusatory *adj.* containing an accusation.

Accuse *v.i.* to bring a charge against; to blame (with of).

Accused *adj.* & *n.* who is charged with the crime.

Accuser *n.* one who accuses another person.

Accustom *v.t.* to make familiar by use; habituate; to make oneself familiar with or accept as normal or usual.

Ace *n.* a unit; a single mark on cards or dice; a hair's breadth.

Acedia *n.* listlessness; laziness or indifference.

Aceldama *n.* scene of bloodshed.

Acephalous *adj.* leaderless.

Acerb *adj.* sour or astringent; sharp.

Acerbate *v.t.* to make sour and bitter.

Acerbity *n.* sourness or harshness (of temper); bitterness.

Acervate *adj.* heaped; growing compactly in clusters.

Acescence, Acescency *ns.* tendency to turn sour.

Acescent *adj.* becoming to tending to be sour.

Acetated *adj.* a salt of acetic acid.

Acetic *adj.* sour; like vinegar; sour acetic acid.

Acetify *v.t.* to turn into vinegar.

Acetous *adj.* of vinegar; sour.

Acetylene *n.* a gas burning with bright light.

Acharne *adj.* furious; desperate.

Achates *n.* faithful friend.

Ache *v.t.* to suffer continuous or prolonged pain. *n.* prolonged pain.

Achieve *v.t.* to attain; to gain; to accomplish by valour; finish successfully.

Achromatic *adj.* free from colour.

Acid *adj.* sour or biting to the taste; sharp. *n.* a sharp and sour substance.

Acidulated *adj.* made somewhat acid.

Acidulous *adj.* somewhat acid.

Acknowledge *v.t.* to admit the truth of, to confess, to express appreciation of, to announce receipt of.

Aclinic *n.* & *adj.* magnetic equator on which magnetic needle has no dip; without inclination.

Acme *n.* the top of highest point; the perfection of the carrier in anything.

Acne *n.* pimple; disease marked by pimples.

Acock *adv.* in a cocked manner.

Acolyte *n.* a faithful follower; an attendant; inferior officer in church attending priest.

Aconite *n.* a plant which is poisonous.

Acorn *n.* the fruit of seed of oak tree.

Acorn-shell *n.* a marine animal.

Acorus *n.* a type of plant.

Acosmism *n.* the principle of denying the existence of the external world.

Acotyledon *n.* plant with no distinct seed-lobes.

Acotyledonous *adj.* having no seed lobes.

Acoustician *n.* one skilled in the science of hearing.

Acoustics *n.* the science treating of the laws of sound.

Acquaint *v.t.* make familiar or conversant; to inform.

Acquaintance *n.* familiarity, knowledge.

Acquest *n.* a thing acquired (law); property gained otherwise than inherited.

Acquiesce *v.t.* to assent; to agree specially tacitly; to remain satisfied.

Acquirable *adj.* that may be acquired.

Acquire *v.t.* to obtain, to come in possession of.

Acquisition *n.* act of acquiring, gain.

Acquit *v.t.* to free; to release as from an accusation.

Acquittal *n.* release from charge of offence.

Acre *n.* a piece of land measuring 4840 sq. yds.

Acrid *adj.* sharp to the taste; bitter; of bitter temper.

Acrimonious *adj.* full of bitterness; sharp.

Acrimony *n.* harshness in speaking; bitterness of temper and manner.

Acrobat *n.* rope-dancer.

Acromania *n.* incurable madness.

Acronychal *adj.* happening at nightfall or midnight.

Acropolis *n.* a citadel of Athens.

Across *prep.* & *adv.* along from side to side.

Acrostic *n.* a poem in which initial words or letter are taken in order from a word or phrase.

Acrotism *n.* an absence or weakness of the pulse.

Act *v.i.* to be in action, to exert power, to produce effect, to feign, to behave.

Acting *adj.* performance.

Actinic *adj.* pertaining to the rays of the sun.

Actinism *n.* property of sun's rays that produces chemical changes (as in photography).

Actinium *n.* an element that turns dark in sunlight.

Actinometer *n.* an instrument for measuring the intensity of sun's actinic rays.

Action *n.* performance, deed, exploit, battle, engagement, law-suit.

Active *adj.* busy; practical; agile; nimble; operative; working; energetic.

Actor *n.* a stage-player.

Actress (*fem.*) *n.* a female actress.

Actual *adj.* real; effective; current.

Actually *adv.* in actual fact; really; for the time being.

Actuary *n.* a clerk, a registrar.

Actuate *v.t.* to give motion to; to urge; to incite; to communicate motion to.

Acuity *n.* sharpness; acuteness.

Aculeated *adj.* having prickles or sharp point.

Acumen *n.* sharpness of intelligence; mental acuteness or penetration.

Acute *adj.* sharp, pointed, keen, shrill, critical.

Acuteness *n.* sagacity; sharpness.

Acyclic *adj. Bot.* not forming cycles.

Ad. *n.* advertisement.

Adage *n.* proverb; an old saying.

Adagio *adv.* slowly; with grace.

Adam *n.* the first man.

Adamant *n.* a very hard stone, diamond.

Adamite *v.t.* a descendant of Adam.

Adapt *v.t.* to make suitable; to modify; to adjust; to make fit.

Add *v.t.* & *i.* to join; to sum up; to increase; to unite.

Addendum *n.* addition, a thing to be added, appendix.

Adder *n.* one who adds; an appendix; small venomous snake.

Addict *v.t.* to devote; to apply habitually; fall into bad habit; apply to.

Addition *n.* a process of adding; anything added; joining; increase.

Additive *adj.* that is added; showing addition.

Addle *adj.* rotten; muddled; empty; vain.

Address *v.t.* to communicate with; to speak; to direct; to make a suit to.

Adduce *v.t.* to cite; to bring to notice; to quote; to bring forward.

Adduct *v.t.* (of muscles) draw to a common centre.

Adeem *v.t.* to award; to adjudge; to deem.

Adenectomy *n.* excision of a gland.

Adeno *n.* Greek work meaning gland.

Adenoids *n. pl.* glandlike; small growth in the back part of the throat in children.

Adept *adj.* proficient, well-skilled. *n.* one skilled in art.

Adequacy *n.* sufficiency; state of being adequate.

Adhere *v.i.* to be attached to remain firm; to stick fast to.

Adhesion *n.* close connections; steady attachment.

Adhesive *adj.* tenacious; apt to stick; gummed.

Adhibit *v.t.* to apply; to affix (one's signature).

Adiantum *n.* kinds of fern, esp. the black maiden hair.

Adiaphorous *adj.* indifferent; neither right nor wrong morally.

Adieu *int.* & *n.* good-bye; farewell.

Adipose *adj.* fatty, containing fat.

Adit *n.* an approach; access; a horizontal entrance or passage.

Adjacent *adj.* lying near to; contiguous.

Adjective *n.* a word which qualifies a noun.

Adjoin *v.i.* to join, to unite, to append. *v.t.* to lie in contract with.

Adjourn *v.t.* & *i.* to put off; to postpone; to suspend.

Adjudge *v.t.* to decide; to settle; to condemn; to award.

Adjudicate *v.t.* to pronounce judgement to sit in judgement.

Adjunct *n.* joined or added; accompaniment; predicate etc.

Adjure *v.t.* to charge under oath or penalty, to request earnestly.

Adjust *v.t.* to fit to settle; to regulate; to harmonise.

Adjustment *n.* settlement; arrangement.

Adjutage *n.* a tube or nozzle.

Adjutant *n.* an assistant officer in the army, gigantic Indian strok.

Adjutant-general *n.* the executive officer of the commander-in-chief.

Admeasure *v.t.* to apportion; to measure.

Admeasurement *n.* measure; weight.

Administer *v.t.* & *i.* to manage; to execute; to supply; to provide with.

Admirable *adj.* worthy of admiration, excellent.

Admiral *n.* a naval officer of the highest rank; the commander of the fleet.

Admiralty *n.* office of admiral; branch of the executive that superintends the navy.

Admire *v.t.* to look on; to contemplate; to wonder at; to have high esteem.

Admissible *adj.* capable of being admitted or allowed.

Admission *n.* introduction, access; enrolment; acknowledgement.

Admit *v.t.* & *i.* to permit; to allow; to enter; to grant.

Admix *v.t.* to mix with something else.

Admonish *v.t.* to reprove mildly; to advise; to warn.

Admonitory *adj.* containing admonition.

Adnoun *n.* an adjective when used as a collective noun.

Ado *n.* bustle, trouble, fuss, difficulty.

Adobe *n.* unburnt brick dried in the sun.

Adolescence *n.* youth; the period of ripening; state of growing; puberty.

Adonis *n.* a beautiful youth loved by venus; dandy.

Adopt *v.t.* to take as ones own child; to take oneself by a choice or approval.

Adorable *adj.* deserving the utmost love and admiration; worthy of love.

Adoration *n.* homage; veneration; worship.

Adore *v.t.* to worship; to love intensely; to reverse.

Adorer *n.* an admirer; lover.

Adorn *v.t.* to decorate; to furnish with ornaments; to embellish.

Adown *adv.* & *prep.* down, downward.

Adrenal *adj.* near the kidney.

Adrenalin or Adrenaline *n.* a secretion of the adrenal ductless glands extracted from animals for medicinal use.

Adrift *adv. adj.* floating at random; moving without direction at the mercy of wind and tide or of circumstances.

Adroit *adj.* dexterious; skilful.

Adroitness *n.* dexterity; skill.

Adry *adj* & *adv.* dry, thirsty.

Adsorb *v.t.* to attract and hold a gas or liquid to its surface.

Adulate *v.t.* to flatter or praise excessively.

Adult *n.* & *adj.* grown up person, a man of mature age.

Adumbral *adj.* overshadowing; shady.

Adumbrant *adj.* adumbrative; adumbrating or giving a faint shadow.

Adumbrate *v.t.* sketch in outline; to indicate faintly.

Adumbration *n.* matter shadowed out; imperfect representation.

Aduncous *adj.* hooked; bent or made in the form of a hook.

Adust *adj.* burnt; parched; sun burnt; having great heat; gloomy.

Advance *v.t.* & *i.* to move; to put forward; to move further.

Advantage *n.* benefit; profit; precedence; favourable occasion.

Advection *n.* transferring of heat by horizontal motion of air currents.

Advent *n.* coming or arrival as of any important person; the birth of Christ; the four weeks before the Christmas.

Adventure *n.* risk, enterprise of hazard. *v.i.* to risk or hazard.

Adverb *n.* a word that modifies or limits the meaning of an adjective.

Adverbial *adj.* pertaining to adverb.

Adversary *n.* an antagonist; an enemy.

Adverse *adj.* opposing or opposed.

Adversity *n.* trouble; calamity.

Advert *v.i.* to draw the attention to, to refer to.

Advertence *n.* heedfulness; attention; regard.

Advertent *adj.* attentive; heedful.

Advertise *v.t.* & *i.* also (advertize) to inform; to publish, to announce.

Advice *n.* counsel, news (*in. pl.*) formal notice, communication from a distance.

Advise *v.t.* & *i.* to give advice to; to counsel; to warn; to recommend.

Advisory *adj.* containing advice.

Advocate *n.* one who pleads; one who defends or vindicates; counsellor.

Advowson *n.* right of presentation to a benefice.

Adynamia *n.* weakness caused by disease.

Adytum *n.* a sacred place; an inner or secret place; shrine in some ancient places of worship; sanctum.

Adze *n.* a tool like axe.

Aegis *n.* protection; sponsorship.

Aegrotat *n.* a medical certificate certifying that a person is unfit to attend his duties.

Aeolian *adj.* the God of air.

Aeon *n.* the age of the universe; a very long period of time.

Aerate *v.t.* to charge with air or gas; to oxygenate the blood; purifying air by exposure; to put air into.

Aerial *adj.* belonging to air, imaginary, atmosphere, lofty, elevated. *n.* a conductor used in wireless telegraph.

Aerobatics *n. pl.* aerial maneuvres; tricks or stunt of flying.

Aerodrome *n.* an area of land set apart for landing of aeroplanes.

Aeronaut *n.* one who ascends in a balloon; or pilots a plane; an aerial navigator.

Aeroplane *n.* airplane or aircraft; a flying machine heavier than air.

Aerostat *n.* any aircraft lighter than air; balloon; an airship.

Aesthesia *n.* capacity for sensation or feeling.

Aesthete *n.* professed appreciator of the beautiful.

Aestheticism *n.* doctrines of aesthetics; the principles of good taste.

Aestival *adj.* pertaining to summer.

Aestivate *adj.* to spend the summer at a specific place.

Aetiology *n.* science of the causes of disease; the doctrine of causation.

Afar *adj.* at a distance.

Affair *n.* bussiness, event, concern, matter, minor battle, (*pl.*) pursuits of life.

Affect *v.t.* to act upon; to aim at; to influence; to move the feelings.

Affection *n.* attachment; kindness; sympathy; a dispositon of mind; love.

Affiance *n.* contact or pledge of marriage; trust; faith.

Affiant *n.* one who submits an affidavit.

Affidavit *n.* a written document of oath in the court before a magistrate.

Affiliate *v.t.* to receive into a family, to adopt, to connect, to receive into a society as member.

Affinity *n.* relation by marriage; resemblance; relationship.

Affirm *v.t.* & *i.* to say with confidence; to assert positively; to maintain a statement; to ratify.

Affirmatory *adj.* that affirms; positive; dogmatic.

Affix *v.t.* to attach to; to fix; to fasten.

Afflatus *n.* inspiration; from above; super-natural knowledge.

Afflict *v.t.* to harass; to trouble, to grieve; to cause suffering.

Affluence *n.* wealth; abundance; flow; opulence; riches.

Affluent *adj.* abounding in riches; rich; wealthy. *n.* tributary stream.

Afflux *n.* a flow towards a point.

Afforce *v.t.* to strengthen.

Afford *v.t.* to have enough money, time, space to spend, sell, expand for a particular pourpose.

Afforest *v.t.* to convert baseland into a forest; to declare subject to forest law.

Affranchise *v.t.* to liberate; to enfranchise.

Affray *n.* fray, noisy quarrel, distribution, a brawl.

Affright *v.t.* to frighten; to impress with sudden fear; to alarm.

Affront *v.t.* to insult openly; to offend; to face defiantly.

Affusion *n.* pouring or sprinkling specially in baptism.

Affy *v.t.* & *i.* to trust; to betrothe; to affiance.

Afield *adv.* in or on the field.

Afire *adv.* & *adj.* on fire.

Aflame *adv.* glowing; flaming; ablaze.

Afloat *adv.* in a floating state; foaming.

Afond *adv.* to the bottom; thoroughly.

Afoot *adv.* able to walk; in motion; on the move.

Afore *adv.* & *prep.* before, in front of, previously.

Aforesaid *adj.* previously said.

Aforetime *adv.* in time past; previously.

Afraid *adj.* frightened, alarmed.

Afresh *adv.* a new; again; with a fresh start.

Afrit *n.* Arabian powerful monster.

Aft *adv.* near; close to or towards the stern of a ship.

After *adv.* later; following. *adv.* later in time; behind in place.

Afternoon *n.* time between noon and evening.

Afterpains *n.* pains of the child-birth.

Afterthought *n.* idea etc. that occurs to one later.

Afterwards *adv.* later; subsequently.

Again *adv.* another occasion, moreover, besides, in return.

Agamous *adj.* without sexual organ.

Agaric *n.* medicine used for relief of night sweats.

Agate *n.* a kind of precious stone used in jewellery.

Agaze *adv.* gazing.

Age *n.* period of life; maturity of years; period of history; generation.

Aged *adj.* old.

Ageless *adj.* never growing old.

Agency *n.* the office of an agent; place of business; the state of being in action.

Agenda *n. pl.* things to be done, memoranda.

Agent *n.* one who acts or has power to act; an efficient cause of anything.

Agglomerate *v.t.* & *i.* to collect into mass.

Agglutinate *v.t.* & *i.* to cause; to adhere or join with glue; to unite with glue.

Agglutination *n.* adhesion of parts.

Aggrandize *v.t.* (also aggrandise) to increase wealth, honour or rank; exalt; to exaggerate.

Aggravate *v.t.* to make worse; to provoke to exasperate; to tease.

Aggravator *n.* one who aggravates.

Aggregate *v.t.* to collect together, to accumulate. *adj.* collected into a body.

Aggression *n.* the first attack; the first act leading to war.

Aggressive *adj.* making the first attack; one who aggresses.

Aggressor *n.* one who invades; or an assaulter.

Aggrieve *v.t.* to give pain or sorrow; to injure one's right.

Aghast *adj.* stupified with sudden fright; struck with amazement.

Agile *adj.* quick witted; active; nimble.

Agility *n.* the state of being agile.

Agio *n.* exchange premium; the premium payable on exchange of one currency for another.

Agiotage *n.* exchange business.

Agist *v.t.* to take cattle of others to graze at a certain sum.

Agitate *v.t.* to move, to shake, to disturb, to discuss.

Agitation *n.* violent motion; discussion; disturbance.

Agitator *n.* one who excites or keeps up a public agitation.

Aglet *n.* a metal tag at the end of a lace or point formerly worn on dresses.

Aglimmer *adv.* in a glimmering manner.

Aglitter *adj.* & *adv.* shiny.

Aglow *adj.* glowing; in a glow; red hot.

Agnail *n.* torn skin at the root of finger-nail, whitlow, corn.

Agnate *n.* & *adj.* any relation of the father's side; akin.

Agnomen *n.* additional name or epithet of a person.

Ago *adv.* past; gone by; since.

Agog *adv.* eager; astir; highly excited.

Agoing *adv.* going on; in motion.

Agonic *adj.* forming or having no angle.

Agonist *n.* one who contest in public games and competitions.

Agonistics *n.* the scientific study of athletics.

Agonize *v.t.* & *i.* to suffer intirely; to make desperate efforts.

Agony *n.* extreme bodily or mental pain; struggle before natural death.

Agoraphobia *n.* morbid fear of public places.

Agrarian *adj.* pertaining to agriculture; relating to landed property.

Agree *v.i.* to be in harmony with; to accede; to occur; to suit.

Agrestic *adj.* rural; rustic; of the country.

Agriculture *n.* cultivation of soil.

Agrology *n.* the science of soils dealing *esp.* with the production of crops.

Agronomy *n.* rural economy.

Agrostography *n.* a scientific description of grass.

Aground *adv.* stranded; on the ground; run ashore.

Ague *n.* a periodical malaria fever accompanied with shivering.

Aguise *v.t.* to adorn.

Aguish *adj.* shivering with fever.

Ah *inter.* an exclamation expressing pain, joy, pity, contempt etc.

Ahead *adv.* in advance; in front; further.

Aheap *adv.* heaped together.

Aheight *adv.* at the top.

Ahem *inter.* exclamation indicating surprise or disbelief.

Aid *v.t.* to assist, to help.

Aids (Acquired Immune Deficiency Syndrome) It is a fatal disease which mainly spreads through sexual contact, infected blood or needles.

Aiglet *n.* metal tag of a lace; a young eagle.

Aigrette *n.* tuft of feathers of hair; spray of gems, etc.

Aiguille *n.* a slender perforating drill; name given to the needle, like tops of rocks.

Ail *v.t.* & *i.* to feel pain, to be in trouble.

Aileron *n.* the control flap behind the wings of an aeroplane.

Aim *v.t.* & *i.* to direct a missile towards an object; to aspire.

Air *n.* the atmosphere, a light breeze, outward appearance, a song.

Aircraft *n.* a kind of craft designed for the air.

Airless *adj.* stuffy; still; calm.

Airman *n.* aviator.

Airplane *n.* aeroplane.

Airway *n.* a passage for air-ventilating passage in mine.

Airy *adj.* pertaining to air; gay; ventilated; unsubstantial; delicate.

Aitchbone *n.* the rump bone in a cattle.

Ajar *adj.* slightly open; out of tune; at variance.

Akimbo *adv.* with hands on hips and elbows turned out.

Akin *adj.* similar; related by blood; allied.

Alabaster *n.* a soft lime-like mineral; gypsum.

Alack, Alack-a-day *interjs.* exclamation expressing sorrow.

Alacrity *n.* promptitude; cheerfulness; briskness; readiness.

A la mode *adv.* & *adj.* according to fashion.

Alamort *n.* dejected; dispirited. **Alar (-y)** *adjs.* pertaining to the wings.

Alarm *n.* summons of arms; warning of danger; a sudden surprise.

Alarmism *n.* panic-mongering; fostering a panic.

Alarmist *n.* easily frightened; a panic-monger.

Alarum *n.* an alarm clock; signal of alarm.

Alas *inter.* expressing grief, pity, sorrow or concern.

Albacore *n.* large sea-fish of the runny kind.

Albatros *n.* a large web-footed sea-bird mostly found in Southern Ocean.

Albeit *conj.* even if; notwithstanding; although it be that.

Albescent *adj.* growing white.

Albino *n.* person (or animal) with white hair and skin and eyes of pink colour.

Album *n.* a blank bound book to store up photograph, stamps etc.

Albumen *n.* a thick white substance as in the egg.

Alburnum *n.* sapwood.

Alchemist *n.* one that practises alchemy.

Alchemy *n.* the art which transmutes base metals into gold.

Alcohol *n.* pure spirit of wine; any liquor containing alcohol.

Alcoholic *adj.* like alcohol; or one given to excessive drinking.

Alder *n.* tree related to birth.

Alderman *n.* magistrate in English and Irish cities.

Alderin *n.* a white chlorinatid hydro-carbon substance used in insecticide.

Ale *n.* beverage made from malt.

Al-bench *n.* a bench outside the ale-house.

Ale-house *n.* place where ale is retailed.

Aleatory *adj.* depending on luck or chance. **Alee** *adj.* towards the lee-side.

Aleft *adj.* to the left hand.

Alembic *n.* apparatus formerly used in distilling.

Alength *adj.* at full length.

Alepine *n.* a mixed fabric of wool and silk.

Alert *adj.* watchful; vigilant; wide-awake, nimble.

Alexandrine *n.* & *adj.* a rhyming verse of twelve syllables.

Alexia *n.* loss of power to read.

Alfresco *adv.* & *adj.* in the fresh open air.

Algae *n. pl.* sea-weed.

Algebra *n.* a branch of mathematics in which general symbols are employed to calculate.

Algid *adj.* of cold stage; to ague.

Algorithm *n.* set of rules or procedures that must be followed in solving a problem.

Alias *adj.* assumed name.

Alibi *n.* a plea that a alleged accused was elsewhere at the time of the occurrence of the crime.

Alien *n.* different in character and nature; incompatible.

Alienee *n.* one to whom transfer of property is made.

Alienism *n.* the position of being a foreigner.

Alienist *n.* doctor who treats mad men.

Alight *v.i.* to dismount; to descend.

Align *v.t.* to lay in a line, to bring troops in a line.

Alike *adj*. same in appearance, size or character.

Aliment *n*. support; nourishment.

Alimony *n*. maintenance; allowance due to a wife for support.

Aliquot *adj*. that divides without remainder.

Alive *adj*. vigorous; lively; sensitive.

Alkalescent *adj*. slightly alkaline.

Alkali *adj*. substance that neutralizes acids.

Alkaline *adj*. of the nature of an alkali. **Alkalize** *v.t.* to make alkali.

Alkaloid *n*. having some resemblance with alkali.

Alkanet *n*. a plant whose roots yield a red dye.

All *n*. whole; entire; the highest possible, the whole world, everything.

Allay *n*. to reduce; to lessen pain.

Allegation *n*. assertion which has not been proved or accepted.

Allege *v.t.* plead; state or advance as a fact; affirm.

Allegiance *n*. duty owed by a subject to his government; loyalty.

Allegoric *adj*. in the manner of an allegory; figurative.

Allegorize *v.t.* to treat in form of an allegory.

Allegretto *adv*. & *n*. light; graceful and moderately fast in tempo.

Allegro *adj*. & *adv*. gay, briskly, gaily.

Alleluia *n*. song sung in praise of God.

Allergy *n*. hypersensitivity; abnormally sensitive.

Alleviate *v.t.* to comfort; to relieve; to mitigate.

Alleviation *n*. act of relieving or making light.

Alley cat *n*. stray cat.

Alleyed *adj*. having narrow lanes.

All-father *n*. The Almighty God.

Alliance *n*. a state of being allied; friendship; affinity; union by marriage.

Alligate *v.t.* to join together.

Alligator *n*. crocodile; a kind of large lizard.

Alliteration *n*. figure of speech of several words in sentence with same letters.

Alliterative *adj*. pertaining to alliteration.

Allocate *v.t.* to apportion; to assign; to place.

Allocution *n*. an address, a formal address.

Allodial *adj*. absolute ownership.

Allogamy *n*. cross fertilization in plants.

Allograph *n*. a writing made by one person for another.

Allopathy *n*. a western system of medicine.

Allot *v.t.* to distribute by lot or proportion, to assign to.

Allottee *n.* one to whom a share is apportioned; a plot-holder.

All-over *adv.* everywhere.

Allow *v.t. & i.* to grant; to give; to permit; to approve.

Allowance *n.* grant; permission.

Alloy *n.* inferior ingredients mixed with silver or gold.

All-purpose *adj.* useful in many ways.

All-right *adj.* acceptable; satisfaction.

All-round *adj.* with ability in all departments.

All-spice *n.* Jamaica pepper.

Allude *v.i.* to make an indirect reference.

Allure *v.t.* to entice; to tempt by alure.

Allusion *n.* indirect reference; hint.

Allusive *adj.* having allusion; hinting at.

Alluvial *adj.* full of deposit of earth, left by flood.

Alluvion *n.* land gained from the sea or river by washing up of sand and earth.

Alluvium *n.* deposit of flood.

Ally *v.t.* to form a relation by marriage, friendship, treaty, co-operation, assimilation.

Almanac *n.* an astrological annual calender.

Almighty *adj.* invincibly powerful; omnipotent.

Almirah *n.* cupboard; chest of drawers, etc.

Almond *n.* fruit of the almond tree.

Almost *adv.* early; quite nearly.

Alms *n.* money, clothes, food given to the poor.

Aloe *n.* plant with erect spikes of flowers and bitter juice.

Aloft *adv. & prep.* upward; above; on the top; at the apex of the mast.

Alone *adj.* without anybody in company; solitary; single.

Along *prep.* lengthwise; throughout; from this end to that.

Aloof *adv.* apart; at a respectable distance.

Aloud *adv.* noisily; with a loud noise.

Alow *adv.* in a lower point or place.

Alp *n.* high mountain; (*pl.*) loftly ranges of Switzerland.

Alpaca *n.* llama with long wooly hair; wool of llama; fabric made from the wool of llama.

Alpenstock *n.* an iron stick used in climbing Alps.

Alpha *n.* first letter in Greek alphabet.

Alphabet *n.* the set letters of a language; first elements.

Alpine *adj.* of the Alps; lofty.

Already *adv.* previously; by the given time in question.

Alsation *n.* a large breed of dog.

Also *adv.* likewise; in addition to.

Altar *n.* a raised platform used for sacrifice or offering.

Alter *v.t. & i.* to modify; to differentiate.

Altercate *v.i.* to wrangle; to argue with heat or anger.

Alterity *n.* an altered situation.

Alternate *v.t.* to cause by turns; to interchange.

Alternation *n.* reciprocal succession.

Although *conj.* though; admit all that.

Altimeter *n.* aeronautical instrument showing height above sea-level.

Altitude *n.* height; elevation; a high point; height above sea-level.

Alto *n.* highest male voice.

Altogether *adv.* wholly; completely; entirely; in total.

Altruism *n.* the principle of having consideration for the good of others.

Alum *adj.* oxide of aluminium.

Aluminium *n.* a kind of light silvery metal.

Alumnus *n.* pupil of school or university; graduate.

Always *adv.* at all times; on all occasions.

Amain *adv.* with force; in haste.

Amalgam *n.* mixture of a metal with mercury.

Amanuensis *n.* one who copies or writes to dictation.

Amaranth *n.* kinds of plant with coloured foliage.

Amass *v.t.* to accumulate; to heap.

Amateur *n.* one who cultivates an art, game etc. for one's hobby's sake.

Amative *adj.* full of love, amorous.

Amatol *n.* a kind of explosive.

Amatory *n.* amorous; expressive of love.

Amaurosis *n.* blindness.

Amaze *v.t.* to confound with astonishment.

Amazing *adj.* exciting amazement or surprise.

Ambages *n. pl.* round-about ways.

Ambassador *n.* a diplomat of the highest order.

Amber *n.* a kind of yellow fossil resin.

Ambergris *n.* a fragrant substance of an ash-gray colour obtained from the sperm-whale.

Ambidexter *adj.* one who uses both hands alike.

Ambient *adj.* surrounding; investing.

Ambiguity *n.* doubtfulness; equivocal; uncertainty of signification.

Ambiguous *adj.* undermined; doubtful; indistinct.

Ambit *n.* circuit, bounds, extent.

Ambition *n.* ardent aspiration; keen desire.

Amble *v.i.* to move without jolts or jerks.

Ambrosia *n.* thing delightful to taste or smell; food of the gods.

Ambsace *n.* bad luck, worthlessness.

Ambulance *n.* mobile van for the sick or injured; a hospital on wheels.

Ambuscade *n.* a body of troops in concealment; a hiding to attack by surprise; the hidden place of ambush.

Ambush *n.* ambushment (concealment); troops for an attack.

Ambustion *n.* a burn or a scald.

Ameliorate *v.t.* & *i.* to make better.

Amelioration *n.* the condition of being made better; improvement.

Amen *inter.* so be it.

Amend *v.t.* & *i.* to correct; to improve.

Amende *n.* French, a penalty.

Amends *n.* (*pl.*) compensation; separation.

Amenity *n.* a pleasing way, feature, object, situation; civility.

Amenorrhoea *n.* stoppage of menstruation.

Amerce *v.t.* to fine, to punish.

American *n.* & *adj.* pertaining to the U.S.A., a citizen of America.

Amerind *n.* aboriginal Indian or American.

Amethyst *n.* a quartz of bluish violet colour; coloured like amethyst.

Amiable *adj.* friendliness; lovable; inspiring.

Amicable *adj.* done in a friendly manner; friendly.

Amicably *adv.* in a friendly manner.

Amid, Amidst *prep.* in the middle of; among.

Amiss *adv.* & *adj.* wrongly; improperly; faultily; wrong; unsuitable.

Amity *n.* friendship, friendly relation, goodwill.

Ammeter *n.* an instrument for measuring force of electric currents.

Ammonia *n.* a compound of nitrogen and hydrogen.

Amnesia *n.* loss of memory; forgetfulness.

Amnesty *n.* general pardon of political offenders.

Amoeba *n.* microscopic animalcule perpetually changing shape.

Among, Amongst *prep.* amidst; in comparison with; in the company of.

Amoral *adj.* out of the sphere of morals.

Amort *adj.* dejected.

Amount *v.i.* to result in, to be equivalent to. *n.* full value.

Amour *n.* love-affair, discreditable love; intrigue.

Ampelopsis *n.* kinds of vine-creeper.

Ampere *n.* unit of electric current.

Amphibian *adj.* & *n.* (animal) living both on land and in water. (aeroplane) designed to rise from and alight on either land or water.

Amphora *n.* two handled vessel.

Ample *adj.* copious; wide; abundant; large; bulky; spacious, extensive.

Amplify *v.t.* & *i.* to expatiate; to enhance; to enlarge.

Amplitude *n.* abundance, extent, dignity.

Amputee *n.* one who has lost one or more limbs by amputation.

Amuck *adv.* in a frenzy; (run about) in frenzied thirst for blood.

Amuse *v.t.* to attract attention; to excite the risible faculty.

Amusedly *adj.* in an amusing way.

Amuser *n.* one that amuses.

Amusing *adj.* pleasing.

An *adj.* any one; the indefinite article used before a vowel sound.

Anachronism *n.* fixing wrong period for any event; out of date things.

Anaclastic *adj.* pertaining to refraction.

Anadem *n.* a wreath; a garland.

Anadromous *adj.* fishes ascending rivers.

Anaemia *n.* lack of blood; paleness; unhealthy pallor.

Anaesthesia *n.* insensible condition.

Anaesthetize *v.t.* to make insensible.

Anagoge *n.* a spiritual interpretation or application of words, as of scriptures.

Anagram *n.* new word or phrase formed by transposition of another word etc.

Anal *adj.* relating to anus or near anus; under the tail; pertaining to the anus.

Analeptic *adj.* & *n.* restorative (medicine).

Analgesia *n.* absence of pain.

Analogical *adj.* expressing an analogy; analogous; according to analogy.

Analogue *adj.* that which is analogous to something.

Analogy *adj.* resemblance; likeness; proportion; parallelism, similarity.

Analphabet(e) *adj.* who cannot read or write.

Analyse *v.t.* to break into components and examine; to ascertain the elements of.

Analysable *adj.* able to be analysed.

Analysis *n.* breaking into parts and examining.

Analyst *n.* one who analyses.

Analytic, Analytical *adjs.* pertaining to analysis; employing the analytic method.

Anamorphosis *n.* deformed figure which appears regular in certain way.

Anapaest *n.* a metrical foot of three syllables.

Anarchic -chical *adjs.* lawless; without government.

Anarchy *n.* absence of law and go-vernment; disorder; disorder.

Anasarca *n.* dropsy.

Anastomosis *n.* cross connection of arteries, branches, rivers, etc.

Anastrophe *n.* inversion; change of order.

Anathema *n.* a divine curse; person so cursed. **Anathematize,** *v.t.* to curse.

Anatomical *n.* belonging to anatomy; structural.

Anatomy *n.* science of bodily structure and of dissection; dissection.

Ancestor *n.* line of ancestors; lineage; forefather.

Anchor *n.* heavy iron piece to which ships are chained.

Anchorage *n.* place for ship lying at anchor.

Ancient *n.* belonging to past times.

Ancillary *adj.* helping; auxiliary; advisory; extra; subservient; subordinate.

Ancon *n.* elbow.

Ancora *adv.* call for repetition of any item.

And *conj.* connecting words, clauses, and sentences.

Andante *adj.* (of Music) moderately slow.

Andiron *adj.* a firedog for supporting burning wood on an open hearth.

Androphagi *n. pl.* cannibals.

Anear *prep.* near.

Anecdote *n.* short narration; biographical narration.

Anemometer *n.* instrument for measuring force of wind.

Anemone *n.* a woodland flower; wild-flower.

Anent *prep.* regarding, concerning; about; respecting.

Aneroid *adj.* without liquid; not employing fluid.

Anethole *n.* oil of anise.

Anew *adv.* afresh; again; once more.

Anfractuous *adj.* intricate; involved.

Angary *n.* right of belligerents to use the properties of neutrals.

Angel *n.* a good spirit; God's messenger; good man with divine qualities.

Angelica *n.* a wild or garden aromatic plant.

Anger *n.* fury; indignations; wrath; hot displeasure.

Angle *n.* a meeting point of two lines; a corner; fish hook.

Angler *n.* a fisher.

Anglicize *v.i.* & *v.t.* to make English.

Angrily *adv.* in anger.

Angry *adj.* furious; annoyed; provoked; full of anger; enraged.

Anguine *adj.* pertaining to or like a serpant.

Anguish *n.* mental or bodily agony.

Angular *adj.* having angles or a corner; lean in body; awkward.

Anigh *prep.* & *adv.* near; at hand.

Anil *n.* indigo plant.

Aniline *n.* a coaltar product from which dyes are made.

Animadversion *n.* remarks by way of criticism or reproof; blame.

Animadvert *v.t.* to consider minutely; to censure; to criticise.

Animal *n.* organised being having life and motion; a living being; beast.

Animalcule *n.* small animal; microscopic animal.

Animality *n.* state of being an animal; animal nature.

Animate *v.t.* to give life to; to inspirit; to encourage.

Animation *n.* state of being alive; act of giving life; enlivenment; ardour.

Animism *n.* theory that soul is most important, spiritualism.

Animosity *n.* enimity; bitter hatred.

Animus *n.* hostile spirit or intention.

Anise *n.* plant with aromatic seed with very useful seeds.

Aniseed *n.* seed of anise.

Ankle *n.* joint connecting foot and leg.

Anna *n.* one sixteenth of a Rupee.

Annalist *n.* writer of annals.

Annals *n. pl.* yearly narrative, historical records generally.

Anneal *v.t.* to temper by heat; to fix colours by heating.

Annex *v.t.* to add at the end; to take possession of; to affix.

Annihilate *v.t.* to remove; to destroy.

Anniversary *n.* an annual celebration of an event; yearly return of a date.

Annotate *v.t.* & *i.* to write notes on, etc.; make notes on.

Announce *v.t.* proclaim; declare; make down.

Annoy *v.t.* to irritate; to trouble; to tease; to harm; to cause annoyance.

Annual *adj.* reckoned by the year; recurring yearly.

Annuitant *n.* one who holds an annuity.

Annuity *n.* payments made annually; yearly grant or sum.

Annul *v.t.* to abolish; to cancel.

Annular *adj.* of the shape of ring.

Annunciation *n.* announcement.

Anode *n.* the positive pole; the path by which electric current leaves the positive pole.

Anodyne *adj.* pain killing; soothing.

Anoint *v.t.* to apply oil or ointment.

Anomalous *adj.* full of anomaly; abnormal; irregular.

Anomaly *n.* irregularity.

Anon *adv.* at once; again; coming; soon; presently.

Anonymity *n.* state of being anonymous.

Anopheles *n.* a kind of mosquito.

Another *adj.* an additional (one); some other; a different (one).

Anserine *adj.* stupid.

Answer *n.* anything done in return, reply, a solution. *v.t.* to make a reply.

Ant *n.* a small insect. *White ant, Red Ant.*

Antagonism *n.* active opposition; contrariety of things or principles.

Antarctic *adj.* of south polar regions.

Ante *adv.* in the sense of 'before'.

Antecedence *n.* prior happening; precedence; priority.

Antechamber *n.* room leading to the chief apartment.

Antedate *v.t.* date before actual time; affix or assign an earlier than the true date to.

Antediluvian *adj.* before the flood; antiquated.

Antelope *n.* deer-like ruminant.

Antelucan *adj.* before dawn.

Antemeridian *adj.* before noon.

Antemundane *adj.* existing or occurring before creation of the world.

Antepenult, Antepenultimate *adjs.* the last syllable of a word except two.

Antenatal *adj.* existing or happening before birth.

Antenna *n.* feeler of insects; apparatus for transmitting or receiving electric waves; aerial.

Anteprandial *adj.* before dinner.

Anterior *adj.* before time or before place; infront; away from.

Anteroom *n.* room leading to another.

Anthem *n.* song of praise, to prose composition set of sacred music.

Anther *n.* part of stamen containing pollen.

Ant-hill *n.* a mound over ants' nest.

Anthoid *adj.* flower-like.

Anthology *n.* collection of small choice poems; epigrams.

Anthrax *n.* malignant boil; a malignant disease of sheep and cattle.

Anthropoid *adj.* man-like; resembling man.

Anthropology *n.* whole science of man; study of man as an animal.

Anthropophagous *adj.* man-eating.

Anti- *prep.* opposite; against.

Antic *n.* grotesque posture or trick.

Anticipate *v.t.* to expect; to know or see before happening.

Anticlimax *n.* lame conclusion to anything promising a climax.

Antilogy *n.* a contradiction in terms.

Antimonarchical *adj.* opposed to monarchy.

Anti-national *adj.* hostile to one's nation.

Antimomy *n.* a brittle metallic silver-white element used in medicine, etc.

Antinomy *n.* a conflict of authority.

Antipathy *n.* constitutional or settled aversion to.

Antiphon *n.* verse or sentence sung by one choir in answer to another.

Antiphonal *adj.* sung alternately.

Antiphonary *n.* a book of antiphons.

Antiphony *n.* echo; response; antiphonal singing.
Anitpodes *n. pl.* those who lives on opposite sides of globe.
Antipole *n.* the opposite pole.
Antipyretic *n.* preventing fever.
Antiquary *n.* fond of relics of past; student or collector of antiquities.
Antiquate *v.t.* to make obsolete or old.
Antique *adj.* ancient; old fashioned; of or dating from old times.
Antiquity *n.* before the middle ages; ancient times; ancient persons.
Antiscorbutic *adj.* & *n.* (a medicine) against scurvy.
Antiseptic *adj.* preventing decay or growth of bacteria; putrefaction.
Antisocial *adj.* opposed to the principles of society.
Antithesis *n.* counterthesis; opposition of word; contrast.
Antitype *n.* something which a symbol represents.
Antler *n.* stage horns and their branches.
Antonym *n.* word with opposite meaning.
Antrum *n.* a cave, a den, a large cavity.
Anurous *adj.* without tail.
Anus *adj.* posterior opening of alimentary canal in animals.
Anvil *adj.* steel block on which hot iron is beaten to give it shape.
Anxiety *n.* uneasiness; longing; worry; restlessness; troubled state of mind.
Any *adj.* one; some; every.
Anybody *n.* or *pron.* any person.
Anyhow *adv.* in any way whatever; at least; in any case; at any rate.
Anything *n.* thing of any type; something; anything.
Anyway *adv.* in any manner; anyhow; at least; at any rate.
Anyways, -wise *adv.* in any way.
Anywhere *adv.* at or to any place.
Aorist *adv.* indefinite; a past tense denoting occurrence merely.
Aorta *n.* great artery issuing from left ventricle of heart.
Apace *adv.* quickly; hastily; swiftly; with a quick pace.
Apache *n.* or (Opache) Red Indian; a lawless hooligan; a street ruffian.
Apanage *n.* provision for younger children; dependency; perquisite.
Apart *adv.* separately; asunder; aside; away from others.
Apartheid *n.* policy of racial segregation.
Apartment *n.* a single room; *pl.* a lodging; suite of rooms.
Apathetic *n.* insensible to emotion; indifferent; without feeling; listless.
Apathy *n.* want of interest; mental indolence; insensibility; indifference.
Ape *n.* a tailless monkey; imitator.
Apeak *adv.* vertically, on peak.

Apercu *n.* summary exposition; a short outline; survey or sketch.

Aperient *adj.* laxative.

Aperture *n.* opening.

Apery *n.* mimicry.

Apex *n.* summit; tip; point; vertex or peak; topmost point; pointed end.

Aphelion *n.* a planet's farthest point from the sun.

Aphorism *n.* definition; short pithy maxim; saying.

Aphrodisiac *n.* & *adj.* medicine producing sexual desire.

Apiary *n.* a place for keeping bees.

Apical *adj.* belonging to apex.

Apiece *adv.* individually; each, severally.

Apish *adj.* imitative; like an ape; of or like an ape; foolish.

Aplomb *n.* perpendicularity; self-possession.

Apocope *n.* cutting off an end of a word.

Apocryphal *adj.* doubtful; sham; false.

Apodosis *adj.* consequent clause in conditional sentence.

Apogee *n.* opposite to perigee; the point of heavenly body's farthest distance from the earth.

Apograph *n.* an exact copy.

Apollyon *n.* Satan, the devil.

Apologetic *adj.* of the nature of an apology; regretfully acknowledging fault.

Apologue *n.* a beast-fable; moral fable or allegory.

Apology *n.* regretful acknowledgement of fault; explanation.

Apophthegm *n.* terse of pithy saying.

Apoplexy *n.* a malady suddenly arresting powers of sense and motion.

Apostopesis *n.* sudden breaking off in speech.

Apostasy *n.* abandonment of one's religion, principle or party etc.

Apostate *n.* a renegade; one guilty of apostasy.

Apostil *n.* a marginal note.

Apostle *n.* one sent to preach Gospel.

Apostrophiz (s) e *v.t.* to deliver an exclamatory address.

Apothecary *n.* chemist; druggist.

Apotheosis *n.* glorification; deification; canonization.

Appal *v.t.* to turn faint; to abate; to horrify; to dismay.

Apparatus *n.* instrument or tools; mechanical appliances; appliances for scientific or other work.

Apparel *v.t.* to adorn; to dress.

Apparition *n.* an appearance; a phantom; a ghost.

Apparitor *n.* herald; usher.

Appeal *n.* to demand judgement from higher court; to call attention; to make an earnest request.

Appear *v.i.* to be visible; to come into view; to be manifest; to seem.

Appease *v.t.* to satisfy; to pacify; to soothe.

Appellant *n.* one who appeals to high court.

Appellate *adj.* (Court) hearing appeals.

Append *v.t.* to add; to annex; to attach.

Appendage *n.* accompaniment.

Appendicitis *n.* inflammation of vermiform; appendix of intestine of the caecum.

Appendix *n.* something appended or annexed; a supplement; subsidiary addition.

Appendicitis *n.* a disease of the intestines.

Apperception *n.* mind's perception of itself.

Appertain *v.t.* belong to as a right, possession or attribute; relate to.

Appetence *n.* desire; longing.

Appetite *n.* desire or craving for food, pleasure, etc.; hunger; relish for food.

Applaud *v.t.* & *i.* to commend; to express approval (esp. by clapping).

Applause *n.* acclamation; praise; loud approbation.

Apple *n.* the forbidden Fruit in the garden of Eden; fruit of the apple tree.

Appliance *n.* compliance; apparatus; thing applied; instrument; device.

Application *n.* a petition, request bearing of a thing.

Apply *v.t.* & *i.* to lay; to put; to administer; to make request.

Appoint *v.t.* to fix; to settle; to assign; to nominate; to ordain; to prescribe.

Apportion *v.t.* to portion out; to divide; to adjust in portion; to assign as share.

Appose *v.t.* to apply; to place side by side; to confront.

Appraise *v.t.* to fix the price of; to estimate the worth of.

Apprehend *v.t.* to understand; to recognise; to consider; to fear.

Apprehension *n.* act of understanding; arrest; fear.

Apprentice *n.* a novice; learner bound to employer for specified term.

Apprise *v.t.* to give notice of; to inform.

Apprize *v.t.* to value; to appreciate.

Approach *v.t.* & *i.* to come near; to resemble; to make proposals to.

Approbate *v.t.* to approve of as valid; to sanction.

Approve *v.t.* & *i.* to be pleased with, to sanction, to commend.

Approximate *adj.* nearing correctness; nearly exact; fairly correct; near to.

Approximation *n.* tolerably exact estimate or amount; close approach

Appurtenance *n.* appendage; that which belongs to something else.

Appurtenant *adj.* appertaining.

Apricate *v.t.* & *i.* to bask.
Apricot *n.* a kind of fruit; orange-coloured stone-fruit allied to plum.
April *n.* the fourth month of the calendar.
Apron *n.* a piece of cloth or leather worn by surgeons; garment worn infront of body.
Apropos *adv.* to the purpose; to the point or purpose.
Apse *n.* a semicircular recess.
Apsis *n.* an apse; aphelion or perihelion of planet.
Apt *adj.* suitable; liable; fit; appropriate; prompt; quick; clever, ready; inclined.
Aptly *adv.* in a fit manner.
Aptitude *n.* fitness; talent.
Apterous *adj.* wingless.
Aqua *n.* a liquid solution, water.
Aquarium *n.* tank for nursing acquatic animals or plants.
Aquarius *n.* the eleventh sign of the zodiac.
Aquatic *n.* living in or near water.
Aquatint *n.* engraving on copper.
Aqueduct *n.* conduit; artificial channel for water.
Aqueous *n.* of water; of the nature of water; watery.
Aquiline *n.* curved and hooked like the beak of an eagle.
Arab *n.* a native of Arabia.
Arable *adj.* fit for tillage.
Arbiter *adj.* a judge; an umpire; arbitrator.
Arbitrary *n.* not according to rules; despotic; capricious; discretionary.
Arbitrate *v.t.* & *i.* to decide; to judge; to settle dispute; to determine.
Arboraceous *adj.* tree-like.
Arboreal *adj.* belonging or pertaining to trees.
Arboreous *adj.* pertaining to trees.
Arborescent *adj.* tree-like in growth or general.
Arboretum *n.* a botanical tree garden.
Arboriculture *n.* cultivation of trees and shrubs.
Arbour *n.* grass plot; park; shady nook; bower of creepers.
Arc *n.* part of circumference of circle.
Arcade *n.* way through arches; covered walk lined with shops; row of arches.
Arcadia, Arcady *ns.* rustic, paradise.
Arcadian *n.* simple; rustic; backward.
Arcanum *n.* a mystery; a magical drug.
Arch *n.* curved construction.
Archaeology *n.* study of antiquities or of prehistoric remains.
Archaic *adj.* old; antiquated; out of date; primitive; no longer in common use.
Archangel *n.* noblest angel; a kind of pigeon; chief angel; angel of the highest rank or order.

Archbishop *n.* a big bishop; chief bishop; metropolitan.

Archdeacon *n.* Church dignitary next below bishop.

Archduke *n.* Duke/Duchess of the highest rank formerly the son of emperor of Austria.

Archer *n.* one who uses bow and arrows.

Archetype *n.* prototype.

Archimage *n.* a great magician.

Archipelago *n.* group of islands; sea with many island.

Architect *n.* one who designs buildings; one who prepares plans for building.

Archives *n. pl.* parts that surround a door or window; public records; place where public records are kept.

Archlike *adj.* built like an arch.

Archway *n.* way under arch; arched entrance; vaulted passage.

Archwise *adv.* in the form of an arch; like an arch.

Arctic *adj.* pertaining to region round north pole; or to poles star.

Arcuate *adj.* bent like an arch.

Ardent *adj.* earnest; fiery; eager; zealous; fervent; glowing; burning.

Ardour *n.* heat, warmth of affection, zeal.

Are *v.* plural of is.

Area *n.* extent of surface; region; sunk court before basement of house.

Areca *n.* betelnut genus of palms; a kind of palm.

Arefaction *n.* act of drying.

Arena *n.* combat field; scene of action; centre of amphitheater.

Arenaceous *n.* sandy.

Argent *n.* like silver.

Argentiferous *n.* yielding silver.

Argentine *n.* silvery, like silver.

Argil *n.* potter's clay.

Argilaceous *n.* of the nature of clay.

Argol *n.* reddish wine bottle crust.

Argon *n.* a gas; an inert constituent of the atmosphere.

Argosy *n.* merchant ship; richly laden ship.

Arguable *n.* doubtful; capable of being argued.

Argue *v.t.* & *i.* to prove; to maintain by reasoning; to debate; to indicate.

Argufy *v.i.* to argue wrongly; to argue for the sake of controversy.

Argument *n.* reasoning; reason advanced; debate.

Argus *n.* a fabulous person with hundred eyes; any observant or vigilant person.

Argute *adj.* sharp; shrewd.

Aria *n.* melody.

Arid *adj.* dry; barren; heated; parched; dull; uninteresting.

Aries *n.* the Ram, first zodiacal constellation.

Aright *adv.* rightly; on the right side as opposed to left; justly; duly.

Arise *v.i.* to awake; to become known; to come out as a sequence.

Aristocrat *n.* a person of high privileged group; haughty person; member of aristocracy.

Arithmetic *n.* computation; use of figures; science of numbers.

Ark *n.* chest; large boat; a coffier; Noah's ark or a toy like that.

Arm *n.* limb from shoulder to hand; upper limb of human body; sleeve.

Armada *n.* a fleet of armed ships; fleet of warships.

Armature *n.* any equipment for defence; a tool in electric generator and motor.

Armlet *n.* a small inlet of sea or branch of a river; a band worn round arm.

Armorial *adj.* of heraldic arms belonging to coats of arms.

Armory *n.* heraldry; armour or arms.

Armour *n.* protective dress used in battle; heraldic marks; protective steel or iron covering of warship.

Armourer *n.* manufacturers; repairer of arms and armour; maker of arms.

Army *n.* organised group of men with arms; land forces of a State.

Aromatic *n.* fragrant.

Around *prep.* & *adv.* on all sides; near; round; about; in every direction; on every side, all round.

Arouse *v.t.* & *i.* to awaken; to rouse; to shake up; to excite.

Arow *adv.* in a row.

Arraign *v.t.* to accuse; to impeach; to indict; to find fault with.

Arrange *v.t.* & *i.* to set according to system; to instruct; to settle; to manage.

Arras *n.* having tapestry; hangings of tapestry.

Array *v.t.* to adorn; to put in order; to dress oneself. *n.* dress; adorn; equip.

Arrear *n.* that which is behind. (*pl.*) outstanding debts, work etc. in which one is behind hand.

Arrearage *n.* being in arrears; debt.

Arrect *adj.* alert; upright.

Arrest *v.t.* to stop; to seize by authority; to apprehend; to catch attention.

Arret *n.* judgement; decision; award.

Arrival *n.* act of reaching; that which or who arrives; appearance; appearance on scene.

Arrive *v.t.* to reach a place, or end of journey; to attain an object; to establish one's position.

Arrogance *v.t.* insolence of bearing.

Arrow *n.* pointed stick shot from a bow; branch of tree. mark or sign (®) used to show direction.

Arrowy *adj.* formed or moving like an arrow.

Arsenal *n.* armoury; ordnance depot; dockyard; a place where weapons and explosives are made or stored.

Arsenious *adj.* containing arsenic.

Arson *n.* burning anything knowingly; wilful setting on fire of houses or other property.

Art *n.* practical skill; creative work of beauty; branch of knowledge.

Arterial *adj.* of the nature of an artery.

Arterialize *v.t.* furnish with arterial system.

Artery *n.* tube which carries blood from heart to other parts of body.

Artful *adj.* crafty.

Arthritis *n.* inflammation of joints.

Artichoke *n.* an edible vegetable.

Article *n.* joint; segment; critical opinion; juncture; separate substance or thing; separate para etc.

Articulate *adj.* joint; distinct; clear; divided into words or syllables.

Artifice *n.* crafty; fraud; the action or a means of deceiving or tracking somebody in a clever way.

Artificial *n.* created not by nature but by art; not real; false; feigned.

Artillery *n.* heavier machines for discharging missiles; the army unit in charge of these machines.

Artisan *n.* handicraftsman; mechanic, a worker who is skilled at making things.

Artist *n.* one who practices any fine art.

Artiste *n.* professional entertainer, singer, dancer, etc.

Artistic *adj.* conformed to art; according to art; having or showing natural skill in the arts.

Artless *adj.* without deception; lacking art; simple and natural.

Arts *n. pl.* branches of learning requiring skill and ingenuity.

As *adv. & conj.* for example: in the same degree; seeing that; similarly; while, when; since.

Asafoetida *n.* resinous gum with smell of garlic, also asafetida.

Ascendancy *n.* powerful influence; the position of having dominant power or control.

Ascension *n.* act of ascending; going up to heaven; ascent.

Ascent *n.* act of ascending; upward movement; rise.

Ascertain *v.t.* to prove; to find out precisely; to determine.

Ascetic *adj.* severely abstinent; severe in self-discipline.

Asceticism *n.* self-mortification; the practice of ascetics.

Ascribe *v.t.* to attribute; to impute; to assign.

Asepsis *n.* the state of being free from pathogenic organisms.

Aseptic *n.* preventing putrefaction.

Ash *n.* residue left after burning; a timber tree; volcanic rock or dust.

Ashen *adj.* of ash; like ashes; pale-grey.

Ashamed *adj.* affected with shame; feeling shame and embarrassment about something.

Ashlar *n.* ashlar work; masonry of squarehewn stones.

Ashore *n.* to, on, the shore; on the land.

Ashy *adj.* of or like ashes, especially in colour, pale.

Asiatic *adj.* pertaining to Asia.

Aside *adv.* pull the curtain aside, away, apart, to one side; out of the way.

Asinine *adj.* of asses; very stupid.

Ask *v.t. & i.* to invite; to demand; to request; to inquire.

Askance, Askant *advs.* with suspicion, mistrust or disapproval; with a side glance; obliquely.

Aslant *adv.* obliquely. *prep.* slantingly across.

Asleep *adv.& prep. adj.* in state of sleep; benumbed.

Aslope *adv.* on a slope; cross-wise.

Asp *n.* a tiny snake; small venomous serpent; a small poisonous snake found especially in Egypt and Libya.

Asparagus *n.* a plant whose young green shoots are cooked and eaten as a vegetable.

Aspect *n.* look; appearance; expression.

Asperity *n.* roughness; harshness; bitter coldness; the quality of being harsh or severe.

Asperse *v.t.* to defame somebody.

Aspersion *n.* unpleasant remarks that may damage somebody's reputation; calumny; slander; a sprinkling.

Asphalt *n.* a mixture of coal-tar and sand. *v.t.* to pave with this.

Asphodel *n.* a kind of plant of the lily family.

Asphyxia *n.* suspended animation due to lack of oxygen in blood.

Aphyxiate *v.t.* to cause asphyxia; to suffocate.

Aspirate *v.t.* (consonant) pronounced with a breathing blended with sound of 'h'.

Aspire *v.t.* be filled with high ambition; to desire earnestly.

Aspiring *adj.* ambitious.

Asquint *adv.* looking askance; with a squint; toward one side.

Ass *n.* (also donkey) a donkey; an animal with long ears related to the horse.

Assail *v.t.* to attack somebody violently.

Assailant *n.* one who assails; one that attacks.

Assassin *n.* a murderer; one hired to kill another treacherously.

Assault *n.* unlawful personal attack; a violent attack; a sudden attack.

Assay *v.t.* to try the purity of (precious metals); to attempt; to draw result.

Assemble *v.t.* & *i.* fit together parts of; to come together.

Assembly *n.* gathering of persons (esp. of deliberative body).

Assent *v.t.* to give consent; to agree; to concur.

Assert *v.t.* to urge; to declare; to affirm; to say forcefully.

Assertion *n.* affirmation; positive statement; the action of claiming or starting something forcefully.

Assertor *n.* one who asserts; advocate (of).

Assess *v.t.* to valuate; to estimate; to determine the value of.

Assets *n. pl.* estate of a deceased person; the property of an insolvent debtor.

Asservate *v.t.* to declare solemnly.

Asseveration *n.* solemn affirmation.

Assibilate *v.t.* to utter a hissing sound, to make sibilant.

Assiduity *n.* constant attention.

Assiduous *adj.* unremitting; diligent.

Assign *v.t.* to give to; confer; to allot.

Assignee *n.* one to whom property or right is legally transferred.

Assimilate *v.t.* & *i.* to absorb ideas, information, make or become like.

Assist *v.t.* & *i.* to support; to help; be present at.

Assistance *v.t.* & *i.* support; succour; help; aid.

Assize *n. pl.* periodical courts of justice held by judges on circuit.

Assizer *n.* one who assizes or fixes price.

Associate *v.t.* & *i.* to link; to make partner; to join; to unite with.

Association *n.* fellowship; organization; company; union; a link or connection between people or organizations.

Assoil *v.t.* pardon; acquit.

Assonance *n.* resemblance of sound between two syllables rhyme depending on identity of vowel-sounds only.

Assort *v.t.* & *i.* to arrange into group; to select; to agree.

Assuage *v.t.* to appease; to soften; to abate; to calm; to soothe; to ease.

Assume *v.t.* to take as true; to take upon oneself; to adopt; to usurp authority.

Assurance *adj.* surety; declaration; certainty; insurance; self-confidence; positive assertion.

Assure *v.t.* to make believe; to insure; to make safe or certain; to satisfy.

Assurgent *adv.* rising; obliquely; ascending; aggressive.

Astare *adv.* gazing.

Aster *adv.* a kind of flower; a star; a starlike mark; kinds of plant with showy radiated flower.

Asterisk *n.* star mark; star used to mark words for reference or distinction.*

Asterism *n.* a constellation; a small cluster of stars. ***

Asteroid *n.* any of the small planets revolving round the sun between orbits of Mars and Jupiter.

Asthenia *n.* debility; lack of power.

Asthma *n.* disease causing difficulty in breathing; a disease marked by difficulty in breathing.

Astigmatism *n.* defect in eye preventing proper focussing.

Astir *n.* in motion; out of bed.

Astonish *v.t.* to astound; to amaze; to surprise greatly.

Astonishing *adj.* surprising; amazing.

Astound *v.t.* to cause fear; to amaze; to astonish; to surprise very much.

Astraddle *adv.* with one leg on each side.

Astragal *n.* bar which holds panes of window.

Astral *adj.* pertaining to stars; starry, spiritual; star-like; of stars.

Astray *adv.* & *adj.* out of right path; out of the right ways; away from the correct path.

Astrict *v.t.* to bind; to compress; to contract.

Astride *adv.* with legs wide apart or one on each side.

Astringent *n.* & *adj.* austere; severe; causing contraction or compression.

Astrolable *n.* instrument formerly used in taking altitudes etc.

Astrology *adj.* study about the influence of heavenly bodies on human being.

Astronomer *adj.* one skilled in astronomy; a student of astronomy.

Astronomy *adj.* science of the heavenly bodies.

Astute *adj.* crafty; shrewd; clever.

Asunder *adv.* apart; widely separated.

Aswarm *adv.* in swarms; teeming.

Aswoon *adv.* in a swoon; in a faining fit.

Asylum *adv.* shelter; place of refuge; institution for afflicted persons.

At *prep.* in; by; near; to; towards.

Atavism *prep.* similarity of off-springs to a remote ancestor than parents; reversion to earlier type.

Ataxia *n.* loss of coordination of the muscles, *esp.* of the extremities.

Ate *n.* the Greek goddess of mischief.

Atelier *n.* studio.

Atheism *n.* disbelief in the existence of God.

Athenaeum *n.* an institution for the propagation of literature and art.

Athirst *n.* thirsty; wanting drink; eager for.

Athlete *n.* one trained in exercise of strength; a wrestler; a champion in public games; a person who trains to compete in physical exercises.

Athwart *adv.* & *prep.* across (esp. obliquely).

Atlas *adv.* & *prep.* a bound book of maps.

Atmosphere *n.* the volume of air that surrounds the earth; mental or moral surroundings; the mixture of gases that surrounds the earth.

Atoll *adj.* an island made of coral and shaped like a ring with a lake of salt water in the middle.

Atom *n.* an extremely small particle of matter.

Atomize *v.t.* to reduce something to atoms or very small pieces.

Atomy *n.* an atom; a skeleton; atom, tiny being; emaciated body.

Atone *v.t.* to make amends; to reconcile; make up for; to act in a way that compensates for a previous wrong.

Atop *adv.* at or on the top of something.

Atrabilious *adj.* gloomy; splenetic.

Atrocious *adj.* extremely heinous; horrible; wicked.

Atrocity *adj.* wicked deed; heinous wickedness.

Atrophy *adj.* emaciation; a wasting of flesh with loss of strength; wasting away for lack of nourishment.

Attach *v.t.* & *i.* to fasten; to bind in friendship; to adhere; to seize by legal authority.

Attache *n.* one attached to ambassador's suite; a small rectangular box for carrying documents.

Attack *v.t.* to set upon; to begin battle or conflict with; to assault; to blame.

Attain *v.t.* & *i.* to gain or reach by efforts; to achieve; to accomplish.

Attaint *v.t.* to succeed in getting something; to infect; to sully.

Attar *n.* perfume which is extracted from flowers.

Attempt *v.t.* to try; to attack; to make an effort to succeed at something to try to do something.

Attend *v.t.* & *i.* to be present with; to wait on; to serve; to accompany.

Attention *n.* heed; care; politeness; the action of turning one's mind to something.

Attenuate *v.t.* to make something thin; reduce in force or value.

Attest *v.t.* to put on solemn oath; to bear witness to.

Attestation *n.* a solemn declaration verbal or written in support of fact.

Attic *n.* the highest storey of a house or a room in this history.

Attire *v.t.* to adorn with garments; to array; to dress.

Attitude *n.* position or posture of a person; gesture; condition.

Attitudinize *v.t.* to assume attitudes; to show affectation.

Attorney *n.* one legally appointed to act for another.

Attract *v.t.* to entice; to allure somebody; to win.

Attraction *n.* the act of attracting; allurement; the power of attracting.

Attribute *v.t.* to ascribe; to assign; to impute, to regard something as belonging to, to consider as due.

Attribution *n.* that which is ascribed; ascription.

Attributive *adj.* qualifying; expressing an attribute. *n.* word denoting an attribute or quality.

Attrited *adj.* worn by friction.

Attrition *n.* abrasion; smoothed by friction; worn down; wearing out.

Auburn *adj.* reddish brown generally.

Auction *adj.* a public sale of property to the highest bidder.

Auctioneer *n.* one who auctions; holder of auctions.

Audacious *adj.* showing a willingness to take risks.

Audacity *n.* boldness; impudence.

Audible *adj.* loud enough to be heard; capable of being heard.

Audibly *adv.* in a audible manner.

Audience *n.* the act of listening; an assembly of hearers; a hearers attention.

Audit *n.* an examination of accounts; persons appointed for the examination of accounts.

Audition *n.* power of hearing; listening.

Auditor *n.* a person appointed to examine the accounts.

Auditorial *n.* connected with an audit.

Auditorium *n.* a place where audience assemble.

Auditory *adj.* concerned with hearing.

Augean *adj.* difficult, filthy.

Auger *n.* a carpenter's boring tool.

Aught *n.* anything part or item; the figure '0' or cypher.

Augment *v.t.* & *i.* to make bigger; to enlarge in size or extent; to swell.

Augur *n.* soothsayer; a prophet; a fore-tellor.

Augury *n.* omen; that which predicts; a sign of what will happen in the future.

August *adj.* venerable; imposing. the eight month of English Calender.

Auk *n.* a northern sea-bird with short wings used as paddles.

Aunt *n.* father or mother's sister; the wife of an uncle.

Aural *adj.* relating to ear; concerning the ear or hearing.

Aureola *n.* a celestial crown; a halo.

Aureole *n.* a halo of lights seen in eclipses; gold disk or circle of light depicted round the head.

Auric *adj.* pertaining to gold.

Auricle *adj.* the external ear; either upper cavity of the heart.

Auricular *adj.* told privately in the ear.

Auriferous *adj.* yielding gold.

Aurora *n.* goddess of dawn.

Auscultation *n.* act of listening to movement of the heart.

Auspicate *v.t.* to foreshow.

Auspice *n.* protection; favourable influence; an omen drawn from birds; patronage.

Austere *adj.* sever and morally strict; having no pleasures or comforts.

Austerely *adv.* rigidly, harshly.

Austerity *n.* discipline; rigour.

Austral *adj.* southern.

Authentic *adj.* genuine; reliable; valid; authoritative; known to be true.

Author *n.* the first mover of anything; the writer of book.

Authoritative *adj.* commanding; possessing; imperative.

Authority *n.* power to command or act; control; right; evidence; an expert person; having influence.

Auto *pref.* in the sense of 'one's own' 'by itself', 'indepently.' *e.g.* Autocar.

Autobiography *n.* one's life written by oneself; the story of a person's life written by that person.

Autocar *n.* a carriage driven by a motor carried with it.

Autocracy *n.* absolute uncontrolled rule; government of a country by one person with absolute power.

Autocrat *n.* absolute ruler; an absolute sovereign.

Autograph *n.* signature; a person's own handwriting; author's own manuscript.

Autogyro *n.* a form of aeroplane that can be descend vertically by means of a windmill revolving freely on its own shaft.

Automatic *adj.* having the power of self motion; acting mechanically.

Automation *n.* the use of automatic equipment and machines to do work previously done by people.

Automatism *n.* involuntary action; mechanical routine.

Automobile *n.* an auto-car or similar vehicle.

Autonomy *n.* the power, right or condition of self-government.

Autopsy *n.* an examination of a dead body to discover the cause of death.

Autotype *n.* a photographic process by which pictures are reproduced in monochrome in a carbon pigment.

Autumn *n.* season of incipient decay; third season of the year coming between summer and winter.

Auxiliary *adj.* giving help or support; additional; subsidiary.

Avail *v.t.* & *i.* to assist, aid or profit; to be of value or advantage; to utilize.

Available *adj.* obtainable; advantageous; attainable; capable of being used; accessible.

Avalanche *n.* a mass of snow with ice and rock descending a mountain side; falling mass of snow.

Avarice *n.* greediness; inordinate desire for wealth; eager to get or keep.

Avaricious *adj.* extremely greedy.

Avast *inter. Naut.* stop! cease!

Avaunt *inter.* depart! away! begone!

Aveint *n.* farewell; hail; welcome.

Avenge *v.t.* to punish.

Avenue *n.* a passage; a wide street; roadway lined with trees; an entrance.

Aver *v.t.* to assert; to affirm with confidence; to declare; to prove (*a plea*).

Average *n.* an ordinary standard, prevailing rate or amount.

Averment *n.* positive assertion.

Averse *adj.* turned away from; unwilling; disinclined; not liking something.

Avert *v.t.* to turn away from; to keep off; to ward off; to turn away (*eyes, thoughts*) from.

Avian *adj.* belonging to birds.

Aviary *n.* large cage or building for keeping birds.

Aviate *v.t.* travel in aircraft.

Aviation *n.* the art of flying aeroplanes; manufacture and operation of aircraft.

Aviator *n.* the pilot of an aeroplane; one who aviates or travels in aircraft.

Aviatik *n.* a kind of German military aeroplane.

Avid *adj.* eager, enthusiastic; keen.

Aviette *n.* engineless man-worked aeroplane.

Avocate *v.t.* to call away; to remove from lower court to higher court.

Avocation *n.* vocation, calling, minor occupation.

Avoid *v.t.* to keep away; to shun to evade; to make void; to make oneself away from somebody.

Avoirdupois *n.* system of weights used for ordinary goods.

Avouch *v.t.* to maintain; to acknowledge; to affirm openly; to guarantee.

Avow *v.t.* to declare openly; to admit; to confess; to acknowledge.

Avowedly *adv.* clearly and openly.

Avulsion *n.* forcible separation; tearing away.

Await *v.t.* to wait or look for; to expect; to attend; to be ready for something.

Awake *v.t. & i.* to rouse from sleep; to put into action or new life; to stop or make somebody stop sleeping.

Awaken *v.t. & i.* to spring into being; to become or make something active again.

Award *v.t.* to adjudge; to determine; especially as a prize, payment, compensation; to grant

Aware *v.t.* informed; conscious; cognizant; apprised.

Awareness *n.* knowing something.

Awash *adj.* & *adv.* washed by waves, especially sea water.

Away *adv* & *inter.* absent; at a distance; apart; begone. *n.* distant.

Awe *n.* dread; fear mingled with terrible; awe inspiring; a feeling of respect combined with fear or wonder.

Awe-inspiring *adj.* impression, making you feel respect and admiration.

Awesome *adj.* very impressive or very difficult and perhaps rather frightening an awesome sight awesome beauty power.

Awestruck *adj.* suddenly filled with wonder and respect or fear.

Awful *adj.* filling with dread; terrible.

Awhile *adv.* for a short time.

Awkward *adj.* clumsy; uncouth.

Awl *n.* a pointed instrument for boring small hole; a shoe maker's tool.

Awn *n.* the beard of corn, grain, etc.

Awning *n.* a covering or canvas or other cloth spread over as a protection from the sun's rays or rain; canvas roof.

Awol *abbr.* absent without leave (used especially in the armed forces when someone has left their group without permission).

Awry *adv.* a wry position; crooked.

Axe *n.* an instrument, for chopping wood or hewing timber.

Axial *adj.* pertaining to an axis.

Axilla *n.* the armpit.

Axiom *n.* a self evident truthart.

Axiomatic *adjs.* characterized by axioms; self-evident; full of maxims.

Axis *n.* an imaginary line round which a body rotates; the axle.

Axile *adj.* in the axis of anything.

Ayatollah *n.* a religious leader of Shite (Shiya) Muslims in Iran.

Ay, Aye *ns.* vote in support of a motion at a meeting; supporter.

Ayes *n. pl.* those persons who vote for a motion.

Azimuth *n.* used to determine the position of a star, planet.

Azure *n.* faint blue; sky coloured; clear; a bright blue colour, like the sky.

Azygous *n.* single; not. existing in pairs.

Azymous *n.* unfermented, azym.

B

B the second letter of English alphabet.

Baa *n.* bleating; the cry of a sheep or lamb.

Babble *v.i.* & *t.* to speak like a baby; to talk quickly and in a way that is difficult or impossible to understand.

Babe *n.* infant; young inexperienced person; baby.

Babel *n.* high building; confused noise; a scene of noisy talking and confusion.

Babish *adj.* childish; foolish.

Baboon *n.* a kind of large monkey; a large African or Arabian monkey with a face like a dog.

Babcuche *n.* a kind of slipper.

Baby *n.* infant; child; doll; a very young child; childish person.

Babylon *n.* any great expire or vicious city; the capital of Chaldean empire.

Baccarat *n.* & *adj.* game of cards played by any number of players.

Bacchanal *adj.* of Bacchus or riotous and drunken.

Bacchant *n.* priest or votary of Bacchus.

Bacchus *adj.* Greek god of wine.

Baccy *n.* tabacoo.

Bachelor *n.* unmarried man; one who has taken his first degree from University.

Back *n.* the hinder surface of the body, part of a thing opposed to the front.

Backache *n.* a continuous pain in the back.

Backbite *v.t.* to speak evil behind one's back; to slander.

Back-blocks *n.* furthermost fringe of settlement.

Backbone *n.* firmness of character; the line of bones down the middle of the back from the skull to the hips.

Backfire *n.* to have the opposite effect on the one intended with bad or dangerous result.

Backer *n.* one who bets.

Backgammon *n.* a game for two players who throw dice and move pieces around a specially marked board.

Background *n.* previous history; hind portion.

Backhand *n.* writing which is leaning to left.

Backing *n.* help; support; the people who support; succour.

Backlash *n.* a strong negative reaction by a large number of people, for example to something that has recently changed in society.

Backstage *adv.* in the part of the theatre where the actors are artists get ready and wait to perform.

Backstairs *n. pl.* stairs in the back part of a house.

Backsword *n.* one edged sword; single-stick; a backward glance.

Backveld *n.* remoter parts of the veld.

Backward *adj.* unwilling, dilatory, dull, behind the time.

Backwoods *n. pl.* remote forest land that has not been cleared.

Bacon *n.* swine's flesh fried and salted; cured meat from the back or sides of the pig.

Bacterial *adj.* connected with or caused by bacteria.

Bad *adj.* worthless; of poor quality; inferior; incorrect; not valid.

Badge *n.* emblem; a mark to distinguish the rank or party.

Badger *n.* bear like animal; brush made of badger's hair; a hawker (*esp.* of provisions).

Badminton *n.* a game played with rackets and shuttlecocks.

Baffle *v.t.* to foil; to frustrate; to defeat.

Baffy *n.* wooden golf club.

Baft *n.* coarse cheap cotton fabric.

Bag *n.* small sack; pouch. *v.t.* to swell or bulge; to hang loosely; to kill game.

Bagful *n.* quantity which a bag can contain; a full bag.

Baggage *n.* luggage; portable equipment of army; a saucy girl.

Baggy *adj.* puffed out; hanging; in loose threads; hanging loosely.

Bagman *n.* a packman; a commercial traveller.

Bagnio *n.* a bathing house; oriental prison; brothel.

Bagpipe *n.* a musical wind instrument.

Bail *n.* security for a prisoner's appearance, a barrier, a bar placed on stumps of cricket.

Bail, Bale *v.t.* to throw water out of boat with buckets.

Bailable *adj.* admitting of bail (offence).

Bailee *n.* one to whom goods are entrusted.

Bailey *n.* outer wall of castle; court inside the walls.

Bailiff *n.* an officer under a sherrif.

Bailiwick *n.* the district or jurisdiction of bailiff.

Bailor *n.* one who delivers goods to another for a stated purpose.

Bairn *n.* a child.

Bait *v.t.* & *i.* to tempt to prey; to put food on a hook to catch an animal or fish; to worry by setting dogs.

Baize *n.* table cloth; lining; a thick, coarse woollen stuff used for coverings.

Bake *v.t.* & *i.* to dry; to make hard by beating; to cook something by dry heat; to be or become baked.

Bakery *n.* shop of baker; bakehouse; a place where bread is baked for sale.

Baking *n.* the act of cooking a thing.

Baking-powder *n.* a substitute for yeast; a mixture of powders used to make cakes, etc. rise and become light as they are baked.

Balance *n.* weighing instrument; act of weighing; harmony; equilibrium.

Balcony *n.* platform projecting out of wall; a place for sitting in theatres.

Bald *adj.* hairless; with less hair.

Baldachin *n.* brocade; canopy over altar; throne.

Balderdash *n.* mixed liquid; senseless talk; jumbled things; obscene language or writing.

Baldhead *n.* a man bald on the head.

Bale *n.* bail; injury; mischief; sorrow; a package; bundle; evil; a large mass of paper.

Baleful *adj.* sorrowful; painful; hurtful; threatening evil or harm; pernicious.

Balk, Baulk *ns.* stumbling-block; sanctuary area on billiard table; roughly squared timber beam.

Ball *n.* spherical thing; bullet; heavenly bodies; solid, used especially for kicking, hitting or throwing in games.

Ballad *n.* dance song; short song; song of adventure; popular songs.

Ballad-monger *n.* an inferior poet; dealer in ballads.

Balladry *n.* ballad poetry.

Ballet *n.* performance of dancing on stage; dancing in group.

Ballistic *adj.* pertaining to the throwing fo missiles.

Ballonet *n.* one of the interior gas-bags of an airship.

Balloon *n.* gas-bag which flies in air; anything empty and inflated.

Ballot *n.* small balls or tickets used in voting. *n.* a small bale. **Ballot box,** *n.* box used in voting.

Bally *adj.* & *adv.* (*sl.*) disgust; it expresses speaker's impatience.

Ballyrag *v.t.* & *i.* to make a fool; to laugh at; to play practical jokes.

Balm *n.* fragrant and healing ointment; an oil that is obtained from certain trees and plants.

Balmy *adj.* fragrant; mild; of or like balm; soothing.

Balsam *adj.* a kind of oily healing substance; any of various trees from which balm is obtained.

Baluster *adj.* post supporting handrail of staircase; any of the short pillars forming a balustrade.

Bam *adj.* falsehood, a hoax.

Bamboo *adj.* a tall plant of the grass family with hard hollow stems that are used for making furniture.

Ban *adj.* prohibition; condemnation; banishment. *v.t.* to prohibit; to curse.

Banal *adj.* ordinary; common-place.

Banana *n.* plantation fruit; a fruit tree; its finger shaped fruit.

Band *n.* that which binds or connects moral bond; a number of persons having a common purpose; flat strip of thin material; belt.

Bandage *n.* a strip of material used for tying round and protecting a wound or an injury.

Bandeau *n.* woman's hair band; hat band; fitting band inside woman's hat.

Bandit *n.* a member of an armed gang that robs people; brigand; robber.

Bandog *n.* chained dog; mastiff.

Bandoleer *n.* shoulder with cartridge loops.

Bandoline *n.* moustache gum; gummy preparation for fixing the hair.

Bandy *v.t.* to throw to and fro. *n.* hockey.

Bane *n.* destruction; death poison; evil; cause of ruin; a cause of great trouble or annoyance.

Bang *v.t.* & *i.* to make sound as of blow or explosion; to hit something or put something somewhere so as to make a loud noise; to strike or shut noisily.

Bangle *n.* a ring worn in hand etc.

Banian, Banyan *ns.* Indian flannel jacket; Indian fig whose branches root themselves over large area.

Banish *v.t.* to exile; to dismiss; to drive away.

Banister *n.* stair; baluster.

Banjo *n.* a musical instrument guitar having five strings.

Banjoist *n.* a banjo player.

Bank *n.* raised ground on the side of a sea or river-bed, a flat cloud, sloping edge of river.

Banker *n.* proprietor or director of a bank; a person who owns or manages a bank.

Banket *n.* auriferous conglomerate like pudding-stone found in South Africa.

Bankrupt *n.* unable to pay his debt, whose property is then taken by the court to repay those debts.

Bankshall *n.* the office of a harbour-master or port authority.

Banksia *n.* a flowering shrub.

Banner *n.* the flag of a country, military standard, a symbol of any principle.

Banneret *n.* one knighted on field for valour.

Bannerol *n.* banner, borne at great men's funerals and placed over tomb.

Banns *n. pl.* pre-announce of coming marriage to.

Banquet *n.* a large formal meal, usually for a special event at which speeches are often made.

Banshee *n.* a female spirit that cries loudly and is thought by some to warn of death.

Bantam *n.* a dwarf fowl, a short-man.

Banter *n.* humorous ridicule; a playful friendly exchange of remarks.

Bantling *n.* a little child.

Baptist *n.* one of a sect objecting to infant baptism and practising immersion.

Baptize *v.t.* to administer baptism to.

Bar *n.* a rod or pole, a barrier, bank of sand, a particular court, a pole for fastening a door, hindrance.

Barb *n.* the point of an arrow; a swift horse; a dark pegion; recurved point (of arrow, fish-hook, etc.).

Barbarian *adj.* a foreigner (*historical*) uncivilized person; anyone without refinement; wild.

Barbaric *adj.* rude; uncultured.

Barbarism *adj.* savageness; harshness; life of barbarians.

Barbarous *adj.* uncivilised; uneducated; harsh; wild or savage.

Barbecue *n.* a metal frame for cooking meat; framework for smoking or broiling etc. over an open fire.

Barbel *n.* a large European fresh-water fish with fleshy filaments hanging from mouth.

Barber *n.* a person whose trade is cutting men's hair and sometimes shaving them; a hair-dresser.

Barberry *n.* the oblong red berry of the shrub; red berried hedge.

Barbet *n.* a bird with bristle-tufts at base of bill.

Barbette *n.* platform within fort or in ship from which guns fire over; parapet.

Barbican *n.* outer defence to city or castle. (*esp.* tower over gate).

Barcarole *n.* a gondolier's song; boat song.

Bard *n.* singer; poet; cover to protect; minstrel; a poet.

Bardic *adj.* pertaining to bards or their poetry.

Bare *adj.* to uncover, to reveal. *adj.* uncovered, bald, unprotected, empty.

Bare-faced *adj.* shameless; insolent; beardless; without any cover on face.

Barely *adv.* hardly; scarcely; just this much; in a bare way.

Bargain *n.* agreement; favourable transaction; compact.

Barge *n.* flat-bottomed boat for carrying heavy burden.

Bargee *n.* driver of barge; a man in charge of a barge.

Baritone *adj.* a voice between tenor and bars. *n.* a singer with such a voice.

Barlum *n.* a white metallic element.

Bark, Barque *ns.* a three-masted vessel; small boat.

Bark *n.* outer cover of tree trunk and branches; outer skin.

Barley *n.* a grain; recess in games.

Barm *n.* yeast; forth on fermenting malt liquor.

Barmaid *n.* a women who serves drinks at a bar; a woman attendant at a bar.

Barman *n.* a man who serves drinks at a bar; an attendant at refreshment bar.

Barmecide *adj.* disappointing; illusory; imaginary. *n.* giver of illusory gifts.

Barn *n.* place for storing grain.

Barn-door (*fig.*) *n.* target too large to be missed.

Barnacle (*usu. pl.*) *n.* a kind of goose; a companion who does not leave us.

Barology *n.* science of weight.

Baron *n.* a peer, one of the lowest order of nobility.

Baronage *n.* book with list of barons, the barons.

Baroness *n.* baron's wife, a female baron, lady holding the same rank as a baron.

Baronet *n.* one of the lowest hereditary titled order.

Baronetage *n.* book with list of barons; baronets collectively.

Baronial *adj.* of a baron; suitable for a baron.

Barony *n.* (in Ireland) a territorial division; a large minor.

Baroque *adj.* especially architecture, grotesque; having the highly decorated and elaborate style.

Baroscope *n.* instrument for measuring density of air.

Barouche *n.* a kind of double-seated four-wheeled carriage.

Barque *n.* a small vessel, boat; a sailing ship with 3, 4 or 5 masts and sails.

Barrack *n.* the quarters for army-men; building of severely dull appearance.

Barracoon *n.* slaves house; set of sheds or enclosure (for slaves, convicts, etc.)

Barrage *n.* a dam.

Barrator, -er *n.* malicious raiser of discord; one who excites suits at law.

Barratry *n.* false litigation; fraud or gross negligence of shipmaster or crew in the management of his ship.

Barrel *n.* a round wooden vessel, a cask, the revolving cylinder of a watch, belly of a horse, the tube of a gun, a measure of wine.

Barren *adj.* unproductive; dull; a woman incapable of bearing child.

Barricade *n.* barrier, obstruction.

Barrier *n.* fence to bar passage; an obstacle placed to divide.

Barrister *n.* one who gets a degree of law from U.K.; a lawyer entitled to practise in the superior courts.

Barrow *n.* a two-wheeled truck for carrying loads, an infant's sleeveless coat.

Barter *v.t.* & *i.* to exchange goods for other goods, without using money.

Barton *n.* a farmyard; outhouse.

Basal *adj.* relating to base; situated at base; low; levelled; basic.

Basalt *n.* a kind of brown rock.

Bascule *n.* a kind of lever or drawbridge.

Base *n.* foundation support; bottom lower part; the base of a pillar/column/lamp.

Basement *n.* storey below ground floor, partly or completely below ground level; lowest part of structure.

Bash *v.t.* to strike heavily so as to smash in; to hit something with great force.

Basial *v.t.* pertaining to kissing.

Basic *adj.* of the base, or forming the base; fundamental.

Basil *n.* a kind of herb.

Basilica *n.* an oblong public hall used for law courts or assembles.

Basilicon *n.* black pitch and resin; an ointment composed of yellow wax.

Basilisk *n.* a lizard with crest inflated at will.

Basin *n.* a shallow hollow vessel, a tract of country drained by rivers.

Basis *n.* foundation; base; fundamental principal; beginning.

Bask *v.t.* to enjoy sunshine; to sit or lie, enjoying the warmth or light of something.

Basket *n.* a net in game; back part of coach.

Bas-relief *n.* shallow carving of sculpture on background; a form of sculpture or carving in which the figure or design projects only slightly from its background.

Bass, Bast *ns.* a low music tone; inner bark of lime tree; grave.

Basset *n.* a dog with short legs, used in hunting.

Bassinet *n.* a hooded wicker cradle or perambulator.

Bassoon *n.* a wooden double-reed instrument (used as bass); a musical instrument like a large wooden tube.

Bast *n.* inner bark of lime tree; other flexible fibrous barks.

Bastard *adj.* an illegitimate child.

Bastardy *n.* illegitimateness, child by putative father.

Baste *v.t.* to beat with stick; to pour fat or juices over meat etc. during cooking; to stich slightly.

Bastille *n.* a fortress prison.

Bastinado *v.t.* canning or to cane on soles of feet.

Bastion *n.* defence; fortification tower.

Bat *n.* a mouse-like animal with wings, flat club used in cricket.

Batata *n.* sweet potato.

Batch *n.* a set; a group of things prepared at one time.

Bate *v.t. & i.* to strife; to fall off in force; to let down; to deduct.

Bath *n.* washing; an act of washing the whole body

Bathe *v.t. & i.* to wash or moisten; to apply water to something.

Bathos *n.* a ludicrous descent from the elevated to the mean in writing or speech.

Baton *v.t.* a staff, a constable's truncheon, to strike with a baton.

Batrachian *adj.* of frogs or other animals that discard gills and tail.

Battalion *n.* an infantry group; a large body of men in battle-array.

Batten *n.* a long strip of wood used especially to keep other building materials in place on a wall or roof.

Batter *v.t.* & *i.* to deface; to attack with artillery; to strike repeatedly so as to brusie or break.

Battery *n.* beating; row of cannon; place for artillery; a set of cells.

Batting *n.* prepared cotton sheets for quilting, the management of a bat in playing games.

Battle *n.* a fight; contest between armies, ships or planes; combat (*esp.* of organized forces).

Battledore *n.* a bat for striking shuttlecock; a wooden instrument used in washing.

Bauble *n.* toy; childish plaything; a stick of ass's ear.

Baulk *n.* hindrance; roughly squared wood beam used in house.

Baw-bee *n.* a half penny.

Bawd *n.* a procurer or procuress, a hare.

Bawdy *n.* & *adj.* dealing with sexual matters in an amusing way; obscene.

Bawl *v.t.* & *i.* to noise; to speak noisily; to shout or cry loudly.

Bay *n.* a kind of tree, a recess in sea or mountain, a division of wall, the large barking of dogs, a reddish brown horse.

Bayard *n.* a brave of chivalrous person.

Bayberry *n.* the fruit of a west-Indian tree.

Bayrum *n.* a perfume distilled from bayberry leaves.

Bays *n. pl.* honorary garland of victory.

Baysalt *n.* salt got from sea-water by evaporation.

Bayou *n.* marshy place near lake or river; a part of river away from the main stream that moves slowly and contains many water plants.

Be *v.i.* to live; to exist; to remain; to occur; to continue.

Beach *n.* sea shore or lake shore; sandy or pebby shore of sea.

Beacon *n.* signal fire (signal station), a light house. *v.t.* to show light, to guide, to signal.

Bead *n.* small ball used in rosary; small balls in necklace.

Beadle *n.* Parish officer; church or court officer; mace-bearer.

Beadsman *n.* pensioner who has to pay to benefactor; a person who is bound to pray for benefactor; almsman.

Beady *adj.* bead-like.

Beagle *adj.* small hound used for hunting hares; spy; bailiff.

Beak *n.* a bird's bill; pointed thing; magistrate; school master.

Beaker *n.* a bowl or cup; a small timber like vessel used in laboratories.

Beam *n.* a long piece of timber used in building, the bar of a balance, ray of light, bright look, smile.

Bean *n.* a seed used as food and its plant; any of various smooth seeds that grow in long pods.

Beano *n.* bean-feast; jubilation; disturbance; any frolicsome enjoyment.

Bear *n.* thick-furred quadruped, an unmannerly person.

Bear *n.* to carry, to sustain weight etc., to strive, to produce, to give birth to, to behave, to produce fall in price.

Beard *n.* barb of arrow; a tuft of hair; hair of grain; hair growing on the chin and the lower cheeks of a man's face; awn of grass.

Bearish *adj.* like a bear, churlish, uncouth.

Beast *n.* quadruped animal; brutal person; an animal especially a large one with four feet.

Beat *v.t.* & *i.* to strike repeatedly, to thrash, to bruise by pounding, to agitate by beating, to baffle, to harass, to vanquish, to throb.

Beater *n.* a person employed to drive birds and animals out of bushes; a man employed to rouse game.

Beatitude *n.* supreme bliss of heaven; blessedness.

Beau *n.* fashionable person; fop; a lover; a rich fashionable young man who is fond of fine dress.

Beauideal *n.* one's highest type of excellence or beauty.

Beautiful *n.* handsome; praise-worthy; charming; delicious; having beauty.

Beautify *v.t.* to make beautiful; to adorn; to make somebody beautiful.

Beauty *n.* hand-someness; charm; a handsome lady.

Beaver *n.* an amphibious rodent. *n.* the face-guard of a helmet.

Becall *v.t.* to abuse; to call (person) names.

Becalm *v.t.* to make calm; to deprive a ship of wind.

Became *p.t.* of Become. to come to be; to grow to be.

Because *adv.* due to the cause; by reason of.

Bechance *v.t.* to befall, to happen.

Beck *n.* a brook; mountain stream; sign by nod of head or movement of finger.

Beckon *v.t.* & *i.* to call by nod, arm or head, usually to make them come nearer or to follow.

Becloud *v.t.* to cover with clouds.

Become *v.t.* & *i.* to come to be; to come into existence; to happen; to suit.

Bed *n.* a thing to sleep on, a layer of earth, floor, mattress, bottom of a river.

Bedaub *v.t.* to smear with paint, etc.

Bedding *n.* mattres and bed-clothes.

Bedeck *v.t.* to adorn.

Bedel *n.* an official with duties chiefly processional.

Bedevil *v.t.* to cause somebody great trouble continually; to treat very cruelly; to bewitch,

Bedew *v.t.* to moisten gently.

Bed-fellow *n.* a sharer of the bed; a person with whom one shares a bed.

Bedim *v.t.* to make dim.

Bedizen *n.* to dress out gaudily.

Bedlam *n.* a hospital for lunatics, a madhouse. *adj.* fit for a madhouse.

Bedlamite *n.* a lunatic; a mad-man.

Bedouin *n.* of the desert; gipsy.

Bedplate *n.* garden plot filled with plants; bottom of sea, river; metal plate forming the base of a machine, etc.

Bedpost *n.* the post of a bedstead; the corners of a bed (especially old-fashioned type).

Bedrabbled *adj.* dirty with rain and mud.

Bedraggle *v.t.* to soil by drawing along on mud.

Bedrench *v.t.* to saturate, to drench.

Bee *n.* insect that gathers honey; persons gathered for combined labour.

Beech *n.* a common forest tree; a type of tree with smooth bark, shiny leaves and small nuts or wood of this tree.

Beech-mast *n.* the mast or nuts of the beech-tree.

Beef *n.* the flesh of a cow, a bull, or an ox; oxen fattend for beef.

Bee-hive *adj.* article dwelling for bees.

Beeline *n.* the direct line or nearest distance between two places.

Bee-master *n.* the keeper of bees.

Beer *n.* a kind of barley wine; an alcoholic drink made from malt and flavoured with hops.

Beery *adj.* like or smelling of beer; influenced by the drinking of beer.

Bees-wax *n.* wax prepared by bees; wax made by bees and used for making wood polish, candles, etc.

Beeswing *n.* old wine; second crust in long-kept port.

Beet *n.* a kind of vegetable used for food.

Beetle *n.* any of several types of insect, often large and black, with hard wing-case; a kind of insect.

Befall *v.t. & i.* to happen; to occur; to come; to pass.

Befit *v.t. & i.* to be suitable to, to become.

Befool *v.t.* to make a fool of; to dupe.

Before *adv.* ahead, previously, in the past.

Befoul *v.t.* to make foul; to defy; to make dirty.

Befriend *v.t.* to favour, to help, to assit.

Beg *v.t. & i.* live by begging; to ask for favour; to request; to beseech; to ask for something by way of alms.

Beget *v.t.* to procreate; to give rise to; to generate.

Beggar *n.* a person who lives by begging; poor or penniless person; one who begs.

Begin *v.t. & i.* to set about; to make a start with; to do the first part of something; to start; to originate.

Beginning *n.* the place or time at which something starts.

Begird *v.t.* to encircle, to surround.

Begone *inter.* go away.

Begonia *inter.* a plant with petalless flowers and ornamental foliage.

Begrime *v.t.* to make grimy; to soil deeply.

Begrudge *v.t.* to show dissatisfaction.

Beguile *v.t.* to deceive; to dupe; to deviate; to amuse.

Begun past participle of Begin.

Behalf *n.* favour; advantage; support; interest.

Behave *v.t.* to treat with good manners; to act or react in the specified way.

Behaviour *n.* conduct; actions; manners; treatment; the way somebody behaves.

Behead *v.t.* to cut off the head of, to kill in this way.

Behemoth *v.t.* a huge creature.

Behind *adv. & prep.* opposite of before; backward; after; inferior.

Behold *v.t.* to see; to view; to observe; to take notice.

Beholden *v.t.* obliged; indebted; under obligation to.

Behoof *v.t.* advantage; convenience; profit; use.

Behove, Behoove *v.t.* to befit; to become; to be proper; to be incumbent on; to be necessary.

Beige *n.* a kind of dress material of undyed unbleached wool of a very light yellowish brown colour.

Being *n.* existence; any thing existing or living; nature; substance.

Bejewelled *adj.* wearing several jewels.

Belabour *v.t.* to hit somebody hard and repeatedly; to beat soundly.

Belated *adj.* old-fashioned; out-of-date; coming very late or too late.

Belaud *v.t.* to praise highly; to heap praises on; to load with praise.

Belay *v.t.* to fix a rope round a peg to coil rope (round cleat, etc.) to secure it, in climbing and sailing.

Belch *v.i. & t.* to emit wind from throat, to utter noisily.

Belcher *n.* a parti-coloured neckerchief.

Beldam, Beldame *ns.* old woman; an angry woman; virago.

Beleaguer *v.t.* to surround; to besiege.

Belemnite *v.t.* a tapering sharp-pointed fossil bone of extinct cuttlefish.

Belfry *n.* the part of a church tower in which bells hang; bell tower.

Belial *n.* the devil. *adj.* wicked.

Belie *v.t.* to falsify; to fail to confirm or act up to; to give false picture of.

Belief *n.* assurance; surity; trust; faith; opinion; a feeling that somebody is real and true.

Believe *v.t.* & *i.* to trust; to take as true; to feel sure of the truth of something.

Believer *n.* one who believes, or has faith, (*esp.*) adherent of one's religion.

Belittle *v.t.* to make small, to depreciate, to discharge.

Bell *n.* any thing bell shaped; bubble of water; a hollow metal object.

Bell *n.* sound of bell as a time signal; the baying cry of certain animals.

Belladonna *adj.* deadly night-shade.

Belle *n.* a handsome woman; reigning beauty.

Belles-letters *n.* studies or writing of purely literary kind.

Bellicose *adj.* of fighting nature; war-like; showing eagerness to fight.

Belligerency *n.* status of a nation etc. engaged in conflict or war.

Bellman *n.* a public crier who uses a bell.

Bellmetal *n.* alloy of tin and copper. (used for making bells.)

Bellona *n.* Roman Goddess of war; a vigorous woman; a woman of commanding presence.

Bellow *v.i.* & *t.* to roar violently; to shout with pain.

Bellows *n. pl.* an apparatus for blowing air into or through something.

Bellwether *n.* leading sheep of flock with a bell on the neck; a ring leader.

Belly *n.* stomach; front part; middle bulging part of pot; womb; abdomen.

Bellygod (a glutton).

Belong *v.t.* to be connected with; to be property of or member of or citizen of, etc.

Beloved *adj.* dearly loved.

Belt *n.* a distinctive geographic region; strip; a fixable bank used in machines.

Belting *n.* belts connectd with machinery.

Belvedere *n.* high turret on house; a house on high place.

Bema *n.* a platform in ancient Athenian public assembly; platform for delivering speeches.

Bemask *v.i.* to conceal, to mask.

Bemire *v.t.* to spoil with mud; to cover with mire; to drag or sink in the mire.

Bemoan *v.t.* to express sorrow for; to express one's sorrow or disappoint- ment about something.

Bemuse *v.t.* to stupefy, to confuse.

Bench *n.* a wooden seat; working table of carpenter, etc.

Bencher *n.* senior member (sharing management) of Inns of Court.

Bend *v.t.* & *i.* to give a curved shape; to slant; to turn downward; to bow.

Bender *n.* one that bends; an instrument used for bending.

Beneath *adv.* & *prep.* below; behind; at a lower level; not befitting; in or to a lower position than somebody.

Benedick *adv.* & *prep.* newly-married man (*esp.* confirmed bachelor who marries).

Benediction *n.* a prayer of blessing, especially one utterances before a meal or at the end of a church service; utterance of a blessing.

Benefaction *n.* good work done for any one; the action of giving something for a good cause or of doing good.

Benefactor *n.* hospital, charity, etc.; one who has given friendly aid.

Benefice *n.* a church living.

Beneficent *adj.* giving benefit; showing active kindness.

Beneficiary *n.* the main beneficiary of a will, connected with the receipt of benefits; profits or advantages.

Benefit *n.* advantage, favour.

Benevolence *n.* charity; kind act; generosity; gift to help poor.

Benight *v.t.* to cover with darkness.

Benighted *adj.* ignorant; without moral or intellectual understanding; overtaken by night; involved in intellectual or moral darkness.

Benign *adj.* kind; favourable; gentle; not likely to spread or occur again after treatment.

Benignity *n.* kindliness; graciousness.

Benison *n.* a blessing, a benediction.

Benjamin *n.* youngest son; dearest son; an old fashioned chester.

Bent *adj.* inclination, tendency, ready grass.

Benumb *v.t.* to make numb or senseless; to perplex; to paralyse; to deprive of sensation.

Benzene *n.* a mixture of mineral oils etc. used for removing stains.

Benzine *n.* a mineral oil used as motor fuel and used for removing stains.

Benzoin *n.* an aromatic resin.

Benzoline *n.* benzine.

Bequeath *v.t.* to leave after death; to give in trust; to arrange, by making a will, to give property, money.

Bequest *n.* property left by will, a legacy.

Berate *v.t.* to chide very much; to speak to or criticize somebody angrily.

Bere *n.* barley.

Bereave *v.t.* to deprive of any thing, or any relative.

Beret *n.* a round flat cap with no peak, usually made of soft cloth.

Bereft *adj.* bereaved.

Berg *n.* ceberg; mountain.

Bergamot *n.* a tree of orange kind; a kind of pear.

Berry *n.* any small round juicy containing stoneless fruit.

Berserk *n.* wild; crazy; in a violentraze.

Berth *n.* sleeping place in aircraft, ship or train; any alloted place.

Berthage *n.* money paid for the accomodation of a ship in a dock.

Beseech *v.t.* to ask earnestly for; to pray; to request; to solicit; to ask in an urgent begging way; to beg eagerly for.

Beseem *v.t.* to become; to suit; to be fitting; to be worthy of.

Beset *v.i.* to encircle; to trouble or threaten somebody constantly and from all sides.

Beshame *v.t.* to make ashamed.

Beshrew *v.t.* to execrate; to wish a curse to.

Beside *prep.* near; by the side of; at the side of somebody; apart from; over and above; next to somebody.

Besides *adv. & prep.* in addition to; otherwise than; as well; also; else.

Besieger *n.* one who lays a siege.

Beslaver *v.t.* to flatter fulsomely; to cover with slaver.

Beslobber *v.t.* to besmear with spittle; to kiss badly.

Besmear *v.t.* with greasy or sticky to smear all over; to soil.

Besmirch *v.t.* to damage the reputation of somebody in the opinion of others.

Besom *n.* a kind of broom.

Besot *v.t.* to stupefy mentally or morally.

Besotted *adj.* stupefied with drink.

Besought *v.t.*

Bespangle *v.t.* to cover with spangles; to sprinkle with something brilliant.

Bespatter *v.t.* to spatter all over; to cover with abuse of flattery.

Bespeak *v.t.* to engage beforehand.

Bespeed *v.t.* to hurry up.

Besprinkle *v.t.* to sprinkle or strew over with; to scatter over.

Best *adj.* of the highest quality, excellence or standing.

Bestain *v.t.* to mark with spots or strains.

Bestead *v.t. & i.* to be of use of; to avail; to help; to assist.

Bested *adj.* (with all, hard, sore, etc.) circumstanced; pressed.

Bestial *adj.* brutish, rude, barbarous.

Bestiality *n.* sexual activity between a human animal; beastliness.

Bestiary *n.* one of those books written in the middle ages treating fancifully of the qualities of beasts.

Bestill *v.t.* to make still or quite.

Bestir *v.t.* to rouse oneself; to become active or busy.

Bestow *v.t.* to confer; to place; to deposit; to confer upon; to present something as a gift to somebody.

Bestowal *n.* disposal.

Bestrew *n.* to scatter about.

Bestride *v.t.* to sit astride on (horse, chair, *etc.*); to stand; to astride over.

Bestud *v.t.* to adorn with studs.

Bet *v.i.* & *t.* to stake; to wager; to risk money on a race or some other event of which the result is doubtful.

Betake *v.t.* to go to; to have recourse to; to resort.

Betel *n.* leaf of a plant chewed with areca nut.

Betal-nut *n.* areca nut.

Beteem *v.t.* to bring forth, to shed.

Bethel *n.* Christian sect; a Churchship; hallowed spot.

Bethink *n.* to recollect; to think over; to ponder; to take into one's head to.

Betide *v.i.* & *i.* to happen; to befall.

Betimes *adv.* early, in good time.

Betoken *v.t.* to suggest; to show by sign; to symbolise; to indicate.

Beteem *v.t.* to bring forth, to shed.

Betray *v.t.* to let down; to prove treacherous to; disclose; to act basely to seduce.

Betrayal *n.* betraying; a breach of trust; an act of treachery.

Betroth *v.t.* to make as marriage contract; to bind with promise to marry.

Better *adj.* superior; more excellent or desirable; having good qualities.

Better, Bettor *ns.* one who bets.

Betters *n. pl.* superiors.

Between *prep.* along; reciprocally, on the part of; in or into the space separating two or more points.

Betwixt *prep.* & *adv.* between.

Bevel *n.* a tool for making sloping edges or surfaces on wood or stone.

Beverl-gear *n.* cogged wheels revolving in different directions.

Beverage *n.* liquor; tea; wine; drink; any type of drink except water; beer.

Bevy *n.* a group of ladies; a flock of roes, larks; a company (of ladies, roes, quails, larks).

Bewail *v.t.* & *i.* to complain about something.

Beware *v.t.* & *t.* to take precaution; to be one's guard; to be cautions of somebody.

Bewet *v.t.* to wet, to moisten.

Bewilder *v.t.* to puzzle; lead astray; to confound; to confuse somebody.

Bewitch *v.t.* to allure; to enchant; to fascinate; to please.

Bewitching *adj.* fascinating; charming; enchanting; attractive and delightful; captivating.

Bewary *v.t.* to betray; to reveal or disclose perfidiously.

Bey *n.* Turkish Governor.

Beyond *adv. & prep.* at the farthest side; above; outside.

Bezel *n.* the sloped edge of a chisel, upper part of the collect of a ring.

Bezique *n.* a card game.

Bi *pref.* in the sense of, "twice, doubly, twofold".

Bias *n.* in the game of bowling greater weight kept on one side of the bowl so that the bowl turns more to one side.

Biaxial *adj.* with two axes.

Bib *v.i. & t.* to sip; to tripple; to drink frequently.

Bibber *n.* one given to drinking.

Bible *n.* the Scriptures consisting of the Old and New Testaments; the sacred writings of the Christian Church.

Bibliomania *n.* a rage for collecting rare and curious books.

Bibulous *adj.* absorbent; excessively fond of alcoholic drink; addicted to drink.

Bicameral *adj.* having two chambers (of a legislative body).

Bice *n.* a green paint; a dull blue or green pigment.

Bicephalus *adj.* two headed.

Biceps *n.* a two headed muscle, which bends the elbow.

Bicker *v.i.* to quarrel, to run quickly.

Bickering *n.* quarrelling; wrangling.

Bicuspid *n.* two-cusped; (tooth) with two cups or points.

Bicycle *n.* a two wheeled vehicle propelled by feet.

Bid *v.t. & i.* to command; to propose; to offer; to offer a price in order to buy something; to proclaim.

Biddable *adj.* obedient; docile; capable of being bid.

Bidder *n.* one who bids; one who offers a price at an action.

Biddery, Bidree *ns.* tin; lead and zinc; an alloy of copper.

Bidding *n.* command, order.

Bide *v.t. & i.* to endure; to dwell; to wait; to remain; to wait for a good opportunity.

Bidental *adj.* having two teeth.

Bield *n.* a sheltered place.

Biennial *adj.* appearing or recurring once in two years.

Bier *n.* a wooden frame or carriage to carry the dead to the grave.

Bifacial *adj.* having two opposite faces alike.

Biff *n.* a smart blow, especially with the fist.

Biffin *n.* a red cooking apple.

Bifold *adj.* folded into two.

Bifurcate *v.t. & i.* to fork; to divide into or have two branches.

Bifurcation *n.* a division into two parts or branches.

Big *n.* grown up; large; pregnant; great; full; important; magnanimous.

Bigamist *n.* one who has married two husbands or two wives at a time.

Bigamous *adj.* guilty of or involving bigamy.

Bigential *n.* of two tribes.

Bight *n.* a curve; bend or coil; a wide bay, coast etc.; small bay.

Bigot *n.* a blind and obstinate; follower or adherent of one's faith.

Bigoted *n.* having the character of a bigot.

Bigotry *n.* narrow-minded zeal for one's creed or party.

Bijouterie *n.* jewelry.

Bike *n.* (colloq.) a short term used for bicycle; a nest of bees or wasps.

Bilateral *adj.* having two sides.

Bilberry *adj.* a shrub with a deep-blue edible fruit.

Bilbo *n.* a rapier; a sword.

Bilboes *n. pl.* an iron bar with sliding shackles for prisoners.

Bile *n.* a bitter fluid secreted by the liver.

Bilge *n.* the nearly horizontal part of a ship's bottom; broadest part of a ship's bottom.

Biliary *adj.* of the bile.

Bilingual *adj.* speaking or using two languages.

Bilious *adj.* pertaining to or affected with excess of bile, melancholic.

Biliteral *adj.* consisting of two letters.

Bilk *v.t.* to evade; to cheat; to elude; to evade payment; to give the slip to.

Bill *n.* a bird's beak, draft of a proposed act, note of charge for goods, a placard, a kind of long-handled axe.

Billet *n.* a thick piece of wood, a small bar of metal, soldier's quarters. *v.t.* to quarter of lodge soldiers.

Billiards *n.* a kind of game played with cues and ivory balls on cloth-covered table.

Billingsgate *n.* abuse, foul language.

Billion *n.* a million millions.

Billow *n.* a great wave of sea. *v.t.* & *i.* to rise or roll like waves.

Billy *n.* in Australia it is used as tea pot or boiling pan.

Billycock *n.* a kind of felt hat, a bowler.

Billy-goat *n.* a male goat.

Bimensal *adj.* occurring once in two months.

Bimetallic *adj.* of using both gold and silver as standard in currency.

Bimetallist *n.* one who favours bimetallism.

Bimonthly *adj.* occurring once in every two month.

Bin *n.* receptacle for dust; a place for storing corn and bottle wine; a large container for coal, etc or for putting rubbish in, usually with a lid.

Binary *adj.* two-fold; of pairs; of two dual.

Bind *v.t.* & *i.* to fasten, to attach, to restrain, to subject to legal obligation, to be obligatory, to impose restraint.

Binder *n.* a book-binder; a cover for holding sheets of paper.

Binding *n.* the act of one that binds; the cover that holds together the pages of a book.

Binnacle *n.* the compass box on deck; the box of ship's compass.

Binocular *adj.* suitable for use with both eyes; relating to, used by, or involving both eyes simultaneously.

Binomial *adj.* consisting of two terms, of two names.

Biograph *n.* continuous photographic representation.

Biographer *n.* writer of biography.

Biological *adj.* relating to biology; pertaining to biology.

Bioplasm *n.* germinal matter; the substance constituting the living matter of the elementary cell in plants and animals.

Bioplast *n.* small separate portion of bioplasm.

Bioscope *n.* a cinematograph.

Bipartite *adj.* having two correspondent part; divided into two parts.

Bipartition *n.* involving two political parties; the act of making or state of being bipartite.

Biped *adj.* a creature with two feet.

Bipedal *adj.* having two feet.

Biplane *n.* an early type of aircarft with two sets of wings, one above the other, two-planed aeroplane.

Birch *adj.* a kind of tree or its twigs used for punishment, with smooth bark and thin branches.

Bird *n.* a feathered vertebrate.

Biretta *n.* a square cap of the roman Catholic and other clerics.

Birth *n.* bringing forth of a baby; coming into the world; begining; origin.

Biscuit *n.* a thin; hard bread in cakes; a small flat thin piece of pastry baked until it is crisp.

Bisect *v.t.* to divide something into two (usually equal) parts.

Bisection *n.* division of any line or two equal parts.

Bisector *n.* something that bisects; a bisecting line.

Bisexual *adj.* hermaphrodite; sexually attracted to both men and women.

Bishop *n.* a consecrated clergyman, one of the pieces or men in chess, a tasteful hot drink mixed with red wine.

Bisk *n.* rich soup made by boiling birds etc.

Bismuth *n.* a reddish-white metal used as alloy etc.

Bison *n.* large wild animal like ox.

Bisque *n.* right of scoring unearned point at tennis, or playing extra turn at croquet, etc.

Bissextile *adj.* containing the extra day of leap year.

Bistoury *n.* a surgeon's narrow knife.

Bistre *n.* a dark-brown pigment prepared from the soot of wood.

Bistro *n.* a small restaurant.

Bit *n.* a small piece; iron mouth-piece in bridle; a morsel of food or bite.

Bitch *n.* wolf, or fox; a female dog or other animal of the dog family.

Bite *v.t. & i.* to tear with teeth; to penetrate; to eat; to grip.

Biter *n.* one who bites, a thief.

Biting *adj.* stinging; sarcastic; severe; sharp; pungent; causing a sharp pain.

Bitingly *adv.* in a biting manner.

Bitter *adj.* acrimonious testing bitter and acid; painful; having a sharp and often unpleasant taste.

Bitts *n. pl.* pair of posts for fastening cables.

Bitumen *n.* a name applied to various inflammable mineral substances, used for covering roads or roof.

Bivalve *adj.* with two valves, and shellfish with a double shell.

Bivouac *n.* a temporary camp without tents or any other cover, used especially by soldiers or people climbing mountains.

Bi-weekly *adj.* twice in every week.

Bizarre *adj.* fantastic; odd; extravagant; of fantastic appearance or effect.

Blab *v.t. & i.* to tell stories blunder; to reveal a secret, especially by talking carelessly, foolish talk.

Black *adj.* dark coloured, dirty, gloomy, wicked, dismal.

Blackbeetle *n.* cockroach.

Blackberry *n.* a plant of the bramble kind, which is of black colour.

Black board *n.* a black board used in schools and such places to write with chalk.

Blacken *v.t. & i.* to make black, to darken.

Black guardly *adj.* rascal; characteristic of a black guard; villainous.

Blacking *n.* paste used for blacking shoes.

Black-lead *n.* a kind of lead.

Black-leg *n.* a swindler *esp.* on the turf; a workman who works for an employer whose men are on strike.

Blackmail *n.* money given as tribute to robbers; hush-money.

Blackshirt *n.* a member of a fascist (Fascism) organization, especially one with a black shirt as part of its uniform.

Blacksmith *n.* iron smith; a smith working in iron.

Blackthorn *n.* a shrub bearing sloes; a pickly shrub with white flowers and purple fruit.

Blackwood *n.* various species of trees and their timber.

Bladder *n.* membraneous bag containing urine, anything inflated, windbag.

Blade *n.* a leaf of grass; the sharp parts of a knife.

Blaeberry *n.* bilberry.

Blain *n.* a boil; an inflated sore.

Blamable *adj.* deserving of blame.

Blame *v.t.* to find fault with; to fix the responsibility on; to censure.

Blanch *v.t.* & *i.* to turn white; to whiten; to make white with something.

Bland *adj.* gentle in manner; polite; mild; balmy; suave.

Blandish *v.t.* to cajole; to flatter.

Bladishment *n.* flattery; enticing expressions or actions.

Blank *adj.* not written upon, empty, void, white.

Blanket *n.* woolen sheet used for covering. *v.t.* to cover with a blanket.

Blankly *adv.* in a blank manner; helplessly; flatly.

Blare *v.t.* & *i.* to roar, to make a loud harsh sound like a trumpet

Blarney *n.* friendly but empty talk; pleasant or convincing talk that is intended to flatter or persuade.

Blaspheme *v.t.* & *i.* to speak in a very rude way about God or sacred things.

Blasphemy *n.* impious speech.

Blast *n.* a strong gust of wind; sound of a wind instrument; explosion.

Blastoderm *n.* the germinal skin or superficial layer of an embryo in its earliest condition.

Blatant *n.* vulgarly clamorous; done openly and without shame.

Blather *v.i.* to talk foolishly.

Blatter *v.t.* to patter, to talk over much.

Blauwbok *n.* a south-African large antelope with bluish hair.

Blaze *n.* bright flame or fire, glow, white mark on cow's head, mark made on the bark of trees.

Blazer *n.* one who spreads news; that which blazes.

Blazon *v.t.* coat of arms.

Blazonry *n.* art of describing or painting heraldic devices.

Bleach *v.t.* & *i.* to wash white; to become or cause something to become white or pale by a chemical process or the effect or sunlight.

Bleak *adj.* bare, chilly, dreary, dull and cheerless, a small white river fish.

Blear *v.t.* to blur; to make dull; to make dim sighted.

Bleat *v.t.* & *i.* to cry like a sheep, goat or calf; to speak foolishly.

Bleed *v.t.* & *i.* to emit blood; to draw blood, to die by slaughter, to feel pity for.

Blemish *n.* flaw; reproach; defect; a mark or fault spoiling something that is otherwise beautiful or perfect.

Blench *v.i.* to flinch; to shrink; to start aside; to quail; to close the eyes to.

Blend *v.t.* & *i.* to mix together, to mingle, to confound. *n.* a mixture.

Blende *n.* native sulphide of zinc.

Bless *v.t.* to invoke blessings or good fortune; to glorify.

Blessed, Blest *adjs.* holy; honoured in the Roman Catholic Church; fortunate; revered; in paradise.

Blether *v.i.* & *n.* to talk nonsense; non-sensical talk.

Blewit *v.i.* & *n.* a late edible mushroom with lilac stem.

Blight *n.* disease of plants and vegetables; rust; damp.

Blighty *v.i.* & *n.* deep wound necessitating one's return to his own native country.

Blimey *inter.* an exclamation expressing surprise, or annoyance.

Blind *adj.* without sight, without intelligence, heedless, inconsiderate.

Blindage *n.* sieges, screen for troops in fortification, etc.

Blindfold *adj.* & *adv.* to cover eyes with bandage so as not to see.

Blindworm *n.* a small harmless worm-like reptile.

Blink *v.t* & *i.* to wink, to ignore *n.* glance, glimmer, wink.

Blinkers *n. pl.* leather pieces fixed on a horse's bridle to prevent the horse from seeing sideways.

Bliss *n.* highest happiness or blessedness; heavenly happiness; great joy.

Blister *adj.* swelling on skin filled with serum. *v.t.* to raise a blister.

Blithe *adj.* gay; cheerful; sprightly; jocund; happy and not anxious.

Blizzard *n.* a severe snowstorm with strong winds, intense cold and fine drifting snow; a snow-squall.

Bloat *v.t.* & *i.* to inflate or swell, to puff off, to grow turgid.

Bloater *n.* a herring that has been preserved with salt and wood smoke.

Blob *n.* a drop of liquid; a globule; a small round mass or spot of colour.

Block *n.* a large piece of wood, solid piece of wood on which figures are cut or engraved, a continuous row of buildings, mould, a bulky piece, a pulley, an obstruction.

Blond, Blonde *ns.* a person of fare complexion and light coloured hair.

Blood *n.* the red liquid which circulates in the veins and arteries of men and animals, offspring, murder, temperament, family.

Blood-relation *n.* of common ancestry; one related by blood (not by marriage).

Bloody *n.* covered with blood; bleeding; pertaining to blood; involving bloodshed; cruel.

Bloom *n.* a bud, flower, freshness, prime, perfection.

Bloomer *n.* (*slang*) a serious mistake.

Bloomers *n.* short loose trousers gathered at the knee for riding bicycles, etc.

Blore *n.* a voilent gust of wind.

Blossom *n.* flower, early growth.

Blot *n.* a drop of ink; a blemish; a kind of game; weak point in anything; a spawn; a mushroom.

Blotch *n.* an eruption upon the skin.

Blotter *n.* pad of blotting-paper.

Blotting-paper *n.* absorbent paper drying ink-marks.

Blouse *n.* a kind of bodice worn by the women (like the smock-froch), grid up at the waist; a garment like a shirt.

Blow *v.t.* & *i.* blowing of flute etc., blossoming, a hard stroke, shock.

Blower *n.* a contrivance for producing current of air into a furnace.

Blowfly *n.* a meat fly.

Blowpipe *n.* a tube for heating flame by blowing air into it.

Blowy *adj.* windy; windswept.

Blub *v.i.* (School *sl*ang) to shed tears.

Blubber *n.* fat of a whale.

Bluchers *n. pl.* old-fashioned low-cut or high laced boots.

Bludgeon *n.* a short thick stick with a heavy end used as a weapon.

Blue *adj.* of colour of the sky; greyish; scholarly; obsence; blue as symbol.

Bluff *adj.* outspoken; rough and coarse; hearty; blunt; braver, than one really is.

Blunder *v.t.* & *i.* a gross of stupid mistake. *v.i.* to make a gross mistake.

Blunt *adj.* dull; rough; outspoken; barren; without a sharp edge or a point; plain-spoken.

Blur *n.* a stain, a spot, a blemish. *v.t.* to smear, to disfigure, to blemish.

Blurb *n.* (*sl.*) publishers comments on the book commonly printed on the jacket of the book.

Blurt *v.t.* to speak out suddenly; to utter abruptly or tactlessly (*usu.* blurt out); to say something suddenly and without careful consideration.

Blush *v.i.* to become red with shame, joy etc., to be ashamed.

Bluster *v.i.* & *t.* to storm rage; to talk in an aggressive way; to storm boisterously (of wind, waves, persons).

Boa *n.* a large S. American snake that kills animals for food by winding its long body round them and crushing them; a woman's long fur throat warp.

Boanerges *n.* a loud-voiced preacher or orator.

Boar *n.* a male pig (*fem.* Sow).

Boarish *adj.* brutal, cruel.

Board *n.* strip of timber; stift paper; table; supply of food.

Boarder *n.* one who lives in another's house, one who boards with another.

Boast *v.i.* self-exaltation. *v.i.* brag, to be proud of.

Boat *n.* a small craft moved by oars.

Boater *n.* a hard straw hat with a flat top.

Boat-house *n.* a shed at water's edge for keeping boats.

Boatswain *n.* ship's officer in charge of sails, etc.

Boatyard *n.* a place where boats are kept, hired out, repaired, etc.

Bob *n.* weight on pendulum, knot of hair, short jerking, motion, worm-bait for fish.

Bobbin *n.* a spool for holding thread.

Bobby *n.* (*sl.*) a policemen (used in slang).

Bobolink *n.* the song-bird of the United States (so called from its cry).

Bobstay *n.* a rope holding bow-spirit down.

Bobtail *n.* tail cut short, the rabble.

Bobwig *adj.* short-curled. not full-bottomed.

Boche *n.* & *adj.* German.

Bode *v.t.* & *i.* to prophecy to foretell; to foresee; to be a good/ bad sign for somebody.

Bodeful *adj.* ominous; threatening; foreboding.

Bodice *n.* a women's (close fitting) garment, corset.

Bodkin *n.* a long thick-eyed pin.

Body *n.* main or whole part of animal or man; main part of anything.

Body-guard *n.* a guardian, escort.

Boer *n.* a South-African of Dutch descent. *adj.* of Boers.

Bog *n.* quagmire; mud; morass; piece of wet spongy ground.

Boggle *v.i.* to start with fear, to hesitate.

Bog-trotter *n.* an Irish-man.

Boggy *adj.* (of land) soft and wet; spongy; marshy; miry.

Bogie *n.* a railway car; an undercarriage, with two or more wheel-pairs, pivoted below the end of a locomotive.

Bogus *adj.* sham; fictitious; without any substance; not genuine.

Bogy *adj.* the devil; goblin; bugbear; (in golf) the score of one over the standard for a hole.

Bohea *adj.* black tea of lowest quality (last crop of the season).

Bohemian *adj.* & *n.* a man of free and easy habits, manners.

Boil *n.* a hard tumour, boiling point.

Boiling *n.* at boiling point; angry; food prepared by boiling.

Boiling-point *n.* temperature at which anything boils (water at sea-level, 212° F., 100°C.); high excitement.

Boisterous *adj.* (of people or behaviour) noisy; lively and cheerful.

Bold *adj.* brave, courageous, daring, immodest, rude.

Bole *n.* the main stem or trunk of a tree.

Bolero *n.* a type of Spanish dance. a woman's short loose jacket with or without sleeves.

Boll *n.* a cotton seed; the part of cotton plant that contains the seeds.

Bollard *n.* a short thick post on a ship or on land close to water, to which a ship's rope may be tied.

Bolster *n.* a round long stuffed pillow.

Bolt *n.* a short arrow, quarrel, discharge of lightning, screwed metal pin with head and nut, a door fastener, sudden start.

Bolt, Boult *v.t.* to sift; to investigate.

Bolter *n.* a sieve.

Bolus *n.* a bit pill.

Boma *n.* enclosure with fencing.

Bomb *n.* hollow shell containing explosives; lava mass thrown by volcano.

Bombard *v.t.* to batter with bombs.

Bombasine *n.* a twilled fabric (ordinary black) of worsted with silk or cotton or alone (much used for mourning).

Bombast *n.* high-sounding words; cotton wool; inflated talk.

Bonafide *adj.* & *adv.* with good faith, genuine.

Bonanza *n.* gold mass; mine of wealth; good luck; a rich mine.

Bonbon *n.* sweetmeat; a Christmas cracker.

Bond *n.* anything that binds, restraining, force, agreement, link or connection, obligation in writing.

Bondage *n.* serfdom or slavery; the state of being a slave or prisoner; confinement; constraint.

Bondsman *n.* a serf; slave; one bound to service without wages.

Bone *n.* a white hard substance which constitutes the skeleton of a body.

Bongo *n.* either of a pair of small drums played with the fingers.

Bonhomie *n.* frankness; free and easy manner; cheerful; friendliness.

Boniface *n.* an inkeeper.

Bonnet *n.* woman's headdress, a protective cap.

Bonny *adj.* comely; healthy-looking; attractive or beautiful; satisfactory.

Bontebok *adj.* a South African antelope (also called Pied Antelope).

Bonus *adj.* something given by way of bargain, extra dividend given to shareholders.

Bony *adj.* full of bones; thin; having much bone; bigboned.

Bonze *adj.* a Japanese or Chinese Buddhist priest.

Boo *inter.* & *n.* make sound of disapproval.

Boob *inter.* & *n.* a stupid mistake; dunce; one easily misled.

Boodle money acquired by bad means *i.e.* by fraud or bribe; crowd.

Book *n.* a literary composition, the Bible, division of a poem.

Bookie *n.* a betting bookmaker.

Booking-office *n.* an office for sale of tickets.

Bookish *adj.* fond of or familiar with books only, not experienced in worldy affairs.

Book-keeper *n.* a person whose job is keeping a record of the financial affairs of a business.

Book muslin *n.* a fine kind of muslin folded like a book.

Book-plate *n.* a special label with owner's name, for pasting into books.

Book-post *n.* printed matter which is sent by post at a lower charge.

Book-shop *n.* a shop which sells mainly books.

Book-work *n.* the study of rules, etc. (as opposed to practice).

Book-worm *n.* a great reader; a book-destroying maggot.

Boom *n.* a long spar which extends to the bottom of a sail.

Boomerang *n.* an Australian missile of curved wood that can be so thrown as to return to the thrower.

Boon *n.* a request; present; blessing; a favour; gift.

Boor *n.* farmer; villager; rude or uncultured fellow; South African Dutch; a rough or rude person; rustic.

Boost *v.t.* to help or encourage somebody; to lift-up; to increase the strength or value of something.

Boosy *adj.* a little intoxicated.

Boot *n.* a covering for foot; profit; advantage; compensation.

Bootee *n.* short boots of women; woollen boots of children.

Booth *n.* temporary shelter, a tent in a fair.

Booty *n.* spoils; goods that have been stolen; pillage, especially by an enemy in war.

Booze *v.i.* to drink heavily; to drink alcohol, especially in large quantities.

Boozy *adj.* addicted to drink.

Bo-peep *n.* a game of hide and seek; a game of hiding and suddenly appearing.

Boracic *adj.* of borax.

Borage *adj.* a blue-flowered plant (used to flavour claret-cup, etc.)

Borax *adj.* a mineral; borate of soda; a salt used as antiseptic and in soldering.

Bordeaux *adj.* claret; a delicious wine of South France; a southern French wine.

Border *adj.* the outer edge, boundary.

Bore *v.t.* & *i.* a great tide-wave, a nuisance, a tiresome person, hollow of a gun-barrel, deep hole in earth.

Boreas *n.* the north wind.

Boreal *adj.* pertaining to North wind.

Boredom *n.* being bored; the state of being bored.

Boric *n.* pertaining to borax.

Born *v.t.* & *adj.* to come into the world by birth; destined from birth.

Boron *n.* a non-metallic solid element (a dark-brown powder).

Borough *n.* a town sending members to Parliament.

Borrow *v.t.* & *i.* to take loan; to imitate; to take and use something that belongs to someone else, usually with their permission and with the intention of returning it; to plagiarize; (Golf) to allow for the wind or slope.

Borstal *n.* a disciplinary institution for offenders aged from 15 to 21.

Bort *n.* fragments or dust of diamond.

Borzoi *n.* a Russian wolf-hound.

Boscage, Boskage *ns.* masses of trees or shrubs.

Bosch *n.* (South African) a wood, a bush.

Boschbok *n.* a antelope; a bushbuck.

Boschvard *n.* species of wild pig.

Bosh *n.* & *int.* (colloq.) a foolish talk; nonsense.

Bosky *adj.* with shrubs or trees; bushy; wooded.

Bosom *adj.* the brest of man, interior parts.

Boss *adj.* projection; knob stud; leader; chief.

Botany *n.* study of plants etc.; fine wool; the science of plants.

Botch *n.* blemish; clumsy patch; a swelling; pimple; boil; ill finished work.

Both *adj.* one and the other; two together; the two.

Bother *v.t.* & *i.* to worry, to trouble oneself. *n.* worry; trouble.

Bothy, Bothie *ns.* a small hut, especially one for farm workers to live in.

Bo-tree *n.* bodhi tree; pipal tree; tree of knowledge; the name given in Ceylon to the Pipal tree (allied to the Banian).

Bottle *n.* narrow necked glass vessel for holding liquids, bundle of hay.

Bottom *n.* the lowest part, ground under water, low and, inmost point, keel, basis, foundations.

Bottomry *n.* borrowing of money by the owner on the security of a ship.

Botulism *n.* a severe illness caused by bacteria in badly preserved food.

Boudoir *n.* a lady's private small chamber; a woman's bedroom or small private room.

Bough *n.* the branch of a tree, the bow of a ship, the gallows.

Bougie *n.* wax candle; a surgical instrument for exploring passages of the body.

Bouillon *n.* a type of thin clear soup.

Boulder *n.* a large waterworn rounded stone.

Boulevard *n.* broad road with trees on both sides; a broad street with lines or rows of trees.

Bounce *v.t.* & *i.* to bound, to boast, to burst noisily, to knock, to beat.

Bound *n.* limit; boundary; springing; a high jump; encircling boundary; recoil of ball, etc.

Bounder *n.* one who bounds; immoral person; a cheerful or nosily ill-bred person.

Bounteous *adjs.* generous; showing bounty; in large quantities.

Bounty *n.* generosity; gift; inducement; given generously as a gift or a reward; a premium to encourage trade or industry; charitable gifts.

Bouquet *n.* a bunch of flowers, nosegay.

Bouquetin *n.* the Alpine wild goat.

Bourbon *n.* a stubborn conservative; kentucky whisky; a type of whisky mainly made in the USA.

Bourgeois *adj.* & *n.* a citizen; middle class person; business man.

Bourgeoisie *n.* the middle classes in society.

Bourn *n.* a small stream or brook.

Bourse *n.* money market; exchange; a stock exchange.

Bout *n.* a spell or turn; a short period of intense activity; a trial of strength.

Bovine *adj.* dull and stupid; relating to cattle.

Bovril *n.* extract of beef; a meat extract used like beef-ten.

Bow *n.* a curve, weapon for shooting arrows, fore-end of a ship, rainbow.

Bow *v.i.* & *t.* respect, consent.

Bowdlerize *v.t.* to remove words or scenes that are considered likely to offend or shock from a book.

Bower *n.* arbour, a shady recess in a garden, the private room of a lady, knave in card-game.

Bow-head *n.* Greenland whale.

Bowl *v.t.* & *i.* to roll; to play with bowls; to play with ball; to move in vehicle.

Bowler *n.* one who throws a ball.

Bowline *n.* a rope fixed to bow of ship; a knot in making fixed the end loop.

Bowling *n.* throwing of ball; the game of skittles.

Bowman *n.* an archer.

Bowsprit *n.* a spar running forwards from a ship's bow.

Bowyer *n.* one who makes bows; one who uses a bow.

Box *n.* a chest; compartment in thea- tre or cinema.
Boxer *n.* one who fights with his fists.
Boxing n. the sport of fighting with the fists.
Boxing-gloves *n.* padded gloves used in boxing.
Box-office *n.* office for booking tickets of cinemas etc. where tickets are bought or reserved.
Boy *n.* a male child.
Boycott *v.t.* to refuse to have social intercourse with; to refuse to hold relation with.
Boyish *adj.* like a boy, puerile.
Boyhood *n.* boyish age.
Boyfriend *adj.* a boy whom a girl loves or likes.
Boyscouts *n.* member of scouts organisation who promotes alertness and sense of service and good character.
Brabble *n.* a broil, quarrel.
Brace *n.* a couple; tightening thing; bandage; armour for arm; bracket.
Bracelet *n.* an ornament for wrist.
Bracer *n.* a tonic; one which tightens.
Brach *n.* a bitch hound.
Brachial *adj.* of the arm; like an arm.
Brachycephalic *adj.* short-headed.
Bracing *adj.* giving strength.
Bracken *adj.* a fern; a kind of plant.
Bracket *adj.* a projection from a wall serving as a support; corbel; a wooden or metal support fixed to or built into a wall to hold a shelf; an angular support for something fastened to a wall; marks (such as [ ], {}) used in pairs for enclosing word or figures. *v.t.* to enclose in brackets.
Brackish *adj.* (of water) slightly salty.
Bract *n.* a small leaf of scale below calyx.
Bracteate *n.* thin beaten plates of gold or silver, having bracts.
Brad *n.* small nail not having a head but a side projection on the top.
Bradawl *n.* a boring tool.
Brae *n.* a steep slope.
Brag *v.i. & t.* to talk with too much pride (about something); to boast.
Braggadocio *n.* bragging talk; empty vaunting; a boaster.
Braggart *n.* a boaster.
Brahmin *n.* a member of the Hindu priestly caste.
Braid *adj.* a plait of hair; embroidery; hair band; threads of silk, cotton, etc. woven together in a narrow strip for decorating clothes and material.
Brain *n.* seat of understanding and intellect; nervous centre in skull.
Brainy *adj.* mentally smart, inventive.
Braise *v.t.* to stew in closed vessel; to cook slowly with very little liquid in a closed container.

Brake *n.* a device for slowing or stopping a car; heavy harrow; brushwood.

Brake-van *n.* a railway carriage or a guard's compartment from which the train-brake is controlled.

Bramah *n.* a kind of lock; a key of that lock.

Bramble *n.* wild bush having thorns; any wild prickly shrub.

Bran *adj.* husks of ground corn.

Branch *n.* arm of tree; any sub-division, department etc.

Branched, Branchy *adjs.* with many branches; having branches.

Brand *n.* a piece of burning or partly burnt wood, mark made by hot iron, trade mark, a sword.

Brandish *v.t.* to wave about.

Brand-new *adj.* quite new; conspicuously new.

Brandy *n.* a strong wine concentrate; a strong alcoholic drink usually made from wine.

Brash *n.* loose and broken ice or rock; sudden rain; slight illness.

Brass *n.* an alloy of copper and zinc.

Brassard *n.* a badge worn on the arm.

Brat *n.* bad child; especially one that behaves; over-garment; apron.

Bravado *n.* boast; show of courage; threat; a display of bold talk or behaviour to impress other people.

Brave *n.* courageous, fearless, valiant, finely, dressed, honest, showy.

Bravo *n.* a bandit; daring villain; shout of approval; hired assassin or bully.

Bravura *n.* a passage of music requiring exceptional powers.

Brawl *n.* to engage in a noisy quarrel, murmur.

Brawn *n.* boar's flesh; muscle; strength; any prepared meat; lean flesh.

Braxy *n.* splenic of sheep; sheep having that disease; its flesh; mutton of a sheep dying from the disease.

Bray *n.* the cry of an ass, to cry like an ass. *v.t.* to pound.

Braze *n.* to solder with brass or colour with brass.

Brazier *n.* brass-worker, burning coal-pan.

Breach *n.* a break, neglect of contract, violation of law, a quarrel, injury, gap.

Bread *n.* cooked or baked food or loaf; a food made of flour; livelihood.

Breadth *n.* broadness, width.

Break *v.t.* & *i.* to divide into parts; to tear to pieces; to disperse; to become feeble.

Breakage *n.* allowance for things broken accidentally, act of breaking.

Breakdown *n.* a collapse; failure of health; a mechanical failure.

Breaker *n.* big wave of sea which breaks the shore; a person or thing that breaks something; small water-cask.

Breakfast *n.* morning meal; first meal of day.

Breakneck *adj.* very fast and dangerous.

Breakwater *adj.* a dam to break the force of waves.

Bream *n.* fresh water fish found in rivers and lakes.

Breast *n.* part of human body above the belly; mammary glands in women (small in men) or animal; conscience; affection.

Breath *n.* slight movement of air, air inhaled and exhaled, breeze, life.

Breathe *v.i.* & *t.* to live, to take breath, to utter softly, to inhale.

Breech *adj.* lower part of body.

Breeches *n.* trousers.

Breed *v.t.* & *i.* to give birth to; to arise; to bear, generate; to produce off-spring; to bring up.

Breeding *n.* act of generating; good manners and behavior.

Breeze *n.* gentle wind.

Breezy *adj.* pleasantly windy; fresh; having light winds.

Brent *n.* a smallest kind of wild goose (visiting Britain in winter).

Brer *n.* (negro dial.) brother.

Brethern *plural* of Brother. of 'brother' fellow member of religious society.

Breve *n.* sign for a short vowel sound, a letter of the pope.

Brevet *n.* a document conferring nominal rank on an army officer.

Breviary *n.* a book containing the Divine office of the R.C. Church for each day (to recited by those in orders.)

Brevier *n.* a special size of type; of 8 point type.

Brevity *n.* shortness of expression; the quality of being brief and exact in speaking or writing; conciseness; a short span (of life).

Brew *v.t.* & *i.* to make beer, to bring about, to gather forces, to mingle. *n.* the amount brewed at once.

Brewer *n.* one who brews; a person or a company that makes beer.

Brew-house *n.* a building in which beer is brewed.

Brewster (arch.) *n.* brewer.

Brewster sessions the court for issue of licenses to trade in alcoholic liquors.

Bribe *n.* an illegal reward given to someone. *v.t.* to give bribe.

Brick *n.* clay moulded, shaped and baked. *v.t.* to block or cover with bricks; to build with bricks.

Brickbat *n.* a piece of a brick (*esp.* used as a missile).

Bridal *n.* & *adj.* belonging to bride or marriage, a wedding feast.

Bride *n.* recently married woman; a woman about to be married.

Bride-groom *n.* recently married; a newly married man.

Brides-maid *n.* a young woman or girl accompanying and helping a bride at her wedding.

Bridge *n.* a structure build across a stream, a kind of card-game.

Bridle *n.* the head-gear of a horse's harness, restraint. *v.t.* to put a bridle on a horse, to bring under control.

Bridlewise *adj.* trained to obey reins.

Brief *adj.* summary of law points for a case; any short statement; a writ.

Brier (Briar) *n.* a prickly bush, especially wild rose bush.

Brig *n.* a vessel having two masts; bridge.

Brigade *n.* a subdivision of an army; organised people.

Brigadier *n.* officer commanding a brigade; an officer with a high rank in the British Army.

Brigand *n.* a robber or free-booter.

Brigandage *n.* pillage; a highway robbery by brigands; plunder.

Brigantine *n.* a two-masted vessel.

Bright *adj.* shining, vivid, clear, illustrious, quick-witted.

Brighten *v.t.* to make bright; to make cheerful; to clear.

Brilliance, Brilliancy *n.* splendour; great brightness; lustre.

Brilliant *adj.* bright, spiendid, showy, shining. *n.* a diamond of the finest cut.

Brills *n.* the hair on the eyelids of a horse.

Brim *n.* upper edge; brink of river; edge of hat, bowl, glass, etc.; a projecting rim of the hat.

Brimmer *n.* a full cup; a hat.

Brimstone *n.* sulphur.

Brindle (d) *adjs.* tawny, brownish.

Brine *n.* sea; salt water; tears; slat and water for prickling.

Bring *v.t.* to fetch; to adduce; to convey in one's hand.

Brink *n.* edge; border; brim; the extreme edge of land, *e.g.* at the top of a cliff or beside a river.

Brinjal, Brinjaul *ns.* the fruit of the egg-plant.

Brinjarry *n.* corrupt form of Hindi word Banjara; a travelling grain and salt merchant of the Deccan.

Briny *adj.* of brine or sea, salt.

Briquette *n.* a small hard block made from coal dust and used as fuel.

Brisk *adj.* active, lively, full of spirit.

Briskly *adv.* in a brisk manner.

Brisket *n.* meat cut from the breast of an animal.

Bristle *n.* stiff hair; one of the short stiff hairs in brush.

Bristling *n.* a small sardine-like fish.

Bristol (attrib.) *n.* a kind of card-board for drawing on.

Britannia *n.* Britain personified.

Britannic *adj.* of Britain.
British *adj.* United Kingdom (of Great Britain and Northern Ireland) or its inhabitants.
Briton *n.* real inhabitants of Britain before advent of English; now generally all citizens; British person.
Brittle *n.* hard but easily broken.
Broach *n.* a boring bit. *v.t* to pierce, to open up, to begin discussion.
Broad *adj.* vast, wide, large, extensive, clear, outspoken, explicit.
Broadly *adv.* fully; widely; plainly.
Broadcast *v.t.* to transmit news, music &c. by wireless.
Broadcloth *v.t.* fine double-width woollen cloth.
Broaden *v.t.* & *i.* to render more comprehensive; to make broader or extensive.
Broadsheet *n.* a newspaper printed on a large size of paper.
Broadside *n.* side of a ship above water; guns on one side of ship; discharge of them.
Brocade *n.* fabric with raised patern in gold-thread or silk.
Broccoli *n.* cabbage with a fruit which is eaten as vegetable.
Brochure *n.* a stitched pamphlet; small book or magazine containing pictures and information about something or advertising something.
Brock *n.* a badger; dirty, smelling fellow; a stinking fellow.
Brocket *n.* a stag which is two years old.
Brogue *n.* a strong outdoor shoe; a marked Irish or other accent.
Broil *n.* to be greatly heated; to cook meat on a fire or over metal bars.
Broken *p.p.* & *adj.* crushed, humbled, tame, rough, ruined, incomplete.
Broker *n.* middle man in bargain who charges commission; second hand dealer; petty reputeless businessman.
Brokerage *n.* commission.
Brolly (*sl.*) *n.* an umbrella.
Bromate, Bromide *ns.* kinds of compound of bromine.
Bromic *adj.* containing bromine.
Bromine (Chem.) *n.* a liquid element used in sedative.
Bromism *n.* morbid state due to the use of bromine.
Bronchial *adj.* pertaining to bronchi.
Bronchitis *n.* slight pneumonia; inflammation of the bronchial membrane.
Bronco *n.* a wild or half tamed horse.
Bronze *n.* brown alloy of copper and tin.
Brooch *n.* an ornament worn for fastening of dress.
Brood *n.* hatch of birds or animals, offspring.
Broody *adj.* (of a hen) wanting to brood.

Brook *v.t.* (usually with a negative) to tolerate something.

Broom *n.* a bush whose twigs are used for besom; sweeping brush or twigs.

Broomstick *n.* a broom-handle.

Broth *n.* water in which meat &c has been boiled.

Brothel *n.* house of ill-fame or prostitution; a house where men pay to have sex with prostitutes.

Brother *n.* son of same parents or having one parent in common; closely united person.

Brotherhood *n.* companion, ship fraternity, an association.

Brother-in-law *n.* brother of one's husband or wife; sister's husband.

Brougham *n.* a type of closed carriage with four wheels, pulled by one horse.

Brow *n.* arch of hair over eye, forehead, edge, projection.

Brow-beat *v.t.* to frighten somebody with severe looks and words.

Brown *adj.* of dusky or dark colour; having the colour of chocolate or coffee mixed with milk.

Brownie *n.* a domestic elf.

Brownie *n.* a junior girl guide.

Brownish *adj.* somewhat brown.

Browse *v.t. & i.* to examine books or other goods in a casual way; to graze.

Bruin *n.* a bear.

Bruise *n.* an injury caused by a blow to the body, making a mark on the skin but not breaking it.

Bruiser *n.* one who bruises, a boxer.

Bruit *v.t.* to noise about; to spread about. *n.* a report; rumour.

Brumal *adj.* belonging to the winter.

Brummagem *adj.* counterfeit; cheap and showy.

Brumous *adj.* foggy, wintry.

Brunette *adj.* & *n.* dark complexioned lady with brown hair and dark eyes; a white woman with dark hair.

Brunt *n.* blow; fierce shock or attack; chief crisis.

Brush *n.* an implement of hair or bristles for cleaning hair, clothes, bottles or floor etc.

Brusque *adj.* using few words in a rude or abrupt way.

Brustal *v.i.* to rustle, to crackle.

Brutal *adj.* rude; cruel; barbarous; sensual; stupid; coarsely; callously cruel.

Brute *adj.* cruel or passionate person; stupid fellow; a beast, especially a large or fierce one.

Bryony *n.* a climbing hedge plant.

Bubble *n.* an air-filled cavity in water, an unsubstantial project or scheme.

Bubo *n.* an inflammatory swelling of a lymph gland in the groin armpit; especially due to veneral diseases.

Bubonic *adj.* accompanied by buboes.

Buccal *adj.* pertaining to the cheek.

Buccaneering *adj.* piratical.

Bucephalus *n.* the charger of Alexander of Macedon; a riding horse.

Buck *n.* male deer, chamois, a fob. *v.t.* to jump vertically.

Bucket *n.* a vessel for drawing or carrying water.

Bucolic *adj.* pastoral; rustic.

Bud *n.* first leaf, shoot or flower, anything undeveloped.

Budge *v.t.* to give way; to make slightest movement.

Budget *n.* annual estimate of accounts; a stock.

Budlet *n.* a small bud (unopened flower.)

Buff *n.* leather of buffalo or oxhide, a blow.

Buffer *n.* apparatus for deadening shock of railway vans.

Buffoon *n.* a jestler; one without self respect; a ridiculus but amusing person.

Bug *n.* an object of terror; a small insect or a small blood-sucking insect infesting beds.

Bugaboo *n.* an object of baseless terror.

Bugbear *n.* an object of imaginary terror; a dreaded event.

Buggy *n.* a four-wheeled light carriage.

Bughouse *adj.* mentally unsound.

Bug-hunter *n.* any small insect; Entomologist.

Bugle *n.* a brass musical instrument like a small trumpet, used for giving military signals.

Bugler *n.* a bugle-signaller.

Buglet *n.* a bicyclist's small bugle.

Bugloss *n.* a rough-leaved plant.

Buhl *n.* an inlaid work on brass or other metal.

Build *v.t.* & *i.* to erect a house; to construct; to frame; to rear; to settle or establish; to be busy making one's house or nest.

Building *n.* the thing built; edifice; a structure with a roof and walls.

Built *adj.* formed, constructed.

Bulb *n.* the rounded part of head of a plant formed beneath the surface of the ground as onion; a vacuum.

Bulbous *adj.* bulb-shaped; having a bulb or bulbs.

Bulbul *n.* an Eastern song-thrush; a singer.

Bulge *n.* an irregular swelling. *v.t.* to swell out.

Bulger *n.* a wooden golf-club with a bulging face.

Bulginess *n.* protuberance or swelling.

Bulgy *n.* swollen.

Bulk *n.* a cargo; magnitude; the main part; the major portion.

Bulky *adj.* large, of great size.

Bull *n.* elephant; whale; the male of any animal in the cow family, and other large animals.

Bulldog *n.* a kind of English dog.

Bullet *n.* a little ball; an iron ball; discharged from a cannon.

Bulletin *n.* a short official statements of news.

Bullfinch *n.* a small bird with a strong curved beak and a pink breast; quickset hedge with ditch.

Bullion *n.* solid gold or silver. *n.* a fringe of gold-thread.

Bullock *n.* a bull that has been castrated.

Bully *n.* a noisy fellow, a tyrant. *v.i.* to oppress, to tease.

Bulrush *n.* a type of tall plant like a red that grows in or near water.

Bulwark *n.* a rampart; fortification, something that defends or protects.

Bum *n.* (*sl.*) back side, the buttocks. *v.i.* to make a humming sound like bees.

Bum-bailiff *n.* a sheriff's officer employed for arrests (from touching debtor on the back.)

Bum-boat *n.* a boat plying with fresh provisions for a ship.

Bumble-bee *n.* a large hairy bee that makes a loud noise as it flies.

Bumbledom *n.* consequential minor officials and their ways.

Bummalo *n.* a small fish found off Southern Asia.

Bummer *n.* a worthless; loafer.

Bump *v.t.* & *i.* to push against, to hurt. *adv.* suddenly.

Bumper *n.* anything that pumps; a bar on a motor-car buffer; anything large or generous in measure.

Bumpkin *n.* a clown; an awkward clumsy rustic; a person from the country who is not sophisticated.

Bumptious *adj.* noisily self-assertive.

Bumpy *adj.* abounding in bumps.

Bun *n.* a kind of sweet cake; a dry stalk; a playful name for rabbit.

Bunchy *adj.* forming a bunch.

Bunco *v.t.* (*sl.*) to swindle.

Bund *n.* an embankment or dike; a thorough fare on a waterfront; esplanade; a confederation.

Bunder *n.* a landing-place as in Bombay; Appolo Bunder; harbour.

Bundle *n.* a collection of things fastened together loosely.

Bung *n.* the stopper for the large hole in a barrel; the hole itself; a piece of cork, used for closing the hole in container.

Bungalow *n.* a country house with a veranda and one storey; now loosely used for one storey house.

Bungle *n.* & *v.t.* clumsy work confusion, to accomplish awkwardly, to blunder over.

Bungler *n.* a clumsy workmen.

Bunion *n.* an inflamed swelling on the first joint of the great toe; foot.

Bunk *n.* a wooden box or case serving as a seat in the day and as a bed at night.

Bunker *n.* a place for storing coal, a window seat and chest, a bomber proof shelter.

Bunkum, Buncombe *ns.* nonsense, sophistry; an insincere talk; humbug.

Bunny *n.* a pet name for rabbit.

Bunsen burner *n.* an invention for burning mixed air and gas, giving great heat.

Bunt *n.* the baggy middle part of sail; a disease of grains.

Bunting *n. n.* stuff for flags.

Buoy *n.* a float moored on a dangerous rock at the edge of a channel, as a guide to navigators.

Buoyage *n.* providing of buoys

Buoyancy *n.* the floating power of liquids.

Buoyant *adj.* apt to float.

Bur *n.* a protuberance; lump; a knot on a tree; the rough sound of 'r' pronounced in the throat.

Burberry *n.* a waterproof material.

Burble *v.t.* to trouble, to confuse.

Burbot *n.* an eel-like flat-headed bearded fresh-water fish.

Burden *n.* a load, responsibility, cargo, refrain. *v.t.* to load.

Burdock *n.* a coarse plant with prickly flowers and dock-like leaves.

Bureau *n.* a writing desk, office, department.

Bureaucracy *n.* a system of government; a system of government by departments which are managed by state officials, not by elected representatives.

Burette *n.* a graduated glass tube for measuring liquids.

Burg *n.* (*sl.*) fortress; a walled town.

Burgee *n.* a flag which ends in two points; a kind of small coal suitable for burning in furnaces.

Burgeon *v.i.* to grow forth, to sprout.

Burgess *n.* an inhabitant of a borough with full municipal rights.

Burgh *n.* a Scotch borough.

Burglar *n.* a house-breaker, a thief.

Burglarious *adj.* pertaining to burglary.

Burglary *n.* breaking into the house for the purpose of stealing.

Burgle *v.t. & i.* to commit burglary; to enter or rob (a house).

Burgomaste *n.* the mayor of Dutch or Flemish town.

Burgonet *n.* a steel cap or helmet.

Burgund *n.* a kind of wine.

Burial *n.* funeral; ceremonies of placing the dead body in a grave.

Burin *n.* a tool for engraving on copper.

Burk *v.t.* to avoid, to suppress, to hush up.

Burke *v.t.* to suppress; to avoid; to hush up; to murder (*esp.* by stifling).

Burlesque *n.* & *adj.* mockery caricature, imitative, comical.

Burly *adj*. of stout sturdy built; corpulent.

Burn *n*. injury caused by fire.

Burner *n*. a device by which a flame is controlled.

Burnt *adj*. treated with fire.

Burr *n*. the sound of a strongly pronounced.

Burrow *n*. a hole or tunnel made in the ground and used as a home or shelter by rabbits, foxes, etc.

Bursar *n*. a treasurer, purser.

Bursa *n*. a sac like body cavity.

Bursarial *adj*. of a bursary; of a bursar.

Bursary *n*. a college bursar's office; an allowance to a poor scholar.

Burst *n*. a rent, a sprint, a sudden explosion.

Bury *v.t.* to enter; to forget; to place in a grave.

Bus *n*. an omni-bus.

Busby *n*. a tall fur cap with a cloth bag on the right side.

Bush *n*. a shrub, woodland, a metal lining of axle-hole.

Bushel *n*. a dry measure of eight gallons.

Bushy *adj*. like a bush; abounding in bushes; growing thickly.

Business *n*. task, duty, employment, occupation, profession, concern.

Busk *v.t.* to entertain by dancing or singing on the street.

Buskin *n*. a boot reaching up to the knee.

Buskined *adj*. wearing a buskin.

Buss *n*. a kiss; a small two masted Dutch vessel used in fisheries.

Bust *n*. a statue of a person's head, neck and shoulders.

Bustard *n*. a large swift running bird.

Buster *n*. used to speak to a man you do not like.

Bustle *v.i.* & *t.* to stir oneself noisily to hurry; to make show of activity.

Bustup *n*. a bad company or very angry disagreement.

Busy *adj*. full of activity; working with concentrated attention.

But *prep.* except. *conj*. unless. *n*. an objection.

Butcher *n*. one whose trade is to kill animals for food.

Butcherly *adj*. & *adv.* in the way of a butcher; cruelly.

Buchery *n*. business of a butcher, the place where animals are killed.

Butea *n*. a dhak, a king of tree.

Butler *n*. a man-servant in charge of wine; a head servant.

Butlery *n*. a larder.

Butt *n*. a barrel, wine-cask, thicker end of a tool, trunk of a tree, a mound behind target, aim, object of ridicule.

Butte *n*. an isolated hill or peak rising abruptly.

Butter *n*. a fatty substance obtained from cream.

Butterfly *n.* an erect winged insect, a showy person.
Buttock *n.* the rump. *v.t.* to throw by using buttock.
Button *n.* flat object made of bone; a knob to fasten dress; the knob of an electric bell; anything of small value.
Buttress *n.* a construction, usually of brick, built against a wall to support it.
Buxom *adj.* gay; jolly; yielding; elastic; plump.
Buy (*bi*,) *v.t.* to purchase, to serve, to procure, to get by some sacrifice, to gain by bribe.
Buyer *n.* one who purchases.
Buzz *n.* stale news, the hum of a bee.
By *adv.* near; close to; through or with; according to; by authority; via; in oaths; with the witness of.
By-blow *n.* a side blow at some one other than an enemy, a bastard child.
By, Bye *n.* anything of minor impor- tance; a run made in cricket without ball being struck by the batsman.
Bye *interj.* good-bye.
Bygone *adj.* past, gone by, departed.
Bylaw, Byelaw *ns.* a law of a private corporation or local authority.
By-pass *n.* a piece of new road relieving traffic by connecting two points.
By-product *n.* a substance produced during the making of something else.
Byre *n.* a cow-house.
By-road *n.* a little frequented road.
Bystander *n.* one who stands near one; a looker-on; a spectator.
Byte *n.* a unit of information stored in a computer, equal to 8 bits. A computer's memory is measured in bytes.
By-way *n.* a short cut; less known department of any subject.
Bywork *n.* work for leisure hours.
Byzant *n.* a gold coin.

C the third letter of the English alphabet.
Caaba *n.* the sacred building at Mecca, Mohammedan Holy of Holies containing the black stone.
Cab *n.* & *v.t.* a carriage for hire; the driver's seat.
Cabal *n.* a secret political plot; a group of people involved in this.
Cabala *n.* secret knowledge; the ancient Jewish tradition.
Caballer *n.* an intrigurer.
Cabaret *n.* a tavern.
Cabbage *n.* a kind of vegetable; edible vegetable of various palms.
Cabby *n.* (colloq.) a cabman who drives a horse-driven carriage; the taxi driver.

Caber *n.* a long heavy wooden pole, it is thrown in the air as a trial of strength in the Scottish sport of tossing the cober.

Cabin *n.* cottage or hut; a small room in a ship; a small house or shelter, usually made of wood.

Cable *n* & *v.t.* submarine telegraph; a rope measuring 100 fathoms.

Cablet *n.* a little cable, a tow rope.

Cabobs *n. pl.* roast meat; meat roasted in small pieces on skewers.

Caboodle *n.* (*sl.*) whole.

Cabstand *n.* a place where cabs are stationed for hire.

Cacao *n.* the tree or its seed giving cocoa and chocolate.

Cache *n.* a secret or hidden place for storing ammunition; stores hidden in this manner.

Cachectic (-al) *adjs.* having ill-condition of body, sick.

Cachet *n.* respect or admiration marks of authenticity.

Cachexy *n.* ill-condition of body or mind.

Cachinnate *v.i.* to laugh loudly or immoderately.

Cachou *n.* a pill used by smokers to sweaten the breath.

Cacique *n.* an aboriginal chief of the West Indies and tropical America.

Cackle *n.* a loud noise that a hen makes, especially after laying an egg.

Cackling *n.* idle talk.

Cacoethes *n.* a bad habit; an itch for doing something unadvisable.

Cacographer *n.* one who writes incorrectly.

Cacology *n.* bad pronunciation.

Cacophony *n.* a harsh or disagreeble sound; a discord.

Cacophonous *adj.* an ugly sound.

Cactus *n.* plant having fleshy usually prickly stems but no leaves.

Cad *n.* a person of mean nature and manners.

Caddish *adj.* behaving like a cad.

Cadaverous *adj.* (of a person) very pale and thin.

Caddie *n.* (in golf) a person who helps a player by carrying her or his clubs during a game.

Caddy *n.* a small box for holding tea.

Cadet *n.* young son; one studying for the commission in the army, navy or airforce.

Cadge *v.i.* & *t.* to beg or go about begging; to get something from somebody by asking, often unfairly.

Cadger *n.* a hawker who collects country produce for reselling; a pedlar.

Cadre *n.* scheme, framework.

Caducous *adj.* perishable; fleeting; falling off when work is done.

Caecum *n.* the blind gut or first part of the large intestine.

Caesarism *n.* belief in autocracy.

Caesura *n.* a pause near the middle of a line of poetry.

Cafe *n.* a small restaurant serving cheap meals and drinks or a coffee-house.

Caffeine *n.* a kind of toxic substance present in tea or coffee that stimulates the body.

Cage *n.* a structure made of bars or wires in which birds or animals are kept or carried.

Cahoot *n.* company partnership.

Cairn *n.* a heap of stones raised over a grave.

Cairngorm *n.* a yellow or wine coloured gem-stone.

Caisson *n.* a chest containing explosive and ammunition.

Caitiff *n.* a base or cowardly person.

Cajole *v.t.* to coax; to make somebody do something by cleverly persuading, deceiving or flattering them.

Cake *n.* a kind of sweet bread; a sweet food of various sizes and shapes.

Calabash *n.* a vessel made from the dry gourd and used as tobacco-pipe etc.

Calaboose *n.* (colloq.) a prison.

Calamity *n.* a misfortune; an event that causes great harm or damage; adversity; deep distress; grave disaster.

Calamitous *adj.* disastrous.

Calash *n.* a hooded carriage; a two-wheeled one-seated vehicle with the driver's seat on the splash-board.

Calcareous *adj.* containing carbonate of lime; of limestone.

Calcify *v.t.* & *i.* to replace by lime; petrify.

Calcine *v.t.* & *i.* to turn into a calx by heating.

Calculate *v.t.* & *i.* to count; to think in a mathematical way.

Calculator *n.* one who or that which calculates.

Calculus *n.* a system of computation applied in higher mathematics.

Caldron *n.* a large boiling vessel.

Calender *n.* a table with months, weeks, festivals &c., an almanac.

Calender *v.t.* to press paper, cloth etc., in a roller machine for smoothing.

Calf *n.* the young of a domestic cow, a stupid fellow.

Calibre *n.* the width of the inside of a tube or the barrel of gun; quality.

Calico *n.* white unprinted cloth.

Caliph, Calif *ns.* Mohammedan chief, civil and religious ruler; a title used, especially formerly by the successor of Muhammed.

Calipers *n. pl.* compasses with curved legs for measuring (inner or outer) diameter of round bodies.

Calix *n.* (Anat.) cuplike cavity or organ.

Calk *n.* a kind of pointed piece added in the horse-shoe to prevent it from slipping.

Calkin *n.* the turned down edge of a horse-shoe.

Call *v.t. & i.* to cry out, to shout, to summon, to address by name, to pay bried visit.

Call-boy *n.* one who calls the actors on the stage.

Caller *n.* a visitor.

Calligraphy *n.* done with a special pen or brush; good handwriting.

Calling *n.* a profession; an occupation.

Callisthenics *n. pl.* exercises to develop strong and graceful bodies.

Callosity *n.* hardened part; abnormal hardness and thickness or skin.

Callous *adj.* having or showing no sympathy for other people's feelings or suffering.

Callousness *n.* hardened; harny; unfeeling; unsympathetic.

Callow *adj.* not covered with feathers, inexperienced.

Callus *n.* thickened part of skin.

Calm *adj.* nervous or troubled; tranquil; not excited; unagitated.

Calomel *n.* a purgative medicine.

Caloric *n.* heat; bodily warmth.

Calorie *n.* driven by hot air.

Caltrop *n.* a kind of instrument used to obstruct the enemy; a kind of fruit; in plural it means a kind of water chestnut.

Calve *v.i.* to produce a calf; to throw off mass of ice.

Calx *n.* ashes left after smelting.

Calyx *n.* whorl or leaves called sepals forming outer case of a bud.

Cam *n.* a portion on a revolving shaft that gives motion.

Camber *n.* a slight upward curve on the surface of something; the convexity of a ship's planks.

Camel *n.* a kind of animal of light brown colour and a very short tail.

Cameleer *n.* a camel driver.

Camelopard *n.* the giraffe.

Camembert *n.* a soft rich cheese with a strong flavour.

Cameo *n.* relief carving in stone.

Camera *n.* a kind of camera used by photographers; legislative chamber for parliamentary legislation.

Camion *n.* a conveyance for transporting guns.

Camisole *n.* an under bodice.

Camlet *n.* a woolen cloth made chiefly from goat's hair; a light cloth of various materials.

Cammock *n.* broad rest horrow.

Camomile *n.* a kind of herbal plant known as chrysanthemum used chiefly in medicines.

Camouflage *n.* artful concealment of military objects from enemy attack.

Camp *n.* a place where tents are pitched; temporary habitation of travellers.

Campaign *n.* time of military operations, organized course of action, time which an army keeps.

Campanology *n.* the study of bells and the art or practice of ringing bells.

Campanula *n.* kinds of plant with bell-shaped flowers (*usu.* blue or white).

Camphorate *v.t.* to impregnate or treat with Camphor.

Campion *n.* a wild flowering plant.

Campus *n.* the grounds and buildings of a university or college.

Can *n.* a metal or plastic container for holding or carrying liquids. *v.t.* to be able; to have skill in.

Can *n.* a vessel for keeping liquids.

Canadian *adj.* & *n.* an inhabitant of Canada.

Canal *n.* an artificial water course constructed for irrigational and navigational purposes.

Canard *n.* a false report or rumour; a unfounded rumour.

Canary *n.* a special kind of wine; a kind of bird; a special kind of dance.

Canaster *n.* tobacco-leaf dried and broken up.

Cancel *v.t.* & *i.* to annul; to suppress; to abolish; to compensate; to cross out.

Cancer *n.* the fourth sign of the zodiac, a malignant tumour.

Cancroid *adj.* like cancer; crab like.

Candelabrum *n.* a large ornamental holder with several branches for candles.

Candid *adj.* fair; impartial; unprejudiced; clear; frant.

Candidate *n.* one who appears in an examination interview etc..

Candied *adj.* coated with sugar; (Fig.) sugared; preserved by boiling in sugar; honeyed; flattering.

Candle *n.* a thing of cylinder shape surrounding a wick and made of tallow or wax etc.

Candlestick *n.* a kind of portable stand; a holder for one or more candles.

Candy *n.* sweetmeat prepared from sugar by boiling it into a paste and crystallising.

Cane *n.* trunk-portion of a certain kind of plant; a slender stick used for beating.

Canine *adj.* like a dog; like or relating to dogs.

Canker *n.* a disease of mouth, diseases of plants, corrupting influence.

Canna *n.* a kind of Indian plant with bright yellow, red, or orange flowers and ornamental leaves.

Cannel *n.* bituminous coal burning with bright flame and used in making coal oils and gas.

Cannibal *n.* one who eats flesh of his own species; a man or animal that feeds on his own species.

Cannibalism *n.* murderous cruelty, practice of eating human flesh.

Cannikin *n.* a pigmy size can; a small can.

Cannon *n.* large gun; an old type of large heavy gun that fired solid metal balls; a mounted gun throwing projectile large than bullet.

Cannonade *n.* a continuous firing of heavy guns.

Cannula *n.* a surgeon's metallic tube.

Canny *adj.* gentle; skilful; shrewd; innocent; thrifty.

Cannon *n.* a deep ravine; an ecclesiastical rule of law; list of Bible books accepted by Church.

Canon *n.* a law or rule, a kind of type, church decree.

Canonical *adj.* appointed by canon law; authoritative or accepted.

Canonize *v.t.* to admit formally to the calendar of saints; to regard as a saint; to recognize (a book) as canonical.

Canopy *n.* covering that shades a stall; altar niche; statue, grave, tomb, etc.

Canorous *adj.* melodious; musical; ringing.

Cant *n.* a bevel or oblique face, titled movement, a jerk, peculiar language of a class, jargon, sale by auction.

Cantab *n.* & *adj.* (member) of Cambridge University.

Cantaloup *n.* a small melon.

Cantabank *n.* a road singer.

Cantankerous *adj.* quarrelsome; bad tempered and tending to argue about unimportant things.

Canteen *n.* soldier's refreshment of traven situated in a barrack.

Canter *n.* an easy gallop, a beggar.

Canterbury *n.* a stand for holding books etc.; a stand with partitions for portfolios, music, etc.

Canticle *n.* a little hymn; song on chant.

Cantilever *n.* a strong bracket that gives support to balconies, stairs etc.

Canting *adj.* hypocritical whining.

Cantle *n.* hind part of a saddle; slice.

Canto *n.* part (division) of a long poem; any of the main divisions of a long poem.

Canton *n.* a square division less than a quarter in the upper corner of a shield; a corner.

Cantorial *adj.* the presentor's side of the choir.

Canvas *n.* a kind of coarse cloth used for painting, sail or tent purposes.

Canvass *v.t.* & *i.* Shakespearean usage-to examine; to toss about; to dabate.

Canyon *n.* a deep gorge with stream.

Caoutchouc *n.* Indian rubber.

Cap *n.* a head-dress for man or woman; a symbolic head-dress as on a student, athelete etc.

Capable *adj.* qualified; able; gifted; having the ability or quality necessary for doing something.

Capacious *adj.* roomy; wide; extensive; (of things) that can hold a lot; of large content.

Capacitate *v.t.* to qualify; to make able or capable (*for, to do*).

Capacity *n.* holding power, cubic content, faculty, capability, ability, opportunity.

Cap-a-pie *adj.* from head to foot.

Cape *n.* a coat without sleeves; a strip of land going in water; a headland; a loose garment; a promontory.

Capful *n.* enough to fill a cap.

Capillary *adj.* pertaining to hair; hair like.

Capital *n.* the head of a pillar, principal thing, chief city in a state, a large letter (in Eng.)

Capitular *adj.* of a Cathedral chapter; (Physiol.) of a terminal protuberance of a bone.

Caporal *n.* a French tobacco.

Capot *n.* winning of all tricks in picket. *v.t.* to win all tricks against an opponent.

Capric *adj.* obtained from butter or oil.

Caprine *adj.* of or like a goat.

Capriole *n.* a leap without going forward; a caper.

Capsicum *n.* a kind of shrub found in tropics which give cayenne pepper.

Capsize *v.t.* & *i.* (especially of a boat) to overturn in the water; to upset.

Capstan *n.* a revolving barrel for winding a cable on it.

Capsular *adj.* pertaining to capsule.

Capsule *n.* a small gelatine case for containing medicines.

Captain *n.* head or chief; commander of a ship; leader.

Caption *n.* legal arrest; words printed with a picture, a heading, photograph or cartoon.

Captious *adj.* censorious; fond of taking exception.

Captive *n.* & *adj.* taken prisoner; unable to escape; not free.

Captor *n.* a person who captures a person or an animal; one who takes a captive or prize.

Capture *n.* seizing, arrest, a prize.

Car *n.* a wheeled vehicle, chariot.

Carabinner *n.* a horse-soldier armed with a carbine.

Caracole *n.* a trained horse's half turn to the right or left.

Carafe *n.* a glass container in which wine or water are served at meals.

Carat *n.* a sign or mark; a unit of weight for precious stones and fineness for gold; a measure of purity of gold (pure gold being 24 carat).

Caravan *n.* a company of merchants or pilgrims especially in crossing deserts.

Caravan serai *n.* resting-place for travelling merchants.

Caravel, Carvel *ns.* a small light fast ship (chiefly Spanish and Portuguese of 15th-17th centuries).

Caraway *n.* cakes; a plant with seeds that have strong taste and are used for giving flavour to bread.

Carbide *n.* a compound of carbon with an element.

Carbine *n.* a short light automatic rifle.

Carbon *n.* a non-metallic element.

Carbonari *n. pl.* members of Italian secret republican society.

Caborundum *n.* a compound of carbon and silicon used for polishing by abrasion.

Carboy *n.* a large round glass or plastic bottle usually protected by an outer frame of wood, etc.

Carbuncle *n.* a precious stone; a malignant ulcer; a garnet cut in boss shape.

Carburet *v.t.* to combine (any element) chemically with carbon.

Carcass *n.* a framework; the dead body of an animal, especially one ready for cutting up as meat.

Card *n.* a cleanse wool or hemp.

Cardamom *n.* spice from seed capsules of East Indian plants.

Cardiac *adj.* relating to the heart or heart disease.

Cardigan *n.* a knitted woolen jacket, usually with no collar and fastened with buttons at the front.

Cardialgia *n.* heat-burn.

Cardinal *adj.* on which a thing hinges; fundamental; of a deep colour.

Care *n.* anxiety; heed; heedfulness; caution; protection.

Careen *v.t. & i.* to lay a ship on her side for repairing.

Careenage *n.* place for careening a ship; expense of repairing a ship.

Career *n.* progress through life; course of life; a job or profession.

Carefree *adj.* without responsibilities or worries.

Careful *adj.* anxious, cautious.

Careless *adj.* without care; unconcerned.

Caress *n.* fondling touch; kiss.

Caret *n.* the mark (^) placed below a line to show the place of omission.

Careworn *adj.* showing effects of anxiety.

Cargo *n.* freight that a ship carries; (a load of) goods carried in a ship or an aircraft.

Carib *n.* an aboriginal inhabitant of Southern West-Indian islands.

Caribou *n.* North-American reindeer.

Caricature *n.* a ridiculous likeness of a thing presented in a distorted form.

Caries *n.* decay of tooth or bone.
Carillon *n.* air played on bells.
Carious *adj.* affected with caries; decayed (*esp.* of bones, teeth).
Cark *n.* care. *v.i.* to be careful.
Carking *adj.* that which causes anxiety; burdensome (always with *care*).
Carman *n.* a van-driver; a man who drives a car.
Carminative *n.* & *adj.* curing flatulence; inducing expulsion of gas from the stomach and intestines.
Carmine *n.* a deep red colour; a vivid or crimson pigment or colour.
Carnage *n.* slaughter; the killing of many people.
Carnal *n.* sexual; sensual; material; bodily; unspiritual; murderous.
Carnify *v.t.* to reduce into flesh.
Carnival *n.* a riotous festival, revelry.
Carnivora *n. pl.* an animal that eats meat or plants; a beat of prey.
Carnivorous *adj.* flesh-eating; eating or feeding on flesh. (L. *caro, carnis,* flesh and *vorare,* to devour).
Carol *n.* a Christmas song; a joyous song. *v.t.* to utter such songs.
Carom *n.* a kind of game.
Carouse *n.* a drinking bout.
Carp *v.i.* to find fault; to complain continually about unimportant matters.
Carpal *n.* pertaining to wrist.
Carpel *n.* the central ovule-bearing female organ of a flower.
Carpenter *n.* a person whose job is making or repairing wooden objects and structures; a kind of ant or bee boring into trees.
Carpet *n.* a woven covering of floors or stairs etc.; a rool of carpet.
Carping *n.* cavilling, fault-finding.
Carpus *n.* the small bones connecting the hand and forearm, wrist; horse's knee.
Carriage *n.* transport; act of carrying; cost or carrying.
Carrier *n.* one who carries (on hire).
Carriole *n.* a small open carriage for one.
Carrion *n.* dead flesh of any animal; dead and decaying flesh; garbage.
Carrot *n.* a kind of vegetable; a plant with tapering red coloured and yellow edible root.
Carry *v.t.* & *i.* range of gun, position of carrying.
Cart *n.* a country-made vehicle for carrying heavy loads.
Cartage *n.* act or cost of caring.
Carter *n.* driver of a cart.
Carte *n.* in the game of fencing fourth position of the wrist; bill of fare; Scot's usage-card; a bill of fare.
Cartilage *n.* firm elastic tissue, gristle.

Cartilaginous *adj.* of or like cartilage.

Cartographer *n.* a person who draws maps and charts.

Cartography *n.* art of map-drawing.

Cartogram *n.* map.

Cartomancy *n.* fortune-telling by playing-cards.

Cartoon *n.* a comic illustration (as in films); a satirical or comic sketch of current social and political happenings; a drawing on strong paper for reproduction.

Cartridge *n.* a case of paper containing the charge of a firearm.

Cart-wright *n.* carpenter.

Caruncle *n.* an outgrowth of a seed; a fleshy lump.

Carve *v.t.* & *i.* to shape or make by cutting; to form something by cutting away material from wood or stone, into slices; to apportion.

Carver *n.* a person who carves; carving knife and fork.

Caryatid *n.* female figure used as a pillar; a statue of a female figure used as a supporting pillar in a building.

Cascade *n.* a small waterfall; a thing that falls or hangs in a way that suggests a waterfall.

Case *n.* occurance, position, condition, suit, (*gram*) inflextion of nouns etc.

Casein *n.* the cheesy substance of milk.

Caseous *adj.* like cheese.

Cash *n.* ready money; money; coin; money in the form of coin or bank-notes.

Cashier *n.* one who keeps accouts.

Cashew *n.* a kind of tropical tree with cashew-nuts; a tropical American tree.

Cashmere *n.* a fine soft wool, especially that made from the hair of a type of Asian goat.

Casing *n.* enclosing material.

Casino *n.* a public building or room where people play gambling games for money or dancing room.

Cask *n.* a wooden vessel for holding liquiors.

Casque *n.* a helmet; a head-piece wanting a vizor.

Cassation *n.* according to French law quashing a court's decision; annulment; an act of nulling.

Cassava *n.* a tropical plant; a type of flour made from the thick roots of this plant.

Cassia *n.* an inferior variety of cinnamon.

Cassock *n.* a kind of loose dress prevalent in olden times now only used by the clergy and cloister.

Cassowary *n.* a large running bird related to ostrich.

Cast *v.t.* & *i.* direction, a throw of dice, motion of the eye, guidance, chance, shape, mould, inclination.

Castaway *n.* an outcast; a person who has been shipwrecked and left in a lonely place.

Caste *n.* rank; any exclusive social class; a social system based on differences in family origin, wealth, etc.

Castellan *n.* governor of a castle; a castle-warden.

Castigate *v.t.* to comment and criticise badly; to amend; to punish.

Castle *n.* a stronghold; a fortress; a large residential mansion for a prince.

Castor *n.* a bright Gemini star; a swivelling wheel; a pot with a perforated top to sprinkle water; a kind of plant.

Castral *adj.* pertaining or belonging to a camp.

Castrate *v.t.* to emasculate.

Castration *n.* the act of castrating.

Casual *adj.* unforseen; unmethodical.

Casuist *n.* a person who examines special cases as affected by conflicting moral rules, relating to cases of conscience or conduct.

Cat *n.* a small carnivorous domestic animal, a spiteful woman.

Cataclysm *n.* a great flood, deluge.

Catacomb *n.* a series of underground tunnels used for burying dead people.

Catafalque *n.* a decorated platform on which the dead body of a famous person is placed before or during a funeral.

Catalectic *n.* system of motor vehicles to reduce the damage caused to the environment.

Catalepsy *n.* a disease in which trances occur.

Catalogue *n.* a systematic list showing books etc.

Catalpa *n.* a kind of tree with heart-shaped leaves and trumpet-shaped flowers.

Catamaran *n.* a raft of float of logs.

Cataplasm *n.* a poultice.

Cataract *n.* a disease of the eye; a waterfall; a down pour.

Catarrh *n.* a disease of common cold; inflammation of the mucous membrane.

Catarrhal *adj.* pertaining to catarrh.

Catastrophe *n.* climax of action in a drama; a sudden calamity.

Catch *v.t. & i.* to capture, to ensnare, to overtake, to take hold, to be entangled.

Catchable *adj.* able to be caught.

Catcher *n.* one who cathes.

Catchment *n.* a basin from which rainfall flows into a river.

Catch penny *n.* a useless publication merely to earn profit.

Catchword *n.* an influential temporary phrase (in politics, etc.)

Catchy *adj.* (of a tune) pleasant and easy to remember.

Cate *n.* (arch) choice food or dainty; rich luxurious food.

Catechism *n.* instruction by question and answer.

Catechismal *adj.* pertaining, to catechism.

Catechist *n.* one who catechizes.

Catechu *n.* a substance extracted from a certain bark.

Catechumen *n.* a beginner who is being taught the rudiments of Christianity.

Categorical *adj.* explicit; positive; absolute; direct; plain-speaking, bidding of conscience as ultimate moral law.

Category *n.* a class; order of division; a class or group of people or thing regarded as having certain features.

Catena *n.* a chain or connected series.

Catenary *n.* a curve formed by a hanging chain.

Catenate *v.t.* to connect by a chain.

Cater *v.i.* to provide foor or amusement.

Cateran *n.* a Highland marauder; a fighting-man.

Caterpillar *n.* a larva of butterfly or moth.

Caterwaul *v.i.* to scream like cats; to quarrel like cats.

Catgut *n.* twisted intestines of certain animals used as a string for instrument etc.

Catharsis *n.* purification; the process of releasing strong feeling.

Cathartic *adj.* purgative *n.* purgative drug.

Cathedra *n.* throne of a bishop, a professor's chair.

Cathedral *n.* the principal church of a diocese with the bishop's throne.

Catherine-wheel *n.* somersault turned sideways; a circular spoked window or window compartment.

Catheter *n.* a tube inside the body that helps in passing gas and urine.

Cathode *n.* the negative pole of an electric battery.

Catholic *adj.* & *n.* universal; orthodox; all embracing the Christians as such; tolerant, broad-minded.

Catholicity *n.* freedom rom prejudice.

Catholicism *n.* adherence to the Catholic Church.

Catholicity *n.* universality; comprehensiveness; wide prevalence; freedom from prejudice.

Catkin *n.* a small thin bunch of soft flowers that grows on the branches of certain tree *e.g.* willow.

Catling *n.* a small cat, surgeon's dismembering knife.

Catoptric *adj.* pertaining to mirror.

Catsup *n.* a sauce made of mushrooms, tomatoes, etc.

Cattle *n.* beasts such as cows, bulls and oxen and horse and sheep etc.; live stock, *esp.* oxen; contemptible people.

Caucus *n.* a local committee for political party organization.

Caudal *adj.* pertaining.

Caudate *adj.* tailed; having a tail.

Caudle *n.* warm gruel for invalids or for women in childbed.

Caudillo *n.* leader dictator.

Caul *n.* membrane that contains a child's head at the time of birth; a kind of cap.

Cauldron *n.* a large boiling vessel.

Cauliflower *n.* a kind of edible cabbage; a vegetable with green leaves around a large hard white head of flowers.

Caulk *v.t.* to watertight seams of a ship; to stop up seams of a ship with oakum and melled pitch.

Causal *adj.* expressing cause; relating to cause and effect.

Causality *n.* the relation of cause and effect; the working of a cause (a doctrine).

Causative *adj.* expressing cause, productive of cause, (*gram*) acting as cause.

Cause *n.* ground or reason or motive for action; justification; the case of a party to a law-suit; what produces an effect; a person or thing that makes something happen.

Causerie *n.* newspaper or magazine article of an informal kind (*esp.* on literary subjects).

Causeway *n.* a raised way or road over a marshy ground, especially across low or wet ground.

Caustic *adj.* capable of burning, corroding or destroying living tissue; biting; sarcastic. *n.* a caustic substance.

Cauerisation *n.* act of burning or searing.

Cautery *n.* metal instrument for searing tissue.

Caution *n.* prudence, warning, avoidance of rashness.

Cautionary *adj.* given as a pledge; conveying warning or advice.

Cautious *adj.* watchful; disposed to or exhibiting caution.

Cavalcade *n.* a company of persons on horseback.

Cavalier *n.* a gallant; a horseman; a lady's protector or escort.

Cavalry *n.* a troop of horsemen; soldiers fighting on horses (especially formerly) or in armoured vehicles.

Cavation *n.* digging of earth for the foundation of a building.

Cave *n.* a hollow cavity in a rock; a hollow place in the side of a cliff or hill, or underground.

Caveat *n.* (Law) a process to suspend proceedings.

Cavern *n.* a deep and hollow place in a rock; a cave, especially a large or dark one.

Caverned *adj.* full of caverns; like a cavern; with caverns.

Cavernous *adj.* full of caverns, hollow.

Caviar *n.* the specially prepared eggs of a sturgeon or certain other large fish; pickled sturgeon-roe (eaten as relish).

Cavil *v.i.* to make false charges; to take exception at.

Cavity *n.* a opening; a hollow place; an empty space within something solid, *e.g.* a hole in a tooth.

Cavort *v.t.* to bound; to jump or dance about in an excited way.

Caw *n.* the cry of a crow. *v.t.* to cry like a crow.

Cayman, Caiman *ns.* a South-American reptile like a crocodile.

Cayenne *n.* very pungent red pepper.

Cease *v.i. & i.* to stop; to end; to give over; to desist from.

Ceaseless *adj.* incessant; continual; perpetual; not stopping; without end; continuous.

Cecils *n. pl.* fried balls of minced meat, bread pieces and onion etc.

Cecity *n.* loss of sight, blindness.

Cedar *n.* a kind of tree which remains evergreen and its wood is durable and fragrant particularly used in furniture.

Cede *v.t.* to yield; to give up; to submit; to surrender.

Ceiling *n.* inner roof of a room; upper limit; the upper inside lining of plaster-work at the top of a room.

Celandine *n.* kinds of yellow spring flower.

Celanese *n.* a kind of artificial silk.

Celebrant *n.* one who celebrates; a priest leading a church service, or a person attending it.

Celebrate *v.t.* to praise, to publish, to make famous, to perform religious ceremony.

Celebration *n.* an occasion of celebrating.

Celery *n.* pale green stems that are eaten raw or cooked as a vegetable; a garden plant with crisp.

Celeste *adj.* sky-blue.

Celestial *n.* pertaining to heaven; divin; handsome; as opposed to temporal.

Celibacy *n.* unmarried life.

Celibate *n. & adj.* unmarried and chaste; of chastity; practising celibacy.

Cell *n.* a small room in a monastery or prison, compartment in a bee's comb, an electrical apparatus, enclosed cavity in an organism, underground room.

Cellar *n.* an underground room for storing things, wine, etc.

Cellarage *n.* charge for storing something in a cellar.

Cellarer *n.* a keeper of monastery's wine and food.

Cellaret *n.* a case or sideboard for keeping wine-bottles in dining-room.

Cellular *adj.* having small cavities.

Cellule *n.* cavity-cell or cell of protoplasm; a small cell.

Celluloid *n.* an artificial substance resembling ivory; a hard elastic substance made chiefly of cellulose.

Cellulose *n.* a natural substance that forms the main part of all plants and trees and is used in making plastics.

Celt *n.* people who are Celtic speaking a branch of Indo-Germanic family of language.

Cement *n.* strong mortar of calcinated lime and clay, anything used or sticking things.

Cemetery *n.* a place for burials: graveyard; an area of land used for burying dead people.

Cenotaph *n.* monument raised in the memory of a person who is buried elsewhere, especially soldiers killed in war.

Cense *v.t.* to perfume with incense; to think; to assess; to adore or perfume with incense.

Censer *n.* a small stand or vessel in which incense is burnt.

Censor *n.* a vessel in which incense is burnt.

Censorial *adj.* severaly critical; given to judging others; tending to find faults in people or things; fault-finding; overcritical.

Censual *adj.* pertaining of censure.

Censure *n.* expression of disapproval; depreciation; reproof; a judgement which is unfavourable; adverse judgement; reprimand.

Census *n.* an official numbering of population.

Cent *n.* one-100th part of a US dollor or of certain other metric units of currency; metal coin of this value.

Cental *n.* weight of 100lb. used for corn.

Centaur *n.* a figure in western mythology—half man and half horse.

Centenarian *n.* a person aged 100 years or more.

Centenary *adj.* commemoration atter one hundred years.

Centennial *adj.* happening once in hundred years; having lived or lasted for one hundred years.

Center *n.* a waist-belt.

Centesimal *adj.* one hundredth part; reckoning or reckoned by hundredths.

Centigrade *adj.* divided into hundred; having a 100 degrees (of Celsius thermometer, with freezing point 0 and boiling point 100).

Centillion *n.* the hundred power of million.

Centipede *n.* a many footed crawling wingless animal.

Cento *n.* a poem or other composition derived mostly form pieces of other authors and not original.

Central *adj.* pertaining to centre; principle; leading; near the centre; dominant.

Centre *n.* the middle point or part of something; a point that is equally distant from all sides of something; a place from which administration is organized.

Centrebit *n.* a boring instrument; a tool of burglar; a kind of boring-tool.

Centreboard *n.* a movable board that can be lowered through a hole in the bottom of a sailing-boat to keep it steady when sailing.

Centric, Centrical *adjs.* at or near the centre; from a centre.

Centrifugal *adj.* tending to fly off from centre.

Centripetal *adj.* moving or tending to move towards a centre.

Centuple *adj.* a hundredfold.

Centuplicate *v.t.* to make a hundredfold.

Centurion *n.* one who scores or achieves a century; commander of 100 soldiers in Rome.

Century *n.* a hundred of something, one hundred successive years.

Cephalic *adj.* pertaining to the head.

Ceramic *adj.* of the art of pottery.

Cerastium *n.* a hoary-leaved herb.

Cerated *adj.* covered with wax.

Cerberus *n.* in western mythology a three or more headed dog who guards the gate of hell.

Cere *n.* naked wax-like membrane at the base of some birds' beaks.

Cereal *adj.* of corn. *n.* (*usu. pl.*) kinds of edible grain (used for human food).

Cerebellum *n.* little or hinder brain.

Cerebral *adj.* pertaining to brain particularly to cerebrum; of the consonant sounds.

Cerebration *n.* the action of cerebrum, working of the brain.

Cerebro-spinal *adj.* of the brain and the spine.

Cerebrum *n.* the front part of the brain; the brain proper.

Cerement *n.* (*usu. pl.*) grave clothes.

Ceremonial *adj.* with ceremony or ritual, formal. *n.* formality.

Ceremonious *adj.* addicted or showing addiction to ceremony; behaving or performed in a formal or elaborate way.

Ceremony *n.* religious or solemn observance.

Ceres *n.* the Roman goddess of growth.

Ceriph *n.* stroke; cross line.

Cerise *n.* & *adj.* (of) a light clear red.

Cerography *n.* the art of engraving on wax.

Certain *adj.* settled; sure; indisputable; reliable; assured; any; inevitable; regular; some one.

Certes *adv.* certainly; assuredly; without doubt.

Certificate *n.* testimony in writing; voucher; testimony of good character or qualification.

Certifier *n.* one who certifies.

Certify *v.t.* to make known as certain; to assure; to bear testimony to attest formally; to inform.

Certitude *n.* a feeling of certainty, conviction.

Cerulean *adj.* skyblue; deep-blue.

Cerumen *n.* wax secreted by the ear.

Ceruse *n.* a white paint from carbonate and hydrate of lead (*esp.* as a cosmetic), white lead.

Cervical *adj.* of the neck.

Cervine *adj.* relating to or like deer.

Cess *n.* an additional tax; local tax on goods.

Cessation *n.* rest; pause; ceasing; end; the action or act of stopping.

Cesspool *n.* a well sunk for drainage.

Cesspit *n.* a covered hole or container in the ground into which liquid waste from a building flows.

Cestoid *n.* a ribbon-like worm.

Cetacean *adj.* & *n.* (of) the *Cetacea* or marine mammals.

Ceterach *n.* kinds of fern with frond-backs covered with scales.

Chablis *n.* famous white wine of France; a dry white wine from E. France.

Chafe *v.t.* & *i.* to rub, to irritate, to make angry, to fret.

Chafer *n.* a chafing-dish in which cooking is done on coal; a kind of beetle.

Chaff *n.* hust of grain; fodder; worthless thing; the outer covering of any grain used as food, *e.g.* corn, wheat, etc.

Chaffinch *n.* a common British small bird whose pleasant song is heard from early spring to the middle of summer.

Chagrin *n.* a feeling of disappointment or annoyance at having failed, made a mistake, etc.

Chain *n.* a connected series of links, fetters, necklace, a length of 66 feet. 66 *v.t.* to connect in links; to tie in chains.

Chair *n.* a portable seat for one, professorship, office, a chairman.

Chairman *n.* one who presides over a meeting.

Chaise *n.* a pleasure carriage.

Chalcedony *n.* chrysoprase; cornelian; a precious stone of quartz kind with many varieties as agate.

Charldron *n.* a coal measure, 36 bushels.

Chalice *n.* goblet, a cup of bowl.

Chalk *n.* calcium carbonate; a soft white substance used for writing; a type of soft white rock.

Challenge *n.* call for contest, or fight; calling to account; demand; claim; accusation; objection.

Chamber *n.* a room, judge's private room, bedroom, one of the houses of Parliament, enclosed space.

Chameleon *n.* a kind of long lizard famous for changing its colour; a person of inconsistent habits.

Chamfer *v.t.* to bevel or slope in a symmetrical manner.

Chamois *n.* wild antelope found on mountains and whose leather is used for shoes; leather made from the hide of chamois.

Champ *v.t. & i.* (especially of horses) to bite or eat something noisily.

Champagne *n.* a kind of French wine.

Champaign *n.* open level country; an expense of open country.

Champion *n.* one who fights for another or for a cause, a hero. *v.t.* to support; to defend; to challenge (obsolete); to maintain the cause of.

Chance *n.* fortune, opportunity, possibility, accident, risk, absence of design, course of events.

Chancellery *n.* the position, department or official residence of a chancellor; the staff in the department of a chancellor.

Chancellor *n.* head of a church; head of university; secretary; a senior state or law official of various kinds.

Chancery *n.* the highest court of justice.

Chancy *adj.* uncertain; risky; lucky; (*sl.*) bringing luck.

Chandelier *n.* a hanging light with branches for several electric bulbs or candles.

Chandler *n.* a dealer in soaps, candles, paints etc.; candle-maker.

Change *n.* alteration; variation; variety, small coins given for a higher one.

Channel *n.* a wooden or iron piece on ship's side; bed of flowing water; passage for water or other liquids; sea strip between land lock; course.

Chant *n.* song. *v.i & t.* to sing; to utter musically; to intone.

Chanter *n.* singer; musician (male) whether oral or instrumental.

Chanticleer *n.* a domestic cock.

Chantress *n.* a female singer (archaic of poet).

Chantry *n.* place where chanting of masses takes place; usually in a portion of chapel.

Chanty *n.* a song sung by sailors while hauling; sailors' song in heaving.

Chaos *n.* formless void, utter confusion, disorder.

Chaotic *adj.* utterly without order; confused; in a state of chaos.

Chap *n.* the jaw; a fellow, a boy; a man; a customer; check.

Chap-book *n.* cheap books (of tales, ballads, tracts, etc.) that were formerly much sold among the people by chapmen.

Chapel *n.* a place of Christian worship.

Chaperon *n.* an elderly lady who looks after and accompanies and unmarried girl; a hood or cap.

Chaplain *n.* priest in charge of a chapel; a clergyman attached to a family or institution.

Chaplet *n.* a gold ornament for head; garland of flowers; prayer-bead; a circle of leaves.

Chapman *n.* one who sells wares by going from house to house; a purchaser; a hawker; a pedlar.

Chappy *adj.* full of chaps or clefts.

Chapter *n.* a main division of a book; an association of priests; Roman numeral on the dial of clock.

Chapter-house *n.* a building used for the meetings of a chapter.

Char *v.t.* & *i.* to burn and turn into charcoal; to do; to accomplish; to become or make something black by burning; to scorch.

Char-a-bane *n.* an early type of bus used especially for pleasure trips, with many seats looking forward, for holiday excursions.

Character *n.* a distinctive mark, characteristics, a person's handwriting, style, moral strength, reputation, an actor.

Characteristic *adj.* & *n.* peculiar; forming part of the character of a person or thing.

Charade *n.* a game of guessing word from wirtten clue, a riddle.

Charcoal *n.* coal prepared by charring wood; a black substance made by burning wood slowly in an oven with a little air.

Chare (*usu. pl.*) *n.* household or domestic work; odd jobs of house-work.

Charge *n.* load, weight, right, quantity put into a thing, expense, duty, care, custody, thing entrusted, injunction duty, accusation, signal for attack.

Chargeable *n.* accusable, imputable.

Charger *n.* a horse ridden by a soldier in battle; an apparatus for charging a battery.

Charge-sheet a list of offenders and their offences.

Chariot *n.* a state car drawn by horses; a car in which war is fought or triumphal march is staged.

Charitable *n.* bountiful; philanthropic; showing charity; of charity.

Charity *n.* kindness; alms; liberality; love for all; habit of doing good to others; lenience in judging others.

Charivari *n.* medley of sounds; hurly-burly.

Charlaton *n.* quack; an impostor pretending knowledge or skill.

Charleston *n.* a fast dance, popular in the 1920s, in which the knees are turned inwards and the legs kicked sideways.

Charlock *n.* field mustard.

Charlotte *n.* a dish containing apple and bread crumbs or any other fruit; pudding of cooked fruit under bread-crumbs.

Charm *n.* words or characters acting as a spell, amulet, attractiveness.

Charmer *n.* magician; one who creates spells or fascinates; one with the power of charms.

Charnel-house *n.* (especially formerly) a place for keeping dead human bodies or bones.

Chart *n.* navigator's map, a tabulated sheet. *v.t.* to make a chart.

Charter *n.* a written statement describing the rights that a certain group of people have or should have.

Chartography *n.* the art or business of map-making, cartography.

Charwoman *n.* woman hired for doing domestic work during day; a woman employed to clean a house.

Chary *adj.* careful; cautious; miser; not extravagant; frugal.

Chase *n.* pursuit, an open park, a hunted animal, an iron frame for holding composed types, part of a gun.

Chaser *n.* hunter; one who chases; a pursuer; a chasing aircraft; a woman who hunts men.

Chasing *n.* the art of engraving.

Chasm *n.* gap; opening; a deep cleft; gulf; fissure; wide difference (of feelings or interest or position); blank.

Chassis *n.* underbody or frame of motor car or of gun-carriage.

Chaste *adj.* virgin, pure, simple unadorned.

Chasten *v.t.* to make chaste; to purify; to correct; to refine.

Chastise *v.t.* to correct; to force to obey; to punish; to beat.

Chastiser *n.* one who punishes.

Chastity *n.* good conduct; purity; virginity; restraint; moderation; refinement.

Chasuble *n.* a loose garment worn over all other clothes by a priest at certain religious functions.

Chat *v.i.* indulge in easy talk. *n.* an idle talk; gossip; a kind of small birds.

Chateau *n.* a country house; a castle; a castle or large country house in France.

Chattel *n.* movable possession, goods; leasehold property.

Chatter *v.t.* & *i.* an idle talk. *n.* useless talk; sound of teeth striking against each other.

Chatty *adj.* talkative; fond of chat.

Chauffer *n.* a small portable furnace.

Chauvinism *n.* an aggressive and unreasonable belief that one's own country is better than all others; bellicose or exaggerated patriotism.

Cheap *adj.* low in price; not costly; worthless.

Cheaply *adj.* at a small price.

Cheat *v.t.* & *i.* to deceive; to deprive of anything; to be sexually unfaithful to one's wife; to get be fraud.

Cheatry *n.* fraud.

Cheating *adj.* deceptive, fraudulent.

Check *v.t.* & *i.* (Chess) to subject (an opponent or his king) to check; to stop; to revise and correct.

Check-book *n.* containing blank cheques.

Checkmate *n.* final defeat in chessgame; final defeat in any enterprise; complete overthrow.

Cheddar *n.* a kind of cheese.

Cheek *n.* outer wall of mouth or face; side of door or window; impudence; (colloq.) saucy speech; either of the buttocks.

Cheeky *adj.* stylish; saucy; showing lack of respect; impudent, rude and daring.

Cheep *v.i.* to chip or pipe like a young bird.

Cheer *n.* praise; support or encouragement to somebody; a mood of happiness.

Cheerful *adj.* pleasant, hopeful, gay, lively. **Cheerfully,** *adv.* in good spirits.

Cheerio *int.* a slang type of good-bye; a word of encouragement.

Cheerly *adv.* in a cheerfull manner; with will.

Cheery *adj.* lively and cheerful.

Cheese *n.* food made of pressed curds.

Chef *n.* a professional cook, especially the chief cook in a restaurant.

Cheliform *adj.* of the form of a claw.

Chemical *adj.* relating to chemistry; specialist in chemistry; studying chemistry; produced by or using chemistry or chemicals.

Chemise *n.* ladies shirt or an under-garment; a loose dress that hangs straight from the shoulders, worn by women.

Chemist *n.* a dealer in medical drugs, a person who is skilled in chemisty.

Chemistry *n.* a science which deals with matter, its properties and the combination of particles and their reaction to each others, and how they behave under different conditions.

Cheque *n.* a written order to banker for payment of money.

Chequer, Checker *ns.* a pattern consisting of squares often alternately coloured. *v.t.* to mark with chequers.

Cherish *v.t.* to hold dear; to love and want to protect somebody; to nurse; to foster to treat with tenderness and affection; to cling to.

Cheroot *n.* a kind of cigar not pointed at either end, root of the shaya tree grown in Madras.

Cherry *n.* a plum tree and its fruit which grows in mountains and has pulpy drupe; other fruits in general.

Cherub *n.* a kind of angel with wings and human shape; a beautiful child in figurative sense.

Chervil *n.* a garden herb whose leaves are used for giving flavour to soups, salads.

Chess *n.* a game of two player played on board divided into sixty-four squares with pieces called 'chessmen'.

Chessel *n.* a mould for making cheese.

Chest *n.* large box; a large strong usually wooden box for keeping or moving things in; treasury.

Chesterfield *n.* a kind of overcoat; a kind of couch.

Chestnut *n.* a tree or its edible fruit.

Chevalier *n.* a gallant; a cavalry man; a knight; a member of certain orders of knighthood.

Cheviot *n.* wool or cloth of sheep of cheviot hill.

Chevy *n.* shout noise; shout hunting cry; pursuit. *v.t.* & *i.* to chase or run; to throw.

Chew *v.t.* & *i.* to grind with teeth; to masticate; to cut; to meditate; to ruminate over.

Chiaroscuro *n.* light and shade in painting.

Chibouk *n.* a long Turkish tobacco-pipe.

Chic *adj.* attractive and fashionable in style. *n.* style and elegance in dress; modishness; fashionableness.

Chicane *v.t.* & *t.* to defraud or cheat; to cheat. *n.* a strick; a special card in game of bridge.

Chicanery *n.* trickery, pettifogging, artifice.

Chick *n.* a young one of a bird, particularly of hen.

Chicken *n.* young one owl; a child; a girl of tender years.

Chicken-hearted *adj.* fearful; timid; cowardly; not brave.

Chicken-pox *n.* a contagious pustulous disease.

Chick-pea *n.* a pale yellow seed, similar in size to a pea.

Chick-weed *n.* a small plant.

Chicory *n.* roots of a plant, used with or instead of coffee.

Chief *n.* a leader of ruler; first in importance; most important; principal; leading highest in office.

Chieftain *n.* a captain, the head of a tribe.

Chiffon *n.* a cloth having gauze used making dresses especially of females; thin gauze.

Chignon *n.* women's back hair, specially when folded up and raised rounded a pad of artificial hair.

Chigoe *n.* a species of flea of the West Indies and South America (burrowing into skin).

Chilblain *n.* a painful inflammation of skin on hand or feet.

Child *n.* an infant; son or daughter of any age; a young person from birth to the age of full physical development.

Childermas *n.* the festival of Holy Innocents celebrated on 28th December.

Childhood *n.* infancy.

Childish *adj.* pertaining to child; what is proper for childhood; like a child; trifling; ignorant; weak; silly.

Chiliad *n.* a thousand years.

Chill *n.* coldness; absence of heat; feeling of being damped; discouraging influence; depression of mind; an unpleasant coldness in the air.

Chilli *n.* a kind of guinea pepper or capsicum.

Chilly *adj.* feeling cold; sensitive to cold; cold-mannered.

Chime *n.* the series of notes sounded by a set of bells; agreement of relation or of sound, rhyme and harmony.

Chimera *n.* an imaginary creature composed of the parts of several different animals.

Chimney *n.* the long passage for escape of smoke in a factory; the glass cover of lantern of flame of any kind.

Chimpanzee *n.* an ape of Africa which is the nearest kin of man and most developed.

Chin *n.* the front part of the face below the mouth.

China *n.* the earthenware first made in China; a fine baked white clay used in making cups, plates, etc.

Chinchilla *n.* a grey fur.

Chine *n.* spine; backbone; ridge; ravine; the joint of meat from the backbone; a hill-ridge.

Chinese *adj.* Chinese language; inhabitant of China.

Chink *n.* a sound produced by the striking of coins or glasses; a crevice; peephole; a narrow opening.

Chintz *n.* glazed printed cotton cloth.

Chip *n.* a thin piece; slice of fruit or vegetable; a trick in wrestling; a sovereign; piece of dried cow dung; a key or musical instrument.

Chipmuck *n.* a small North American animal similar to a squirrel but with black and white marking along its back.

Chippendale *n.* a light style of drawing-room furniture.

Chippy *adj.* full of chips, uninteresting.

Chirography *n.* handwriting.

Chirology *n.* the art of practice of talking with signs made by hands and fingers.

Chiromancy *n.* fortune telling by seeing the hand.

Chiropody *n.* treatment of hands, corns, nails, feet, etc.

Chirp *n.* a short sharp sound made by small birds or certain insects.

Chirpy *adj.* cheerful; lively; chatting; merry.

Chirr *v.t.* to make trilling sound, to chrip like a cricket.

Chirrup *v.t.* to cheer up; to make a sound with the mouth for urging a horse.

Chisel *n.* a tool with a sharp flat edge at the end used by sculptor for cutting for shaping wood, stone or metal.

Chit *n.* a young child; young woman; small piece of paper; a girl.

Chitty *n.* like a babe, childish.

Chitchat *n.* idle talking; chatting, light conversation; gossip.

Chivalric *adj.* worthy of a kinght, courteous.

Chivalry *n.* gallantary, a kinght's characteristics.

Chive *n.* a herb like onions and other leaves used in soup; a bulb of small size.

Chloral *n.* a liquid of oily nature having no colour; a white substance used for making unconscious.

Chlorosis *n.* disease of women of young age in which blood becomes scarce; blanching of green parts of plants and leaves due to scarcity of oxygen.

Chock *n.* a block of wood. *v.t.* to fasten; to block; to make fast with a chock. *adv.* tightly, closely.

Chock-full *adj.* completely full.

Chocolate *n.* a sweet eaten by children mostly containing sugar, cocoa in paste form, or cake form; a tea-like drink prepared with this paste.

Choice *n.* act or power of choosing, the thing chosen, selection, alternative.

Choir *n.* a band or singers in a church or elsewhere; birds singing.

Choke *v.t. & i.* to suffocate, to become speechless, to stifle, to block up.

Choker *n.* one who or which chokes; high collar; a necklace or band of material worn closely round the throat by women.

Choky *n.* & *adj.* tending to choke or exert pressure; a custom or toll station; a lock-up.

Choler *n.* bile, biliousness, anger.

Cholera *n.* an infectious disease in which vomiting takes place accompanied by diarrhoea.

Choose *v.t.* & *i.* to select; to determine to decide; to think fit.

Chop *n.* a small piece of meat; a crack; a cleft; an exchange; jaw; person with fat cheeks; a seal; an act of killing somebody. *v.i.* to cut by a blow; to exchange.

Chopper *n.* a butcher's cleaver, a short axe.

Choppy *adj.* full of crags or clefts.

Chopstick *n.* (*pl.*) two sticks with which the Chinese and Japanese take rice etc. usually either of a pair of thin sticks made of wood.

Choral *adj.* fit for singing in chorus; composed for or sung by a choir.

Chorale *n.* a simple tune of hymn.

Choralist *n.* a choral singer.

Chord *n.* the string of a muscial instrument, a straight line joining the ends of an arc.

Chore *n.* household work like cooking; a task done as part of a routine; an unpleasant or boring task.

Chorion *n.* the outer membraneous envelope of foetus.

Chorister *n.* a person, especially a boy, who sings in a choir.

Choroid *n.* the membrane which lines the eye-ball.

Chortle *v.i.* to make noise like a loud chuckle.

Chorus *n.* a band of singers; a choir; the line in a song repeated by all the singers, usually large group of singers.

Chou *n.* ornamental knot of ribbon.

Chough *n.* a crow with red leg; a jack daw.

Chouse *v.t.* & *n.* one who cheats; one easily deceived; a trick; to swindle.

Chowder *n.* fish and vegetables cooked together in milk.

Chrism *n.* an unguent, holy oil.

Christ *n.* the man who founded the Christian religion and who Christians believe is the son of God; the Messiah.

Christendom *n.* Christians, Christain countries.

Christening *n.* the ceremony of baptism.

Christlike *adj.* partaking of the nature and attributes of Christ; like Christ in character of action.

Christmas *n.* the festival of Christ's birth which falls on the 25th of December.

Chrome *n.* a yellow pigment got from the compounds of chromium.

Chromolithograph *n.* a picture lithographed in colours.

Chronic *adj.* old; lingering (spoken of diseases) constitutional; happening confirmed; permanent; bad; intense.

Chronograph *n.* an instrument to record time with great accuracy.

Chronologer *n.* one versed in the science of chronology.

Chronology *n.* the science and method of computing time and dates.

Chronoscope *n.* an instrument for measuring velocities of time.

Chrysalis *n.* the form of an insect (especially a butterfly or moth) while it is changing into a adult and is enclosed in a hard case.

Chrysanthemum *n.* a kind of flower; a garden plant with brightly coloured flowers.

Chrysolite *n.* a kind of green or yellow gem.

Cyrysology *n.* the branch of political economy which treats of production of wealth.

Chub *n.* a kind of river fish with coarse flesh and skin; a small fish with a thick body, living in rivers.

Chuck *n.* the call of fowl, term of enderment, jerk under the chin, a contrivance in lathe.

Chucker *n.* each of the periods into which the game of polo is divided.

Chuckle *n.* a partly suppressed laugh. *v.i.* to laugh in a suppressed manner; to show signs of cheer.

Chuffy *adj.* with swollen cheeks.

Chum *n.* a chamber fellow; an old friend; a good friend.

Chump *n.* a heavy piece of wood, the thick end, a blockhead.

Chunk *n.* a thick slice of bread; thick piece of wood; a thick solid piece that has been cut or broken of something.

Church *n.* a building for public, Christian worship, an organised Christian society, the clergy.

Churchyard *n.* often used for burials; the graveyard attached to a church; the enclosed area of land round a church.

Churl *n.* an ill-bred fellow, a rustic.

Churn *n.* a machine in which milk or cream is shaken to make butter; container in which milk is carried from a farm.

Chute *n.* fall of water with speed and rush; sloping passage.

Chyle *n.* a milk-like fluid which is separated in the small intestine from the food eaten.

Chyme *n.* food converted into acid pulp.

Cicada *n.* a tree-insect which makes a loud noise.

Cicatrize *v.i.* & *t.* to skin over; to heal up.

Cicerone *n.* a guide who shows the strange things or places to outsiders.

Ciceronian *adj.* pure as cicero Latin, *n.* an expert in Cicero.

CID *n.* (in Britain) Criminal Investigation Department (the department of the police force responsible for solving crimes).

Cider *n.* a fermented drink from apple juice.

Cigar *n.* roll of tobacco leaf containing tobacco used for smoking like cheroot.

Cigarette *n.* tobacco rolled in fine paper in small sizes for smoking.

Cilia *n. pl.* eye-lashes.

Ciliary *adj.* pertaining to the eye-lids.

Cilice *n.* a garment of hair-cloth.

Cimmerian *adj.* extremely dark; relating to a tribe mentioned in old books which lived in darkness.

Cinch *n.* & *v.t.* girth of saddle; a certainty; an easy task; advantage; a sure hold, to fasten firmly; to girth tightly up.

Cinchona *n.* a tree from the bark of which quinine is extracted.

Cincture *n.* border; belt round the back; a girdle; belt; fillet.

Cinder *n.* ash; remaining portion of coal after burning; a chemical mixed with tea and soda to make it strong; wood, etc. that is no longer burning but may still be hot.

Cinder-path *n.* a running track.

Cindery *adj.* composed of cinders.

Cinema *n.* a play of moving pictures; a moving film; a building in which films are shown.

Cinematograph *n.* art and science of preparing cinematograph films; an apparatus producing pictures of motion.

Cinephone *n.* a gramophone fitted with some device to synchronize cinematograph with the sounds produced by it.

Cinerary *adj.* & *n.* pertaining to ashes.

Cinereous *adj.* ashy grey.

Cingalese *n.* & *adj.* a native of or belonging to Ceylon.

Cinnabar *n.* red mercuric sulphide; vermillion.

Cinnamon *n.* a spice made from the inner bark of a SE Asian tree, used especially to give flavour to sweet foods.

Cinque *n.* number five in cards; number five in dice.

Cinquefoil *n.* a plant with five-lobed leaves.

Cipher (Cypher) *n.* the symbol (0); person of no importance, secret writing.

Circa *prep.* & *adv.* about, around.

Circean *adj.* degrading; pertaining to a goddess who made men into swines by magic; enchanting; tempting.

Circle *n.* a figure on plane surface bounded by line and having a centre; a round body.

Circuit *n.* a line enclosing a circle; journey; path of electric current;

an apparatus through which an electric current flows.

Circular *adj.* in the shape of a circle, round. *n.* a letter or printed notice, a coy of which is sent to several persons.

Circum *pref.* in the sense of 'round about'.

Circumambient *adj.* surrounding; encompassing; being on all sides.

Circumcise *v.t.* to cut off the foreskin of a boy or man for religious or medical reasons.

Circumcision *n.* Jewish religious rite or surgical operation of cutting of the foreskin.

Circumference *n.* the line encompassing a circle.

Circumflex *adj.* & *n.* state of bending round; the mark (^) put over a vowel in French and some other languages to show how it is pronounced. (^).

Circmfluence *n.* flowing round on all sides.

Circumfuse *v.t.* to bathe; to pour round; to surround.

Circumgyration *n.* turning this way and that; turning round.

Circumjacent *adj.* which is lying round; bordering on every side; surrounding; situated around.

Circumlocution *n.* using many words for one, roundabout expression.

Circumlocutory *adj.* involving circumlocution.

Circumnavigate *v.t.* to sail round the globe or anything else, especially the world.

Circumoral *adj.* placed round the mouth.

Circumscribe *v.t.* to enclose in a line drawn around; to draw a circle round another space so that it touches all the outside points or corners.

Circumsolar *adj.* being near the sun; revolving round the sun.

Circumspect *adj.* cautious; considering everything carefully before acting; taking everything into account.

Circumspection *n.* thoughtfulness; exercise of caution.

Circumstance *n.* event, incident, occurance, situation, (*pl.*) state o of things, event.

Circumstantial *adj.* accidental; inferred from the circumstances of the case; with many details.

Circumvallation *n.* a rampart or entrenchments made round a place.

Circumvent *v.t.* to entrap, to cheat.

Circumvolution *n.* the act of rolling round, a coil.

Circus *n.* a circular space; an open circle with streets converging on it; play ground; place for exhibiting.

Cirque *n.* an arena; a natural amphi theatre.

Cirrus *n.* form of cloud like distended locks of hair, a tendril.

Cist *n.* a stone chest, a grave of prehistoric times.

Cistern *n.* a reservoir for storing water, especially one connected to a toilet or in the roof of a house supplying water to the rooms below.

Cistus *n.* rock-rose; kind of flowering shrub.

Citable *adj.* able to be cited or quoted.

Citadel *n.* a fortress protecting or dominating a city.

Citation *n.* reverence; an official summons to appear as before a court; mention; a enumeration.

Cite *v.t.* to quote, to summon, to mention as example.

Cithern *n.* a lute; a guitar.

Citizen *n.* an inhabitant of a state; a townman; a person who has full rights as a member of a country.

Citrate *n.* salt of citric acid.

Citric acid *n.* an acid existing in the juice of the citron.

Citrine *adj.* lemon coloured, yellow.

Citron *n.* a large lemon like fruit; the fruit of lemon kind but larger.

City *n.* a town with special rights given by a king or queen and usually containing a cathedral.

Civet *n.* a kind of perfume; a strong-smelling substance obtained from a civet and used in making perfume.

Civic *adj.* proper to citizens, of city, municipal, civil.

Civies *n.* civilian clothes.

Civil *adj.* relating to people, becoming a citizen, political, polite, not criminal.

Clack *n.* rattle; chatter; a short sharp sound made by hard objects hitting each other. *v.t.* to clap; to cackle as a hen; to utter heedlessly.

Clad *adj.* clothed; covered; adorned; endowed with.

Claim *v.t.* to demand as one's due, to profess to be.

Claimant *n.* one who makes a claim; a claiming party; one who asserts a right or title.

Clairvoyance *n.* the faculty of seeing mentally what is happening elsewhere.

Clam *n.* a clamp as of bricks; a gripping of instruments; an uncommunicative person.

Clamant *adj.* insistent calling for help or remedy; clamourous resounding; insistent; urgent.

Clamber *v.i.* to climb with difficulty.

Clammy *adj.* moist and sticky; noisy confusion of loud voices; a continuous vehement objective or demanding adhesive.

Clamorous *adj.* vociferous; noisy with the tongue.

Clamour *n.* a loud confused noise, made especially by many people shouting.

Clamp *n.* a clasp or hand used to hold things together. *v.t.* to put a clamp on; to strengthen or bind with clamps.

Clan *n.* a united group of families or relatives having a common ancestor; one hereditary chieftain.

Clandestine *adj.* hidden, secret.

Clang *v.t.* to make a metallic sound.

Clangour *n.* a continuous loud ringing noise or disturbance.

Clank *n.* a short harsh metalic sound; a sound as of a heavy chain shaken.

Clanship *n.* prevalence of a clannish feeling.

Clansman *n.* the member of a clan or tribe.

Clap *n.* a sharp sudden noise as of two hard flat objects coming together.

Clapboard *n.* a narrow board for weather-boarding.

Clap net *n.* a net closed by a pulling strip.

Clapper *n.* one who claps, the tongue of a bell.

Clapper-claw *v.t.* to scratch and hit; to abuse; to criticize spitefully.

Claptrap *n.* language or doings meant to catch applause; worthless; insincere or stupid talk.

Claque *n.* a ground of hired applauders; a hired body of applauders.

Clarence *n.* a four-wheeled closed carriage.

Clarendon *n.* a type with heavy face.

Claret *n.* the name given to red wines.

Clarification *n.* the act of clarifying.

Clarify *v.t. & i.* to make something clear especially a fact.

Clarine *n.* a wooden single reed muscial instrument.

Clarion *n.* a shrill trumpet; a rousing call to action.

Clarionet *n.* a clarinet; a reed instrument with holes and keys.

Clarity *n.* purity, clearness.

Clarkia *n.* a garden flower.

Clash *n.* a confused resounding metalic noise; opposition.

Clasp *n.* a contrivance for fastening, embrace, reach.

Class *n.* a rank or order of society, a scientific division, a set of students taught together.

Classic *adj.* of the highest quality; of enduring interest, quality or style; of literary or historical fame.

Classical *adj.* (of music) serious and traditional in style.

Classicism *n.* a Greek or Latin idiom; classical scholastic.

Classification *n.* the placing of animals and plants into groups according to their structure, origin.

Classify *v.t.* to arrange something in categories or groups or distribute in classes; to arrange in classes.

Classy *adj.* elegant; grand; superior.

Clatter *n.* a sound; a noisy talk.

Clatterer *n.* a babbler.

Clause *n.* part of a sentence with subject and predicate; a separate statement in a legal or state document.

Claustral *adj.* narrow; of the cloister monastic.

Clavichard *n.* the first string instrument with a keyboard predecessor of piano.

Clavicle *n.* collar-bone; merry thought of birds.

Claw *n.* the thorny nail of a beast.

Clay *n.* tenacious earth; earth of various colours brittle when dry and sticky when wet.

Claymore *n.* a large sword with two sharp edges, formerly used in Scotland.

Clean *adj.* free from dirt or blemish, clear, pure, guiltless, holy.

Clear *adj.* & *adv.* unclouded, bright, lustrous, distinct, intelligible, manifest, decided, free, unobstructed, sharply, intelligent, quite.

Clearance *n.* the act of clearing; a certificate for a vessel to sail.

Clearing *n.* act of making clear, a piece of land cleared of trees for cultivation, a method of changing cheques & drafts in bank.

Clearly *adv.* in a clear manner; no doubt; explicitly.

Cleat *n.* a wedge or piece of wood for fastening.

Cleavable *adj.* that may be broken up, divided or split.

Cleavage *n.* a line along which material such as rock or wood splits; the division between a woman's breasts that can be seen above a dress which does not completely cover them.

Cleave *v.t.* to split; to break; to chop. *v.i.* to stick fast.

Cleaver *n.* a heavy knife with a broad blade used for chopping meat.

Cleek *n.* a large hook; a narrow iron headed golf club.

Clef *n.* in musical notation; a character placed upon the staff to determine the pitch; a symbol at the beginning of a line of printed music showing the pitch of the notes on it.

Cleft *adj.* a fissure, a crack, a split. *n.* a fissure; a crack; a split.

Cleg *n.* gadfly; a large grey fly; a horse-fly.

Clem *v.t.* & *i.* to starve.

Clematis *n.* a climbing plant with white, purple or pink flowers.

Clemency *n.* mildness of temper.

Clement *adj.* mild (*esp.* of weather); kind; gentle; merciful; lenient.

Clench *v.t.* & *i.* to clinch; to grasp; to close tight; to make conclusive.

Clerestory *n.* the upper part of a wall in a large church with a row of windows in it.

Clergy *n.* the clerical order, the ministers of Gospel. **Clergyman,** *n.* a man in holy orders.

Cleric *n.* a clergyman; a religious leader in any religion. *adj.* of clergy.

Clerical *adj.* of a clergyman; belonging to the clergy or a clerk; of or done by a clerk.

Clerk *n.* one who works in an office as writing letters, keeping accounts etc., as a bank clerk; a salesman in a store.

Clever *adj.* dexterous; skilful; ingenious.

Clew *n.* a ball of thread, that guide through a labyrinth; any thing that points towards the solution of a mystery; the corner of a sail.

Cliche *n.* the impression made by a die on any soft metal; a stereotyped phrase; a phrase or an idea which is used so often that it is no longer interesting.

Click *n.* a catch in machinery, a sharp short sound.

Client *n.* one in whose interest a lawyer acts; one who engages the services of a lawyer.

Cliff *n.* the stop and rugged face of a rocky mass; a headland; a precipice, especially at the edge of the sea.

Climatology *n.* the science of climates, meterology.

Climax *n.* the last and most important of a number of ideas, events, expressions; the highest point of sexual pleasure.

Climb *v.t.* to ascend, to mount. *n.* one who climbs; creeper.

Clime *n.* a tract or region of a country, climate.

Clinch *v.t.* to secure firmly, as a nail by bending down the protruding point; to confirm as a bargain or an argument.

Cling *v.i.* to hold on to something firmly as grasping or embracing; to remain together; to resist separation.

Clingstone *n.* a kind of peach or nectarine in which flesh adheres to stone.

Clinic *n.* the teaching of medicines or surgery by treatment or by operating the patients in the presence of the students.

Clink *n.* a sharp ringing sound like that made by small pieces of metal or glass knocking together.

Clinometer *n.* an instrument for measuring slopes.

Clip *v.t.* the wool of a season's sheep, shearing, a device for gripping or clasping or holding things together.

Clique *n.* a small exclusive party or action, a gang.

Cloak *n.* loose garment; something which covers or hides; a disguise.

Clock *n*. any clock-like device for recording distance etc.
Clod *n*. a lump of earth, a lout.
Clog *n*. anything that impedes motion as a block attached to animal or vehicle.
Cloggy *adj*. knotty, sticky.
Cloister *n*. an arched way or covered walk running round the walls of certain portions or monastic and collegiate building.
Close *adj*. conclusion, end.
Closet *n*. a cupboard or small room for storing things.
Closeted *adj*. in private consultation.
Closure *n*. the act of closing; the stopping of debate by vote.
Clot *n*. a semi-solid lump.
Cloth *n*. a woven fabric of wool, silk, cotton, rayon etc.; clerical attire.
Clothier *n*. a cloth-maker; a dealer in cloth or clothes.
Clothing *n*. clothes; apparel; dress.
Clotted *adj*. coagulated.
Cloud *n*. a mass of visible vapour or an aggregation of water or icy particles, floating in the atmosphere at various heights, exhibiting a large variety of shapes which partly aid the determination of weather conditions.
Clough *n*. a gorge; a ravine; a steep valley.
Clout *n*. a piece of cloth or leather for mending, a rag, an iron plate, nails for shoe soles, centre of target, a knock.
Clove *n*. a dried flower bud of a tropical evergreen tree used as a spice.
Clover *n*. a kind of grass.
Clown *n*. a rustic, an ill-bred person, a buffoon.
Cloy *v.t.* & *i.* to overfeed, to disgust, to weary, to cause distaste, to become distasteful owing to excess.
Club *n*. a stout stick or staff; cudgel; a staff with curved head used in golf, hockey etc.; a three lobed mark on a playing card.
Clubfooted *adj*. crooked in the feet; having short deformed feet.
Cluck *n*. call of a hen to her chickens. *v.t.* to make noise of a brooding hen.
Clue *n*. a guiding principle, the thread of a story, train of thought.
Clumber *n*. a kind of spaniel; a breed of spaniel.
Clump *n*. a thick cluster; lump; a dull sound as of heavy tramping; an irregular thick piece of mass.
Clumsy *adj*. shapeless; consisting of clumps; awkward in movement or shape; ill-contrived; ill-conceived; tactless.
Cluster *n*. a group of bunch, as of grapes, dropped simultaneously; an assembly.
Clutch *v.t.* & *i.* to grasp and hold firmly; to close the hands on; to hatch; to seize somebody eagerly.

Clutter *v.t.* to run with confused noise. *n.* confused noise, bustle.

Clypeus *n.* shield-like part of insect's head.

Clyster *n.* enema.

Coacervation *n.* the act of heaping together; a pile.

Coach *n.* a large four-wheeled carriage, a private tutor, a passanger railway train.

Coaching *n.* driving of a coach, instruction (*esp.* for examination).

Coachman *n.* the driver of a carriage pulled by horses.

Co-act *v.t.* & *i.* (obs.) to act together; to compel.

Co-adjust *v.t.* to adjust with other object.

Coadjutant *n.* an assistant, a colleague.

Coagulant *n.* coagulating agent.

Coagulate *v.i.* & *t.* to curdle, to solidify.

Coagulation *n.* the act of clotting.

Coal *n.* a black, brittle compact amorphous substance of variable physical and chemical composition produced by the decomposition of prehistoric vegetation, found in veins of the earth and used as fuel.

Coalesce *v.i.* to grow or come together as one; to fuse; to blend; to unite; to come together and form one group, substance.

Coalescence *n.* union, fusion.

Coalescent *adj.* uniting.

Coalition *n.* a temporary union of separate political parties; fusion into one whole, usually in order to form a government.

Coalmine, Coal-pit *ns.* a mine or a place underground where coal is dug.

Coalmouse *n.* small dark-coloured bird.

Coaming *n.* raised work about the edges of ship to keep water out.

Coarse *adj.* common, inferior, rough, unrefined, vulgar, large in texture.

Coarsely *adv.* roughly, vulgarly.

Coarseness *n.* rough nature, vulgarity.

Coarsen *v.t.* & *i.* to make or become coarse.

Coast *n.* the land next to the sea; the seashore; a region; a boundary (used chiefly in *pl.*).

Coastal *adj.* relating to coast.

Coastwise *adj.* & *adv.* along the coast; by way of the coast.

Coat *n.* an outer and upper garment with sleeves generally used by men; any outer covering, as the fur of the animal.

Coating a layer of paint, cloth for coats.

Coax *v.t.* to pet; to caress; to persuade; to persuade somebody gently or gradually; to force gently.

Cob *n.* a roundish mass of heap as a piece of coal; the woody spike of a corn.

Cobalt *n.* a metal like nickel.

Cobble *n.* a rounded stone generally used for paving.

Cobbler *n.* one who mends shoes; a person who repairs shoes.

Coble *n.* a kind of fishing boat.

Cobra *n.* a venomous hooded snake.

Cobswan *n.* a male swan.

Cobweb *n.* a spider's web or net; any device intended to trap.

Cocaine *n.* a drug producing local insensibility.

Coccyx *n.* a small bone at the bottom of the spine in humans; similar part in birds.

Cochineal *n.* dried insects used for making scarlet dye & carmine.

Cock *n.* a male bird, male of a domestic fowl, tapped spout, lever in gun.

Cock-hoop *adj.* exultant.

Cockade *n.* a rosette worn in hat.

Cockatoo *n.* a crested parrot.

Cockatrice *n.* a basilisk (zool.).

Cockboat *n.* a small boat.

Cockcrow *n.* the early morning, dawn.

Cocker *n.* one who follows cockfighting; a small spaniel employed in wood cock shooting.

Cockerel *n.* a young cock; a fighting youth.

Cockle *v.i.* to bulge, to pucker or wrinkle.

Cockney *n.* a native of London; London English, the way of speaking typically used by Cockneys.

Cockpit *n.* a pit or ring for cock fighting; an apartment for the wounded in a warship.

Cockroach *n.* the black beetle.

Cock-comb, Coxcomb *ns.* cock's crest; (Bot.) kinds of plant; a dandy.

Cocksure *adj.* dogmatic; very confident; quite convinced of; in a way that annoys other people.

Cock-tail *n.* & *adj.* (a horse) of racing stamp but not thorough-bred; a kind of beetle; an alcoholic drink.

Cocky, Cocksy (Coxy) *adjs.* conceited.

Coco *n.* the palm tree that produces coconut; a tropical palm bearing coconut.

Cocoa *n.* powder of crushed cacao seeds; drink made from cocoa.

Coconut *n.* a large edible nut mostly found in India near sea shores.

Cocoon *n.* the silky case spun by a silk-worm.

Cocoonery *n.* the place where silkworms are reared.

Cod *n.* a kind of food-fish found bet- ween Newfoundland and Norway.

Coddle *v.t.* & *i.* to fondle; to pamper; to treat somebody with great care and sympathy.

Code *n.* a systematic collection of laws, a secret language.

Codex *n.* a medieval manuscript in leaf form; ancient manuscript volume.

Codger *n.* (*sl.*) a chap; a queer fellow.

Codicil *n.* a supplement codifying or revoking a will.

Codify *v.t.* to put in the form of a code; to digest; to systematise; to frame laws into a code.

Codifier *n.* a codist, one who codifies.

Codlin (g) *n.* a variety of apple.

Codling *n.* a small cod-fish.

Co-ed *n.* (U.S., *sl.*) a young woman being educated at the same institution with young men.

Co-education *n.* of or relating to the system of educating girls and boys together.

Co-efficient *n.* a joint factor, a number or quantity that multiplies another number.

Coequal *adj.* & *n.* equal.

Coerce *v.t.* to restrain by force; to compel; to use coercive measures.

Coercion *n.* controlling by force.

Coercive *adj.* of or exercising coercion.

Coessential *adj.* of the same substance or essence.

Coetaneous *adj.* coeval; of the same age.

Coeternal *adj.* equally eternal with another; alike eternal.

Coeval *adj.* of the same age or duration. *n.* one of equal or same age.

Coexist *v.t.* to exist together at the same time or in the same place; (of opposing countries or groups) to exist together without fighting.

Coffee *n.* the berries or the ground seeds of a tree mostly found in India; a drink made from it.

Coffer *n.* a box for valuables, (*pl.*) treasury.

Coffin *n.* the chest or box in which a human body is buried or deposited in a vault; a casing of paste for a pie.

Cog *n.* the tooth of a wheel by which it drives another wheel or body or any similar mechanical contrivance.

Cogence also **Cogency** *n.* force; strength.

Cogent *adj.* (of reasoning, etc.) compelling assent; convincing.

Cogitable *adj.* capable of being thought; capable of being conceived.

Cogitate *adj.* to think deeply; to devise; to meditate.

Cognac *n.* a type of fine brandy made in W. France.

Cognate *adj.* kindered; allied by blood; radical characteristics; derivation from the same source.

Cognation *n.* cognate relationship.

Cognition *n.* perception, sensation, knowledge.

Cognomen *n.* nickname; surname.

Cognovit *n.* defendant's acknowledgement that plaintiff's cause is just.

Cohabit *v.i.* to dwell together as husband and wife.

Coheir *n.* a male joint heir.

Cohere *v.i.* to hold firmly together; to be logically connected or consistent; to be consistent as a part of an address; to agree.

Coherence *n.* consistency.

Coherent *adj.* holding together; not inconsistent; (of a person) able to talk clearly.

Cohesion *n.* union; the act of cohering; in physics that force by which the molecules of the same kind of substance are held together so that the substance resists disintegration.

Cohesive *adj.* producing union.

Cohibit *v.t.* to restrian.

Cohort *n.* a body of soldiers; a legion; a person; tenth part of Roman army.

Coif *n.* a kind of cap.

Coiffure *n.* a hair-dresser.

Coign *n.* a corner or external angle; a wedge.

Coil *v.t.* & *i.* to wind or twist oneself/something round and round in circles or loops, through which an electric current can pass.

Coin *n.* metal money. *v.t.* & *i.* to make money by stamping metal.

Coinage *n.* coining; coins; system of coins in use; the process of making coins.

Coincide *v.t.* to occupy the same position in space, to agree.

Coiner *n.* one who coins; a maker of money often of base coin.

Co-inhere *v.i.* to exist or inhere together.

Coir *n.* coconut-husk fibre; rough material made from the outer part of coconuts; used for making ropes, mats.

Coition *n.* a coming together, especially sexual intercourse.

Coke *v.t.* to convert coal into solid substance. *n.* a kind of coal.

Col *n.* a depression between two mountains; a gap in a ridge serving as a pass from one valley to another.

Cola *n.* a carbonate soft drink having a syrup base.

Colander *v.t.* to pass through a perforated vessel. *n.* a sieve.

Colatitude *n.* (Astron.) complement of latitude.

Cold *adj.* of a relatively low temperature; too rapid a loss of heat from the body.

Cole *n.* kinds of cabbage.

Colic *n.* griping belly-pain; a severe pain in the stomach, suffered *esp.* by babies.

Collaborate *v.t.* to cooperate or labour with another, especially in scientific and literary persuits.

Collapsible *adj.* able to be pressed down.

Collapse *n.* a sinking or falling together; extreme prostration; ruin.

Collapsable, Collapsible *adjs.* able to be pressed down; folding.

Collar *n.* a neckband, a connecting band. *v.t.* to seize by collar.

Collarette *n.* woman's collar of lace, etc.

Collate *v.t.* to bring together and compare.

Collateral *adj.* side by side, contributory, of common descent, corresponding.

Collation *n.* a light meal; collating; bestowing, especially at an unusual time.

Colleague *n.* an associate in office; a person with whom one works.

Collect *v.t.* & *i.* to assemble, to accumulate, to secure, to concentrate, to recover, to infer. *n.* a short prayer.

Collected *adj.* gathered together; not distracted.

Collection *n.* collecting; a group of objects that have been collected; set of collected specimens.

Colleen *n.* a pretty Irish girl; a girl or young woman.

College *n.* an incorporated school for instructions in the liberal arts or professional studies; a school of higher learning; building of any college.

Collegian *n.* member of a college, a University man.

Collide *v.t.* to meet and strike violently; to clash; to come into collision.

Collie *n.* a dog with long hair and a long pointed nose.

Collier *n.* coal-miner; coalship member of its crew.

Collision *n.* conflict, opposition.

Collocation *n.* position; arrangement; relative situation.

Collocutor *n.* one of the speakers in a dialogue; one's partner in colloquy.

Collodian *n.* a gluey solution of gun-cotton.

Collogue *v.t.* (*Colloq.*) to plot together; to show belief in its absence.

Colloid *adj.* & *n.* gluey (substance); (a substance) of non-crystalline semi-solid kind.

Collop *n.* a slice of meat (fried or unbaked).

Colloquial *adj.* not literary; proper or peculiar to everyday talk.

Colloquially *adv.*

Colloquy *n.* conversation; talk.

Collotype *n.* a gelatine photographic plate that can be printed from or in ink.

Collude *v.i.* to conspire in fraud.

Collusion *n.* secret agreement or understanding between two or more people with the aim of deceiving or cheating other.

Collyrium *n.* eye salve.

Colocynth *n.* a kind of bitter apple.

Colon *n.* a punctuation mark indicating a pause greater than a semicolon but less than a period.

Colonitis *n.* inflammation of the colon.

Colonel the highest regimental officer.

Colonelcy *n.* the status of a colonel.

Colonial *n.* & *adj.* characteristics of colonial times; a person living in a colony.

Colonize *v.t.* to establish a colony.

Colonnade *n.* a series or range of columns, a row of trees.

Colony *n.* an independent city or state founded by emigrants, settlers in a new country.

Colophon *n.* a printer's name, place of publication and date formerly put at the conclusion of a book.

Colophony *n.* kind of dark resin obtained from turpentine.

Coloration *n.* disposition of colours.

Colorific *n.* colour-producing.

Colossal *adj.* huge; enormous; tremendous; like a colossus; gigantic.

Colossus *n.* a gigantic statue; a person or thing or very great size, importance.

Colour *n.* a particular hue, appearance, pretence.

Colourable *adj.* plausible; counterfeit.

Colouring *n.* a beautiful appearance, any thing used to give colour, manner of applying colours.

Colporteur *n.* a book-hawker (*esp.* one employed by society to distribute bibles.)

Colt *n.* a young horse, especially a young male horse.

Columbine *n.* female character in pantomime.

Column *n.* a cylindrical pillar, support, mass, vertical division of a page, body of troops.

Columnar *adj.* like a column.

Colza *n.* cole-seed; oil made from colza-seed and used in lamps.

Coma *n.* stupor, unnatural heavy sleep, lethargy, a tuft of soft silken hair over some seeds, the head of tree, the nebulous envelope round a comet.

Comatose *adj.* in a condition of coma.

Comb *n.* an instrument used for arranging and cleaning the hair.

Combat *v.t.* to struggle, to contest, to fight. *n.* a battle.

Combatant *n.* a person involved in fighting in a war.

Comber *n.* one who combs, one who combs wool, a kind of fish.

Combination *n.* the state of being joined or mixed together.

Combine *v.t.* & *i.* to join together; to co-operate; to possess in combination.

Combiner *n.* he, who or that which combines.

Combustion *n.* the process of burning; destruction by fire.

Come *v.i.* to arrive to a point; to happen; to appear; to become.

Comedian *n.* the writer of a comedy.

Comedienne *n.* a comedy actress.

Comedy *n.* an entertaining drama, usually with a happy ending.

Comely *adj.* pleasant to look at, graceful.

Comer *n.* one who comes.

Comestibles *n.* things to eat.

Comet *n.* an object that moves round the sun and looks like a bright star with a tail.

Cometary *adj.* pertaining to a comet.

Comfit *n.* a dry sweetmeat; confection.

Comfort *n.* freedom or relief from pain, sorrow, distress; consolation.

Comfrey *n.* a rough hairy herb of the borage family or its root.

Comic *adj.* pertaining to a comedy; provoking mirth; ludicrous; funny.

Coming *n.* approach. *adj.* expected to come.

Comity *n.* courtesy; civility.

Comma *n.* indicating separation in ideas or construction in a sentence.

Command *v.t. & i.* to order, to have control over, to be supreme, to restrain, to have at disposal. *n.* the right to command; order; biding.

Commandant *n.* the military governor of a fortress.

Commander *n.* the commanding officer.

Commander-in-chief *n.* supreme military commander; the highest staff appointment in the army.

Commanding *adj.* exalted, dignified.

Commando *n.* a body of troops; a party called out for military service.

Commemorate *v.t.* to preserve in memory by some celebration.

Commemorative *adj.* serving to commemorate.

Commence *v.t. & i.* to have first existence; to take origin; to begin or make something begin; to start.

Commend *v.t.* to praise; to recommend; to deliver; to give one's complements to.

Commensurable *adj.* measurable by the same standard; proportionate to.

Commensal *adj. & n.* one who eats at the same table.

Comment *n.* a remark or an observation; a note intended to explain a difficult passage of an author.

Commentary *n.* remarks on a speech or performance; running comments on a book.

Commerce *n.* exchange of merchandise.

Commination *n.* a denunciation or vengeance; threatening of divine vengeance.

Commingle *v.t.* & *i.* to mix; to unite.

Comminute *v.t.* to reduce to podwer.

Commiserate *v.t.* to feel or say that one feels sympathy; to express sorrow for another's troubles.

Commissariat *n.* food and store department of army; family's or person's food supply.

Commissary *n.* a person deputed by superior power; head of commissariat.

Commission *n.* command, authority, warrant, conferring authority, percentage on an amout, a comittee of enquiry. *v.t.* to authorize.

Commissioner *n.* the head of an executive department of a government, especially one with particular duties; representative of supreme authority in a district or Government department; member of a permanent Government board or other commission; a public official of high rank.

Commissure *n.* a place where two bodies unite.

Commit *v.t.* to perpetrate; to consign; to devote; to pledge; to compromise.

Committal *n.* act of committing.

Committee *n.* a person or persons appointed by a large number to act upon something.

Commix *v.t.* & *i.* to mix together.

Commode *n.* a chest of drawers, a night-stool, a tall head-dress for ladies, a procuress.

Commodious *adj.* well adopted to serve the purpose for supplying needs, especially affording ample accommodation.

Commodity *n.* a useful or valuable thing, an article that meets needs or can be traded in.

Commodore *n.* the commander of a squadron of ships; the senior caption of several ships sailing together.

Common *adj.* frequent or usual; often occurring; pertaining to two or more things; general; belonging to the public.

Commonage *n.* right of common; land held in common.

Commonalty *n.* the common people; the bulk of mankind.

Commonly *adv.* frequently; usually; very often; ordinarily; for the most part.

Commons *n. pl.* the common people; food; diet.

Commonwealth *n.* the whole body of people in a state.

Commotion *n.* a violent agitation; excitement; physical disturbance; confusion; agitated stir.

Commove *v.t.* to excite, to agitate.

Communal *adj.* involving different groups in a community.

Commune *n.* a small territorial district; intimate intercourse. *v.i.* to hold intimate intercourse with.

Communicable *adj.* that can be communicated.

Communicate *v.t. & i.* to exchange information; to impart to others, news, ideas etc. with somebody.

Communication *n.* act of imparting news etc., intercourse, information given, correspondence.

Communicator *n.* that which communicates, part of a telegraphic transmitter.

Communion *n.* common participation; intercourse; exchange of thoughts and feelings.

Communique *n.* an official message, announcement etc.

Communism *n.* a social and economic system in which the state owns and controls the means of production on behalf of the people.

Community *n.* society, association, joint ownership, communion, fellowship.

Commutator *n.* a device for altering the course of electric current.

Commute *v.t. & i.* to interchange; to put something less severe in place of, as prisoner's sentence.

Compact *adj.* an agreement between parties, a treaty. *v.t.* to make compact; to join firmly. *n.* agreement.

Compages *n.* a framework or structure.

Companion *n.* a person with similar tastes; a comrade; a mate; a friend.

Company *n.* body of persons combined for commercial or other end; party of players; persons assembled together; guest.

Comparable *adj.* able or suitable to be compared with somebody else; susceptible of comparison with; fit to be compared to.

Compare *v.t. & i.* to examine in respect of similarity or dissimilarity; to represent as analogous or equal.

Comparison *n.* the state of being compared; an act of comparing; resemblance.

Compartment *n.* a separate part, partition of a railway carriage.

Compass *n.* a device with a needle that always points to the north; circuit extent, area, range.

Compatible *adj.* suitable; agreeable; that can exist together without problems or conflict; consistent.

Compatriot *n.* patriotic; a fellow-countryman.

Compeer *n.* associate; an equal, peer; comrade.

Compel *v.t.* to constrain; to subdue; to force to yield; to exact; to seize; to overpower.

Compendious *adj.* concise, brief.

Compendium *n.* an abridgement or summary; epitome.

Compensate *v.t.* & *i.* to recompense; to give equal value to; to counter balance to make up for.

Compete *v.i.* to contend; to be a rival to; to contest; to strive with or against.

Competence *n.* competent ability; capacity; suitableness; fitness.

Competent *adj.* adequate, suitable, properly qualified, permissible.

Competition *n.* rivalry; contest; the act of competing; those competing against somebody; a contest; activity in which people complete.

Competitor *n.* one who competes, a rival.

Compilation *n.* the action of compiling something; that which is compiled.

Compile *v.t.* to gather in to a volume (from other works); to collect and arrange facts together.

Complacency *n.* gratification; pleasure; self-satisfaction.

Complacent *adj.* self-satisfied; satisfied with oneself; in pleasant mood.

Complain *v.i.* to find fault; to express grief; to state; to bewail.

Complaint *n.* a formal charge; expression of grief; an ailment.

Complaisance *n.* politeness, civility.

Complaisant *adj.* courteous; obliging; pleasing in manners.

Complaisantly *adv.* obligingly.

Complement *n.* fullness; that which completes; (in an angle) the amount by it falls short 90º.

Complementary *adj.* being a complement to; combining well to form a balanced or attractive group or whole.

Complete *adj.* entire, finished. *v.t.* to finish, to make whole, to accomplish.

Completion *n.* fulfillment; completeness; the formal completing of a contract of sale.

Complex *adj.* having many parts connected together in a particular pattern; complicated; intricate.

Compliance *n.* consent; submission; acquiescence.

Compliant *adj.* willing to agree with other people; yielding.

Complicacy *n.* quality or state of being complicated, a complicated structure.

Complicate *v.t.* to make something more difficult to do; to entangle.

Compliment *n.* polite expression of praise, praise, favour. *v.t.* to praise; to congratulate.

Complin *n.* last service of the day.

Comply *v.i.* to act according to request or command or rules.

Component *adj.* forming part of a whole.

Comport *v.t.* & *i.* to behave or conduct oneself; to be compatible or in harmony with.

Compose *v.t.* & *t.* to frame; to place the types in order to print; to write like authors; to construct in one's mind; to become tranquil.

Composite *adj.* made of distinct element; consisting of different parts or materials.

Compost *n.* a mixture of manures; combination.

Composure *n.* calmness; quietness; the state of being calm in mind or behaviour.

Compote *n.* fruit preserved in syrup.

Compound *v. t.* & *i.* to combine; to settle amicably; to mix together.

Comprehend *v.t.* to seize; to take into the mind; to grasp; to include.

Comprehension *n.* the capacity to understand the act of including; grasp.

Comprehensive *adj.* large in scope; (of education) for pupils of all abilities in the same school; full.

Compress *v.t.* to press together; to condense; to compact; to press or squeeze something into a smaller space; to bring into smaller compass.

Comprise *v.t.* to consist of; to be composed of; to have somebody as parts or members; to include.

Compromise *n.* the giving up of particular demands by each side in a dispute; agreement attained by mutual concessions.

Comprovincial *adj.* & *n.* of the same province.

Comptroller *n.* one who checks the accounts of a state by counter-rolls.

Compulsion *n.* obligation, constraint.

Compulsory *adj.* that which must be done; done or acting under compulsion; brought about by force.

Compunction *n.* a sense of guilt; remorse; contrition; pricking of conscience; sorrow for a cruel act.

Compunctious *adj.* remorseful, repentant.

Compurgation *n.* the clearing from a charge, vindication.

Computable *adj.* that may be calculated or reckoned.

Computation *n.* estimate, reckoning.

Compute *v.t.* to count; to calculate, especially with a computer; to estimate.

Computer *n.* an electronic device for storing and analysing information fed into it, or for controlling machinery automatically.

Comrade *n.* a mate or fellow; a companion or associate. **Comradeship,** *n.* friendship.

Con *v.t.* to study carefully; to learn by heart; to direct steering of ship.

Conation *n.* the exertion of willing that desire or aversion shall issue in action.

Concatenate *v.t.* to link together.

Concatenation *n.* a series of things or events linked together; connexion as of chain-links; a chain of events.

Concave *adj.* curved towards; curved inward; (of an outline or a surface) curved inwards like the inner surface of a ball.

Conceal *v.t.* to keep something from being seen or known about; to withdraw form observation.

Concede *v.t.* to allow; to admit; to agree to; to yield; to give up; to give something away.

Conceit *n.* personal vanity, fanciful notion.

Conceited *adj.* having a high notion or too good an opinion of oneself.

Conceive *v.t. & i.* to form in the mind; to become pregnant; to receive in womb; to think; to fancy.

Concent *n.* harmony.

Concentrate *v.t. & i.* to bring to bear or bring together (*e.g.* soldiers) on one point; to direct one's attention, not thinking about other less important thing.

Concentration *n.* the ability to concentrate; a close gathering of people or thing; mental faculty or exclusive attention.

Concentre *v.t. & i.* to come or bring to a common centre, to coincide.

Concept *n.* general notion; a thing conceived; an idea or a principle relating to something abstract.

Conception *n.* formation of foetus, act of conceiving idea.

Conceptual *adj.* of mental conception; of or based on concepts.

Concern *n.* business, interest, anxiety, an object. *v.t.* to be relevant to somebody to affect somebody.

Concerning *prep.* about.

Concernment *n.* affair, interest, importance.

Concert *n.* agreement; union; musical entertainment.

Concertina *n.* a musical instrument like a small accordion.

Concerto *n.* a composition for solo instrument accompanied by orchestra.

Concession *n.* something conceded or given; an argument, especially after discussion.

Conch *n.* the shell-fish, shell-trumpet, external ear.

Conchology *n.* study of shells and shell-fish.

Conciliate *v.t.* to pacify; to win over; to reconcile; to make somebody less angry or more friendly.

Conciliation *n.* use of conciliating measures; bringing of opponents into harmony; reconcilement.

Concise *adj.* brief and comprehensive; giving a lot of information in few word.

Conclave *n.* a meeting for secret consultation; a private meeting place; the meeting-place of assembly of cardinals to the election of Pope.

Conclude *v.t. & i.* to finish; to end; to draw an inference; to arrange.

Conclusion *n.* the end; final result; inference; a belief or an opinion that is the result of reasoning; final opinion.

Conclusive *n.* convincing; ending doubt; decisive; final.

Concoct *v.t.* to devise; to compound; to make something by mixing ingredients (especially ones that do not usually go together).

Concoction *n.* devising.

Concolorous *adj.* of uniform colour.

Concomitance *n.* being together; co-existence.

Concomitant *adj.* going together; happening at the same time as something else; accompanying.

Concord *n.* absence of quarrelling; peace and harmony between people; agreement (in gender, person, etc.) between words.

Concordance *n.* agreement; an alphabetical index.

Concourse *n.* confluence, a crowd, an assembly.

Concrete *adj.* existing in form that can be touched, seen; not abstract, real.

Concubinage *n.* the state of being a concubine.

Concubine *n.* a woman who cohabits with a man without marriage.

Conculate *v.t.* to trample under feet.

Concur *v.i.* to occur together; to coincide; to agree to coincide; to act.

Concurrence *n.* agreement.

Concussion *n.* damage to somebody's brain caused by a blow; a violent shaking or shock.

Condemn *v.t.* to blame, to give judgement against, to doom.

Condensation *n.* drops of water that form on a cold surface when steam or water vapour touches it.

Condense *v.t. & i.* to compress, to concentrate, to reduce into a denser form.

Condenser *n.* a device for cooling vapour and making it change into a liquid; a curved glass which brings light together into a beam.

Condescend *v.t.* to do something that one clearly thinks is below one's dignity or level of importance; to stoop from dignity.

Condescension *n.* patronizing manner.

Condign *adj.* adequate; having merit; deserved; fit.

Condigness *n.* agreeableness, fitness.

Condiment *n.* matter added to food to make its taste nicer.

Condite *v.t.* to preserve, to pickle.

Condition *n.* state of body; attribute; a thing on which another thing depends.

Condolatory *adj.* expressing grief for others.

Condole *v.t.* to express sympathy in sorrow with; to express pity for.

Condolence *n.* expression of sympathy in another's sorrow.

Condone *v.t.* to accept wrong behaviour or to treat it as if it were not serious; to ignore something.

Conduce *v.t.* to lead; to contribute; to help to produce or effect.

Conduct *n.* a person's behaviour; the action or manner of directing or management.

Conductor *n.* a person who conducts; a leader; a manager; in charge of bus.

Conduit *n.* a pipe or channel for conveying liquids.

Confabulate *v.t.* to take familiarly together; to chat.

Confection *n.* preserved sweetmeat.

Confederacy *n.* alliance; league of confederate States; conspiracy.

Confederation *n.* an organization consisting of countries, etc. that have joined together for mutual benefit.

Confess *v.t.* & *i.* to acknowledge or admit one's sins or guilt.

Confessor *n.* one who confesses.

Confession *n.* a formal statement admitting that one is guilty of a crime, etc.; acknowledgement.

Confide *v.t.* & *i.* to trust, to impart secret to.

Confidence *n.* self-reliance; boldness; telling of secrets; confidence in oneself; a feeling or belief that one can firmly trust or rely on somebody.

Configuration *n.* mode of arrangement, outline.

Confine *v.t.* to limit; to imprison; to put restrictions around; to enclose; to be adjacent; to be on border of.

Confirm *v.t.* to ratify, to corroborate, to establish.

Conflation *n.* fusing together of two different readings or metals.

Conflict *n.* a struggle of ideas in the mind; a big collision; a contest.

Confluence *n.* a meeting of confluents; a concourse.

Confluent *adj.* flowing together.

Conflux *n.* a confluence, a crowd.

Conformation *n.* the shape or structure of something.

Conformist *n.* one who conforms to the usages of the church of England.

Conformity *n.* likeness, congruity, compliance.

Confraternity *n.* a brotherhood (*esp.* religious or charitable); a body, gang.

Confrere *n.* a fellow worker.

Confront *v.t.* to meet face to face, to oppose, to compare.

Confrontation *n.* act of bringing face to face.

Confusable *adj.* able to be confused.

Confuse *v.t.* to mix up; to create disorder; to perplex; to throw into disorder.

Confused *adj.* perplexed.

Confusion *n.* confusedness; disorder; perplexion; a state of uncertainty about what is happening.

Confutation *n.* act of confusing, refutation.

Confute *v.t.* to prove to be false; to show to be wrong; to disprove.

Conge *n.* dismissal.

Congeal *v.t. & i.* to solidify by freezing or otherwise; to become or make something thick or solid.

Congener *adj.* akin, allied.

Congenial *adj.* of kindred temper, etc. that are similar to one's own interests; suiting one's likes and dislikes.

Conger *n.* a large type of eel; a large snake-like fish caught for food, living in the sea.

Congest *v.i.* to accumulate to excess.

Conglobate *v.t.* to collect or form into a ball.

Conglomerate *n.* a mass of pebbles cemented into a kind of stone.

Conglutinate *v.t.* to stick together with glue.

Congratulate *v.t.* to offer congratulations to; to express pleasure at another's good fortune.

Congratulation *n.* the action of congratulating somebody or of being congratulated.

Congregate *v.t. & i.* to collect together; to assemble; to meet in a crowd.

Congregate *v.t. & i.* to collect or gather together, to come together, to assemble.

Congress *n.* a formal meeting or series of meetings for discussion between representatives.

Congressite, Congressman, *ns.* member of a congress.

Congruence *n.* agreement; consistency.

Congruent *adj.* able to be fitted one on the top of another; harmonious; having the same size and shape.

Congruity *n.* accordance; harmonious relation; correspondence.

Congrous *adj.* suitable, fitting.

Congrously, *adv.* in a consistent manner.

Conic, Conical *adjs.* cone-shaped; having the form of a cone.

Conifer *n.* a type of tree that bears cones.

Conjecture *n.* guessing; guesswork.

Conjectural *adj.* imaginary.

Conjoin *v.t.* & *i.* to join or make somebody join together.

Conjoint *adj.* united, associated.

Conjugal *adj.* of marriage or the relationship between a husband and a wife; between married persons.

Conjugate *v.t.* & *i.* to mix and unite; to unite sexually; to marry.

Conjunct *adj.* joint; conjoined; associated with or assisting another.

Conjunction *n.* word used to connect sentences and words together.

Conjunctive *adj.* a combination of events, occasion, a crisis.

Conjuncture *n.* position of affairs at a particular moment.

Conjuration *adj.* enhancement; increase; conspiracy.

Conjure *v.t.* & *i.* to appeal in solemn manner; to practise magic.

Conjurer *n.* a juggler; a magician; an adept at sleight-of-hand.

Conk *n.* the head; the nose; a blow.

Connate *adj.* innate, born together.

Connatural *adj.* congenital; of the same nature.

Connect *v.t.* & *i.* to relate with anything; to join together.

Connective *adj.* serving as connexion; that connects things; something that connects.

Connection, Connexion *ns.* relation; act of connecting; something which connects.

Connivance *n.* conniving at a wrong action; pretence of being unaware.

Connive *v.i.* wink at.

Connotate *v.t.* to include in the meaning, to imply as a consequence.

Connote *v.t.* to imply; to include in its meaning; to suggest something in addition to the main meaning.

Connotation *n.* inference; implied meaning; an idea suggested or implied by a word in addition to its main meaning.

Connubial *adj.* of marriage; conjugal; matrimonial.

Conoid *adj.* more or less conical.

Conquer *v.t.* & *i.* to win; to gain by force; to obtain by effort; to defeat.

Conqueror *n.* a person who conquers.

Conquest *n.* act of conquering; that which is acquired by force.

Consanguineous *adj.* of the same blood of family; related by birth; near of kin.

Consanguinity *n.* kinship; blood-relationship.

Conscience *n.* moral sense of right and wrong.

Conscientious *adj.* obedient to the dictates of conscience.

Conscious *adj.* in senses, aware; knowing.

Conscribe *v.t.* to enlist unvoluntarily in armed forces by compulsion.

Conscript *n. n.* enrolled in army by conscription; new recruitment.

Consecrate *v.t.* to devote to sacred purpose.

Consecration *n.* dedication; setting apart for sacred purposes.

Consecution *n.* sequence of events.

Consensus *n.* oneness; agreement of parts; unanimity in opinion.

Consent *v.i.* to agree, to comply; to yield; to concur.

Consentaneous *adj.* a result or and effect of something else; importance; done by common consent.

Consequence *n.* importance; that which comes from any cause or principle; influential position.

Consequent *adj.* following something as a result or an effect.

Conservancy *n.* official preservation; a group of officials controlling a port; a board controlling a river or a port, an area of land, etc.

Conservation *n.* continuance; the prevention of loss; keeping from decay or from being destroyed.

Conservative *adj.* & *n.* preservative, moderate, disposed to maintain existing institutions.

Conservatoire *n.* a school of music, drama, *esp.* in Europe.

Conservator *n.* one who preserves from injury.

Conservatory *n.* a green-house for tender plants; a room with glass walls and a glass roof built on the side of a house.

Conserve *v.t.* to save from injury; to prevent something from being changed; to preserve.

Consider *v.t.* to contemplate, to reflect, to reckon, to be of opinion, to regard.

Consideration *n.* thoughtfulness; meditation; deliberation; payment or compensation for a thing acquired.

Consign *v.t.* to sign; to denote; to transfer; to entrust; to commit; to deliver.

Consignee *adjs.* a person to whom or by whom goods are consigned.

Consignment *n.* goods consigned.

Consist *v.t.* to be composed of; to be comprised of; to exist.

Consistence *n.* firmness; solidity; degree of density (in liquid etc.); self-consistency.

Consistent *adj.* compatible, firm.

Consolation *n.* comfort or compensation; alleviation of grief or disappointment; a person or thing that comforts.

Consolatory *adj.* tending to console.

Console *v.t.* to bring consolation to; to give comfort or sympathy to somebody who is unhappy.

Consolidate *v.t.* & *i.* to combine and forge a union; to make one out of many.

Consols *n. pl.* Government consolidated stock.

Consonance *n.* agreement, harmony, concord.

Consonant *adj.* full of harmony; having same sound; suitable.

Consort *n.* a husband or wife, especially of a ruler; a partner.

Conspecific *adj.* of the same species.

Conspectus *n.* a short account of a whole subject; a general view.

Conspicuous *adj.* attracting notice; striking to the eye; noticeable; readily seen; remarkable.

Conspiracy *n.* a plot hatched to harm someone; a group of people united for a bad purpose.

Conspirator *n.* a man engaged in a conspiracy.

Conspire *v.t.* & *i.* to plot, to devise.

Conspue *v.i.* to express hatred.

Constable *n.* a great officer of the royal house-hold.

Constabulary *n.* the body of constables; the police force.

Constancy *n.* tenacious adherence; the quality of being firm and not changing; steadiness.

Constant *adj.* firm, resolute, faithful.

Constantly *adv.* regularly; in a constant manner; invariably.

Constellate *v.t.* to form stars into fixed groups, to cluster together.

Consternate *v.t.* to dismay.

Consternation *n.* anxiety or mental confusion; paralysing sense of calamity; a feeling of great surprise and fear.

Constipate *v.t.* to confine bowels; to make costive.

Constipation *n.* difficulty in evacuating the bowels.

Constituency *n.* a body of people electing a representative to the government; the place represented.

Constituent *adj.* & *n.* composing, appointing, a component part, a voter.

Constitute *v.t.* to form; to establish.

Constitution *n.* the method of governing a country; book containing the system prescribed for governance.

Constitutive *adj.* constructive; essential; component.

Constrain *v.t.* to compel; to put under detention; to violent.

Constraint *n.* restraint, compulsion.

Constrict *v.t.* to compress; to contract; to press together tightly.

Constringe *v.t.* to draw together, to contract, to constrict.

Construct *v.t.* to frame; to draw; to make; to build something.

Construction *n.* act of constructing; building; meaning; interpretation.

Constructive *adj.* tending to construction; having a useful purpose.

Construe *v.t.* to analyse; to translate; to explain, to interpret.

Consubstantial *adj.* of one substance; of the same substance.

Consul *n.* the title of magistrate in Roman Republic; the State agent in a foreign town.

Consular *adj.* of a consul; relating to a consul.

Consulate *n.* the house and office of a consul.

Consult *v.t.* & *i.* to take advice from; to consider; to ask for information.

Consultative *adj.* deliberative; giving advice or making suggestions.

Consume *v.t.* & *i.* to spend; to waste; to use and utilise; to eat or drink; to destroy; to be exhausted.

Consumedly *adv.* excessively.

Consumer *n.* one who consumes; a user.

Consummation *n.* the action or moment of completing; making perfect.

Consumption *n.* act of consuming; destruction; excessive spending; a wasting disease (*esp.* tuberculosis).

Contact *n.* condition of touching, close uion.

Contagion *n.* a disease that can be spread by contact; communication of disease by contact.

Contagious *adj.* spreading by contact; catching; infectious.

Contagiously, *adv.* in an infectious manner.

Contain *v.t.* to comprise; to keep from moving; to restrict; to be equal.

Contaminate *v.t.* to pollute; to make dirty; to corrupt; to tarnish.

Contemn *v.t.* to hate; to disregard; to depise; to feel contempt for.

Contemplation *n.* meditation; the action of looking at something in a calm/careful way.

Contemplator *n.* one who contemplates or meditates.

Contemporary *adj.* belonging to the same period; equal in age.

Contempt *n.* the feeling that somebody is completely worthless and cannot be respected.

Contend *v.i.* & *t.* to argue; to strive; to enter into competition; to oppose.

Contended *adj.* satisfied; enjoying contentment; easy in mind.

Content *adj.* satisfied; having limited desires; not wanting more.

Contention *n.* dispute, strife, quarrel

Contentious *adj.* given to or involving contention; likely to cause disagreement.

Contents *n.* a list of subjects dealt within book.

Conterminous *adj.* having a common boundary or end.

Contest *v.t.* & *i.* to take part in and try to win something; to contend or compete for.

Context *n.* the place from which a passage has been quoted; circumstances in which something is to be considered.

Contexure *n.* structure, composition.
Contiguity *n.* proximity; contact.
Contiguous *adj.* touching; next to; adjoining; near; neighbouring.
Continence *n.* abstinence; self restraint in sexual matters; chastity.
Continency *n.* restraint upon desires.
Continent *n.* & *adj.* a main continuous land; one of the six parts of land or earth.
Continental *adj.* belonging to or typical of a continent.
Contingency *n.* contingent event; a possibility; being contingent.
Contingent *adj.* dependent on something that may not happen; happening without known cause.
Continual *n.* seeming incessant; occurring on every occasion.
Continuance *n.* continuing in existence or operation; duration.
Continue *v.t.* & *i.* to preservere; to take up again; to extend; to prolong.
Continuous *n.* uninterrupted; joined together; connected without break.
Contort *v.t.* to become or make something twisted out of its natural shape.
Contour *n.* outline; general aspect; boundary line; a line marking a level or special characteristic in a map.
Contra *pref.* in the sense of against.
Contraception *n.* prevention of conception.
Contract *n.* an agreement; terms of agreement; a bond; a betrothal.
Contractile *adj.* tending to contract.
Contraction *n.* act of contracting abbreviation of a word or phrase.
Contractor *n.* one who enters into an agreement; one who undertakes to execute a work at a fixed rate.
Contradict *v.t.* & *i.* to deny; to say a contrary thing; to oppose verbally.
Contradistinction *n.* distinction by opposite qualities; distinction by contrast.
Contradistinguish *v.t.* to distinguish by opposite qualities.
Contralto *n.* lowest musical voice in women; the women having such a voice.
Contraption *n.* a machine or device, especially an unusual or complicated one.
Contrapose *v.t.* to place over against a thing.
Contrariety *n.* opposition in nature, disagreement, inconsistency.
Contrariwise *adv.* on the other hand.
Contrary *adj.* unfavourable; opposite in nature or tendency. *n.* opposite.
Contrast *n.* exhibition of difference; comparison with a view to find unlikeness.

Contravene *v.t.* to oppose; to infringe to violate; to conflict with; to act or to be contrary to a law.

Contretemps *n.* an unlucky accident; an unexpected and an unfortunate event or disagreement.

Contribute *v.t. & i.* to pay a share, to help or bring about.

Contribution *n.* act of giving for a common cause.

Contrite *adj.* broken-hearted due to sin; doing penance; filled with or showing deep regret for having done wrong.

Contrition *n.* sorrow for sin.

Contrivable *adj.* what may be contrived.

Contrivance *n.* a clever or complicated device or tool; contriving.

Contrive *v.t. & i.* to invent; to design to plan or make a plan.

Control *v.t.* command, check, device to bring under restraint.

Controversial *adj.* open to controversy; causing or likely to cause controversy.

Controversy *n.* dispute; different opinions on a subject expressed in press.

Contumacious *adj.* insubordinate; disobedient (*esp.* to the order of a court).

Contumacy *n.* wilful and obstinate resistance; perverseness.

Contumelious *adj.* insolent.

Contumely *n.* insulting language or treatment; disgrace.

Contuse *v.t.* to beat; to crush; to injure the body by a blow without breaking the skin.

Contusion *n.* act of bruising; state of being bruised; an injury to part of the body that does not break the skin.

Conundrum *n.* a riddle, a puzzle.

Convalesce *v.i.* to recover from weakness and to regain health.

Convection *n.* act of conveying heat or electricity.

Convene *v.t. & i.* to come together for a meeting; to call together.

Convenience *n.* suitableness; a useful appliance; (*pl.*) comforts.

Convenient *adj.* suitable, commodious.

Convent *n.* association of religious devotees; their residence; a building in which a community of nuns live.

Conventicle *n.* a religious assembly; a secret meeting.

Convention *n.* an agreement; a usage or custom; fashion; a meeting or conference; act of convening.

Coverage *v.i. & t.* to meet at one point to acquire; to move towards and meet at the same place.

Conversable *adj.* fond of or pleasant in conversation; fit for social intercourse.

Conversant *adj.* well acquainted with a subject; having knowledge of something; familiar.

Conversation *n.* intercourse; a usually informal talk, especially one involving a small group of people or only two.

Conversazione *n.* a social meeting of scientific or artistic kind.

Converse *v.t.* to talk, to hold intercourse with.

Conversion *n.* change from one condition to another.

Convert *n.* to change from one opinion, religion, party or condition to another one.

Convex *adj.* rising in the central portion and thining at edges

Convey *v.t.* to carry; to give; to steal; to transfer; to impart or communicate; to take from one place to another.

Conveyance *n.* the process of taking somebody from one place to another.

Convict *v.t.* to prove guilty; to adjudge as guilty and to sentence.

Conviction *n.* the action of finding somebody guilty or of being found guilty of a crime in a law court.

Convince *v.t.* to carry conviction by giving evidence.

Convivial *adj.* befitting a feast, jovial.

Conviviality *n.* a convivial temper; good humour; mirth.

Convocation *n.* act of calling a students gathering at Universities to award degrees.

Convoke *v.t.* to assemble; to call together; to hold a meeting; to summon to an assembly.

Convolute *adj.* rolled up; rolled together; coiled.

Convolution *n.* a fold; a coiling; a thing that is very complicated and difficult to follow.

Convolve *v.t.* to roll or wind together.

Convolvulus *n.* a climbing plant with flowers shaped like a trumpet.

Convoy *v.t.* to escort; to accompany as a protect or guard, especially one that is accompanied by armed troops.

Convulse *v.t.* to shake violently, to draw or contract.

Convulsion *n.* the act of convulsing; a violent disturbance; laughter.

Cony *n.* a wild rabbit; its skin.

Coo *v.t.* to make a low sweet sound like pigeon or dove; to talk fondly.

Cook *n.* one who prepars food for eating.

Cooker *n.* a kind of stone used for cooking; a vessel in which food is cooked.

Cook-house *n.* an outdoor kitchen.

Cookie *n.* the U.S. word for biscuit; a dry thin, sweet cake.

Cool *adj.* anything cold; coolness; not excited, angry or emotional.

Cooler *n.* a machine used for cooling the room; a vessel for cooling.

Coolie *n.* a labour hired for any purpose; a person who carries weight.

Coomb, Combe *ns.* a steep valley; a hollow on the flank of a hill.

Coon *n.* an American dog; a worthless fellow; a black person.

Coop *n.* a basket placed over fowls, a fishing-basket. *v.t.* to confine in coop.

Cooper *v.i.* one who makes or repairs the tubs or casks.

Co-operant *adj.* co-operating.

Co-operate *v.i.* to work or act together with another or others for a common purpose.

Co-operation *n.* working together for a common purpose; willingness to be helpful and do as one is asked.

Co-opt *v.t.* to elect into a body by the votes of existing members.

Co-ordinate *adj.* equal in rank of the same order.

Coot *n.* a water fowl, a stupid fellow.

Cop *v.t.* to capture; to catch or arrest somebody in the act of doing something wrong.

Co-partner *n.* a joint partner with others in some business.

Cope *n.* a long loose garment worn by priests on special occasions; the vault (of heaven).

Coper *n.* (a horse-dealer.

Copier *n.* one who copies.

Copious *adj.* produced in large quantities; abounding in words.

Copper *n.* metallic element used for making coins and utensils.

Copperas *n.* green vitriol.

Coppice *n.* small trees grown as thicket and cut periodically wood of small trees grown for periodical cutting.

Copra *n.* dried kernels of coconut.

Coprology *n.* moral impurity in art and literature.

Copula *n.* a part which connects; in logic a word of predication.

Copulate *v.t.* to have sexual intercourse; to unite sexually.

Copulative *adj.* serving as copula; connecting predicate with subject.

Copy *n.* reproduction, imitation, transcript. *v.t.* to transcribe from original.

Copy-book *n.* a book used by students for taking copies of notes.

Copyist *n.* a person who makes copies, especially in art; an imitator.

Copyright *n.* exclusive right to produce copies and to control an original literary, musical or artistic work.

Coquet *n.* a woman who behaves in a playful way that is intended to be attractive to men.

Coquetry *n.* coquet as noun; a woman who firts; coquettish appearance.

Coquettish *adj.* practising, coquetry.

Coracle *n.* a small light boat made of a framework of sticks covered with watertight material.

Coral *n.* a hard submarine substance secreted by many species of polyps.

Coralline *adj.* of coral; like coral; coral-red.

Corbel *n.* a piece of stone or wood that projects from a wall to support something.

Corbie *n.* a raven; a carrion crow.

Cord *n.* a rope of small diameter or thick string; a measure for wood.

Cordage *n.* a number of cords or ropes.

Cordial *adj.* hearty, stimulating, sincere, warm, friendly, an exhilarating medicine.

Cordiality *n.* sincerity; warm affection.

Cordite *n.* a smokeless explosive.

Cordon *n.* a string course; a chain of military posts.

Corduroy *n.* a strong cotton cloth covered with parallel soft raised ridges.

Cordwainer *n.* a shoe-maker.

Core *n.* the heart of innermost part of anything.

Co-regent *n.* a joint ruler.

Co-religionist *n.* a person of the same religion.

Coreopsis *n.* a plant with yellow flowers.

Co-respondent *n.* a person accused of committing adultery with the husband or wife or somebody who is seeking a divorce.

Corf *n.* a basket in which fishes are kept alive, a coal-miner's basket.

Coriaceous *adj.* leathery; made of leather.

Coriander *adj.* a plant with fruit used as flavouring.

Co-rival *n.* a fellow rival.

Cork *n.* a bark of the cork-tree; a bottle stopper.

Corkage *n.* corking or uncorking of bottles.

Cork-screw *n.* a steel screw for drawing cork from bottle.

Corky *adj.* buoyant; lively.

Cormorant *n.* a large black bird with a long neck which lives near water and eats fish.

Corn *n.* a grain seed; small hard seed of hernel; a thorny tumour on feet.

Cornea *n.* the interior transparent membrane of the eye-ball.

Corneous *adj.* horny, like horn, hard.

Corner *n.* the place or point where two lines or planes meets.

Cornet *n.* a brass musical instrument like a trumpet but smaller.

Cornice *n.* the projection under which curtains hang; the moulding of a room wall just below ceiling.

Cornicle *n.* a little horn.

Cornucopia *n.* the representation of horn filled with fruit, flowers and grain and used as a symbol of plenty and peace.

Corolla *n.* the flower's inner part consisting of petals.

Corollary *n.* a proposition that follows without the need of a separate proof from the one proved.

Corona *n.* a small disk of light round the sun moon or stars, round chandelier hung from the roof of a church, ths stalk of a daffodil.

Coronation *n.* a ceremony at which a crown is formally put on the head of new king or queen.

Coronal *n.* a circlet for the head.

Cornated *adj.* furnished with a crown-shaped ornament.

Coronet *n.* a small crown worn on formal occasions by a member of the peerage peer.

Corporal *n.* pertaining to the body, material.

Corporality *n.* being or having a body.

Corporate *adj.* united in a group and given power by law to do business acting as one person.

Corporator *n.* member of a corporation.

Corporeal *adj.* bodily, material.

Corposant *n.* a ball of light seen on a ship in a storm.

Corps *n.* a division; a branch; a department of army; a consolidated body.

Corpse *n.* the dead body of a human being.

Corpulence *n.* excessive fatness; bulkiness of the body.

Corpulent *adj.* bulky of body, fat.

Corpus *n.* a body; collections of literature or writing; any special structure in animal body.

Corpuscle *n.* atom; a minute body forming part of the organism, especially those that forms the major part of the blood in the backbone.

Corral *n.* an enclosure in which wild animals are captured.

Correct *v.t.* to make or set right; to remove faults.

Correction *n.* act of correction; punishment; amendment.

Correctitude *n.* correctness of conduct; correct behaviour.

Correlate *v.t.* & *i.* thing related to each other. *n.* each of two related things.

Correspond *v.i.* to be in harmony with or to; to be similar or analogous.

Corridor *n.* the strip to reach the port; the main passage of a large building on which many rooms open.

Corrigendum *n.* a thing to be corrected.

Corrigible *adj.* capable of being corrected.

Corroborant *adj.* & *n.* strengthening.

Corroborate *v.t.* to strengthen; to establish; to make certain.

Corrode *v.t.* to wear away gradually, to rust.

Corrosion *n.* wearing away from the surface inwards.

Corrosive *adj.* producing corrosion; consuming.

Corrugate *v.t.* & *i.* to wrinkle; to draw into folds; to mark or bend into ridge.

Corrupt *adj.* wicked, depraved, rotten, bribed. *v.t.* & *i.* to make corrupt.

Corruption *n.* the form of a word, etc. which has been changed from its original form in an unusual way.

Corsage *n.* a woman's bust-dress, a bodice.

Corsair *n.* a private ship conferred to seize and plunder an enemy's ship.

Corse *n.* (*poet*) corpse.

Corset *n.* corsage; a tight fitting garment worn under the outer garments to shape the body.

Corslet, Corselet *ns.* a piece of armour coverning the brest.

Cortege *n.* a train of servants; a procession; also a funeral procession.

Cortex *n.* the outer layer of an organ of the body, especially the brain.

Cortical *adj.* pertaining to the outer part of animal body.

Coruscate *v.t.* to sparkle to flash; to shine.

Coruscation *n.* a flash; quick vibration of light.

Corvee *n.* an obligation to labour without being paid for the feudal lord or sovereign.

Corvine *adj.* of the raven or crow.

Cosaque *n.* a cracker bonbon.

Cosher *v.t.* to pamper; to coddle; to chat in a friendly way.

Co-signatory *n.* a person or state signing a formal document that is also signed by others.

Cosine *n.* (of an angle) the ratio of the shorter side next to this angle in a right angled triangle to the longest side.

Cosmetic *n.* a preparation used for beautifying the hair, skin or complexion.

Cosmic *adj.* of a whole universe.

Cosmogony *n.* the principle of creation of universe; the theory of the origin of universe.

Cosmolatry *n.* the worship of the universe.

Cosmology *n.* the study of the universe in all its parts.

Cosmopolitan *n.* & *adj.* a citizen of the world; an international person free from local or national prejudice.

Cosmos *n.* the universe, seen as an ordered system.

Cossack *n.* a Russian soldier.

Cosset *v.t.* to pamper somebody; to give somebody a lot of care and protection from harm.

Cost *v.t.* to be valuable; to include expenditure.

Costal *adj.* pertaining to ribs or side of body.

Costard *n.* a large ribbed apple; the head of human beings.

Coster, Costermonger *ns.* a man who sells (fruit, fish, etc.) from barrow in a street; a hawker.

Costive *adj.* constipated; having confined bowels.

Costliness *n.* dearness, expensiveness.

Costly *adj.* of great value expensive.

Costume *n.* a style of dressing; dress; clothes; fancy dress.

Costumier *n.* one who makes and sells women's dresses.

Cosy, Cozy *adjs.* sheltered; snug; comfortable.

Cot *n.* a small dwelling cottage for shelter; children's bed or crib; a bed in the hospital.

Cote *n.* small cottage; a shelter for animals.

Co-tangent *n.* the tangent of the complement of an arc or angle.

Coterie *n.* a small group of people with shared activities.

Cottage *n.* a small dwelling house; single storey house; a small hut.

Cottar *n.* a Scottish peasant occupying a cottage on a farm and labouring on the farm at a fixed rate when required.

Cotter *n.* a pin or wedge for fastening; kinds of key.

Cotton *n.* a soft substance like wool; plant of cotton; cloth made of cotton.

Cotyloid *adj.* of the shape or a cup.

Cotyledon *n.* the primary or seed leaf in plant embryos.

Couch *v.t.* & *i.* to lie down; to lower; to spread; to level.

Couchant *adj.* lying with the body resting on the legs and the head raised.

Cough *v.i.* to force something out of the throat or lung by coughing.

Coulter *n.* the iron blade of a plough.

Council *n.* an assembly called for deliberation, advice or administration.

Councillor *n.* the member of a council.

Counsel *n.* consultation; advice; a secret matter; plan.

Counsellor *n.* one who deliberates or gives his advice, especially one who has professional training.

Count *n.* the number counted; a charge in a criminal case.

Countenance *n.* the face; expressions on face.

Counter *n.* a small piece of metal used for keeping accounts, a banker's table, the part of a horse's brest between shoulders and neck, curved part of stern, back part of shoe.

Counteract *v.t.* to defeat; to act against and reduce the force or effect of something; to neutralise.

Counter-agent *n.* a counteracting force or agent.

Counter-attack *n.* attack for an attack; an attack made in response to an enemy's attack.

Counterbalance *v.t.* to weigh against with an equal weight.

Counterfeit *adj.* & *n.* anything made in imitation, not genuine, forged.

Counterfoil *n.* the corresponding part of any cheque.

Countermand *n.* an order issued in revocation of previous one.

Countermarch *n.* & *v.t.* & *i.* to march in a contrary direction so that previously followed.

Countermark *n.* an additional mark marked on goods fixed for greater security.

Countermine *n.* a mine dug to destroy that of an enemy.

Counterpane *n.* a coverlet or quilt of bed.

Counterpart *n.* a duplicate complimentary part.

Counterplot *n.* a plot devised to defeat another.

Counterpoise *n.* equilibrium; a counterbalancing weight of force.

Countersink *v.t.* to sink the head of a screw in a hole which is bevelled off.

Countervail *v.t.* & *i.* to avail against to counter-balance.

Counterwork *n.* an opposing work.

Countess *n.* the wife or widow of a count or an earl.

Counting-house *n.* the business office.

Countless *adj.* numberless, innumerable, too many to be count.

Countrified *adj.* in appearance; like or made like the countryside or the people who live there.

Country *n.* an area of land that forms a politically independent unit.

County *n.* a territorial division in Great Britain and Ireland.

Coup *n.* a blow or stroke; a surprising and successful action; a successful piece of business.

Coupe *n.* a four wheeled carriage having an accommodation for two persons inside and the driver; one side seated railway.

Couple *n.* a pair, a man and wife. *v.t.* & *i.* to link or fasten or associate together.

Coupon *n.* a billet; a detachable ticket or a voucher entitling the holder to periodical payments.

Courage *n.* bravery, boldness.

Courier *n.* a messenger; one appointed to attend travelling arrangements; a messenger who transports parcels or important papers.

Course *v.t. & i.* to hunt, to pursue, to cause to run about, to run quickly.

Courser *n.* a swift horse.

Court *n.* a space enclosed by walls marked out for tennis or similar games.

Courteous *adj.* kind, wellbred, civil, polite.

Courtesan *n.* a refined or high-placed harlot; a prostitute with wealthy or noble clients.

Courtesy *n.* good manners; polite behaviour; a polite remark or act.

Courtier *n.* a flatterer; a sovereign; a courtman; a nobleman; frequenter of royal court.

Courtly *adj.* polished in manners, flattering.

Courtship *n.* the act of wooing with a view to marriage.

Courtyard *n.* enclosed ground before a house, especially forming part of a castle.

Cousin *n.* a child of one's uncle or aunt.

Cove *n.* a small opening in the sea; a bay; a rocky sheltered recess; curved concave arch; a customer.

Covenant *n.* a compact, a bargain, a mutual agreement or contract.

Covenanted *adj.* bound by a covenant.

Cover *v.t.* to overspread, to overlay, to shelter, to extend over.

Coverlet *n.* the outer covering of a bed; counter-pane.

Coverpoint *n.* (Crick.) the fielder behind the point to stop balls.

Covert *adj.* an area of thick low bushes or trees among which animals live, especially hunted animals.

Coverture *n.* a cover, a shelter, a defence.

Covet *v.t.* to desire ardently, that belongs to somebody else.

Covetous *adj.* greedy or eager for gain.

Covey *n.* brood of partridges; a group of birds (*esp.* those shot for food.)

Cow *n.* female of bull; a large female animal kept on farms to produce milk or beef.

Coward *n.* a person who lacks courage when facing a dangerous or unpleasant situation and tries to avoid it.

Cowardice *n.* the fear of and desire to avoid dangerous or unpleasant situations; timidity; cowardly conduct.

Cowboy *n.* boy who takes charge of cows.

Cower *v.t.* to couch from fear; to bend down and move backwards with your head lowered because of fear or distress.

Cowherd *n.* one who tends cows at pasture.

Cowl *n.* a monk's hooded garment, hood-shaped covering, a tub for water.

Coowrie *n.* a small sea shell.

Cowslip *n.* a yellow-flowered plant growing in pastures.

Cox *n.* coxswain, *esp.* of a racing boat.

Coxcomb *n.* a conceited showy person, a fop.

Coxswain *n.* one in charge of ship's boat; a crew of a boat; a boat's helmsman.

Coy *adj.* bashful; shy; retiring; gengle; pretending to be shy or modest.

Coze *v.i.* to have a chat.

Cozen *v.t.* & *i.* to flatter; to cheat; to defraud.

Crab *n.* a crustaceans having a short tail and ten feet; cancer or zodiac constellation; a portable roller.

Crack *n.* a sharp sudden, a sharp blow, a partial fracture; (*pl.*) news.

Cracker *n.* a firework, exploding with a sharp sound.

Crackle *n.* a sound of repeated slight cracking.

Cracknel *n.* a crisp soft biscuit.

Cracksman *n.* a burglar; a thief who breaks into houses.

Cradle *n.* a rocking bed or cot for infants. *v.t.* to rock in crade.

Cradling *n.* nursing a baby; a wood or iron framework used in building.

Craft *n.* cunning; art; artifice; skill; trade; occupation; a kind of ship; a boat or vessel.

Crafty *adj.* deceitful; wily; cunning; artful.

Crag *n.* a steep rugged point or rock; throat; neck.

Cragsman *n.* a skilled climber of rocks.

Cram *v.t.* & *i.* to fill overfull, to learn, to get by heart, to stuff.

Crambo *n.* a game in which one player gives a word to which another finds a rhyme.

Cramp *n.* a contraction of muscles from sudden chill, usually caused by cold or too much exercise, making movement difficult.

Crampons *n. pl.* a metal plate with pointed pieces of metal on one side.

Cranberry *n.* a small red fruit.

Crane *n.* a large wading bird with long legs, a machine for lifting heavy weights.

Cranium *n.* the hard part of the head enclosing the brain; the skull.

Crank *n.* whim; a fanciful speech; a projected arm on the shaft for signal purposes.

Cranog *n.* lake dwelling; an ancient lake-dwelling in Scotland or Ireland.

Cranny *n.* a very small hole or opening.

Crape *n.* a gauzy wrinkled fabric, *usu.* of black silk.

Crapulence *n.* sickness caused by excessive drinking or eating.

Crapulent *adj.* suffering or sick from intemperance.

Crash *n.* a noise caused by falling; a sound caused by the meeting of two bodies.

Crass *adj.* thick; gross; stupid; empty; dense.

Cratch *n.* a rack for feeding beasts, a manager, a disease in the feet of horse and sheep, a form of itch.

Crate *n.* a kind of basket for packing crockery etc.

Crater *n.* a large hole in the top of a volcano.

Cravat *n.* a kind of neck-cloth worn by men, folded inside the collar of a shirt.

Crave *v.i.* & *i.* to beg earnestly; to ask eagerly; to have a strong desire for something.

Craven *n.* & *adj.* a coward and a spiritless fellow; without courage; cowardly.

Craw *n.* the crop or throat or stomach of insects or birds.

Crawl *v.t.* to move slowly on the ground; to creep.

Crayon *n.* a pencil made of clay; a coloured pencil or stick of soft coloured chalk or wax.

Craze *v.t.* to render insane, to produce small cracks.

Creak *n.* & *v.i.* to make a sharp strident sound (as is heard when door opens fixed on a hinge.).

Cream *n.* the fatty part of milk which gathers on the top, the best part of anything. *v.t.* to skim off the cream.

Crease *n.* a mark left by folding, pressing or doubling anything.

Create *v.t.* to bring into existence, to originate, to beget.

Creation *n.* the action or process of creating something; the act of creating universe; the universe.

Creator *n.* the Supreme Being; one who creates.

Creature *n.* a kind of wine known as alcoholic liquor.

Creche *n.* a day-nursery for children when their parents are at work.

Credence *n.* credit; trust; belief; a small table in a church for bread and wine.

Credent *adj.* having credit.

Credentials *n. pl.* papers which prove that one may be trusted.

Credible *adj.* that can be believed; convincing; worthy of belief.

Credit *n.* good reputation; trust; honour; good character; sales done on credit basis.

Creditable *adj.* worthy of honour.

Credo *n.* a set of beliefs; creed.

Creed *n.* a religious belief, a set opinion on any subject.

Creek *n.* a small opening, inlet, bay etc.; the tidal estuary of a river.

Creep *v.i.* to move slowly (as a reptile) sweeping the ground with the bell.

Cremate *v.t.* to place on the pyre and burn the dead body.

Cremation *n.* the act of putting on the pyre and setting fire so that the body may be burned to ashes.

Crematorium *n.* a building or place where dead bodies are cremated.

Creosote *n.* a kind of coal-tar; an oily liquid obtained from coal (used for killing seeds of disease and protecting things from decay).

Crepe *n.* a gauge-like fabric.

Crepitate *v.t.* to make a crackling noise.

Crepuscular *adj.* at twilight; of twilight; dim.

Crescendo *n.* a gradual increase in force, volume or loudness.

Crescent *n.*the increasing moon, the Turkish power.

Cress *n.* a plant with pungent edible leaves.

Cresset *n.* a fire-basket slung to give light.

Crest *n.* a tuft on animal's head as cock and a kind of sparrow etc.

Cretaceous *adj.* of the nature of chalk; chalky.

Cretin *n.* one suffering from a serious disease of the mind known as cretinism; a very stupid person or deformed idiot.

Cretinism *n.* combination of idiocy and deformity.

Cretonne *n.* an unglazed colour-printed cotton cloth.

Crevasse *n.* a deep open split or chasm in a great mass of ice on a mountain side.

Crevice *n.* a chink; a small fissure.

Crew *n.* a ship's company; a squad, company or gang; a mob.

Crib *n.* a receptacle for storing fodder for the cattle; a crate; a plagiarism.

Cribbage *n.* a game played with cards and a board with many holes in it.

Cribble *n.* a coarse sieve.

Crick *n.* a cramping of muscles, especially of the neck; a sudden stiffness.

Cricket *n.* a kind of grasshopper or an insect; a kind of outdoor game played with the wickets on both ends.

Crier *n.* one who cries; an officer's peon who makes public announcements.

Crime *n.* a punishable act, sin.

Criminal *adj.* pertaining to crime; of or involving crime; relating to crimes.

Criminology *n.* the scientific study of crime and criminals.

Crimple *v.t.* to contract or shrink, to curl.

Crimson *adj.* & *n.* a red colour in general; a special type of deep red colour having a blue tinge.

Crinal *adj.* belonging to the hair.

Cringe *v.t.* to submit; to fawn; to bow servilely; to bend; to move back or lower one's body in fear.

Cringing *adj.* servile.

Crinkle *n.* a wrinkle; a short bend or turn.

Crinoid *n.* & *adj.* a feather-star, lily-shaped.

Crinoline *n.* a kind of device to keep the cloth stiff; a basket to keep the skirt hooped all round.

Cripple *n.* a lame person.

Crisis *n.* turning or decisive point; especially of a disease; moment of suspense or danger.

Crisp *adj.* fragile; curling; having corrugated surface; brittle.

Crisply *adv.* in a crisp manner.

Cristate *adj.* having a crest.

Criterion *n.* a principle taken as standard in judging; a measure; a test.

Critic *n.* a reviewer by profession; a fault-finder; a person who attempts or is skilled in criticism.

Critical *adj.* skilful, fault-finding, involving risk, belonging to criticism.

Criticaster *n.* a feeble critic.

Criticism *n.* a critical observation or examination; judging of merit.

Critique *n.* a critical essay, art of criticism, a review.

Croak *n.* to grumble; to foretell evil; to cry like a frog.

Croceate, Croceous *adjs.* saffron-coloured.

Croaker *n.* a prophet of ill.

Crochet *n.* a knitting work done with the help of a cooked needle; an ornamental work done with a small instrument.

Crock *n.* an earthenware; a jar; a man of loose character; an aged ewe; a pot or pitcher.

Crockery *n.* earthen ware. china dishes.

Crocket *n.* (in architecture) a chisel work in the stone.

Crocodile *n.* a kind of large water reptile, that lives especially in rivers and lakes in hot parts of the world.

Croesus *n.* saffron colour; a wealthy man.

Croft *n.* a small farm; a small piece of arable land close to house.

Crone *n.* an old hog or an old woman; a withered old woman; an ugly old woman.

Crony *n.* an intimate friend.

Crook *n.* bowing of one's body out of reverence; artifice; a trick.

Crooked *adj.* not straight or level; straightforward.

Croon *v.t.* & *i.* to hum. *n.* a low undertone.

Crop *n.* a gullet of birds for storing food for digestion; a whip; a handle; style of having short hair.

Cropper *n.* a person or thing that crops; (*sl.*) a heavy fall.

Croquet *n.* a kind of game played with the help of large wooden sticks and woolen balls, by passing them through a number of arches, and mallets.

Croquette *n.* a fried ball of rice, potato, meat etc.

Crore *n.* one hundred lakhs or ten million.

Crosier, Crozier *ns.* a long ceremonial stick, carried by a bishop, usually with a hook at one end.

Cross *n.* an upright stake with a transverse bar, the cross on which Christ was crucified, the Christian religion, affliction, intermixture.

Cross-country *adj.* across fields or open country rather than on main roads.

Cross-examination *n.* the examination of a witness by the opposite party or counsel with a view to shaking his evidence.

Crossing *n.* cross-breeding; place where roads meet; act of going across; an act by which a sign of the cross is made.

Cross-question *n.* a question put in cross examination.

Cross-road *n.* one that crosses another or joins two.

Cross-word *n.* cross-word puzzle in which left out square are to be filled with the help of clues given separately.

Crotchet *n.* (music) a note equal to half a minim; a whimsical fancy.

Croton *n.* a genus of plants.

Crouch *v.i.* to stoop, to bend timidly, to cringe, to fawn.

Croup, Croupe *ns.* a kind of disease of the children known as diphtheria.

Croupier *n.* a person in charge of a gambling table who deals cards, collects and pays out money etc.

Crow *n.* a large black bird, the crowing of the cock.

Crowbar *n.* a straight iron bar, usually with a curved end, used as a lever.

Crowd *n.* a musical instrument; a large number of persons gathered closely together; multitude or rabble.

Crown *n.* the diadem; the royal of honour; a head dress worn by heads of the state; the sovereign; kingship.

Croydon *n.* a two-wheeled carriage like a gig.

Crucial *adj.* decisive; searching; critical; severe; very important; of the shape of the cross.

Crucible *n.* a pot in which metals are melted; a severe test or trial.

Cruciferous *adj.* with four equal petals arranged crosswise or in the form of a cross.

Crucifix *n.* image of Christ on the cross.

Crucifixion *n.* the mode of putting to death by nailing or the killing of somebody by fastening them to a cross.

Cruciform *adj.* having the shape of a cross.

Crucify *v.t.* to punish; to torment; to bind behind a cart and draw (as a military punishment).

Crude *adj.* raw; unrefined; unprepared; not digested; unripe; ill-digested; unpolished.

Cruel *adj.* savage; severe; merciless; not careful of others pain; taking pleasure in giving pain to others.

Cruet *n.* a small container for salt, pepper; a set of small glass bottles (for vinegar, oil, etc.) used on the table at meals.

Cruise *n.* cruising voyage; a journey by sea. *v.i.* to make a trip by sea for pleasure; to sail to travel over; to search far enemy vessels in a warship.

Crumb *n.* a loaf of bread; a morsel; particle of anything; that part of a bread which is soft; a small piece or amount.

Crumble *v.t.* & *i.* to break or fall into crumbs or fragments; to begin to fail or lose strength; to come slowly to an end.

Crummy *adj.* of very bad quality; plump; rich; comely; jolly.

Crump *adj.* crooked. *v.t.* to hit hard.

Crumpet *n.* a soft piece of bread; a small flat round cake.

Crumple *v.t.* & *i.* to crush into crooks; to cause to collapse; to collapse; to wrinkle; to become creased.

Crunch *v.t.* to crunch noisily with teeth.

Crupper *n.* the hind portion of a horse.

Crusade *n.* a daring and adventurous undertaking.

Cruse *n.* an earthenware pot or bottle.

Crush *v.t.* to subdue; to ruin; to overwhelm; to beat.

Crushed *adj.* crumpled.

Crust *n.* the outer and hard part of a bread; covering of a pie.

Crustacean *n.* a hard-shelled water creature.

Crutch *n.* the staff with a cross-piece on the head used by lame persons.

Crux *n.* anything that puzzles greatly; the most important or difficult part of a problem.

Cry *v.i.* & *t.* to lament; to bawl; to weep; to utter a shrill cry; to produce tears; to announce for sale.

Cryogen *n.* a freezing mixture.

Crypt *n.* a vault, *esp.* one below the church used as a burial-place.

Cryptic *adj.* veiled in obscurity; secret; with a meaning that is hidden or not easily understood; mysterious.

Cryptogram, Cryptograph *ns.* a thing written in cipher.

Crystal *n.* a clear and transparent mineral resembling ice; rock crystal; a superior kind of glass, or a cut glass.

Crystalline *adj.* having the structure and part of a crystal; of or like or clear as crystal.

Crystalloid *adj.* crystal-like; of crystalline structure.

Cub *n.* a chest; young of a fox or certain other animals; a whelp; a wolf-cub; a boy-scout; a young-boy.

Cube *n.* a block having six sides (six equal squares); third power of a given quantity; the product of a number multiplied by its square.

Cubiform *adj.* cub-shaped.

Cubit *n.* the length of the forearm from the elbow to the tip of the middle finger; an old measure.

Cuckold *n.* the husband of an unfaithful wife.

Cuckoldom *n.* the act of adultry.

Cuckoo *n.* an empty person; a silly person; a bird with a call that sounds like its name.

Cuculiate *adj.* of the form of a hood.

Cucumber *n.* a long fleshy fruit of a creeping plant; the plant.

Cucrubit *n.* the gourd.

Cud *n.* the food that cattle bring back from the stomach into the mouth to chew again.

Cudbear *n.* a dyestuff.

Cuddle *v.t.* & *i.* to fondle; to love; to embrace; to nestle together.

Cuddy *n.* a cabin on a boat, a donkey, a fool, an ass.

Cudgel *n.* a heavy stick of bamboo. *v.t.* to strike; to beat with a cudge.

Cue *n.* a pig tail of hair at the back of head; an intimation; an example of how to behave.

Cuff *n.* the open extreme end of the sleeve; light blow with open hand.

Cuirass *n.* the brest-plate of leather or iron.

Cuirassier *n.* a horse soldier wearing armour on the breast and back.

Cuisine *n.* cookery; a department where cooking work is done; kitchen arrangement.

Culinary *adj.* having to do with cooking; used in kitchens.

Cull *n.* diseased and unsuitable animals separated from the herd.

Cullet *v.t.* refuse glass for remelting.

Culminate *v.i.* to reach highest and last point of development.

Culpable *adj.* criminal; responsible and deserving blame for having done something wrong; guilty.

Culprit *n.* a criminal; offender; a person who has done something wrong or against the law.

Cult *n.* system of religious worship or belief; devotion to a person or thing; lover for a teacher or idea.

Cultrate *adj.* shaped like a edge of a knife.

Culture *n.* refinement; tillage; intellectual development; rearing of (bees, fish, silk germs, bacteria and oysters).

Culverin *n.* a large cannon; a small firearm.

Culvert *n.* an arched channel carrying water under or over a road.

Cumber *v.t.* to stand in the way of; to trouble; to hinder; to load up with useless things, and so to prevent easy movement; to hamper.

Cummerbund *n.* a wide band of cloth worn round the waist.

Cummin, Cumin *ns.* a plant with seeds that are used as a spice in cooking.

Cumulate *adj.* heaped up, amassed.

Cumulative *adj.* representing the sum of many items; increasing in amount, force, etc.

Cumulus *n.* a type of cloud formation consisting of round masses on a flat base.

Cuneal *adj.* of the shape of a wedge.

Cuneiform *adj.* shaped like an arrow-head; (of inscriptions) composed of cuneiform marks.

Cunning *n.* skill; art; ability; dexterity.

Cup *n.* drinking vessel, rounded cavity of anything, portion, experience, fate.

Cup-board *n.* a set of shelves with a door or doors in front.

Cupel *n.* a circular dish used by goldsmiths in assaying gold.

Cupid *n.* The Roman God of love; a beautiful boy.

Cupola *n.* a dome; an internal part of a dome; a turret to protect a gun; a kind of iron foundry furnace.

Cupreous, Cupric *adjs.* of copper; coppery.

Cur *n.* a scoundrel; a dog of low breed; sully or cowardly fellow.

Curacy *n.* the curate's office.

Curate *n.* the Parish priests who help the priest in charge of a church.

Curative *adj.* tending to cure; helping to make sick persons well.

Curator *n.* superintendent of a museum; incharge of anything; a board that selects university professors.

Curb *n.* a chain or strap passing under the lower jaw of a horse, check, restraint.

Curcuma *n.* turmeric.

Curd *n.* cheesy part of milk; thickened milk coagulated with acid; a kind of fatty matter found in salmon fish.

Curdle *v.t.* & *i.* to thicken; to coagulate; to form or make something into curds.

Cure *n.* the act of healing, that which heals, a remedy.

Curette *n.* a surgeon's scraping instrument.

Curfew *n.* the ringing of a bell at fixed evening hours after which inhabiants are not allowed to stir abroad.

Curio *n.* a curious object of art, a rare object.

Curion *n.* a curious object of art; an article of curiosity.

Curiosity *n.* a desire to know; inquisitiveness; a strange or rare thing.

Curious *adj.* having or showing too much interest in the affairs of others; eager to know or learn.

Curl *v.t.* & *i.* to coil into a spiral shape, especially a small bunch of hair; to proceed in a curve.

Curly *adj.* having curls.

Curmudgeon *n.* a churlish fellow; a miser; an avaricious.

Currant *n.* a grape of levant of black colour and seedless.

Currency *n.* current money, circulation, prevalence.

Current *adj.* flowing (as water); running (as stream); in circulation or general use; course (as of events) belonging to the moment or period of time now running.

Curricle *n.* a light two-wheeled two-horse carriage.

Curriculum *n.* the subjects included in a course of study or taught at a particular school, college, etc.

Currier *n.* a leather-dresser.

Curry *n.* a kind of Indian dish made from a mixture of curd, turmeric, and other condiments etc.

Curse *n.* an utterance of destruction, divine vengeance.

Cursive *adj.* & *n.* written with a running of flowing hand.

Cursory *adj.* hasty; hurried; superficial; without attention to details; rapid; done quickly and not thoroughly.

Curt *adj.* summarised; brief; concise.

Curtly *adv.* briefly.

Curtail *v.t.* to abridge; to cut short; to chop off; to reduce something.

Curtain *n.* drapery cloth used as a screen at the door or window or around the bed etc.

Curtilage *n.* a field, garden etc. attached to a dwelling-house.

Curvated *adj.* bent.

Curvature *n.* curving; curved shape; the bending of a line.

Curve *n.* anything with a bend; a curved line; a graph; a curved surface; an arch (of a building or a bridge etc.) a line of which no part is straight.

Curvet *n.* a frolic, a kind of horse's leap.

Curvilinear *adj.* of curved lines, bounded by curved lines.

Cushat *n.* a wood pigeon.

Cushion *n.* a stuffed bag for sitting, reclining or sleeping. *v.t.* to supply with cushions.

Cusp *n.* a point of the moon; a point made by the meeting of two curved lines; an instrument.

Custard *n.* a drink made by mixing milk and egg, and with a small dose of sweet.

Custodial *adj.* pertaining to guardianship.

Custodian *n.* a person who takes responsibility for or who looks after something.

Custody *n.* a keeping; a guarding; a watching; care; locking up or imprisonment; security.

Custom *n.* usual practice, established usage. *n.* (*pl.*) duty levied on import.

Customer *n.* a buyer; one who is accustomed to visit a certain market; Shakespeare's usage—a harlot, a prostitute; as a slang—a person; an accustomed purchaser.

Cut *n.* a stroke or blow, a notch, excision, act of speech which wounds the feelings, refusal to recognize, fashion.

Cutaneous *adj.* pertaining to skin.

Cutchery *n.* a court-house, a public house.

Cute *adj.* clever; attractive; pretty and charming; ingeneous.

Cuticle *n.* a thin skin; the piece of hard skin at the base of a nail on a person's finger or toe.

Cutlass *n.* a short sword with a slightly curved blade, used formerly by sailors.

Cutler *n.* one who makes and sells knives and similar tools.

Cutlet *n.* cooked meat from the neck of an animal.

Cutpurse *n.* a pickpocket.

Cutter *n.* a tailor's cutting-out hand; a person or thing that cuts; a warship's rowing and sailing boat.

Cutting *n.* an article, story etc. cut from a newspaper or magazine and kept for reference.

Cuttle, Cuttlefish *ns.* a sea animal with ten arms.

Cutty *n.* a short clay pipe.

Cut-water *n.* the fore part of a ship's prow which cuts water.

Cuvette *n.* a trench sunk along the middle of a dry ditch.

CV *abbr.* a written record of your education and employment that you send when you are applying for a job; curriculum vitae.

Cyan *n.* a greenish-blue colour.

Cyanic *adj.* of or containing cyanogen.

Cyber *n.* combining form (in nouns and adjectives) connected with electronic communication networks, especially the Internet.

Cyborg *n.* a creature that is part of human par machine.

Cycle *n.* a series of events or phenomenon which recur in the same order, a long period, a series of songs etc.

Cycle-line *n.* a part of a road or path that only bicycles are allowed to use.

Cycloid *n.* a curve traced by a point on the circumference of a circle as the circle rolls along a straight line.

Cyclometer *n.* an instrument for measuring circular arcs.

Cyclone *n.* a violent hurricane.

Cyclopaedia, Cyclopedia *n.* a short form of the word encyclopedia; a book or set of books supplying knowledge on all subjects.

Cyclolpaedic *adj.* pertaining to an encylopaedia.

Cyclop(s) one-eyed giant; one-eyed person.

Cyclorama *n.* circular panorama.

Cyclosis *n.* circulation of blood.

Cyclostyle *n.* a apparatus for making many copies from a stencil.

Cyder *n.* apple-wine.

Cygnet *n.* a young swan.

Cygnus *n.* swan.

Cylinder *n.* anything roller shaped, hollow or sold; the cylindrical part of a machine.

Cymar *n.* woman's under garment.

Cymbal *n.* a round brass plate used as a musical instrument.

Cymbalist *n.* one who plays cymbals.

Cymbolo *n.* a kind of stringed musical instrument which is played with hammers, one who plays on a cymbal.

Cymbiform *adj.* of the form of a boat.

Cyme *n.* an inflorescence in which each flower-stem ends in a flower.

Cymric *adj.* & *n.* pertaining to the Welsh, the Welsh language.

Cynic *n.* snarling; surely or dog-like; characteristic of cynic philosophers.

Cynical *adj.* of or like a cynic; concerned only with one's own interests.

Cynicism *n.* surliness.

Cynosure *n.* Little Bear; a guiding star; an object at which every one looks.

Cypher *n.* nought.

Cypress *n.* a kind of tree having a very hard wood; a symbol of mourning.

Cyprus *n.* a thin transparent black stuff similar to crape.

Cyst *n.* a bladder; a bag; a bladder having morbid secretion or any other matter.

Cystic *adj.* the urinary bladder.

Cystic fibrosis *n.* a serious medical condition that some people are born with, in which glands in the lungs and other organs do not work correctly.

Czar, Tsar, Tzar *n.* the title of the Emperor of Russia, a king.

Czarevna *n.* the daughter of a Czar.

Czarina (Tsarina) *n.* the title of the wife of Czar (of Russia).

Czecho-Slovak *n.* a native of Czechoslovakia.

Czech *n.* a language of Czechoslovakia.

D the fourth letter of the English alphabet, (*muc.*) the second note of natural major scale.

Dab *v.t.* & *i.* to strike gently with something soft or moist; to smear.

Dabble *v.i.* & *t.* to shake about in liquid; to take part in something without serious intentions.

Dabchick *n.* a kind of water-bird.

Dace *n.* a small silvery fresh-water fish.

Dacha *n.* a Russian country house.

Dachshund *n.* a German dog with a long body and short legs.

Dacapo *adv.* once.

Dacoit *n.* a member of a robber band.

Dactyl *n.* a digit; a metrical foot.

Dad, Dada, Daddy *ns.* father; (often as a form of address); (used *esp.* by and when speaking to young children).

Dado *n.* the lower part of the wall of a room, when it is different from the upper part in colour or material.

Daedal *adj.* inventive; skilful.

Daemon *n.* demigod, giant.

Daffodil *n.* a yellow flower with a tall stem that grows from a bulb.

Daft *adj.* silly; insane; unreasonably merry; foolish; reckless; mad.

Dagger *n.* a short sharp pointed sword; a disk; a stiletto; a pointed and edged blade.

Daggle *v.t.* & *i.* to run through mud and water; to smear mud.

Dago *n.* a foreign person with dark skin, Spanish or Portuguese or Italian.

Daily *adv.* happening or being every day; constantly.

Dainty *n.* something nice and delicate to the taste; a delicacry.

Daintily *adv.* deliciously.

Dairy *n.* the place where milk is converted into butter or cheese; a shop where milk butter etc. are sold.

Dairymaid *n.fem.* a female servant in a dairy.

Dais *n.* a raised platform, *esp.* at one end of a room, for somebody to make a speech from.

Daisy *n.* a well-known composite plant, having a white flower with a tinge or red and yellow centre; a general term of admiration, often ironical.

Dak *n.* transmitting letters etc. by post.

Dak bungalow *n.* a house for travellers in India.

Dak, Dawk *ns.* the mail-post; letters.

Dale *n.* the low place between hills; a valley.

Dalesman *n.* a dweller in dales.

Dalliance *n.* behaviour that involves dallying with somebody; fonding; love-making; delay; delaying.

Dally *v.t.* to waste time in effeminate or voluptuous pleasures; to toy.

Dalmatian *n.* a large dog with short white hair marked with dark spots.

Dalt *n.* a foster child.

Daltonism *n.* colour blindness.

Dam *n.* an embankment to restrain water; mother (*usu.* of beast).

Damage *n.* hurt; harm caused to something; injury; loss; the value of what is lost.

Damascene *v.t.* to ornament metal with inlaid silver or gold.

Damask *n.* kinds of woven material of silk or linen; a fine steel made in Damascus; a light rose colour.

Dame *n.* a lady of rank; the wife of a knight or baronet; a woman of mature years; a matron.

Dammar *n.* the cat's-eye resin; name of various resins.

Damn *v.t.* & *i.* to send to hell; to condemn; to censure severely; to curse or swear at; to doom to eternal torment.

Damnify *v.t.* to cause an injury to.

Damp *n.* moisture in air; chill; discouragement. *adj.* slightly wet. *v.t.* to moisten; to chill; to deject.

Damper *n.* that which makes the fire burn more slowly; a person or thing that depresses; a thin cake or flour and water.

Damsel *n.* a young women who is not married.

Damson *n.* a small dark-coloured plum.

Dance *v.i.* & *t.* to leap and frisk about to move with short abrupt rapid movements; to make to dance.

Dander *n.* indignation; anger; temper.

Dandiacal *adj.* inclined to be dandy.

Dandie *n.* a kind of terrier.

Dandify *v.t.* to dress like or cause to resemble a dandy.

Dandle *v.t.* to shake or jolt on the knees, as an infant; to fondle.

Dandruff, Dandriff *ns.* the dead skin in small scales among the hair.

Dandy *n.* a person devoted to smartness of costume; a foppish fellow.

Dane *n.* a native of Denmark.

Danger *n.* peril; risk; hazard; insecurity; loss; pain or other evil; liability or a chance of suffering damage.

Dangerous *adj.* full of danger; perilous; hazardous; unsafe.

Dangle *v.t.* & *i.* to hang loose; to hang and swing; to hang on any one.

Dangler *n.* one who dangles.
Daniel *n.* an upright judge; a very wise man.
Danish *adj.* & *n.* of Danes, the language of Denmark.
Dank *n.* moist; damp; cold and wet.
Dap *v.i.* to dip lightly; to bounce.
Daphne *n.* a flowering shrub.
Dapper *adj.* neat; (usually of a small man) neat and elegant in appearance and often quick in movement.
Dapple *v.t.* to variegate; to be variegated with spots.
Dare *n.* to be bold enough; to have courage or impudence for any purpose.
Daredevil *adj.* a desperado; reckless. *n.* a reckless person; a person who is foolishly bold and seems not to care about danger.
Daring *adj.* bold; courageous; intrepid; fearless; brave. *n.* courage.
Dark *n.* absence of light.
Darken *v.t.* & *i.* to make dark; to obscure; to cloud; to dim; to deprive of bodily or mental vision.
Darkle *v.i.* to lie concealed.
Darkness *n.* wickedness; absence of light; ignorance.
Darksome *adj.* gloomy; obscure.
Darling *n.* dearly beloved, lovable.
Darn *v.t.* to mend by imitating the texture of the stuff with thread and a needle; to sew together with thread.
Dart *n.* a light javelin in other pointed missile; insect's sting.
Darwinism *n.* a belief in the theory of Charles Darwin about the evolution of species, evolution.
Dash *v.t.* & *i.* to knock or cause to strike suddenly or violently; to mix slightly; to form hastily.
Dashing *adj.* having dash; impetuous; spirited; showy; active.
Dastard *n.* cowardly fellow.
Data *n.* things certainly known; facts given from which other facts are deduced.
Date *n.* a statement of time or time and place of writing; tending, executing, as on a letter.
Dative *adj.* the case in grammar which signifies the person or object to which something is given.
Datum *n.* something known or assumed as basis for inference; fixed starting-point (of scale, & etc.).
Daub *v.t.* & *i.* to coat with clay or palster; to smear; to stain; to paint inartistically.
Daughter *n.* one's female child; the female offspring of animal or plant; female member of a family.
Daughter-in-law *n.* a son's wife.
Daunt *v.t.* to discourage; to intimidate.

Dauphin *n*. (formerly) the title of the king of France's eldest son.

Davenport *n*. a small ornamental writing desk.

Davit *n*. a crane for suspending a hip's boat.

Davy-Lamp *n*. a miner's safety lamp.

Daw *n*. a kind of small crow; a jackdaw.

Dawdle *v.t.* to be slow; to stand about doing nothing; to waste time; to trifle.

Dawn *v.t.* to begin to show intellectual light or knowledge; to glimmer obscurely; to begin to open or appear.

Day *n*. the time between the rise and setting of the Sun.

Daze *v.t.* to stupefy; to stun; to dazzle. *n*. bewilderment.

Dazzle *v.t.* to over-power with a bright or intense light; to dim or blind by a glare of light or with show or display of any kind

Dead *n*. the time when things are most still, those deceased. *adv.* thoroughly.

Dead-beat *n*. very tired; a person who has no job and no money and has lost the will to live an active life.

Deaden *v.t.* & *i*. to diminish the force of; to deprive of vitality; to blunt; to remove gloss or brilliancy.

Dead-heat *n*. a race in which the runners come all to the winning post at the same time, to that no one is the winner.

Dead-letter *n*. a law no longer observed; an unclaimed letter at the post-office.

Dead-lift a heavy weight.

Dead loss *n*. a loss without any compensation.

Dead-shot a good marksman.

Deadly *adj*. causing death; mortal; fatal; murderous; extremely effective; implacable.

Deaf *adj*. dull of hearing; unable to hear at all; not inclined to hear; inattentive.

Deafen *v.t.* to make deaf; to make somebody feel that they cannot hear sounds around them by making a very loud noise.

Deafly *adv.* without sense of sounds.

Deal *n*. a portion or part; an indefinite quantity; degree, or extent, generally implying that the amount is considerable.

Dealer *n*. one who deals; a trader; a merchant; one who distributes cards; a trafficker.

Dealings *n. pl.* manner of acting towards others.

Deambulation *n*. the act of walking.

Dean *n*. the head of a cathedral, the head of a faculty in a college.

Deanery *n*. the office, jurisdiction of a dean.

Dear *adj.* high in price; valuable; expensive; precious to.

Dearth *n.* the quantity of being dear; scarcity; want; need.

Death *n.* end of life; want of spiritual life annihilation.

Debacle *n.* sudden breaking up of ice on a river; a sudden outbreak of water; a confused rout; a stampede; a crash in social or political world.

Debar *v.t.* to prevent; to hinder; to obstruct; to exclude from admission.

Debark *v.t. & i.* to disembark.

Debarkation *n.* disembarkation; landing from a ship.

Debase *v.t.* to bring low; to lower to sink; to cast down; to reduce; to depress.

Debatable *adj.* liable to be questioned, subject to discussion.

Debate *n.* formal discussion; deliberation; consideration.

Debauch *v.t.* to corrupt; to vitiate; to pollute; to defile; to pervert from virtue; to mislead.

Debauchery *n.* habitual lewdness.

Debel *v.t.* to conquer in war.

Debenture *n.* a certificate of drawback of customs duties on the exportation of certain goods.

Debilitate *v.t.* to make faint or languid; to weaken; to enfeeble; to cause debility in.

Debit *n.* a sum withdrawn from an account; a written note in an account of a sum owed or paid out.

Debonair *adj.* (usually of men) confident and charming; kind; genial; having nice manners.

Debouch *v.i.* to come out of a wood or ravine.

Debris *n.* fragment; rubbish; (geology) fragments of rock and other substance piled up.

Debt *n.* that which is due from one person to another; due; obligation.

Debtor *n.* one who owes a sum of duty.

Debus *v.t. & i.* to unload or alight from motor vehicles.

Debut *n.* entrance upon anything; first appearance before the public, as of an actor or public speaker.

Decade *n.* a series of ten years.

Decadence *n.* a state or behaviour that shows a fall to a lower level in morals, art, literature, etc.

Decagon *n.* a plane figure bounded by ten lines.

Decagonal *adj.* having ten sides.

Decalcify *v.t.* to deprive (bone) of lime.

Decalogue *n.* the Ten Commandments in the Bible.

Decameter *n.* ten metres.

Decamp *v.t.* to abscond; to march off; to break up or leave camp.

Decanal *adj.* pertaining to a dean.

Decant *v.t.* to pour off leaving sediment, etc.

Decapitate *v.t.* to behead; to cut off the head.

Decapitation *n.* a deceiving trick, a sham.

Decapod *n.* a shell-fish having ten feet.

Decay *v.i.* & *t.* to fall away from a state of health or excellence; to become or make something bad.

Decease *n.* death; departure from life.

Deceit *n.* the quality or act of deceiving; deception; fraud; artifice; guile.

Deceive *v.t.* to mislead the mind intentionally; to cause to believe what is false or disbelieve what is true.

Decency *n.* propriety of behaviour; respectability; modesty.

Decennary *n.* a period of ten years.

Decennial *adj.* recurring every ten years.

Decent *adj.* becoming; seemly; fit; suitable; comely; not gaudy or ostentatious; decorous; proper; modest.

Deception *n.* act of deceiving or misleading; state of being deceived or mislead; deceit.

Deceptive *adj.* likely to deceive; misleading.

Decide *v.t.* & *i.* to settle; to give judgement; to com to a resolution.

Deciduous *adj.* shedding leaves, teeth etc. periodically.

Decigram *n.* one tenth of a gram.

Decimal *adj.* numbered or proceeding by tenths; of tenths.

Decimate *v.t.* to destroy a tenth part.

Decimeter *n.* equal to one-tenth of metre; a unit of length in the metric system.

Decipher *v.t.* to explain what is written in ciphers; to succeed in understanding something such as a code.

Decision *n.* a settlement, judgement, conclusion, resolve.

Deck *v.t.* to dress; to clothe; to dress elegantly; to array; to adorn; to embellish; to ornament.

Declaim *v.t.* to speak rhetorically.

Declaration *n.* an emphatic or deliberate or formal statement.

Declarative *adj.* making a declaration.

Declare *v.t.*& *i.* to make known; to proclaim; publicly; to reveal.

Declension *n.* a falling-off from a standard; descent; in English Grammar.

Declination *n.* angular distance of star; downward bend; deflexion of compass-needle.

Decline *v.t.* & *i.* to droop, (to bend); to draw to a close; to decrease; to refuse; to infect.

Declivity *n.* downwards slope (of a mountain-side, etc.)

Declutch *v.i.* to disengage a clutch.

Decoction *n.* an extract; extraction of essence got by boiling.

Decode *v.t.* to translate from a code; to find the meaning of something; to interpret something.

Decompose *v.t.* to separate into original elements.

Decontrol *v.t.* to release (trade, etc.) from government control.

Decorate *v.t.* to furnish with ornaments; to beautify.

Decoration *n.* decorating or being decorated; an ornament, etc. given and worn as an honour.

Decorator *n.* one who decorates or embellishes.

Decorous *adj.* fitting and polite; not offending against decency or seemliness; dignified and decent.

Decorticate *v.t.* to strip off bark.

Decorum *n.* etiquette; seemliness; propriety; decency.

Decoy *n.* an enticement; an apparatus of hoops and network for trapping wild-ducks, a bird or an animal.

Decrease *v.t.* & *i.* to lessen; to deminish gradually. *n.* gradual diminution.

Decree *n.* an ordinance or edict; a decision of court; a judgement; a predetermined purpose.

Decrement *n.* decrease; waste.

Decrepit *adj.* worn out with old age; in the last stage of decay; infirm.

Decrepitate *v.i.* to crackle by heat.

Decrescent *adj.* decreasing, warning.

Decretal *n.* papal decree.

Decry *v.t.* to cry down; to condemn; to censure as worthless; to blame; to say bad things about.

Decuple *adj.* tenfold. *n.* a tenfold amount.

Dedicate *v.t.* to devote to the service of God; to devote with solemn rites; to inscribe; to patron.

Deduce *v.t.* to trace descent of; to draw from; to infer as a conclusion.

Deduct *v.t.* to subtract; to take away an amount or a part.

Deductive *adj.* of or reasoning by deduction.

Deed *n.* an actual fact; a performance; an exploit; a written or printed instrument for legal disposition.

Deem *v.t.* to think; to believe; (not in the continuous tenses) to consider.

Deemster *n.* one of the two judges of the Isle of man.

Deep *n.* going far down from top; profound; absorbed; intense; extreme; hidden; secret.

Deepen *v.t.* & *i.* to make deep or deeper; to become deep.

Deer *n.* a kind of animal with branching horns.

Deface *v.t.* to destroy the face; to obliterate.

Defacto *adj.* & *adv.* whether or not it is justified; existing or doing something in actual fact.

Defalcate *v.t.* to deduct a part of; to be guilty of defalcation; to use other people's money for one's own purposes.

Defame *v.t.* to destroy the reputation; to speak evil of.

Defamation *n.* act of defaming; calumny; slander.

Default *n.* defect; a fault or failure; neglect of duty; failure to account for money entrusted to one's charge offence.

Defeat *v.t.* to undo; to frustrate; to disfigure; to win a victory over; to ruin.

Defect *n.* fault; a blemish; deficiency; imperfection; error; a shortcoming.

Defection *n.* deserting a leader; abandonment of one's leader or cause.

Defence *n.* the action of defending somebody from attack or of fighting against attack; justification.

Defend *v.t. & i.* to guard; to protect; to speak in favour.

Defensible *adj.* justifiable; that can be defended.

Defensive *adj.* serving in defence; protective. *n.* a safeguard.

Defensivel *adv.* in a defensive manner.

Defer *v.t.* to put off to another time; to postpone; to delay; to submit respectfully.

Deference *n.* regard; respect; submission. *adj.* expressing respect.

Defiance *n.* act of defying; a challenge to fight; open disobedience.

Defiant *adj.* fearlessly refusing to obey; showing no fear or respect.

Deficiency *n.* a thing wanting; the state of lacking something necessary or shortage.

Deficit *n.* deficiency (in a sum of money, & etc.), excess of liabilities over assets; falling short.

Defile *v.i.* to march off in file or line or file by file. *n.* a gorge or pass.

Define *v.t.* to bring to an end; to decide; to fix the limits of; to make clear; to describe accurately.

Definite *adj.* distinct; clear; that cannot be determinate; precise.

Definition *n.* description of a thing by its qualities; a brief explanation.

Definitive *adj.* done with authority and not to be questioned or changed.

Deflate *v.t.* to reduce from a state of inflation.

Deflect *v.t. & i.* to turn aside; to deviate from a right line or proper course; to change direction.

Deflower *v.t.* to deprive of flowers; to deprive of grace and beauty, or virginity; to ravish; to spoil.

Deform *v.t.* to make ugly; to put out of shape.

Defraud *v.t.* to deprive by fraud; to cheat or deceive; to get something, especially money, from somebody by deception and illegally.

Defray *v.t.* to discharge by payment; to pay.

Deft *adj.* handy; clever; dexterous; skilful and quick in one's movements, especially of the hands.

Defunct *adj.* having finished the course of life; dead; no longer existing without any force; obsolete.

Defy *v.t.* to challenge; to resist openly; to disregard; to present obstacles.

Degeneracy *n.* growing worse or inferior; degenerate state; meanness.

Degenerate *adj.* having lost high quality of race; corrupt.

Deglutition *n.* swallowing.

Degradation *n.* thing that degrades; degrading; disgrace.

Degrade *v.t.* to lower in rank or dignity; to deprive of office or dignity.

Degree *n.* row, stage, step, rank, relative condition, academic rank, 360th part of a circle, 90th part of a right angle, unit of temperature.

Dehort *v.i.* to dissuade; to exhort.

Dehiscent *adj.* gaping, bursting open (seed-vessels).

Dehumanize *v.t.* to deprive or human characterisitics.

Deify *v.t.* to exalt to the rank of a god; to worship as a deity; to make god-like.

Deign *v.t.* & *i.* to do something in a way that shows one thinks one is too important to do it.

Deism *n.* a belief in the existence of God without accepting revelation.

Deity *n.* godhood; a god or goddess; the Supreme Being.

Deject *v.t.* to dishearten; to sadden; to cast down; to depress.

Dejection *n.* lowness of spirits.

Dejure *adj.* & *adv.* rightful; by right; according to law.

Delaine *n.* a light dress-fabric.

Delate *v.t.* to inform against; to charge with a crime.

Delay *v.t.* & *i.* to put off to another time; to defer; to hinder.

Delectable *adj.* pleasing; delightful; very pleasant.

Delectation *n.* enjoyment; entertainment.

Delegacy *n.* appointment as a delegate.

Delegation *n.* delegating; a group of delegates, representatives.

Delegate *v.t.* to entrust; to send as a delegate.

Delete *v.t.* to blot or strike out; to erase.

Deleterious *adj.* harmful; injurious.

Delf *n.* a kind of earthenware.

Deliberate *v.i.* & *t.* to weigh well in one's mind; to think or talk carefully; to take counsel.

Deliberation *n.* a careful consideration; a weighing in mind.

Delicacy *n.* a dainty; delicateness; refined feeling.

Delicacies *n. pl.* objects delicate to taste.

Delicate *adj.* dainty; tender; soft; delightful; nice; elegant; light.

Delicately *adv.* daintily; tenderly.

Delicious *adj.* a highly pleasing to the taste; very pleasing; giving pleasure to the senses of taste or smell.

Delict *n.* a violation of law; misdemeanour.

Delight *v.t. & i.* to please highly; to take great pleasure.

Delimitation *n.* assigning of limits or boundaries.

Delineate *v.t.* to show something by drawing or describing it in detail.

Delinquency *n.* a fault; a crime.

Delinquent *n.* guilty; offender; young people showing a tendency to commit crimes.

Deliquesce *v.i.* to melt away; to undergo change to liquid form.

Delirium *n.* a disordered state of the brain.

Deliver *v.t.* to save; to set free from danger; to rescue from evil or fear; to give up or part with; to hand over.

Deliverable *adj.* that can be delivered.

Delivery *n.* delivering or being delivered; person's manner of delivering a speech or a ball that is thrown.

Dell *n.* a small valley covered over with trees.

Delphain, Delphic *adjs.* of the oracle of Delphi; oracular; obscure, ambiguous.

Delta *n.* the fourth letter of the Greek alphabet [D]; an alluvial triangular tract at the mouth of a river.

Deludable *adj.* able to be deluded.

Delude *v.t.* to play to impose upon; to deceive.

Deluge *n.* a great flood; a heavy rainfall; a heavy downpour or water.

Delusion *n.* a false impression or opinion; deception; fallacy.

Delusive *adj.* beguiling; not real; raising vain hopes; deceptive.

Delusory *adj.* apt of deceive.

Delve *v.t.* to dig with a spade; to make deep research; to try very hard to find information about something.

Demagogue *n.* a political leader who tries to win people's support by using arguments which are emotional and often not reasonable.

Demand *n.* a rightful claim; an earnest enquiry. *v.t.* to ask authoritatively.

Demarcate *v.t.* to fix the boundary.

Demean *v.t.* to behave; to conduct oneself; to make mean; to ill-treat; to lower the dignity of; to degrade.

Demeanour *n.* the outward bearing; behaviour.

Demented *adj.* beside oneself; mad.

Dementia *n.* a kind of insanity.

Demerit *n.* a fault; a bad point of character; a defect.

Demesne *n.* possession of land with unrestricted rights; a landed estate round a great house.

Demigod *n.* the son of a god and mortal; a deified man.

Demijohn *n.* a large wicker-cased bottle.

Demi-monde *n.* a class of woman of doubtful reputation.

Demi-rep *n.* a woman of suspected chastity.

Demise *v.t.* to bequeath by will or lease; to transmit. *n.* a transferring, death.

Demit *v.t.* to resign.

Demobilize *v.t.* to disband; to release somebody from military service.

Democracy *n.* a government of the people, for the people and by the people; a representative government.

Democrat *n.* an advocate of popular government.

Demolish *v.t.* to destroy; to lay in ruins; to ruin; to pull down.

Demolition *n.* ruin; destruction.

Demon *n.* an evil spirit; a devil; a cruel person or an energetic or aggressive person.

Demoniac *adjs.* influenced by demons.

Demoniacal *adj.* devilish; cruel or malignant.

Demonic *n.* demoniac; abnormal.

Demonolatry *n.* the worship of demons.

Demonology *n.* a branch of learning concerned with demons.

Demonstrate *v.t.* & *i.* to describe and explain; to prove with certainty; to prove logically; to make or take part in a demonstration.

Demonstrator *n.* a person who teaches or explains by showing how something works.

Demote *n.* to reduce in rank; to move down into a lower class.

Demur *v.i.* to create doubts or difficulties; to object; to delay; to take exception to.

Demurrant *n.* one who demurs.

Demurrage *n.* an allowance made for undue detention of goods; the amount payable for delay in loading or discharging ships or railway trucks.

Demurrer *n.* exception taken to opponent's point.

Den *n.* a wild beast's lair; a hiding place of thieves; a dirty small room.

Denary *adj.* of ten; decimal.

Dene *n.* a sandy tract; a deep wooded valley.

Dengue *n.* a severe tropical fever accompanied by acute pain in this joints.

Denial *n.* refusal; rejection; contradiction.

Denim *n.* a strong cotton cloth, used for making jeans, etc. usually blue in colour.

Denizen *n.* an inhabitant; an occupant; one admitted to the rights of a citizen; a wild plant.

Denominate *v.t.* to give a name to; to call; to describe.

Denotation *n.* denoting; the exact meaning of a word; term's primary meaning; designation.

Denote *v.t.* to note or mark off; to indicate by a sign; to signify or mean; to distinguish.

Denounement *n.* the untravelling of a plot.

Denounce *v.t.* to inform against or accuse publicly; to prophesy evil; to notify termination to treaties.

Dense *adj.* thick; close; compact; stupid; (of people and things) crowded together in great numbers.

Density *n.* the quality of being dense.

Dent *n.* a hollow place in a hard even surface made by a blow or pressure.

Dental *adj.* pertaining to the teeth or dentistry; produced by the aid of the teeth.

Dentate *adj.* toothed; notched.

Dentifrice *n.* a powder or paste used for cleaning the teeth.

Dentine *n.* the hard tissue forming the main part of the teeth.

Dentist *n.* a tooth-doctor.

Dentistry *n.* the art or profession of a dentist.

Dentition *n.* teething; characteristic arrangement of teeth.

Denture *n.* a plate holding one or more artificial teeth.

Denudation *n.* making nude or bare.

Denude *v.t.* to make naked or nude; to lay bare; to stripe of clothing.

Denunciation *n.* (an instance of) denouncing a person, policy, etc.

Deny *v.t.* to declare untrue; to contradict; to reject; to refuse to admit.

Deodorize *v.t.* to deprive of smell or odour; to disinfect.

Deontology *n.* the science of duty or morality, ethics.

Depart *v.t.* & *i.* to quit or leave; to die; to go away or leave, especially when starting a journey.

Departure *n.* an action or a course of action different from what is usual; the action of departing.

Department *n.* separate part of a complex whole; branch of a business or of municipal or State administration.

Depend *v.i.* to hang down; to rely upon; to be connected with.

Depict *v.t.* to paint; to describe in words.

Depilate *v.t.* extirpation of hair (from the face, & etc.)

Deplete *v.t.* to empty; to reduce greatly the quantity, power or value of something; to use until little or none is left.

Deplorable *adj.* sad, miserable; lamentable; much to be regretted; pitiable.

Deplore *v.t.* to bewail; to feel deep grief over; to regret.

Deploy *v.t. & i.* to unfold; to open out to extend; to move or cause troops to move into position for military action.

Deplume *v.t.* to strip off feathers.

Deponent *n.* one who says certain facts in a court of law declaring them to be true.

Depopulate *v.t.* to reduce the number of people living in a place.

Depopulation *n.* act of dispeopling.

Deport *v.t.* to banish; to send a person out of a country as a punishment.

Deportation *n.* banishment.

Deportment *n.* a person's way of standing and walking; graceful movement and behaviour; conduct; demeanour.

Depose *v.t. & i.* to dethrone; to remove from office; to testify.

Deposit *n.* that which is stored or entrusted, accumulation of mud, gravel etc.

Depositary *n.* a trustee; a person with whom a thing is deposited.

Deposition *n.* dethronement; a piece of sworn evidence; depositing.

Depository *n.* a storehouse.

Depot *n.* a place of deposit; a building for storage or sale.

Depravation *n.* degeneration; corruption; debasement.

Deprave *v.t.* to corrupt; to vitiate; to make somebody morally bad.

Depravity *n.* wickedness; the state of being depraved; moral corruption.

Deprecate *v.t.* to try to ward off by prayer; to desire earnestly the prevention or removal of; to regret deeply.

Depress *v.t.* to lower; to let down; to cause to sink; to humble; to make subject.

Depression *n.* a lowering; a reduction in vitality; a hollow.

Deprivation *n.* the action or process of depriving somebody or of being deprived of something.

Depth *n.* state of being deep; abstruseness, (*pl.*) deep water, middle.

Deputation *n.* a group of people given the right to act or speak on behalf of others.

Depute *v.t.* to appoint as one's substitute.

Deputize *v.t.* to act as deputy for.

Deputy *n.* one deputed or appointed for an other.

Derail *v.t.* to cause a train to leave the rails; to make (train) leave the rails.

Derange *v.t.* to put of place or order; to displace; to confuse; to disorganize.

Derby *n.* a famous horse-race in England (at Epsom); an important sports contest; a hard hat with a round top; a strong type of boot.

Derelict *adj.* not used or cared for and in bad condition; left ownerless; neglectful of duty.

Dereliction *n.* abandoning; desertion; neglect (of duty).

Deride *v.t.* to laugh at in contempt; to mock.

Derision *n.* scoffing; ridicule; a laughing-stock.

Derisive *adj.* unkind and mocking.

Derisory *adj.* mocking; ridiculing.

Derivation *n.* a source to which a thing is traced; descent.

Derivative *adj.* & *n.* of a derived kind; not primitive.

Derive *v.t.* & *i.* to trace from; to get; to obtain; to have origin from.

Dermatology *n.* the medical study of the skin and its diseases.

Derogate *v.t.* to detract; to lessen in value; to depreciate.

Derogatory *adj.* involving or causing loss of respect.

Derrick *n.* a large crane for moving or lifting heavy weights, *esp.* on ship.

Derringer *n.* a small pistol.

Dervish *n.* a Mohammedan friar.

Descant *v.t.* to discourse at large; to comment freely; to talk at large.

Descend *v.t.* & *i.* to come down; to climb down; to sink; to slope downwards; to be derived from.

Descendant *n.* a person or an animal that has another as an ancestor.

Descent *n.* a discourse or discussion; a song. *v.t.* to discourse at large; to comment freely.

Describe *v.t.* to give description of; to give a picture in words.

Description *n.* a verbal portraiture; kind or class (of a thing).

Descry *v.t.* to catch sight of; to detect; to succeed in discerning.

Desecrate *v.t.* to violate the sanctity of; to treat a sacred thing or place badly or without respect.

Desert *n.* reward or punishment that is deserved; conduct or qualities deserving reward or punishment; merit.

Desert *adj.* & *n.* a large area of land that has very little water and very few plants growing on it; uninhabited and barren.

Deserter *n.* one who forsakes a cause or a duty.

Desertion *n.* deserting or being deserted.

Deserve *v.t.* & *i.* to merit; to be entitled as worthy of.

Desiccate *v.t.* to exhaust of moisture, (especially of food) dried especially in order to preserve it.

Desiderate *v.t.* to long for or earnestly desired; to want or miss; to regret the absence of.

Desideratum *n.* a very necessary thing; a thing missing; something much wanted.

Design *v.t.* to indicate; to draw; to form a plan of; to contrive; to intend; to set apart; to purpose.

Designate *adj.* appointed to office. *v.t.* to specify; to serve as a mark.

Designedly *adv.* by design; intentionally; purposely.

Designer *n.* a plotter; one who draws design; a contriver.

Designing *adj.* cunning; crafty; scheming; artful.

Desire *n.* wish; longing; craving; request. *v.t.* to with to long for.

Desist *v.i.* to abandon a course; to leave off; to discontinue.

Desk *n.* a piece of furniture with a flat or slopping top and often with drawers.

Desolate *v.t.* to make lonely or forlorn; to make joyless; to deprive of inhabitants; to lay waste; to destroy.

Despair *v.t.* to be without hope; to lose all hope; to despond.

Desperado *n.* a person given to criminal undertaking.

Desperate *adj.* hopelessly bad; difficult or dangerous.

Despicable *adj.* very unpleasant or evil; contemptible; deserving contempt.

Despise *v.t.* to look down upon; to scorner; to disdain.

Despiser *n.* a scorner.

Despite *n.* a looking down with contempt; anger; offended pride.

Despoil *v.t.* to spoil completely; to rob; to deprive; to take away by force; to plunder; to steal.

Despond *v.t.* to despair; to be cast down; to lose hope; to be dejected.

Despot *n.* an absolute ruler; a tyrant; an oppressor.

Despotic *adj.* of or like a despot.

Despotism *n.* the rule of a despot; tyrannical conduct; an autocratic government.

Desquamate *v.i.* & *t.* to throw off scale; to scale off.

Dessert *n.* any sweet or fruit served at the end of a meal; the course in which this dish is served.

Destination *n.* end or purpose; appointed place for which a thing or person is boudn or appointed.

Destine *v.t.* to ordain; to appoint; to fix; to sentence; to mark out beforehand.

Destiny *n.* ultimate lot; invincible necessity; fate; the power believed to control events.

Destitute *adj.* wanting; devoid of.

Destroy *v.t.* to annihilate; to demolish; to break down.

Destructible *adj.* destroyable; liable to destruction.

Destruction *n.* ruin; overthrow; death; slaughter; the action of destroying something or of being destroyed.

Destructive *adj*. destroying; causing ruin.

Destructor *n*. a furnace that burns refuse; one who destroys.

Desuetude *n*. state of disuse; discontinuance of practice.

Desultory *adj*. without a definite plan or purpose and without enthusiasm; going from one thing to another.

Detach *v.t.* to unfasten; to remove; to free; to send on a separate mission.

Detached *adj*. separated; standing apart; isolated.

Detachment *n*. a group of soldiers sent away from larger group, *esp.* to do special duties.

Detail *v.t.* to give particulars of; to relate.

Detailed *adj*. minutely related.

Detain *v.t.* to hold; to withhold; to stop; to keep, to keep in custody or confinement.

Detect *v.t.* to discover; to find out.

Detective *adj*. a person employed in or concerned with detection.

Detector *n*. a device by which high-frequency oscillations are rectified in a wireless receiver.

Detention *n*. a check; restraint; dealy.

Deter *v.t.* to frighten from; to prevent; to make somebody decide not to do something; to hinder.

Detergent *n*. a substance that removes dirt, *e.g.* from the surface of clothes or dishes. *adj.* cleansing; purifying.

Determinant *adj*. & *n*. decisive; a decisive factor.

Determination *n*. that which is determined or resolved on; ascertainment; resolution.

Determinative *adj*. that which defines.

Determine *v.t.* & *i.* to put an end to; to define; to limit; to decide; to resolve; to cause to resolve.

Determinism *n*. the theory that action is determined by motives themselves which are determined by cause independent of the will.

Deterrent *adj*. a thing that deters or is meant to deter somebody.

Detest *v.t.* to dislike extremely; to abhor.

Detestable *adj*. that one detests.

Detestation *n*. very strong dislike.

Dethrone *v.t.* to remove a ruler from power; to depose (a sovereign).

Detonate *v.t.* & *i.* to explode or cause to explode rapidly and loudly.

Detour *n*. a circuitous or round about way.

Detract *v.t.* & *i.* to take away; to defame; to withdraw.

Detrain *n*. to get off a train; to alight (troops) from a train.

Detriment *n*. injury; harm; damage; mischief.

Detrimental *adj.* causing loss; injurious; hurtful; harmful.

Detrition *n.* a wearing away by rubbing.

Deuce *n.* the two at dice and cards; the devil; mischief; bad luck; (in tennis) a score of 40-40.

Devastate *v.t.* to lay waste; to ravage.

Develop *v.t.* & *i.* to grow larger; to unroll; to unfold.

Deviate *v.i.* to trun from the way; to diverge.

Deviation *n.* deflection; the action of deviating.

Deviator *n.* one who deviates.

Device *n.* stratagem; contrivance; power of devising; artifice; a moto.

Devil *n.* the supreme spirt of evil; a very wicked person; an enemy of God.

Devilish *adj.* monstrously cruel or wicked.

Devilry *n.* black magic; iniquity; reckless; daring.

Devious *adj.* winding; rambling; erring; round-about.

Devise *v.t.* to consider; to imagine; to contrive; to give by will.

Devitalize *v.t.* to make lifeless.

Devoid *adj.* without something; destitute; empty of; lacking.

Devoir *n.* duty; due act of respect; one's best.

Devolution *n.* a passing from one person to another; a handling over of powers; a modified home-rule.

Devolve *v.t.* & *i.* to fall by succession; to descend; to deliver over.

Devote *v.t.* to set apart or dedicate by a vow or solemn act; to engage wholly or chiefly.

Devotee *n.* a votary; a bigot.

Devotion *n.* the act of devoting; divine or religious worship; devoutness; piety; prayer; ardour.

Devour *v.t.* to swallow; to eat up; to consume or waste; to destroy; to kill.

Devout *adj.* pious; religious; reverential.

Dew *n.* moisture found on leaves and ground at the end of the night; beaded moisture resembling it.

Dewlap *n.* the loose skin hanging from the throat; (*esp.* in cattle).

Dewy *adj.* full of dew; wet or moist with dew.

Dexter *adj.* on the right hand side.

Dexterity *n.* adroitness; cleverness; right-handedness.

Dhow *n.* a sailing boat used by the Arabs.

Diabetes *n.* a kind of disease marked by excessive discharge of urine and with excessive sugar in urine.

Diablerie *n.* the devillore; magic; sorcery; uncanny proceedings.

Diabolic *adj.* devilish; fiendish.

Diadem *n.* sovereignty; regal power; a band of precious stones worn on the head.

Diagnose *v.t.* to identity the nature of a problem.
Diagnosis *n.* identification of disease by its distinctive marks.
Diagonal *n.* a straight line drawn from one corner to another corner of a four or more sided figure.
Diagram *n.* a figure made of lines; sketch showing the features of object to be explained.
Dial *n.* the face of a clock or watch; a circular plate on which an index finger indicates degress etc.
Dialect *n.* a language modified by local; peculiar mode of speech or pronunciation distinguished from literary or standard speech.
Dialectic *n.* (*pl.*) the art of discovering and testing truths by discussion and logical argument.
Dialogue *n.* a conversation in which two or more persons take part.
Diameter *n.* the straight line passing through the centre of a circle terminating at circumference dividing it into two equal parts.
Diamond *n.* mineral of great hardness and refractive power consisting of crystallised carbon.
Diapason *n.* a volume of concord sounds.
Diaper *n.* a small towel; a napkin; reticulated decorative work.
Diaphanous *adj.* (of fabric) light, very fine and almost transparent.
Diaphoretic *adj.* & *n.* promoting sweet.
Diaphragm *n.* the muscle separating the chest from the abdomen.
Diarchy *n.* a form of government in which two persons are jointly invested with supreme powers.
Diarrhoea *n.* an illness in which waste matter is emptied from the bowels frequently and in a liquid form.
Diary *n.* a daily record of events; a journal.
Diathesis *n.* a particular habit of body.
Diatom *n.* a very small creature or plant living in water.
Diatribe *n.* a denunciatory harangue; a bitter criticism; a fierce speech attacking person or thing.
Dibble *n.* implements for digging holes in the ground for sowing.
Dice *n.* a game with dice.
Dicer *n.* one who plays at dice.
Dichotomy *n.* division into two parts.
Dicky, Dickey *ns.* a third seat at the back in a two-seated motor-car.
Dictaphone *n.* an instrument for setting down the sounds of the voice on wax and producing them again later.
Dictate *v.i.* to read aloud words to be taken down; to communicate with authority; to command.
Dictation *n.* the matter or material dictated; a test in which people

have to write down a passage that is read aloud.

Dictator *n.* an absolute ruler, one who dictates to a writer.

Dictatorial *adj.* rude and commanding in manner; absolute.

Diction *n.* the choice and use of words in speech or writing.

Dictionary *n.* a book containing the words of a language arranged alphabetically with their meanings, a word book.

Dictum *n.* a formal saying; a maxim.

Didactic *adj.* designed for the purpose of teaching something.

Didactyl *adj.* having two fingers or two toes.

Didapper *n.* a diving bird.

Didder *v.t.* to shiver with cold.

Diddle *v.t.* to cheat; to take in.

Dido *n.* a fantastic leap or trick; prank; caper.

Die *v.t.* a small cube used in gaming; plinth.

Diehard *n.* a person who resists to the end.

Diet *n.* way of feeding as prescribed by a physician; a legislative body; a congress.

Dietary *adj.* rules of diet.

Differ *v.t.* to be unlike; to disagree; to be distinguishable from; to dispute with; to be not the same as somebody; to diverge in opinion.

Difference *n.* distinction; unlikeness; a quarrel; the remainder after deduction; disagreement in opinion.

Differential *adj.* marked by a difference; distinctive.

Differentiate *v.t.* & *i.* to constitute the difference between, to discriminate; to make different.

Difficult *adj.* hard to understand; perplexing; hard to do.

Difficulty *n.* hardness to be done; an obstacle; a hindrance.

Diffidence *n.* self-distrust; shyness; modesty; reserve.

Diffident *adj.* wanting in self-confidence; not having or showing much confidence in one's own abilities.

Diffract *v.t.* to deflect; to break up a beam of light into a series of dark and light bands or into the different colours of the spectrum.

Diffuse *v.t.* to spread in all directions; to circulate; to spread by diffusion; to cause to intermingle.

Diffusive *adj.* to spread out; to scatter.

Dig *v.t.* to excavate; to hollow out by digging; to make a research. *n.* a digging.

Digamy *n.* a second legal marriage.

Digest *v.t.* & *i.* to arrange in proper head or titles; to arrange methodically in mind; to think out.

Digestion *n.* dissolving of food in the stomach; the process of digesting food; the ability of digest food.

Digestive *adj*. promoting digestion.

Dight *n*. to put in order; to array; to dress. *adj*. adorned.

Digit *n*. a finger's breadth; any one to the ten Arabic numeral symbols, *i.e.*, 1 to 9; (Atsron.) twelfth part of the sun's or moon's diameter.

Digitalin *n*. a medicine which makes the heart beat more slowly.

Dignify *v.t.* to honour; to speak highly of.

Dignitary *n*. a holder of a high office; (*esp.* in the Church).

Dignity *n*. nobleness of mind; honourable rank; loftiness.

Digraph *n*. a union of two vowels or two consonants giving a single sound as 'ea' in 'head'.

Digress *v.i.* to stray; to depart from the main subject.

Dike, Dyke *ns*. an embankment for protection of low land from inundation; a bank formed by excavation of ditch; a causeway.

Dilapidation *n*. state of bad repair; falling into decay.

Dilapidated *adj*. falling to pieces; in a bad state of repair.

Dilate *v.t.* & *i.* to expand; to extend; to widen; to enlarge.

Dilatory *adj*. tardy; tending to cause delay; slow in acting.

Dilemma *n*. a situation in which one has to chose between two things, both bad or unfavourable.

Dilettante *n*. lover of fine arrs; an armature.

Diligence *n*. industry; proper attention; care; a four wheeled stage coach divided into three apartments.

Diligent *adj*. industrious; painstaking; showing care and effort in one's work or duties; working with care and not wasting time.

Dill *n*. an umbelliferous medicinal plant.

Dilly-dally *v.t.* to loiter; to delay; to procrastinate; to trifle.

Dilute *v.t.* to make thinner; to weaken the force; to reduce in strength by addition of water.

Diluvial *adj*. pertaining to floods.

Dim *adj*. fainty visible; tarnished; indistinct; obscure.

Dime *n*. a coin of the USA and Canada worth ten cents.

Dimension *n*. measurement of length, breadth, height etc.

Diminish *v.t.* & *i.* to make less; to impair; to degrade.

Diminution *n*. lessening; degradation.

Diminutive *adj*. tiny; very small; tending to diminish; expressing diminished size; undersized.

Dimity *n*. a stout woven and painted fabric with a corded effect, used for dresses or bed room hangings; a king of cotton fabric.

Dimple *n.* a small hollow in cheek or chin. *v.i.* to produce dimples.

Din *n.* a continuing loud unpleasant noise. *v.t.* to stun with a noise; to harass with clamour.

Dine *v.t.* & *i.* to take dinner or give a dinner; to entertain at dinner.

Ding *v.t.* & *i.* to throw with violence; to break; to dash; to hurl; to ring (as a bell); to tell again and again in a wearisome way.

Dingle *n.* a small dale; a narrow valley.

Dingo *n.* an Australian wild dog.

Dingy *adj.* dull coloured; dark brown.

Dinky *adj.* pretty; neat; of attractive appearance.

Dinner *n.* the chief meal of the day whether taken during the middle of day or in the evening.

Dinosaur *n.* a person or thing that is old fashioned and cannot adapt to changing conditions.

Dint *n.* a blow; stroke; effort.

Diocese *n.* the part of the country in the charge of a bishop.

Diorama *n.* a spectacular painting.

Dioxide *n.* oxide with two parts of oxygen to one of the metal.

Dip *v.t.* & *i.* to immerse into a liquid; to plunge.

Diphtheria *n.* a serious and easily spread disease of the throat.

Diphthong *n.* union of two vowels in one sound; digraph; ligature.

Diploma *n.* an official written or printed paper, usually under seal showing that a person has completed a course of study, usually at a school or college.

Diplomat *n.* one employed or skilled in diplomacy; one who has skill in securing advantages.

Dipper *n.* one who dips; a ladle.

Dipsomania *n.* mad desire for a strong drink.

Dipteral *adj.* with double columns.

Dipterous *adj.* two-winged; (Bot.) with two wing-like appendages.

Dire *adj.* fearful; dread; terrible; very serious or urgent; very bad.

Direct *v.t.* & *i.* to order; to address; to control; to guide.

Direction *n.* course; aim; an address; management; guidance.

Directly *adv.* in a direct manner; immediately; at once; without delay.

Director *n.* a member of a board directing affairs of a company; superintendent.

Directorate *n.* the office of a director.

Directory *n.* a book of reference; a guide; a list of names of people with their addresses and other details.

Direful *adj.* dreadful.

Dirge *n.* a funeral song; a song sung at a burial or for a dead person; any slow sad song or piece of music.

Dirigible *n.* which can be steered and guided as a balloon or airship.

Dirk *n.* a kind of dagger or poniard.

Dirt *n.* filth; worthless things or people; mud; unpleasant; mire; earth, soil; unkind or harmful talk or words.

Dirty *adj.* soiled; foul; obscene; filthy; mean; despicable; unclean.

Disable *v.t.* unable to act or move; to incapacitate.

Disabuse *v.t.* to undeceive; to free from wrong ideas.

Disaccord *n.* to be at variance.

Disadvantage *n.* injury; detriment; unfavorable conditions.

Disaffection *n.* disloyalty; dislike; ill-will; discontentedness.

Disagree *v.i.* to have a different opinion from somebody; to fail to agree with; to argue slightly; to quarrel.

Disallow *v.t.* to refuse to accept as reasonable; to reject; to prohibit.

Disappear *v.i.* to vanish; to pass from sight; to become invisible.

Disappoint *v.t.* to defeat the hopes of; to break appointment with; to prevent a hope; to frustrate.

Disapprobation *n.* disapproval.

Disapprove *n.* to hold a bad opinion of; to have unfavourable opinion of.

Disarm *v.t.* to pacify hostility or suspicions of; to take weapons away from somebody.

Disarray *v.t.* to throw into disorder.

Disaster *n.* terrible accident; a calamity; adversity; a mishap; a sudden or great misfortune.

Disastrous *adj.* calamitous; full of great misfortune; gloomy.

Disavow *v.t.* to undo what is attached.

Disband *v.t.* & *i.* to dismiss from military service; to break up as body of men; to disperse; to be broken up; to let soldiers go out of the army.

Disbelieve *v.t.* & *i.* to refuse to accept the existence of something; to refuse or be unable to believe somebody.

Disburden *v.t.* & *i.* to relive of burden; to get rid of.

Disburse *v.t.* & *i.* to distribute or scatter; to spend out; to expend; to pay out money; to make an outlay.

Discard *v.t.* & *i.* to turn of as undesirable; to reject; to dismiss; to throw out from one's hand in card playing.

Discern *v.t.* to distinguish difference; to judge; to preceive clearly.

Discernment *n.* insight; critical sagacity.

Discharge *v.t.* & *i.* to unload from ship; to give or send out; to fire as a gun; to take away or give off electricity.

Disciple *n.* one who gets instruction from another; a learner; a follower.

Disciplinary *adj.* intended for discipline; of or promtong discipline.

Discipline *n.* self-control; training of mind and character; a state of order and obedience; punishment.

Disclaim *v.t.* & *i.* a renounce claim; to disown or disavow.

Disclose *v.t.* to lay open to the view; to cause to appear; to make known.

Disclosure *n.* anything disclosed; the act of disclosing; utterance of what was secret.

Discolour *v.t.* & *i.* to stain; to tarnish.

Discomfit *v.t.* to frustrate; to rout; to vanquish; to defeat.

Discomfiture *n.* the state of being discomfited; defeat; rout.

Discomfort *n.* pain; worry; uneasiness; disturbance of peace; annoyance; lack of comfort.

Discommon *v.t.* to enclose common land.

Discompose *v.t.* to distrub; to agitate; to ruffle.

Disconcert *v.t.* to confuse; to disarrange; to embarrass; to disturb; to ruffle; to derange or upset.

Disconnect *v.t.* to detach something from something; to separate; to undo a connection; to disjoin.

Disconsolate *adj.* unhappy; disappointed.

Discontent *n.* lack of satisfaction; unsatisfied state of mind; uneasiness of mind. *v.t.* to make dissatisfied.

Discontinue *v.t.* to stop doing or providing something; to leave off; not to go on with.

Discord *n.* strife; absence of friendliness; lack of harmony; disagreement; quarrelling; harsh noise.

Discount *n.* a deduction from the amount due, allowance.

Discourage *v.t.* to reduce the confidence or spirits of; to cause one to lose courage.

Discourse *n.* a talk; conversation; sermon.

Discourteous *adj.* void of courtesy; uncivil; not polite; rude.

Discover *v.t.* to find and bring to the knowledge of the world; to disclose; to reveal.

Discovert *n.* (Legal) an unmarried or widowed (woman).

Discovery *n.* finding out; revealing.

Discredit *v.t.* to refuse belief to; to bring disbelief or disrepute on.

Discreet *adj.* prudent; separate; discontinuous; distinct; cautious in speech or action.

Discrepancy *n.* difference; failure to tally; divergence.

Discretion *n.* freedom to act at pleasure; prudence; judgement.

Discretive *adj.* disjunctive.

Discriminate *v.t.* & *i.* to observe a difference; to distinguish; to treat unfairly; to choose with judgement.

Discursive *adj.* digressive; argumentative; desultory; proceeding by argument.

Discursory *adj.* digressive.

Discus *n.* a disc; a heavy disc thrown as a sport; the event in which this is done.

Discuss *n.* to debate; to reason upon; to test by eating or drinking; to talk about together; to examine.

Disdain *v.t.* to scorn; to deem as worthless; to contempt; to condemn; to treat as unworthy.

Disease *n.* illness; malady; bodily or mental derangement.

Disembark *v.t.* & *i.* to put or go ashore; (of people) to leave a ship or an aircraft.

Disembody *v.t.* to set free from the body.

Disembosom *v.t.* to unburden oneself; to reveal.

Disembowel *v.t.* to remove or cut out bowels from the body; to rip up.

Disenchant *v.t.* to disillusion; to free from the effect of magic.

Disengaged *adj.* at leisure; vacant.

Disentangle *v.t.* to unravel; to untie a knot; to extricate; to untwist.

Disenthral *v.t.* to free from bondage.

Disfavour *n.* disapproval; dislike; being disliked.

Disfigure *v.t.* to spoil; to deform; to harm the beauty or shape of; to spoil the appearance of somebody; to sully.

Disfranchise *v.t.* to deprive of right of electing or voting.

Disgorge *v.t.* & *i.* to emit from the throat; to give up unjustly seized gains.

Disgrace *n.* disfavour; condition of shame; cause of shame.

Disgruntled *adj.* discontented; in a bad temper.

Disguise *v.t.* to conceal; to misrepresent.

Disgust *n.* aversion; distaste; disfavour; a strong feeling of dislike, a violent distaste; a keen disappointment.

Dish *n.* a shallow flat-bottomed vessel for holding food at meals.

Dishabille *n.* not fully dressed state; undress garment.

Dishearten *v.t.* to depress; to discourage; to deject; to lose hope.

Dishevelled *adj.* with discordered hair.

Dishonest *adj.* insincere; fraudulent.

Dishonour *v.t.* to bring dishonour upon; to violate the chastity of; to refuse to honour or pay.

Disillusion *v.t.* freedom from illusion.

Disinclination *n.* slight dislike or unwillingness.

Disincline *v.t.* to inspire with disinclination; to make disaffected.

Disinfect *v.t.* to cleanse of infection; to make clean and free from all seeds of disease.

Disinherit *v.t.* to deprive of inheritance.

Disintegrate *v.t. & i.* to lose cohesion; to separate into the component parts; to break into pieces.

Disinter *v.t.* to dig out from ground; to unbury; to exhume; to take out of a grave; to unearth.

Disjoin *v.t.* to prevent from joining; to separate; to disunite.

Disjunction *n.* disjoining; separation.

Disk, Disc *ns.* a flat and circular surface; a thin flat circular object or semblance of this; a circular plate on which data can be recorded in form that can be used by a computer.

Dislike *v.t.* to consider somebody unpleasant; to feel aversion to. *n.* a feeling of aversion; disinclination

Dislocate *v.t.* to put out of joint; to displace.

Dislodge *v.t.* to drive away from a place of defence; to drive from the place occupied; to remove from the place.

Disloyal *adj.* not true to allegiance; false; faithless; false in love.

Dismal *adj.* dark; not bright; gloomy; sad; frightful; dreary; sorrowful.

Dismantle *v.t.* to strip off dress; to deprive of covering.

Dismantlement *n.* the act of dismantling anything.

Dismasted *adj.* having lost its masts.

Dismay *n.* loss of courage; amazement. *v.t.* to affect with loss of courage; to reduce to despair.

Dismember *v.t.* to divide a country; to cut or tear off the limbs of a person or an animal.

Dismiss *v.t.* to send away; to allow; to go; to discharge from office or service; to put out of thoughts.

Dismount *v.i. & t.* to come down; to come off or to alight from horseback; to take down a thing from that upon which it is mounted.

Disobedience *n.* violation of orders; failure or refusal to obey.

Disobey *v.t. & i.* to break rules; to disregard orders; to fail to obey a person; an order.

Disorder *n.* breach of peace, want or order; confusion; bodily or mental ailment; disturbance of public order.

Disorganize *v.t.* to break the structure of.

Disparage *v.t.* to discourage; to undervalue; to reduce in esteem; to indignify; to lower in rank.

Disparity *n.* inequality; unequal state or degrees; disproportion.

Dispassionate *adj.* cool; calm; impartial.

Dispatch, Despatch *v.t.* to send off messengers or letters; to send to destination; to send off quickly; to get business done promptly.

Dispel *v.t.* to disperse; to scatter.

Dispensary *n.* place where medicines are dispensed with or sold away.

Dispensation *n.* distribution; administration; a certain order, system, or arrangement; doing without something.

Disperse *v.t.* & *i.* to scatter; to dispel; to diffuse.

Dispirit *v.t.* to discourage; to depress; to dishearten; to deject.

Dispirited *adj.* sad and without hope.

Displace *v.t.* to change the place; to put out of place; to disorder; to remove; to overthrow; to replace.

Display *v.t.* to show; to exhibit; to unfold; to spread out; to view; to put something in a place where people can see it easily.

Displease *v.t.* to offend or make angry; to annoy.

Displeasure *n.* indignation; vexation; resentment; annoyance; disfavour.

Displume *v.t.* to deprive of feathers, honour etc.

Disposal *n.* sale; management; distribution; right of bestowing.

Dispose *v.t.* & *i.* to place; to bestow; to arrange; to settle; to finish; to distribute; to give mind to.

Disposition *n.* bestowal; management; temper; distribution.

Dispossess *v.t.* to put out of possession.

Dispraise *v.t.* to blame or censure.

Disproof *n.* refutation; proving of an error.

Disprove *v.t.* to reject; to give an unfavourable opinion; to show the fallacy of.

Disputable *adj.* controvertible, uncertain.

Disputant *n.* one who disputes; a controversialist.

Disputation *n.* a discourse or treatise; an argumentative debate; (an instance of) disputing.

Disputatious *adj.* quarrelsome; fond of argument.

Dispute *v.t.* & *i.* to contend for; to argue; to discuss.

Disqualify *v.t.* to deprive of the requisite quality; to disable; to debar; to unfit.

Disquiet *v.t.* to deprive of peace; to worry.

Disquisition *n.* an inquiry; a long speech; a treatise; a long written report about some subject.

Disregard *v.t.* to pay no heed to; to disobey; to be uninfluenced by; to treat something as unimportant.

Disreputable *adj.* dishonourable; disgraceful.

Disreputation *n.* disrepute; disgrace.

Disrepute *n.* disrespect; shame; dishonour; ill-repute; discredit.

Disrespect *n.* lack of deference; incivility; want of respect or reverence.

Disrobe *v.t.* & *i.* to take off the clothes or dress; to undress.

Disrupt *v.t.* to shatter.

Dissatisfaction *n.* want of satisfaction.

Dissatisfy *v.t.* to make discontented; to fail to satisfy.

Dissect *v.t.* to cut as under; to cut to examine in detail; to examine and criticize; to anatomize.

Dissemble *v.t.* & *i.* to hide one's feeling; to conceal or disguise; to be hypocritical.

Disseminate *v.t.* to scatter abroad; to sow in different places.

Dissension *n.* contention; disunion; strife.

Dissent *v.t.* to differ in opinion; to disagree; to discord.

Dissenter *n.* one who dissents or does not agree with the teachings of the church of England.

Dissentient *adj* & *n.* dissenting; not agreeing.

Dissertation *n.* a formal discourse.

Disservice *n.* a bad turn done to a person or cause a harmful action.

Dissever *v.t.* & *i.* to cut apart; to disunite; to separate.

Dissidence *n.* disagreement.

Dissident *adj.* not in agreement conflicting.

Dissimilar *adj.* unlike.

Dissimulate *v.t.* & *i.* to pretend falsely; to hide or disguise one's thoughts and feeling; to practise deceit.

Dissipate *v.t.* & *i.* to fritter away; to dispel; to squander; to waste something foolishly.

Dissociate *v.t.* to disconnect; to separate.

Dissolubility *n.* capacity of being dissolved.

Dissolve *v.t.* & *i.* to decompose; to break; to vanish; to disperse.

Dissonant *adj.* disagreeing; jarring; discordant; clashing; not agreeing in sound.

Dissuade *v.t.* to advise against doing; to divert.

Distaff *n.* a cleft that holds fast the bunch of flax or wool in spinning.

Distance *n.* remoteness; a remote place; opposition; space between two objects; time intervals.

Distant *adj.* remote; far off.

Distaste *n.* dislike; a feeling that somebody is unpleasant or unacceptable; aversion.

Distasteful *n.* disagreeable to the taste; causing dislike.

Distemper *n.* ailment; derangement of temper; a waterpaint for walls; a disordered condition.

Distend *v.t.* to swell out; to extend.

Distich *n.* a couplet.

Distil *v.t.* & *i.* to fall in drops; to flow smoothly and gently.

Distillery *n.* place of distillation; an establishment where whisky is made.

Distinct *adj.* different; separate; clearly perceptible; definite.

Distinction *n.* difference; an excellence; a thing that differentiates; a mark of honour; individuality.

Distinctive *adj.* distinguishing; characteristic.

Distinguish *v.t.* & *i.* to draw distinction; to recognise; to make oneself prominent.

Distort *v.t.* to spoil shape of; to turn from the true meaning; to give a false account of something.

Distract *v.t.* to confuse; to perplex; to draw away the attention; to take somebody's attention away from something.

Distraction *n.* interruption; confusion; diversion; anger; perplexity.

Distrain *v.i.* to seize goods for debt.

Distraint *n.* legal seizure of goods as payment for debt.

Distress *n.* extreme pain of body or mind; misfortune; act of distraining goods; mental pain.

Distribute *v.t.* to divide the share to each of a number; to scatter; to arrange.

Distributive *adj.* concerned in distribution; that which distributes; referring to each individual of a class.

District *n.* a part of a state, city etc., marked out for a special purpose; a tract; a region; a province; a territory.

Distrust *n.* want to trust; doubt.

Disturb *v.t.* to agitate; to trouble.

Disturbance *n.* tumult; trouble; the action of disturbing somebody or process of being disturbed; disturbed state.

Disunion *n.* dissension; separation; want of union.

Disunite *v.t.* & *i.* to divide; to separate or become separate.

Disuse *n.* neglect of use. *v.t.* to cease to use.

Disyllable *n.* a word or metrical foot of two syllables.

Ditch *n.* a trench in the earth made for carrying water; a deep water channel for carrying off water.

Dither *v.t.* to quiver; to tremble.

Ditto *n.* the same; a substitute for repetition of word or phrase.

Ditty *n.* a short simple song.

Diurnal *adj.* daily; belonging to day time; in or of the day.

Divagate *v.t.* to wander about.

Dive *v.i.* to go deeply into any matter; to move quickly in a specified direction.

Diver *n.* one who dives.

Diverge *v.t.* to differ; to turn apart; to deviate; to take a different direction; to go off sideways; to digress.

Divers *adj.* sundry; various; several.

Diverse *adj.* of differing kinds; differing form.

Diversify *v.t.* to variegate; to modify.

Diversion *n.* amusement; diverting; deviation.
Diversity *n.* diverseness; variety.
Divert *v.t.* to change the course off; to please; to amuse; to turn aside; to get rid of.
Diverting *adj.* amusing.
Divest *v.t.* to unclothe; to deprive or strip off.
Divide *v.t.* & *i.* to separate into parts; to break into two or more parts; to arrange in separate groups.
Dividend *n.* a share; the number to be divided by a divisor.
Divider *n.* that which divides; (*pl.*) a pair of measuring compasses.
Divination *n.* the act of telling the unknown or the future by the aid of magic.
Divine *adj.* belonging to or proceeding from God; sacred; excellent; beautiful.
Divining-rod *n.* a switch used by dowser to detect underground water or minerals.
Divinity *n.* the deity; a celestial being.
Divisible *adj.* that can be divided.
Division *n.* the act of dividing; distribution; separation; a class or section.
Divorce *n.* dissolution of marriage; a separation between things that should go together.
Do *n.* the first note in music.
Do *v.t., i.* & *aux.* to impart; to perform; to give; to finish.
Docile *adj.* (of a person or an animal) easy to control; easy to teach and willing to obey; easily taught or led.
Dock *n.* part of animal's tail containing flesh; part of a port where loading and unloading takes place; a place for prisoners in court.
Docket *n.* a register of judgements; a document.
Dockyard *n.* a naval establishment; an enclosure for building and repairing ships.
Doctor *n.* a teacher or learned man; the highest university degree.
Doctorate *n.* degree beyond Master's degree like Ph.D., D.Sc.; persons holding the doctor's degree.
Doctrinaire *n.* an unpractical theoriser.
Doctrine *n.* a body of tenets, beliefs and instructions, dogmas etc.; teaching.
Document *n.* a deed; a writing; something that furnishes evidence; a legal deed or other piece of writing.
Dodder *v.t.* to tremble; to totter; to shake.
Dodecagon *n.* a plane figure of twelve sides.
Dodge *n.* a trick; a quick movement to avoid somebody; a swerving or zigzag movement; a piece of duplicity.

Dodo *n.* a clumsy bird of Mauritious, now extinct.

Doe *n.* a female of deer or buck.

Doff *v.t.* to abandon; to take off; to remove; to take off one's hat.

Dog *n.* a domestic quadruped. *v.t.* to follow as a dog; to pursue.

Dogma *n.* a principle; a tenet; a doctrine.

Dogmatic *adjs.* one who follow dogmas; authoritative; insisting that one's beliefs are right and that others should accept them.

Dogmatism *n.* dogmatizing temper; the tendency to be dogmatic.

Dogmatize *v.i.* to assert positively.

Dogrose *n.* the wild rose.

Dog-star *n.* the brightest star in the heavens.

Dog-tired *n.* very tired.

Doily *n.* a small ornamental napkin.

Doings *n. pl.* things done; events; behaviour.

Doit *n.* a very small sum.

Doldrums *n. pl.* parts of the ocean near the Equator where there is little or no wind and ships with sails cannot move.

Dole *n.* destiny; charitable; distribution; grief.

Doleful *adj.* sad; miserable.

Doll *n.* a toy baby; a puppet.

Dollish *adj.* innocent.

Dollar *n.* a banknote or coin worth one dollar; a coin and money of account in U.S. Canada, and elsewhere.

Dolorous *adj.* sad; painful; dismal.

Dolour *n.* sorrow; distress.

Dolphin *n.* a fish of whale type; a sea animal six to eight feet long.

Dolt *adj.* a dull fellow; a blockhead.

Domain *n.* estate; scope; field; dominion; lands as held or ruled over.

Dome *n.* roof or round shape; a big building; judgement; sentence.

Domestic *adj.* belonging to household; native; tame.

Domesticate *v.t.* to naturalize (plant); to make somebody used to or fond of home life and doing jobs around the house.

Domesticated *adj.* tamed.

Domicile *n.* a dwelling place; a place of permanent residence.

Dominant *adj.* powerful or prominent; dominating; established in power; ruling; very influencial.

Dominate *v.t. & i.* to rule; to prevail over; to keep under bondage.

Domination *n.* ascendancy; supremacy; authority.

Domineer *v.i.* to rule with violence; to tyrannize; to bluster.

Dominical *adj.* relating to Lord.

Dominie *n.* a schoolmaster in Scotland.

Dominion *n.* sovereignty; authority; control; country under the authority; government; domination

Domino *n.* a hooded cap worn by priests; a game played with dice.

Don *v.t.* to put on clothes etc.

Donate *v.t.* to give as a gift or in charity; to subscribe; to make a donation.

Donation *n.* a gift; gift to a fund or institution; a bestowal; a thing that is donated; the act of donating something; benefaction.

Donative *adj.* vested or vesting by gift.

Donee *n.* the person to whom a gift is made.

Donjon *n.* central defence; great tower or keep of castle.

Donkey *n.* an ass; a stupid fellow; an animal of the horse family.

Donna *n.* an Italian, Spanish or Portuguese lady.

Donor *n.* the giver of a gift.

Do-nothing *adj.* & *n.* doing nothing; an idler.

Don't 'do not'

Doom *n.* judicial sentence; death or ruin; any terrible fate.

Doomsday *n.* the day of the Last Judgement.

Door *n.* entrance; access; a barrier for closing the access to a place.

Dope *n.* a kind of thick varnish; a fool; a secret informations, especially one that is smoked; an illegal drug.

Dormant *adj.* lying inactive as in sleep; concealed; not active or growing, through.

Dormer-window *n.* an upright window set in a sloping roof.

Dormitory *n.* a large sleeping room or chamber.

Dormouse *n.* a small mouse-like animal with a long furry tail.

Dorothy-bag *n.* a lady's open topped hand-bag hung at wrist.

Dorsal *adj.* pertaining to the back.

Dory *n.* a flat-bottomed boat; a sea-fish.

Dose *n.* the amount of medicine to be taken by a patient at one time.

Doss *v.i.* a bed; place for sleeping; especially when one has not got a proper bed.

Dossier *n.* brief documents of a case; a collection of documents containing information about a person, an event or a subject; a file.

Dot *n.* the money a woman brings with her at marriage; a small round mark; a small child; a tiny object.

Dotage *n.* excessive fondness; senility.

Dotard *n.* a man in his dotage; an old fool.

Dote *v.i.* to feel or show great or too much affection for somebody.

Doting *adj.* regarding with extreme fondness.

Dotterel *n.* a kind of shore bird.

Dottle *n.* plug of tobacco left after smoking a pipe.

Double *adj.* & *adv.* consisting of two forming a pair; two-fold; deceitful.

Doublet *n.* tightly fitting jacket worn by men in former times; a short.

Doubloon *n.* a gold coin in Spain (worth slightly over £ 1).

Doubt *n.* a state not allowing of certainty; a feeling of not being certain or not believing something.

Doubtful *adj.* ambiguous; uncertain.

Doubtless *adv.* very probably; certainly.

Douceur *n.* gratuity; a present; a bribe.

Douche *n.* a jet of water forced into any part of the body externally or internally.

Dough *n.* flour mixed with water ready for baking.

Dour *adj.* severe and threatening; silent and unwilling to change an idea; gloomy.

Douse *v.t.* & *i.* to plunge or fail into water; to strike a blow.

Dove *n.* a kind of pigeon-like bird; a word of endearment for beloved.

Dovecot *n.* a kind of cage for keeping and breeding fowls, especially doves; a pigeon-house.

Dovetail *n.* & *v.t.* a tenon having a shape of a dove's spread tail; to unite with such tenons.

Dowager *n.* a widow of a rich person who has left her a lot of estate.

Dowdy *adj.* (of clothes) dull; lacking smartness; not fashionable.

Dower *n.* share that widow gets at her husband's death; gift; dowry; a natural gift or talent.

Down *n.* soft feathers of birds; short tender hair; high open hand.

Downcast *adj.* very low in spirits; (of eyes) looking down; (of person) dejected.

Downfall *n.* falling down; ruin.

Downhearted *adj.* depressed; in low spirits.

Downhill *n.* a downward slope.

Downpour *n.* heavy fall of rain.

Downright *adj.* outspoken; tactless; straight forward; blunt; plain; undisguised.

Downs *n. pl.* low hill covered with grass.

Downstairs *adv.* in the lower part of a house.

Downtrodden *adj.* trampled down.

Downy *adj.* covered with down; soft.

Dowry *n.* the property brought by a wife at marriage.

Dowser *n.* a man who finds underground water by means of a dowsing-rod.

Doxology *n.* a short song of praise to God.

Doyen *n.* a senior and greatly respected member of a group; the oldest member (of a body of colleagues).

Doze *v.i.* to sleep lightly or drowsily. *n.* a slumber.

Dozen *n.* twelve things of one kind; a set of twelve.

Drab *n.* an unchaste woman; a prostitute. *adj.* of light brown colour; dull; not interesting.

Drachm, Dram *ns.* a unit of weight 1/16 oz. 1/8 oz; a unit of money in Greece.

Draff *n.* refuse of wine; dregs.

Draft *n.* drawing of money by written order; a bill of excahnge; a summary. *v.t.* to draw off; to prepare.

Draftsman *n.* one who prepares a draft; a designer; a man who draws plans.

Drag *v.t. & i.* to pull with force along the ground; to trail or go heavily; to draw along with force.

Dragnet *n.* a net drawn on the bottom of a river or pond to catch fishes.

Dragoman *n.* an interpreter and travellers guide.

Dragon *n.* a big snake having wings mentioned in western mythology; a dangerous person.

Dragon-fly *n.* a long-bodied flying insects.

Dragoon *n.* a cavalryman, a rough fierce fellow. *v.t.* to harass; to persecute.

Drain *n.* a ditch; a sewer. *v.t.* to draw off gradully; to filter; to dry.

Drake *n.* the male of duck; a fly used in fishing.

Dram *n.* a small weight; a small measure of wine; a small draught of strong drink.

Drama *n.* a play on the stage; a theatre; literature which can be played like drama on stage; the dramatic art; play-like series of events.

Draper *n.* a dealer in cloth or ready-made garments; a shopkeeper selling cloth and clothing.

Drastic *adj.* vigorous; powerful; strongly purgative.

Drat *v.t.* an oath; "God rot" to curse; to bother.

Draught *n.* act of drawing; dose of liquid medicine; the amount of liquor drink at one time; current of air; a sketch or outline. *v.t.* to make a plan.

Draughts *n.* a game played by two people each with 12 round pieces on a chess-board of 64 squares.

Draughtsman *n.* one who makes or designs drawings.

Draughty *adj.* full of currents of air.

Draw *n.* act of drawing; strain; end of game without any decision.

Drawback *n.* a deduction; a disadvantage; an amount of excise or import duty remitted or repaid on exports.

Drawbridge *n.* a bridge which ma be raised up or drawn aside.

Drawee *n.* a person in whose favour a bill is drawn.

Drawer *n.* one who draws; a kind of box which slides in table; a two-legged undergarment.

Drawing *n.* the art of representing any object in lines; dragging or hauling; act of pulling; a picture drawn with a pencil; a sketch.

Drawl *v.t.* & *i.* to speak in a low tone.

Drawler *n.* one who mutters.

Drawlingly *adv.* a low or slow tone.

Draw-well *n.* a well with a rope and a bucket for drawing water.

Dray *n.* a low cart having wheels; a low heavy four-wheeled cart; a squirrel's nest.

Dread *v.t.* & *i.* to be afraid; to make afraid; to fear something greatly. *n.* an object of terror; fear; awe.

Dreadnought *n.* a kind of thick cloth; a kind of warship; one who fears nothing.

Dream *n.* vision which seen in sleep; imagination; fancies; reverie; a day dream.

Dreamland *n.* imaginary fancies.

Dreary, Drear *adjs.* dismal; cheerless; sad; gloomy; dull.

Dredge *n.* a net for talking out oysters; any instrument used to gather or take by dragging; an apparatus for clearing mud.

Dredger *n.* one who fishes with a dredge; a box for spreading powder.

Dree *v.t.* to endue.

Dreg *n.* (*pl.*) grounds; sediment; refuse; (sing.) a small remnant.

Dreggy *n. pl.* sediment; refuse.

Drench *v.t.* to wetten completely; to soak; to force (a beast) to take a dose.

Dress *v.t.* & *i.* to array; to provide oneself with clothes; to apply dressing to (wound etc.) to cleanse; to prune.

Dress-circle *n.* a person who dresses in a specified way; a large piece of kitchen furniture with shelves for dishes and cupboards below.

Dressing *n.* bandage; ointment; manure; scolding or thrashing.

Dribble *v.t.* & *i.* to trickle to run in mouth; to work ball forward with repeated touches of feet; to flow or let flow in drops.

Driblet *n.* a small instalment; a small amount (of liquid).

Drift *n.* a slow current; tendency; purpose; accumulation.

Drifter a boat which is used for catching fish.

Driftwood *n.* wood floating on the sea or washed on the shore.

Drill *n.* a boring tool; a kind of thick cloth; military exercise; a small furrow for sowing seeds.

Drink *v.t.* & *i.* to swallow a liquid; to absorb; to lisen; to empty. *n.* anything for drinking; the act of drinking.

Drinker *n.* one who drinks.

Drip *v.i.* & *t.* to fall or let fall in drops.

Dripping *n.* that which falls in drops.

Drive *v.t.* & *i.* to urge with violence; to convey vehicle; to throw; to conclude.

Drivel *n.* a silly senseless talk; slaver.

Driver *n.* one who drives a car; a coachman.

Drizzle *v.i.* to drop in small drops; to fall in fine dense rain.

Droil *v.t.* to work slowly.

Droll *adj.* amusing, surprising. *n.* a jester.

Dromedary *n.* a camel having one hump.

Drone *n.* a male of the bee; an idler; a deep monotonous hum.

Droop *v.t.* & *i.* to hung down; to loose heart; to bend.

Drop *n.* a globule of water or other liquid; the smallest quantity of a liquid; a hanging ornament, act of dropping.

Drop *v.t.* & *i.* to fall or shed in drops; to disappear; to be finished; to leave hold of; to sink to lower level.

Dropcurtain *n.* a curtain let down between the acts in a theatre.

Droplet *n.* a little drop.

Dropping *adj.* falling in drops.

Dropsy *n.* a disease in which watery fluid collects in the tissues of the body.

Drosky, Droshky *ns.* a light four wheeled horse-carriage used in Russia.

Dross *n.* a waste of coal or metal; material without value or worth.

Drought *n.* thirst; continuous dry weather.

Drove *n.* of drive; a herd; a moving herd or flock; a crowd in motion.

Drover *n.* cattle dealer.

Drown *v.t.* & *i.* to submerge in water; to perish in water; overpower by immersion; to drench of flood.

Drowse *v.i.* to be dull and sleepy; to doze.

Drowsy *adj.* half asleep; sleepy.

Drub *v.t.* to beat with a stick. *n.* one who drubs.

Drudge *v.i.* to work hard at distasteful tasks.

Drug *n.* anything used to prepare medicine; a substance that stimulates the nervous system, cocaine or heroin.

Druggist *n.* a dealer in drugs.

Druid *n.* a priest of the ancient Celts; an ancient French or British priest.

Drum *n.* (music) an instrument for making heavy sounds; inner part of ear.

Drummer *n.* a player of a drum.

Drunk, Drunken *v.t.* intoxicated.

Drunkard *n.* a person who often drinks too much wine; addicted to a strong drink.

Drupe *n.* a stone-fruit.

Dry *adj.* where no rains fall; (cows) not giving milk; thirsty; not loving; where wine is prohibited; damp or sticky.

Dryad *n.* a female nymph of wood and groves.

Dry-dock *n.* a place in which a ship is taken out of water for repair.

Dryer *adj.* more dry. *n.* (especially in compounds) a machine that dries.

Dry-goods *n.* non-liquid goods.

Dry-nurse *n.* a nurse who brings up a child without milk from the brest.

Dry-rot *n.* wood that has decayed and turned to powder.

Dry-shod *adj.* without feet dry.

Duad *n.* a union of two.

Dual *adj.* consisting of two things; double; twofold; of double nature; forming a pair.

Dualism *n.* duality recognition of two independent principles or powers.

Dub *v.t.* to confer the title of knight; striking the shoulder with a sword; to smooth or dress; to smear.

Dubber *n.* a large leather vessel used for holding or transporting oil or ghee.

Dubiety *n.* a feeling of doubt.

Dubious *adj.* vague; doubtful.

Dubitation *n.* the act of doubting.

Dubitative *adj.* inclined to doubt.

Ducal *adj.* having to do with a duke or nobleman.

Ducat *n.* an old European gold coin.

Duchess *n.* a woman who holds the rank of duke in her own right; the wife or widow of a duke.

Duchy *n.* territory of a duke; the part of a country under the control of a duke.

Duck *n.* a waterfowl. *v.i.* to plunge into water.

Ducky *n.* darling.

Duct *n.* a tube or pipe in body.

Ductless *adj.* without a duct.

Ductile *adj.* which can be drawn into wires; flexible; plastic; docile.

Dud *n. pl.* ragged clothes; futile plan; scarecorw. *adj.* useless.

Dudder *v.t.* to deafen with noise; to shake.

Dude *n.* a city person; a man who loves to wear fine clothes.

Dudgeon *n.* resentment; envy; state of wrath or indignation; anger.

Due *adj.* & *adv.* payable; appropriate; proper; calculated; exactly; directly. *n.* what one owes.

Duel *n.* a fight or competition between two people, using swords or guns, especially to settle a point of honour.

Duenna *n.* old lady who looks after a young woman; a female guardian.

Duet *n.* a piece of music for two players or singers.

Duff *n.* dough.

Duffer *n.* useless old fellow; useless mine; bad coin; an idiot; a person who is stupid or unable to do anything well.

Dug *n.* nipple of a cow or other beast; teat.

Dug-out *n.* a very old army officer recalled to serve in war; a boat made by hollowing out a tree; an underground shelter in war-time.

Dugong *n.* also called 'sea-cow'; a large fish-like creature found in the sea.

Duke *n.* a person holding the highest order of nobility in England.

Dulcet *adj.* sweet and soothing; sounding sweet; pleasing to the ear.

Dulcify *v.t.* to sweeten.

Dulcimer *n.* a musical instrument with strings hit with a striker.

Dull *adj.* who is low in understanding; sad; blunt; stupid; lacking interest or excitement; not bright or clear; (of pain) not felt sharply.

Dullard *n.* a stupid person.

Dully *adj.* & *adv.* dull; in a dull manner.

Dumb *adj.* unable to speak; silent; mute.

Dumb-bell *n.* a wood or iron weight used in exercising the arms; a short bar used in pairs to exercise muscles.

Dumbfound *v.t.* to cause one to lose the power of speech; to confound to dumbness.

Dumb-waiter *n.* a movable table used for serving food.

Dummy *n.* a man of straw; a blockhead; a lay figure.

Dump *v.t.* to throw down; to sell at a low price. *n.* dullness of mind; a place in the open for storing goods; a place for throwing waste matter.

Dumps *n. pl.* depression; low spirits.

Dumpy *adj.* short and stout.

Dun *adj.* of dark grey colour; of dull greyish brown. *v.t.* to demand a debt. *n.* a debt collector.

Dunce *n.* a bad learner; a dullard.

Dunderhead *n.* a fool; a blockhead.

Dune *n.* a mound of sand on a coast; a sandhill.

Dung *n.* excrement of animals; manure. *v.t.* to manure.

Dungaree *n.* a coarse Indian cloth.

Dungeon *n.* dark underground cell for prisoners. *v.t.* to imprison in a dungeon.

Duodecimo *n.* a form folded to make twelve leaves.

Dupable *adj.* that can be duped or decived.

Dupe *v.t.* to cheat; to deceive and make use of. *n.* one who is unknowingly used by another for a wrong purpose.

Duplex *adj.* & *n.* two-fold; a second copy; anything dubled; a building divided into two homes.

Duplicate *adj.* double; two fold.

Duplicity *n.* the act of being dishonest; deceitfulness; double-minded-ness.

Durability *adj.* permanence.

Durable *adj.* resisting wear; capable of lasting; lasting a long time.

Duramater *n.* outer membrane of the brain.

Durance *n.* imprisonment.

Duration *n.* continuance of time; the length of existence; the time a thing lasts.

Durbar *n.* a special meeting of a ruler and the important men of his government in India.

Duress, Duresse *n.* threats or force used to make somebody do something; forcible restraint; stress; hardship; imprisonment.

During *prep.* continuing in the course of; throughout.

Durst *p.t.* past tense of Dare.

Dusk *n.* shade; darkness; evening; the time when daylight is fading; partial daudness.

Dusky *adj.* not bright; dark; dark-coloured.

Dust *n.* fine particles of anything; powdered earth; powder made up of fine particles of waste matter; the grave.

Dust-bin *n.* a receptacle for rubbish.

Dust bowl *n.* an area of land that has been turned into desert by lack of rain or too much farming.

Dust cart *n.* a vehicle for collecting rubbish/garbage from outside houses etc.

Duster *n.* a cloth or brush to clear off dust.

Dusting *n.* clearing of dust; thrashing; tossing at sea.

Dusty *adj.* full of dust.

Dutch *adj.* the people of Holland; the name of their language.

Duteous *adj.* obeying his call of duty; obeying regularly and willingly.

Dutiable *adj.* on which one must pay duty; liable to customs duties.

Dutiful *adj.* regular and willing in the discharge of duty.

Duty *n.* expression of respect; behaviour due to a superior; payment of public revenue; moral obligation.

Dutyfree *n.* exempt from customs duty.

Dux *n.* the top boy in a class.

DVD *n.* a disk on which large amounts of information, especially photograph and video.

Dwarf *n.* one who is below the size of ordinary beings of its kind; an animal or a plant that is much smaller than the normal size.

Dwarfism *n.* the medical condition of being a dwarf.

Dweeb *n.* a person, especially a boy or a man, who does not have good social skills and is not fashionable.

Dwell *v.t.* to live; to speak lengthily on a subject; to spend one's time; to keep one's attention fixed.

Dweller *n.* an inhabitant.

Dwelling *n.* a place of residence; a habitation; a house.

Dwelt *p.t.* of Dwell.

Dwindle *v.i.* to shrink; to lose importance; to decline; to grow weak.

Dyad *n.* group of two things; set of two.

Dyarchy *n.* government by two.

Dye *n.* a colour produced by dying; hue; matter used to dye with.

Dyeing *n.* the process of fixing colours to a fabric.

Dying *adj.* mortal; declining at the time of death.

Dynamic *adj.* of motive force; active; energetic.

Dynamite *n.* a powerful explosive (used to break up rocks).

Dynamo *n.* a machine for making electricity; a generator.

Dynamometer *n.* an instrument measuring energy spent.

Dynast *n.* a ruler.

Dynastic, Dynastical *adjs.* belonging to a line of kings.

Dynasty *n.* line of succession; the time during which number of kings of the same family rule a country.

Dyne *n.* the unit of force. (C.G.S. system)

Dysenteric *n.* pertaining to or accompanied by dysentery.

Dysfunctional *n.* an infection of the bowels that causes severe Diarrhoea with loss of blood.

Dyslexia *n.* a slight disorder of the brain that causes difficulty in reading and spelling, for example, but does not affect intelligence.

Dyspeptic *adj.* affected with dyspepsia.

Dysphagia *n.* difficulty in swallowing.

Dysphonia *n.* difficulty in producing sounds.

Dysuria *n.* difficulty in passing uring.

Dyvour *n.* bankrupt.

Dysteleology *n.* a doctrine denying the existence of a final cause or purpose.

E

E the fifth letter of the English alphabet, the third note of the natural scale.

Each *adj.* one of the two considered separately.

Eager *adj.* strongly desirous; earnest; keen; severe; ardent; vehement.

Eagle *n.* a large bird or prey; an ensign of French army.

Eagre *n.* a rise of tide in a river.

Ean *v.i.* to bring forth young; to yean.

Ear *n.* the organ of hearing; an ear-shaped thing; a sense of hearing.

Earache *n.* pain in ears.

Ear-drop *n.* an earring with a pendant.

Earmdrum *n.* the tympanum.

Earmark *n.* & *v.t.* an identification mark on lamb ear.

Ear-shot *n.* distance at which sounds can be heard.

Earwax *n.* cerumen.

Eared *adj.* pointed; having ears.

Earl *n.* a British nobleman ranking between a marquis and a viscount.

Earlobe *n.* a soft part at the bottom of the ear.

Early *adj.* & *adv.* near the beginning of a time; period; series; soon.

Earmark *v.t.* to assign (a fund) to some definite purpose.

Earn *v.t.* to gain by labour; to acquire; to deserve; to bring to one.

Earned *adj.* having ears, pointed.

Earnest *adj.* intent; sincere; zealous; eager; serious; honest; not trifling; ardent.

Earth *n.* the planet we live on; ground; the world.

Earthen-ware *n.* baked clay; vessels made of baked clay.

Earthquake *n.* a heaving of the ground; shaking of the earth's surface which often destroys buildings.

Earthwards *adv.* towards the earth.

Ear-wig *n.* a small harmless insect with pincers at the back end of its body.

Earthworm *n.* worm that lives in the ground; a mean wretch.

Ease *n.* freedom from pain or disturbance; anxiety; rest; facility.

Easeful *adj.* comfortable; quiet.

Easel *n.* a wooden frame for holding a black board, or a picture while it is being painted.

East *n.* & *adj.* the part of horizon where the sun rises.

Easter *n.* a festival of Christ's resurrection; a feast-day in memory of Christ's rising from the dead.

Eastern *adj.* of or in the east.

Easy *adj.* not difficult; free from pain; tranquil; unconstrained; giving ease; yielding; not tight; not strict; easily gained (money); compliant.

Eat *v.t.* & *i.* to take into body by the mouth as food to consume; to corrode; to take food; to destroy.

Eater *n.* one who eats.

Eau *n.* a French word for water.

Ebb *n.* reflux to tide; decline; decay. *v.i.* to flow back; to recede.

Ebon *adj.* black as ebony.

Ebonist *n.* a worker in ebony.

Ebony *n.* a kind of wood as heavy and hard as stone, usually black; a negro.

Ebonite *n.* black vulcanised rubber; a hard black form of rubber.

Ebriety *n.* drunkness.

Ebullient *adj.* in a state of boiling; over-enthusiastic; exuberant.

Ebullition *n.* action of boiling; effervescence.

Eburine *adj.* like ivory.

Ecarate *n.* a card-game for two.

Eccalebion *n.* a kind of hatching machine.

Eccentric *adj.* departing from the centre; not having the same centre as another.

Ecclesiast *n.* the preacher; a clertyman; an author of one the old testaments.

Ecdemic *adj.* of foreign origin.

Echo *n.* the repetition of soudn caused by reflection of sound waves. *v.i.* & *t.* to resound with an echo; to imitate.

Eclat *n.* general applaude; splendour; social distinction; striking success; acclamation.

Eclectic *adj.* selecting or borrowing; choosing the best out of everything; drawing one's philosophy from various schools.

Eclogue *n.* a short pastoral poem.

Ecology *n.* the relation of plants and living creatures to each other and to their environment; or the study of this.

Economic *adjs.* pertaining to economy; frugal.

Economics *n.* a science of wealth in relation to man.

Economist *n.* a thirsty person; the manager or user (of money **etc.**); writer on political economy.

Economy *n.* administration and management of household matters; frugality.

Ecstasy *n.* joy, enthusiasm or any exalted feeling; poetic frenzy.

Ecstatic *adj.* of or in ecstasies; delightful beyond measure.

ECT *abbr.* Electro Convulsive Therapy.

Eczema *n.* an inflammatory disease of the skin of various kinds.

Edacious *adj.* fond of eating; greedy.

Eddy *n.* a small whirlpool; a movement of water or air in a circle.

Edelweiss *n.* a plant with a white flower found only on high mountains.

Eden *n.* the garden of Adam and Eve; a Paradise; a delightful place or state.

Edenic *adj.* pertaining to Eden.

Edentate *adj.* a toothless animal.

Edge *n.* sharp; border of a thing; a ridge; keenness; a surface or an area; a boundary-line.

Edible *adj.* fit to be eaten; suitable for human food.

Edict *n.* an order proclaimed by authority; an order issued by a king; proclamation; decree.

Edification *n.* improvement of the mind.

Edifice *n.* a large building or structure.

Edify *v.t.* to build; to benefit spiritually to improve the mind of; to instruct.

Edit *v.t.* to prepare a film, radio or television programme, or book by arranging separate items or parts in a suitable sequence.

Edition *n.* a form in which a book is published; the whole number of copies published at a time.

Editor *n.* one who conducts a newspaper.

Editorial *adj.* pertaining to editing; of an editor. *n.* a leading article in a newspaper written by an editor.

Educate *v.t.* to teach; to train; to give moral and intellectual training.

Education *n.* systematic instruction.

Educator *n.* one who gives education.

Educe *v.t.* to draw out; to develop; to extract; to bring out; to infer; to form some judgement from facts.

Educt *n.* a body separated from another.

EEC *abbr.* European Economic Community.

Eel *n.* a snake like fish; a long thin fish that resembles a snake.

E'en E'er *adjs.* (poet) for Even; Ever.

Eerie, Eery *adjs.* strange and fearful.

Effable *adj.* capable of being expressed; utterable; explicable.

Efface *v.t.* to destroy; to rub out; to crease or expunge; to cause something to fade.

Effaceable *adj.* that may be effaced.

Effect *n.* result; intent; force; impression; consequence; a change produced by an action or a cause.

Effective *adj.* powerful in effect.

Effectuate *v.i.* to accomplish to achieve.

Effeminate *adj.* womanish; cowardly; unmanly; weak.

Effendi *n.* a title given in Turkey or Egypt to an officer of a government or to a gentleman.

Efferent *adj.* conveying or carrying outwards.

Effervesce *v.t.* to exhibit signs or excitement; to give off bubbles of gas.

Effete *adj.* worn out; spent; exhausted; vigourless; incapable; having the energies worn out; feeble.

Efficacious *adj.* producing desired effect.

Efficient *adj.* producing the desired effect; effective; competent.

Effigy *n.* a portrait or image of a person or thing; statue; head or impression on a coin.

Efforesce *v.t.* to burst into flower; to become hard and powdery on the surface.

Effluence *n.* flowing out.

Effluent *adj.* a river or stream flowing out of a large river or of a lake.

Effluvium *n.* an unpleasant smell.

Efflux *n.* that which flows out; effusion.

Effodient *adj.* accustomed to dig.

Effort *n.* exertion of strength; an attempt.

Effrontery *n.* shamelessness; insolence; imprudence; audacity; bold or rude behaviour without any feeling of shame.

Effulgence *n.* lustre; brightness.

Effulgence *n.* great lustre; a flood of light.

Effuse *v.t.* to power forth as a liquid.

Eft *n.* a newt; a water lizard.

Egg *n.* an oval body produced by the female of birds; spawn; germ.

Egis *n.* shield; protection.

Eglantine *n.* a sweet briar; the wild rose bush.

Ego *n.* egotism; self importance; an individual's idea of herself or himself, especially in relation to other people or to the outside world.

Egoism *n.* the theory that we have proof of nothing but one's own existence; selfishness.

Egregious *adj.* extraordinary; uncommon; distinguished (now depreciatory).

Egress *n.* the act of going or issuing out; the way out.

Egression *n.* going from a place.

Egret *n.* a white bird with a long white tail and black feathers; hairy crown of seeds.

Eider *n.* a large wild duck living on sea coasts.

Eight *n.* one more than seven; one less than nine; a set of eight things or persons.

Eikon *n.* a small likeness of some holy person or object; an image.

Either *adj.* & *pron.* one of two each of two; every one; or.

Ejaculate *v.t.* to utter suddenly; to eject from body.

Eject *v.t.* to cast out; to dismiss; to turn out; to expel; to emit; to throw out; to force somebody to leave a place.

Eke *v.t.* to increase; to supplement; to add; to lengthen.

Elaborate *v.t.* to proudce by labour; to work out in detail. *adj.* carefully worked out.

Elaborative *adj.* giving out details.

E'land *n.* a large South African deer.

Elapse *v.t.* (of time) to pass.

Elastic *adj.* having the power or tendency to resume its normal bulk or shape; flexible; springing back.

Elate *v.t.* to stimulate; to swell; to make proud. *adj.* in high spirits; very happy.

Elbow *n.* the joint where the arm bends; or the outer part of this.

Elder *adj.* older; prior in origin.

Elderly *adj.* (of people) rather old; past middle age.

Eldest *adj.* first-born or oldest surviving; most advanced in age.

El-Dorado *n.* an imaginary country full of gold; a dream land of wealth.

Elect *v.t.* to choose or decide to do something; to choose somebody by vote; to pick out.

Election *n.* the action or an instance of choosing by vote one or more of the candidates for a position.

Electoral, Electorial *adjs.* pertaining to elections.

Elective *adj.* pertaining to the right of election; appointed by election; entitled to elect; optional.

Elector *n.* one who elects; one who has a right of vote in election.

Electric *adj.* charged with or able to develop electricity.

Electricity *n.* the energy of charged elementary particles, supplied as electric current for lighting, heating, driving machines.

Electrify *v.t.* to convert (railways, transport) to electric working; to charge with electricity.

Electrocute *v.t.* to execute (a criminal) by electricity.

Electrocution *n.* killing by electricity.

Electroplate *v.t.* to put a thin covering of metal on another metal object by means of electricity.

Electron *n.* an elementary particle in all atoms.

Electotype *n.* a printing plate made by electricty.

Electrum *n.* an alloy of silver and gold.

Eleemosynary *adj.* of alms; dependent on alms; charitable.

Elegance *n.* purity, beauty; neatness.

Elegant *adj.* neat; refined; pretty; graceful and attractive in appearance or manner, etc.

Elegiac *adj.* expressing sorrow, especially about the past.

Elegist *n.* a writer of elegles.

Elegy *n.* a poem or song expressing sorrow, especially for the dead.

Element *n.* a first principle; one of the essential parts of anything; any one of the four substances—fire, air, earth and water; a component part.

Elementary *adj.* of a single element; primary; rudimentary; simple.

Elemi *n.* a resinous exudation from certain trees.

Elephant *n.* a huge quadruped with a long trunk and two tusks.

Elephantiasis *n.* a disease which causes a part of the body (usually the legs) to swell up and grow very large.

Elevate *v.t.* to lift up; to raise to a higher level or rank; to cheer.

Elevated *adj.* exalted; dignified; elated; fine; noble.

Elevation *n.* angle; the height above a given level; raising aloft; exaltation; dignity; the altitude.

Elevator *n.* machine for hoisting.

Eleven *n.* one and ten; a team of eleven; the eleventh hour after noon or midnight.

Elf *n.* a supernatural being; a small fairly; a dwarf; a small or mischievous creature.

Elicit *v.t.* to deduce or to draw out; to bring to light.

Elide *v.t.* to rebut; to cut off as a syllable; to leave out a letter or sound.

Eligible *adj.* fit or worthy to be chosen; legally qualified; desirable; having the right or proper qualification.

Eliminate *v.t.* to get rid of; to expel; to extract; to set at liberty.

Elite *n.* a selected part of anything; the best people in any group.

Elixir *n.* a cordial; quintessence; a panacea; a strong tincture; an imaginary liquid designed to change metal into gold.

Elk *n.* a kind of large deer; the hopper swan.

Ell *n.* a measure of length equal to 45 inches.

Ellipse *n.* a regular oval figure.

Ellipsoid *n.* an ellipitcal spheroid.

Elm *n.* a kind of forest tree; a tall tree with board leaves which is loses in winter.

Elocution *n.* oratory; eloquence; the art or style of speaking clearly and effectively, especially in public.

Elodes *n.* the sweating sickness.

Elogium, Elogy *ns.* a speech praising a (dead) person.

Eloin *v.t.* to banish to a distance.

Elongate *n.* to lengthen; to draw out; to stretch out so as to be longer; to make something longer; to extend.

Elope *v.i.* to escape privately, especailly with a lover; to run away, especially to get married; to abscond.

Eloquence *n.* the art or power of delivering fluent speech.

Eloquent *adj.* having the power of fluent speech; strongly expressive; having or showing eloquence; exciting emotion or interest.

Else *adv.* other (in addition or instead) otherwise; besides; instead.

Elucidate *v.t.* to make lucid or clear; to throw light upon; to illustrate.

Elude *v.t.* to escape by stratagem; to baffle, especially by a clever trick; to escape somebody; to avoid somebody.

Elusion *n.* deception.

Elysium *n.* the abode of the blessed; any delightful place; (place of) ideal happiness or exquisite felicity.

Em *n.* the letter M, the unit of measurement in estimating a line of composed types.

Emaciate *v.t.* to make lean; to waste; to lose freshness gradually.

Emanate *v.t.* to flow out from anything; to issue; to originate; to produce and give something out from oneself.

Emanation *n.* act of emanating.

Emancipate *v.t.* to make free; to free from legal, social or other restraint.

Emarginate *v.t.* to notch the edge.

Emasculate *v.t.* to castrate; to deprive of masculine vigour; to effeminate.

Embale *v.t.* to make up inot a bundle or bale.

Embalm *v.t.* to preserve from decay with spices; to perfume; to fill with sweet scent.

Embank *v.t.* to enclose; to confine; to defend with a bank or mounds.

Embar *v.t.* to fasten with a bar.

Embargo *n.* a prohibition of ships to leave or enter a port; a stoppage of trade for short time by authority.

Embark *v.t.* & *i.* to go or put on board a ship; to enter upon an enterprise; to venture.

Embarrass *v.t.* to perplex; to render intricate; to encumber with debt; to make somebody feel awkward, ashamed or self-conscious; to make movement difficult.

Embassy *n.* the charge or the function of an ambassador; deputation to a king; an ambassador's residence.

Embattle *v.t.* to set in battle array.

Embay *v.t.* to enclose a ship in a bay.

Embed *v.t.* to fix something deeply and firmly in a mass of something.

Ember (*usu. pl.*) *n.* a piece of live coal or wood.

Embezzle *v.t.* to appropriate other's entrusted money fraudulently; to use money placed on one's care wrongly, especially so as to benefit oneself.

Embitter *v.t.* to make bitter; to aggravate; to exasperate; to fill somebody with deep feelings of disappointment; to make hatred or anger worse.

Emblazon *v.t.* to decorate; to celebrate.

Emblem *n.* a type or symbol; a device or picture; an object that represents something; a symbolic figure.

Embody *v.t.* to give a concrete form; to include; to incorporate.

Embolden *v.t.* to give boldness or courage; to encourage.

Embosom *v.t.* to embrace; to surround.

Emboss *v.t.* to cover with bosses; to carve or to ornament with relief; to clothe; to warp; to enclose.

Embottle *v.t.* to mouth of a river.

Embowel *v.t.* to take out or remove bowels from the body.

Embrace *v.t.* to take in the arms; to press to the bosom with affection; to adopt; to enclose; to accept or believe an idea, etc.

Embrangle *v.t.* to confuse; to entangle.

Embrasure *n.* an opening in a wall of a fort for gun.

Embrocate *v.t.* to moisten and rub, as with a lotion; to bathe; to foment.

Embroidery *n.* embroidered work; adventitious ornament.

Embroil *v.t.* to entangle; to distract; to involve in trouble; to draw (a person) into a quarrel.

Embryo *n.* a thing in its rudimentary stage.

Embus *v.t.* to put inot a bus; lorry or motor vehicle.

Emend *v.t.* to remove faults; to correct or improve.

Emerald *n.* a very precious stone of beautiful green colour; a bright-green precious stone; a blue-green colour.

Emerge *v.t.* to issue or proceed from; to come into view.

Emergency *n.* an unexpected event; a sudden happening needing prompt action.

Emeritus *adj.* who is no longer holding office; retired.

Emersion *n.* emerging; reappearance.

Emery *n.* a hard metal which is used as a powder for polishing and grinding.

Emetic *adj.* & *n.* (a medicine) causing one to bring food back up from the stomach and through the mouth.

Emication *n.* a spark.

Emigrant *n.* having emigrated; one who quits one's country to another as a place of adobe.

Eminence *n.* height; superiority; distinction; fame; renown; (shake.) advantage; upper hand.

Eminent *adj.* exalted in rank; distinguished.

Emissary *n.* a secret missionary; a spy; an underground outlet, especially from one nation to another.

Emission *n.* the act of issuing or emitting, *e.g.* light, heat, gas matter.

Emit *v.t.* to give out; to send forth; to throw out.

Emollient *adj.* softening. *n.* a medicine which softens animal's texture.

Emolument (*n. pl.*) profit from employment; salary.

Emotion *n.* excited mental stage; feeling.

Empanel *v.t.* to put the name of a person on a list of person who will serve on a jury.

Emperor *n.* the ruler of an empire.

Emphasis *n.* significant stress on words or syllables; forcible or impressive expression.

Emphatic *adj.* forcible, strong; (of words) bearing the emphasis.

Emphractic *adj.* closing or stopping the pores of the skin.

Empire *n.* the territory of an emperor; supreme control or dominion; the government and office of an emperor; the time of its duration.

Emplane *v.i.* to go on board (to ride) an aeroplane.

Employ *v.t.* to keep in one's service, to keep occupied; to give work.

Employee *n.* a person employed for wages.

Employer *n.* one who employs labour.

Employment *n.* work, *esp.* in return for regular payment; one's trade; the action of employing somebody; business entrusted to one.

Emporium *n.* a place of trade; a centre of commerce; a shop selling a variety of goods.

Empoverish *v.t.* to make poor.

Empower *v.t.* to authorize; to have power over; to licence.

Empress *n.* the wife of an emperor; the female ruler of an empire.

Empty *adj.* containing nothing; not filled; devoid of inmates; meaningless.

Empurple *v.t.* to redden; to make purple.

Empyrean *n.* the highest heaven as sphere of fire or abode of God.

Emu *n.* a large Australian bird that runs quickly but cannot fly.

Emulation *n.* rivalry.

Emulatress *n. fem.* a female who emulates.

Emulous *adj.* desirous of fame; zealously imitative of.

Emulsion *n.* a milky fluid made by rubbing almonds or other seeds with water; (phy. chem.) a suspension of fine particles or globules of a liquid in another.

Emulsive *adj.* milk-like.

Enable *v.t.* to supply with means (to do); to cause to be able; to empower; to make something possible.

Enact *v.t.* to establish by law; to make into a law; to ordain; to decree; to play (part).

Enactor *n.* one who enacts.

Enamel *n.* a smooth hard metallic coating; a work of art in enamel; a substance used to cover the surface of metal, pots, etc. for decoration or as protection.

Enamour *v.t.* to inspire with love; to make fond of.

Enate *adj.* protruding; growing out.

Enbloc *adv.* wholesale; in a lump.

Encage *v.t.* to put in a cage.

Encamp *v.t.* & *i.* to form into a camp; to settle in a camp; to lodge in tents.

Encase *v.t.* to put into a case.

Encash *v.t.* to convert into a cash.

Encave *v.t.* to hide in a cave or recess.

Enceinte *adj.* pregnant; with child. *n.* an enclosure.

Enchain *v.t.* to chain up; to link together; to hold fast.

Encircle *v.t.* to enclose; to surround; to encompass.

Enclasp *v.t.* to clasp; to embrace.

Enclose *v.t.* to fence in; to shut up; to put in; to surround.

Enclosure *n.* a thing enclosed; enclosing; an enclosed land.

Encomiast *n.* one who praises another.

Encomium *n.* formal or highflown praise; an expression of praise; eulogy.

Encompass *v.t.* to shut in; to encircle; to environ; to surround; to include something.

Encore *inter.* (called out by an audience to ask for a further performance of something by somebody) again! more!; once more!

Encounter *n.* a meeting in conflict.

Encourage *v.t.* to put courage in; to inspire with hope; to patronise; to cherish; to further; to make hold; to give support; to urge out; to promote.

Encradle *v.t.* to lay in a cradle.

Encrust *v.t.* & *i.* to cover with a thin hard outer covering.

Encumber *v.t.* to impede.

Encumbrance *n.* a burden; an impediment;

Encyclop(a)edia *n.* a book or set of books of information on all branches of knowledge.

End *n.* limit; extremity; to utmost point; remnant; conclusion; death; purpose; thing aimed at.

Endanger *v.t.* to cause danger to; to expose to danger; loss or injury.

Endear *v.t.* to make dear; to cause to be loved.

Endeavour *n.* effort; exertion; attempt. *v.t.* & *i.* to try or to make an attempt; to strive; to try to achieve.

Endecagon *n.* a plane figure which has eleven sides.

Endemic *adj.* regularly found in a particular country or area, or among a particular group of people.

Endive *n.* a bitter plant used for food.

Endless *adj.* unending; without end; continual.

Endmost *adj.* farthest; at the extreme end.

Endogamy *n.* the custom forbidding marriage outside one's own group; inbreeding; pollination between two flowers on the same plant; union of female gametes.

Endorse *v.t.* to give one's approval or support to a claim; to write on the back of a document; to confirm; to agree with what has been said or done.

Endow *v.t.* to give a dowry or marriage gift; to provide permanent means of support for; to enrich with any gift; to present.

Endue *v.t.* to put on clothes; to give; to put in stomach or mind; to digest.

Endurance *n.* forbearance; submission; fortitude; the ability or willingness to suffer patiently and without complaining or to tolerate a difficult situation for a long time.

Endure *v.t.* & *i.* to submit; to bear; to undergo; to last; to remain.

Endways *adv.* in an upright position.

Enema *n.* an injection of liquid into the rectum; an instrument for doing this.

Enemy *n.* a foe; a hostile person; an opponent; one who is unfriendly.

Energetic *adj.* active; vigorous; powerful.

Energy *n.* power of doing work; force; power; vigour; ability; efficacy.

Enervate *v.t.* to deprive of force or strength or courage; to weaken.

Enface *v.t.* to write or stamp a bill on the face.

Enfeeble *v.t.* to make feeble.

Enfeeter *v.t.* to bind in fetters.

Enfilade *n.* a number of things arranged in series.

Enfold *v.t.* to give force or effect to; to urge; to compel.

Enforce *v.t.* to give force to; to impose; to compel; to gain by force; to give effect to; to urge; to impress.

Enframe *v.t.* to set or put (a picture) in a frame.

Enfranchise *v.t.* to set free; to franchise; to give the right to elect members to government.

Engage *v.t.* & *i.* to hire; to encounter; to occupy; to bind by promise; to embark in any business.

Engagement *n.* bethrothal; an appointment; a promise to marry; a battle; obligation; binding condition.

Engender *v.t.* to beget; to bring about; to breed; to cause to bring forth; to produce.

Engild *v.t.* to brighten; to gild.

Engine *n.* a device; a mechanical contrivance; locomotive; a military machine; any instrument or device.

Engineer *n.* one who designs an engine. *v.t.* & *i.* to construct; to manage or to act as an engineer.

English *adj*. belonging to England or its inhabitants or language.

Englut *v.t.* to swallow; to fill.

Engorge *v.t.* to devour; to glut.

Engraft *v.t.* to insert; to implant; to incorporate; to add.

Engrain *v.t.* to dye with a fast colour; to infix deeply.

Engrave *v.t.* to carve; to cut designs in metal; to deposit in a grave.

Engross *v.t.* to write in bold letters; to buy whole stock; to monopolize; to take wholly oneself to occupy.

Engulf *v.t.* to swallow up completely; to overwhelm.

Enhance *v.t.* to raise; to advance; to increase; to exaggerate; to raise price & etc.

Enigma *n.* a statement with a hidden meaning; a riddle; a puzzle.

Enjoin *v.t.* to prescribe; to command; to order or direct with authority or urgency; (law) to forbid to prohibit.

Enjoy *v.t.* to take delight in; to experience pleasure.

Enkindle *v.t.* to set on fire; to kindle into ardour.

Enlace *v.t.* to encircle; to embrace; to enfold; to entwine; to entangle.

Enlarge *v.t.* & *i.* to increase; to widen; to expand; to grow larger.

Enlighten *v.t.* to inform; to give light to; to make free from prejudice; to make clear to the mind; to impart knowledge; to cause to understand.

Enlist *v.t.* & *i.* to enrol; to employ in advancing an object; to engage or be engaged for military service; to get the support of.

Enliven *v.t.* to animate; to inspirit; to amke cheerful.

Enlock *v.t.* to lock up.

Enmasse *adv.* all together; in a body.

Enmesh *v.t.* to catch in a net.

Enmity *n.* hatred; hostility.

Ennui *n.* feeling of boredom; tiredness caused by lack of interest.

Enode *adj.* knotless; without knots.

Enormity *n.* great wickedness; a great crime; outrage; iniquity; the great size, extent or scale of something.

Enormous *adj.* excessive; huge; very large; immense.

Enough *n.* sufficient; as much as need; beyond measure; to a necessary desirable or acceptable extent.

Enquire *v.t.* & *i.* to ask about.

Enrage *v.t.* to make angry or furious; to excite rage in; to exasperate.

Enrank *v.t.* to place in order.

Enrapture *v.t.* to transport with pleasure; to delight intensely.

Enrich *v.t.* to make rich or wealthy; to fertilize; to adorn; to enhance.

Enrol, Enroll *v.t.* to register a student on a course, etc.; to become or make somebody a member of a group.

Enroot *v.t.* to fix by the root; to fix fast.

Enroute *adv.* on the way.

Enshrine *n.* to enclose in shrine; to preserve as sacred; to cherish.

Enshroud *v.t.* to cover completely.

Ensign *n.* a badge; banner; flag; standard-bearer.

Ensilage *n.* green food or fodder for cattle preserved in air-tight chamber and used during the winter.

Enslave *v.t.* to make a slave or to reduce to a slavery or bondage; to subject to the influence of.

Ensnare *v.t.* to entrap.

Ensober *v.t.* to make sober.

Ensue *v.t.* & *i.* to result from; to happen later.

Ensure *v.t.* & *i.* to make certain; to make safe; to betroth; to secure.

Entablature *n.* the part of an order above the column.

Entail *n.* settlement of an estate may not dispose of.

Entangle *v.t.* to catch in a snare; to involve in difficulties; to perlex; to bewilder.

Entame *v.t.* to tame.

Enter *v.t.* & *i.* to come or go in; to come upon a stage; to penetrate; to record; to admit; to enrol; to insert.

Enteric *adj.* pertaining to bowels; of the intestines.

Enterprise *n.* an undertaking; a bold or dangerous undertaking; an adventure; readiness.

Entertain *v.t.* to maintain; to amuse; to cherish; to receive guests.

Entertainment *n.* a public performance; hospitality; an amusement.

Enthral *v.t.* to capture the whole of somebody's attention; to bring into bondage; to enslave.

Enthrone *v.t.* to place on a throne or royal seat.

Enthusiasm *n.* a strong feeling of admiration for someone or something; ardent zeal.

Entice *v.t.* to allure; to attract; to tempt.

Entire *adj.* whole; complete; full; firm; intact; unimpaired; unmingled; unbroken; undamaged.

Entitle *v.t.* to give a title or claim to.

Entity *n.* being; existence; a reality; a real substance; essence; an existing thing; any real thing.

Entoil *v.t.* to entanglel; to ensnare.

Entomb *v.t.* to place in a tomb; to serve as a tomb for.

Entomology *n.* the science that deals with insects; the study of insects.

Entails *n. pl.* the inner parts of an animals.

Entrain *v.t.* & *i.* to get into a train; to put (troops) into a train.

Entrammel *v.t.* to entangle; to obstruct.

Entrance *v.t.* a coming or going in; act of entering; entry; right of admission.

Entrant *n.* a person or an animal that enters a race, a competition or an examination.

Entrap *v.t.* to catch somebody in a trap or place from which they cannot escape.

Entreat *v.t.* to ask earnestly; to pray for; to beg for; to beseech to treat; to deal with.

Entrench *v.t.* to protect a place or an army with trenches.

Entrust *v.t.* to give responsibility for somebody to somebody; to charge with (duty); to confide to (thing, secret); to give in trust.

Entry *n.* act of entering; a passage; taking possession of; list of competitors.

Entune *v.t.* to sing.

Entwine *v.t.* to twist round and round; to interweave; to embrace.

Enumerate *v.t.* to count the number of; to specify; to name one by one.

Enuciable *adj.* capale of being enunciated.

Enunciate *v.t.* to state formally; to declare; to announce; to utter an idea.

Enure *v.t.* to practise habitually.

Envelop *v.t.* to wrap up; to cover; to surround (enemy).

Envelope *n.* cover of a letter; (bot.) one of the coverings or a flower; corola; the gas bag of a baloon or airship.

Envenom *v.t.* to infuse poison or venom into; to corrupt the mind.

Enviable *adj.* worthy of envy; calculated to excite envy.

Envious *adj.* full of envy.

Environment *n.* surrounding; a surrounding object.

Environs *n. pl.* the outskirts of a city; neighbourhood; the region surrounding a place, especially a town.

Envisage *v.t.* to face; to consider; to form a mental picture; to view; to contemplate.

Envoy *n.* a messenger; a representative.

Envy *n.* ill will; hostility; odium; a feeling of mortification at another's good; malice; malignity; rivalry.

Enwind *v.t.* to wind itself round something.

Enwomb *v.t.* to hide in a pit etc. to bury.

Enwrap *v.t.* to envelop; to perplex; to wrap; to enfold.

Enzyme *n.* (Chem.) an unorganized ferment.

Eoan *adj.* pertaining to dawn.

Epaulet, Epaulette *ns.* an ornament worn on the shoulders by soldiers, ship's officers and others.

Ephemeral *adj.* short-lived; transitory.

Epic *n.* a long film, story, etc. dealing with brave deeds and exciting adventures; an epic poem.

Epicure *n.* one who is given to sensual enjoyment.

Epidemic *n.* prevalent for the time among community.

Epidermal *adj.* pertaining to the outer skin.

Epigene *adj.* formed on the surface of the earth.

Epidermi *n.* the outside part of the skin.

Epigram *n.* a few words expressing a clever or amusing thought; a short poem with witty ending.

Epigraph *n.* an inscription; a quotation or a motto.

Epigraphy *n.* the study of inscriptions.

Epilepsy *n.* a disease of the brain in which person falls down unconscious with spasms and foaming.

Epilogue *n.* the concluding part of a book; a speech or short poem delivered at the end of play.

Epiphora *n.* a disease in which tears collect in the eyes.

Epiphyte *n.* a plant which grows on another plant.

Episcopal *adj.* having to do with bishops.

Episode *n.* an incidental story.

Epistle *n.* a writing sent to a person; a letter; a literary work; a verse composition in letter from, usually long and important.

Epistolary *adj.* of or carried on by letters.

Epitaph *n.* words inscribed on a monument or tombstone; a brief poem or other writing in praise of a deceased person.

Epithet *n.* an adjective expressing some quality; a descriptive term.

Epitome *n.* an abridgement or brief summary.

Epitomist *n.* a writer of epitome.

Epitomize *v.t.* to summarize.

Epoch *n.* beginning of an era, date, period of life or events.

Epochal *adj.* making and epoch.

Epode *n.* the last part of an ode.

Epopee *n.* epic; poetry; an epic poem.

Equable *adj.* neither very hot nor very cold; uniform; even.

Equal *adj.* identical; adequate; uniform. *n.* one of the same age, rank etc.

Equanimity *n.* evenness of mind; composure; calm.

Equate *v.t.* to reduce to an average or to a common standard of comparison; to state as equal.

Equation *n.* reduction of equality.

Equator *n.* an imaginary line round the middle of the earth halfway between the north and south poles.

Equerry *n.* an officer of old days; incharge of royal horses; an official in attendance upon a prince or personage.

Equestrian *n.* & *adj.* a man on horseback; pertaining to horsemanship.

Equidistant *adj.* at equal distance.

Equilibrium *n.* a state of balance; a state in which a thing is held level or steady because there is equal weight on both the sides; mental balance.

Equine *adj.* pertaining to horse.

Equinoctial *adj.* of equal day and night.

Equinox *n.* the time at which the sun crosses equator (about March 31 and September 22) and day and night are equal.

Equip *v.t.* to supply with the requisites; to fit out; to furnish; to dress for journey.

Equipage *n.* equipment; outfit furniture required for operation; retinue; a carriage and attendants.

Equitable *adj.* fair; just.

Equitation *n.* the art of horse riding.

Equity *n.* moral; justice; fairness.

Equivalent *adj.* equal in value, amount, power, meaning, importance.

Equivocal *adj.* of double or doubtful meaning.

Equivocate *v.i.* to use doubtful wards in order to mislead; to use words ambiguously.

Era *n.* series of years commencing from some remarkable event or particular point of time.

Eradicate *v.t.* to pull up by the root; to root out; to extirpate; to exterminate; to destroy completely.

Erase *v.t.* to rub out; to obliterate.

Ere *prep.* & *conj.* before; sooner than.

Erect *v.t.* to raise upright; to build.

Erection *n.* the action of erecting.

Erectile *adj.* which can be made to stand up straight.

Eremite *n.* a hermit; one who leads a solitary.

Ergo *adv.* therefore.

Ergot *n.* a disease of plants.

Erne *n.* the golden eagle.

Erode *v.t.* gnaw away; wear out; corrode.

Erosion *n.* the act of eating away.

Erotic *adj.* of love; amatory.

Err *v.t.* & *i.* to sin; to make a mistake; to be incorrect.

Errand *n.* a short journey made to carry a commission.

Errant *adj.* wandering; roving; wild; roaming in quest of adventure; itinerant; erring.

Erratic *adj.* uncertain; irregular; wandering.

Erratum *n.* an error in printing.

Erroneous *adj.* incorrect.

Error *n.* deviation from truth mistake; a wrong opinion; transgression.

Erst, Erstwhile *adj.* & *adv.* former; formerly.

Eructate *v.t.* to belch out.

Erudite *adj.* deeply read; learned.

Erudition *n.* knowledge gained by the study of books; learning.

Erupt *v.t.* & *i.* to burst forth; to cast out.

Eruption *n.* an outbreak (of volcano; anger); rash; pimples.

Erysipelas *n.* a serious disease producing red colour on the skin.

Escalade *n.* an attack or asssult of troops on a fortified place.

Escalator *n.* a moving staircase.

Escapade *n.* an incident that involves excitement or adventure, usually one that is disapproved of or that one later regret.

Escape *v.t.* & *i.* to get free; to avoid; to get clear away from.

Escarp *n.* a steep slope just below the wall of a fort.

Eschatology *n.* the doctrine of death and judgement.

Escheat *n.* lapsing of property to the state for want of an heir.

Eschew *v.t.* to abstain from; to shun; to avoid; to fly from.

Escort *n.* a body of armed men as guard; a person accompanying another as protection.

Escritoire *n.* a small writing-desk with a top which opens downward for writing and is closed when not in use.

Esculent *adj.* & *n.* fit to be used for food.

Escutcheon *n.* a shield on which the signs of titled families are painted; a pivoted keyhole cover.

Eskimo *n.* a member of a North American race.

Esoteric *adj.* secret; initiated; private; confidential.

Especial *adj.* special; chief; more than ordinary; particular; principle.

Esperanto *n.* an artificial language designed to be used as a medium for the people of all nations.

Espier *n.* one who watches like a spy.

Espionage *n.* the practice of employing spies.

Esplanade *n.* a level space between a town and the first houses of it; any level space for walking or driving in, one used as promenade.

Espousal *n.* betrothal.

Espouse *v.t.* to give or take in marriage or betrothal; to embrace.

Esprit *n.* sprightliness; wit.

Espy *v.t.* & *i.* to see at a distance; to detect; to spy.

Esquire *n.* a squire of shield bearer; an attendant on a knight; a landed proprietor; a gentleman acting as escort; a general title of respect in addressing letters; a title of courtesy; a squire.

Essay *n.* an attempt; trial; test; a literary composition. *v.t.* to try; to test.

Essence *n.* existence; intrinsic nature; the extracted qualities of a medicine; perfume. *v.t.* to perfume.

Essential *adj.* very necessary; of or constituting a thing's essence; indispensable. *n.* an indispensable element.

Establish *v.t.* to settle on permanent basis; to set and fix firmly; to found; to place beyong dispute.

Estate *n.* condition; rank; landed total possession; wordly condition; property; one's assets and liabilities.

Esteem *v.t.* to think highly of; to regard. *n.* respect; estimation; high regard; a favourable opinion.

Estimate *n.* reputation; an opinion or judgement about the value of a thing; a rough calculation.

Estimation *n.* reckoning; honour; opinion; esteem; judgement.

Estop *v.t.* to stop by one's own act.

Estrange *v.t.* to treat as an alien; to withhold.

Estuary *n.* the broad mouth of river into which the sea flows; a firth.

Et cetera (short form of etc.) and others; of the like kind; and the rest; and so on.

Etch *v.t.* & *i.* to engrave on metal plates by hand or by the helo of acids.

Eternal *adj.* constant; without beginning or end of existence; everlasting; ceaseless; unchangeable.

Ether *n.* a very fine matter supposed to fill all space; the pure upper air; a colourless transparent volatile liquid.

Ethereal *adj.* airy; heavenly; very light; like air.

Ethic *adj.* relating to morals.

Ethics *n.* the science of morals; a treatise on morals.

Ethnic, Ethnical *adj.* pertaining or race or nations; pertaining to gentile of the heathen; having to do with races of people.

Ethnology *n.* the science of races; the study of the races of man.

Etiquette *n.* conventional rules of manners; rules of good behaviour; unwritten code of professional conduct.

Ethmology *n.* facts relating to the origin, history, formation and meaning of words.

Eucalptus *n.* a tree which produces a strong smelling oil used in medicine.

Euchre *n.* an American card-game.

Eugenic *adj.* pertaining to the production of fine offsprings.

Eulogize *v.t.* to speak well of; to extol; to praise highly.

Eulogy *n.* speech or writing in praise of person; praise.

Eunuch *n.* a castrated male person.

Euonym *n.* a fitting or proper name for a thing.

Euphemism *n.* a pleasant way of saying an unpleasant truth; the substitution of a mild for blunt expression.

Euphonic *adj.* agreeable in sound.

Euphony *n.* pleasing or agreeable sound.

Euphuism *n.* high-flown diction; high-flown style of writing.

Eurasian *adj.* one who is of mixed European and Asiatic parentage.

European *adj.* & *n.* belonging to Europe; a native of Europe.

Euthanasia *n.* any painless and easy death.

Evacuate *v.t.* to make empty or clear; to discharge; to withdraw.

Evade *v.t.* to find a way of not doing something, especially something that legally or morally ought to be done; to escape from; to avoid.

Evanescent *adj.* quickly disappearing; fleeing.

Evangelist *n.* a writer of one of the four Gospels (books of the Bible which tell the life of Christ); a teacher of good news.

Evaporative *adj.* pertainting to evaporation.

Evaporator *n.* an apparatus for evaporation of vegetable juices.

Evasion *n.* act of evading; an attempt to escape the force of an argument of accusation.

Evasive *adj.* that evades or seeks to evade; elusive; not straight forward; shuffling; trying to avoid.

Eve *n.* the time just preceding any event, especially a religious festival or holiday.

Even *n.* (*poet.*) evening.

Evening *n.* the close of the day time; the decline or end of life.

Event *n.* that which happens; incident.

Eventide *n.* the evening.

Eventiliate *v.t.* to winnow; to fan.

Eventual *adj.* happening under certain conditions; last.

Ever *adv.* always; at all times; at any time; eternally; continually; on record; in any degree; at all.

Evergreen *n.* a tree or shrub that is green throughout the year; any tree or plant which does not leave its leaves in winter.

Evert *v.t.* to turn outwards or inside out.

Every *adj.* each of a number; one of a whole; all.

Evict *v.t.* to expel by legal process; to dispossess.

Evidence *n.* testimony; witness; that which makes evident; any thing which helps to prove a fact.

Evil *adj.* wicked; mischievous; bad; disagreeable; unfortunate; harmful. *n.* an evil thing; a sin; harm.

Evince *v.t.* to show; to prove; to indicate clearly.

Evirate *v.t.* to castrate; to emasculate.

Eviscerate *v.t.* to prove beyond doubt; to make a evident; to indicate clearly; to cut out the inner parts of the body.

Evocation *n.* act of calling out.

Evoke *v.t.* to call up; to summon; to bring an image, a feeling, a memory, etc. into one's mind.

Evolution *n.* the act of process of opening out; appearance in succession.

Evolve *v.t.* & *i.* to unroll; to disclose; to unfold; to open out; to set forth in order; to develop naturally and usually gradually.

Evulsion *n.* extraction by force.

Ewe *n.* a female sheep.

Ewer *n.* a kind of pitcher; a large water-pot with handle; a water-jug.

Exact *adj.* precise; accruate; strictly correct.

Exacting *adj.* requiring great effort and attention to detail; making great demands; demanding unreasonable.

Exactitude *n.* exactness; great care in being correct.

Exactly *adv.* accurate; quite so; just so.

Exaggerate *v.t.* to carry beyond truth; to overstate.

Exalt *v.t.* to raise to a high rank; to praise; to extol.

Exaltation *n.* elevation in rank; high estate; a state of great excitement and of pleasure; elation; rapture.

Exalted *adj.* high; noble.

Examination *n.* testing of knowledge; investigation.

Examinee *n.* one who is examined.

Example *n.* an illustration; a copy of a book; fact; instance; a pattern; a warning; a model; a specimen.

Exasperate *v.t.* to irritate (a person); to aggravate (pain).

Excavate *v.t.* to dig out; to hollow out; to remove soil by digging.

Exceed *v.t.* & *i.* to surpass; to excel; to be greater than; to go beyond what is necessary or allowed.

Excel *v.t.* & *i.* to go beyond; to surpass; to be pre eminent.

Excellence *n.* great; merit.

Excelsior *adj.* still higher.

Except *v.t.* & *i.* to make objection against; to exclude (from general statement).

Excerpt *v.t.* to extract; to quote. *n.* a short interesting passage taken out of a book.

Excess *n.* intemperance; superfluity; that which exceeds; the amount by which a thing exceeds; the fact of exceeding.

Exchange *n.* barter; money changer's trade; standard value of comage. *v.t.* & *i.* to interchange; to barter; to give and take mutually.

Exchequer *n.* the department of public service empowered for issuing receipts and to deposit revenue.

Excise *n.* a duty or tax on certain commodities made and consumed in the country; a tax on licences for certain trades.

Excision *n.* a cutting out or off of any kind of a part of the body.

Excitable *adj.* able to be excited or irritated.

Excite *v.t.* to call into activity; to rouse up; to stir up; to energise; to provoke; to incite; to irritate.

Excitement *n.* a thing that excites; an exciting incident.

Exclamation *n.* outcry; a loud utterance; the mark expressing this (!) an interjection.

Exclude *v.t.* to expel; to reject or evict; to shut out; to make impossible; to preclude.

Exclusion *n.* act of shutting out or rejecting.

Exclusive *adj.* kept for a special class; excluding; not inclusive.

Excogitate *v.t.* to think out; to contrive carefully.

Excommunicate *v.t.* to exclude a person from a society; to expel from fellowship; to cut off from a community.

Excrement *n.* useless matter discharged from animal body; dung.

Excrescene *n.* an abnormal or morbid outgrowth on animal or vegetable body; (fig.) an incumbrance.

Excrescent *adj.* abnormally growing; redundant.

Excreta *n. pl.* matters discharged from the animal body; waste thrown out from body.

Excrete *v.t.* to discharge waste matter from the body.

Excruciate *v.t.* to toment or torture; to give pain to.

Exculpate *v.t.* to clear from a charge of a crime or fault; to free from blame; to vindicate.

Excursion *n.* an expedition; a ramble; a trip for pleasure or health.

Excursive *adj.* digressive.

Excursus *adj.* detailed discussion of the special point in a book, *esp.* in appendix.

Excuse *v.t.* to free from guilt; to forgive; to make an apology for; to pardon.

Excusable *adj.* that may be excused.

Exeat *n.* (in school etc.) leave of absence.

Execrable *adj.* abominable.

Execrate *v.t. & i.* to curse; to hate; to detest.

Executant *n.* performer.

Execute *v.t.* to carry into effect; to perform; to complete.

Execution *n.* carrying out; accomplishment; seizure of a doctor's property in default of payment.

Executive *adj.* pertaining to the execution of law; administrative; concerned with execution *esp.* of laws and sentences.

Executor *n. mas.* a man appointed to carry out the provisions of one's will.

Exegesis *n.* exposition, *esp.* of scripture.

Exemplar *n.* an ideal; a model; a pattern; the ideal model of an artist.

Exemplary *adj.* typical; illustrative.

Exemplify *v.t.* to illustrate by giving example; to make an attested copy of; to prove by an attested copy.

Exempt *v.t.* to set apart; to free from control; to make exempt.

Exempted *adj.* not included.

Exemption *n.* the act of exempting; freedom from any service, duty, burden etc.; immunity; privilege.

Exequies *n. pl.* funeral rites.

Exercise *n.* putting in practice; bodily exertion; discipline; employment; a lesson for practice.

Exert *v.t.* to do or perform; to bring into operation; to exercise; to make an effort; to put forth.

Exertion *n.* striving; activity; exerting oneself or something; efforts.

Exeunt *v.t.* (stage direction in plays) actors leaving the stage.

Exfoliate *v.t.* to come off in scales or layers.

Exhalation *n.* puffing off of breath.

Exhale *v.t.& i.* to breath forth to emit as vapour; to give off or be given off in vapour.

Exhaust *v.t.* to draw off air; to empty of contents; to tire out.

Exhaustion *n.* arrival at a conclusion by eliminating alternatives; exhausting; total loss of strength.

Exhaustive *adj.* tending to exhaust; comprehensive.

Exhibit *v.t.* to hold to view; to display; to manifest; to present formally; to show publicly.

Exhibition *n.* act of exhibiting; a display; a public show; a grant or gift.

Exhibitor *n.* one who exhibits.

Exhilarate *v.t. & i.* to cheer up; to gladden; to enliven; to become joyous.

Exhort *v.t.* to urge strongly and earnestly; to counsel; to caution.

Exhortation *n.* admonition; good advice; counsel.

Exhume *v.t.* to dig out; to unearth.

Exigence, Exigency *ns.* an urgent need or demand; an emergency.

Exigent *adj.* urgent; exacting.

Exigible *adj.* capable of being exacted; that may be exacted (*against, from*, person).

Exiguous *adj.* scanty; small.

Exile *v.t.* to expel from one's country; to banish.

Exist *v.t.* to have a reality; to continue to be or live; to occur under certain circumstances; to sustain life.

Existence *n.* state of being; life; fact or mode of living; a manner of living; especially when this is difficult, boring etc.

Exit *n.* departure of a player from the stage; a pasage to go out; death.

Exlibris *n.* a book-plate.

Exodus *n.* a going out or departure; going forth.

Ex-officio *adv.* & *adj.* in virtue of one's office, because of one's position, office or rank.

Exogamy *n.* marriage outside the tribe.

Exogenous *adj.* (Bot.) growing outside.

Exonerate *v.t.* to free from blame; to absolve; to acquit of a fault; to exculpate; to release (from duty).

Exorcize *v.t.* to expel evil spirits by calling forth holy names.

Exordium *n.* an introductory part of a discourse or treatise.

Exoteric *adj.* ordinary; external; easily intelligible; public, (of disciples) not admitted to esoteric teaching.

Exotic *n.* & *adj.* anything of foreign origin; extraneous.

Expand *v.t.* & *i.* to spread out; to lay open; to enlarge; to dilate; to express at length; to develop into.

Expanse *n.* wide extent; expansion.

Expansile *n.* (capable) of expansion.

Expansion *n.* act of expanding; state of being expanded; increase; extension; space.

Expansive *adj.* extensive; able or tending to expand; comprehensive; genial.

Exparte *adv.* & *adj.* (Law) on or in the interest of one side only.

Expatriate *v.t.* to banish from one's home.

Expect *v.t.* to await; to hope to; to reckon on; to anticipate.

Expectant *adj.* waiting; looking for.

Expectation *n.* hope; that which is expected; prospect of future good.

Expectorant *adj.* & *n.* (medicine) which promotes expectoration.

Expectorate *v.t.* & *i.* to eject phlegm from the chest.

Expedient *adj.* suitable; advisable; fit; advantageous.

Expedite *v.t.* to free from obstacles; to dispatch. *adj.* speedy.

Expel *v.t.* to drive or force out; to banish; to discharge; to throw out; to eject; to force to leave.

Expend *v.t.* to spend; to consume; to use up; to waste.

Expenditure *n.* act of expending; amount which is expended disbursement.

Expense *n.* outlay; cost; (*usu. pl.*) money used or needed for something.

Expensive *adj.* costly; valuable; costing a lot of money.

Experience *n.* wisdom derived from the varied changes and trial of life.

Experiment *n.* a trial or test done to prove a theory or discover some thing new; procedure tried on the chance of success or as a test.

Expert *adj.* taught by practical; having a thorough knowledge; skillful; adroit.

Expiate *v.t.* to make complete atonement for; to make reparation or satisfaction for; to pay the plenty of; to make amends for (sin).

Expire *v.t.* & *i.* to breath out; to die; to come to end; (of fire) to die out; (of period) to come to an end; (of law etc.) to become void, or extinct.

Expiry *n.* termination; end.

Expiscate *v.t.* to find out by skilful means.

Explain *v.t.* to make plain or intelligible; to clear the meaning of.

Expletive *adj.* & *n.* serving to fill out sentence; a filling word; oath.

Explicable *adj.* explainable.

Explicate *n.* to unfold, to explain; to interpret.

Explode *v.t.* & *i.* to cry down; to bring into disrepute and reject; to blow up.

Exploit *n.* a heroic achievement; a feat.

Explore *v.t.* to search for the purpose or discovery; to examine thoroughly; to examine (wound) by touch; to inquire into.

Explosion *n.* outbreak (of anger); going off with loud noise.

Exponent *adj.* & *n.* one who explains or points out; an expounder; an inxed in Algebra.

Export *v.t.* to send out of the country; to send goods to another country.

Expose *v.t.* to lay forth; to view; to deprive of protection; to make bare.

Exposition *n.* decscription; commentary; interpretation; explanation.

Expositor *n.* a person, thing that expounds.

Expostfacto *adj.* (-law) retrospective.

Expostulate *v.i.* to make (*esp.* friendly) remonstrance.

Exposure *n.* act of exposing; subjection to sun or wind; openness to danger.

Expound *v.t.* to expose; to explain the meaning of; to explain in a certain way.

Express *v.t.* to squeeze out; to utter; to write; to state one's opinion.

Expression *n.* act of forcing out by pressure; representation; giving utterance.

Expropriate *v.t.* to dispossess.

Expulsion *n.* the act of expelling; banishment; driving away by violence.

Expugn *v.t.* to conquer.

Expunge *v.t.* to wipe out; to mark of deletion; to remove; to omit.

Expurgate *v.t.* to purge; to purify; to remove objectionable matter (from book etc.).

Exquisite *adj.* of great excellence; select; acute; keen; fastidious; delicate.

Exsanguine *adj.* without blood; anemic; lacking blood.

Exscind *v.t.* to cut off; to excise.

Exsert *v.t.* (Biol.) to protrude; to put forth.

Ex-service *adj.* that has been formerly in fighting services.

Exsiccate *v.t.* to dry up; to drain.

Extant *adj.* (*esp.* of documents) still in existence; existing.

Extempore *adv.* without previous preparation; suddenly.

Extend *v.t.* & *i.* to enlarge; to expand or dilate; to prolong; to spread out.

Extensile *adj.* that can be enlarged or stretched out.

Extension *n.* extent; enlargement.

Extensor *n.* a muscle that straightens a joint.

Extent *n.* space covered; large space or tract; size.

Extenuate *v.t.* to diminish; to lessen; to weaken the force of.

Exterior *adj.* on or from the outside; foreign; external; interior; outer; outward.

Exterminate *v.t.* to drive out to destroy utterly; to put on end to; to root out.

Exterminator *n.* one who exterminates.

External *adj.* exterior; lying outside; outward; belonging to the world of outward things.

Exterritorial *adj.* (of ambassadors etc.) free from the jurisdiction of the territory one resides in.

Extersion *n.* act of wiping or rubbing.

Extinct *adj.* put out; extinguished; no longer existing; dead; no longer burning; quenched.

Extinguish *v.t.* to put out; to quench; to obscure; to eclipse; to wipe out (debt).

Extirpate *v.t.* to root out; to destroy utterly; to eradicate.

Extort *v.t.* to get by force; to exact by compulsion (*from*).

Extra *adv.*, *adj.* & *n.* additional; more than usual; in addition to fixed charge.

Extract *v.t.* to draw out by force or otherwise; to choose out or select; to find out; to derive; to extort.

Extradite *v.t.* to give up (a fugitive or prisnor) to another state or authority.

Extrajudicial *adj.* not made in court; not legally authorized.

Extramundane *adj.* outside the world.

Extraneous *adj.* of external origin; not essential; foreign.

Extra-official *adj.* not pertaining to an office.

Extraordinary *adj.* beyond ordinary; not usual or regular.

Extravagance *n.* excess; irregularity.

Extravagant *adj.* exceeding due limits; irregular; excessive; unrestrained; wasteful.

Extravaganza *n.* extravagant speech; an extravagant musical, dramatic, or literary production.

Extravasate *v.t.* & *i.* to force out (fluid etc.) from its vessel.

Extreme *adj.* outermost; remote; last; most pressing; excessive.

Extremism *n.* revolution.

Extremist *n.* an advocate of extreme measure.

Extricate *v.t.* to release; to set free; to send out; to disentangle; to free from difficulties.

Extrinsic *adj.* lying outside; not essential.

Extrorse *adj.* (Bot.) turned outward; opening toward the outside of the flower; facing outwards.

Extrovert *n.* a person not given to introspection.

Extrude *v.t.* to expel; to thrust out.

Exuberance *n.* overgrowth.

Exuberant *adj.* especially of people and their behaviour filled with or showing great happiness and excitement.

Exuberate *v.t.* to abound.

Exudation *n.* the act of exuding.

Exude *v.t.* & *i.* to discharge by sweating; to discharge through pores or incisions.

Exult *v.i.* to rejoice exceedingly; to triumph.

Exultant *adj.* triumphantly rejoicing.

Exultation *n.* rapturous delight.

Exuviae *n. pl.* animal's cast skin shell.

Exuvial *adj.* containing exuviae.

Exuviate *v.i.* to shed slough.

Exvoto *n.* prayer for something.

Eyas *n.* an unstrained hawk; a young hawk not yet completely trained.

Eye *n.* the organ of sight; power of seeing; presence; a small hole; anything like an eye; sprout of a plant.

Eyelash *n.* hair (s) on eyelid.

Eyelet *n.* a loop hole; a small eye; a small hole in cloth, sail, etc. for lace, ring etc.

Eyelid *n.* either cover of eye.

Eyot *n.* a small island.

Eyre *n.* a journey; a circuit court.

F

F sixth letter of the English and Latin alphabet.

Fa *n.* the fourth note of an octave.

Fabaceous *adj.* like a bean.

Fabian *adj.* practising dilatory policy; awaiting opportunity.

Fable *n.* a fiction; a myth; a factious tale or narrative story, in which even inanimate characters are made to speak to teach morals.

Fabliau *n.* a metrical tale.

Fabric *n.* texture; a structure; construction; workmanship.

Fabulist *n.* a composer of fables; a lair.

Facade *n.* the exterior of a building; face of building towards street or open space.

Face *n.* the front part of head; outside appearance; aspect; look.

Facer *n.* one who assumes a false face; a blow in face; sudden difficulty.

Facet *n.* the plane surface of a crystal; a little face.

Facia *n.* a plate over shop front with name etc.

Facial *adj.* of the face.

Facile *adj.* affable; yielding; pliant; easily persuaded.

Facility *n.* anything that is easy in performance; absence of difficulty; dexterity; (*usu. pl.*) convenient opportunities; pliancy.

Facsimile *n.* an exact copy or representation of writing, picture etc.

Fact *n.* an act; a deed; a truth; anything that happens; assertion.

Faction *n.* a company of bad people; self interested or unscrupulous party (*esp.* in politics).

Factitive *adj.* of a verb, expressing idea of making to be something.

Factor *n.* a commercial agent; a deputy; a component part of a number.

Factory *n.* a manufactory; merchant company's foreign trading station.

Factotum *n.* a man who does miscellaneous types of work for another; a man of all work.

Facula *n.* (Astron.) a bright spot or streak on the sun.

Facultative *adj.* of a faculty; permissive.

Faculty *n.* inherent power in a body or organ; power to act; power of the mind; department of a University.

Fad *n.* a fashion; an interest; a reference; an enthusiasm, etc.

Fade *v.t. & i.* to lose freshness, wit, brightness etc.; to droop.

Faces *n. pl.* the excrements of the bowels.

Faffle *v.i.* to stammer.

Fag *v.t. & t.* to become weary; to toil; to grow or make weary; to work hard.

Faggot *n.* bundle of sticks used as fuel; a bundle of steel and iron bars.

Fahrenheit *adj.* the name used for a thermometer in which the freezing point is represented by 32° and boiling point by 212°.

Fail *v.t. & i.* to decay, die and fall away; to miss; to fall short; to become bankrupt; to be missing.

Failing *n.* a penchant; a weakness; deficiency; failure; fault; shortcoming.

Failure *n.* bankruptcy; decay; a falling short.

Fain *adv.* & *adj.* with pleasure; gladly.

Faineant *adj.* idle; inactive.

Faint *adj.* wanting in strength; fading; not bright.

Fair *adj.* bright and clear; pure; beautiful; handsome; satisfactory; abundant; moderately good.

Fairing *n.* a present which is bought at a fair.

Fairly *adv.* reasonably; justly; clearly; neatly; beautifully; painly.

Fairplay *n.* equal opportunities; just treatment.

Fairtrade *n.* free trade conditional on reciprocity.

Fairy *n. adj.* fairly-like; unreal.

Faith *n.* reliance; confidence; trust; fidelity; belief in the revealed religion.

Faithful *adj.* loyal in one's faith or belief; trustworthy; true; accurate.

Faithless *adj.* delusive; inconstant; adulterous; disloyal.

Fake *n.* a coil of rope; a cheat.

Falcate *adj.* bent like a sickle.

Falchion *n.* a kind of short broad curved sword.

Falciform *adj.* shaped like a sickle.

Falcon *n.* a bird of prey; a bird of the Folco genus; a canon.

Faldstool *n.* bishop's armless chair; a small desk for kneeling at.

Fall *v.t.* to descend; to drop; to come down; to be diminished in weight or value; to come to an end suddenly; to sink to a lower level.

Fallacious *adj.* deceitful; misleading; containing a fallacy; delusive.

Fallacy *n.* misleading argument; error; deceptive appearance; delusion.

Fallal *n.* a kind of ornament; a piece of finery.

Fallow *adj.* uncultivated (land); of pale brownish colour.

False *adj.* & *n.* untrue; wrong; erroneous; incorrect; not genuine; counterfeit; artificial.

Falsetto *n.* voice above one's natural range; an unusually high voice, especially when singing.

Falsify *v.t.* to misrepresent; to prove to be false.

Falsity *n.* the quality of being false; false assertion.

Falter *v.i.* & *t.* to stagger; to stammer; to stumble; to finch.

Fame *n.* renown; reputation; celebrity; public report; rumour; reputation.

Familiar *adj.* in close friendship; well acquainted with, well known; usual.

Family *n.* the members of a household; parents and children living together.

Famine *n.* hunger; starvation; a time when there is very little food in a region.

Famish *v.t.* & *i.* to starve; to die of extreme hunger; to reduce (or to be reduced) to extreme hunger.

Famous *adj.* distinguished; noted; renowned; celebrated; (colloq.) very good; excellent.

Famulus *n.* one who attends on a magician.

Fan *n.* a winnowing machine; a totating apparatus for giving current of air.

Fanatic *adj.* unreasonably zealous in religion; filled with mistaken enthusiasm.

Fanaticism *n.* extravagant zeal.

Fancier *n.* one who keeps and breeds for sale birds and animals.

Fanciful *adj.* including in fancies; unreal; odd-looking; capricious.

Fancy *n.* the faculty of forming images in the mind; imagination.

Fane *n.* a weather cock; a temple.

Fanfare *n.* a flourish of trumpets, bugles, etc.

Fanfaronade *n.* brag; fanfare.

Fang *n.* a long sharp tooth, especially of a dog or snake.

Fanon *n.* a napkin; scart.

Fantasia *n.* a musical composition governed by it's own rules; a musical composition in which form is subservient to fancy.

Far *adv.* & *n.* remote; at a great distance; very much; distance.

Farad *n.* the electro-magnetic unit of capacity.

Farce *n.* a dramatic piece intended to excite laughter.

Fardel *n.* (arch.) a bundle; burden.

Fare *n.* the cost of conveying passengers; fod; provisions for the table.

Farewell *inter.* good-bye. *n.* leave-taking; act of departure.

Farfetched *adj.* not obvious; forced; strained.

Farl *n.* thick-cake.

Farm *n.* land used for cultivation. *v.i.* & *i.* to grow crops or keep animals; to till the soil; to take proceeds of (tax, office) on payment of fixed sum.

Farmer *n.* one whose work is to cultivate land; one who farms land.

Faro *n.* a kind of game played for the sake of gambling.

Farrago *n.* a confused collection; a mixture; medley; hotchpotch.

Farrier *n.* a veterinary doctor; a shoeing-smith.

Farrow *n.* a litter of pigs.

Fart *n.* & *v.i.* to let air from the bowels come out through the anus.

Farther *adj.* & *adv.* more remote and distant; more far; in addition to.

Farthing *n.* quarter of a penny; a very small price.

Fascia *n.* long flat surface; band.

Fascicle *n.* bunch bundle; part of a book.

Fascinate *v.t.* to captivate; to enchant; to charm.

Fascine *n.* a long faggot used for engineering purposes and for lining trenches.

Fascism, Fascismo *ns.* principles and organization of the patriotic movement in Italy under Mussolini.

Fash *v.t.* to annoy; to bother; to take pains; to trouble.

Fashion *n.* style; model; manner; shape of dress; pattern; prevailing custom.

Fast *v.t.* to abstain from food; to go without food. *n.* the act of fasting.

Fasten *v.t.* & *i.* to attach; to fix; to secure; to close or join something.

Fasti *n. pl.* a day in the ancient Roman calendar opposite to Nofasti; records.

Fasting *n.* act of abstaining from food.

Fastness *n.* a stronghold; a usually remote place that has been strengthened against attack; rapidity.

Fat *adj.* corpulent; fertile; plump; thick; oily; fleshy; fulsome; profitable.

Fatal *adj.* appointed by fate; mortal.

Fatalism *n.* the belief that events are decided by fate; the acceptance of all that happens as inevitable.

Fatality *n.* supremacy of fate; calamity; death by accident.

Fate *n.* destiny; appointed lot; doom; death.

Father *n.* a male parent; fore-father; a word or respect used for an old man; origination.

Father-in-law *n.* wife's or husband's father.

Fathom *n.* a measure of six feet. *v.t.* to measure the depth of water.

Fatidical *adj.* gifted with prophetic power.

Fatigue *n.* weariness due to exertion; toil; weakness due to hard work and repeated stress; the condition of being very tired.

Fatiguing *adj.* tiring.

Fatling *n.* a young animal fattened for slaughter.

Fatten *v.t.* & *i.* to make or grow fat; to enrich (soil).

Fatty *adj.* of or like fat.

Fatuous *adj.* foolish; impotent; stupid and silly; senseless.

Fault *n.* blemish; defect; mistake; error; imperfection.

Faun *n.* (in Roman myths) a god of the fields and wood, with a human body and a goat's horns and legs.

Fauna *n. pl.* animal life of a region.

Favour *n.* kind; regard; good will; approval; undue kindness.

Fawn *n.* young of a deer; light brown colour; mean flattery.

Fay *n.* (Poet.) fairy; faith; dross.

FBI Federal Bureau of Investigation.

Fealty *n.* loyalty; faithful adherence.

Fear *n.* awe; alarm; dread; painful emotion due to danger; painful emotion caused by impending evil.

Fearsome *n.* formidable.

Feasible *adj.* that can be done; practical; possible; plausible

Feast *n.* a banquet; a sumprous meal; a festiva; gratification.

Feat *n.* an extraordinary act which shows great strength, skill and courage of the performer.

Feather *n.* the outer covering over a bird's skin. *v.t.* to furnish with fethers.

Feature *n.* (*usu. pl.*) appearance distinctive parts of the body or face; external appearance; characteristic part of a thing.

Febrifuge *n.* a medicine to reduce fever; cooling drink.

Febrile *adj.* pertaining to fever.

February *n.* second month of the English year.

Feckless *adj.* feeble; weak; not able to manage things properly or look after oneself; not responsible or efficient.

Fecula *n.* starch obtained by pounding green plants.

Feculence *n.* turbidness; dregs.

Fecundate *v.t.* to make fruitful; to impregnate.

Federal *adj.* pertaining to a covenant, (of States) united, but independent in internal affairs.

Federate *v.t.* & *i.* to unite on federal basis or for common object.

Fee *n.* the sum paid to a public officer for performing his function; remuneration paid to a doctor or lawyer.

Feeble *adj.* wanting in strength; weak; wanting in character or intelligence or lacking force or not effective.

Feed *v.t.* & *i.* to nourish; to feed; to administer food; to supply with food.

Feeder *n.* one who eats; a tributary; one who feeds a machine; child's feeding-bottle or bib.

Feel *v.t.* & *i.* to perceive or explore by touch; to ascertain; to have pity.

Feeler *n.* tentative suggestion; an organ of touch in some animals.

Feeling *n.* sense of touch; physical sensation; emotion; (*pl*) susceptibilities; opinion.

Feeze *v.t.* to twist; to screw.

Feign *v.t.* & *i.* to invent; to forge; to pretend; to imagine.

Feint *n.* pretence; a sham attack, blow, etc. to deceive opponent.

Feist *n.* (U.S.) a small dog.

Feldspar *n.* a kind of mineral.

Feline *adj.* of cats; cat like.

Fell *n.* skin fleece; a mountain; a barren hill. *v.t.* to strike down; to cut down (a tree).

Felloe, Felly *ns.* outer circle, or section of circumference; of wheel.

Fellow *n.* an associate or comrade; a companion; equal; male; member of a university; an individual.

Felodese *n.* self murderer; self-murder.

Felon *n.* one who is guilty of felony; a convic; a malefactor; a murderer.

Felonious *adj.* criminal; (Law) of involving felony.

Felony *n.* a crime graver than misdemeanour.

Felt *n.* cloth of matted wool etc.

Felucca *n.* a small coasting vessel with oars or sails or both.

Female *n.* & *adj.* of the female sex.

Feminal *adj.* pertaining to a woman.

Feminality *n.* female nature or peculiarity.

Feminine *adj.* of women; womanly; effeminate; having the gender proper to women's names.

Feminism *n.* belief in or advocacy in influence of women.

Fen *n.* low marshy land; a marsh.

Fence *n.* a hedge for keeping animals away; a structure of rails.

Fenceless *adj.* not enclosed; (poet.) unfortified; defenceless.

Fencer *n.* one who fences.

Fencible *n.* a soldier liable only for home defence.

Fend *v.t.* & *i.* to ward; ɔff; to maintain; to repal; to act in opposition.

Fenestra *n.* small hole or opening.

Fenestrate *adj.* (Bot., Zool.) with small window-like perforations.

Fennel *n.* a plant of the genus of dill.

Fenny *adj.* marshy.

Fenugreek *n.* leguminous plant with seeds.

Feoff *n.* fief; territory held in fee.

Feral, Ferine *adjs.* living wild; uncultivated, especially after escaping from life as a pet, from a farm etc.; brutal.

Ferement *v.t.* to effervesce; to stir up; to excite.

Feretory *adj.* a shrine; tomb.

Ferial *adj.* (of day) ordinary.

Ferment *n.* fermenting agent; agitation; excitement; tumult.

Ferret *n.* a half-tamed variety of polecat. *v.t.* to clear out; to searh out.

Ferriage *n.* fare paid at a ferry.

Ferrotype *n.* positive photograph on thin iron plate; this process.

Ferruginous *adj.* of iron rust; rust-coloured.

Ferrule *n.* a metal ring or cap for strengthening the end of a tube.

Ferry *v.t.* & *i.* to convery in a boat across a river or lake. *n.* a place for ferrying.

Fertile *adj.* fertilising; inventive; (of land or soil) that can produce good crops.

Ferule *n.* a cane; a rod or flat ruler which is used for striking children.

Fervent *adj.* warm; ardent; zealous; hot; glowing; intense.

Fervid *adj.* ardent.

Fescue *n.* teacher's pointer; kind of grass.

Festal *adj.* joyous; of a feast; gay.

Fester *v.i.* to rankle; to rot; to generate matter. *n.* an inflamed tumour.

Festival *n.* joyful celebration; merry making; a feast.

Festoon *n.* a chain of flowers; ribbons, & etc.).

Fetching *adj.* attractive.

Fete *n.* a festival, usually to raise money for a special purpose.

Feticide *n.* destroying of foetus in the womb.

Fetid *adj.* smelling very unpleasant; stinking.

Fetish, Fetich *n.* inanimate objects worshipped by savages.

Fetlock *n.* part of horse's leg where tuft of hair grows.

Fetter *n.* a shackle for the feet; a band; (*pl.*) captivity; restraint.

Fettle *n.* fit and cheerful condition.

Fetus *n.* the young animal in the womb.

Feu *n.* perpetual lease at fixed rent; piece of land so held.

Feud *n.* a bloody strife; lasting mutual hostility; territory held in fee.

Feudal *n.* belonging to a feud.

Feudatory *adj.* & *n.* a feudal vassal; feudally subject to.

Fever *n.* a disease with high temperature; thirst and quick pulse; agitation; great; excitement.

Feverfew *n.* a herb formerly used as febrifuge.

Few *adj.* & *n.* not many; small in number.

Fey *adj.* with the mind in abnormal state; fated to die.

Fez *n.* a tasselled red Turkish cap.

Fiance *n.* one's betrothed (male).

Fiancee *n.* girl engaged to be married.

Fiasco *n.* an ignominious and notorious failure; break-down.

Fiat *n.* authorization; decree.

Fib *n.* & *v.t.* (to tell) a trivial lie; to tell a lie.

Fibre *n.* a thread-like animal or vegetable tissue.

Fibrill *n.* small fibre.

Fibrin *n.* coagulable lymph found in animals and plants.

Fibroid *adj.* fibre-like. *n.* fibroid uterine tumour.

Fibroma *n.* fibrous tumour.

Fibula *n.* an outer bone of the leg from ankle to the knee; splint bone on outer side of leg; brooch.

Fickle *adj.* irresolute; changeable; inconstant.

Fictile *adj.* made by a potter; of pottery.

Fiction *n.* a thing feigned or imagined; romance; an imaginary story or novel; invented statement or narrative.

Fictive *adj.* created by imagination.

Fidelity *n.* honesty; faithfulness (of a wife or husband); firmness; loyalty.

Fidget *n.* restlessness. *v.i.* to move restlessly.

Fidibus *n.* a paper spill for lighting candles, etc.

Fiducial *adj.* having the nature of trust or reliance.

Fiduciary *adj.* held or given in trust.

Fie *inter.* expressing sense of outraged propriety.

Fief *n.* a land held on condition of military service.

Field *n.* a piece of land or open country in general; a ground for battle; a ground for tillage or pasture; the battle itself; range of vision.

Fiend *n.* an evil spirit; a demon; an extremely wicket person.

Fiendish *adj.* diabolical; malicious.

Fierce *adj.* violent in hostility; raging; vehement; intense.

Fiery *adj.* consisting of fire; flaming; ardent.

Fife *n.* a small shrill flute.

Fig *n.* a soft pear-shaped many-seeded fruit.

Fight *v.i.* & *t.* to contend in war or single combat; to set to fight.

Figment *n.* an imaginary statement; a fiction.

Figurant *n.* a ballet dancer.

Figuration *n.* an act of formation; shape.

Figurative *adj.* representing people, etc. as they are; metaphorical; emblematic.

Figure *n.* shape; external form; space enclosed by lines; a person as seen.

Figurine *n.* a small figure.

Filament *n.* thread-like body; fibre; part of stamen that supports another.

Filature *n.* reeling silk from cocoons.

Filch *v.t.* to steal; to pilfer.

File *n.* a wire or flap of card board for keeping papers in order.

Filial *adj.* of or befitting a son or daughter.

Filibuster *n.* own who wages unauthorized warfare against foreign state.

Filigree *n.* silver or copper wire; fine tracery of gold; anything delicate, light and showy.

Fill *n.* full supply. *v.t.* & *i.* to make or become full; to stock ot supply with abudnace; to pervade.

Filler *n.* one who or that which fills.

Fillet *n.* a little band to tie about the hair; thin narrow strip.

Fillip *n.* stimulus; mere trifle; smart stroke given with the finger.

Filly *n.* a female foal; a young charming girl.

Film *n.* a movie; a thin coating; thin skin or layer; coating on photographic paper or plate.

Filter *n.* a contrivance for cleaning liquids.

Filth *n.* garbage; disgusting dirt; very rude and offensive words.

Fin *n.* a thin flat part of a fish that sticks out from its body.

Final *adj.* conclusive ultimate; coming last.

Finale *n.* last movement of instrumental composition; close of opera etc.

Find *v.t.* to discover; to obtain; to receive; to experience; to succeed.

Fine *adj.* clear; refined; thin; slender; beautiful; delicate; pure; nice; excellent; satisfactory.

Finesse *n.* delicate manipulation; artfulness.

Finger *n.* one of the five terminating members of hand (except thumb).

Finial *n.* (Archit.) ornamental top to gable, canopy, etc.

Finical *adj.* fastidious; precise; over-nice.

Finis *n.* conclusion; the end.

Finish *v.i.* & *t.* to come to an end; to bring to an end; to complete.

Finite *adj.* limited; not infinite.

Finny *adj.* like or having fins; of fish.

Fiord *n.* long narrow arm of the sea between cliffs as in Norway.

Fir *n.* fir tree; kinds of coniferous; their wood.

Fire *n.* heat and light caused by burning; flame; conflagration; light.

Firearm *n.* a gun; pistol.

Firebrand *n.* piece of burning wood; kindler of strife.

Firing *n.* discharge of fire arms.

Firkin *n.* a small cask; half kilderkin.

Firm *n.* business; business house.

Firmly *adv.* strongly.

First *adj.* foremost; earliest in place; time or degree; chief.

Firstlings *n. pl.* first fruits.

Firth *n.* an estuary; a narrow stretch of the sea.

Fisc, Fisk *ns.* treasury of ancient Rome; (rare) exchequer.

Fiscal *adj.* of public revenue.

Fish *n.* an animal living in water; flesh of fish; (colloq.) a person (*usu.* with *queer, cool*), *v.i.* to catch fishes.

Fissile *adj.* tending to split; capable of nuclear fission.

Fissure *n.* cleft; split; (Bot., Anat.) narrow opening in organ; a long deep crack in rock or in the earth; cleavage.

Fist *n.* the clenched hand. *v.t.* to strike with fist; (Naut.) handle (sail etc.)

Fistula *n.* a natural pipe or spout (in whales, insects, etc.); a pipe-like ulcer.

Fit, Fytte *ns.* section of a poem.

Fit *n.* a sudden attack of illness; sudden unconsciousness; paroxysm; sudden transitory condition.

Fitter *n.* one who fits, specially in various trades.

Fix *v.t* & *i.* to make firm; to establish; to fasten; to secure.

Fixation *n.* process of combining gas with solid; being fixed; coagulation.

Fixedly *adv.* intently.
Fixity *n.* fixed state.
Fixture *n.* fixing; fixedness.
Fizz *v.i.* (of a liquid) to produce bubbles of gas; to hiss.
Fizzle *v.i.* to hiss feebly.
Flabbergast *v.t.* to shock or surprise somebody very much; to astonish somebody completely.
Flabby *adj.* soft; limp; loose; feeble.
Flabellate *adjs.* (Bot, Zool.) fan-shaped.
Flaccid *adj.* soft and weak; flabby.
Flag *n.* a king of plant growing on moist ground; a flat slab for paving.
Flagellant *n.* one who whips himself.
Flagellate *v.t.* to whip or scourage.
Flagitious *adj.* heinous; deeply criminal.
Flagon *n.* a large vessel with handle to hold liqour.
Flagrant *adj.* glaring; notorious.
Flag-staff *n.* a long pole on which a flag is flown.
Flair *n.* a natural aptitude; paying; selective instinct for what is good.
Flake *n.* a layer; portion of ignited matter thrown off.
Flam *n.* a sham story; hoax.
Flambeau *n.* a lighted torch.
Flame *n.* blaze of a fire; rage; warmth of affection.
Flamen *n.* a god's priest.
Flamingo *n.* a bird with long legs and neck.
Flammenwerfer *n.* a machine spouting liquid fire in war.
Flaneur *n.* an idler.
Flange *n.* a projecting edge or rim.
Flank *n.* fleshy part of the side of an animal or man; belly; side of a building; side of an army; a wing.
Flannel *n.* a soft woolen cloth.
Flap *v.t.* & *i.* to strike with something broad; to sway about; to flutter.
Flapper *n.* a flat fly-killer; a flap; a young wild duck etc.; a fashionable and lively young woman.
Flare *v.i.* to glitter or burn with a bright unsteady flame; to widen out.
Flaring *adj.* glaring.
Flash *v.t.* & *i.* to gleam; to appear or occur suddenly; to break into a flame of sparks; to fill or flood with water.
Flask *n.* pocket-bottle of metal or glass, gunpowder case.
Flat *adj.* level; insipid; dull; dejected; slow-witted; wanting relief.
Flatten *v.t.* & *i.* to make or become flat.
Flatulent *adj.* inflated; attended with wind.
Flaunt *v.i.* & *t.* to wave proudly; to display oneself.
Flavin *n.* surgical antiseptic and yellow dye.
Flavour *n.* aroma; relish; distinctive taste; savour.

Flaw *n.* defect; blemish; a crack; a rent; defect in document, etc.

Flax *n.* a plant known for its textile fibre and its seeds.

Flaxen *adj.* made of flax; pale yellow.

Flay *v.t.* to strip off the skin or hide; to plunder.

Flea *n.* a small wingless jumping insect; a small or contemptible person.

Fleck *n.* skin-spot; a patch (of colour, & etc.); a small piece or grain of something; freckle; a speck.

Fledge *v.t.* able to fly; (of birds) having mature wing feathers for flying.

Flee *v.i & t.* to run away; to leave abruptly; to hasten; to shun.

Fleece *n.* woolly covering (*esp.* of sheep); wool shorn from a sheep; white cloud etc.

Fleer *v.i.* to laugh impudently or mockingly; to jeer.

Fleet *v.t. & i.* to laugh mockingly; to sneer; to float. *n.* mockery.

Fleming *n.* an inhabitant of Flanders.

Flench, Flense *v.t.* to cut up (whale); flay (seal.)

Flesh *n.* the muscular part of animal body; animal food.

Flessless *adj.* without flesh.

Fleshmonger *n. pl.* one who sells meat.

Fleshy *adj.* plump; of or like flesh.

Flexible *adj.* easily bent; pliable; supple.

Flexion *n.* bending; bent state; a bent part.

Flexor *n.* a muscle which bends a joint.

Flexuous *adj.* bending.

Fley, Flay *v.t.* to cause to fly; to terrify.

Flick *n.* a light blow or jerk.

Flicker *v.t.* to flutter; to shine or burn unsteadily.

Flight *n.* act of flying through air; flock of birds or insects; swift passage.

Flimsy *adj.* frail; slight; paltry; (of cloth or material) light and thin; weak; not convincing; shallow.

Flinch *v.i.* to give way; to shrink.

Fling *v.i. & t.* (*flung*) to throw; to rush; to move oneself or part of one's body suddenly or forcefully; to go violently.

Flint *n.* anything very hard; a very hard stone formerly used for striking fire.

Flip *v.t. & i.* to strike; to turn over or make something turn over onto its side or back with a sudden sharp movement.

Flippancy *n.* fluency of speech.

Flippant *adj.* not showing a serious attitude or sufficient respect.

Flipper *n.* limb used by turtle etc. in swimming.

Flirt *v.t. & i.* to send with a jerk; to move briskly; to jeer.

Flit *v.i.* to depart; to fly lightly.

Flitch *n.* a slice of timber from tree-trunk; side of hog salted.

Float *n.* a raft; something that swims; a tool for smoothing plaster.

Floatage *n.* part of ship above water-line; floating (wreckage), ships etc.; a float on river.

Flock *n.* a number of animals, birds etc.; number of pupils; powdered wool or cloth for making wall-paper.

Floe *n.* a large sheet of floating ice in the ocean.

Flog *v.t.* to beat with a whip or cane; to lash.

Flood *n.* an inundation; river; stream; inflow of tide; downpour; sea.

Floor *n.* a story of a building; lower surface of a room; bottom of sea.

Floorer *n.* paper or question hard to answer; a knock-down blow.

Flop *v.t. & i.* to sit or lie down heavily and awkwardly because of being tired.

Flora *n.* plants of a particular region.

Florentine *adj. & n.* (an inhabitant) of Florence; kind of twilled silk.

Florescence *n.* flowering season or condition; blossoming.

Floret *n.* a small flower; any of the small flowers of a composite flower.

Floriculture *n.* cultivation of flowers.

Florid *adj.* high-coloured ornate; flowery; showy; ruddy.

Floriform *adj.* of the form of a flower.

Florin *n.* an English coin worth two shillings.

Florist *n.* one who cultivates and deals in flowers.

Floruit *n.* period at which a person lived.

Floss *n.* a silky substance found in the husks of certain plants.

Flotilla *n.* a group of boats or small ships sailing together.

Flotsam *n.* a floating wreckage; oyster-spawn.

Flounce *v.i.& n.* to go or move abruptly or impatiently.

Flounder *n.* a small flat-fish.

Flour *n.* a fine powder obtained by grinding grain, used for making bread, cakes etc.; finer part of meal got by bolting. *v.t.* to sprinkle with flour.

Flout *v.t & i.* to express contempt for by word or act.

Flow *v.i.* to flow as water; to glide along as a stream; (of the sea tide) to come in; to gush out; to circulate.

Flower *n.* the blossom of a plant, often brightly coloured and lasting only a short time.

Fluctuate *v.i.* to be unstable; to rise and fall; to move up and down like waves.

Flue *n.* fluff of cotton, etc.; a fishing-net; tube for conducting heat.

Fluency *n.* flowering ready speech.

Fluent *adj.* able to perform an action smoothly and easily.

Fluff *n.* feathery stuff given off by blankets, etc.; theatrical part imperfectly known.

Fluid *n.* any liquid substance.

Fluke *n.* the triangular arm of an anchor. *v.t.* to make an accidental hit.

Flume *n.* artificial channel of water.

Flump *v.i.* to fall with a dull sound.

Flunkey *n.*

Fluorine *n.* a non-metallic element.

Fluor *n.* menstrual flux.

Fluorescence *n.* coloured luminosity produced by direct action of light.

Flurry *n.* sudden gust; agitation; excitement. *v.t.* to agitate.

Flush *v.t. & i.* to make even a game of cards; (of a person's face) to become red because of a rush of blood to the skin.

Flute *n.* semi-cylindrical groove; a musical instrument with blow-hole and finger-holes or keys.

Fluvial, Fluviatile *adjs.* of or found in rivers.

Flux *n.* copious flow; excrement. *v.i. & t.* to flow copiously.

Fluxion *n.* flowing; continuous change (rare); (Math.) rate of change of a continuously varying quantity.

Fly *n.* a small flying insect with two wings; a part of flag; a distance flown; a one-horse hackney carriage; a lap on garment to cover button-holes; speed-regulating device in machines.

Flying *n.* moving in air or on wings. *adj.* hurried; fleeting; hanging; waving.

Foal *n.* the young of a horse or of a related animal; *e.g.* a donkey.

Foam *n.* froth; spume; fury; air bubbles formed in or on a liquid; any of various chemical substances forming a thick mass of bubbles and used for different purposes.

Fob *n.* a small pocket for watch.

Focal *adj.* pertaining to or of a focus.

Focus *n.* a point of concentration; a point where rays meat after being reflected; a central point.

Fodder *n.* dried food for horses or cattle.

Foe *n.* an enemy; an opponent.

Foetal *adj.* pertaining to foetus.

Foeticide *n.* criminal abortion.

Foetus, Fotus *ns.* developed embryo in womb or egg.

Fog *n.* a thick mist; cloudy weather; a grass that grows up after hay is cut.

Foible *n.* a weak point; a fault.

Foil *n.* a person or thing that contrasts with the qualities of another, and so emphasizes.

Foist *v.t.* to bring by stealth; to pass off as genuine.

Fold *n.* an enclosure for cattles; doubling of a substance.

Foliaceous *adj.* with organs like leaves; of or like leaves; laminated.

Foliage *n.* leaves; leafage.

Foliar *adj.* of leaves.

Foliate *adj.* of leaves. *v.t. & i.* to decorate (arch, door-head) with foils; to split into laminae; to number leaves of (book) consecutively.

Folio *n.* a book formed by sheets of paper which are folded once.

Folk *n.* the people in general; a race or nation of ones own family; folk music.

Folklore *n.* legendary traditions.

Follicle *n.* (Bot.) a root surrounding a hair-root; small sack; cocoon.

Follow *v.t.* to go or come after; to imitate; to pursue; to accompany.

Folly *n.* a foolish thing; weakness of mind; foolishness; a foolish act.

Foment *v.t.* to bathe with warm medicated lotion; to foster; to encourage.

Fond *adj.* loving; tender; doting; foolishly credulous.

Font *n.* a receptacle for holy water; assortment of type of one sort.

Fontal *adj.* original; baptismal.

Fontanel, Fontanelle *ns.* membranous space in infant's head.

Food *n.* that which can be eaten for nourishment to maintain life and growth; any substance that people or animals eat or drink; a specific type of food.

Fool *n.* a silly person; one destitute of intellect; a jester. *v.i. & t.* to deceive; to cheat; to trifle.

Foot *n.* the leg; step; oace; infantry; lower end of bed; metrical unit; lineal measure of twelve inches; bottom.

Football *n.* a large round or elliptical inflated ball.

Footbridge *n.* a narrow bridge for the use of people who are walking and not for cars etc.

Fop *n.* a vain showy person; a dandy.

For *prep.* because; with a reason of; with a view to; in place of; with reference to; to the extent to; in spite of.

Forage *n.* food for horses and cattle. *v.i. & t.* to go in search of food; to ravage.

Foray *n.* an incursion; a raid.

Forbear *v.t. & i.* to cease; to refrain from proceeding; to pause; to delay.

Forbearance *n.* command of temper; long-suffering.

Forbid *v.t.* to order not to do; to prohibit; to exclude; to hinder; to prevent.

Force *n.* strength; energy; pwoer; intense effort; an army or navy; influence; vitality.

Forceps *n.* surgical pincers; (Zool.) forceps-like organ.

Forcible *adj.* that may be inforced; powerful; involving force; strong.

Forcite *n.* an explosive.

Ford *n.* a shallow part of a river which can be waded; a shallow place (where river, etc. may be crossed).

Fordone *adj.* utterly wearied.

Fore *adj.* situated in front; former.

Forebode *v.t.* to foretell; to predict; to betoken; to portend; to have presentment of.

Forecast *v.t.* to calculate beforehand; to predict; to foresee; to estimate for.

Foreclose *v.t.* to preclude; to prevent; to stop.

Fore-closure *n.* the act of foreclosing.

Forefather *n.* (*pl.*) the earlier generation; those from whom one's father or mother is descended.

Forefinger *n.* first or index finger; the finger next to the thumb.

Forefront *n.* very front; foremost part.

Forego *v.t. & i.* to precede in place of time; to give up.

Foreground *n.* the part of the head; confidence; audacity.

Forehand *n.* the part of a horse before rider; a forehand stroke.

Forehead *n.* the front part of the face above the eyes; modesty.

Foreign *adj.* not native; alien; connected with other countries.

Forejudge *v.t.* to judge before hearing evidence.

Foreknow *v.t.* to foresee; to know beforehand.

Foreland *n.* a cape or headland.

Forelay *v.t.* to lie in wait for.

Foreleg *n.* beast's front leg.

Forelock *n.* lock of hair just above the forehead; a linchpin.

Foreman *n.* the spokesman of a jury; the chief man; principal workman.

Foremast *n.* the forward lower mast (near the blow of a ship).

Foremost *adj.* first in place or order; chief; best.

Forenoon *n.* day till noon.

Forensic *adj.* of courts of law.

Foreordain *v.t.* to appoint beforehand.

Forerun *v.t.* to be a precursor of; to foreshadow.

Forerunner *n.* harbinger or messanger.

Foresay *v.t.* to predict.

Foresee *v.t.* to see or know beforehand; to foreknow.

Foreshadow *v.t.* to prefigure; to show or indicate beforehand.

Foreshore *n.* shore between high and low water marks.

Foreshorten *v.t.* to portray or show (object) with the apparent shortening due to visual perspective.

Foreshow *v.t.* to foretell; to portend; to predict.

Foresight *n.* a looking forward; thoughtful care for the future; foreseeing; foreknowledge; provident care.

Forespeak *v.t.* to foretell; to predict.

Foreskin *n.* a loose fold of skin covering the end of penis; prepuce.

Forest *n.* a large area covered with trees etc.; something like a forest. *v.t.* to plant with trees; to make into a forest.

Forestall *v.t.* to be beforehand with; to anticipate.

Forester *n.* an officer who is in charge of a forest.

Foretaste *n.* a taste beforehand; partial enjoyment or suffering (of) in advance; anticipation.

Foretell *v.t.* to tell in advance; to predict; to prophecy; to be the precursor of.

Forewarn *v.t.* to warn or give notice before hand.

Foreword *n.* an introduction; a preface; introductory remarks in a book.

Forfeit *n.* a thing lost by way of penalty; lost owing to crime or fault.

Forfend *v.t.* (*God forfend* !) to prevent; to forbid; to avert.

Forgather *v.i.* to meet; to assemble; to associate; to converse.

Forge *v.t.* to shape by heating; to counterfeit; to move ahead.

Forgery *n.* forging or falsifying of document.

Forget *v.t. & i.* to lose remembrance of; to neglect; to put out of mind.

Forgive *v.t.* to excuse; to forego penalty for; to pardon (as an offence).

Forgo *v.t.* to omit; to let go; to go without; to relinquish.

Fork *n.* a two, three or four pronged instrument.

Forlorn *adj.* quite lost; neglected; wretched; forsaken.

Form *n.* the shape or external appearance; appearance to the eye.

Formal *adj.* according to established method; strictly ceremonious; methodical.

Formality *n.* precise observance of forms; established order.

Forme *n.* body of type locked up in chasis for printing.

Former *adj. & pron.* before in time; long past; first mentioned; of the past.

Formerly *adv.* in former times.

Formic *adj.* pertaining to ants.

Formidable *adj.* exciting fear; dangerous to encounter; difficult to accomplish; causing fear.

Formless *adj.* shapeless; without regular form.

Formula *n.* a set of rule; a formal statement.

Fornicate *v.t.* to commit adultery.

Forsake *n.* to give up; to renounce; to withdraw; to abandon.

Forsooth *adv.* in very truth; no doubt; indeed; certainly.

Forspend *v.t.* to tired out.

Forswear *v.t.* to abjure; to renounce; to perjure oneself.

Fort *n.* a fortified place; a castle.

Forte *n.* a person's strong point.

Forth *adv.* & *prep.* forward; out of doors; onwards in time.

Forthcoming *adj.* about to happen or appear in the near future.

Forthwith *adv.* at once; without delay; immediately.

Fortification *n.* the art or science of fortifying; the action of fortifying or strengthening something.

Fortify *v.t.* & *i.* to strengthen by forts; to encourage with; to provide means of defence.

Fortitude *n.* courage in pain or adversity.

Fortnight *n.* two weeks.

Fortnightly *adv.* once a fortnight. *adj.* appearing once a fortnight.

Fortress *n.* a military stronghold.

Fortuitous *adj.* casual; accidental.

Fortuity *n.* a chance; occurrence.

Fortunate *adj.* having good fortune; lucky; prosperous; successful; auspicious.

Fortune *n.* chance; luck; lot; success; wealth; riches.

Forum *n.* a market place; a court of a law; a place of public discussion; the law courts.

Forward *adj.* & *n.* towards the front; onward; relating to future; well-advanced; prompt; ardent.

Forworn *adj.* tired out.

Fosse *n.* canal; ditch or moat.

Fossil *adj.* & *n.* dug up from earth; petrified remains of animals under the earth.

Fossorial *adj.* (Zool.) (used in) burrowing.

Foster *v.t.* to nourish; to hear; to sustain; to cherish; to encourage; to harbour (feeling); to help the development of something.

Foul *adj.* dirty; filthy; impure; wicked; offensive; loathsome; stinking; soiled.

Foulard *n.* thin flexible material of silk; handkerchief of it.

Foully *adv.* in a cruel way; wickedly.

Foumart *n.* a pole-cat.

Found *v.t.* & *i.* to begin building of; to set up or establish; to construct; to fix firmly; to cast a meal; to melt.

Fount *n.* a fountain; any source; a complete set of printing types of one size and face.

Fountain *n.* a water spring; a jet of water; source.

Fowl *n.* kinds of bird kept to supply eggs and flesh for food; a bird.

Fox *n.* an animal allied to the dog; a sly; a cunning fellow.

Foxy *adj.* like a fox in appearance.

Frab *v.t.* to worry.

Fracas *n.* a noisy quarrel; an uproar; a brawl.

Fraction *n.* a numerical quantity that is not integer.

Fracture *n.* a crack in bone; a rapture; the breaking or breakage (*esp.* of bone or cartilage).

Fragile *adj.* easily shattered; weak; perishabel; delicate; brittle.

Fragment *n.* a part broken off; a peace of something incomplete or unfinished; a small detached portion.

Fragrance *n.* sweetness of smell.

Frail *adj.* fragile; weak; infirm.

Frame *v.t.* & *i.* to put together; to arrange; to shape; to put a border.

Franchise *n.* exemption from burden; right to vote.

Frank *adj.* open; generous; free in expression; candid; sincere; undisguised.

Franklin *n.* an old English freeholder.

Frantic *adj.* wildly excited (by pain, joy, & etc.); violent.

Frap *v.t.* to bind tightly (ropes etc.)

Fraternal *adj.* belonging to brother of or like a brother or brothers.

Fraternity *n.* a group of male students at a university who form a social club; brotherliness.

Fratricide *n.* brother or sister slayer; murder of a brother or sister.

Frau *n.* a woman; a wife.

Fraud *n.* a deceit; an imposture; a cheat; criminal deception.

Fraught *adj.* full off; involving.

Fray *n.* a noisy quarrel; a broil; a fight; a contest or an argument.

Freak *n.* whim; caprice; produce of sportive fancy.

Freckle *n.* a light brown spot on the skin.

Free *adj.* not in bondage; loose; not confined or imprisoned; unimpeded; unconnected.

Freebooter *n.* a pirate; a robber.

Freedom *n.* civil liberty; frankness; facility.

Freehold *n.* tenure in fee simple or fee tail.

Freeze *v.t.* & *i.* to convert into ice; to become chilled; to feel very cold.

Freight *n.* a cargo of a ship; the charge of transporting of goods through land or water.

Fremescent *adj.* raging; riotous.

French *adj.* belonging to France; of France; of its people.

Frenetic *adj.* mad; frantic.

Frenzy *n.* wild folly; delirious fury.

Frequency *n.* repeated occurrence of anything; frequent occurrence.

Frequent *adj.* addicted; often occurring; common; habitual.

Fresco *n.* a process of painting pictures on wall before plaster is dry.

Fresh *adj.* healthy and strong; new; not previously known; additional.

Freshet *n.* flood of river; rush of fresh water flowing into the sea.

Fret *n.* an ornamental pattern made of straight lines.

Freudian *adj.* of Freud's theory of psycho-analysis.

Friable *adj.* easily crumbled.

Friar *n.* a monk; member of a religious order.

Fribble *v.i.* to trifle; to be frivolous.

Friction *n.* rubbing of two bodies; attrition; diagreement.

Friday *n.* the day before Saturday; the sixth day of the week.

Friend *n.* an intimate associate; a helper; patron; companion.

Frieze *n.* coarse woollen cloth with nap on one side. band of decoration.

Frigate *n.* a warship; a cruise.

Fright *n.* a sudden fear; terror; a ridiculous appearance causing terror; alarm.

Frighten *v.t.* to fill with terror; to alarm; to throw into fright; to terrify into doing.

Frigid *adj.* wanting heat; wanting warmth of affection; (of a woman) not showing any sexual desire or responses.

Frill *n.* a ruffle; an ornamental border on a garment or piece of cloth, especially one gathered in a number of small folds at one edge.

Fringe *n.* border; edging; trimmings of hanging threads.

Frippery *n.* finery; a showy ornament; useless things; trumpery; unnecessary items of ornament or decoration.

Frisette *n.* artificial curls on fore-head.

Frisk *v.i.* to gambol; to move sportively.

Frisket *n.* (Print.) the light iron frame which holds a sheet of paper in position before it is printed.

Frit *n.* a mixture of sand, flint etc. used in glass-making.

Frith *n.* a wooded country; sanctuary; a narrow inlet of the sea.

Fritter *n.* a small pancake.

Fritz *n.* not operating; in need of repair.

Frivol *v.i.* to triffle; to act foolishly.

Frivolity *n.* foolish thoughts; a foolish action.

Friz (z) *v.t.* to form into small curls; to crisp hair; to dress (leather).

Frizzle *v.i.* to make sputtering noise while boiling.

Fro *adv.* from; back; away; backward.

Frock *n.* a long robe worn by monks; a loose garments worn by workmen; child's skirt and bodice.

Frog *n.* a tailess amphibious creature.

Frolic *adj.* merry; frankly; mirthful; sportive.

Frolicsome *adj.* lively and playful.

From *prep.* expressing separation; starting point; source; motive; out of; away; at a distance; by reason of.

Frond *n.* (Bot.) a leaf-like part of a palm tree; a leaf-like organ, *esp.* in ferns; (Zool.) an organ like a leaf.

Front *n.* the forehead; face; line of battle towards the enemy.

Frontage *n.* front of building; land abutting on street or water.

Frontal *adj.* of or on front; of forehead. (Anat.) any of several parts in the frontal region.

Frontier *n.* a boundary of any territory; bordering.

Frontlet *n.* a fillet worn on the forehead.

Frontward *adv.* towards the front part.

Frost *n.* frozen dew or vapour; chilling influence.

Froth *n.* a foam; empty talk; a chatter; scum; idle talk; mere words.

Froward *adj.* perverse; unreasonable; refractory; ungovernable.

Frown *v.t.* & *i.* to contract brow in anger; to drive away with a frown.

Frowst *v.i.* & *n.* (to stay in) fusty heat in a room.

Frozy *n.* ill-smelling; close; unkempt.

Fructiferous *adj.* bearing or producing fruit.

Fructify *v.i.* & *t.* to bear fruit; to make fruitful.

Fructose *n.* fruit sugar.

Fructuous *adj.* fruitful; fertile.

Frugal *adj.* sparing; thirfty; economical.

Fruit *n.* a product of a tree; produce; effect; result; profit; produce; produce of action.

Fruition *n.* attainment; enjoyment; gratification; realization of hopes.

Fruitless *adj.* devoid of fruits; barren; useless.

Fruitlet *n.* a small fruit.

Frumenty *n.* hulled wheat boiled in milk and sweetened.

Frump *n.* a bad tempered, old fashioned female; a dowdy.

Frustrate *v.t.* to baffle; to disappoint; to defeat. *adv.* vain.

Frustration *adj.* tending to defeat.

Frustum the lower part of a solid formed by cutting if off parallel to the base.

Frutescent, Fruticose *adjs.* shrub-like; shrubby.

Frutex *n.* a shrub.

Fry *v.t.* & *i.* to cook into butter by roasting in a pan over fire; to simmer; to be agitated in feelings; to cook something in very hot fat or oil.

Fudge *n.* nonsense. *v.t.* to patch up; to cheat.

Fuel *n.* that which is used to feed fire; any material burned to produce heat or power e.g. wood, coal or oil.

Fugitive *adj.* apt to flee away; violate; flying; fleeting; transient.

Fugleman *n.* soldier placed before regiment at drill to show motions; leader.

Fulfil *v.t.* to complete; to accomplish; to bring to pass.

Fulgent *adj.* shining; brilliant.

Full *adj.* filled up; complete; crowded; engrossed; abundant; copious; entire; perfect.

Fulminant *adj.* fulminating; (of disease) developing suddenly.

Fulminate *v.t.* & *i.* to flash; to explode.

Fumarole *n.* crevice in cone of volcano through which vapour comes out.

Fumble *v.i.* & *t.* to handle clumsily; to fail to catch a ball.

Fume *n.* smoke; any odorous smoke or vapour; mental heat; rage.

Fumigate *v.t.* to subject to smoke or fumes; to perfume; to purify by subjecting to fumes.

Fun *n.* frolic; a joke; sport; amusement. *v.t.* (rare) to joke.

Function *n.* peformance; a social gathering; office.

Fund *n.* a stock; stock or supply always ready for use.

Fundamental *adj.* pertaining to the groundwork or root of matter.

Funeral *n.* the burial or burning of the dead; burial procession.

Fungicide *n.* fungus destroying substance.

Fungus *n.* mushroom; a kind of spongy plant.

Funicular *adj.* of a rope or its tension.

Funk *n.* an offensive smell; timidity; fear.

Funnel *n.* a mouthed conical vessel terminating in a tube for filling closed neck vessels.

Funny *adj.* full of fun; sportive.

Fur *n.* the soft, the hairy coat covering the skin of many animals.

Furcate *adj.* forked; branched.

Furious *adj.* very angry; raging; frantic; uproarious.

Furl *v.t.* & *i.* to fold; to wrap up; to relinquish; to contract.

Furlong *n.* one-eighth of a mile.

Furnace *n.* an apparatus for melting metals; a fireplace; severe; test.

Furnish *v.t.* to provid; to afford; to supply; to equip.

Furniture *n.* the movables with which a house is equipped; equipment; decorations; articles.

Furor *n.* rage; excitement.

Furrow *n.* a narrow trench made by ploughing; a groove; track; rut; wrinkle. *v.t.* to plough; to make furrow in.

Further *adv.* in addition; at or to a greater distance in space or time; more remote.

Furtive *adj.* sly; obtained by theft; stealthy.

Furuncle *n.* a boil; a tumour.

Fury *n.* rage; violent passion; madness; a passionate woman; fierce passion.

Furze *n.* thorny evergreen flower; spiny yellow-flowered shrub; gorse; whin.

Fuscous *adj.* dark in colour.

Fuse *v.t.* & *i.* to melt with great heat; to amalgamate.

Fuselage *n.* the frame-work of an aeroplane.

Fusible *adj.* that may be melted.

Fusiform *adj.* shaped like a spindle; tapering on both ends.

Fusil *n.* a light musket.

Fusillade *n.* continuous discharge of firearms.

Fusion *n.* the act of melting by heat; fusing; fused mass; coalition.

Fuss *n.* bustle; tumult; abundance of detail. *v.i.* to make a fuss.

Fusspot *n.* a person who is often worried about unimportant things and is difficult to please.

Fustian *n.* a twilled cotton cloth; bombast.

Fustic *n.* wood yielding a yellow dye.

Fusty *adj.* stale-smelling; antiquated.

Futility *n.* worthlessness.

Futile *adj.* useless; frivolous; worthless; of no effect; trivial.

Future *adj.* pertaining time to come; that is to happen hereafter; (Gram., of tense) describing event yet to happen. *n.* time to come.

Fuze fuse. *n.* (see fuse)

Fuzz *n.* to fluff; to fly off in minute particles. *v.t.* to fluffy.

Fylfot, Filfot *n.* a kind of equal armed cross («).

Fyrd *n.* a nation's full military force.

G

G the seventth letter of the English aiphabet.

Gab *n.* idle talk; prattling; chatter.

Gabarage *n.* coarse packing cloth.

Gabardine *n.* a strong fabric used especially for making raincoats.

Gabble *v.t.* & *t.* to utter too fast; to talk inarticulately or too fast.

Gabelle *n.* a tax or duty.

Gabfest *n.* an informal meeting to talk and exchange news.

Gabion *n.* a cylindrical basket filled with earth used in fortification.

Gable *n.* the triangular end of a wall at the end of ridged roof.

Gaby *n.* a simpleton.

Gad *v.i.* to go about idly; to wander. *n.* the point of a spear; a goad.

Gadfly *n.* a fly that bites cattle; a worrying person, an irritating person.

Gadgetry *n.* a small tool or device that does something useful.

Gadling *n.* a loitering person.

Gaff *n.* a barbed fishing-spear.

Gaffer *n.* an old fellow; foreman of a gang; an old rustic.

Gag *v.t.* to stop mouth forcibly, to silence.

Gaga *adj.* slightly crazy because you are very excited about someone/something, or very much in love.

Gage *n.* something thrown down as a symbol to fight; pledge; security; a challenge.

Gaiety *n.* mirth; amusement; merry-making; finery.

Gaily *adv.* in a gav or lively manner.

Gain *v.t. & i.* to obtain; to acquire; to earn; to have as profit; to reach.

Gainable *adj.* able to be gained.

Gainer *n.* one who gains profit.

Gainsay *v.t.* to deny; to controvert; to contradict; to oppose in words.

Gait *n.* manner of walking; pace.

Gaiter *n.* covering of leather, etc. for leg or ankle.

Gala *n.* pomp; show; festive occasion.

Galanty-show *n.* pantomime on screen made by shadows of puppets.

Galatic *adj.* pertaining to milk or the Milky Way.

Galaxy *n.* a luminous land of small stars like a girdle; the Milky Way.

Gale *n.* strong wind; a storm; a gentle breeze.

Galea *n.* a structure like helmet in shape.

Gailmatias *n.* confused or meaningless talk; nonsense.

Galipot *n.* resin from hardened turpentine.

Gall *n.* a malignity; bile; blister; painful swelling; asperity; rancour.

Gallant *adj.* grand; fine; brave; showy; attentive to women.

Gallery *n.* a long and narrow passage, balcony with rails around it; corridor; room for showing works or art.

Galley *n.* a low flat one decked vessel *usu.* rowed; a light open boat. (Print.) an oblong tray in which types are transferred after composing.

Gallipot, Galipot *ns.* a small glazed cup for holding medicines; small vessel.

Gall-nut *n.* gall used in the making of ink.

Gallon *n.* a liquid measure of 3.8 litres.

Gallon *n.* a narrow woven braid or lace.

Gallop *n.* horse's swiftest pace.

Galloway *n.* a horse of small size; a small breed of horse.

Galop *n.* a lively dance.

Galore *adv.* in plenty. *n.* abundance.

Galosh *n.* shoe worn over another in rainy season.

Galvanic *adj.* pertaining to producing electricity; produced by galvanism.

Gam herd of whales; a tooth or tusk.

Gamble *v.i.* to play games of chance for money stake; to take great risks. *n.* a risky undertaking.

Gamboge *n.* a gum-resin yellow pigment.

Gambol *v.i.* to dance and skip about in sport. *n.* a leaping about in frolic; a caper.

Gambrel *n.* the angle above the hoof of a horse's hind leg.

Game *n.* jest; sport; diversion; a hunted animal. (*pl.*) tricks.

Gamma *n.* the third letter of the Greek alphabet.

Gammer *n.* an old woman

Gammon *n.* the thigh of hog; deception; ridiculous nonsense.

Gamut *n.* the whole series of musical notes; the hole scope of anything.

Gamy *adj.* abounding in or full of games.

Gander *n.* a male goose, a fool.

Gang *n.* a band of criminals; a number of labourers working together.

Ganger *n.* the foreman of a gang.

Ganging *n.* a method of completing two coils in a radio set so that both may be operated on one dial.

Ganglion *n.* a knot of nervous matter, centre of force or interest.

Gangrene *n.* mortification of part of body; decomposition of flesh.

Gangway *n.* the narrow passage on a ship; a narrow way between rows of seats.

Gannet *n.* a kind of sea-bird.

Gantry *n.* a fourfooted stand for barrels, railway signals etc.

Gaoler *n.* a warder in gaol.

Gap *n.* a gorge; a blank; a cleft; defect.

Gape *v.i.* to open mouth wide; to split; to stare at; to yawn, to split.

Garage *n.* place for storing motor cars.

Garb *n.* clothes, dress of nation or class; costume; fashion (of speech). *v.t.* to clothe; to dress.

Garble *v.t.* to pick up the best.

Garden *n.* a piece of ground for growing flowers, fruits or vegetable.

Garfish *n.* a fish with long spear-like snout and green bones.

Gargle *v.t.* & *i.* to wash throat with liquid. *n.* a liquid preparation for washing the mouth and throat.

Gargoyle *n.* a spout projecting from gutter to carry rain water.

Garibaldi *n.* a blouse; a kind of biscuit.

Garish *adj.* gandy; dazzling; showy.

Garland *n.* a wreath or chaplet of flowers; distinction; prize for victory; an anthology. *v.t.* to crown with a garland.

Garlic *n.* a plant with bulbous strong-smelling pungent root.

Garment *n.* an article of dress.

Garner *n.* a storehouse for corn; granary; a bin. *v.t.* to store in a granary.

Garnet *n.* a red mineral of which gems are made.

Garnish *v.t.* to decorate (*esp.* a dish of food); to embellish; to adorn.

Garret *n.* a room on the top floor. *v.t.* to insert small pieces of stone.

Garrison *n.* military force stationed in town or a fortified place.

Garron *n.* a small horse.

Garrot *n.* a kind of sea-duck.

Garrulity *n.* loquacity; talkativeness.

Garrulous *adj.* talkative; (of bird) chattering.

Garter *n.* a band to keep stocking up; highest order of kinghthood.

Garth *n.* a garden, yard.

Gas *n.* any aeriform or completely elastic fluid; coal gas used for light or heat.

Gasconade *n.* bragging; boasting.

Gaselier *n.* a gas lamp with several burners.

Gash *n.* a long deep cut or wound; a cleft. *v.t.* to make a deep cut.

Gasify *v.t.* to convert into gas.

Gasiform *adj.* of the form of gas.

Gasoline *n.* an inflammable liquid obtained by distilling petroleum.

Gasp *v.i.* to catch breath with open mouth. *n.* convulsed effort to catch breath.

Gate *n.* an opening of entrance or exit, mountain pass, passage, way, framework hung on hinges.

Gather *v.t.* & *i.* to bring together; to amass; to collect; to acquire; to deduce; to draw together; to pick up; to develop.

Gauche *adj.* lefthanded; awkward tactless; clumsy.

Gaud *n.* something showy, gaudy ornament. *adj.* showy, brilliant.

Gaudery *n.* ornaments.

Gaudy *adj.* gay, showy.

Gauge *n.* a standard of measure; capacity; extent; criterion; distance between rails.

Gaul *n.* the name of ancient France.

Gault *n.* clay and marl beds.

Gaunt *adj.* lean; thin; haggard.

Gauntlet *n.* armoured glove; glove with long loose wrist.

Gauze *n.* a thin fabric of silk, cotton, fine wire etc.

Gavel *n.* an auctioneer's hammer; a tribute or rent.

Gavial *n.* a kind of alligator found in the Ganga.

Gawk *n.* a awkward person; a fool.

Gay *adj.* sportive; lively; light-hearter; merry; showy; mirthful; brilliant; finely dressed.

Gaze *v.i.* to look fixedly at. *n.* an intent look; look of admiration.

Gazebo *n.* a structure from which the view of a distant object may be had.

Gazelle *n.* small graceful soft-eyed kinds of antelope.

Gazette *n.* a newspaper (*esp.* an official journal). *v.t.* to publish in an official gazette.

Gear *n.* equipment, appliances, tools etc. arrangement connecting a motor with its parts.

Gearing *n.* harness, a train of toothed wheels.

Gecko *n.* a house-lizard found in warm climates.

Gee *n.* a horse. *inter.* word of command to horse to go on, to move on, to get on well.

Geezer *n.* (*sl.*) an old person.

Gelatine *n.* a transparent animal substance obtained from skins, tendons etc.

Gelation *n.* making solid by freezing.

Geld *v.t.* to deprive of generative powers; to castrate.

Gelid *adj.* ice-cold; cool.

Gelignite *n.* a nitroglycerine explosive.

Gelsemium *n.* a kind of American jasmine.

Gem *n.* a precious stone; object of great worth. *v.t.* to adorn as with gems.

Geminate *v.t.* to double; to repeat; to arrange in pairs.

Gemini *n.* the third sign of the Zodiac; the twins.

Gemma *n.* a leaf-bud. *v.t.* to put forth buds.

Gemmy *adj.* full of gems.

Gender *n.* grammatical classification of sexes. *v.t.* to beget; to copulate.

Genealogy *n.* the account of descent from ancestors; pedigree; lineage.

General *adj.* widespread; relating to a whole class; usual; vague; lacking detail. *n.* chief, head, commander of an army.

Generally *adv.* in a general sense; in most respects; usually.

Generate *v.t.* to bring into existence; to beget; to produce.

Generation *n.* procreation; begetting; production; race; period of about 30 years.

Generator *adj.* he who or that which generates.

Generic *adj.* relating to a genus or class; general; not special.

Generous *adj.* noble-mindend; magnanimous; bestowing gifts; liberal.

Genesis *n.* the first book of the Old Testament, origin.

Genet *n.* a kind of civet cat; its fur.

Genetic *adj.* pertaining to the origin.

Genetics *n. pl.* the science of heredity.

Genial *adj.* kindly; cheering; jovial.

Genie *n.* a sprite or goblin of Arabian tales.

Genista *n.* kinds of yellow flowered shrub.

Geniculate *adj.* having joints like the knee.

Genital *adj.* pertaining to generation.

Genii *n. pl.* of Genius, evil spirits.

Genitive *adj.* indicating source, origin, or possession.

Genius *n.* great natural ability; mental endowments; a person having special intellectual powers.

Genius spirit; a demon.

Genteel *adj.* blonging to polite or well-bred persons; elegant.

Gentian *n.* kinds of *usu.* blue-flowered plant.

Gentility *.ı.* gentle birth; social superiority; upper-class habits.

Gentle *adj.* honourable, noble, courteous, mild, moderate.

Gentleman *n.* a man of good birth.

Gently *adv.* mildly; kindly; quietly; softly; slowly.

Gentry *n.* the class of people below the nobility and above the bulgar.

Genual *adj.* of the knee.

Genuflect *v.i.* to bend the knee in worship.

Genuflector *n.* one who bends the knee..

Genuine *adj.* pure-bred; not sham; real; authentic; unadulterated.

Genus *n.* a class of objects divided in to several subordinate species; (loosely) a kind or class.

Geocyclic *adj.* pertaining to the revolution of the earth.

Geode *n.* (a stone containing) cavity lined with crystals.

Geodesy *n.* study of the earth and its parts (a branch of mathematics).

Geognosy *n.* a study of the materials of the earth substance.

Geolatry *n.* earth worship.

Geology *n.* science of earth's crust, its strata and their relations.

Geomancer *n.* one who is versed in geomancy.

Geomancy *n.* divination by lines drawn on the earth.

Geometer *n.* a person skilled in geometry; a kind of caterpillar.

Geomtric, Geometrical *adjs.* pertaining to or according to geometry.

Geometry *n.* science of properties and relations of magnitudes in space.

Geonomy *n.* the science of the physical conditions of the earth.

Geoponic *adj.* pertaining to agriculture.

Georgette *n.* a thin silk dress material.

Geranium *n.* a kind of plant.

Germ *n.* rudimentary form of a living plant or animal; a plant ovary.

German *adj.* pertaining to Germany; its language or inhabitants.

Germicide *adj.* pertaining to the destruction of germs.

Germinate *v.i.* & *t.* to sprout, to shoot up; to develop.

Gerontocracy *n.* government by old men.

Gerrymander *v.t.* to manipulate constituency so as to give undue influence to some class.

Gerund *n.* English verbal noun in 'ing'. 'ing' **Gerundial,** *adj.* pertaining to or like a gerund.

Gesso *n.* plaster of Paris; gypsum, as used in painting and sculpture.

Gestation *n.* duration of pregnancy; carrying in the womb between conception and birth.

Gestic *adj.* legendary.

Gesticulate *v.i.* & *t.* to use expressive motion of limbs with or instead of speech.

Gestural *adj.* pertaining to gesture.

Gesture *n.* a motion of limb or body expressing sentiments.

Get *v.t.* & *i.* to gain possession of; to beget; to learn; to prevail to; to go; to arrive; to become.

Gewgaw *n.* gaudy play-thing or ornament; a trifle.

Geyser *n.* a hot spring; an apparatus for heating water.

Ghastly *adj.* horrible; death-like; pale; frightful.

Gherkin *n.* young or small cucumber for pickling.

Ghost *n.* an apparition; spectre; spirit; shadowy outline.

Giant *n.* a being of superhuman size, a very tall person or animal.

Gibber *v.i.* to chatter like an ape.

Gibbet *n.* a post on which an executed criminal was exposed.

Gibbous *adj.* convex; hunch-backed; protuberant.

Gibe *v.t.* & *i.* to flout; to jeer; to mock (at); a taunt. *n.* taunt; scoff.

Giblets *n. pl.* liver, gizzard, feet etc. of a bird removed before cooking.

Gibus *n.* opera or crush hat.

Giddy *adj.* frivolous; dizzy; inconstant, unsteady; circling with bewildering speed; mentally intoxicated.

Gift *n.* a present; talent; natural endowment; donation.

Gig *n.* a light two-wheeled one-horse carriage; a rowing-boat *esp.* for racing; a kind of fish-spear.

Gigantic *adj.* enormous; prodigious; mighty; huge; giant-like.

Giggle *v.t.* to laugh like a silly person; to have suppressed laughter.

Gill *n.* (*usu. pl.*) the respiratory organ of fish; a deep ravine; flesh below person's jaws and ears.

Gillaroo *n.* a kind of fish.

Gimbal *n.* (*pl.*) a contrivance *usu.* of rings and pivots for keeping things horizontal at sea.

Gimcrack *n.* a useless ornament; a toy.

Gimlet *n.* a small boring-tool.

Gin *n.* net; a snare; a trap; a machine separating cotton from seeds. *v.t.* to trap; to clear of seeds.

Gingall *n.* a kind of gun.

Ginger *n.* a plant with spicy hot root.

Gingerade *n.* an aerated drink with ginger taste.

Gingham *n.* a kind of cotton or linen cloth in stripes; an umbrella.

Gingival *adj.* pertaining to gums.

Ginglymus *n.* a hinge-like joint in the body.

Ginning *n.* the operation by which cotton is separated from its seeds.

Gipsy *n.* a member of a wandering race; a dark-complexioned woman.

Giraffe *n.* an African ruminant quadruped with spotted skin and long neck and legs.

Girandole *n.* a revolving fire-work, or jet of water.

Gird *v.t.* to bind with a belt; to fasten on; to equip; to encircle; to surround.

Girdle *n.* a belt; bony support; a ring round a tree. *v.t.* to bind with a girdle; to enclose.

Girl *n.* an unmarried woman; a maid-servant; daughter; a man's sweet-heart.

Girlish *adj.* like a girl.

Girt *n.* measurement across the surface.

Girth *n.* the band tightened round the body of a horse; measurement round a cylindrical object.

Gist *n.* the real point or ground; substance or pith of a matter.

Give *v.t. & i.* to estow; to hand over; to impart; to pay; to bequeath; to deliver; to entrust.

Gizzard *n.* the second stomach of birds and fish.

Glabrous *adj.* smooth skinned.

Glacial *adj.* of ice; icy.

Glacier *n.* a slowly moving river or mass of ice.

Glacis *n.* a bank sloping down from fort.

Glad *adj.* pleased; joyful; cheerful.

Gladden *v.t.* to make glad; to cheer.

Glade *n.* an open space between trees in a forest; a passage made through a wood.

Gladiate *adj.* of the form of a sword.

Gladiator *n.* a trained fighter in ancient Roman shows; political controversialist.

Gladly *adv.* with pleasure.

Gladsome *adj.* joyful; cheerful.

Glair *n.* the white of egg; mud, any viscous substance.

Glaive *n.* a broad sword.

Glamour *n.* magic; enchantment; delusive or alluring beauty.

Glance *v.t.* to pass quickly over; to flash; to gleam; to cast a momentary look at.

Gland *n.* organ that produces and secrets substance in the body.

Glanders *n. pl.* a contagious horse-disease.

Glandiform *adj.* of form of a gland.

Glandular *adj.* pertaining to glands.

Glare *n.* strong fierce light; brilliance.

Glary *adj.* dazzling; brilliant.

Glasnost a policy of freedom of information and publicly accountable government.

Glass *n.* a hard and brittle usually transparent substance; a vessel of glass; a mirror. *v.t.* to fit with glass; glaze.

Glassy *adj.* like glass; (of eye) dull; fixed.

Glaucoma *n.* an eye-disease.

Glaucous *adj.* of dull blue, covered with bloom as of grapes.

Glaze *v.t. & i.* to fit with a glass; to give a lustrous coating to; to cover with glossy substance or glaze.

Glazier *n.* one whose business is to glaze windows.

Gleam *n.* a small beam or glow of light; dim light; temporary show of some quality.

Gleamy *adj.* shedding beams of light.

Glean *v.t.* & *i.* to gather corn left by reapers; to pick up (facts, etc.) in small quantities. *n.* that which is gleaned.

Gleaner *n.* one who gathers.

Glebe *n.* earth; land; clod; land yielding revenue to a Parish church.

Glee *n.* mirth, cheerfulness, delight, song sung by three or more men.

Gleeful *adjs.* joyous; gay.

Gleet *n.* thin morbid discharge from wound.

Gleety *adj.* thin.

Glen *n.* a narrow valley.

Glenoid *adj.* pertaining to the small; cavity on bone receiving projection of other bone to form a joint.

Glib *adj.* fluent; slippery; voluble; smooth.

Glide *v.i.* & *t.* to pass by smooth continuous movement; to go stealthily.

Glider *n.* an engineless aeroplane; a fast boat used for hunting submarines.

Glim *n.* (*sl.*) a light; candle; lantern.

Glimmer *v.t.* to shine faintly.

Glimpse *n.* faint transient appearance; a sudden flash; brief view.

Glint *v.i.* & *t.* to flash; to sparkle; to reflect (light). *n.* a flash; glitter.

Glissade *v.i.* to slide on ice.

Glisten *v.i.* to shine; to glitter; to sparkle with light.

Glister *v.i.* glitter.

Gloaming *n.* twilight, especially of evening.

Gloat *v.i.* to look at with wicked gladness; to feast eyes or mind lustfully, greedily, malignantly etc. up, upon or over.

Globe *n.* a spherical solid body; spherical chart of the earth of the constellations, spherical lamp-shade.

Globoid *adj.* of the form of a globe.

Globular *adj.* globe shaped; composed of globules.

Globule *n.* a small globe; a pill.

Globulin *n.* protein found in blood; constituent of haemoglobin.

Glomerate *adj.* clustered compactly together.

Glomeration *n.* the act of gathering into a ball.

Glomerous *adj.* gathered into a round mass.

Gloom *n.* semidarkness; melancholy; depression; obscurity.

Glorify *v.t.* to honour; to praise; to extol; to invest with beauty.

Gloriole *n.* an aureole; a circle of light; a halo.

Glory *n.* renown; fame; pride; resplendent; beauty; splendour; magnificence. *v.i.* to take a pride.

Gloss *n.* glossary; a comment; a marginal explanation.
Glossary *n.* a dictionary of technical or special words.
Glossitis *n.* inflammation of the tongue.
Glossology *n.* terminology.
Glottis *n.* the opening at the upper part of wind-pipe.
Glove *n.* covering for the hand. *v.t.* to provide with gloves.
Glow *v.i.* to throw light and heat without a flame; to burn with bodily heat; to show warm colour. *n.* a shining heat; ardour of passion.
Glowing *adj.* shining with heat.
Glow-worm *n.* an insect female of which emits green light at tall.
Gloze *v.t.* & *i.* to flatter; to misinterpret; to palliate; to comment up upon. *n.* flattery.
Glucose *n.* grape-sugar.
Glue *n.* hard gelatin obtained from hides; and hoofs of animals.
Gluey *adj.* looking sullen or displeased.
Glum *adj.* dejected; sullen; looking displeased.
Glume *n.* husk of grain.
Glut *v.t.* to satiate; to overload the stomach with food; to swallow greedily; to fill to excess.
Glutton *n.* an excessive eater; a person with great appetite.
Gluttonish *adjs.* given to gluttony.
Glycerine *n.* colourless sweet liquid which is obtained from oils.
Glycogen *n.* a substance producing sugar in animal tissue.
Gnash *v.t.* to grind tooth together.
Gnarl *v.i.* to growl; to snarl.
Gnash *v.i.* to gring teeth together.
Gnat *n.* a small two-winged fly.
Gnaw *v.t.* to bite persistently; to corrode; to torture.
Gnawing *n.* chewing; biting.
Gnome *n.* a maxim; a dwarf; an aphorism; a diminutive spirit guarding treasures of earth.
Gnomic *adj.* pertaining to maxims; sententious.
Gnomon *n.* the rod or pin of sun-dial; (Geom.) the part of a parallelogram left when similar one has been taken off from its corner.
Gnosis *n.* knowledge of spiritual mysteries; gnosticism.
Go *v.t.* to walk; to move; to depart; to circulate; to advance; to pass; to travel; to proceed; to make regular journey.
Goad *n.* a pointed stick used for urging cattle; a stimulus; thing that incites or torments. *v.t.* to drive with a goad.
Goal *n.* a point where race ends, object of effort; aim; purpose; final end.
Goat *n.* a horned ruminant quadruped.
Goatee *n.* part of man's beard on the chin like goat's beard.

Goatsucker *n.* a nocturnal bird resembling swift; a nightjar.

Gob *n.* a clot of slimy matter spittle.

Gobbet *n.* a small piece. *v.t.* to swallow in bits; to divide in bits.

Gobble *v.t. & i.* to make gurgling sound in throat; to eat hurriedly with noise.

Goblet *n.* a bowl-shaped drinking-cup without handle.

Goblin *n.* a mischievous demon.

Goby *n.* kinds of small fish.

Go-cart *n.* a wheeled-appliance to teach babies to walk.

God *n.* a divinity; image possessing divine power; the Supreme Being.

Godown *n.* a warehouse or storeroom.

Godsend *n.* precious things.

Golden *adj.* made of or consisting of gold; shining like gold; valuable.

Goldfinch *n.* a song-bird with yellow on wings; gold coin; sovereign.

Goldsmith *n.* a worker in gold.

Golf *n.* a game played with small hard ball and clubs.

Golliwog *n.* a grotesque doll; a doll with black face and thick stiff hair.

Gondola *n.* a long narrow boat.

Gong *n.* a heavy metal disk giving resonant note when struck with a mallet.

Goniometer *n.* an instrument for measuring angles.

Gonorrhoea *n.* inflammatory discharge of mucus from urethra or vagina.

Good *adj.* having the right qualities, adequate; of an acceptable standard; worthy; right; excellent.

Goose *n.* a web-footed bird; female of this; its flesh; a simpleton; a silly creature; tailor's smoothing iron.

Gooseberry *n.* a thorny shrub; its edible berry; wine make of gooseberries.

Goosery *n.* a place for geese; stupidity.

Gopher *n.* kinds of squirrel; a kind of wood.

Gordian *adj.* intricate; difficult.

Gore *n.* thick or clotted blood; a triangular piece of cloth.

Gorge *n.* the internal part of throat; a narrow opening between hill.

Gorgeous *adj.* richly coloured; (of diction) splendid; magnificent; dazzling. *adv.* in a gorgeous manner.

Gorget *n.* a piece of armour for throat; a necklace.

Gorgon *n.* a fabulous snake-haired women, an ugly woman.

Gorilla *n.* A large powerful African ape.

Gorse *n.* a prickly yellow flowered shrub; furze.

Gory *adj.* covered with blood; of blood; blood-like.

Goshen *n.* place of light and plenty.

Gosling *n.* a young goose.

Gospel *n.* glad tidings; the teachings of Jesus Christ. *v.t.* to instruct.

Gossamer *n.* the web of a spider floating in the air; delicate gauze.

Gossip *n.* an idle or trifling talk; unconstrained talk. *v.i.* to talk idly; to chat.

Gossoon *n.* a lad.

Gotha *n.* a type of large German aeroplane.

Gotham *n.* a town of foolishness.

Gothamite *n.* a great fool.

Gothic *adj.* in the pointed-arch style; barbarous; (of type) German; black-letter. *n.* gothic language; type architecture.

Gouge *n.* a hollow bladed chisel used by carpenters.

Gourd *n.* a climbing plant with large fleshy fruit.

Gourmand *n.* a lover of delicacies. *adj.* gluttonous.

Gourmandism *n.* gluttony.

Gout *n.* a disease with inflammation of the smaller joints; swelling of the joints.

Gouty *adj.* disease or swollen with gout.

Govern *v.t.* & *i.* to rule with authority, to regulate; to determine.

Governance *n.* control; government.

Governess *n.* a female teacher; an instructress.

Government *n.* form of polity; the portion of a country ruled by a governor; control.

Gowk *n.* a half-witted person; a fool.

Gown *n.* a loose upper garment, a long robe; official uniform.

Gowned *adj.* dressed in a gown.

Grab *v.t.* & *i.* to seize suddenly; to appropriate greedily; to arrest; to capture; to make snatch at.

Grabble *v.i.* to grope about.

Grabby *n.* a soldier.

Grace *n.* beauty; mercy; divine influence; pardon; elegance of manners; favour; goodwill.

Gracious *adj.* friendly; agreeable; pleasing; kindly; merciful.

Gradate *v.t.* & *i.* to arrange in gradations.

Gradation *n.* progression; orderly arrangement; arrangement in grades.

Gradatory *adj.* proceeding step by step.

Grade *n.* a degree in rank; merit; group; order; relative position.

Gradient *n.* amount of inclination; a proportional rise and fall in thermometer or barometer in passing from one region to another.

Gradine *n.* a kind of toothed chisel used by sculptors; a rising tier of seats as in an amphitheatre.

Gradual *adj.* happening by degrees; progressive; not steep or abrupt.

Graduate *v.t.* & *i.* to take or admit to academic degree to arrange in gradations; to concentrate (solution) by evaporation.

Graduation *n.* a regular progression; state of receiving a degree.

Graffito *n.* a drawing made by scratching.

Graft *n.* a shoot inserted into the stock of another tree. *v.t.* to insert graft; to transplant living tissue.

Grail *n.* comb-maker's file.

Grain *n.* a fruit of a cereal; corn; a small minute particle.

Gram *n.* chick-pea; a unit of weight in metric system.

Gram *n.* anger; grief; trouble.

Grama *n.* a kind of low grass.

Gramarye *n.* witchcraft; necromancy.

Graminaceous *adj.* like grass; grassy.

Grammalogue *n.* (short hand) word represented by single sign; such sign.

Grammar *n.* branch of linguistics dealing with the form, function and order of the words.

Gramme *n.* a unit weight in metric system.

Gramophone *n.* a kind of phonograph reproducing sound from record disks.

Grampus *n.* sea mammal.

Granary *n.* a storehouse for thrashed grain.

Grand *adj.* of highest rank; of chief importance; imposing; lofty.

Grandee *n.* foreign noble of high rank, great personage.

Grandeur *n.* high rank; eminence; majesty; splendour.

Grandiloquent *adj.* speaking bombastically.

Grandiose *n.* imposing; splendid; bombastic; pompous; on a large scale.

Grange *n.* a country-house with farm buildings.

Granite *n.* a crystalline rock used for a building.

Granivorous *adj.* eating grains of corn.

Granny *n.* grand-mother; reef-knot crossed the wrong way.

Grant *v.t.* to allow; to bestow to admit as true; to consent to give; to concede; to allow; to permit; to admit as true.

Grantable *adj.* that may be granted.

Granular *adj.* of or like grains; with granulated surface.

Granule *n.* a small grain.

Grape *n.* the fruit growing on the vine.

Grapery *n.* vinery.

Graph *n.* symbolic diagram expressing mathematical or chemical connection. *suf.* in sense of "writer or written".

Graphite *n.* soft black form of carbon used in pencil leads.

Graphy *suf.* sense of "style of drawing or writing".

Grapnel *n.* a small anchor with several flukes.

Grapple *v.t. & i.* to take hold of (to seize); to fasten; to struggle. *n.* a close fight.

Grasp *v.t.* to try to seize; to hold; to comprehend. *n.* a grip of the hand; a hold; power of intellect.

Grass *n.* a common type of plant with jointed stems and long narrow leaves; herbage. *v.t.* to cover with grass.

Grasshopper *n.* a straight winged insect of the locust family.

Grassy *adj.* full of or covered with grass; green.

Grate *n.* a frame of metal bars for holding coal in a fireplace.

Gratify *v.t.* to please; to oblige; to delight; to bribe.

Grating *n.* a framework of parallel bars.

Gratis *adv.* given free of charge.

Gratitude *n.* being thankful for and ready to return kindness.

Gratuitous *adj.* given free; unwarranted; without motive.

Gratuity *n.* a free gift money present for services; a bounty to soldiers; tip.

Gravamen *n.* a grievance; essence of accusation.

Grave *n.* an excavation in which a corpse is laid. *v.t.* to engrave; to carve.

Gravely *adv.* seriously.

Gravel *n.* water-worn pebbles; a disease with urinary crystals.

Gravid *adj.* pregnant.

Graver *n.* an engraving instrument; burin; engraver.

Gravity *n.* solemnity; importance; serious demeanour; a body's attraction to the centre of the earth.

Gravy *n.* juice that comes out of flash during or after cooking for food.

Graze *v.t. & i.* to feed on growing grass; to pasture cattle; to touch lightly to abrade skin etc. in rubbing past.

Grease *n.* fat, oily matter. *v.t.* to lubricate; to bribe.

Great *adj.* large; big; many; much; important; pre-eminent; of great ability; hard; difficult; familiar.

Greatcoat *n.* an overcoat.

Greaves *n.* piece of armour for legs.

Grebe *n.* a diving bird; its plumage.

Grecian *adj.* pertaining to Greace.

Greed *n.* insatiate desire specially for wealth; avarice.

Greedy *adj.* gluttonous; ravenous; avaricious.

Greek *n.* a native of Greece; Greek language. *adj.* of Greece or its people.

Green *adj.* of the colour of grass; or sea water; unripe young and tender; fresh.

Greet *v.t.* to meet with expressions of welcome; to receive in a specified manner.

Gregarious *adj.* living in flocks or communities; growing in clusters; fond of company.

Gremial *n.* the silk apron of a bishop. *adj.* belonging to the lap.

Grenade *n.* a hollow shell filled with gunpowder thrown by hand or shot from a rifle.

Greves *n. pl.* armour for the legs.

Grey, Gray *adj.* coloured like ashes or lead; clouded; dull.

Greyhound *n.* a tall, very slender swift dog kept for the chase.

Grid *n.* a frame of bars; a grating.

Gridiron *n.* a frame of iron bars for broiling; a structure over stage.

Grief *n.* deep sorrow; regret; deep trouble.

Grievance *n.* cause of grief; ground of complaint; injury; hardship.

Grieve *v.t.* & *i.* to cause to feel grief; to be in pain; to mourn.

Grievous *adj.* exciting grief; injurious.

Griffin *n.* a fabulous creature half lion and half eagle; a new European in India; a kind of vulture, a coarse-haired dog.

Grig *n.* a small eel; a grass-hopper; a cricket.

Grill *v.t.* to broil on a gridiron; to torment. *n.* a gridiron.

Grilse *n.* a young salmon.

Grim *adj.* stern; severe; horrible; merciless; of harsh aspect.

Grimace *n.* disgust; an affected expression of the face. *v.t.* to make grimaces.

Grimalkin *n.* an old she-cat; a spiteful old woman.

Grime *n.* ingrained dirt or soot. *v.t.* to blacken; to soil with grime; to dirt.

Grin *v.i.* & *n.* to show teeth in pain or in smile affected laugh.

Grind *v.t.* & *i.* to crush to small particles; to sharpen; to harass with exactions.

Grinder *n.* one who or that which grinds.

Grip *n.* grasp; a firm hold; mastery; control of a subject.

Gripper *n.* that which grips.

Gripe *v.t.* to hold fast; to pinch; to grip; to grasp; to oppress.

Grippe *n.* influenza.

Grisly *adj.* causing terror; frightful.

Grist *n.* corn for grinding; malt crushed for brewing; size or thickness of yarn or rope; flexible tissue.

Grit *n.* small particles of dirt etc. which clog machinery; rough hard particles.

Gritty *adj.* consisting of small hard particles.

Groan *v.t.* & *i.* to make sound expressing grief of pain; to be oppressed, long for. *n.* a deep mournful sound.

Groat *n.* a silver coin worth four pence; small sum.

Grocer *n.* a shopkeeper selling foodstuffs; a dealer in spices, tea, sugar and domestic store.

Grog *n.* a drink of spirit and water.
Grogram *n.* coarse fabric of silk, mohair; often stiffened with gum.
Groin *n.* the part of the body between belly and thigh; edge formed by intersecting vault.
Groom *n.* a servant who takes care of horses a bridegroom.
Groove *n.* a long, narrow cut occurring in a surface by some means.
Grope *v.i.* to feel bout as in dark; to search blindly.
Grosheak *n.* kinds of small bird with a large strong beak.
Gross *adj.* vulgar; not refind; luxuriant; total, not net; dense; rude.
Grot *n.* a grotio.
Grotesque *n.* a style of decorative art; distorted figure.
Grotto *n.* a picturesque cave; a place of retreat; a structure imitating a cave.
Ground *n.* the surface of land; bottom of the sea; base.
Grounding *n.* drill in the elements of subject; a thorough preparatory instruction.
Groundling *n.* a dwarf plant or creeper.
Groundsel *n.* kinds of weed; the threshold.
Groundwork *n.* foundation; chief ingredient; fundamentals.
Group *n.* a number of persons or things belonging to a class; cluster; assembly; crowd.
Grout *n.* thin fluid mortar for filling joints of masonry and brick work.
Grove *n.* a small shady wood; a group of growing trees.
Grovel *v.t.* to lie prostrate; to humble oneself; to be low or mean.
Grow *v.t. & i.* to germinate; to vegetate; to increase; to advance.
Growable *adj.* that may be grown.
Grower *n.* one who grows fruit etc.; plant that grows in a specified way.
Growl *v.i.* to make a low rumbling sound.
Growth *n.* development; increase; what has grown.
Groyne *n.* a wall built out from the shore to control erosion.
Grub *n.* a caterpillar; food larva of an insect.
Grudge *v.t. & i.* to regard with envy and discontent; to murmur at.
Gruel *n.* liquid food as of oat etc.; severe punishment.
Gruesome *adj.* horrible; frightful.
Gruff *adj.* harsh; surly; laconic; rough-mannered; rough-voiced.
Grumble *v.t. & i.* to protest irritatingly; to growl.
Grume *n.* a clot of blood; viscous fluid.
Grumpy, Grumpish *adjs.* ill-tempered; of a surly temper.

Grunt *v.t.* & *i.* & *n.* to utter a harsh sound like hogs; to express discontent; such a sound.

Guana *n.* kind of large lizard.

Guano *n.* excrement of sea-fowl used as manure; artificial manure.

Guarantee *n.* one who gives security; thing given as security; recipient of guaranty.

Guard *n.* vigilant state; watch; a protector; a sentry; escort; (*pl.*) house-hold troops.

Guardian *n.* one who takes care or protects; a defender; custodian.

Guava *n.* a tropical tree and its fruit.

Gudgeon *n.* a kind of fresh-water fish; the pivot on which a wheel revolves; a person easily duped.

Guebre *n.* a fire-worshipper.

Guerdon *n.* reward; recompense.

Guernsey *n.* thick knitted woollen (*usu.* blue) outer tunic or jersey worn by sailors, workman, and children.

Guerilla, Guerrilla *ns.* an irregular war conducted by a small party of men.

Guess *v.t.* & *i.* to make an estimate without detail; to form a hypothesis.

Guesser *n.* one who guesses.

Guest *n.* one who entertained at another's house; a person lodging at a hotel or boarding-house.

Guff *n.* an empty talk.

Guffaw *n.* a crude and boisterous laugh.

Guidable *adj.* that may be guided.

Guidance *n.* direction; act of guiding.

Guide *n.* one who directs the way; a conductor, that which guides; an adviser; a book of information.

Guideless *adj.* destitute of a guide.

Guidon *n.* a small flag narrowing to point at free end.

Guile *n.* duplicity; cunning; artifice; deceit.

Guillemot *n.* a kind of sea-bird.

Guilloche *n.* an architectural ornament imitating braided ribbons.

Guileless *adj.* craftless.

Guillotine *n.* a machine for beheading. *v.t.* to behead with guillotine.

Guilt *n.* criminality; sin.

Guiltless *adj.* free from guilt; innocent.

Guilty *adj.* having committed a crime.

Guise *n.* appearance; style of dress; pretence.

Guitar *n.* a six-stringed musical instrument. *v.t.* to play on a guitar.

Gular *adj.* pertaining to the upper throat.

Gulch *n.* a ravine, *esp.* one with gold deposit.

Gulf *n.* a large deep bay; a deep hollow chasm; an impassable dividing line.

Gull *n.* dupe; fool; large long winged sea bird. *v.t.* to cheat; to deceive.

Gullet *n.* the throat; the passage for food from the mouth to the stomach.

Gully *n.* a ravine or channel worn by water; a gutter; a drain.

Gulosity *n.* greediness.

Gulp *v.t.* & *i.* to swallow hastily; to gasp; to choke.

Gum *n.* firm flesh in which the teeth stand.

Gum *n.* a sticky substance that comes out of certain trees, used for making glue; a tree that is a source of gum; the wood of such a tree.

Gumption *n.* informed courage; informal resourcefulness.

Gun *n.* the singal to begin a race; made by firing a starting pistol; member of shooting party.

Gunnel *n.* a small sea-fish.

Gunner *n.* a member of the armed forces trained to maintain and fire guns; game-shooter.

Gunning *n.* firing with guns.

Gunny *n.* sack, of jute fibre; coarse sacking.

Gunter *n.* (*Gunter's scale*) flat 2 ft. rule with scales etc. for solving problems in surveying.

Grugitation *n.* bubbling sound or motion.

Gurgle *v.i.* to make a bubbling sound as of water from a bottle.

Gush *n.* an amount of liquid suddenly flowing or pouring out of something.

Gusset *n.* a triangular piece of cloth set into a garment to strengthen or enlarge.

Gust *n.* a sudden violent rush of wind; a sudden strong expression of a feeling or an emotion; burst (of rain, smoke, anger, etc.)

Gusto *n.* special flavour; taste; zest; enjoyment.

Gut *n.* belly as seat of appetitie; material for fishing-lines (made from intestines of sild-worm).

Gutter *n.* a channel in a street carrying off water; a passage made from running water.

Guttle *v.t.* to eat gluttonously.

Guttural *adj.* deep and rough; (of a sound) being or seeming to be produced in the throat.

Gutty *n.* gutta-percha ball.

Guy *n.* a rope to hold a tent. *v.t.* to attach a tent by ropes.

Guzzle *v.t.* & *i.* to drink, eat, greedily.

Gym *n. esp.* at school; (*sl.*) physical exercises in a gymnasium; a gymnasium.

Gymkhana *n.* a place for display of athletic sports.

Gymnasium *n.* a place which is used for practising gymnastics.

Gymnical *adj.* pertaining to athletic exercises.

Gym-slip *n.* a dress without sleeves worn over a shirt as a school uniform for girls, especially in the past.

Gynaeceum *n.* a woman's apartment in a house.

Gynaechy *n.* government by a female.

Gynarchy *n.* government by a female.

Gyneolatry *n.* the worship of woman.

Gynethasia *n.* the offering of woman in sacrifice.

Gyp *v.t.* & *i.* to swindle; cheat. *n.* an act of cheating or swindling; a person who gyps.

Gypsy *n.* gipsy; a deceitful woman.

Gyrate *v.i.* to move in circle or spiral. *adj.* arranged in the form of rings.

Gyre *n.* a circular motion.

Gyrose *adj.* folded like waves.

Gyve *v.t.* to fetter; to shackle; to chain. *n.* a fetter.

H

H the eighth letter of the English alphabet.

Haberdasher *n.* a dealer in small articles of dress etc.

Habergeon *n.* sleeveless coat of male.

Habile *adj.* skilful.

Habilitate *v.t.* to furnish with capital; to equip; to qualify.

Habit *n.* fixed practice; mental or bodily constitution; mode of growth; dress; settled tendency. *v.t.* to clothe.

Habitat *n.* the natural home of a plant or animal. a place where something is commonly found.

Habitual *adj.* given to some habit; regular; usual.

Habituation *n.* the state of being habituated.

Habitue *n.* a habitual visitor or resident.

Hachures *n. pl.* lines used in hill-shading to indicate the slope.

Hacienda *n.* land/property given to someone by ruler.

Hack *n.* a wound; a cut or notch; horse which is let on hire; a tool of instrument for breaking or chopping.

Hackette *n.* female journalist.

Hackle *n.* a steel flax-comb; long feathers on the neck of a domestic cock; a finishing-fly dressed with hackle.

Haddock *n.* a fish allied to cod.

Hades *n.* abode of the dead.

Haemal *adj.* of the blood; situated on same side of body as the heart and blood-vessels.

Haematic *adj.* & *n.* of or containing blood; a medicine which acts on blood.

Haematite *n.* a red or brown iron ore.

Haemoglobin *n.* red substances found in the corpuscles of blood.

Haemorrhage *n.* the discharge of blood from blood-vessels.

Haft *n.* the handle of knife, dagger etc. *v.t.* to furnish with a handle.

Hag *n.* an ugly old woman; a witch; a malicious.

Haggle *v.t.* & *i.* to raise difficulties in bargaining; to mangle; to wrangle.

Hail *n.* salutation; a large number of things coming with force; frozen vapour falling down in pellets (*hail-stones*); a shower of missiles; curses etc.

Hair *n.* dry elastic filaments growing from the skin.

Hake *n.* a fish like the cod.

Halberd *n.* a kind of military weapon.

Halcyon *n.* a fabled bird which made its nest on sea; the kingfisher.

Hale *adj.* healthy; robust; vigorous.

Half *n.* a school-term; Half-back playing (at) left half; either two (*esp.* equal) parts into which a thing is divided. *adj.* amounting to half.

Halibut *n.* a large flat fish used for food.

Haliography *n.* a description of the sea.

Hall *n.* a building or large room for meeting; meals; concerts etc.

Hallo, Halloa *interjs.* calling attention or expressing surprise. *v.i.* to cry for attracting attention.

Hallow *v.t.* & *i.* to chase with shouts; to incite with shouts; to shout to incite dogs etc.

Hallucination *n.* an illusion; the apparent perception of an object not present; a mistake.

Halo *n.* a circle (round the sun, moon, etc.); disk of light round head of saint; ideal glory.

Halt *n.* temporary stoppage on journey. *v.t.* & *i.* to bring to a stand.

Halting *adj.* hesitating.

Halter *n.* a rope or strap which is used for tying horses or cattle or for hanging criminals.

Halve *v.t.* to reduce to a half; to share equally; to divide in halves.

Halyard *n.* a rope for raising or lowering sails.

Ham *n.* the back of thigh; the bend of the knee; an actor who overacts; an amateur.

Hames *n. pl.* two curved pieces of wood or metal in the harness of a draught horse.

Hamlet *n.* a small village.

Hammer *n.* a metal ball attached to a wire for throwing.

Hammock *n.* a hanging bed which is used in ships.

Hamper *v.t.* to obstruct movement of; to perplex; to impede; to hinder.

Hamshackle *v.t.* to fasten a cow or house by a rope joined to the head and forelegs.

Hamster *n.* an animal like a large mouse; kept as a pet.

Hamstring *n.* the tendon of the thigh.

Hand *n.* the extremity of human arm below the wrist; authority; side or post.

Handbag *n.* a small bag for money, keys etc. carried especially by a woman.

Handicraft *n.* work performed by the hand; manual art; trade or skill.

Handiwork *n.* work or thing done or made by the hands or by any one's personal agency.

Handkerchief *n.* a small piece of cloth or paper tissue for blowing the nose into wiping the face, etc.

Handle *n.* the part of a thing by which it is held; a fact that may be taken advantage of.

Handloom *n.* a loom worked by hand.

Handmaid *n.* a female servant.

Handpress *n.* a press worked by hand.

Handsaw *n.* a saw used with one hand.

Handsel *n.* earnest money; first instalment; a foretaste; a present of the new year.

Handsome *adj.* good looking; pretty; generous; considerable.

Handwriting *n.* way a person writes; the peculiar way of writing.

Handy *adj.* ready to the hand; convenient to handle; dexterous; near.

Hang *v.t.* & *i.* to droop; to hover; to rest upon.

Hangar *n.* a shed for housing aeroplane.

Hangman *n.* a public executioner.

Hank *n.* a circular loop or coil of thread.

Hanker *v.i.* to long for; to desire earnestly; to crave after.

Hap *n.* a chance; luck; lot; accident; occurrence. *v.i.* to happen; to befall by chance.

Haphazard *n.* accident; mere chance; random. *adj.* without order or plan.

Haply *adv.* perhaps; by chance.

Happen *v.i.* to fall out; to take place; to do or be something as a result of chance.

Happy *adj.* lucky; fortunate; content; glad; blessed; felicitous.

Harangue *n.* speech to assembly; vehement address. *v.t.* & *i.* to address in a vehement manner.

Harass *v.t.* to trouble; to worry; to attack repeatedly.

Harbour *n.* a place of shelter for ships; a lodging; a shelter.

Hard *adj.* firm, solid, difficult, laborious, harsh, not easily understood.

Harden *v.t.* & *i.* to make or grow hard; to become hard; callous or robust.

Hardihood *n.* audacity; boldness.

Hardly *adv.* with difficulty; severely; rigorously; scarcely.

Hardship *n.* oppression; affliction; injustice; severe suffering or privation.

Hardy *adj.* bold; resolute; robust; capable of resisting exposure.

Hare *n.* a small timid rodent with long ears, short tail and divided upper lip.

Harem *n.* the apartment in a dwelling house which is allotted to women.

Haricot *n.* ragout *usu.* of mutton.

Hark *v.i.* (as call to hounds) go (forward) into; to listen (to); to lend the ear; to hear to. *inter.* listen.

Harl(e) *n.* the fibre of flax or hemp.

Harlequin *n.* stock comic character; a breed of spotted dogs; a buffoon.

Harlot *n.* a prostitute.

Harm *n.* & *v.t.* damage; injury; moral wrong doing.

Harmonic *n.* of, in, harmony. *adj.* harmonious; concordant.

Harmonium *n.* a keyboard instrument with metal reeds.

Harmony *n.* agreement, sweet or melodious sound; peace; concord.

Harness *n.* equipment of a horse or other animal.

Harp *n.* stringed musical instrument.

Harpoon *n.* a spear to strike whales, used for catching whales.

Harpsichord *n.* a stringed instrument with a key-board.

Harpy *n.* a rapacious person; a rapacious monster.

Harquebus *n.* an old type of portable gun.

Harridan *n.* a haggard old vixen.

Harrier *n.* a hound for hunting hares; a kind of hawk.

Harrow *n.* an instrument for breaking clods on ploughed land.

Harry *v.t.* to harass; to plunder; to spoil (land, people).

Harsh *adj.* rough; severe; cruel; austere; peevish.

Hart *n.* the male of deer.

Harum-scarum *adj.* & *n.* reckless; unsteady; rash.

Harvest *n.* the conequences of an action; a season's yield; (a season for) reaping and storing of grain etc.

Hash *v.t.* to cut in small pieces.

Hasp *n.* part of a fastening for a door, box, etc. *v.t.* to fasten with a hasp.

Haste *n.* urgency of movement; hurry; rapidity; rashness. *v.t.* to hasten.

Hasten *v.t.* & *i.* to make or cause to make haste; to accelerate.

Hat *n.* a covering for the head. *v.t.* to put hat on.

Hatch *v.t.* & *i.* to bring or come forth from egg.

Hatchet *n.* a short-handled light axe.

Hate *v.t.* to dislike strongly; to detest; to loathe; to bear malice to.

Hauberk *n.* (hist). coat of mail.

Haugh *n.* a piece of flat alluvial land by river.

Haul *v.t.* & *i.* to turn a ship's course; (of wind) to shift; to pull or drag forcibly.

Hauler *n.* one who hauls.

Haulm *n.* stalks of beans; peas.

Haunch *n.* part of the body between ribs and thigh.

Haunt *v.t.* & *i.* to frequent company of (a person); to visit frequently, to stay habitually.

Hauteur *n.* haughtiness of manner.

Have *v.t.* to hold in possession; to contain; to permit; to know; to be obliged.

Haven *n.* a port of harbour; a place of safety.

Haversack *n.* a soldier's canvas bag for provisions.

Having *n.* property; belongings.

Havoc *n.* devastation; waste.

Haw-Haw *inter.* & *n.* & *v.i.* a boisterous laugh.

Hawk *n.* a rapacious person; a bird of prey used in falconry.

Hawse *n.* a hawse-hole; situation of the cables when a vessel is moored with two anchors.

Hawser *n.* a thick rope or steel cable used on a ship.

Hawthorn *n.* a throny shrub bearing haws.

Hay *n.* grass cut and dried for use as animal food.

Hazard *n.* a game at dice with complicated chances; risk; chance.

Haze *n.* fog; mistiness; dimness; mental obscurity. *v.t.* make hazy.

Haze *v.t.* to make somebody nervous or worried by playing tricks on them or giving them unpleasant tasks to do.

Hazel *n.* a bush with fruit; its wood; stick; reddish brown colour.

Hazy *n.* vague; misty; indistinct; slightly drunk.

He *pron.* the male person or animal in question; third person singular.

Head *n.* that part of the body which contains the brain.

Headache *n.* pain in the head.

Header *n.* a plunge into water head first.

Headland *n.* a strip of land left unploughed at the en l of field.

Headlong *adv.* precipitately; rashly; with the head foremost.

Headpiece *n.* an ornamental engraving at the head of chapter etc.

Headquarters *n. pl.* centre of operations; commander in-chief's residence.

Headstrong *adj.* self-willed; obstinate.

Headway *n.* progress; motion.

Headwork *n.* metal or intellectual labour.

Heady *adj.* intoxicating; rash; impetuous.

Heal *v.t.* & *i.* to restore to health, to become sound; to cure; to reconcile.

Health *n.* a sound state of mind; soundness of body; condition of body.

Heap *n.* group or mass of things lying one on another; a pile; a large number of amount.

Hear *v.t.* & *i.* to listen or pay attention to somebody; to perceive with ear.

Hearken *v.i.* to listen to; to hark.

Hearsay *n.* a gossip; a report; a rumour.

Hearse *n.* a car for conveying the dead to the grave; a bier.

Heart *n.* the hollow organ in one's chest that pumps blook through the body; soul; mind; courage.

Hearth *n.* floor of fireplace.

Heartly *adj.* in hearty manner; genial.

Hearty *adj.* genial; vigorous sincere; (*esp.* or older people) strong and healthy.

Heat *n.* energy; hotness; inflamed state of body; anger; warmth of feeling.

Heath *n.* a waste of land which is covered with shrubs; kinds of shrub.

Heathen *n.* a pagan; an unenlightened person; a barbarous person.

Heather *n.* kinds of shrub; a heath.

Heave *v.t.* & *i.* to lift; to throw; to rise; to sigh; to pant.

Heaven *n.* the sky; the abode of God and his angels; place of bliss.

Heavily *adv.* sorrowfully; dejectedly; weightily; with pounderousness.

Heavy *adj.* weighty; ponderous; of great specific gravity; abundant; striking.

Hebe *n.* the goddess of youth; a waitress.

Hebetate *v.t.* & *i.* to make or become dull.

Hebraic *adj.* pertaining to a Jew.

Hebrew *n.* the language of the ancient Hebrews.

Hecatomb *n.* a great public sacrifice.

Heck *n.* (used to express mild annoyance or surprise or for emphasis) hell.

Heckle *v.t.* to interrupt a public speaker with questions, taunts and comments.

Hectare *n.* measurement equal to 10,000 square metres (2.471 acres).

Hectic *adj.* consumptive; wild; morbidly flushed; exciting.

Hecto *pref.* in the sense of 'hundred'.

Hector *n.* a bully; a blustering fellow.

Heddles *n. pl.* small cords or wires through which the warp is passed in a loom before going through the reed.

Hedge *n.* a row of bushes or small trees planted close together and forming a boundary for a field, garden, etc.

Hedge-born *adj.* of low birth.

Hedgehog *n.* a small animal with stift spines covering its back.

Hedonic *adj.* pertaining to pleasure.

Hedonism *n.* the doctrine that pleasure is the chief good.

Heed *v.t.* to attend to; to take notice of. *n.* careful attention.

Heedless *adj.* inattentive; thoughless; negligent.

Heehaw *n.* to bray like an ass.

Heel *n.* the hinder part of human foot; a hinder part of hoof, spur.

Heft *n.* the handle of a tool.

Hegomonic *adj.* ruling; supreme.

Heifer *n.* a young cow that has not had a calf.

Heigh *int.* an expression of encouragement or inquiry.

Height *n.* elevation above ground or sea level; the main point or highest degree of something.

Heighten *v.t.* & *i.* to rise; to make or raise higher; to intensity.

Heinous *adj.* atrocious; hateful; extremely wicked.

Heir *n.* a person who inherits a successor; one to whom something is due.

Helicon *n.* the mountain sacred to Muses; the source of poetic inspiration.

Helicopter *n.* a flying machine that should rise vertically by airscrews.

Helio *pref.* in the sense of 'concentric', 'with the sun as centre'.

Heliosis *n.* exposure to the sun.

Heliotrope a kind of flower.

Helium *n.* a transparent gas first inferred in sun's atmosphere.

Helix *n.* a spiral form or structure; the external part of the ear; a snail-shell.

Hell *n.* a state of misery; a gamin-house.

Hellebore *n.* kinds of plant.

Hellene *n.* a native of ancient or modern Greece.

Helm *n.* the wheel by which a rudder is manipulated; cloud over mountain during storm.

Helmet *n.* the upper part of retort; a defensive head-cover.

Helminth *n.* worm.

Helot *n.* a serf of ancient Sparta.

Help *v.t.* to assit; to aid; to remedy; to avoid; to prevent.

Helpful *adj.* useful; that gives assistance; serviceable.

Helpless *adj.* wanting help.

Helpmate *n.* a wife; a helpful companion.

Helter-skelter *adv.* in disordered haste; in a hurry.

Helve *n.* handle of a cutting tool.

Hem *n.* the border of a garment turned down and sewed; a border; margin.

Hemi *pref.* (in composition) half.

Hemicrania *n.* headache confined to one part of the head.

Hemiopia *n.* blindness of half of the vision.

Hemiplegia *n.* paralysis of one side of the face or body.

Hemisphere *n.* half of the globe; half the celestial sphere; half the earth.

Hemistich *n.* a verse not completed; half line of a verse.

Hemlock *n.* a poisonous plant used as sedative; poison got from this.

Hemp *n.* a plant whose fibres are used for rope-making. *n.* narcotic like bhang, hashish, ganja.

Hem-stitch *n.* & *v.t.* a kind of ornamental stich.

Hen *n.* female of birds of the common domestic fowl; any female bird.

Henbane *n.* narcotic and poisonous drug; a poisonous plant.

Hence *adv.* from here; from this time; therefore.

Hendecagon *n.* a plane figure of eleven angles or sides.

Henpecked *adj.* domineered over by one's wife; governed by one's wife.

Hepta *pref.* in comb., meaning 'seven'.

Heptad *n.* a set or group of seven.

Heptarchy *n.* a government by seven rulers.

Her *pron.* objective or possessive case of 'She'.

Herald *n.* state-officer who makes proclamations and bears messages; a proclaimer.

Herb *n.* a plant whose leaves or seeds, etc. are used to give flavour to food or for their scent or in medicines.

Herbage *n.* herbs; pasturage; green food for beasts.

Herbal *adj.* pertaining to herbs.

Herculean *adj.* very hard to perform; of extraordinary strength.

Hercules *n.* a Greek hero famous for his strength; a strong man.

Herd *n.* a company of animals, *esp.* cattle, feeding or travelling together.

Here *adv.* in this place, in this life; now; in this matter; at this point.

Heretofore *adv.* formerly.

Hereditable *adj.* that can be inherited.

Hereditary *adj.* of inheritance; descending by inheritance; transmitted from one generation to another.

Heresy *n.* an opinion contrary to an accepted doctrine.

Heretic *n.* a person who holds an unorthodox opinion.

Heritage *n.* that which is inherited; one's portion or lot; what is or may be inherited.

Heritor *n.* one who inherits.

Hermaphrodite *n.* a human being, animal, or plant with characteristics of both sexes.

Hermes *n.* a messenger of the gods; god of science; eloquence.

Hermit *n.* a person who has withdrawn from society and lives completely alone.

Hermitage *n.* hermit's abode; a solitary abode.

Hernia *n.* a rupture, *esp.* of the abdomen.

Hero *n.* a man of superhuman power; a man admired for great or noble deeds; a very brave man; chief person in a play.

Heroic *adj.* (of poetry) dealing with heroes; worthy of; having qualities of; a hero; bold.

Heroine *n.* principal female actor; chief woman in a poem.

Heron, Hern *ns.* a long-legged wading bird.

Herpes *n.* a disease of the skin characterised by patches; netlerash.

Herring *n.* a small sea fish much used for food.

Hesitate *v.i.* to speak or act with indecision; to waver; to be doubtful.

Hesitator *n.* one who hesitates.

Hesperian *adj.* (poet.) western.

Hesperus *n.* the evening star.

Hessian *n.* a strong coarse cloth of hemp or jute.

Hest *n.* (*arch.*) behest.

Hetaera, Hetaira *ns.* a courtesan; a harlot.

Hetero *pref.* in the sense of other; different.

Heterodox *adj.* not orthodox; contrary to established opinions.

Heterodyne *n.* the pulsation due to simultaneous sounding of waves that are nearly of same length.

Heterogeneous *adj.* composed of diverse elements; diverse in kind or race.

Heterosexual *n.* a person who is sexually attracted to members of opposite sex.

Heuristic *adj.* serving to discover.

Hew *v.t.* & *i.* to cut or chop with an axe or sword; to cut coal from seam.

Hexa *pref.* in the sense of 'six'.

Hex-, Hexa- in comb., six. **Hexad,** *n.* a set or group of six.

Hexahedron a figure having six faces.

Hexagon *n.* a plain figure having six angles and six sides.

Hexameter *n.* a verse which consists of six metrical feet.

Hiatus *n.* a break in continuity; an opening; a gap or chasm; a break between two vowels.

Hibernate *v.t.* to pass the winter in torpor or (of person) in mild climate.

Hibernian *adj.* & *n.* or Ireland; Irish (man).

Hiccup *n.* spasm of respiratory organs.

Hick *n.* a farmer; countryman.

Hide *n.* animal's skin, raw or dressed.

Hide *v.t. & i.* to keep out of sight; to keep secret; to conceal oneself.

Hideous *adj.* horrible; repulsive; frightful; revolting.

Hie *v.i.* to go quickly; to hasten.

Hiemal *adj.* wintry; pertaining to winter.

Hierarch *n.* the chief priest; a ruler in holy matters; an archbishop.

Hierarchy *n.* priestly government.

Hieroglyph *n.* the sacred characters of the ancient Egyptian language.

Higgle *v.i.* to be tedious and nice in bargaining; to dispute about terms to chaffer.

Higgledy-piggledy *n.* an utter confusion.

High *adj.* powerful; strong; intense; lofty; tall; loud; deer in price; honourable; elevated in rank; arrogant.

Highly *adv.* greatly; in a high or great degree; at a high rate.

High-school *n.* the chief public school in a town providing secondary education.

Highway *n.* a public road; main road; main route.

Hilarious *adj.* merry; cheerful; mirthful.

Hilarity *n.* mirthfulness; merriment.

Hill *n.* heap of earth; an elevation of the earth's surface; a small mountain.

Hillock *n.* a small hill; a mound.

Hilt *n.* the handle of a sword or dragger.

Him *pron.* objective case; subjective case of He.

Hindrance *n.* obstruction.

Hing *n.* the drug asafoetida.

Hinge *n.* a movable joint of a door; a natural joint doing similar work; a main principle.

Hip *n.* projection of pelvis and upper part of thigh-bone; the thigh joint.

Hippiatric *adj.* pertaining to the treatment of the diseases of horses.

Hippocampus *n.* kinds of small fish; a sea-horse.

Hippocras *n.* spiced wine.

Hippodrome *n.* a course for chariot races etc.; a circus.

Hippogriff *n.* a fabulous griffin-like creature with horse's body.

Hippopotamus *n.* African riverhorse.

Hircine *adj.* goat-like.

Hire *n.* payment for use of a thing; wages.

Hireling *n.* one engaged on hire; mercenary person.

Hirsute *adj.* hairy; rough with hair; shaggy.

His *pron.* possessive of He.

Hispid *adj.* shaggy; bristly.

Hisk *v.t.* to breathe with difficulty.

Hiss *n.* a sharp hissing sound.

Hist *inter.* demanding silence and attention.

Histo *n.* in comb. web, tissue.

Histogram *n.* a figure that represents a frequency distribution.

Historian *n.* writer of history.

Historic *adj.* history.

Historical *adj.* based on history; happening in the past.

History *n.* a methodical record of public events; past events; narration of facts; study of these; an eventful career.

Histrion *n.* a stage-player.

Histrionic *adj.* (of behaviour) very dramatic and intended to attract attention; of acting or the theatre.

Hit *v.t. & i.* to strike; to deliver a blow at; to find; to affect sensible; to suit, to arrive at; to fall in with.

Hitch *v.t. & i.* to move with a jerk; to fasten with loop; to shift.

Hive *n.* the habitation of bees.

Hoar *adj.* grey-haired; white with age; hoariness.

Hoarfrost *n.* white frost; white particles of frozen dew.

Hoard *n.* a store; a treasure; a stock. *v.t. & i.* to keep in hoard; to treasure up; to amass.

Hoarse *adj.* husky; rough; having a hoarse voice.

Hoax *v.t.* to deceive by way of joke; to play a trick upon.

Hob *n.* a projection on the side of a fire-place; a rustic; a peg; the hub of a wheel.

Hobble *v.t. & i.* to walk limpingly; to proceed haltingly; to tie the legs of animals so that they may not run away.

Hobby *n.* a small horse; a favourite activity that a person does for pleasure and not as her or his regular business; a small falcon.

Hobgoblin *n.* an elf; a bogy.

Hobnail *n.* large-headed nail for boot soles; short nail with a heavy head.

Hobo *n.* a wandering workman or tramp.

Hockey *n.* a game with ball and curved sticks between goals.

Hocus *v.t.* to haox; to stupefy a man with drug.

Hocus-pocus *n.* a deception; jugglery; trickery used by conjurers.

Hod *n.* a trough for carrying mortar, bricks etc.

Hodden *n.* a coarse woollen cloth.

Hodge *n.* an English farm-labourer.

Hodge-podge *n.* hotch-potch; a confused mass.

Hodman *n.* a man who carries a hod.

Hodometer *n.* an instrument for measuring distance travelled by a wheeled vehicle.

Hoe *n.* a garden tool with a long handle and a blade.

Hog *n.* a swine; a castrated boar; young sheep before first shearing; a greedy person.

Hoggish *adj.* like a hog; filthy.

Hoiden *n.* a rude bold girl.

Hoist *v.t.* to lift; to raise aloft to raise with a tackle.

Hold *v.t. & i.* to defend something against an attacking force; to possess; to restrain;to contain.

Holder *n.* a tenant; one who holds anything.

Holding *n.* tenure of land; land or stocks.

Holdback *n.* hindrance; check.

Holdfast *n.* a contrivance of securing nail, etc.

Hole *n.* a hollow place; an excavation, animal's burrow.

Holiday *n.* a day of cessation from work or of recreation; (*pl.*) vacation.

Holily *adv.* in a holy manner.

Holiness *n.* freedom from sin; sanctity.

Hollow *adj.* excavated; vacant; empty; false; unreal; having a hole. *n.* hole; a hollow place; a void.

Holly *n.* an evergreen shrub with red berries.

Hollyhock *n.* a tall plant with large showy flowers.

Holm *n.* an islet in a river.

Holo *n.* in comb., Gk. *holos,* whole.

Holocaust *n.* a wholly burnt sacrifice.

Holster *n.* a leather case for pistol fixed to a saddle.

Holt *n.* a wood; wooded hill.

Holy *adj.* a high moral or spiritual excellence; regarded as sacred.

Holystone *n.* a sandstone for scouring decks. *v.t.*

Hom *n.* an inlet in a river.

Homage *n.* acknowledgment of allegiance; tribute paid to a person or merit; dutiful reverence.

Home *n.* a place where one lives, *esp.* with one's family; a house, flat, etc.

Homely *adj.* plain; unpretending; not beautiful primitive.

Homeopath *n.* one who practises homeopathy.

Homeopathy *n.* Hahnemann's system of curing diseases by minute doses of drugs.

Homeward *adj.* & *adv.* towards home or one's native land.

Homicide *n.* one who kills a human being; the killing of one person by another.

Homing *adj.* that goes home; (of pigeons) trained to fly milk.

Homo *n.* a man.

Homo *pref.* in the sense of; the same; common.

Homonym *n.* a ward of the same form as another but of different sense.

Homophobia *n.* fear of homosexuals.

Homosexual *n.* sexually attracted to member of the same sex.

Hone *n.* whetstone.

Honest *adj.* telling the truth; good, worth; showing or resulting from an honest mind or attitude.

Honesty *n.* truthfulness; uprightness; a kind of plant with purple flowers.

Honey *n.* sweet fluid collected from flowers by bees.

Honeymoon *n.* a month's holiday spent by newly married couple after marriage.

Honeysuckle *n.* name of sweet scented flower of clover.

Hong *n.* (in China) a set of buildings used as a factory; foreign trading establishment.

Honk *n.* wild goose's cry, sound of a motor horn.

Honorarium *n.* the fee paid for professional services.

Honorary *adj.* conferred by way of honour; given as an honour.

Honorific *adj.* implying or conferring respect.

Honour *n.* high respect; dignity; high reputation chastity; good name.

Hood *n.* covering for the head and neck; a badge worn over the gown to show university degree.

Hoodlum *n.* gangster; lawless youth; a street rowdy.

Hoof *n.* the horny part of beast's foot.

Hook *n.* bent piece of metal; bent wire used for catching fish; a snare; a trap.

Hooker *n.* kinds of small sailing-ships.

Hooligan *n.* one of a gang of street roughs.

Hoop *n.* a large ring used at a circus for riders or animals to jump through or as a chil's toy.

Hoop *v.t.* to utter a hooping sound. *n.*

Hoot *v.t.* & *i.* to make a loud sound especially in contempt; to drive away by hooting.

Hoover *n.* vacuum cleaner.

Hop *n.* a kind of perennial creeper; hopping; jump; dance.

Hope *n.* a desire combined with expectation; anticipation; probability.

Hopper *n.* an inverted pyramid or cone; a hopping-insect; a device for filing grain into mill.

Hopple *v.t.* to fasten together legs of (a horse etc.).

Horde *v.t.* a band of nomads; a gang; troop; multitude.

Horizon *n.* the line at which the earth and the sky appear to meet; a boundary of mental outlook.

Hormone *n.* a chemical secretion from certain glands of the body.

Horn *n.* hard and pointed excrescence on the head of cattle.

Hornblende *n.* a mineral of various colours found in granite.

Horner *n.* one who deals in horns.

Hornet *n.* a large species of wasp.

Hornpipe *n.* an old wind instrument; a lively dance, *esp.* of sailors.

Horny *adj.* like a horn; hard as horn; callous.

Horologe *n.* a time-piece; a clock; a dial.

Horology *n.* the art of making clocks.

Horoscope *n.* configuration of the heavens at certain moment, *esp.* at one's birth.

Horrent *adj.* bristling.

Horrible *adj.* fit to excite horror; hideous; shocking; unpleasant.

Horrid *adj.* frightful; horrible; terrible; unpleasing.

Horrific *adj.* causing horror.

Horror *n.* shuddering; a dreadful shivering, terror, intense dislike or fear.

Horse *n.* a large animal with four long legs, a mane and a tail.

Hortative *adj.* serving to exhort; advisory.

Horticulture *n.* the art of gardening; the art of cultivating gardens.

Hose *n.* a flexible tube made of rubber, plasic or canvas used for directing water into fires, gardens etc.

Hosier *n.* one who deals in hosiery.

Hospice *n.* a traveller's house of rest kept by religious order.

Hospital *n.* an institution for care of the sick and wounded.

Host *n.* a large of people or thing.

Hostage *n.* a person or thing given as a pledge; a pledge; security.

Hostel *n.* a house or residence for students; a lodging house.

Hostile *adj.* opposed; inimical; adverse; unfriendly.

Hostility *n.* enmity; warfare.

Hostler *n.* one who takes care of horses at an inn.

Hot *adj.* intense and exciting, and involving a lot of activity, argument or strong feeling.

Hotchkiss *n.* a kind of machine-gun.

Hotchpotch *n.* a confused mass of ingredients mixed together; jumble; medlay.

Hotel *n.* a large inn; a house for travellers.

Hottentot *n.* a member of a South Africa race; a person of inferior intellect or culture.

Hough *n.* the joint on the hind-leg of a quadruped between the knee and fetlock.

Hound *n.* a dog for the chase.

Hour *n.* duration of 60 minutes or twenty-fourth part of day; an occasion.

Houri *n.* a nymph of Mohammedan paradise.

Hourly *adv.* every hour.

House *n.* a building for habitation or for some specified purpose; a family.

Housewife *n.* the mistress of a house; domestic manager.

Hovel *n.* a small house that is not fit to live in, *esp.* because it is dirty, damp, etc.

Hover *v.i.* to hang in the air; to loiter about. *n.* a walk.

How *adv.* in what manner or way; by what means; to what extent?

Howbeit *adv.* nevertheless.

Howitzer *n.* a short gun firing shells at high elevation.

Howl *v.t.* & *i.* to roar; to utter loud doleful cry; to cry like a dog or wolf.

Howling *n.* a roaring cry.

Hoy *n.* a small coasting vessel, carrying passengers and goods. *inter.* ho!

Hoya *n.* a genus of climbing flower plants.

Hub *n.* central part of a wheel, from which spokes radiate.

Huckle *n.* the hip; the haunch.

Huckster *n.* a pedlar or hawker; a mercenary person.

Huddle *v.t.* & *i.* to curl one's body up into a small space; to crowd together, *esp.* in a small space and often because of cold or fear.

Hue *n.* colour; tint; a variety of colour caused by admixture of another.

Huff *v.t.* & *i.* to bully; to storm at; to offend; to take offence. *n.* anger.

Huffish *adj.* petulant.

Hug *v.t.* to embrace closely; to delight in; to hold fast; to keep close to the shore; to cling to.

Huge *adj.* very large; immense; enormous.

Hugeous *adj.* huge; enormous.

Hulk *n.* a very large and often threatening object.

Hull *n.* the outer covering of a fruit; the frame of a ship.

Hullabaloo *n.* an uproar.

Hum *v.i.* & *t.* to smell unpleasantly; to make a buzzing sound like bee or top.

Hum *n.* a sham; hoax.

Human *adj.* having the qualities of a man; belonging to the human race.

Humble *adj.* of lowly condition; modest; meek; submissive; having or showing low estimate of one's importance.

Humdrum *adj.* & *n.* dull; trite; commonplace; a stupid fellow.

Humeral *adj.* of the shoulder.

Humerus *n.* the bone of the upper arm in man; similar bone in other vertebrates.

Humid *adj.* damp; moist.

Humidity *n.* moisture.

Humming *n.* murmuring.

Humoral *adj.* pertaining to humours.

Humorist *n.* a facetious talker.

Humorous *adj.* full of humour; funny; adapted to excite laughter.

Humour *n.* a turn of mind; inclination; wit; facetiousness; comically; jocose imagination; (Med.) fluid of the body.

Hump *n.* the protuberance on the back of an animal; hunch.

Humph *int.* denoting doubt or dissatisfaction.

Humpy *n.* a kind of Australian hut.

Humus *n.* rick dark material formed by the decay of dead leaves, etc. that makes the soil more fertile.

Hunch *n.* hump; a thick piece; suspicion. *v.t.* to bend; to form a hump.

Hunchbacked *adj.* having a humpback.

Hunger *n.* an uneasy sensation caused by want of food; an earnest desire.

Hungry *adj.* showing hunger; inducing hunger; lean; greedy.

Hunk *n.* a clumsy piece. *pl.* a miser.

Hunt *v.t.* & *i.* to pursue wild animals for food or sport.

Hunter *n.* one who hunts; a horse for hunting; a watch with cover protecting glass.

Hurdle *n.* wooden sticks woven together for temporary frame.

Hurl *v.t.* to throw (a missile etc.); to shout something forcefully; to throw violently from some position.

Hurricane *n.* a cyclone; a violent storm

Hurry *n.* eager; haste; the need or wish to get something done quickly.

Hurt *v.t.* & *i.* to damage; to give pain; to distress; to injure. *n.* a wound; an injury; harm; wrong.

Hurtle *v.t.* & *i.* to move rapidly or violently; to strike against; to hurl swiftly.

Husband *n.* a man married to a woman; a man to whom a woman is betrothed.

Husbandman *n.* a farmer.

Husbandry *n.* agriculture; farming; domestic economy; thrift.

Hush *n.* silence; stillness. *v.t.* to calm; to silence.

Hussar *n.* a soldier of light cavalry.

Hustings *n.* a platform for the nomination of candidates; election proceedings.

Hustle *v.t.* & *i.* to push roughly; to jostle; to bustle; to hurry.

Hut *n.* a small mean house; a small simply built house or shelter; usually made of wood, mud or metal.

Hutch *n.* an enclosure for rabbits; a small house.

Huzza *inter.* expressing joy or applause.

Hyacinth *n.* a precious stone; a bulbous plant with a bell-shaped flower.

Hyades *n. pl.* the group of stars near Pleiades.

Hyaena *n.* a carnivorous animal.

Hyaline *adj.* glassy, transparent, vitreous.

Hyalite *n.* a colourless variety of opal.

Hybrid *n.* & *adj.* an offspring of two different species or varieties, heterogeneous.

Hydatid *n.* a watery cyst sometimes found in animal bodies.

Hydra *n.* a serpent with many heads; a water-snake.

Hydrangea *n.* kinds of flowering shrub with globular clusters of flowers.

Hydrant *n.* a waterpipe (*esp.* in a street) with nozzle for hose.

Hydraulic *adj.* worked by the pressure of water. *n. pl.* the science of conveyance of liquids, *esp.* of water.

Hydric *adj. chem.* of, containing hydrogen.

Hydro *n. pref.* for 'water'.

Hydro *n.* hotel, inn where hydropathy is available.

Hydrogen *n.* the lightest colourless gas.

Hyena, Hyaena *ns.* a carnivorous quadruped allied to dog; a cruel, treacherous or rapacious person.

Hygeia *n.* health personified; principles of health; goddress of health.

Hygiene *n.* the science of health; sanitary science.

Hygrometer *n.* an instrument for measuring humidity of air or gas.

Hygroscope *n.* an instrument for showing humidity of air.

Hymen *n.* the god of marriage, represented as young man carrying a torch and whale.

Hymen *n.* (Anat.) virginal membrane often found at the orifice of the vagina.

Hymn *n.* a song of praise to God. *v.t.* & *i.* to praise or sing hymns.

Hyper *pref.* in sense of over, above, excessive.

Hyperbola *n.* one of the conic sections.

Hyperbole *n.* an exaggerated statement; a figure of speech much beyond truth.

Hyperborean *adj.* & *n.* of the extreme north of the earth or of a country, an inhabitant of this.

Hypercritic *n.* an overcritical person.

Hypertrophy *n.* enlargement of an organ due to excessive nutrition.

Hyperemesis *n.* too much vomiting.

Hypertrophy *n.* morbid enlargement of an organ.

Hyphen *n.* a short line (-) used to join two words together, as in ex-officer, or to show that a word has been divided between the end of one line and the beginning of the next.

Hypnosis *n.* hypnotic state; artificially produced sleep.

Hypocaust *n.* the hollow space under floor for heating a house or bath from furnace.

Hypochondria *n.* state of causeless depression; a kind of nervous malady.

Hypocrisy *n.* a false pretension; concealment of true character; dissimulation; pretence.

Hypocrite *n.* a pretender; a dissembler.

Hypodermic *adj. Anat.* lying under the skin; introduced beneath the skin.

Hypostasis *n.* excess of blood in the organs of body.

Hypostrophe *n.* a relapse of illness.

Hypotenuse *n.* the side of a right angled triangle opposite the right angle.

Hypotension *n.* abnormally low blood pressure.

Hypothecator *n.* one who pledgs.

Hypothesis *n.* assumption; supposition made as basis for reasoning.

Hypothesize *v.i.* to form assumptions.

Hyson *n.* kind of Chinese green tea.

Hyssop *n.* an aromatic herb formerly used medicinally.

Hysterectomy *n.* a medical operation to remove a woman's womb.

Hysteria *n.* a nervous disorder characterized by anesthesia; a convulsion.

Hysterics *n. pl.* fit of hysteria.

Hysterotomy *n.* the operation of cutting into the uterus.

Hz-hertz unit of frequency.

I

I the ninth letter of the English alphabet.

Ibex *n.* a wild goat of Alps.

Ibid *adj.* in the same book or place, chapter etc.

Ibidem *adv.* (abbr. *ib., ibid*) in the same book, chapter, etc.; in the same place.

Ibis *n.* a bird like stork.

Ice *n.* frozen water, (*pl.*) frozen confection; ice-cream; water-ice.

Iceberg *n.* a vast mass of floating ice in the ocean.

Icicle *n.* a pointed piece of ice that is formed when water piece as it falls down from something such as a roof.

Ichneumon *n.* a small quadruped allied to mongoose.

I'chor *n.* watery discharge from wound.

Icicle *n.* a tapering mass of ice.

Icily *adv.* said of done in a very unfriendly way.

Icon *n.* a painting, carving etc. usually on wood, of a holy person; an image, a statue.

Iconoclasm *n.* breaking of images.

Iconoclast *n.* a breaker or destroyer of images; one who assails cherished belief.

Icosahedron *n.* a solid of twenty faces.

Ictus *n.* metrical stress.

Icy *adj.* abounding or covered wiht ice, very cold.

Ide *n.* a kind of fish.

Idea *n.* a plan; aim; a notion conceived by the mind; conception.

Ideal *adj.* mental; phenomenal; visionary. *n.* a perfect type.

Ideate *v.t. & i.* to imagine; to form ideas.

Idem *n.* (*abbr. id*) in the same.

Identic *adv.* simultaneous and uniformly worded.

Identify *v.t.* to treat a thing or ideas identical.

Identity *n.* sameness; equality; individuality.

Ideograph *n.* a symbol for an idea.

Ideology *n.* manner of thinking of a person; speculation that is imaginary.

Idiocy *n.* perfect imbecility; madness.

Idiom *n.* a specific form of expression of a language.

Idiot *n.* one who is deficient in intellect; a perfect fool; one void of understanding.

Idle *adj.* worthless; indolent; unoccupied; purposeless; useless; trifling; lazy.

Idol *n.* an image of a diety used for worship; an object of devotion; false mental conception.

Idolum *v.t.* mental image; an idea; fallacy.

If *conj.* whether; supposing that; on condition that.

Igloo *n.* dome-shaped hut of an Eskimo.

Igneous *adj.* of fire; fiery; pertaining to or containing fire.

Ignite *v.t. & i.* to make extremely hot; to set fire to; to take fire; to heat to the point of combustion.

Ignoble *adj.* base; of low birth or position; worthless; mean.

Ignominy *n.* public disgrace; dishonour; infamous conduct.

Ignoramus *n.* an ignorant person.

Ignorance *n.* a lack of knowledge or information about something.

Ignore *v.t.* to pay no attention to somebody; to refuse to take notice of; to shut the eyes; to reject.

Iguana *n.* a kind of lizard.

Ill *adj.* evil; harmful; morally bad; out of health, sick; (*arch.*) difficult; faulty; deficient; in an unkind or critical way.

Illation *n.* inference; deduction; conclusion; the thing deduced.

Illative *adj.* that may be inferred; inferential.

Illegal *adj.* contrary to law.

Illegitimacy *n.* the state of being a bastard.

Illegitimate *adj. & n.* not legitimate; unlawful; bastard; born out of wedlock; abnormal.

Illiberal *adj.* vulgar; stingy; narrow-minded; sordid.

Illicit *adj.* unlawful; forbidden.

Illimitable *adj.* infinite; boundless.

Illiteracy *n.* want of learning.

Illiterate *adj. & n.* not learned; not educated.

Illness *n.* a disease; sickness.
Illogical *adj.* contrary to the principle of logic; contrary to sound reasoning.
Illude *v.t.* to deceive; to play artifice upon.
Illume *v.t.* to make bright.
Illumine *v.t.* to enlighten intellectually; (poet.) to light up.
Illusion *n.* a thing that person wrongly believes to exist; a false appearance.
Illusinist *n.* one who does believe in objective existence; a conjurer.
Illusive *adj.* deceiving by false show; fallacious.
Illusory *adj.* illusive; deceptive.
Illustrate *v.t.* to explain; to make clear by examples.
Illustration *n.* elucidation; explanation; a picture designed to explain.
Illustrious *adj.* very well-known; admired and respected; distinguished by the reputation of greatness.
Image *n.* likeness; an immitation; form; semblance; idea. *v.t.* to portray; to reflect; to imagine; to describe vividly.
Imagine *v.t.* to concieve; to form mental image of; to suppose; to think; to fancy.
Imago *n.* the last or perfect state of insect's life.
Imbibe *v.t.* to inhale; to drink something especially alcohol; to absorb something.
Imbricate *v.t.* & *i.* to arrange in heaps, so as to overlap like tiles.
Imbroglio *n.* confused heap or mass; complicated situation.
Imbrue *v.t.* to stain; to wet.
Imbue *v.t.* to dye (with); to fill or inspire somebody with feelings; opinions or qualities.
Imitable *adj.* worthy of imitation.
Imitate *v.t.* to follow the example of; to copy; to mimic.
Immaculate *adj.* pure; faultless; unstained; without blemish; spotless.
Immanent *adj.* inherent (*in*); (of God) pervading the universe.
Immature *adj.* not mature or ripe; premature; not perfect.
Immeasurable *adj.* that cannot be measured.
Immediate *adj.* not separated by an intermediary, direct, promixate.
Immemorial *adj.* beyond memory; very old; of unknown duration.
Immense *adj.* vast, huge; (*sl.*) very good; extremely large or great.
Immensity *n.* the extent that cannot be measured; infinity; vastness.
Immerse *v.t.* to plunge into liquid; to put under water; to involve deeply.
Immersion *n.* the act of immersing.
Immethodical *adj.* without method; irregular.
Immigrate *v.t.* & *i.* to go (or send) to another country as settler.

Imminence *n.* proximity; being imminent; nearness.

Imminent *adj.* (of danger, etc.) about to happen soon; impending.

Immisible *adj.* which cannot be mixed.

Immitigable *adj.* not to be mitigated.

Immixture *n.* mixing up; purity; being involved (in).

Immobile *adj.* immovable; fixed; not mobile; motionless.

Immoderate *adj.* excessive; exorbitant; wanting in moderation.

Immodest *adj.* indecent; shameless; unchaste; obscene; indelicate.

Immolate *v.t.* to sacrifice; to kill in a sacrifice.

Immoral *adj.* dissolute; licentious; contrary to morality; wicked; unjust.

Immovable *n.* & *adj.* incapable of being moved; motionless.

Immune *adj.* & *n.* the system in the body which produces substances to help it to resist disease.

Immunize *v.t.* to render free.

Immure *v.t.* to confine; to enclose within walls; to imprison; to shut up.

Immutable *adj.* unchangeable, not variable.

Imp *n.* a little devil; a mischievous child; a child.

Impact *n.* collision; striking.

Impaction *n.* collision.

Impair *v.t.* to damage; to make worse; to deteriorate; to weaken; to injure.

Impale *v.t.* to put to death by spitting on stakes; to enclose with sailings.

Impalpable *adj.* not to be perceived by touch.

Impanel *v.t.* to enter in a list or on a piece of parchment called a panel.

Imparity *n.* inequality; disproportion.

Impark *v.t.* to enclose in a park; to enclose (land) for a park.

Impart *v.t.* to give a share of; to communicate to.

Impasse *n.* a blind alley; deadlock; a difficult situation; fix.

Impassive *adj.* without feeling; serene; not subject to suffering.

Impaste *v.t.* to make into a paste; to paint with thick colours.

Impatience *n.* want or lack of patience.

Impawn *v.t.* to deposit as a security; to pledge.

Impayable *adj.* not to be paid for going beyond limits.

Impeach *v.t.* to accuse; to find fault with; to call; to account.

Impecunious *adj.* having no money; poor.

Impedance *n.* (Elect.) obstruction in the free flow of.

Impede *v.t.* to retard; to obstruct.

Impediment *n.* hindrance; obstruction.

Impel *v.t.* to drive to do; to force forward; to incite; to instigate.

Impellent *adj.* having the quality of impelling.

Impend *v.t.* to hang or be suspended; to be imminent; to threaten.

Impendent *adj.* imminent; near at hand.

Impending *adj.* threatening.

Impenetrable *adj.* that cannot be entered.

Impenetrate *v.t.* to penetrate deeply.

Impenitent *adj.* not sorry for one's sin; obdurate.

Imperative *adj.* expressing command; authoritative; obligatory; necessary; urgent.

Imperator *n.* commander; an emperor.

Imperceptible *adj.* not perceptible; very slight; subtle.

Impercipient *adj.* lacking perception.

Imperfect *adj.* incomplete; faulty; defective.

Imperforate *adj. Anat.* lacking the normal opening; not perforated.

Imperial *adj.* pertaining to an empire or emperor; supreme; majestic.

Imperialism *n.* imperial rule, its principle & support.

Imperil *v.t.* to put in danger; to endanger.

Imperious *adj.* overbearing; imperative.

Imperishable *adj.* that cannot perish; indestructible.

Imperium *n.* absolute power; empire.

Impermanence *n.* want of permanence.

Impermanent *adj.* not permanent.

Impermeable *adj.* impenetrable.

Impermissible *adj.* not permissible.

Impersonal *adj.* having no personality or personal reference.

Impersonate *v.t.* to pretend to be another person.

Impersonative *adj.* pertaining to personating.

Impertinence *n.* rudeness; impertinent action; incivility.

Impertinent *adj.* insolent; rude; out of place; irrelevant; intrusive; absurd.

Imperturbable *adj.* the quality of being undisturbed; calm.

Impervious *adj.* not allowing water, gas, etc. to pass through; unpassable; not at all affected or influenced by something.

Impetigo *n.* a pustular disease of the skin.

Impetrate *v.t.* to obtain by request; to ask for.

Impetuous *adj.* vehement, furious; moving violently or fast; rash.

Impetus *n.* driving or moving force; momentum; impulse.

Impi *n.* a body of kafir warriors.

Impiety *n.* lack of piety.

Impinge *v.i.* & *t.* to strike or fall against; to make thing dash against.

Impious *adj.* not pious; wicked; profane.

Impish *adj.* of or like an imp.

Impiteous *adj.* pitiless.

Implacable *adj.* not appeasable; inexorable.

Implacental *adj.* with no placenta.

Implant *v.t.* to insert; to ingrant; to fix; to plant ideas in the mind; to instil.

Impledge *v.t.* to put in pledge; to pawn.

Implement *n.* a tool; an articel of dress or furniture; a piece of equipment.

Impletion *n.* the act of filling; fullness.

Implicit *adj.* implied; resting on another's authority; unquestioning.

Implore *v.t.* to beg earnestly; to entreat.

Imply *v.t.* to involve the truth of; to mean; to hint; to signify.

Impolicy *n.* a bad policy.

Impolite *adj.* in a rude manner.

Impone *v.t.* to stake; to impose.

Import *v.t.* to bring from a foreign country; to indicate; to signify.

Importance *n.* weight; significance; dignity.

Important *adj.* of great value or concern; serious; (of a person) having great influence or authority.

Importune *v.t.* to solicit pressingly and repeatedly.

Impose *v.t.* & *i.* to lay on; to exert influence.

Impossible *adj.* not possible; very difficult to endure or deal with.

Impost *n.* a tax; duty; a tribute; the upper course of a pillar.

Imposture *n.* a fraud practised by an impostor; deception; sham.

Impotent *adj.* (of men) unable to have full sex or reach an orgasm; unable to take effective action; helpless; powerless.

Impound *v.t.* to shut up to; take legal possession of; to confiscate.

Impoverish *v.t.* to make poor; to exhaust resources.

Impracticable *adj.* impossible in practice; unmanageable; (of roads) impassable.

Imprecate *v.t.* to invoke a curse or some evil upon.

Impregnable *adj.* impossible to enter or capture because of being strongly built.

Impregnate *v.t.* to make pregnant; to fill; to fecundate.

Impresario *n.* an organizer of public entertainment.

Impress *n.* a seal; a stamp. *v.t.* to imprint; to stamp; to mark; to influence.

Impressive *adj.* capable of making an impression on the mind; able to excite deep feeling.

Imprest *n.* money advanced to a person to be used in State business. *v.t.* to pay in instalment in advance.

Imprimatur *n.* an official license to print a book; a sanction.

Imprimis *adv.* in the first place.

Imprint *v.t.* to impress a mark on; to fix on the mind or memory. *n.* an impression; a stamp; a printer or publisher's name and address on a book.

Imprison *v.t.* to confine; to put into prison; to shut up; to incarcenate.

Improbable *adj.* not likely to be true; incredible.

Improbity *n.* wickedness; dishonesty.

Impromptu *adj.* & *adv.* performed without rehearsal or preparation.

Improper *adj.* inaccurate; wrong; not suitable; indecent.

Impropriate *v.t.* to annex (ecclesiastical benefice) to a corporation or person, as property.

Improvable *adj.* that can be improved; adapted for cultivation.

Improve *v.t.* & *i.* to make good use of (occasion, opportunity); to make or become better.

Improver *n.* one who improves anything; a learner in a trade.

Improvisation *n.* the act of improvising; that which is improvised.

Improvise *v.t.* to utter extempore; to bring about on a sudden; to do anything off-hand.

Imprudent *adj.* incautious; inconsiderate; indiscreet.

Impudent *adj.* bold-faced; shameless; pert; insolent; impertinent.

Impugn *v.t.* to contradict; to assail by word; to call in question.

Impuissant *adj.* impotent; weak.

Impulse *n.* a force suddenly communicated; incitement; influence.

Impulsion *n.* impelling; push; mental impulse; an impetus.

Impulsive *adj.* having power to impel; actuated by impulse.

Impunity *n.* exemption from loss or punishment.

Impure *adj.* dirty; unchaste; defiled; adulterated.

Imputable *adj.* that may be imputed.

Impute *v.t.* to set to the account of; to attribute to; to ascribe.

In *prep.* within; inside of; into; during.

Inability *n.* lack of power; skill or ability; the state of being unable to do something.

Inaccessible *adj.* not to be reached; not obtainable; unapproachable.

Inaccurate *adj.* not accurate; erroneous; untrue.

Inaction *n.* want to action; sluggishness; idleness; inertness.

Inactive *adj.* inert; not active.

Inadequate *adj.* the quality of being inadequate; insufficiency.

Inadhesive *adj.* not sticking or adhesive.

Inadmissible *adj.* that cannot be admitted or allowed; not proper.

Inadvertent *adj.* inattentive, unintentional, heedless.

Inaffable *adj.* reserved; not social.

Inalienable *adj.* not transferable.

Inalterable *adj.* that cannot be changed.

Inane *adj.* empty; void; silly; senseless.

Inanimate *adj.* without life; lifeless; dull.

Inanition *n.* emptiness; exhaustion from want of food.

Inappeallable *adj.* not to be appealed against; unsuitable.

Inappeasable *adj.* that cannot be satisfied.

Inapposite *adj.* in an inappropriate manner; not pertinent; out of place.

Inappreciable *adj.* not appreciable; not worth reckoning; that cannot be appreciated.

Inappropriate *adj.* not suitable.

Inapt *adj.* unskilful; unfit.

Inaptitude, Inaptness *ns.* inappropriateness; lack of skill; want of fitness or desire.

Inaptly *adj.* unfitly.

Inarch *v.t.* to ingraft.

Inarm *v.t.* to embrace.

Inarticulate *adj.* not spoken distinctly; not articulate; indistinct; dumb.

Inartificial *n.* artless; simple; natural.

Inartistic *adj.* unskilled in art; contrary to art.

Inattention *n.* want of attention; heedlessness; negligence.

Inaudible *adj.* not audible; that cannot be heard.

Inaugural *adj.* pertaining to inauguration; introductory.

Inaugurate *v.t.* to admit to office with ceremony; to commence formally; to expose; to view; to open.

Inauspicious *adj.* having signs which show that future success is unlikely; not favourable; ill-omened; not of good omen.

Inboard *adv.* on the deck or board; near the centre of a ship.

Inborn, Inbred *adjs.* inherent by nature; produced within.

Inbreathe *v.t.* to inhale.

Inbred *adj.* innate; natural.

Incamera *n.* in judge's private room; not in the open court.

Incandesce *v.t.* & *i.* to glow or cause to glow, with heat.

Incandescent *adj.* glowing or luminous with heat.

Incantation *n.* magic spell; charm; enchantment.

Incapable *adj.* not capable (of); unable to comprehend.

Incapacitate *v.t.* to make incapable or unfit (*for*).

Incapacity *n.* inability; incompetency; legal disqualification.

Incarcerate *v.t.* to imprison; to confine.

Incarnadine *adj.* to invest with a human farm; (poet.) crimson.

Incarnate *adj.* embodied in the humna form. *v.t.* to put into concrete form; to embody in flesh.

Incautious *adj.* rash; heedless; indiscreet.

Incavate *v.t.* to hollow out.

Incendiarism *n.* practices of maliciously setting fire to houses.

Incendiary *adj.* of or guilty of the malicious setting on fire of property; inflammatory.

Incense *v.t.* to enrage; to make somebody very angry. *n.* the gum; giving sweet smell when burned; praise; flattery.

Incentive *adj.* a thing that encourages somebody to do something; inciting; encouraging; stirring up.

Incessant *adj.* uninterrupted; continual; repeated.

Incest *n.* sexual intercourse with near relatives.

Inch *n.* the twelfth part of a foot; a small degree; a small amount; (*pl.*) stature.

Inchoate *v.t.* to begin; to originate.

Incidence *n.* the direction in which a ray falls on any surface; event; extent.

Incident *adj.* apt to occur; naturally attaching to; falling upon.

Incinerate *v.t.* to consume by fire; to burn to ahes.

Incipient *adj.* beginning; in an initial stage.

Incise *v.t.* to scribe; to engrave.

Incision *n.* a cut; a gash; a notch.

Incisive *adj.* having power of cutting; penetrating; mentally sharp.

Incisor *n.* a front tooth.

Incite *v.t.* to create or cause something.

Incivility *n.* rudeness; want of courtesy.

Incivism *n.* want of good citizenship.

In-clearing *n.* the cheques etc. collectively payable by a bank and received through a clearing house for being settled.

Inclemency *adj.* harshness.

Inclement *adj.* severe; tempestuous; cold or stormy.

Inclinable *adj.* favourable (*to*); that may be inclined; somewhat disposed.

Incline *v.t.* & *i.* to lean; to cause to lean; to bend forward or downward; to be disposed. *n.* an inclined plane; a slope.

Inclinometer *n.* an instrument for determining magnetic inclination.

Include *v.t.* to comprise; to contain; to comprehend; to treat; to regard.

Inclusion *n.* the act of including.

Inclusive *adj.* including; comprising.

Incoginant *adj.* thoughtless.

Incognito *adj.* & *adv.* under a false name; concealed; in disguise.

Incoherent *adj.* inconsistent; inconsequential; unconnected.

Incombustible *adj.* that cannot be consumed by fire.

Income *n.* periodical profits from business; land's revenue.

Incomer *n.* an immigrant; an intruder; a successor.

Incoming *n.* (*pl.* **Incomings**) entrance; arrival; (*pl.*) revenue; income.

Incommensurable *adj.* having no common measure.

Incommode *v.t.* to trouble; to annoy; to hinder.

Incommodious *adj.* not commodious; inconvenient; unsuitable.

Incommunicable *adj.* that cannot be told.

Incommunicative *adj.* not communicative.

Incommutable *adj.* unchangeable; not commutable.

Incompact *adj.* not compact; not solid.

Incomparable *adj.* excellent; matchless.

Incompatible *adj.* incongruous, inconsistent; discordant.

Incompetent *adj.* incapable; wanting adequate power; inability; not legally qualified.

Incomplete *adj.* not complete; not having all its parts; unfinished condition.

Incomprehensible *adj.* not able to be understood; inconceivable; boundless.

Incomprehension *n.* failure to understand.

Incompressible *adj.* that cannot be compressed.

Incomputable *adj.* that cannot be computed or calculated.

Inconceivable *adj.* unthinkable; that cannot be imagined; very remarkable.

Inconclusive *adj.* not conclusive or convincing.

Inconcocted *adj.* not fully digested; not matured; raw.

Incondensable *adj.* that cannot be condensed; not condensable.

Incondite *adj.* badly constructed; unpolished; crude.

Incongruity *n.* disagreement of parts; inconsistency; absurdity.

Incongruous *adj.* inconsistent; out of keeping; absurd.

Inconsecutive *adj.* wanting in sequence; irrelevant.

Inconsequent *adj.* without regular inference; irrelevant; disconnected.

Inconsiderable *adj.* small in size or value; not worth considering.

Inconsiderate *adj.* imprudent; indiscreet; careless; thoughtless; rash.

Inconsistent *adj.* not in harmony with something; containing parts that do not agree with one another.

Inconsolable *adj.* that cannot be consoled or comforted.

Inconsonant *adj.* not harmonizing; disagreeing; discordant.

Inconspicuous *adj.* not noticeable; not conspicuous; scarcely discernible.

Inconstant *adj.* fickle; changeable; variable; irregular.

Inconsumable *adj.* not meant to be consumed in use; that cannot be consumed by fire etc.

Incontaminate *adj.* flawless; pure.

Incontestable *n.* past dispute.

Incontinence *n.* lack of self-restraint; indulgence of just.

Incontinent *adj.* unable to control that bladder or bowels in passing waste matter from the body; wanting in self-restraining; unchaste.

Incontrovertible *adj.* not to be disputed.

Inconvenience *n.* want of convenience; annoyance.

Inconvenient *adj.* inopportune; troublesome.

Inconvertible *adj.* not to be converted.

Inconvincible *adj.* that cannot be convinced.

Incoordination *n.* want of coordination.

Incorporate *v.t.* & *i.* to form into a body; to unite; to combine into one substance. *adj.* united in corporation.

Incorporeal *adj. Law.* existing only in contemplation of law; not composed of matter; of immaterial beings.

Incorrect *adj.* inaccurate; erroneous; faulty.

Incorrigible *adj.* beyond correction; bad; beyond reform.

Incorrupt *adj.* pure; untainted.

Incrassate *adj.* of thick or swollen form.

Increase *v.t.* & *i.* to become greater; to grow; to advance; to make greater or numerous; to intensify.

Incredible *adj.* difficult to believe; that cannot be believed; surprising.

Incredulity *n.* scepticism.

Incredulous *adj.* unbelievable; sceptical.

Increment *n.* an increase; profit.

Incrust *v.t.* to cover with a hard crust; to form a crust.

Incubate *v.t.* & *i.* to hatch eggs; to develop to brood.

Incubator *n.* an apparatus like a box in which small weak babies are cared for.

Incubus *n.* an evil spirit visiting sleeping persons; a nightmare.

Inculcate *v.t.* to impress or inforce; to urge on the mind.

Inculpable *adj.* without blame; faultless.

Inculpate *v.t.* to blame; to censure; to accuse; to involve in a charge.

Inculpatory *adj.* censuring; blaming.

Incult *adj*. unpolished; rude; untilled; coarse.

Incumbent *n*. the holder of a benefice.

Incumbency *n*. the holding of an office or tenure.

Incombent *n*. the holder of a benefice. *adj*. (with on) lying or resting on.

Incur *v.t.* to cause oneself to suffer something bad.

Incurable *adj*. that cannot be cured; irrecoverable.

Incuriosity *n*. want of curiosity.

Incurious *adj*. wanting in curiosity; heedless; uninteresting; careless.

Incursion *n*. an invasion; a sudden attack.

Incurve *v.t.* to bend into a curve; to curve inwards.

Incus *n*. the bone of ear receiving vibration from malleus.

Incuse *adj*. stamped in. *v.t.* mark (a coin) with a figure by stamping.

Indebted *adj*. owing money to; under obligation.

Indecent *adj*. unbecoming; obscene; immodest.

Indecipherable *adj*. that cannot be deciphered.

Indecision *n*. hesitation; want of decision; irresolution.

Indecisive *adj*. hesitating; undecided; irresolute.

Indeciduous *adj*. not deciduous.

Indecision *n*. want of decision; irresolution; hesitation.

Indeclinable *adj*. not inflected; having no inflexions; not variable.

Indecomposable *adj*. that cannot be decomposed or resolved into constituents.

Indeed *adv*. in truth; truly; in fact; in reality; really; expressing surprise; but not disbelief.

Indefatigable *adj*. not tired out; that unremitting; that cannot be fatigued.

Indefeasible *adj*. that cannot be forfeited or done away with.

Indefectible *adj*. not liable to defect; unfailing; faultless.

Indefensible *adj*. not admitting defence; that cannot be justified.

Indefinable *adj*. that cannot be defined or adequately described.

Indefinte *adj*. not precise; uncertain; undefined; unlimited.

Indehiscent *adj*. remaining closed at maturity; not opening along regular lines.

Indelible *adj*. that cannot be blotted out or effaced.

Indelicate *adj*. immodest; tactless; unrefined; coarse.

Indemnify *v.t.* to protect or secure against harm or loss; to compensate.

Indemnity *n*. compensation; legal exemption from penalties etc. incurred.

Indenture *n*. deed made by two or more parties; indented document.

Independence *n.* freedom; political freedom; exemption from control.

Independent *adj.* free; not subject to the control of others; not supported by others.

Indescribable *adj.* vague; indefinite; beyond description.

Indeterminate *adj.* not precise; not certain; vague.

Index *n.* a pointer on instruments; an alphabetical list with references; the guiding principle; an exponent.

Indicate *v.t.* to make known; to show; to suggest; to state briefly.

Indict *v.t.* to accuse; to charge with a crime.

Indifference *n.* unconcern; freedom from prejudice; neutrality.

Indigence *n.* want; poverty.

Indigenous *adj.* native to a country; not exotic; belonging naturally to the soil.

Indigent *adj.* needy; poor.

Indigested *adj.* not digested; shapeless; not thought of before.

Indigestion *n.* want of digestion.

Indignant *adj.* moved by indignation; angry.

Indignation *n.* feeling of anger and scorn.

Indignity *n.* incivility; insult.

Indigo *n.* a deep blue colour; blue powder used as a dye.

Indirect *adj.* not direct; circuitous; not straight.

Indirection *n.* roud-about means; an indirect course.

Indiscernible *adj.* & *n.* that cannot be discerned or distinguished from another; not perceptible.

Indisciplinable *adj.* not capable of discipline.

Indiscreet *adj.* injudicious; imprudent; unwary.

Indiscrete *adj.* not divided into parts or separated.

Indiscriminate *adj.* given or done without careful judgement; or at random.

Indispensable *adj.* that cannot be dispensed with absolutely necessary.

Indispose *v.t.* to render unfit; to disincline; to make averse to.

Indisputable *adj.* incontestable; beyond dispute; incontrovertible.

Indissoluble *adj.* that cannot be dissolved; lasting; stable.

Indistinct *adj.* not clearly defined; obscure; confused.

Indistributable *adj.* that cannot be distributed.

Indite *v.t.* to put into words; to compose; to write.

Indium *n.* a rare metal of lead.

Indivertible *adj.* that cannot be diverted or turned aside.

Individual *adj.* plant or thing, particular; single; separate.

Individuate *v.t.* to form into an individual.

Indivisible *adj.* that cannot be divided. *n.* an infinitely small particle or quantity.

Indo *pref.* in sense of 'Indian'.

Indocile *adj.* intractable; not docile.

Indolence *n.* habitual laziness, sloth.

Indolent *adj.* lazy; slothful; causing no pain.

Indomitable *adj.* un-yielding; not to be subdued; that cannot be defeated or suppressed.

Indoor *adj.* situated or carried on within a house; done within house.

Indoors *adv.* (within the house) in or into a building.

Indorsation *n.* endorsement.

Indorsee *n.* one in whose favour a bill etc. is endorsed.

Indorse *v.t.* to assign by writing on the back of; to approve.

Indraught *n.* the inward flow of a current.

Indubitable *adj.* beyond doubt; certain.

Induce *v.t.* to cause a woman by means of drugs to begin having her baby.

Induct *v.t.* to initiate; to introduce.

Induct *v.t.* to introduce; to initiate.

Inductive *adj.* of electric or magnetic induction; tending to induce.

Inductor *n.* any part of electric induction apparatus.

Indulge *v.t.* & *i.* to gratify; to entertain; to take one's pleasure freely in.

Indurate *v.t.* & *i.* to make or become hard.

Industry *n.* a commercial activity that provides services; the making or production of things in factories.

Indwell *v.t.* & *i.* to dwell in; to inhabit; to occupy.

Inebriate *adj.* drunken. *n.* a drunkard.

Ineffable *adj.* unspeakable; unutterable.

Ineffective *adj.* useless; not producing the desired effect; inefficient; lacking artistic effect.

Inefficacious *adj.* not able to produce effect.

Inefficacy *n.* want of efficacy.

Inefficient *adj.* (of a person or an organization) failing to make the best use of the available time and resources.

Inelegant *adj.* wanting elegance or beauty; mean; ungraceful; unrefined.

Ineligible *adj.* not eligible.

Ineloquent *adj.* not eloquent.

Inequality *n.* want of equality; inadequacy; irregularity; variableness.

Inequitable *adj.* unfair; unjust.

Ineradicable *adj.* not able to be eradicated or rooted out.

Inerrable *adj.* not liable to err.

Inert *adj*. without inherent power; indisposed; sluggish; lazy.

Inertia *n*. inertness; sloth.

Inestimable *adj*. to good or too great to be estimated; priceless.

Inevitability *n*. the state of being inevitable.

Inevitable *adj*. unavoidable; bound to happen or appear; convincing.

Inexact *adj*. not exact.

Inexhaustible *adj*. that cannot be exhausted; unfailing.

Inexorable *adj*. impossible to change or prevent; relentless.

Inexpectant *adj*. not expectant.

Inexpensive *adj*. cheap.

Inexperience *n*. want of experience.

Inexpert *adj*. not having particular skill or knowledge.

Inexpiable *adj*. that cannot be expiated; implacable.

Inexplicable *adj*. that cannot be explained; mysterious.

Inexplicit *adj*. not definitely or clearly expressed.

Inexplosive *adj*. not explosive.

Inexpressible *adj*. that cannot be expressed in words; unutterable.

Inexpressive *adj*. not expressive.

Inextensible *adj*. not extensible; not stretchable.

Inextenso *adj*. in an unabridged form.

Inextricable *adj*. that cannot be disentangled or solved.

Infallible *adj*. not capable to making mistakes or being wrong; never failing; always effective.

Infamize *v.t.* to make infamous.

Infamous *adj*. of ill fame; notorious; scandalous; disgraceful.

Infamy *n*. public disgrace; ill fame; vileness.

Infancy *n*. early childhood.

Infant *n*. a baby; a child under seven years of age; a minor.

Infantile *adj*. of infancy; in its infancy.

Infantry *n*. foot-soldiers.

Infatuate *v.t.* to make foolish; to affect with folly; to excite with passion.

Infeasible *adj*. not practicable.

Infect *v.t.* to fill with a disease; to corrupt; to imbue.

Infection *n*. a disease caught especially by breathing in bacteria, etc. from the air.

Infective *adj*. infectious.

Infelicific *adj*. producing unhappiness.

Infelicitous *adj*. unhappy; not felicitous.

Infelicity *n*. misfortune; misery; unhappiness; inaptness of expression.

Infer *v.t.* to arrive at a conclusion.

Inferior *adj*. less valuable; situated below; lower in rank; of poor quality.

Infernal *adj*. pertaining to hell; hellish; abdominable; diabolical.

Inferno *n.* hell; a large dangerous fire that out of control; a place or situation that is hot; noisy or confused.

Inferrable *adj.* that can be inferred.

Infertile *adj.* not fertile.

Infest *v.t.* to haunt; to harass; to tease.

Infidel *n.* a person who does not believe in what is considered by the speaker to be the true religion.

Infield *n.* a land near a hamlet; land regularly manured and cropped.

Infighting *n.* boxing at closer quarters than an arm's length.

Infiltrate *v.t. & i.* to enter a substance through its pores.

Infinite *adj.* boundless; without limit; very great; unlimited.

Infinitesimal *adj.* infinitely or very small.

Infinitude *n.* boundlessness; infinity.

Infinity *n. Math.* infinite quantity; infinite number or extent; a point far away in space that can never be reached.

Infirm *adj.* physically weak; weak of mind; feeble; irresolute.

Infix *v.t.* to fix or fasten; to impress; to insert in the body of a word.

Inflame *v.t. & i.* to set ablaze; to catch fire; to excite passionately.

Inflate *v.t.* to swell with air or gas; to fill with the breath; to raise (price) artificially.

Inflation *n. Econ.* expansion of money in circulation; the act of inflating or state of being inflated.

Inflator *n.* one who or that which inflates.

Inflect *v.t.* to bend; to curve; to sharpen.

Inflict *v.t.* to lay on; to impasse as punishment; to impose.

Infliction *n.* punishment; trouble.

Inflorescence *n.* collective flowers of a plant; flowering.

Inflow *n.* flowing in.

Influence *n.* the power to produce an effect; action of natural forces.

Influent *adj.* flowing in.

Influential *adj.* having a great influence; possessing power.

Influenza *n.* a kind of contagious cattarrh accompanied by fever.

Influx *n.* flowing in; infusion.

Inform *v.t. & i.* to tell; to communicate, to imbue with; to instruct.

Informal *adj.* (of dress) not for a special or official occasion.

Information *n.* news; intelligence; communication.

Informative *adj.* giving information; having power to inform.

Informed *adj.* intimated; instructed; educated.

Informer *n.* one who informs against another.

Infra *pref.* in sense of below; further on (in book).

Infraction *n.* infringement; violation.

Infranchise *v.t.* to give franchise rights; to set free.

Infrequency *n.* rarity; the state of being infrequent.

Infrugal *adj.* prodigal; extravagant.

Infundibular *adj.* funnel-shaped.

Infuriate *v.t.* to enrage; to fill with fury.

Infuse *v.t. & i.* to prepare a drink or medicine by soaking tea or herbs in a liquid.

Infusion *n.* distillation; the act of infusing.

Ingathering *n.* a gathering in; a harvest.

Ingenious *adj.* (of an ideal) very clever and orginal; (of a hinge) original in design and well suited to its purpose.

Ingenue *n.* an artless girl, *esp.* as stage type.

Ingenuity *n.* power of ready invention skill in contriving.

Ingest *v.t.* to take in (food) to the stomach.

Ingle *n.* fire burning on hearth.

Inglorious *adj.* shameful; obscure.

Ingoing *adj.* going in; entering in. *n.* entrance.

Ingot *n.* a mass of unwrought metal cast in a mould.

Ingrain *adj.* dyed in grain; inveterate, inherent.

Ingrate *adj.* ungrateful (person) *n.* an ungrateful man.

Ingratiate *v.t.* to bring oneself into favour with.

Ingratitude *n.* unthankfulness; want of gratitude.

Ingravescent *adj.* (of disease etc.) growing worse.

Ingredient *n.* any of the things or qualities of which something is made.

Ingress *n.* right of entrance; means of entering.

Ingrowing *adj.* growing inwards; growing into the flesh (*esp.* of nail).

Inguinal *adj.* pertaining to the groin.

Ingurgitate *v.t.* to swallow greedily; to engulf.

Inhabit *v.t.* to live in a place; to occupy something.

Inhabitant *n.* one who resides in a place; a resident; a dweller.

Inhale *v.t.* to take into lungs; to breathe in; to suck in.

Inharmonic *adj.* not harmonic.

Inhere *v.t.* (of rights) to be vested in (a person); (of qualities) to exist.

Inherence *n.* existing in something else.

Inherent *adj.* innate; inseparable.

Inherit *v.t.* to acquire by succession; to succeed as heir.

Inheritor *n.* one who inherits; an heir.

Inhesion *n.* inhering.

Inhibit *v.t.* to restrict or prevent a process or an action; to forbid;to probibit.

Inhibition *n.* obstruction.

Inhibitory *adj.* prohibitory.

Inhospitable *adj.* not affording shelter to strangers; not hospitable.

Inhuman *adj.* brutal; unfeeling; barbarous.

Inhume *v.t.* to bury in the ground.

Inimical *adj.* harmful; unfriendly; prejudicial; hurtful.

Inimitable *adj.* one which defies imitation.

Iniquity *n.* wickedness; gross injustice.

Initial *adj.* & *n.* incipient; of or occurring at the beginning.

Initiate *v.t.* to begin or originate; to admit with introductory rites; to introduce.

Initiative *adj.* originating. *n.* an introductory step.

Initio *adv.* at the beginning.

Injection *n.* the act of injecting; fluid that is forced into the body by a syringe.

Injudicious *adj.* unwise; illjudged; indiscreet.

Injunction *n.* authoritative order; command; legal writ; direction.

Injure *v.t.* to harm; to do wrong to; to impart; to hurt; to damage.

Injurious *adj.* tending to injure; wrongful; harmful; detrimental.

Injury *n.* damage; wrong done to some one.

Injustice *n.* an unjust act; lack of equity.

Ink *n.* a coloured fluid for writing with pen or for printing.

Inland *n.* interior. *adj.* within a country; of the interior of a country.

Inlay *v.t.* to embed one thing into another; to ornament in this way.

Inlet *n.* an entrance; an opening; a creek; a small bay or arm of sea.

Inlier *n.* an underlying formation completely covered by an overlying one.

Inly *adv.* intimately; inwardly; in the heart.

Inlying *adj.* lying inside.

Inmate *n.* any of a number of people living together in an institution.

Inmost *adj.* most inward; most intimate.

Inn *n.* a tavern; a hotel; a lodging place for travellers.

Innate *adj.* inborn; natural.

Innavigable *adj.* not navigable.

Inner *adj.* inside; towards the middle of a place; not near the outside.

Innervate *v.t.* to supplant with nerve force; to stimulate.

Innings *n.* a team's turn of batting in a cricket match; gathering of grains.

Innocence *n.* harmlessness; perfect moral purity; freedom from guilt.

Innocent *adj.* not guilty of wrongdoing; harmless; having little experience of deception.

Innocuity *n.* the quality of being harmless or sinless.

Innocuous *adj.* harmless in effect.

Innominate *adj.* unnamed; without a name.

Innovate *v.i.* to make a change by introducing a novelty.

Innovator *n.* one who introduces a new change.

Innoxious *adj.* harmless; pure.

Innoxiousness *n.* harmlessness.

Innuendo *n.* a side-hint, allusive remark; indirect intimation or reference.

Innumerable *adj.* countless; numberless.

Innutrition *n.* lack of nutrition.

Inobservance *n.* inattention; non-observance (of law etc.).

Inoccupation *n.* want of occupation.

Inoculate *v.t.* to impregnate germs of disease in a person; to insert as bud or eye of a tree in another tree.

Inodorous *adj.* odourless; having no smell.

Inoffensive *adj.* not offending or objectionable; harmless.

Inofficial *adj.* not officious; contrary to moral duty.

Inoperative *adj.* producing no effect; not operative.

Inopportune *adj.* not appropriate or convenient; unseasonable.

Inordinate *adj.* immoderate; excessive; disorderly.

Inorganic *adj.* having no organic structure.

Inornate *adj.* not elaborate.

Inosculate *v.t.* & *i.* to join or unite closely; to blend; to be interwoven.

Inpouring *adj.* pouring in.

Input *n.* information that is put in; the action of putting information into a computer for processing or storage.

Inquest *n.* a legal or judicial inquiry into a matter.

Inquietude *n.* want of metal or bodily rest; uneasiness.

Inquire, Enquire *v.t.* & *i.* to make a search into; to ask for; to examine.

Inquirer *n.* one who makes an inquiry.

Inquiry *n.* asking a question; investigation; search for information.

Inquisition *n.* investigation; inquest; a search; an official inquiry.

Inquisitive *adj.* inquiring; curious; inclined to seek information.

Inquisitor *n.* an investigator.

Inrail *v.t.* to enclose with rails.

Inroad *n.* encroachment; a raid; an attack.

Inrush *n.* a violent influx; rushing in or inflow.

Insalivate *v.t.* to mix food with saliva.

Insalubrious *adj.* unhealthy; unwholesome.

Insane *adj.* deranged in mind; mad; senseless.

Insanity *n.* derangement of mind, madness.

Insatiable *adj.* greedy; that cannot be satisfied or appeased.

Insatiate *adj.* never satisfied.

Inscribe *v.t.* to write on a stone; to enter in a list; to engrave.

Inscrutable *adj.* unsearch-able; mysterious; impenetrable; that cannot be understood or known.

Insect *n.* small invertebrate creeping or flying animal; an insignificant creature.

Insectarium *n.* a place for keeping insects.

Insecure *adj.* unsafe; not secure; liable to give way.

Insecurity *n.* uncertainty; danger; fear.

Inseminate *v.t.* to sow seed.

Insensate *adj.* void of sense; without physical sensation.

Insensible *adj.* void of feeling; without sense or feeling; imperceptible; unconscious.

Insensitive *adj.* not sensitive.

Insentient *adj.* lifeless; inanimate.

Inseparable *adj.* that cannot be separated.

Insert *v.t.* to place or fit one thing into another.

Insertion *n.* ornamental needlework etc. inserted into plain material; inserting.

Inset *n.* extra page or pages or map inserted in a sheet or book.

Insheathe *v.t.* to cover with a sheathe.

Inshore *adv.* close to shore.

Inside *n., adj. & adv.* inner portion; interior; side next to wall; on the inside of, in the interior of.

Insidious *adj.* treacherous; crafty.

Insight *n.* thorough knowledge.

Insignia *n. pl.* badges or distinguishing marks of an office or honour.

Insignificant *adj.* having little or no value; immaterial; trivial; meaningless.

Insicerity *n.* want of sincerity.

Insincere *adj.* false; not sincere; deceitful; hypocritical; trivial.

Insinuate *v.t.* to introduce gradually; to hint indirectly; to instil; to suggest.

Insinuative *adj.* tending to insinutate.

Insinuator *n.* he who insinuates.

Insipid *adj.* having almost no taste of flavour; lifeless; spiritless; dull.

Insipient *adj.* wanting in sense or wisdom.

Insist *v.i. & t.* to emphasize; to assert firmly; to demand persistently.

In situ *adj. & adv. Latin.* in its original place.

Insobriety *n.* want of sobriety; drunkenness; intemperance.

Insolate *v.t.* to dry in the sun.

Insolation *n.* the act or process of exposing to the sun's rays for bleaching.

Insolent *adj.* extremely rude and showing a lack or respect; offensively contemptuous.

Insoluble *adj.* that cannot be dissolved in a fluid.

Insolvable *adj.* that cannot be solved or explained.

Insolvency *n.* inability to pay debts.

Insolvent *adj.* & *n.* relating to insolvent; a debtor who is unable to pay off his debts.

Insomnia *n.* want of sleep; unnatural sleeplessness.

Insomuch *adj.* to such an extent; so that.

Insouciant *adj.* careless; unconcerned.

Inspan *v.t.* & *i.* to yoke oxen to a vehicle; to harness.

Inspect *v.t.* to examine in an official manner; to superintend.

Inspector *n.* a person who inspects.

Inspectorial *adj.* pertaining to an inspector.

Inspiration *n.* a sudden good idea; the act of inspiring; person or thing that inspires; divine influence.

Inspirator *n.* an apparatus for drawing in air or vapour.

Inspiratory *adj.* of breathing in.

Inspire *v.t.* to breathe in; to inhale; to infuse supernatural element into.

Inspirit *v.t.* to put life into; to invigorate; to animate; to encourage.

Inspissate *v.t.* to thicken; condense; by the evaporation moisture.

Instability *n.* want of stability or firmness; fickleness; inconstancy.

Install *v.t.* to place in an office with ceremony; to invest with customary.

Instalment *n.* any one of the parts of a payment spread over a period of time.

Instance *n.* an example; an occurrence; a request; a law suit; process.

Instancy *n.* urgency.

Instant *n.* precise moment; a day of the current month.

Instantaneous *adj.* occurring or done in an instant.

Instantly *adv.* at once; forthwith.

Instate *v.t.* to put in possession; to install; to set or place.

Instead *adj.* as a substitute; in place of.

Instep *n.* the upper or fore-part of the human foot.

Instigate *v.t.* to make something begin or happen.

Instil *v.t.* to put into by drops; to infuse gradually.

Instinct *n.* to innate propensity in animals; intuition; intuitive feeling.

Instictive *adj.* prompted by instict or natural impulse.

Institute *n.* to appoint to an office; to establish or start something, *e.g.* an inquir, a custom or a rule.

Institution *n.* establishment; foundation society; law.

Instruct *v.t.* to teach somebody a skill; to adivise; to give information to; to direct.

Instructor *n.* a teacher; a teacher ranking below a professor.

Instruction *n.* the process of teaching; knowledge or teaching given.

Instrument *n.* a tool or implement, contrivance producing musical sounds; a written deed.

Insubordinate *adj.* refusing to obey instruction or show respect.

Insubstantial *adj.* lacking in reality; unreal.

Insufferable *adj.* greatly arrogant; conceited; intolerable.

Insufficient *adj.* not enough; incompetent; not sufficient.

Insufflate *v.t.* to breathe; to blow air into.

Insular *adj.* narrow minded; having no interest in or contact with people and ideas from outside one's own country or society; belonging to an island.

Insulate *v.t.* to make (land) into an island; to isolate; to keep a part.

Insulin *n.* a protein hormone secreted in the pancreas by the islets of Langerhans.

Insult *n.* abuse in words or action; affront; an insulting speech.

Insuperable *adj.* that cannot be got over; invincible; insurmountable.

Insupportable *adj.* unbearable.

Insurable *adj.* fit to be insured.

Insurance *n.* a contract made by a company or society, or by the state, to provide a gaurantee of compensation for loss, damage, illness, death, etc.

Insure *v.t.* & *i.* to secure against loss by the payment of insurance money.

Insurgent *adj.* risinging in revolt; rebellious. *n.* a rebel.

Insurmountable *adj.* insuperable; unable to be overcome.

Insurrection *n.* an open rebellion; a revolt; a rising against established authority.

Insusceptible *adj.* incapable of being influenced or affected.

Intact *adj.* untouched; uninjured; unimpaired; entire.

Intactable *adj.* not perceptible by touch.

Intagliated *adj.* carved on the surface.

Intaglio *n.* an engraved design; a stone or gem with an incised design.

Intake *n.* the place of taking water into a pipe etc. from a river etc.

Intangible *adj.* that cannot be touched; that cannot be grasped mentally.

Integer *n.* a whole or undivided number; thing complete in itself.

Integral *adj.* complete; whole; entire; not fractional.

Integrant *adj.* making part of a whole.

Integrate *v.t.* & *i.* to make complete; to unite.

Integration *n. Math.* finding the integral of; integrating; the act or instance of combining into an integral whole.

Integrity *n.* entireness; wholesomeness; soundness; honesty; purity.

Integument *n.* outer covering; skin; husk; rind.

Intellect *n.* the faculty of thinking; understanding; person of intellect.

Intelligence *n.* intellect; sagacity; notice; information; news.

Intelligent *adj.* having intellect; quick to learn; skilled; well-informed.

Intelligible *adj.* that can be understood; *Philos.* that can be apprehended only by the intellect, not by the senses.

Intemperance *n.* want of moderation.

Intemperate *adj.* immoderate; excessive in appetite.

Intend *v.t.* to purpose; to desire; to design; to mean.

Intendment *n.* the true meaning of a legal instrument.

Intense *adj.* very great or severe; (of emotion, etc.) very strong; strained; eager; existing in a high degree.

Intensify *v.t.* & *i.* to make or become intense; to heighten to aggravate.

Intension *n.* intensity; high degree; of a quality, strenuous exertion of mind or will.

Intensity *n.* the state of being intense.

Intensive *adj.* concentrated; assiduous; of or in intensity; producing intensity.

Intent *n.* intention; aim; purpose.

Intention *n.* purpose; aim; (*pl.*) purpose in respect of proposal of marriage; conception.

Intentional *adj.* done with some purpose; intended; designed.

Inter *v.t.* to place in earth or tomb; to bury.

Interact *n.* (of people) to work together or communicate; to act or have an effect on each other.

Interactive *adj.* interacting.

Interblend *v.t.* & *i.* to mingle or blend with each other.

Interbreed *v.t.* & *i.* to crossbreed with each other.

Intercalary *adj.* (of day or month) inserted between others to harmonize the calendar with the solar year.

Intercalate *v.t.* to insert a day in a calender to interpose.

Intercede *v.i.* to plead; to act for another; to mediate.

Intercept *v.t.* to check; to stop; to cut off.

Intercession *n.* mediation for reconciliation.

Interchange *v.t.* to exchange with each other; to alternate.

Intercolonial *adj.* existing, carried on between different colonies.

Intercommunity *n.* the state of having in common; being or having things in common to various parties.

Interconnect *v.t.* & *i.* to connect with one another.

Intercontinental *adj.* between continents; capable of travelling from one continent to another.

Intercourse *n.* social communion; commercial communication familiarity.

Intercurrent *adj.* (of disease) occuring during the progress of another; recurring at intervals; intervening.

Interdependent *adj.* mutually dependent.

Interdict *v.t.* to prohibit; to forbid. *n.* an prohibition; injunction.

Interest *n.* profit; advantage; welfare; concern; money paid for a sum lent; excitement of feeling.

Interesting *adj.* exciting emotions; engaging interest.

Interfere *v.i.* to come into collision to meddle; to intervene.

Interfluent *adj.* flowing into each other.

Interfuse *v.t.* & *i.* to blend or mix together.

Intergrowth *n.* growing together.

Interim *n.* meantime; intervening moment.

Interior *adj.* inland; inward; internal; domestic.

Interjacent *adj.* lying between; intermediate.

Interject *v.t.* to interpose abruptly; to remark parenthetically.

Interjection *n.* exclamation.

Interlace *v.t.* & *i.* to mingle together; to entangle; to interweave.

Interlard *v.t.* to mix fat with lean & thin.

Interlay *v.t.* to place between.

Interleaf *n.* an extra leaf inserted between leaves of a book.

Interleave *v.t.* to insert blank leaves between printed leaves in a book.

Interline *v.t.* to insert words between lines; to write in alternate lines.

Interlinear *adj.* written between the lines.

Interlink *v.t.* to connect with links; to join.

Interlock *v.t.* & *i.* to engage or clasp with each other.

Interlocutor *n.* one who takes part in a dialogue or conversation.

Interlocution *n.* dialogue.

Interlope *v.t.* to intrude; to traffic without licence.

Interlude *n.* a period of time coming between two events or between two stages of something.

Intermarriage *n.* reciprocal marriage between members of different families.

Intermarry *v.i.* to become connected by marriage with members of different tribes etc.

Intermeddle *v.i.* to interfere in the affairs of others.

Intermediate *adj.* situated or coming between two people or things in time, space, degree etc.; interposed.

Interment *n.* burial; act of interring.

Intermezzo *n.* a short light dramatic or other performance between acts of drama or opera.

Interminable *adj.* endless; extremely long.

Intermission *n.* a temporary pause or cessation; interval.

Intermit *v.t.* & *i.* to discontinue; to cease for a time; to interrupt; to suspend.

Intermix *v.t.* & *i.* to mix together; to intermingle.

Intern *v.t.* to confine somebdoy, in a prison or within a place, especially for political or military reasons, without allowing them to leave.

Internee *n.* an interned person.

Internal *adj.* situated in the inside; inward; intrinsic.

International *adj.* relating to the relations existing between two or more nations.

Internecine *adj.* causing destruction to both sides; deadly, causing great slaughter.

Internode *n.* part of the stem between two nodes or points of the stem.

Internuncial *adj.* joining different parts of the system.

Interosculate *v.i.* to intermingle with each other to form a connecting link.

Interpage *v.t.* to insert leaf between the pages of a book.

Interpellate *v.t.* (in legislative councils) to interrupt to demand explanation from the Minister concerned.

Interpenetrate *v.t.* & *i.* to penetrate thoroughly or mutually.

Interplace *v.t.* to place between.

Interplay *n.* the operation of two things on one-another.

Interplead *v.t.* to litigate with each other in order to settle a point in which a third party is concerned.

Interpose *v.t.* & *i.* to intervene; to insert; to make an interruption.

Interpret *v.t.* & *i.* to translate or expose the meaning of.

Interpreter *n.* one who translates orally; an expositor.

Interregnum *n.* interval between successive reigns.

Interrelation *n.* mutual relation.

Interrogate *v.t.* to examine by questions; to question closely or formally.

Interrogation *n.* asking questions; a question put.

Interrogative *adj.* & *n.* denoting a question; expressed in the form of a question.

Interrogator *n.* questioner.

Interrogatory *adj.* denoting a question; of inquiry.

Interrupt *v.t.* to block; to break continuity.

Interrupter *n.* one who interrupts.

Interruptive *adj.* tending to interrupt.

Intersect *v.t.* & *i.* to divide (a thing) by crossing it.

Intersection *n.* the act of intersecting; a point or line common to intersecting lines or planes.

Interspace *n.* space between two things.

Interstellar *adj.* between stars.

Interstice *n.* a very small gap or crack; an intervening space.

Interstitial *adj.* occurring in interstices.

Intertwine *v.t.* & *i.* to twine closely together.

Interval *n.* intervening time for space; a pause; a break; a gap.

Intervene *v.i.* (of events or circumstances) to happen in such a way as to dealy or prevent something from being done.

Intervener *n.* one who intervenes.

Intervention *n.* interference; mediation; an interposition.

Interview *n.* meeting of persons face to face for purpose of discussion, business, a formal meeting.

Intervolve *v.t.* to wind; to roll up with each other.

Interweave *v.t.* to weave or twist two or more threads, etc. together; to blend intimately.

Interwind *v.t.* & *i.* to wind together.

Intestate *adj.* & *n.* one who has not made a will.

Intestine *n.* lower part of alimentary canal.

Intimacy *n.* friendship; close familiarity.

Intimate *adj.* (of a relationship) warm and friendly, close.

Intimidate *v.t.* to dishearten; to create fear; to inspire with fear.

Intimity *n.* inwardness.

Into *prep.* expressing entrance or passage within a thing.

Intoed *adj.* having the toes turned inwards.

Intolerable *adj.* enormous; not to be endured.

Intolerant *adj.* not able to bear; not tolerant.

Intolerance *n.* want of toleration.

Intomb *v.t.* to deposit in a tomb.

Intonate, Intone *v.t.* & *i.* to sound musical notes; to recite in a singing voice; to utter with a particular tone.

Intonation *n.* the rice and fall of the voice in speaking.

Intone *v.t. & i.* to chant; to utter a deep sound; to read recitingly.

Intort *v.i.* to twist.

Intortion *n.* a winding or twisting.

Intoxicate *v.t.* to make drunk; to excite; to elate; to exhilarate.

Intra *pref.* in the sense of "within".

Intractable *adj.* not easily controlled or dealt with; hard to manage.

Intrados *n.* interior curve of an arch.

Intramural *adj.* existing; done within the walls.

Intransient *adj.* not passing away suddenly; not transient.

Intransigent *adj.* uncompromising in politics.

Intransitive *adj.* (of verbs) not having an object.

Intrant *n.* one who enters a collage; an assembly & etc.

Intrench *v.t. & i.* to dig up a trench and parapet; to fortify with a ditch.

Intrepid *adj.* fearless; brave.

Intrepidity *n.* fearlessness; undaunted state.

Intricacy *n.* perplexity; complication.

Intricate *adj.* entangled; complicated of many parts put together in a complex way.

Intrigue *n.* a plot; a stratagem.

Intrinsic *adj.* naturally belonging to; inherent; true; essential.

Intro *n.* an introduction to something; especialy to a piece of music or writing.

Introduce *v.t.* to bring in; to bring out; to conduct.

Introduction *n.* the commencing portion of a book; preliminary matter in a book.

Intromit *v.t.* to let in; to admit into; to insert.

Introspect *v.t.* to examine one's own thoughts and feelings; to view the inside.

Introvert *v.t.* to turn (the mind, thought) inward upon itself.

Intrude *v.t. & i.* to thrust; to encroach; to come uninvited.

Intrusion *n.* the act of intruding; an encroachment.

Intrusive *adj.* entering without right, apt to intrude.

Intubate *v.t.* to insert a tube into mouth to keep it open.

Intuitive *adj.* possessing or perceived by intuition.

Intumesce *v.t.* to enlarge with heat; to swell. **Intumescence,** *n. a* swelling.

Inunction *n.* the act of anointing smearing or rubbing with oil.

Inundate *v.t.* to flood; to submerge; to spread or flow over; to deluge.

Inurbane *adj.* rough; discourteous.

Inure, Enure *v.t.* to habituate; to accustom; to come into operation.

Inurn *v.t.* to put the ashes or a dead body into an urn.

Inutile *adj.* useless; out of use.

Invade *v.t.* to assail; to enter a place in large numbers.
Invaginate *v.t.* to put into a sheath.
Invalid *adj.* feeble; weak; enfeebled by illness or injury.
Invalidate *v.t.* to destroy the strength of; to make something invalid.
Invalidity, Invalidness *ns.* want of strength; want of legal force.
Invaluable *adj.* inestimable; priceless.
Invar *n.* an alloy of steel and nickel.
Invariable *adj.* constant, unchangeable; uniform.
Invasion *n.* the action of hostile armed forces entering a country or territory.
Invective *n.* abusive speech; violent words of censure.
Inveigh *v.t.* to speak violently; to reproach.
Inveigle *v.t.* to allure; to entice; to seduce; to wheedle.
Invent *v.t.* to devise; to originate something new; to fabricate; to concoct.
Invention *n.* the action of invention something.
Inveracity *n.* untruthfulness; falsehood.
Inverness *n.* a kind of man's sleeveless cloak.
Inverse *adj.* & *n.* an inverted state; inverted.
Inversion *n.* a change of order; reversal of position.
Invert *v.t.* to turn upside down; to reverse position. *n.* an inverted arch.
Invest *v.t.* & *i.* to endue with qualities, etc.; to clothe; to dress; to use money to buy *e.g.* shares or property.
Investiture *n.* formal investing of a person with an office; enduing with attributes.
Investment *n.* money invested; the investing of money.
Investor *n.* one who invests.
Inveterate *adj.* obstinate; deep-rooted; confirmed.
Invidious *adj.* envious; likely to provoke ill-will.
Invigilate *v.i.* to guard students in an examination.
Invincible *adj.* insurmountable; unconquerable; not to be subdued.
Inviolable *adj.* not to be profaned or injured; not to be violated; to be kept sacred.
Inviolacy *n.* the state of being inviolate.
Inviolate *adj.* not violated; unbroken; unprofaned.
Invisible *adj.* that cannot be seen; unable to be seen; not visible.
Invite *v.t.* to ask politely; to summon; to entice; to tend to bring.
Invocation *n.* an appeal to muse for inspiration or helping in poem.
Invoice *n.* a bill. *v.t.* to make an invoice of (goods).

Invoke *v.t.* to call upon earnestly; to implore; to call to help.

Involuntary *adj.* not done willingly; un-intentional; not having the power of will; done without intention.

Involute *adj.* rolled inwards at edges.

Involution *n.* raising of quantity to any power; curling inwards.

Involve *v.t.* to roll up; to envelop; to complicate.

Invulnerable *adj.* that cannot be harmed or damaged.

Inward *adj.* internal; directed towards the inside; interior; confidential; private; situated within.

Inweave *v.t.* to weave in or together.

Inwrought *adj.* adorned with figures; decorated; wrought or worked in; intimately blended with.

Inyala *n.* a South African antelope.

Iolite *n.* silicate of aluminium, iron, and magnesium, of violet or blue colour.

Ion *n.* a particle of moving matter carrying a unit or unitary charge of positive or negative electricity.

Iota *n.* a very small quantity.

Ipecacuanha *n.* a root of S. American plant used as emetic and purgative.

Ipse dixit *n.* a dictum; a dogmatic statement.

Ipso facto *adv.* by that very fact.

Irascible *adj.* hot-tempered; easily provoked with resentment; irritable

Irate *adj.* angry.

Ire *n.* anger; wrath.

Irenic, Irenical *adjs.* aiming at peace; aimed at peace.

Iridaceous *adj.* (of plants) of the iris kind.

Iridescent *adj.* showing rainbow like colours.

Iridium *n.* a precious white metal like platinum.

Iris *n.* a kind of rock-crystal reflecting.

Irish *adj.* of Ireland of its culture, language or people.

Irk *v.t.* to make tired; to cause trouble; to tire; to disgust; to annoy or irritate somebody.

Iron *n.* a very common hard metal.

Irradiant *adj.* shining brightly.

Irrational *adj.* not unreasonable; illogical; not endowed with reason; contrary to reason; not rational.

Irrecusable *adj.* that cannot be refused; that must be accepted.

Irredeemable *adj.* not to be redeemed; irreclaimable; hopeless.

Irreducible *adj.* that cannot be brought (to desired condition).

Irrefragable *adj.* that cannot be disputed; unanswerable.

Irrefutable *adj.* unanswerable; not to be refuted.

Irregular *adj.* disorderly; contrary to rule; uneven; varying.

Irrelative *adj.* unrelated to absolute; unconnected.

Irrelevant *adj.* not relevant.

Irreligion *n.* hostility to or disregard of religion; impiety.

Irreligious *adj.* impious; un-goldy; profane; hostile or in-different to religion.

Irremediable *adj.* that cannot be remedied or corrected.

Irremissible *adj.* unpardonable; binding.

Irremovable *adj.* that cannot be removed.

Irreparable *adj.* that cannot be made good; irretrievable.

Irreplaceable *adj.* of which the loss cannot be supplied.

Irrepressible *adj.* that cannot be repressed or restrained.

Irreproachable *adj.* innocent; faultless; blameless; unblemished.

Irresolute *adj.* hesitating; undecided; wavering; wanting in resolution.

Irresolvable *adj.* that cannot be resolved into parts.

Irrespective *adj.* without reference to; not having; regard (with of) not taking into account.

Irrestrainable *adj.* that cannot be restrained.

Irretentive *adj.* not retentive.

Irretrievable *adj.* irreparable; not retrievable; irrecoverable.

Irreverent *adj.* feeling or showing no respect for somebody generally respected by others.

Irreversible *adj.* that cannot be reversed or changed back to the original state.

Irrevocable *adj.* that cannot be changed or altered; final.

Irrigate *v.t.* to supply (land) with water; (Med.) to supply (a wound) with constant flow of liquid; (fig.) to refresh.

Irritable *adj.* (of muscles etc.) capable of being excited to vital action by physical stimulus.

Irritancy *n.* irritation; annoyance; the state of being irritant.

Irritant *adj.* causing slight discomfort to a part of the body.

Irupt *v.i.* to attack; to enter forcibly.

Isagogic *adj.* introductory. *n. pl.* the study of literary and external history of Bible.

Ischiatic *adj.* of the hip; sciatic.

Ishmael *n.* an outcast; one at war with society.

Isinglass *n.* gelatinous substance obtained from the air-bladders of the sturgeon and other freshwater fish.

Islam *n.* the Muslim religion, baed on belief in one God and revealed through the Prophet Muhammad.

Island *n.* a piece of land with water all round; a small raised place of safety of the crossing of the street.

Isle *n.* an island.

Islet *n.* a small island; an isolated tract or spot.

Isolate *v.t.* to place apart or alone; to place in a detached situation; *Electr.* to insulate.

Isomeric *adj.* composed of same elements in the same proportions, and having the same molecular weight, but differently grouped.

Isometric, Isometrical *adjs.* of equal measure.

Isomorphism *n.* property of crystallizing in the same or closely related geometric forms.

Isopod *n.* a crustacean with seven pairs of equal and similarly placed legs.

Isosceles *adj.* (of triangle) having two sides equal.

Isoseismal *adj.* & *n.* (a line) of equal earthquake-shock intensity.

Isotherm *n.* line imaginary of equal mean annual temperature.

Issue *n.* result, outcome; a number quantity or set of items supplied and distributed at one time; children; a question, a dispute; an important topic; for discussion or argument.

Istle *n.* a kind of fibre got from species of agave etc.

It *pron.* the thing in question; the person in question.

Itch *n.* an uncomfortable feeling on the skin that causes a desire to scratch; a constant desire to scratch.

Item *n.* an article; a separate particular; a hint; one part of a whole.

Iterance *n.* repetition.

Iterate *v.t.* to repeat; to do again; to do a second time; to state repeatedly.

Iterative *adj.* tending to iterate.

Itenerant *adj.* wandering; travellng from place to place; strolling.

Ivory *n.* a substance like bone forming the tusks or elephat and certain other animals.

Ivy *n.* an evergreen creeping plant.

Ixions wheel *n.* the wheel on which Ixion was condemned to revolve for even in Hades.

Izard *n.* a capriform antelope of Pyrenees.

J

J the tenth letter of the English alphabet.

Jaal-goat *n.* a wild goat.

Jab *v.t.* to thrust or poke roughly; to stab.

Jabber *v.i.* & *t.* to utter indistinctly; to talk rapidly in an excited manner; to chatter. *n.* one who jabbers; chatter; gabble.

Jabiru *n.* a tropical American bird of the stork family.

Jaborandi *n.* a kind of medicine.

Jabot *n.* a kind of lace worn on a woman's bodice.

Jacana *n.* a small tropical wading bird with large straight claws.

Jacinth *n.* a variety of zircon; a reddish-orange gem.

Jack *n.* a device for rasing heavy weights off the ground; a man or fellow.

Jack *n.* the tree; East-Indian fruit.

Jackal *n.* a drudge for another; a wild animal of Africa and Asia that is related to the dog.

Jacket *n.* outside wrapper of a book; skin of a potato; an outer cover round a tank, pipe, etc.

Jacob *n.* a flowering plant with leaves suggesting a ladder.

Jacobin *n.* a kind of pigeon with reversed feathers on the back of neck.

Jacobite *n.* an adherent of the exiled Stuarts.

Jaconet *n.* a thin cotton fabric.

Jactitation *n.* restless tossing of the body in illness; twisting of limbs or muscle.

Jaculate *v.t.* to dart.

Jade *n.* a poor or worn-out horse; a low playful woman or girl.

Jadery *n.* the tricks of a jade.

Jaeger *n.* a huntera low playful woman or girl.

Jag *n.* a sharp point of a rock; a sharp projection.

Jaggery *n.* raw palm-sugar made in India; crude sugar.

Jaguar *n.* a large American carnivorous spotted quadruped of the cat kind.

Jah *n.* Jehovah.

Jailer *n.* keeper of a jail.

Jalap *n.* a purgative drug or medicine.

Jalousie *n.* a shutter, with slats sloped upwards from outside; a blind.

Jam *v.t. & i.* to squeeze; to thrust violently; to crowd.

Jamb *n.* the side post or side of doorway, window, or fireplace or other opening in a wall.

Jampack *v.t.* crowd to full capacity.

Jangle *v.t. & i.* to make a harsh noise; to speak in noisy way.

Janitor *n.* a doorkeeper; an attendant; a caretaker of a building.

January *n.* (abbr. *Jan.*) the first month of the English year.

Japan *n.* an empire on the east of Asia; a hard varnish.

Jape *n.* jest; a joke played on somebody. *v.i.* to joke or jest.

Japonica *n.* kinds of plant from Japan; an ornamental bush with red flowers and pale green fruits.

Jar *n.* a harsh sound; shock; a quarrel.

Jardiniere *n.* an ornamental pot or stand for display of growing flowers.

Jarvey *n.* a hackney coach-man; driver of Irish car.

Jasmin(e) *n.* a shrub with beautiful white fragrant flowers.

Jasper *n.* a red, yellow, or brown opaque quartz.

Jaundice *n.* a disease of the blood characterised by yellowness of skin and eyes from bile pigments; prejudice; jealously. *v.t.* to affect with jaundice.

Jaunt *v.i.* to go from place to place for pleasure; to make excursion.

Jaunty *adj.* feeling or showing that one is cheerful and full of confidence.

Javan *adj.* & *n.* a native of Java.

Jaw *n.* the lower jaw; a bone containing the teeth.

Jay *n.* a chattering bird of brilliant plumage; a wanton woman.

Jaywalk *v.i.* crossing the road in a careless or dangerous manner.

Jazz *n.* noisy music and dancing; garish colouring; a manner of jazz.

Jealous *adj.* envious of; solicitous or resentful or rivalry in the affections.

Jean *n.* a twilled cotton cloth; (*pl.*) a suit made of jean; a garment of jean.

Jeep *n.* a small strong motor vehicle used especially by the army for driving over rough ground.

Jeer *v.t.* & *i.* to sneer; to deride; to laugh and shout rude remarks at somebody.

Jehovah *n.* Hebrew name of God, Scripture name of Supreme Being.

Jehu *n.* a (furious) driver.

Jejune *adj.* empty; barren; spiritless; void of interest; poor; scanty.

Jelly *n.* fruit-juice boiled with sugar; it is made of liquid set with gelatine and shakes when moved.

Jennet *n.* a small Spanish horse.

Jenny *n.* a locomotive crane; a machine for spinning.

Jeopardy *n.* hazard; a danger.

Jerboa *n.* a small jumping rodent of African deserts with long hindlegs.

Jeremiad *n.* wailing; a doleful complaint.

Jericho *n.* a town in Palestine.

Jerid *n.* sharp knife.

Jerk *n.* a sudden, quick sharp movement; spasmodic twitch of muscle; a jerkling throw.

Jerk *v.t.* to curse (*esp.* beef) by drying in sun.

Jerkin *n.* a jacket usually of leather.

Jerry *n.* building of flimsy houses with bad material.

Jersey *n.* a garment of knitted wool or cotton without fastenings.

Jess *n.* a short strap of leather or silk.

Jessamine *n.* jasmine.

Jest *n.* a thing said or done to cause amusement; a joke.

Jester *n.* a buffoon; one who jests.

Jesuit *n.* a crafty person; a member of Society of Jesus.

Jet *n.* a black fossil; stream of water steam, etc. shot from.

Jetsam *n.* goods thrown overboard from a ship to lighten it and washed ashore.

Jetton *n.* a counter with stamped or engraved device.

Jetty *n.* a wall of wooden platform built out into the sea.

Jew *n.* a person of Hebrew race. *v.t.* to cheat.

Jewel *n.* a precious stone; an ornament of great value; a gem.

Jeweller *n.* a dealer in jewels.

Jewing *n.* wattles at the base of beak in some pigeons.

Jewry *n.* the Jews; Jews' quarter in a town.

Jezebel *n.* a shameless woman; an impudent woman;

Jib *n.* the arm of a crane used for lifting things.

Jibe *n.* & *v.t.* & *i.* scoff; taunt; to scoff.

Jiff(y) *n.* a short time, moment.

Jig *n.* a quick lively dance or the music for this.

Jigger *n.* a kind of flea burrowing into skin; a small sail; one who jigs ore.

Jiggle *v.t.* to rock or jerk lightly.

Jihad, Jehad *ns.* religious war of Mohammedans against unbelievers; (fig.) a crusade.

Jill *n.* a young woman.

Jilt *n.* a woman who capriciously discards her lover.

Jim Crow *n.* (U.S.) a negro; an implement for straightening iron bars or rails.

Jimp *adj.* handsome; scanty; elegant.

Jingle *n.* a mingled rattling sound; a clinking sound.

Jingling *adj.* rattling, ringing.

Jingo *n.* a bellicose or blustering patriot.

Jinks *n.* riotous merry making.

Jinx *n.* person or thing bringing bad luck.

Jitters *n. pl.* worried nervousness.

Job *n.* a responsibility; duty or function; a crime, especially stealing.

Jobation *n.* (lengthy) reprimand; a scolding.

Jobber *n.* one who does small jobs.

Jock *n.* (*sl.*) a Highland solider.

Jockey *n.* a professional rider in horse-races. *v.t.* & *i.* to cheat; to trick.

Jocko *n.* a chimpanzee.

Jocose, Jocular *adjs.* sportive; given to jokes and jesting; waggish; humorous.

Jocular *adj.* mirthful, sportive, humorous.

Jocund *n.* merry; sportive; pleasant; cheerful.

Joey *n.* (Austral.) a young kangaroo; a young animal.

Jog *v.t.* & *i.* to move in an unsteady way; to stimulate (memory).

Joggle *v.t.* & *i.* to give a sudden but slight push to; to shake.

Joggle *n.* joints in two pieces of timber or stone.

Jogtrot *n.* a slow regualr pace.

John *n.* a masculline Christian name.

Join *v.t.* & *i.* to unite or be united (in marriage; friendship etc.).

Joinder *n.* (*esp.* law) joining; union.

Joiner *n.* maker of furniture and light woodwork.

Joining *n.* a connection; a joint.

Joint *adj.* combined; shared by two or more; created by combined effort.

Jointly *adv.* unitedly, together.

Jointress *n.* a woman who holds a jointure.

Jointure *n.* an estate settled on wife to be enjoyed by her after her husband's death.

Joist *n.* any of the parallel timbers stretched from wall to wall to support ceiling laths or floor boards.

Joke *n.* a thing said or done to excite laughter; a jest; witticism; a ridiculous circumstance.

Jokul *n.* snow-mountain in Iceland.

Jollify *v.i.* & *t.* to make merry; to make jolly.

Jollity *n.* merrymaking.

Jolly *adj.* mirthful; happy and cheerful; joyful; festive.

Jolt *v.t.* & *i.* to disturb; to shake with a sudden jerk.

Jolting *n.* a shock or jerk.

Jolterhead *n.* a clumsy head.

Jonah *n.* a person who bring ill luck.

Jonquil *n.* a rush-leaved daffodil.

Jordon *n.* a chamber pot; urinal.

Jorum *n.* a large drinking-bowl.

Joseph *n.* woman's long cloak; a chaste man.

Josh *v.t.* (U.S.) to make jokes or mock somebody in a gentle way.

Joskin *n.* (*sl.*) a rustic; a dolt.

Joss *n.* a Chinese idol.

Josser *n.* a blunderer; a foolish person; a fool.

Jostle *v.i.* & *t.* to push or knock against something; to elbow; to struggle with.

Jot *n.* a little; a point; the least quantity; a small amount; whit. *v.t.* to write briefly; to set down in writing.

Joule *n.* (Electr.) a unit of work or energy.

Jounce *v.t.* & *i.* to jolt; to bounce; to bump. *n.* a shake.

Journal *n.* a newspaper or magazine that deals with a particular subject or professional activity.

Journey *n.* a travel, tour of excursion; pleasure trip.

Joust *v.t.* to engage in a combat on horseback.

Jove *n.* Jupiter.

Jovian *adj.* of like Jove; of the planet Jupiter.

Jowl *n.* the jaw; jawbone; the cheek; external prominent throat or neck.

Joy *n.* a feeling of great happiness or pleasure; occasion of great happiness.

Jubate *adj.* having a mane.

Jubilant *adj.* rejoicing; shouting triumphantly.

Juiblance, Jubilation *n.* shout of triumph.

Jubilate *v.i.* to make demonstrations of gladness; to exult; to shout for joy.

Jubilee *n.* a special anniversary of an event; the celebration of this.

Judaic *adj.* relating to Jews.

Judge *n.* a person who decides who has won a competition or contest.

Judicature *n.* court of justice; administration of justice; judge's (term of) office; body of judges.

Judicial *adj.* pertaining to a judge or court of justice; critical; impartial.

Jug *n.* a deep container, with a handle and a lip, for holding and pouring liquids with a handle.

Juggins *n.* (*sl.*) a simpleton.

Juggle *v.t.* & *i.* to throw aset of objects, *e.g.* balls, up into the air and catch them repeatedly.

Jugular *adj.* any of several veins in the neck that carry blood from the head to the heart.

Jugulate *v.t.* to strangulate; to suffocate; to kill.

Juice *n.* the soup of vegetables or fruits; the fluid part of the animal bodies.

Juicy *adj.* containing a lot of juice and enjoyable to eat.

Juke-box *n.* a record-player operated by a coin.

Julep *n.* sweet drink, *esp.* as vehicle for medicine; a medicated drink as a stimulant.

July *n.* the seventh month of the English year.

Jumbal *n.* thin crisp sweet cake.

Jumble *v.t.* & *i.* to mix up; to move in disorder.

Jumbo *n.* a very big thing; a big clumsy person.

Jump *v.t.* & *i.* to spring from the ground; to leap.

Jumpy *adj.* nervous; panicky.

Junction *n.* jointing-point; meeting-place.

Juncture *n.* joining; concurrence of events; point of time.

June *n.* sixth month of the English year.

Jungle *n.* (also Sanskrit word) a forest; a land covered with tangled vegetation.

Junior *adj.* younger; later or inferior in office; less advanced.

Juniper *n.* a evergreen bush that does not lose its leaves in winter.

Junk *n.* discarded material; thing that are considered useless or of little value.

Juno *n.* wife of Jupiter; a woman of excellent beauty

Junto *n.* a faction or clique; secret society; confederacy.

Jupe *n.* skirt.

Jupiter *n.* the largest planet of the solar system, more distant from the sun than the Earth and Mars; king of gods.

Jural *adj.* of law of moral rights and obligations.

Jurassic *adj.* of the Jura mountains; marked like these by the prevalence of oolitic limestone.

Jurisconsult *n.* one learned in law or jurisprudence.

Jurisprudence *n.* the science or knowledge of law.

Jurist *n.* one versed in law; student of law; writer on law; a law graduate.

Juror *n.* one who takes oath.

Jury *n.* a number of persons sworn to enquire into a case and deliver the truth according to evidence.

Jury-mast *n.* a temporary mast in place of a broken or lost one.

Jus *n.* law right.

Jussive *adj.* expressing a command.

Just *adj.* based on or behaving according to accepted moral principles.

Justice *n.* justness; uprightness; just treatment; a judge of the Highcourt or Supreme Court.

Justify *v.t.* to show that somebody is right; reasonable or just; to be a good reason or excuse for something.

Justle *v.t.* to push.

Jut *n.* a projection; a jetting movement; protruding point.

Jute *n.* fibre from the bark of an Indian plant used especially for making bags.

Juvenile *adj.* pertainting to young persons; youthful; puerile.

Juvenile-Court *n.* a court of law that deals with young people who are not yet adults.

Juvenilia *n. pl.* works produced in author's youth.

Juvenility *n.* young age, youth.

Juxtapose *v.t.* to place people or thing next to each other or very close together, especially to show a contrast.

K

K the eleventh letter of the English alphabet; the symbol for potassium in chemistry; used as constant in Mathematics.

Kaaba *n.* Holy stone of Mecca.

Kabaya *n.* a loose shirt.

Kadi *n.* a kind of tent in boat.

Kaftan *n.* a long loose Eastern garment; woman's dress resembling this.

Kago *n.* a Japanese palanquin made of basket-work.

Kail *n.* a kind of cabbage.

Kaiser *n.* the title of the Emperor of Germany or Austria.

Kakemono *n.* a Japanese wall picture with roller.

Kakapo *n.* the ground parrot or owl parrot of New Zealand.

Kale *n.* cabbage.

Kaleidoscope *n.* tube throudh which are seen symmetrical figures.

Kali *n.* a plant from which soda-ash is obtained, Hindu goddess of destruction.

Kangaroo *n.* a kind of Australian quadruped with very long hind-legs and great power of leaping.

Kaolin *n.* China clay.

Kapok *n.* cotton-wool found in the seeds of certain trees.

Kaput *adj.* (not before noun) not working correctly; broken.

Karaoke a sound system with a pre-recorded song track of popular music.

Kedge *n.* small anchor. *v.t.* to change the position of a ship by pulling rope attached to an anchor.

Kedgy *adj.* merry, happy, lively.

Keel *n.* a lower longitudinal timber or iron on which ship's framework is built; a narrow ridge.

Keen *adj.* having a sharp point; eager; of fine edge; strong; severe; bitter; penetrating.

Keen *n.* Irish funeral song accompanied with wailing.

Keep *v.t.* & *i.* to guard; to preserve; to celebrate; to retain possession of.

Keeve *n.* tank.

Keg *n.* a small cask or barrel, especially of beer.

Keif *n.* drowsiness due to intoxicants.

Kelp *n.* a type of large brown sea plant sometimes used as manure.

Kelvin *n.* S.I. unit of temperature.

Ken *v.t.* to descry; to recognize; to know.

Kennel *n.* a shelter for a pet dog; a place where dogs are bred or cared for.

Kepi *n.* a French military cap.

Kept *adj.* & *n.* maintained by a paramour.

Keramic *adj.* pertaining to pottery.

Keratin *n.* fibrous protein found in the hair and nails.

Keratose *adj.* of hornlike structure.

Kerb *n.* the edge of pavement.

Kerchief *n.* a square cloth used for covering head; a handkerchief.

Kermes *n.* red dye-stuff made of its dried body.

Kern *n.* an Irish foot-soldier.

Kernel *n.* a seed within a hard shell; the edible part of a nut; a nucleus; the important part of a thing.

Kerosene *n.* distilled petroleum; lamp-oil got by distillation of petroleum.

Kersey *n.* a kind of coarse narrow woollen cloth.

Kestrel *n.* a kind of small hawk.

Ketch *n.* a small two masted ship.

Ketch up *n.* sauce prepared from mushrooms, tomatoes, etc.

Kettle *n.* a metal vessel with spout and handle for boiling.

Kettle-drum *n.* a large afternoon tea-party; a drum with parchment spread over a brass hemisphere.

Key *n.* an instrument for moving the levers of a lock, that which gives opportunity solution, explanation, system of muscial notes, level pressed by a finger in a musical instrument.

Keyboard *n.* all the black and white keys on a piano; a set of keys that operate a computer or typewriter, etc.

Keyhole *n.* an apparatus for receiving a key.

Kibble *n.* a hoisting bucket used in mines.

Kick *n.* a blow with the foot; a jerk; kicking power; resistance; kicking.

Kicker *n.* a horse which kicks.

Kicshaw *n.* fancy dish of food; toy; tirfle.

Kid *n.* the young of a goat; a child or young person; goat's skin.

Kiddle *n.* a barrier in a river with opening fitted with nets to catch fish.

Kiddy *n.* a small child.

Kidnap *v.t.* to seize and forcibly carry away any person against his will.

Kidnapper *n.* a man-stealer.

Kidney *n.* either one of two glandular bodies in the lumbar region which secrets the urine.

Kier *n.* a vessel in which cloth is boiled for bleaching.

Kill *v.t.* & *i.* to put to death; to slay; to cause the death of; to switch or turn something off.

Kiln *n.* a furnace or oven for calcining lime or baking bricks.

Kilo- in the Metric system for one thousand.

Kilogram *n.* a thousand grams.

Kilt *n.* a skirt, the Highlander's dress.

Kin *n.* a person of the same family; relationship; affinity; kindred.

Kinchin *n.* a child.

Kind *n.* race; style; manner; sort; variety; character; produce; a group of people or things having similar characteristics.

Kindergarten *n.* an infant school in which they are given education by means of toys, games etc.

Kindle *v.t.*& *i.* to inspire; to make somebody start to feel hope.

Kindly *adj.* kind; sympathetic.

Kindred *n.* relationship; relatives; a family relationship; one's family and relations.

Kine *n. pl.* of **Cow.**

Kinematic *adj.* of motion considered without reference to force.

Kinetic *adj.* of motion in relation to force; of or produced by movement.

King *n.* the male sovereign of a nation; the monarch; a hereditary ruler.

Kingcraft *n.* able exercise of royalty.

Kingdom *n.* state or territory ruled by a king; dominion of a king.

Kinship *n.* a close feeling between people that develops as a result of common origins; a family relationship, attitudes, etc.

Kiosk *n.* small booths selling drinks, cigarettes, news papers, etc.

Kip *n.* hide of a young beast or small animal, a pointed hill, a brothel.

Kipper *v.t.* to cure (fish). *n.* salmon fish, preserved with salt; and then dried or smoked; a dried skin.

Kirk *n.* Chruch.

Kirtle *n.* a woman's gown or outer petticoat.

Kiss *n.* a salute given with lips; caress given with lips.

Kit *n.* a small wooden tub; the outfit of necessaries for a soldier, sailor or mechanic; equipments of travellers.

Kitchen *n.* a room or building in which meals are cooked or prepared.

Kite *n.* a bird of prey belonging to falcon family; a rapacious person.

Kith *n.* acquaintance and relative; friend and relations.

Kitten *n.* the young of a cat; playful girl.

Kittle *adj.* difficult to pacify.

Kiwi *n.* a person from New Zealand.

Kloof *n.* a narrow valley; ravine.

Knack *n.* a skill at performing some special task; an ability.

Knag *n.* a knot in wood; a pag.

Knap *v.t.* to break; to snap; to bleak (flints) with a hammer. *n.* a rising ground; summit.

Knar *n.* (also **Gnar**) a knot on a tree.

Knarl *n.* a knot in wood.

Knave *n.* a dishonest person; a scoundrel; a rascal; a villian.

Knavish *adj.* dishonest; faudulent.

Knead *v.t.* to work up into paste or dough; to blend together.

Knee *n.* to touch with knee; to cause (trousers) to bulge at knees; to fasten (framework etc.) with knees.

Kneel *v.t.* to take or be in a position where the body is supported by the knees; to fall or rest on the knees (*esp.* in reverence).

Knell *n.* the sound of a bell, *esp.* one rung at a funeral.

Kinckers *n. pl.* women's under pants.

Knick-knack *n.* a light dainty article; gimerack.

Knickery *n.* trivialness.

Knife *n.* a cutting instrument; a sharp blade with a handle, used for cutting or as a weapon.

Knight *n.* a champion in war; a title of rank; a piece used in a game of chess.

Knightage *n.* the body of knights.

Knit *v.t.* & *i.* to tie together; to join to unite closely; to form into a knot.

Knittle *n.* a small line made of yarn.

Knob *n.* a round handle, especially of a door or drawer.

Knobble *n.* a small knob.

Knock *v.t.* & *i.* to strike; to strike to clash; to put somebody in a certain state or position by hitting them/it.

Knoll *n.* a small hill; a mound. *v.t.* & *i.* to ring or sound (bell); to toll out; to summon by the sound of bell.

Knop *n.* the bud of a flower.

Knot *n.* a tie, a nautical mile (6080 ft.), perplexity, difficulty, cluster, a joint in the stem or root of a plant.

Knotty *n.* full of knots; puzzling; difficult; intricate.

Know *v.t.* & *i.* to perceive clearly; to recognise; to distinguish.

Knowledge *n.* learning; instruction; acquaintance; information.

Knuckle *n.* bone at finger joint.

Knurl *n.* a knot or ridge.

Kobold *n.* dwarf.

Kohl *n.* collysicum.

Kodak *n.* a kind of photographic camera.

Kosher *adj.* conforming to Jewish religious law.

Kowtow *v.i.* to abase oneself.

Kraal a cattle-enclosure.

Kraut *n.* an offensive word for a person from Germany.

Kremlin *n.* Russian citadel, *esp.* imperial palace at Moscow.

Krill *n.* very small shellfish that live in the sea around the Antartic and are eaten by Whales.

Krypton *n.* an inert gas discovered in 1898.

Kudos *n.* fame; glory.

Kyphosis *n.* *adj.* kyphotic.

Kyte *n.* belly.

L

L the twelfth letter of the English alphabet; a symbol for 50 in Roman numerals.

Lab *n.* (abbr.) laboratory.

Labarum *n.* Roman millitary standard.

Labefaction *n.* shaking; weakening; downfall.

Label *n.* stamp; a piece of paper or of any material fastened to an object showing what it is.

Labial *adj.* pronounced chiefly with the lips; of the lips.

Labiate *adj.* having two unequal lips.

Labile *adj.* liable to change.

Labialise *v.t.*

Laborious *n.* toilsome; industrious; diligent; hard-working.

Labour *n.* physical or mental exertion; work; toil; a task; working class collectively; travail.

Labrador *n.* hard physical work that is not skilled.

Laburnum *n.* a small shrub with yellow flowers.

Labyrinth *n.* a confusing network of passage; a network of winding passages; tangled affairs; (Anat.) complex cavity of internal ear.

Lac *n.* a resinous substance mainly produced from banyan-tree; lakh, 100000.

Lace *n.* a cord or string used for fastening; a plaited string; a delicate kind of network.

Lacerate *v.t.* to tear; to torture; to injure flesh by tearing; to wound feelings.

Laches *n.* negligence in performing a legal duty; culpable negligence.

Lachrymal *adj.* of tears.

Lachrymatory *adj.* causing tears to flow. *n.* a tear-bottle.

Lack *n.* want, deficiency, need. *v.i.* & *t.* to be without something; to have less than enough of something.

Lackadaisical *adj.* languidly superior; feebly sentimental.

Lackey *n.* a foot-boy, a man servant. *v.t.* to dance attendance on; to behave servilely to.

Laconic *adj.* expressed in few words; short; pithy.

Laconicism *adj.* brevity of speech; short pithy saying.

Lacquer, Lacker *ns.* a kind of varnish. *v.t.* to smear or varnish with lacquer.

Lactation *n.* secreting and excreting of milk.

Lactiferous *adj.* yielding milk or milky juice.

Lactometer *n.* instrument for testing purity of milk.

Lactose *n.* a form of sugar found in milk and used in some baby foods; sugar of milk.

Lacuna *n.* a missing or empty part, the cavity in a bone.

Lacustrine *adj.* dwelling or growing in lakes.

Lad *n.* a boy; a youth; a lover; a young man.

Ladder *n.* a series of stages by which a person may advance in her or his career etc.

Lade *v.t.* to load (ship); to dip; to take cargo abroad; to ship (goods).

Ladle *n.* a long-handled large-bowled spoon for transferring liquids.

Lady *n.* a well-bread woman; a well-dressed woman; the woman head of house-hold.

Lag *v.t.* & *i.* to take into custody; to go too slow.

Lagoon *n.* salt-water lake parted from sea by sand-bank.

Laid *adj.* press down.

Lair *n.* a place to lie or rest; an enclosure for cattle; a beast's lying-place.

Laird *n.* a house-proprietor.

Lake *n.* a large area of water surrounded by land; a crimson pigment.

Lamb *n.* the young of the sheep; any innocent person; a helpless person.

Lambent *adj.* moving on surface only; playing about; gently brilliant.

Lame *adj.* (of argument, excuse) imperfect, unsatisfactory.

Lament *v.t.* & *i.* to mourn; to wail; to deplore; to express grief.

Lamented *adj.* mourned for (*esp.* conventionally of the dead, as the *late lamented*).

Lamentable *adj.* that is to be regretted; very sad.

Lamentation *n.* expression of sorrow; lamenting; mourning.

Lamina *n.* a thin plate or layer of bone, metal etc.

Laminate *v.t.* to fold in thin plates.

Lamp *n.* source of spiritual or intellectual light.

Lampas *n.* a kind of floral silk.

Lampion *n.* a glass pot holding light for illumination.

Lampoon *n.* a personal satire in writing.

Lance *n.* a weapon with a long wooden handle and a sharp pointed meal head.

Lancer *n.* a soldier of cavalry regiment armed with lances.

Lancet *n.* a two edged knife used by surgeons for opening veins, etc. (architecture) a tall narrow pointed arch or window.

Lances *n.* a soldier armed with a lance.

Lancinate *v.t.* to cut open with a lancet.

Land *n.* the solid part of earth's surface; soil estate.

Landan *n.* a four-wheeled coach or carriage with top whose back and front can be raised and lowered.

Landing *n.* an act of coming or bringing somebody to land; a place for setting on land or disembarking.

Landlady *n.* a woman who owns or manages a guest-house.

Landless *adj.* destitute of land.

Landlocked *adj.* alomost or quite enclosed by land.

Landlord *adj.* person, especially a man, from whom one rents land, a house, a room; a person of whom another holds any tenement, etc. for money; keeper of an inn or lodgings.

Landmark *n.* a notable event; a discovery, an invention, etc.

Landscape *n.* a piece of inland scenery; a picture representing land.

Landslide *n.* a mass of earth, rock, etc. sliding down the side of a mountain or cliff.

Land-tax *n.* tax assessed on landed property.

Landward *adj., adv.* & *n.* towards the land.

Landwind *n.* land-breeze.

Lane *n.* any of the marked sections of track, water, etc. each intended for a competitor in a race; a narrow street.

Language *n.* human speech; style, manner of expression; form of speech used by the people.

Languish *v.i.* to become week; to get exhausted; to whither.

Languor *n.* lassitude; faintness.

Laniary *adj.* tearing; a canine tooth.

Lank *adj.* lean and thin; tall and lean; straight.

Lanolin *n.* extract obtained from sheep's wool used in ointments.

Lantern *n.* a metal lamp, often used outside, whose light is protected from the wind etc by glass.

Lanyard *n.* a short rope used as handle.

Laodicean *n.* a person lacking zeal, *esp.* in religion or politics.

Lap *n.* front of woman's skirt held up as a receptacle; the flat area between the stomach and knees of a person when he or she is sitting.

Lapel *n.* the part of a coat folded back containing the collar.

Lapidary *n.* a cutter of a gem-stones.

Lapislazuli *n.* a bright blue pigment.

Lappet *n.* a flap or fold of garment, etc.

Lapse *n.* a slip, a slight mistake, a falling or gliding.

Lar *n.* a household deity of the Romans.

Larboard *n.* the left-hand side of a ship. (opposite to star-board).

Larcener *n.* a thief; one who steals.

Larceny *n.* robbing the personal goods of others.

Larch *n.* bright-foliaged tree of pine kind; its timber.

Lard *n.* a firm white substance made from the melted fat of pigs and used in cooking.

Lardaceous *adj.* of the nature of lard.

Larder *n.* a room or cupboard for storing meat & other articles.

Lardy *adj.* full of hog's flesh.

Large *adj.* liberal; of considerable or relatively great magnitude; big; great.

Largesse *n.* money or gifts scattered on occasions of rejoicing.

Lark *n.* amusing incident; kinds of small singing bird. *v.t.* to indulge in merry-making.

Larva *n.* the first stage after leaving the egg of an insect.

Laryngeal *adj.* pertaining to the larynx.

Larynx *n.* the upper part of the wind pipe; cavity in throat holding vocal chords.

Laryngitis *n.* inflammation of larynx.

Lascar *n.* a sailor or camp-follower; an East-Indian sea-man.

Lascivious *adj.* exciting voluptuous; emotions; lustful manner.

Lash *v.t.* & *i.* to strike with a whip; to make a sudden movement; to fasten together; to rebuke.

Lasher *n.* one who lashes or whips.

Lassitude *n.* wearing; debility; languor.

Lasso *n.* a noosed rope for catching cattle. *v.t.* to catch with lasso.

Last *adj.* lates, most recent; after all others, coming at the end.

Latch *n.* a contrivance for fastening a door or window.

Latchet *n.* the string that fastens a shoe.

Late *adj.* coming after the appointed time; backward; long delayed.

Latent *adj.* concealed; not manifested, dormant; under the surface.

Latex *n.* milky juice of plants.

Lath *n.* a long thin and narrow piece of wood. *v.t.* to cover with lath.

Lather *n.* a mass of small white bubbles produced by soap or detergent when mixed with water.

Latin *n.* pertaining to the ancient Romans; the old Roman language.

Latitude *n.* the angular distance from the equator; breadth; space.

Latitudinous *adj.* of large extent.

Latrine *n.* a toilet in a camp, etc. especially one made by digging a hole in the ground.

Latter *n.* recent; nearer to the end of a period than to the beginning.

Lattice *n.* interlaced network of wood; a framework of crossed bars with spaces between.

Laud *n.* a praise; a song of praise; hymn; eulogy.

Laudable *adj.* commendable; praise worthy; sound.

Laudanum *n.* opium prepared in spirit of wine; alcoholic tincture of opium.

Luadation *n.* praise; commendation.

Laugh *v.t.* & *i.* to make the sounds and movements of the face and body that express amusement or happiness.

Laughter *n.* the action, sound or manner of laughing.

Launch *v.t.* & *i.* to put something into action; to start something.

Launderer *n.* a washerman.

Laundry *n.* business where clothes, etc. are washed.

Laureate *adj.* wreathed or decked or invested with laure.

Laurel *n.* a plant with bright green leaves; a crown of laurel as sign of distinction.

Laurustinus *n.* an evergreen flowering shrub.

Lava *n.* hot liquid rock that comes out of a volcano.

Lavabo *n.* washing of hands before religious rites.

Lavatory *n.* the place for washing hands and face.

Lave *v.t.* to wash; to bathe; to flow out; to put out; to wash against.

Lavement *n.* (Med.) a washing injection; enema.

Lavender *n.* a plant with sweet-smelling pale purple flowers.

Laver *n.* spiritual cleansing; a large vessel used for ablution.

Laverock *n.* a lark.

Lavish *adj.* profuse; extravagant; wasteful; giving or doing something generously or excessively.

Law *n.* enacted rule recognised by a community; influence of such a rule.

Lawful *adj.* not illegal; legitimate; rightful; permitted or appointed by law.

Lawn *n.* an open space between forests.

Lawny *adj.* covered with lawn.

Lawyer *n.* a person trained and qualified in the law who does legal work for other people, especially a solicitor.

Lax *adj.* slack; loose; soft; weak in control.

Laxative *adj.* having the power of loosening the bowels.

Laxly *adv.* in a lax or loose manner.

Lay *n.* the way or position in which a thing lies or is arranged in relation to other things; a short narrative poem.

Layer *n.* a stratum; bed; shoot embedded in earth; one that lays; thickness of a matter laid over a surface.

Layette *n.* a set of clothes, nappies, etc. for a new baby.

Lazar *n.* a beggar with leprosy.

Lazaretto *n.* a hospital for lepers; a hospital for quarantine.

Lazarus *n.* a begger, a poor man.

Laze *v.t.* to spend time in laziness.

Lazily *adv.* in a lazy manner.

Lazy *adj.* indolent; slothful; sluggish; unwilling to work.

Lea *n.* a piece of meadow or arable or pasture land; a grassy plain.

Lead *v.t. & i.* to be the leader or head of somebody; to force to go with one; to direct or control somebody.

Lead *n.* a heavy soft metal, dull grey in colour; a chemical element used formerly for water pipes or to cover roofs.

Leaden *adj.* consisting of lead; lead-coloured; sombre.

Leader *n.* one who leads; a guide; a conductor; the editorial article in a newspaper; anything to guide the eye.

Leaderette *n.* a short leading article in a newspaper.

Leading *adj.* in first position (s); giving guidance; chief; of most important.

Leaf *n.* the flat green parts of a plant; two pages of a book; a part of the top of a table that can be taken out.

Leafage *n.* leaves collectively, foliage.

Leafless *adj.* devoid of leaves.

Leaflet *n.* a printed sheet of paper, usually folded and free of charge containing information.

League *n.* a group of sports clubs competing against each other.

Leak *n.* a hole or opening caused by wear; an amount of liquid or gas that passes through this.

Leal *adj.* honest; faithful; loyal.

Lean *adj.* slender; thin; without fat; unproductive; small in amount or quality.

Leaning *n.* predilection; inclination; bias; tendency.

Leap *v.t.* & *i.* to spring over; to jump high or a long way.

Leap-Year *n.* a year with 29th Feb. as an intercalary day.

Learn *v.t.* & *i.* to gain knowledge; to become familiar with by studying.

Lease *n.* an agreement by which a person allows another person to use his land or property for a certain period in return for payment.

Leash *n.* a band for tying hounds; a thing for holding dogs.

Least *adj.* smallest.

Leat *n.* an open water-course.

Leatheroid *n.* chemically prepared artificial hide.

Leave *n.* permission; liberty granted; departure; the period or time one is allowed to take as holiday from one's job.

Leaven *n.* a quality or influence that makes people, an atmosphere, etc. less serous or more lively.

Leacher *n.* a man who is always thinking about and looking for sexual pleasure.

Lectern *n.* a high sloping desk for a speaker's notes or a bible in church.

Lection *n.* different reading in a book.

Lecture *n.* a talk giving information about a subject to an audience or a class, often as part of a teaching programme.

Lecturer *n.* one who lecturers.

Led *adj.* under the control of a farm-holder.

Ledge *n.* a narrow shelf sticking out from a wall.

Ledger *n.* a horizontal timber in scaffolding.

Lee *n.* the part or side of something providing shelter against the wind.

Leech *n.* a physician; a blood-sucking worm.

Leek *n.* a bulbous plant similar to the onion.

Leer *v.t.* to glance obliquely. *n.* sidelong look.

Lees *n. pl.* a barrel of beer, etc.; sediment of wine.

Left *adj.* opposed to the right; relatively liberal; of or situated on the side opposite to the right.

Leg *n.* one of the limbs by which an animal walks.

Legacy *n.* that which given to a person by will; a bequest; a thing passed to somebody by people who lived before them or from earlier events.

Legal *adj.* pertaining to law, lawful, required by law, in conformity with law.

Legate *n.* the official representative of the Pope in a foreign country.

Legatee *n.* one to whom a legacy is bequeathed; recipient of a legacy.

Legation *n.* a diplomatic mission; the body of delegates.

Legend *n.* traditional or romantic story, a myth.

Legging *n.* outer covering of leather, usually for lower leg.

Leghorn *n.* breed of fowls; kind of plaited straw for hats; a hat of it.

Legible *adj.* that can be read; distinct; clear.

Legion *n.* a division of armies; a great number; a large number of people who share a characteristic.

Legislate *v.t.* to make laws.

Legislative *adj.* pertaining to or done by legislation.

Legislator *n.* a law-giver; a member of a body that makes laws.

Legislatress, Legistatrix *ns. fem.* a female legislator.

Legislature *n.* legislative body or legislating power of a State.

Legist *n.* a person skilled in law.

Legitimacy *n.* lawfulness; being legitimate; legality.

Legum *adj.* of laws.

Leguminous *adj.* pertaining to or consisting of pulse.

Leisure *n.* unoccupied time; freedom from business; free time.

Leman *n.* a lover; a sweet heart; unlawful lover.

Lemma *n.* the presumed proposition in an argument or in Mathematics; motto.

Lemon *n.* an oval yellow fruit with sour juice; a pale yellow colour.

Lemur *n.* a mammal resembling a monkey, mostly found in Madagascar, lemurs usually live in trees and are active at night.

Lend *v.t.* to give on loan; to let for hire; to bestow; to grant.

Length *n.* the amount something measurers or extends from one end to the other.

Lenience, Leniency, Lenity *ns.* kindness; gentleness; mildness; clemency.

Lenient *adj.* tolerant, mild, relaxing, mitigating, gentle.

Lenitive *adj. & n.* mitigating; smoothing or gently laxative (drug).

Leno *n.* a kind of cotton gauze used for window-curtains.

Lens *n.* a piece of glass spherically convex on one or both sides.

Lent *n.* a fast of 40 days before Easter commemorating the Christ's fast during which some Christians fast in memory or Christ's suffering.

Lenten *adj.* relating to Lent; sparing.

Lentil *n.* usually dried and used as food; a small green, orange or brown seed.

Lentitude *n.* sluggishness.

Lentoid *adj.* of the shape of lens.

Leo *n.* the lion; a sign of zodiac; a person born under the influence of this sign.

Leopard *n.* a large African and S. Asian animal of the cat family with a yellowish coat and dark spots.

Leper *n.* an outcast; a person suffering from leprosy; a person who is rejected and avoided by others.

Lepid *adj.* pleasant.

Leporine *adj.* of the hare-kind.

Lesbian *adj.* pertaining to unnatural crime. *n.* homosexual woman.

Lese-majesty *n.* treason.

Lesion *n.* a wound; an injurious change in the action or texture of an organ.

Less *adj.* a smaller amount; not as much as; of lower rank of degree.

Lesson *n.* that which is learnt by pupil, amount of teaching at a time, precept, example, punishment.

Lest *conj.* for fear that; of the possibility of something happening; in case.

Let *v.t.* & *i.* to allow or enable or cause to; to make it possible for somebody to go or pass in, out, etc.

Let to obstruct; to hinder.

Lethal *adj.* causing death; deadly; harmful or causing damage; causing or designed to cause death.

Lethargy *n.* an extreme lack of energy or enthusiasm for doing anything.

Lethargic *adj.* apathetic; dull.

Lethe *n.* the river of the under world, water causing oblivion.

Letter *n.* a mark used to express sound of speech; a written message.

Lettuce *n.* a composite plant the leaves of which are used as salad.

Leucocyte *n.* the white blood corpuscle of the blood.

Leucoderma *n.* *Path.* a kind of skin disease in which there are patches on the body.

Leucoma *n.* a disease of the eye.

Levant *v.i.* to decamp; to abscond without paying one's debts.

Levee *n.* an assembly of visitors; sovereign's reception for men only.

Level *n.* an instrument for ascertaining the level of a spot; a standard, even, flat, uniform.

Lever *n.* a mean of putting pressure on somebody to do something.

Leviable *adj.* that may be assessed.

Leviathan *n.* a thing of enormous size or power; a sea-monster of immense size.

Levity *n.* unseasonable jocularity; the treatment of a serious matter with humour or lack of respect.

Levy *n.* the act of collecting money by authority or force; the amount collected.

Lewd *adj.* licentious, profligate, indecent, not chaste.

Lewisgun *n.* kind of a machine gun.

Lexical *adj.* pertaining to the words of a language.

Lexicographer *n.* the author or complier of dictionaries.

Lexicography *n.* the theory and practice of writing and editing dictionaries.

Lexicon *n.* a word-book of dictionary.

Lexigraphy *n.* the system of writing in which each symbol represents a word.

Liable *adj.* answerable; reliable; obliged; bound legally; responsible by law.

Liaison *n.* a union; connection; illicit union between sexes.

Liar *n.* one who speaks an untruth.

Libation *n.* an offering to a God; a drink offering.

Libatory *adj.* pertaining to libation.

Libel *n.* a false defamatory statement; a published statement damaging to a person's reputation.

Libellous *adj.* defamatory.

Liberate *v.t.* to release.

Libertine *n.* & *adj.* a licentious man; one free from restraint.

Liberty *n.* freedom from salavary or restraint, right to do as one pleases, privillege.

Libra *n.* a pound weight (lb.) or pound sterling; the seventh sign of the Zodiac.

Library *n.* a reading and writing room in which books are kept; a collection of books.

Librate *v.i.* to oscillate; to quiver; to balance.

Libretto *n.* the song-book of an opera.

Lice *n. pl.* of louse.

Licence *n.* permission; leave; an official document showing that permission has been given to do.

Licentious *adj.* immoral in sexual relations; dissolute.

Lichen *n.* a kind of fungus. *v.t.* to cover with lichens.

Lick *v.t.* to pass the tongue over a thing, to taste it, to lap.

Lickerish *adj.* fond of dainty food; greedy; lecherous.

Licorice *n.* the sweat root of a certain plant.

Lid *n.* the upper and lower covers of eye.

Lie *n.* a false statement; a statement devoid of truth; an intentional false statement; imposture; false belief.

Lief *adv.* with as much or more willingness.

Liege *adj.* faithful. *n.* a lord or superior.

Lien *n.* the right to own another's property till he pays the debt.

Lieu *n.* place; stead.

Lieutenant *n.* a deputy acting for a superior; an officer in the army .

Life *n.* conscious existence; vitality, manner of living.

Lifeline *adj.* a line or rope thrown to rescue somebody in difficulty in water; a line attached to somebody who goes deep under the sea.

Lifelong *adj.* extending throughout one's life.

Lifestyle *n.* the way in which an individual or a group lives.

Lifetime *n.* the length of a person's life or a thing's existence.

Lift *v.t. & i.* to raise; to elevate; to exalt; to hoist; to rise; to disperse.

Ligament *n.* a bond of union; anything that unites.

Ligature *n. & v.t.* anything that binds; a bandage.

Light *n.* a natural agent that makes things visible; a burning candle; brightness of eyes or aspect

Lighthouse *n.* a tower or other structure containing a strong light to warm or guide ships.

Like *adj.* having similar qualities or features or in a similar situation; resembling another or the original.

Liken *v.t.* to compare, to find similarity in, to make like.

Likely *adj.* that seems suitable for a purpose; promising; probable or expected; apparently suitable.

Liking *n.* one's taste; regard or taste of predilection for.

Lilac *n.* a pale purple colour; a bush with sweet-smelling purple or white flowers. *adj.* lilac coloured.

Lilt *v.t.* to sing melodiously. *n.* a regular rising and falling pattern in music.

Lily *n.* kinds of plant with showy and fragrant flower, with large white or coloured flowers.

Limb *n.* leg, arm or wing; branch of a tree, edge.

Limbate *adj.* having different borders.

Limber *n.* the shaft of a vehicle; the detachable part of a gun-carriage.

Lime *n.* a sticky substance, white alkaline earth, a kind of lemon.

Limit *n.* a point or line beyond which something does not extend, a boundary; a terminal point.

Limitation *n.* a lack of ability; a condition, fact or circumstance that limits.

Limn *v.t.* to draw or paint, especially in the water; to paint (picture); to portray.

Limp *v.i.* to go with a lame gait; to walk with difficulty, especially when one foot or leg is hurt or stiff; to halt.

Limpid *adj.* clear; transparent; translucent; pure (of liquids, atmosphere, eyes, literary style).

Limpkin *n.* a kind of crane.

Linchpin *n.* a pin fixed on the end of the axle to keep wheel on.

Linden *n.* the lime-tree.

Line *n.* a fine cord; rail road; wire; a verse; a long thin mark on the surface of something.

Lineage *n.* descent; progeny; family; pedigree; race; ancestry.

Lineal *adj.* in the direct line of descent or ancestry.

Linear *adj.* of lines, narrow.

Linen *adj.* cloth made of flax; resembling linen cloth; household resembling linen cloth.

Liner *n.* a large passenger or cargo ship travelling on a regular route; a piece of material used to line something.

Linger *v.t.* & *i.* to delay; to stay about; to loiter; to stop departure.

Lingerie *n.* women's underclothing; linen articles; (in shop, etc.) women's clothing worn next to the skin.

Lingo *n.* expressions used by a particular group of people; contempt for everything foreign; foreign language.

Lingual *adj.* of the tongue; of speech; pronounced by the tongue.

Lining *n.* a layer of material applied to the inside of a garment, & etc.

Link *n.* one ring of a chain, bend in a river; connecting part, a torch.

Linoleum *n.* a strong cloth coated with a hard shiny substance, used as a floor covering.

Linotype *n.* a machine producing stereotyped lines of type.

Linseed *n.* lint or flax seed, used in paint; an oil made from flax seeds to protect wood, etc.

Linstock *n.* a staff to hold a lighted match for firing canon.

Lintel *n.* horizontal timber over a door.

Liny *adj.* marked with wrinkles or lines.

Lion *n.* a large, fierce loud roaring animal of the cat family; a man of unusual courage.

Lionet *n.* a small lion.

Lip *n.* either edge of the opening into the mouth; the edge of a hollow container or opening.

Lipstic *n.* a substance made into the shape of a small stick, used for colouring the lips.

Liquate *v.t.* to melt; to subject to liquation; to separate or purify (metals) by liquefying.

Liquid *adj.* & *n.* (of sounds) fluent; not discordant; a substance that flows freely, *e.g.* water, milk or oil.

Liquor *n.* a liquid; a liquid secretion; any alcoholic drink or other drink.

Lisp *v.t.* to speak or say something with a lisp.

Lissom *adj.* nimble; agile; thin and graceful in movement.

List *n.* the strip or edge of cloth, enclosing ground, scene of contest, catalogue.

Listen *v.i.* to give ear; to hear something that one is not meant to hear.

Listener *n.* one who listens.

Litany *n.* supplications for use in a church.

Litchi *adj.* a tree, or its fruits, orig. from China, grown in Bengal.

Literacy *n.* ability to read and write.

Literate *adj.* & *n.* able to read and write; lettered; learned.

Literati *n. pl.* educated and intelligent people who enjoy literature.

Literatim *adv.* letter for letter.

Literature *n.* learning, literary production, writing of a country.

Lithe *adj.* moving or bending easily and gracefully.

Lithium *n.* a metallic element.

Lithic *adj.* pertaining to stone. (*esp.* in bladder).

Lithium *n.* metallic element.

Lithograph *n.* & *v.t.* a print from stone; to engrave or draw on stone and print impressions from it.

Lithology *n.* the science of stones and rock.

Lithotomy *n.* (surg.) cutting operation for stone in the bladder.

Litigable *adj.* contestable in law.

Litigant *adj.* a person involved in a claim or dispute brought before a law court; disposed to litigate.

Litigate *v.t.* & *i.* to go to law; to contest at law.

Litigious *adj.* fond of litigation; contentious; quick to argue or to take a case to a law court.

Litre *n.* a unit of capacity in the metric system (about 35 ounces).

Litter *n.* carrying couch; used as a carriage; a heap of straw (for animals to lie upon).

Litterateur *n.* a man of letters.

Little *n., adj.* & *adv.* small, of small size, brief, short, trivial, mean.

Littoral *adj.* of or on the shore; (the part of a country that is) near the coast; close to the sea.

Liturgical *n.* pertaining to litugry.

Liturgics *n.* the theory of ritulas.

Livable *adj.* (of house, room, climate, etc.) fit to live in.

Live *v.t.* & *i.* to pass or spend; to dwell; to conduct oneself in a specified way.

Live *adj.* having life; not dead or fictitious or exhausted.

Lively *adj.* (of a place, an event, etc.) cheerful and full of interest or excitement.

Liven *v.t. & i.* to become or make somebody become more lively.

Liver *n.* a large gland that secrets bile; a peace regarded as a seat of love and courage.

Liveried *adj.* wearing a livery.

Livery *n.* a dispensing or allowance of food or clothes to servants.

Livid *adj.* black and blue; extremely angry.

Living *n.* livelihood, maintenance.

Lixiviate *v.t.* to separate (substance) into soluble and insoluble constituents by percolation of water.

Lizard *n.* scaly reptiles with four short legs and a long tail; a reptile with a rough skin.

Llama *n.* a S. American animal kept for its soft wool or for carrying loads.

Loach *n.* a small river fish of a family Cobitidae.

Load *n.* a lot of something, *esp.* something upleasant or undesirable; a weight of responsibility, worry or grief.

Loaf *n.* a mass of bread shaped and baked in one piece; a shaped and moulded mass of food.

Loam *n.* a muddy soil.

Loan *n.* a sum of money lent, anything borrowed.

Loath, Loth *adjs.* unwilling; averse; disinclined; reluctant.

Loathe *v.t.* to feel great dislike or disgust for somebody; to abominate; to regard with disgust.

Lob *v.t. & i.* to hit or throw a ball or missile in a high curve through the air.

Lobate *adj.* pertaining to lobes.

Lobby *n.* to move clumsily, to run lazily, to bowl underhand.

Lobe *n.* a broad, rounded segmental division.

Lobelia *n.* a kind of flowering plant.

Lobster *n.* a large shellfish with eight legs and two long claws.

Local *adj.* (*esp.* medical) affecting a particular place, not general.

Locale *n.* scene of some event.

Locate *v.t. & i.* to settle or establish at a particular place; to state the locality of.

Location *n.* the action of finding where something is.

Locative *adj.* denoting place; pertaining to a location. *n.* locative case.

Lock *n.* an appliane for fastening door etc.

Lockage *n.* canal-locking.

Locker *n.* a drawer; a small cupboard, *esp.* one reserved for an individual in a bank etc.

Locket *n.* that is worn on a chain round the neck and may hold somebody's picture.

Locomotion *n.* the power for motion from place to place; going from one place to another.

Locular *adj.* pertaining to small recess.

Locus *n.* a line or a curve formed by points satisfying given conditions.

Lode *n.* a line of metal ore found among rocks, *esp.* underground; a vein of metal or a water course.

Lodge *n.* a small house, an outhouse in a garden; a place where Freemason meet.

Lodging *n.* a temporary habitation.

Loft *n.* an attice; a room or space directly under the roof of a house, used for storing things.

Loftily *adv.* in an exalted manner.

Lofty *adj.* haughty; exalted; elevated; dignified; distinguished; too proud; of imposing height; (not of people) very high and impressive.

Log *n.* an official written record of events during a ship's voyage or an aircraft's flight.

Logarithm *n.* a simplified way of arithmetical calculation.

Log-book *n.* a book containing daily record of ship's rate of progress.

Loggia *n.* a room or gallery with one or more open sides, especially one that forms part of a house and has one side open to the garden.

Logic *n.* a way of thinking or explaining something, whether right or wrong.

Logical *adj.* following the rules of logic; capable of thinking clearly and sensibly.

Logician *n.* one who is versed in logic.

Logistics *n.* the art of stationing or moving troops.

Logogram *n.* a sign representing a word.

Logomachy *n.* a controversy about words.

Logomania *n.* craze for speaking.

Loin *n.* the lower part of the human body on both sides below the waist and above the legs.

Loiter *v.t.* to stand in a public place, usually with no particular or obvious purpose.

Loiterer *n.* an idler.

Loll *v.i.* to lie lazily about; to sit or stand in a lazy relaxed way.

Lollipop *n.* a large flat or round sweet on a small stick, held in the hand and sucked.

Lone *adj.* solitary; unfrequented, uninhabited.

Lonely *adj.* not often visited; remote; sad because one has no friends or companions; without companions.

Long *adj.* extended in length or time, protracted, lingering, slow in coming, far-reaching, lengthy.

Longish *adj.* somewhat long.

Longitude *n.* the distance east or west of the Greenwich meridian, measured in degrees.

Look *v.t. & i.* to seem to be; to appear; to face a particular direction.

Looking-glass *n.* a mirror.

Look-out *n.* post of observation; a man stationed to watch.

Loom *n.* a machine for weaving cloth; inner part of an oar, a haze.

Loon *n.* a scamp; an idler; a rascal; a kind of diving bird.

Loop *n.* an endless strip of film or tape that can be repeated continuously.

Loose *adj.* detached or that can be detached from its place, not firmly fixed.

Loosen *v.t.* & *i.* to become or make something loose or looser; to relax.

Loot *n.* goods, especially private, taken from an enemy in war or stolen by thieves.

Lop *v.t.* & *i.* to cut off; to cut away branches or twigs of trees; to hang limply.

Lope *v.i.* to run with a long bouncing stride.

Loquacious *n.* talkative; babbling; talking a lot; fond of talking.

Loquacity *n.* talkativeness.

Lord *n.* a male ruler; a nobleman; husband; master; God. *Lord!* (inter.) expressing wonder etc.

Lords *n.* headquarters of the M.C.C and English cricket; (used for) Lord's cricket ground in London.

Lore *n.* learning, wisdom, scholarship.

Loricate *adj.* having defensive parts.

Lorn *adj.* desolate; forlorn.

Lorry *n.* a long low sideless wagon; a large truck.

Lory *n.* a bird of the parrot kind.

Lose *v.t.* & *i.* to mislay; to suffer loss; to suffer detriment; to become unable to find something.

Loser *n.* one who loses.

Loss *n.* diminution; losing; what is lost; the state of no longer having something.

Lot *n.* the whole number or amount of people or things; a considerable number or amount.

Lothario a risk; a libertine.

Lotion *n.* a wash for wounds or the skin; a liquid medicine or beauty product for use on the skin.

Lottery *n.* gamble in which prizes are won by lot or chance by ticket-holders.

Lotus *n.* a water lilly.

Loud *adj.* noisy; strongly audible; producing much noise.

Loud-speaker *n.* an instrument which is used for magnifying sound.

Lounge *v.i.* to sit or stand in a lazy way; to recline; to stand about lazily; to idle.

Lour *v.i.* to frown; to look sullen; to look gloomy; to be angry.

Louse *n.* a parasitic insect.

Lout *n.* a mean awkward fellow; a hulking or rough-mannered fellow; a man or boy with bad manners.

Loutish *adj.* clumsy.

Louver, Louvre *ns.* each of a set of fixed or movable strips of wood, plastic, etc. designed to let air in while keeping light or rain out.

Lovable *adj.* worthy of love; easy to love; inspiring affection; amiable.

Lovage *n.* a kind of herb.

Love *n.* warm affection, fondness, passion, courtship, the object of love.

Lovelace *n.* a libertine.

Lovely *adj.* enjoyable; pleasant; exquisitely beautiful; attractive.

Lover *n.* a woman's sweetheart.

Love-sick *n.* sick or languishing with love.

Low *n.* the sound made by cows. *v.i.* to utter low.

Low *adj.* & *adv.* not far up; not elevated; depressed; submissive; not loud.

Lower *v.t.* & *i.* to let down; to reduce in value; to diminish height of; to sink; to descend; to decrease.

Lowland *n.* a low-lying country; an area of land that is fairly flat and not very high above sea level.

Lowly *adj.* humble; unpretending; low in status or importance.

Loyal *n.* true and faithful; constant to friends or associates; devoted to the sovereign.

Loyalty *n.* adherence to the sovereign; firm allegiance; fidelity.

Lozenge *n.* rhombus, a small tablet of flavoured sugar.

Lubber *n.* a lout; a clumsy fellow.

Lubric *adj.* unsteady, slippery.

Lubricant *n.* that which lessens friction; substance used to oil machinery.

Lucent *adj.* shining; clear; bright; luminous.

Lucerne *n.* a clovelike fodder plant.

Lucid *adj.* bright; free from obscurity; clearly expressed or arranged.

Lucifer *n.* the planet Venus as a morning star; Satan; a match ignitible by friction.

Luck *n.* chance, *esp.* considered as a force that causes good or bad things to happen.

Lucky *adj.* fortunate, prosperous, auspicious.

Lucrative *adj.* gainful; profitable; yielding considerable profit.

Lucre *n.* as a motive for doing something; pecuniary gain as a motive; profit or money.

Luculent *adj.* clear; lucid.

Lues *n.* contagious disease; plague.

Luff *n.* the broad part of a ship's bow.

Lug *v.t.* & *i.* to carry or drag something with great effort; to pull hard at.

Luggage *n.* a traveller's packages or baggage, bags, cases, etc. containing somebody's belongings and taken on a journey.

Lugubrious *adj.* doleful; sad, full of sorrow.

Lukewarm *adj.* not eager or enthusiastic; neither hold nor cold.

Lull *v.t.* to put to sleep by caresses; to quite; to lessen. *n.* a season of calm.

Lumbago *n.* a pain in the muscles of the lower part of the back, caused by rheumatism.

Lumbar *adj.* of the lower part of the back.

Lumber *v.t.* & *i.* to move clumsily. *n.* piece of furniture, etc.

Lumiere *n.* a colour photography method.

Luminant *adj.* & *n.* giving light; a luminous object.

Luminary *n.* a person who inspires or influences others, especially a leading person in a particular activity.

Luminosity *n.* brightness.

Luminous *adj.* giving out light; shedding light.

Lump *n.* a shapeless mass; a heap; protuberancce; swelling.

Lumpish *adj.* (of a person) heavy; awkward; stupid; clumsy; dull.

Lumpy *adj.* full of lumps.

Lunacy *n.* insanity; folly; very foolish behaviour; extreme mental illness; madness.

Lunar *adj.* pertaining to the moon.

Lunate *adj.* crescent-shaped.

Lunatic *adj.* a person who is mad or severely mentally ill.

Lunation *n.* the time from one new moon to the next.

Lunette *n.* a hole or crescent-shaped space in a ceiling or dome.

Lung *n.* either of the two breathing organs in the chest of humans and many other animals.

Lunge *n.* a horse-breaker's long rope.

Luniform *adj.* crescent-shaped.

Lupine *adj.* of or like wolves.

Lupine *n.* a tall garden plant with a long pointed stem bearing many small flowers, white or yellow flowers.

Lupus *n.* disease of the skin.

Lurch *n.* a sudden unsteady leaning or rolling movement; a forlorn state.

Lurcher *n.* a spy; a cross-bred dog used *esp.* by poachers; a petty thief; a swindler.

Lure *n.* a thing that attracts or is used to attract people or animals.

Lurid *adj.* ghastly; terrible; (in colour, etc.) pale yellow.

Lurk *v.t.* to be hidden in; to escape notice; to lie in wait.

Luscious *adj.* imagery or voluptuous suggestion (of language or literary style).

Lush *adj.* luxuriant; succulent; growing thickly and strongly.

Lust *n.* passionate enjoyment or desire; a strong sexual desire.

Lustration *n.* ceremonial washing or other rite of purification.

Lustre *n.* gloss, brightness, brilliance, fame, radiant beauty, splendour.

Lusty *adj.* vigorous; stout; bulky; healthy and full of life; robust, lively; healthful.

Lustily *adv.* in a lusty manner.

Lute *n.* a musical instrument with strings, played like a guitar.

Luteous *adj.* of deep orange colour.

Lutose *adj.* covered with mud.

Luxate *v.t.* to dislocate a joint; to displace.

Luxurious *adj.* supplied with expensive and enjoyable things; fond of luxury; exuberant.

Luxuriate *v.i.* to enjoy something as a luxury; to grow profusely.

Luxurist *n.* one given to luxury.

Luxury *n.* indulgence in rich and costly pleasures; a thing that is expensive and enjoyable, but not essential.

Lycanthropy *n.* madness in which the patient thinks himself to be a beast.

Lychnis *a.* a genus of plants.

Lycra *n.* an artificial fabric that stretches, used for making clothes that fit close to the body.

Lyddite *n.* an explosive for shells.

Lydian *adj.* soft, effiminate.

Lye *n.* water alkalized with wood, ashes etc. for washing.

Lyke-wake *n.* watch kept at night over a dead body.

Lymph *n.* a colourless fluid in the tissues or animal body.

Lyncean *adj.* keen-sighted.

Lynch *v.t.* (of a group of people) to kill somebody believed to be guilty of a crime without a proper trial.

Lynch-Mob *n.* a crowd of people who gather to lynch someone.

Lynx *n.* a kind of animal of the cat tribe noted for keen sight.

Lyrate *adj.* of the form of a lyre.

Lyre *n.* an ancient musical instrument with strings fixed in a frame shaped like a U. It is played with the fingers.

Lyric *adj.* of the nature of song; (of poetry) expressing the writer's feelings). *n.* a lyric poem.

M

M *abbr.* male, married, metre(s), million(s).

Mab *n.* the queen of the fairies.

Mac *n.* Mackintosh, a water proof cloth.

Macadam *n.* a road surface made of layers of broken stones; broken stone for covering the road.

Macque *n.* an African ape.

Macarise *v.t.* to give blessings and compliments.

Macaroni *n.* an edible paste of wheat flour.

Macaronic *adj.* composed of a mixture of languages; mixed; jumbled.

Macassar-oil *adj.* & *n.* a kind of hair-oil.

Macaw *n.* a kind of parrot, a kind of palm.

Mace *n.* an ornamental rod, carried or displayed as a sign of the authority of an official.

Macerate *v.t.* & *i.* to reduce to soft mass by soaking; to make lean; to mortify by fasting.

Mach *n.* a measurement of speel, used especially for aircraft.

Machete *n.* a broad heavy knife used as a cutting tool and as a weapon.

Machiavel *n.* one who practises duplicity in statecraft; an unscrupulous schemer.

Machination *n. (usu. pl.)* an intrigue or plot; a secret plot or scheme; underhand devices.

Machinator *n.* one who plans a scheme.

Machinal *adj.* pertaining to machines.

Machine *n.* an apparatus for applying mechanical energy, one who acts without intelligence.

Machinery *n.* machines in general; the work of a machine; machines as a group or in general.

Machismo *n.* maleness or virility; male domination.

Mackerel *n.* an edible sea-fish with greenish-blue bands on its body.

Mackintosh *n.* a waterproof cloth.

Mackle *n.* a blur in printing as from a double impression.

Macle *n.* a twin crystal.

Macrame *n.* a fringe of knotted thread.

Macrobiotic *adj.* prolonging life.

Macrocosm *n.* any large complete structure containing smaller structures.

Macrodent *adj.* having abnormally large teeth.

Macrology *n.* verbosity.

Macron *n.* a mark over a vowel to show that it is long. á, ê, î, ô, û.

Macula *n.* a permanent spot on the skin; a spot in the sun; spot of different colour from its surroundings.

Mad *adj.* insane, crazed, wildly excited, disorded to intellect.

Madam *n.* a polite form of address to a woman, whether she is married or not.

Madcap *n.* typical of a person who acts in a dangerous or reckless way.

Madden *v.t.* & *i.* to make or become mad.

Madder *n.* plant whose root yields a red dye; kinds of red dye and plants yielding them.

Made *adj.* to be completely suited to somebody/each other.

Media *n.* a plant similar to sunflower.

Madrigal *n.* a short love song; a pastoral song.

Maelstrom *n.* any large, powerful or violent whirlpool.

Maestro *n.* a master of any art, *esp.* a composer, conductor or teacher of music.

Mafia *n.* an international criminal organization.

Maffick *v.i.* to exult or rejoice in a riotous manner.

Magazine *n.* a place for storing arms, ammunition, provision etc.

Mage *n.* a magician; a learned man.

Magdalen *n.* a repentant prostitute; a place where such prostitutes are kept.

Magenta *n.* a reddish purple colour; a colour between purple and red.

Maggot *n.* larva of a worm; whimsical fancy; whim.

Magic *n.* the art of making things happen by the use of supernatural forces by using spirits

Magisterial *adj.* authoritative; of the rank of a magistrate.

Magnanimity *n.* dignity of spirit; greatness of mind; generosity.

Magnanimous *adj.* high-souled; liberal and honourable.

Magnate *n.* a wealthy or eminent personage.

Magnesia *n.* a carbonate of magnesium used in medicine.

Magnet *n.* a piece of iron which has the property of attracting small bits of iron.

Magnetic *adj.* of or like or acting as a magnet; having the properties of a magnet.

Magnetite *n.* a very common black iron oxide extracted from ore.

Magnificent *adj.* remarkable; impressive; grand in appearance; splendid.

Magnifier *adj.* a magnifying lens; one that magnifies.

Magnify *v.t.* to make a thing appear larger than is actual size; to exaggerate; to speak highly of.

Magniloquent *adj.* lofty in expression; boastfully.

Magnitude *n.* largeness, bulk, size, importance.

Magnolia *n.* a tree with large sweet-smelling, usually white or pink flower.

Magnum *n.* a bottle containing about eighty ounces of liquid.

Magpie *n.* a chattering bird like crow; a chattering person.

Magus *n.* a Eastern magician or wise man.

Mahogany *n.* an American tree much used for furniture.

Maid *n.* a girl; a young unmarried woman; virgin; spinster.

Maiden *n.* girl; young unmarried woman.

Mail *n.* a armour of chainwork; a bag for the conveyance of letters; the postal system; rent; payment.

Mailable *adj.* able to be mailed.

Maim *v.t.* to cripple, mutilate; to injure; to bruise.

Main *adj.* chief; most important; leading; extensive.

Mainmast *n.* principal mast.

Mainsail *n.* the principal sail on a ship; lowest sail of main mast.

Mainspring *n.* the most important part of or reason for something.

Mainstay *n.* the main part of something, enabling it to continue or be effective.

Maintain *v.t.* to keep up; to hold; to support; to continue; to furnish; to uphold; to defend; to assert as true.

Maize *n.* Indian corn; its grain.

Majesty *n.* impressive dignity or beauty; royal power; stateliness of aspect; manner; language.

Major *n.* an officer in rank above a captain; a chief; a person of full age.

Majority *n.* the greater number; more than half.

Make *v.t.* & *i.* to construct; to frame; to draw up; to perfrom; to compose; to execute; to establish.

Maladjustment *n.* faulty adjustment.

Maladministration *n.* faulty or bad administration; the poor or dishonest management of public affairs, business dealings, etc.

Maladroit *adj.* unskillful; clumsy; tactless.

Malady *n.* sickness, disease.

Malaise *n.* uneasiness; a feeling of discomfort; a general feeling of illness.

Malar *adj.* pertaining to the check.

Malaria *n.* a kind of fever caused by a mosquito bite; fever due to or produced by mosquito bites.

Malcontent *adj.* a person who is not satisfied with a situation and complains or causes trouble.

Male *adj.* masculine; pertaining to a sex that begets young; of the impregnating sex.

Malediction *n.* curse; the utterance of a curse.

Malefactor *n.* a person who does something wrong.

Malefic *adj.* (of magical arts, etc.) hurtful, noxious.

Maleficence *n.* evil-doing, ill-will.

Malevolent *adj.* having or showing a wish to do evil or cause harm to others; malicious; spiteful.

Malfeasance *n.* (law) an official misconduct; evil doing.

Malformation *n.* the state of being badly formed or shaped; a badly formed part, *esp.* of the body.

Malice *n.* ill-will; spite; enemity; the desire to harm somebody; hatred for somebody.

Malicious *adj.* caused by hatred; bearing ill-will; intended to harm somebody.

Malign *v.t.* to defame; to say things that are unpleasant or not true about somebody; to traduce; to misrepresent; to slander; to vilify. *adj.* maleficent; (of disease) malignant.

Malignant *adj.* showing a strong desire to harm people; cruel; outrageously malevolent.

Malignity *n.* extreme ill-will or malice.

Malinger *v.i.* to feign sickness in order to avoid duty; to pretend illness; to escape duty (*esp.* to soldiers & sailors).

Malignly *adv.* with mallice or ill-will.

Mall *n.* a shady public walk or promenade.

Malleable *adj.* educable; pliable; (of people, ideas, etc.

Mallet *n.* to beat into a plate or leaf; hammer with large wooden head (for driving pins, chisels, etc.); an implement for striking polo ball.

Malleus *n.* the bone of the ear.

Mallow *n.* kinds of plant.

Malnutrition *n.* under feeding; a condition resulting from a lack of food or the right type of food.

Malodorous *adj.* an offensive stinking; having an unpleasant smell.

Malpractice *n.* wrong doing (*usu.* in *pl.*); wrongful procedure.

Malt *n.* steeped barley or other grain prepared for brewing.

Maltose *n.* sugar which is obtained from starch.

Maltreat *v.t.* to treat a person or an animal with violence or cruelty.

Mamma *n.* mother (used chiefly by young children)

Mammal *n.* any of the class of animals that give birth to live babies and feed their young on milk from the breast.

Mammon *n.* wealth as an object of pursuit, or evil influence.

Mammoth *n.* an extinct elephant; (*attrib.*) huge.

Man *n.* a human being of either sex; the human race; a husband, male lover or boyfriend; ordinary soldier or sailor.

Manage *v.t.* & *i.* to guide by the hand, to conduct carefully, to handle, to contrive.

Manager *n.* a person who trains and organizes a sports team; one who has direction or control.

Manatee *n.* an aquatic animal; the sea-cow.

Manciple *n.* a steward or catering official in colleges, etc.

Mandamus *n.* superior court's writ conveying command to lower one.

Mandrel *n.* an axis on which material revolves in lathe.

Mandrill *n.* a large baboon.

Manducate *v.t.* to chew; to masticate.

Mane *n.* the long hair on the neck of certain animals.
Mange *n.* a skin disease of animals.
Manger *n.* a trough to feed horses or cattle.
Mango *n.* an Indian fruit and tree or a tropical fruit with sweet juicy yellow flesh.
Mangy *adj.* shabby, squalid.
Manhood *n.* adult age in males; manliness; the qualities of a man; strength and sexual power.
Mania *n.* a violent madness; a great enthusiasm.
Maniac *n.* mental derangement, unreasonable or vehement desire for a thing.
Manifest *adj.* clear; obvious; plain; clear to sight or mind; indubitable.
Manifesto *n.* public declaration of principles, policies, aims etc.
Manifold *adj.* of various forms or kinds, complicated.
Manikin *n.* a little man; a lay figure; anatomical model of the body.
Manilla *n.* fibre used for ropes, etc.
Manipulate *v.t.* to handle with skill; to manage skilfully.
Mankind *n.* human race; the human species; all human beings considered together; males, especially those of a household.
Manner *n.* form, mode of life; method, style, outward bearing.
Mannish *adj.* like a man; bold.
Manoeuvre *n.* a planned and controlled movement of armed forces.
Man-of-war *n.* a war-vessel; an armed navy ship.
Manor *n.* the territory of a lord.
Manorial *adj.* pertaining to a manor.
Manse *n.* the house of a minister of the church, especially in Scotland.
Mansion *n.* habitation; abode; dwelling; a large impressive house.
Mansuetude *n.* gentleness; tameness; mild temper.
Mantel *n.* an ornamental structure enclosing the fireplace.
Mantle *n.* a cover round the flame of a gas lamp that becomes very bright when heated; a loose sleeveless cloak.
Mantilla *n.* a large veil, a small mantle.
Manual *adj.* of or done with the hands; requiring bodily exertion.
Manufactory *n.* a building where goods are manufactured; a factory; a workshop.
Manufacture *n.* preparation of things by hand or machinery on a large scale.
Manumission *n.* emancipation; setting free.
Manumit *v.t.* to give freedom to slave.
Manure *n.* anything spread over soil for fertilizing it.

Manurial *adj.* pertaining to manure.

Manuscript *n.* a book or paper written by hand; a document.

Many *adj.* having a great number; numerous; much more than one.

Map *n.* representation on paper; of earth's surface, countries etc.

Maple *n.* a usually tall, deciduous tree or shrub.

Mar *v.t.* to spoil; to interfere; to damage; to disfigure; to impair.

Marasmic *adj.* pertaining to marasmus.

Marathon *n.* a long-distance race usually of 26 miles.

Maraud *v.t.* to make raid; to pillage; to rove in quest of; to plunder; to attack.

Marble *n.* any compact hard limestone capable of taking polish.

March *v.t.* & *i.* to cause to march; to move in order. *n.* the third month of the English year.

Marchioness *n.* the wife or widow of a marquis.

Marchpane *n.* a sweet paste of pounded almond.

Macronigram *n.* a message sent by wireless on Marconi's system.

Mare *n.* the nightmare; the female of the horse or of any other equine animal.

Margin *n.* border, the space on a page between the edge & written matter, reserved amount.

Marginal *adj.* not central; (of land) that cannot produce enough to be profitable except when prices of farm products are high.

Margravine *n. fem.* the wife of a Margrave.

Marigold *n.* a name for several plants bearing yellow flowers.

Marinade *n.* a sauce of wine or herbs in which fish or meat is soaked before cooking.

Marine *adj.* relating to ships, trade by sea, the navy, etc.

Mariner *n.* a seaman or sailor.

Mariolatry *n.* worship of the Virgin.

Marionette *n.* a puppet moved with strings.

Marital *adj.* pertaining to a husband; relating to a marriage.

Maritime *adj.* connected with the sea, situated near the sea.

Marjoram *n.* a plant whose sweet-smelling leaves are used in cooking.

Mark *n.* a target, a desired object, token, sign, seal, a written symbol, distinction, indication, numerical award assigned in an examination, conspicuous character.

Markedly *adv.* remarkably; evidently.

Market *n.* a country, an area, a section of the population, etc.

Marking *n.* an identification mark; pattern of marks.

Marksman *n.* a person skilled in shooting, especially with rifle.

Marl *n.* kind of rich soil or clay often much used for manure.

Marlin *n.* a small rope composed of two strands little twisted, used for winding round ropes to prevent their being chaffed.

Marmalade *n.* a type of jam made from citrus fruit, especially oranges, and usually eaten at breakfast.

Marmoreal *adj.* made of marble; like marble.

Maroon *n.* crimson colour, firework.

Marplot *n.* one who mars a plot by unwarranted interference.

Marquee *n.* a large tent used for public or social events.

Marquis, Marquess *ns.* a peer ranking between a duke and earl.

Marriage *n.* the ceremony by which a man and woman become husband and wife, matrimony, wedlock.

Marrow *n.* a soft substance in the hollow of a bone; pulp of plants.

Marry *v.t.* & *i.* to join persons in wedlock; to enter into the connubial state.

Mart *n.* a place of trade; a market or centre of trade.

Martial *adj.* warlike; brave; belonging to Mars or the god of war.

Martian *n.* an inhabitant of mars.

Martin *n.* a bird of swallow family.

Martinet *n.* a strict disciplinarian.

Martyr *n.* one who undergoes death for his cause. *v.t.* to prosecute as a martyr; to torture.

Marvel *n.* an object of great astonishment; a wonderful thing; a person or thing that fills one with surprise and admiration.

Marvellous *adj.* exciting wonder, astonishing.

Mascot *n.* a talisman; something which brings good luck; a person, an animal or a thing thought to bring good luck.

Masculine *adj.* having the qualities or appearance considered to be typical or of appropriate for men.

Mash *n.* a mixture of boiled grain and bran for horses and cattle.

Mask *n.* a manner or an expression that hides one's true character, emotions, etc.

Mason *n.* builder in stone; a freemason.

Masonry *n.* solid stonework; the art or occupation of a mason.

Masque *n.* a mask; an entertainment in dumb show; dramatic performance in castles, etc. in the 16th and 17th centuries.

Masquerade *n.* a masked ball; a false show, pretence.

Mass *n.* unbroken expense, assembly of people.

Massacre *n.* general slaughter, *esp.* of unresisting persons; a defeat of a team, political party etc.

Massage *n.* stoking or pressing the limbs for the relief of morbid conditions.

Masseur *n.* a massagist. **Masseuse,** *n.*

Massif *n.* a group of mountains within a limited area.

Massive *adj.* exceptionally large; large and heavy or solid; ponderous.

Massy *adj.* solid; weighty.

Mast *n.* an upright for decorations, wireless telegraphy, etc.

Mast *n.* fruit of beech, oak, etc. as food for pigs.

Master *n.* owner, employer, the head of a family, a teacher, a skilled workman.

Masterpiece *n.* best or very fine specimen of an artist's work.

Mastic *n.* gum which is obtained from the bark of certain trees.

Masticate *v.t.* to chew; to grind with the teeth and prepare for digestion.

Mastiff *n.* a kind of large dog.

Mastitis *n.* inflammation of the breast or udder.

Mastodon *n.* an extinct animal allied to elephant.

Mastoid *adj.* shaped like female breast.

Masturbate *v.i.* to give oneself/ somebody sexual pleasure by stimulating the sexual organs, *esp.* by hand.

Mat *n.* a coarse fabric of sedge, rushes, etc.

Match *n.* a person equal to another in some quality, of exact similarity.

Mate *n.* an associate; a companion; a partner; a comrade; an officer in a ship; an assistant.

Material *adj.* unspiritual; considerable; important, essential; relevant; composed of or connected with physical objects rather than the mind or spirit.

Maternal *adj.* motherly, relating to a mother.

Maternity *n.* motherhood; the state of being a mother.

Matey *adj.* sociable; friendly.

Mathematics *n.* quantity and space, of which arithmetic, algebra, trigonometry and geometry are branches.

Matin *n.* a morning song; morning prayer. *adj.* of the morning.

Matinee *n.* an entertainment of the day; an afternoon performance at a cinema or theatre.

Matriarchy *n.* the female head of a family or tribe; social organization in which mother is head of family.

Matricide *n.* the killing of one's mother.

Matriculate *v.t.* & *i.* to admit or enrol as a member of college; to enrol as a member by entering one's name in register.

Matrimony *n.* the state of being married; state of having a husband or wife.

Matrix *n.* the social, political, etc. conditions that govern the existence and development of something.

Matter *n.* a substance from which anything physical is prepared, subject, material, pus.

Matting *n.* rough woven material used for making mats or for packing goods.

Mattock *n.* a kind of pick-axe.

Mattress *n.* a strong cloth-case filled with soft or firm material and used for sleeping on.

Maturate *v.t.* to come to maturation.

Mature *adj.* (of insurance policies, etc.) due to payment.

Maul *n.* a heavy wooden hammer.

Maund *n.* a measure of 40 seers; a measure of weight.

Maunder *v.t.* to move carelessly; to talk ramblingly; to mutter.

Mauser *n.* a kind of military rifle.

Mausoleum *n.* a magnificent monument.

Mauve *n.* & *adj.* a bright purple dye; a pale purple colour.

Maverick *n.* a dissenter, who takes an independent stand apart from his associates.

Maw *n.* the stomach of lower animals; inner parts an animal's stomach or throat.

Mawkish *adj.* disgusting, of faint flavour.

Mawseed *n.* seed of opium, poppy.

Maxillary *adj.* of the jaw.

Maxim *n.* a general principle serving as a guide; a proverb.

Maximum *n.* the greatest number, quantity or value.

Mayor *n.* a head of municipal corporation.

Mazarine *n.* & *adj.* deep blue.

Maze *n.* tangle of facts; a network of paths or hedges designed as a puzzle in which one must find one's way.

Meagre *adj.* lean; having little flesh; barren; without strength; insufficient.

Meal *n.* the eatable part of a grain ground into powder.

Mealie *n.* a kind of African maize.

Mealy *adj.* dry and powdery.

Mean *adj.* low in rank or birth, base, sorbid, of little value, contemptible, poor.

Mean *v.t.* & *i.* to be resolved; to intend; to have in mind to design; to signify.

Meander *n.* wandering of a river (*pl.*) windings, maze.

Measles *n. pl.* an eruptive infectious disease.

Measure *n.* size, limit, degree, quantity, unit of capacity, means to end, a proposal, time in music.

Meatus *n.* passage in the body; a channel.

Mechanic *n.* a skilled worker; a handicraftsman.

Mechanism *n.* the construction of a machine.

Medal *n.* a flat piece of metal, usually shaped like a coin an stamped with words and a design, medals are also sometimes made to celebrate public events, which is awarded to somebody.

Meddle *v.i.* to interfere; to interpose.

Meddlesome *adj.* fond of or in the habit of meddling.

Meddling *adj.* interfering in other's affairs.

Medial *adj.* situated in the middle; of average size.

Median *adj.* situated in the middle. *n.* (Math.) middle or average point, line, number, etc.

Medical *adj.* pertaining to medicine or the art of curing diseases.

Medicaster *n.* a quack.

Medicate *v.t.* to treat medically.

Medicinal *adj.* having healing properties; used for healing.

Medicine *n.* a substance, *esp.* a liquid, taken through the mouth, used in curing illness.

Medico *n. pref.* denoting doctor; a medical student or doctor.

Medieval, Mediaeval *adjs.* of or pertaining to the middle ages, about AD 1100-1400.

Mediocre *adj.* second-rate; not very good; of fairly low quality.

Meditate *v.t.* & *i.* to design; to think; to contemplate.

Mediterranean *adj.* & *n.* surrounded by or in the midst of land.

Medium *n.* a substance or the surrounding in which something exists or moves or is transmitted.

Medley *n.* heterogenous mixture; jumble; a piece of music consisting of passages from other musical works.

Medulla *n.* marrow of the spine; marrow of bones.

Meed *n.* wages; reward, recompense.

Meek *adj.* gentle, humble, submissive.

Meet *v.t.* & *i.* to encounter; to assemble; to go to receive; to find; to satisfy.

Meeting *n.* an interview; an assembly; a crowd; an assembly of people for a particular purpose.

Megaphone *n.* a speaking trumpet.

Megass *n.* residue which is left after extracting juice from sugarcane.

Megrim *n.* half headache, whim, a kind of fish.

Melancholy *n.* & *adj.* mental depression, sad, gloomy, depressing.

Melee *n.* a confused fight or struggle or crowd; a hand-to-hand conflict; lively debate.

Melic *adj.* fit to be sung.

Melinite *n.* an explosive.

Meliorate *v.t.* to make or grow better; to improve; to ameliorate.

Mellow *adj.* soft, juicy, jovial, ripe, intoxicated.

Melodic *adj.* melodious; containing melody.

Melodrama *n.* a sensational drama with music.

Melody *n.* sweetness of sound; sound that delights the ear.

Melon *n.* a kind of gourd eaten as fruit.

Melt *v.t.* & *i.* to become liquid; to pass into liquid condition; to soften.

Member *n.* one of a society; a representative in a legislative body; a member of parliament.

Membrane *n.* a thin tissue covering the inner parts of the body.

Memento *n.* something which serves as a warning.

Memo *n.* a memorandum.

Memoir *n.* a biography sketch; (*pl.*) proceedings of a society; an essay; a memorial account; a written record of somebody's life.

Memorable *adj.* worthly to be remembered.

Memorandum *n.* a note for helping the memory; a document in which terms of contract are recorded.

Memorial *adj.* & *n.* commemorative, serving to preserve memory, a petition or written representation, monumental record.

Memory *n.* power or remembering.

Menace *n.* a threat; apparent danger.

Menage *n.* household arrangement.

Mend *v.t.* & *i.* to repair; to regain health.

Mendacity *n.* beggary.

Mendelism *n.* theory of heredity tending to reduce to numerical law the recurrence of inherited characters.

Menial *n.* a person having a menial job; a servant; (of work) not requiring much skill and often boring.

Meningitis *n.* a serious disease in which the tissues enclosing the brain and spinal cord become infected and swollen.

Menopause *n.* a time when a woman ceases to menstruate usually around the age of 50.

Mensal *adj.* monthly.

Menses *n. pl.* the monthly discharge from the uterus; the flow of blood each month from a woman's uterus.

Menshevik *n.* a member of the Russian socialist party.

Menstrual *adj.* monthly, pertaining to the menses of females.

Menstruate *v.t.* to discharge blood etc. from the uterus, usually once a month.

Mensurable *adj.* measurable; having fixed rhythm.

Mensuration *n.* the art of measuring the dimensions of anything.

Mental *adj.* pertaining to intellect or mind; of or in the mind; mad.

Mention *v.t.* naming; a brief notice; suggestion.

Mentor *n.* a wise or faithful advisor.

Menu *n.* (computing) a list of possible action from which a user can choose.

Mephitis *n.* noxious emanation from below ground.

Mercantile *adj.* commercial; trading.

Mercenary *adj.* working for money or reward; influenced by greed or gain.

Mercer *n.* a dealer in costly textiles; a dealer in silk, velvet and such fabrics.

Merchant *n.* a trader; an exporter or importer of goods.

Merciful *adj.* compassionate; disposed to mercy; kind.

Mercurial *adj.* pertaining to quicksilver, fickle, active, changeful.

Mercury *n.* quicksilver; heavy silver-coloured metal.

Mercy *n.* a kind of forgiving attitude shown towards somebody one has the right or power to punish.

Mere *n.* nothing more; unmixed; pure; absolute; nothing more than; no better or more important than.

Meretricious *adj.* artificial, of a showy nature.

Merganser *n.* a diving fish-eating duck.

Merge *v.t.* & *i.* to fade or change gradually into something else.

Meridian *n.* a conventional circle passing through Celestial Poles and Zenith.

Meridional *adj.* of the south; of a meridian.

Meringue *n.* a mixture of the whites of eggs and sugar baked until crisp and used as a covering over sweet pies.

Merino *n.* a kind of sheep; fine woollen yarn.

Merit *n.* (*usu. pl.*) worth; value; that which one deserves; (in *pl.*) question at issue; commendable quality.

Meritorious *adj.* having merit; deserving praise or reward; praiseworthy.

Merle *n.* a black bird.

Merlin *n.* a kind of falcon; eagle.

Mermaid *n.* a half-human being with head & trunk of woman & tail of a fish.

Merman *n.* man of the sea with fish tail.

Merriment *n.* amusement; enjoyment; gaiety with laughter of noise; mirth.

Merry *adj.* joyous, gay, jovial, mirthful.

Mesalliance *n.* a marriage with person of inferior social position.

Meseems Archaic it seems to me.

Mesh *n.* one of the spaces between the threads of the net; network.

Mesmerism *n.* hypnotism.

Mesmerize, *v.t.* to hypnotize; to enthral.

Mesne *adj.* intermediate.

Mess *n.* mixed food, medley, untidy state of things, group of men taking meal together.

Message *n.* an idea or a statement from *e.g.* a writer or a religious group.

Messrs *n.* title prefixed to name of firm or to a list of gentlemen.

Messuage *n.* a dwelling house without building and land.

Metabolic *adj.* (Biol) of, relating to or exhibiting metabolism.

Metabolism *n.* the process in an organism by which food is built up into living matter.

Metacarpus *n.* the part of hand from the wrist to the finger-roots.

Metal *n.* a substance as gold, silver, copper etc.

Metamorphic *adj.* of transformations.

Metamorphosis *n.* change of character; change of form, *esp.* magic transformation, circumstances, etc.

Metaphor *n.* application of name etc. to an inanimate object.

Metaphysics *n. pl.* the philosophy of being and knowing.

Metatarsus *n.* group of five long bones of foot between tarsus and toes.

Metathesis *n.* transformation of the sound of letters into words.

Mete *n.* to dole; to measure. *n.* boundary; a defeat or bad treatment.

Metempsychosis *n.* migration of soul at death into another body.

Meteoric *adj.* transiently brilliant; brilliant and transitory as a meteor.

Meteorite *n.* an aerolite.

Meteorology *n.* the science of the motions and phenomenon of atmosphere.

Meter *n.* a person, a thing, that measures.

Methinks *v.t.* it appears to me; it seems to me; I think.

Method *n.* orderly or regular arrangement, system, scheme.

Methodize *v.t.* to introduce method into.

Methyl *n.* the base of wood spirit.

Meticulous *adj.* slavishly accurate or correct or proper; giving or showing great care and attention to detail.

Metonymy *n.* a work used in a transferred sense.

Metre *n.* poetic rhythm, measure of a verse. *n.* length of about 39½ incehs.

Metric *adj.* made, measured, etc. according to the metric system.

Metrify *v.i.* to versify.

Metrological *adj.* relating to metrology.

Metrology *n.* science, system, of weights and measures.

Metronome *n.* an instrument for measuring time in music.

Metropolis *n.* chiefy city, capital.

Metropolitan *adj.* belonging to a capital; of a metropolis.

Mettle *n.* temperament; courage; spirit; endurance; the ability to endure difficulties and to face opposition.

Mew *v.i.* & *t.* the soft high-pitched noise that a cake makes.

Mew *n.* a sea-gull; a seafowl.

Mewl *v.t.* to cary feebly.

Mews *n.* a horse-stable.

Mica *n.* an alkali metal; a glittering metal.

Mickle *n.* a great quantity; a large amount, etc.

Microbe *n.* a minute living organism as cause of a disease.

Microcosm *n.* a miniature representation of man or the universe.

Micron *n.* one millionth (million) of a metre.

Microphone *n.* an instrument for intensifying feeble sounds.

Microscope *n.* an instrument for making very small objects appear larger, especially for scientific study.

Mid *adj.* middle, medium, intervening. *prep.* amid.

Midden *n.* a dung-hill; a refuse-heap.

Middle *adj.* equidistant from two extremities, intermediate.

Middling *adj.* fairly well in health; moderately good. *adv.* fairly or moderately.

Midge *n.* a small insect or person.

Midget *n.* diminutive person; photograph of small size.

Midland *adj.* remote from the sea or border. *n.* middle part of country; *(pl.)* the middle countries of England.

Midnight *n.* twelve o'clock at night; the middle of the night.

Midst *adv.* in the middle.

Midsummer *n.* the middle of summer, around 21 June.

Midwife *n.* a person, *esp.* a woman, trained to assist women in having their babies.

Midwifery *n.* obstetrics.

Mien *n.* aspect, bearing, deportment.

Miff *n.* a petty quarrel. *v.t.* to quarrel.

Might *n.* great power of strength or resources; strength; ability; force.

Mignonette *n.* kinds of lase & fine net; a plant with fragrant flowers; greyish green colour of these.

Migrate *v.i.* to move from one place to another.

Mike *v.i.* *(sl.)* to shirk work; to idle. *n.* a contraction of microphone.

Milage *n.* miles travelled, used, etc.; expenses per mile.

Milch *adj.* giving milk.

Mild *adj.* gentle, placid, moderate, not strong, tame, feeble.

Mildew *n.* a tiny white fungus that grows on plants, leather, food, etc. in warm damp conditions.

Mile *n.* a large area or long distance; linear measure, measure of length or distance, 1760 yards.

Mileage *n.* distance travelled, expenses per mile.

Milestone *n.* stone which is fixed to mark miles.

Milieu *n.* environment or surroundings.

Militant *adj.* & *n.* engaged in warfare; fighting; combating.

Militarism *n.* belief in increasing one's military strength to become or remain powerful.

Military *adj.* of or for soldiers or an army. *n.* the armed forces.

Militia *n.* body of men enrolled and drilled as soldiers.

Milk *n.* white fluid secreted by female mammals for nourishing their young ones.

Milky *adj.* mixed with or made of milk, of or like milk.

Mill *n.* an apparatus for grinding, fitting with machinery; a manufactory.

Mill-hand *n.* a factory worker.

Millenarian *adj.* of the age of a thousand years.

Millennium *n.* a period of a thousand years.

Millepede *n.* a long thin small creature; many-legged creature.

Miller *n.* a person who owns or works in a mill for grinding corn.

Millesimal *adj.* thousandth.

Millet *n.* an Indian plant which bears grains.

Milliard *n.* a thousand millions.

Milliner *n.* one who makes up women's hats.

Million *n.* ten hundred thousand.

Millionaire *n.* a very rich person.

Milt *n.* spawn of male fish; spleen in mammals.

Milter *n.* a male fish.

Minaret *n.* a tall thin tower, usually forming part of a mosque from which Muslims are called to prayer.

Mince *v.t.* & *i.* to cut or chop into small pieces, to speak in an affected manner.

Mind *n.* memory; thought; opinion; the seat of consciousness.

Mindful *adj.* attentive; not forgetful; regarding with care; heedful.

Mine *pron.* & *adj.* the one (s) belonging to me. *adv.* belonging to me.

Mine *n.* an excavation in the earth from which coal, salt, metals etc.

Mineral *n.* an inorganic substance; got from the earth by mining.

Minerva *n.* the goddess of Wisdom.

Mingle *v.t.* & *i.* to move around in a place and have contact with other people.

Mini *n.* miniskirt, minidress etc.; very small or minor of its kind.

Miniate *v.t.* to paint with vermilion.

Miniature *n.* painted portrait on small scale or of small dimensions; small-scale representation.

Minify *v.t.* to represent as smaller or less important than it is.

Minim *n.* a creature of the smallest size, the sixtieth part of a dram.

Minimal *adj.* smallest in amount.

Minimalist *n.* a person ready to accept a minimum provisionally.

Minimize *v.t.* to reduce to the smallest amount or degree.

Minimum *n.* the least or smallest amount, degree.

Minimus *n.* the younger of the same name.

Minion *n.* a favourite; mere dependent; slave; an employee.

Minister *n.* a person at the head of a government department of a main branch or one, often a member of the cabinet.

Ministerial *adj.* of a minister or relating to a minister or ministers.

Ministrative *adj.* ministering.

Ministry *n.* agency, body of ministers.

Mink *n.* a kind of furred animal.

Minor *adj.* smaller, less serious or less important than others.

Minority *n.* a small group in community or nation, differing from others in race, religion, language, etc.

Minster *n.* a cathedral; a large chruch.

Minstrel *n.* a travelling musician; a bard; a poet; a medieval singer or musician.

Mint *n.* a place where money is coined; a small plant wiht leaves that have a pleasant fresh taste.

Minuet *n.* a slow graceful dance of the 17th and 18th centuries.

Minus *prep.* less; less by so much with the deduction symbol (–); without or lacking something; below zero. –

Minute *n.* the sixtieth part of an hour, the sixtieth part of a degree, instant, memorandum.

Minx *n.* a girl who is playful or cunning and does not show the proper respect; a sly girl.

Miracle *n.* a supernatural event, a remarkable occurrence, a wonder.

Miraculous *adj.* supernatural; extraordinary; wonderful; like a miracle; remarkable.

Mirage *n.* an illusive atmospheric appearance of water in a sandy desert.

Mire *n.* an area of soft deep mud; wet muddy soil; swampy ground.

Mirror *n.* a looking-glass; a thing that reflects or gives a representation of something.

Mirth *n.* merriment; glee; gladness.

Mis *pref.* in sense of 'badly' 'wrongly.'

Misadventure *n.* an unlucky accident; an undesigned evil result; bad luck; misfortune.

Misalliance *n.* improper connection by marriage; unsuitable marriage.

Misanthrope *n.* a hater of mankind.

Misapply *v.t.* to use something for the wrong purpose or in the wrong way; to apply wrongly.

Misapprehend *v.t.* to misunderstand.

Misappropriate *v.t.* to use somebody else's money wrongly, especially for one's own benefit.

Misarrange *v.t.* to arrange in a wrong order.

Misascribe *v.t.* to ascribe wrongly.

Misbecome *v.t.* to suit ill; to be unbecoming to.

Misbegotten *adj.* illegitimate; bastard; badly planned; not appropriate.

Misbehave *v.i.* to behave in an improper way.

Misbelief *n.* a wrong or erroneous belief; a false opinion.

Miscalculate *v.t.* & *i.* to calculate wrongly.

Miscall *v.t.* to call by wrong name; to abuse.

Miscellanea *n. pl.* literary jumbling.

Miscellaneous *adj.* of various types or from various sources; consisting of various kinds; diversified.

Mischief *n.* a desire or tendency to behave in a playful way, causing trouble or mocking somebody; harm; injury.

Mischievous *adj.* inclined to mischief.

Miscible *adj.* that can be mixed (*with*).

Miscite *v.t.* to quote erroneously or wrongly.

Misclaim *n.* a mistaken claim.

Misconceive *v.t.* & *i.* to conceive erroneously.

Misconception *n.* misapprehension.

Misconduct *n.* improper conduct (*esp.* adultery); unacceptable behaviour.

Misconjecture *n.* a wrong guess or conjecture. *v.t.* to make a wrong guess.

Misconstrue *v.t.* to put a wrong construction on (word, action).

Miscounsel *v.t.* to advise wrongly.

Miscount *v.t.* & *i.* to count something wrongly.

Miscreant *n.* & *adj.* a vile, wretch, an infidel, depraved.

Misdate *v.t.* to date wrongly.

Misdeal *v.i.* to make mistake in dealing (cards).

Misdeed *n.* a crime; an evil deed.

Misdeem *v.t.* & *i.* to have a wrong opinion; to judge wrongly.

Misdemeanour *n.* an indictable but not felonious offence; a minor wrongdoing.

Misdirect *v.t.* to direct in a wrong way.

Misdo *v.t.* to commit a crime.

Misdoing *n.* misdeed.

Miser *n.* a person who loves wealth and spends as little money as possible; a hoarder of money.

Misery *n.* wretchedness, calamity.

Misfeasance *n.* wrongful exercise of lawful authority.

Misfire *v.t.* (of gun, motor engine, etc.) to act.

Misfit *n.* a garment not fitting the person from whom it is made.

Misfortune *n.* an unfortunate condition, accident or event.

Misgive *v.t.* to feel mistrust; to fill with doubt.

Misgovern *v.t.* to govern badly; to administer unfaithfully.

Misguide *v.t.* to mislead; to lead into an error.

Mishandle *v.t.* to handle or to treat something roughly.

Mishap *n.* an unlucky chance or accident, misfortune.

Mishear *v.t.* to hear wrongly.

Misinform *v.t.* to give wrong information to; to mislead.

Misinterpret *v.t.* to assume something wrongly.

Misjudge *v.t.* to judge wrongly or erroneously, to have a wrong opinion of.

Mislay *v.t.* to put something in a wrong place; to put (thing) by accident where it cannot readily be found.

Mislead *v.t.* to cause somebody to have a wrong idea or impression about somebody; to lead astray.

Mismanage *v.t.* to manage badly; to conduct badly.

Misname *v.t.* to call somebody by a wrong name or one that is not appropriate.

Misnomer *n.* a wrong use of a name or term.

Misogamy *n.* hatred of marriage.

Misogynist *n.* a hater of women.

Misplace *v.t.* to put in wrong place.

Misplead *v.t.* to make an error in pleading.

Misprint *v.t.* to make an error in printing. *n.* a mistake in printing.

Misprize *v.t.* to scorn; to undervalue.

Mispronounce *v.t.* to pronounce wrongly.

Misquote *v.t.* to quote wrongly.

Misread *v.t.* to read something wrongly.

Misreckon *v.t.* to reckon wrongly.

Misrepresent *v.t.* to represent somebody wrongly; to falsify.

Misrule *n.* bad government; disorder or confusion. *v.t.* to rule badly.

Miss *v.t.* & *i.* to have a failure; to avoid or to escape something; to feel the absence of; to pass over.

Missel *n.* a kind of thrush.

Mis-shapen *adj.* not formed normally.

Missile *n.* water vapour near the ground in minute droplets limiting visibility, dimmness.

Missing *adj.* not to be found; wanting; lost.

Mission *n.* the act of sending forth, commission, errand, embassy.

Missis, Missus *ns.* (Informal) the mistress of a household; one's wife.

Missive *n.* a letter, especially a long or official one; a letter from sovereign.

Mist *n.* rain in very fine drops, filmy appearance before eyes.

Mistake *v.t. & i.* to suppose wrongly that somebody is somebody else; to come to wrong conclusion about.

Mister *n.* (abbr. Mr.) a title of courtesy prefixed to a man's name.

Mistime *v.t.* to do something out of time.

Mistranslate *v.t.* to translate incorrectly.

Mistress *n. fem.* the female head of a household; a woman loved by.

Mistrial *n.* a trial rendered invalid through some error in the proceedings.

Mistrust *v.t.* to suspend; to have no confidence in.

Misunderstand *v.t. & i.* to misinterpret; to come to a false conclusion about; to take in wrong sense.

Misuse *v.t.* bad treatment; wrong use. *n.* bad treatment; wrong use.

Mite *n.* a tiny creature similar to a spider that lives on plants, animals, carpets, etc.; a very small amount; a small insect found in cheese.

Mithridate *n.* an antidote for poison.

Mitigate *v.t.* to soothe; to appease; to alleviate.

Mix *v.t. & i.* to combine one thing with another; to blend things together.

Mizzle *n.* a fine shower; decamp.

Mnemonic *adj.* designed to help the memory. *n.* the art of memory.

Moan *n.* low murmur of suffering; lamentation.

Moanful *adj.* expressing sorrow.

Moat *v.t.* a deep wide ditch that was dug around a castle, etc.

Mob *n.* the low people; a disorderly crowd.

Mobile *adj.* not fixed, changeable, (of people) able to change class, occupation or place of residence easily.

Moccasin *n.* a flat shoe made from soft leather.

Mock *v.t. & i.* imitation, derision. *n.* thing deserving scorn; imitation; derision.

Modal *adj.* (grammar) a verb that is used with another verb (not a modal) to express possibility, permission, obligation.

Mode *n.* any of several arrangement of musical notes, *e.g.* the major or minor scale system in modern music; a way in which a thing is done.

Model *n.* a representation; a plan or design; a pattern; a figure in clay etc.

Moderate *adj.* not excessive, temperate, avoiding extremes.

Moderation *n.* freedom from restraint; the quality of being moderate; moderating; moderateness.

Modern *adj.* of a current or recent style of art fashion, etc.

Modest *adj.* bashful, humble, net excessive, chaste, unstylish.

Modicum *n.* a small or moderate amount of something; what is barely enough; a little or small quantity.

Modifiable *adj.* able to be modified.

Modify *v.t.* to change the form of; to moderate; to alter in some respect.

Modish *adj.* (sometimes derog.) fashionable.

Modulate *v.t.* & *i.* to regulate; to adjust; to vary the tone of voice.

Module *n.* a unit of a computer program that has a particular function.

Modulus *n.* a constant multiplier.

Modus operandi *n.* method or procedure; a particular method of working or dealing with a task.

Mofussil *n.* rural localities as distinct from the chief station.

Mogul *n.* & *adj.* a very rich, important or influential person.

Mohair *n.* fine wool.

Moider *v.t.* to confuse.

Moire *n.* watered fabric, usually silk.

Moist *adj.* (of season); rainy; (of disease) marked by discharge of matter etc.; slightly wet, humid.

Molar *adj.* (of teeth) serving to grind. *n.* a molar tooth.

Molasses *n.* the thick syrup drained from sugar in the process of refining; treacle.

Mole *n.* a small burrowing animal with short dark fur; a permanent dark excrescence on the skin.

Molecule *n.* the smallest unit, usually consisting of a group of atoms, into which substance can be divided without a change in its chemical nature.

Moleskin *n.* a type of strong cotton cloth with a soft surface; mole's fur; kind of fustian like it, used for making clothes.

Molest *v.t.* to vex; to treat somebody aggressively, often causing them injury.

Mollusc *n.* any of the class of animals that have a soft body, no backbone, and usually a hard shell.

Molly *n.* an effeminate man, a prostitute.

Molten *adj.* melted or made liquid by heating to a very high temperature.

Moment *n.* a very short time; an instant; importance.

Momentum *n.* a impetus gained by a body in motion.

Monad *n.* a unit; a simple organism assumed as the first term in evolution.

Monandry *n.* the custom of having one husband.

Monarch *n.* sovereign, supreme ruler.

Monastery *n.* residence for men who lead a retired life; an abbey.

Monastic *adj.* of monks or monasteries.

Monday *n.* the second day of the week; that is sacred to the moon.

Money *n.* wealth, current coin, bank or government notes (*pl.*) coins.

Monger *n.* dealer; trader (chiefly in combinations.)

Mongoose *n.* a small tropical animal with fur that kills snakes, birds, rats, etc.

Monism *n.* the doctrine that only one being exits.

Monition *n.* a warning of danger; admonition; summons.

Monitor *n.* a senior pupil in a school or class; an instructor; a lizard.

Monk *n.* a hermit; a recluse; a member of a religious community.

Monkey *n.* an ape; a member of the group of animals most similar to humans in appearance.

Monochrome *n.* presenting one colour only; completely colour-blind.

Monocle *n.* a single glass lens for one eye.

Monocular *adj.* one-eyed.

Monodic *adj.* pertaining to monody.

Monodrama *n.* a dramatic performance by one person.

Monody *n.* an ode sung by a single person.

Monogamist *n.* a man who has only one wife.

Monogamy *n.* a custom by which one man or male has one wife or mate.

Monogram *n.* a cypher of two or more letters interwoven into one.

Monograph *n.* a detailed written study of a single subject, usually appearing as a short book.

Monolith *n.* a single block of stone shaped into a pillar.

Monologue *n.* a dramatic composition in which only one person speaks.

Monomania *n.* derangement with reference to a particular subject.

Monomial *adj.* consisting of only one term in Algebra.

Monometallism *n.* use of one metal as standard of currency.

Monoplane *n.* an aircraft with only one set of wings.

Monopoly *n.* exclusive or sole possession of some commodity or the exclusive right of selling it.

Monorail *n.* a railway system in which trains travel along a truck consisting of a single rail, usually placed high above the ground.

Monosaccharide *n.* sugar that cannot be hydrolysed to give a simpler sugar, *e.g.* Glucose.

Monotheism *n.* the belief that there is only one God.

Monotone *n.* an utterance in the same tone or voice.

Monotonous *adj.* in the same tone, without variation, wearisome.

Monotony *n.* absence of variety; sameness of tone or pitch, as in speaking.

Monotype *n.* a type casting and setting machine.

Monseigneur *n.* French title for dignitaries.

Monsoon *n.* a seasonal wind which blows before the rainy season.

Monster *n.* a large, ugly and frightening creature, especially an imaginary one; a person or thing of portentous appearance or size.

Monstrous *adj.* shocking and unacceptable; outrageous; extremely large.

Montane *adj.* inhabiting mountainous country.

Montessori *n.* a form of infant education.

Month *n.* a period to time between a day in one month and the corresponding day in the next month.

Monument *n.* a memorial; a written record.

Monumental *adj.* exceptionally great; impressive and of lasting importance.

Moo *v.t.* & *i.* to make the long deep sound that a cow makes.

Mood *n.* (Gram.) a period of bad temper, anger, etc.

Moon *n.* the earth's satellite; a body that moves round a planet other than the earth.

Moonling *n.* a simpleton; a foolish person.

Moonstruck *adj.* slightly mad; lunatic.

Moor *n.* an open waste ground; a heath; a negro.

Moose *n.* a large North American deer with broad flat antlers (antler).

Moot *n.* an assembly of law students.

Mop *n.* an implement for cleaning floors etc.

Mope *v.t.* to be spiritless or gloomy; to feel very unhappy and full of pity for oneself.

Moral *n.* & *adj.* relating to the distinction between right and wrong, ethical, virtuous, just, conformity with moral rules, lesson taught by a fable.

Morale *n.* discipline and spirit pervading an army or other body of person.

Moralist *n.* one versed in ethics.

Morality *n.* practice of moral duties.

Morass *n.* a dangerous area of low soft wet land; a situation that is confusing and complicated or prevents progress.

Morbid *adj.* sickly, unwholesome, unhealty, diseased.

Morbific *adj.* causing disease.

Mordant *adj.* biting, caustic. *n.* mordant substance.

More *adj.* of greater quantity or amount, additional.

Morgue *n.* haughty temper or demeanour.

Morning *n.* forenoon; the period from midnight to noon.

Morocco *n.* a fine soft leather made from the skins of goats or a similar material used for making shoes and covers for books.

Moron *n.* a person who is mentally subnormal; a very stupid person.

Morone *n.* a deep crimson colour.

Morose *adj.* gloomily or sullenly ill-humoured; unhappy and bad-tempered but not saying much.

Morpheus *n.* God of dreams or sleep.

Morphia, Morphine *ns.* powerful anodyne; narcotic principle of opium.

Morphology *n.* the study of the organic form of animals; the study of the form of words.

Morris *n.* a traditional English dance performed by people wearing special costumes, with bells and sticks.

Morse *n.* a sea-horse; a walrus.

Morsel *n.* a small amount or piece of something, especially food.

Mortal *adj.* subject to death, fatal, deadly.

Mortgage *n.* property laid by a debtor as security. *v.t.* to pledge.

Mortify *v.t.* & *i.* to humble; to bring into subjection by self-denial or discipline; to feel humiliated.

Mortmain *n.* condition of land, etc. held inalienably by a corporation.

Mortuary *n.* a room or building.

Mosque *n.* a building in which Muslims worship.

Mosquito *n.* a small flying insect that sucks the blood of people and animals.

Moss *n.* a very small green or yellow plant without flowers which grows in thick masses on damp surfaces or trees or stones.

Most *adj.* existing in the greatest degree. *n.* the greatest amount.

Mot *n.* a witty saying.

Mote *n.* a speck, a small particle of dust.

Motel *n.* a hotel for motorists, with space for parking cars and other facilities near the rooms.

Moth *n.* a person hovering around temptation.

Mother *n. fem.* a female parent, producer, source.

Motherhood *n.* state of being a mother; office or state of a mother.

Mother-in-law *n.* the mother of one's wife or husband.

Motif *n.* predominating feature or idea.

Motion *n.* change of place, tendency, impulse, gesture, proposal, legal application in court, movement.

Motional *adj.* characterised by motions.

Motive *n.* a reason; what impels a person to action.

Motor *adj.* a device that changes power into movement, used to make machines work; a device that changes fuel.

Mottle *v.t.* to make mottled.

Mould *n.* loose earth; a pattern; a case or matrix.

Moult *v.t.* & *i.* to shed feathers, hair etc.

Mound *n.* a small hill; rampart; a pile or heap; a heap or bank of earth.

Mount *n.* a mountain, a hill, border of a picture, a board on which pictures are mounted.

Mountain *n.* a mass of very high rock, often going up to a point.

Mountaineer *n.* an inhabitant of a mountain; a dweller in mountains.

Mountebank *n.* a quack doctor; a charlatan; a pretender.

Mourn *v.t.* & *i.* to grieve; to show conventional signs of grief for a period after person's death.

Mournful *adj.* doleful; suggestive of mourning.

Mouse *n.* a small rodent animal.

Mouser *n.* a mouse-catcher, *esp.* cat.

Mouse-trap *n.* an appliance for catching mice.

Mousse *n.* a thick liquid put on the hair to shape it or improve its condition.

Moustache *n.* a line of hair allowed to grow on a man's upper lip.

Mouth *n.* the opening in the front part of the head of an animal for eating and vocal utterence, entrance to something.

Mouthpiece *n.* a person commissioned to speak for others.

Mouthy *adj.* railing; ranting; bombastic.

Movable *n.* that can be moved.

Move *n.* changing of the position of a piece in chess; the act of moving.

Movement *n.* motion, excitement, agitation, wheel-work of a clock or watch.

Mover *n.* proposer of motion; source of motion; originator.

Movies *n. pl.* (*sl.*) the film industries; a cinema pictures.

Mow *n.* a pile of hay.

Mow *v.t.* & *i.* to cut grass, etc. using a machine or an implement.

Moya *n.* volcanic mud.

Mr. *n.* an abbreviated form of mister; a title of courtesy prefixed to a man's name.

Mrs. *n. fem.* a title that comes before a married woman's surname or before a her first name and surname together.

Much *adj.* great in quantity or amount; many; existing in great quantity.

Muchness *n.* the state of being much.

Mucid *adj.* musty; slimy.

Mucilage *n.* adhesive gum; viscous substance extracted from plant.

Muck *n.* farm-yard manure, dirt.

Mucus *n.* slimy substance secreted by an organ of the body; a thick fluid secreted by mucous membrane.

Mud *n.* wet, soft earth; mire; moist; mixture of earth with water.

Muddle *v.t.* & *i.* to bewilder; to stupefy; to confuse; to mix disorderly.

Muddy *adj.* full of or covered in mud; (of liquid or colours) coloured by or like mud, not clear.

Muff *n.* soft cover of fur, to wrap the hands in; an awkward person; a fool.

Muffin *n.* a king of light cake.

Muffle *n.* the upper thick lip of animals; a plate placed within a furnace.

Muffler *n.* a cloth worn round the neck for warmth; a scarf; any of various devices for deadening sound.

Mug *n.* a cup; a drinking-vessel.

Mugwump *n.* one who holds aloof from party politics; a great man, boss.

Mulatto *n.* offspring of black & white parents; a person who has one black parent and one white.

Mulberry *n.* a tropical fruit-tree whose leaves are used for feeding silk-worm; its fruit.

Mule *n.* the offspring of a horse and a she-ass; a stupid obstinate person.

Mull *v.t.* to make hot with spices.

Mullet *n.* an edible sea-fish.

Mulligrubs *n. pl.* depression of spirits; stomachache.

Mullion *n.* the vertical bar of a window.

Mullock *n.* refuse, dirt, rubbish.

Multangular *adj.* having several angles.

Multimillionaire *n.* a person with two or more millions of money.

Multipartite *adj.* divided into many parts.

Multiple *n.* several parts or components; a number that divides another without a remainder.

Multiplex *adj.* of several elements; manifold.

Multiplicand *n.* a number or quantity to be multiplied by another.

Multiplication *n.* the act or process of multiplying.

Multiply *v.t.* & *i.* to increase in number; to accumulate.

Multipresence *n.* the spiritual power of being present at several places simultaneously.

Multitude *n.* great number; a large gathering; a crowd.

Multure *n.* the toll of grain or flour given to a mill-owner.

Mum *n. inter.* a mother; enjoining silence or secrecy.

Mumble *v.t.* & *i.* to pronounce or chew (food) like a toothless person.

Mumm *v.t.* to mask; to make diversion with a mask on.

Mummy *n.* an embalmed human body for burial. *n.* (used mainly by or to young children) a mother.

Mump *v.t.* to utter indistinctly; to be silent and sullen; to go about begging.

Munch *v.t.* & *i.* to eat food with much chewing and making sound with the mouth.

Mundane *adj.* worldly; earthly; cosmic; ordinary and with little excitement; terrestrial.

Municipal *adj.* pertaining to the local government of a city or town; relating to home affairs.

Munificence *n.* liberality, bounty, generosity.

Muniments *n. pl.* title deeds and similar records.

Munition *n.* military weapons, implements of war.

Muntjak *n.* a small Asiatic deer.

Murage *n.* a tax levied for building the walls of a town.

Mural *adj.* & *n.* of or pertaining to a wall; a painting, usually a large one, done on a wall.

Murder *v.t.* to kill to slaughter; to torture; to put to death or kill (a human being) unlawfully.

Murderer *n.* a person who murders somebody.

Mure *v.t.* to confine or shut up in a prison.

Murk, Mirk *adjs.* (archaic, poet.) (of night, day, place, etc.) dark; misty; poor light; dense.

Murmur *n.* subdued expression of discontent; a quiet expression of feeling.

Murphy *n.* (*sl.*) a potato.

Murrain *n.* a deadly and infectious disease among cattle or other animals.

Murrey *n.* & *adj.* the colour of a mulberry; of this colour; of purple red colour.

Muscadine *n.* musk flavoured kinds of grape.

Muscle *n.* physical strength; lean flesh or meat of an animal.

Muscovite *n.* common mica.

Muse *v.t.* one of the nine goddesses of poetry, music and other liberal arts, a deep thought, a poet's genius.

Museum *n.* a place or building used for storing curious in nature or art.

Mushroom *n.* the edible spore-producing body of various fungi, with a stem and domed cap.

Music *n.* the art and science of harmonious sounds, rhythmic order, pleasent sound.

Musk *n.* a strong scented substance which is secreted by male musk-deer.

Musket *n.* a male sparrow-hawk.

Musketry *n.* the theory and practice of rifle-shooting.

Muslim *adj.* & *n.* same as **Moslem.**

Muslin *n.* a kind of fine thin cotton fabric; a thin fine cotton cloth used for dresses, curtains, etc.

Muss *v.t.* (with up) to disarrange, to throw into disorder.

Mussel *n.* kinds of bivalve mollusc.

Mussuck *n.* leather water bag.

Must *n.* grape-juice before or during fermentation; new wine.

Must *v. aux.* to be obliged to; to be certain to.

Mustang *n.* a small American wild horse.

Mustard *n.* a plant with only pungent condiment.

Muster *n.* a gathering of men; collection or act of collecting.

Musty *adj.* antiquated; damp and smelling stale or of mould.

Mutable *adj.* that may be changed; subject to change.

Mutant *n.* an animal, organism or gene that has undergone mutation.

Mutation *n.* action of changing, alteration, succession.

Mutatis mutandis *adv.* with due alteration of details (in comparing cases).

Mute *adj.* one remaming silent; incapable of speaking; dumb; (of a letter in a written word) not pronounced when the word is spoken.

Mutilate *v.t.* to separate a limb or organ; to main; to make imperfect.

Mutineer *n.* a partaker in mutiny.

Mutinous *adj.* rebellious; refusing to obey orders or instructions.

Mutiny *n.* a revolt against legal authority, insurrection of soldiers.

Mutt *n.* (*sl.*) a fool; a dog, especially one of no particular breed.

Mutter *v.t.* & *i.* to speak in a low voice; to grumble; to murmer.

Mutton *n.* a sheep's flesh used as food; the meat from a fully grown sheep.

Mutual *adj.* done towards each other; reciprocal, given and recieved.

Muzzle *n.* the projection part of an animal's mouth.

My *adj.* belonging to me.

Myriad *n.* ten thousand, a very large number.

Myriapod *n.* any land-living arthropod; a centipede.

Myrmidon *n.* a base servant.

Myrrh *n.* a sticky substance with a sweet smell but a bitter taste that is obtained from plants and used for making incense and perfume.

Myrtle *n.* a kind of evergreen shrub.

Mystagogue *n.* a teacher of mystical doctrines.

Mysterious *adj.* full of mystery, obscure, secret, incomprehensible.

Mystery *n.* secrecy, obscurity; a person about whom not much is known or can be learned.

Mystery-Play *n.* a type of play that was popular between the 11th and 14th centuries and based on Bible.

Mystic *adj.* of hidden meaning, occult.

Mysticism *n.* profession of spiritual things.

Mystification *n.* bewilderment.

Mystify *v.t.* to bewilder; to puzzle.

Mystique *n.* the quality of being mysterious.

Myth *n.* a fictitious story involving supernatural agency; a creation of the mind.

Mythical *adj.* fabulous.

Mythicism, *n.* mythical description.

Mythicist *n.* one who relates mythical stories.

Mythology *n.* a body of myths relating to heathen deities.

Mythonomy *n.* the laws which govern the evolution of myths.

Mythoplasm *n.* the narration of a fable.

Mythus *n.* a myth.

N

N the fourteenth letter of the English alphabet.

Nab *v.t.* to seize; to catch somebody doing something wrong.

Nacre *n.* a shell yielding mother-of-pearl.

Nag *n.* a pony; a small horse, especially one that is old or ill.

Nagor *n.* a Senegal antelope.

Nah *n.* exclamation (spoken, slang) No.

Naiad *n.* a water nymph.

Nail *n.* horny covering on the ends of human fingers and toes.

Nainsook *n.* fine cotton fabric.

Naive *adj.* amusingly simple; showing lack of experience, wisdom or judgement.

Naked *adj.* without the usual covering; defenceless; not disguised; nude.

Name *n.* a word by which a thing is spoken of; a person known, fame, reputation.

Namesake *n.* one having the same name.

Nankeen *n.* a kind of cotton cloth.

Nanny *n. fem.* a child's nurse; (especially as a form of address) a grandmother.

Nanometer *n.* one thousand millionth of metre.

Nap *n.* a short sleep; smooth hairy surface of cloth.

Naphtha *n.* a kind of inflammable rock oil.

Naphthalene, Napthaline *n.* a white crystalline substance used as disinfectant.

Napkin *n.* a square cloth used for wiping hands etc.

Napoleonic *adj.* characteristic of or like Napoleon I.

Narceine *n.* a sedative got from opium.

Narcissus *n.* a plant bearing sweet-scented flowers.

Narcosis *n.* an insensible state; narcotic action.

Narcotic *adj.* & *n.* a substance causing one to sleep or become very relaxed and feel no pain.

Nark *n.* an informer; a police spy; a person who informs the police about people involved in crimes.

Narrate *v.t.* to relate (as a story); to recite.

Narrow *adj.* small in width in relation to length; with only a small margin, only just achieved.

Nasal *adj.* (of speech) sounded through the nose; of, for or relating to the nose.

Nascent *adj.* growing, just begining to increase.

Nasiform *adj.* of the shape of nose.

Nasturtium *n.* a kind of trailing plant.

Nasty *adj.* filthy; foul; spiteful; unkind; full of spite; morally bad; obscene; repulsively dirty.

Natal *adj.* pertaining to one's birth.

Natation *n.* an act or art of swimming.

Nation *n.* a distinct race, people living under one government.

National *adj.* owned, controlled or financially supported by the State.

Native *n.* a person born in a place, country, etc., and associated with it by birth.

Natron *n.* native carbonate of soda.

Natter *v.i.* to talk casually for a long time, especially about unimportant things; to grumble.

Natty *adj.* trim, tidy, deft-handed.

Natural *adj.* instinctive, normal, inherent, regular, illegitimate, unassumed, unaffected.

Naturalism *n.* the style of art and literature in which things are presented in a real and detailed way.

Nature *n.* person's or animal's innate character, disposition of mind.

Naught *n.* nothing; a nought evil; wickedness; (Arith.) cipher; nought.

Naughty *adj.* worthless; wicked; bad; mischievous; indecent.

Nausea *n.* feeling of sickness, loathing.

Nauseate *v.t.* & *i.* to make somebody feel nausea; to loathe; to disgust.

Nauseous *adj.* disgusting; loathsome; causing nausea.

Nautch *n.* (Hindi) an Indian dance; performance of E. Indian dancing girls.

Nautical *adj.* of ships, sailors or sailing.

Naval *adj.* of a navy; of ships or war.

Nave *n.* a central block of a wheel, main body of a church.

Navel *n.* the depression in the centre of abdomen.

Navicular *adj.* of the shape of a boat.

Navigable *adj.* (of seas, rivers, etc.) suitable for ships, boats, etc. to sail on.

Navigate *v.t.* & *i.* to steer or manage a ship in sailing; to sail.

Navvy *n.* a labourer employed in excavation or cutting canal.

Navy *n.* a fleet of ships, a state's ship of war.

Nay *adv.* no; not only so. *n.* a denial; a vote against; refusal.

Neap *adj.* of the lowest (tide).

Near *adj., prep.* & *adv.* at short distance, within easy access, closely related, almost.

Neat *adj.* (of things) arranged in a tidy way, done carefully; not wasting time and effort, skilful, efficient; nicely arranged.

Neb *n.* nose; a beak; a bill; snout; a nib; tip.

Nebula *n.* a cloudlike appearance before the eyes; a cluster of stars.

Nebulium *n.* element known only as producing green line in spectrum of gaseous nebulae.

Nebulous *adj.* (Astron.) not clear; vague; clouded; turbid; hazy.

Necessary *adj.* requisite, indispensable, essential, inevitable.

Necessity *n.* compulsion, imperative need, want, hardship.

Neck *n.* the part of body which connects the head with the trunk.

Necklace *n.* an ornament of jewels or beads, worn around the neck.

Neckline *n.* at or below the neck; the edge or shape of a garment, especially that of a woman.

Necromancer *n.* one who practises magic; a wizard.

Necrophobia *n.* horror of death.

Necropolis *n.* a cemetery, especially a large ancient one.

Necrosis *n.* mortification of piece of bone or tissue.

Nectar *n.* the drink of the gods, a very pleasant thing.

Nectary *n.* the honey gland contained in a flower.

Need *n.* want, emergency, necessity, time of difficulty, lack, poverty.

Needful *adj.* necessary; requisite.

Needle *n.* small pointed pierced round wire of steel used in sewing, the magnet of a compass, any pointed instrument.

Needs *adv.* of necessity.

Negation *n.* a negative or unreal thing; denying; contradiction; the absence or opposite of something.

Negative *adj.* (of a number or quantity) less than zero; wanting positive attributes.

Negatory *adj.* of the nature of negation.

Neglect *v.t.* not to pay attention to; to leave uncared for; to disregard.

Neglige *n.* free and easy attire.

Negotiator *n.* one who negotiates.

Negress *n.* female Negro.

Negro *n.* a black skinned native of Africa.

Negus *n.* the king of Abyssinia.

Negus *n.* hot sweetened wine and water.

Neigh *v.i.* & *n.* the cry of a horse; to make the long high cry of a horse.

Neighbour *n.* one who lives in the adjacent house in the same lane.

Neither *adv., conj.* & *prep.* not either, not the one or the other.

Nelly *n.* a silly or effeminate person.

Nek *n.* (south Africa) depression in mountain chain.

Nematoid *adj.* similar to thread.

Nemesis *n.* retributive justice Greek goddess of retribution.

Neo *prep.* in sense of 'new'.

Neocracy *n.* government by new men.

Neogamist *n.* a person who is lately married.

Neolithic *adj.* of the later part of the Stone Age.

Neologism *n.* a new doctrine.

Neology *n.* a system of new words, adoption of novel religious views.

Neophyte *n.* beginner; one newly implanted in the church; new convert; religious novice.

Nephew *n.* the son of a brother or sister.

Nephology *n.* study of the clouds.

Nephritic *adj.* of the kidneys; of or for nephritis.

Nepotism *n.* undue favour shown to relations.

Neptune *n.* the god of the sea; the name of a planet, eighth in order from the sun; the sea; a plant.

Nereid *n.* sea centipede; a sea nymph.

Nervate *adj.* pertaining to leaves that have ribs.

Nerve *n.* the organ of sensation and motion in animals sinew, energy, vigur, strength.

Nervine *n.* & *adj.* (Med.) a medicine that relieves the disorders of the nerves; pertaining to such a medicine.

Nervous *adj.* vigorous, strong, muscular, excitable, working on the nerves, easily agitated.

Nervy *adj.* sinewy; impudent; (*colloq.*) in nervous state.

Nescience *n.* absence of knowledge.

Ness *n., suff.* used to express state of condition; promontory; cape; the quality, state or character of being.

Nest *n.* a shelter made by a bird for laying eggs, an animal or insect's abose, bed, a snug retreat, a haunt of robbers, a collection of objects.

Nestle *v.t.* to settle or be settled; to press affectionately; to take shelter.

Nestling *n.* a bird that is too young to leave nest.

Net *n.* loose open material made of string, thread, wire, etc. woven or tied together.

Net *adj.* (of money) remaining when nothing more is to be taken away; (of an effect, etc.).

Nether *adj.* lower.

Netting *n.* string wire etc. woven or tied into a net.

Nettle *n.* a plant with stinging hairs on it.

Network *n.* anything resembling a net.

Nett *adj.* clear of all charges or deductions.

Neural *adj.* of or relating to a nerve or the nervous system.

Neuralgia *n.* nervour pain.

Neurasthenia *n.* nervous debility.

Neuritis *n.* inflammation of a nerve.

Neurosis *n.* derangement due to nervous disorders.

Neurotic *adj.* & *n.* having or showing an abnormal anxiety or obsession about something.

Neuter *adj.* of neither sex, neither male nor female, neutral, indifferent.

Neutral *adj.* indifferent; taking part of neither side; impartial.

New *adj.* (of person) not yet familiar with something because one has only just started, arrived, etc.

Newel *n.* the pillar which supports the hand rails of a staircase; centre pillar of winding stair; post at the top or bottom of a staircase.

News *n. pl.* tidings, fresh account.

Newspaper *n.* periodical publication with the latest news.

Next *n.* nearest in time or place, almost, immediately following.

Nexus *n.* a complex series of connection; a bond; a connection; link.

Nib *n.* something small, and pointed; the point of a pen; the beak of a bird.

Nibble *v.t.* & *i.* to bite in bits; to find fault or error; to criticise.

Nibbler *n.* one who bites; one who finds faults.

Nice *adj.* dainty, delicate, attractive, fine, fastidious, exacting.

Nicety *n.* a fine distinction or detail; unimportant detail; accuracy.

Niche *n.* a recess in a wall.

Nick *n.* a notch; a score for keeping account; a cut; exact point of time.

Nickname *adj.* a by-name; the name added to or substituted for regular name.

Nicotine *n.* an oily substance in tobacoo that is dangerously to one's health.

Nictate, Nictitate *v.i.* to blink; to wink.

Nictation *n.* the act of winking.

Nidificate *v.t.* to build nests.

Nid-nod *v.t.* to go on nodding.

Nidor *n.* the colour of cooked food.

Nidus *n.* the place to origin of a disease, a nest.

Niece *n.* a daughter of one's brother or sister or of one's husband's or wife's brother or sister.

Niello *n.* piece of niello-work; black alloy for filling designs engraved on silver, etc.

Nifty *adj.* (*sl.*) fine smart; stylish; neat; fashionable; simple and effective.

Niggard *n.* & *adj.* a stingy person, a miser, meanly, covetous.

Nigger *n.* a negro.

Niggle *v.i.* to potter; to spend time in petty maters; to fiddle.

Nigh *adv.* & *prep.* near by; near; almost.

Night *n.* the time from sunset to sunrise.

Night-blindness *n.* nyctalopia.

Nightingale *n.* a small brown bird; the male of which has a beautiful song.

Nightmare *n.* a dreadful dream; a horrifying experience.

Nightshade *n.* a kind of poisonous berry.

Nigrescent *adj.* growing black.

Nil *n.* nothing; no number or amount, especially as the score in certain games, zero.

Nimble *adj.* agile, active, quick of movement, clever.

Nimbus *n.* halo of bright light round the head of a saint; cloud of glory.

Nimrod *n.* a sportsman, a hunter.

Nincompoop *n.* a foolish person; blockhead; a feeble person; simpleton.

Nine *adj.* & *n.* eight and one; a symbol representing the number nine (9, IX, etc.)

Ninny *n.* a simpleton; a foolish person.

Nip *v.t.* & *i.* to pinch; to bire; to check the growth of; to vex. *n.* a pinch with nails or teeth.

Nipple *n.* the teat on a woman's breast.

Nisi *conj.* unless before.

Nit *n.* the egg or young form of a louse or other insect, especially the type that lives in human and animal hair; a stupid person.

Nitrate *n.* a compound made of nitric acid and alcohol.

Nitre *n.* nitrate of potassium; potassium nitrate or saltpetre.

Nitrify *v.t.* & *i.* to make or become nitrous.

Nitrogen *n.* a kind of gas.

Nitrous *adj.* of, derived from, or containing nitrogen, *esp.* in a low valency state.

Nix *inter.* give warning or approach of master etc.

No *adj.* not any. *adv.* not at all; by no amount.

Nob *n.* a member of the upper class or a wealthy person; the head.

Nobble *v.t.* to obtain by dishonesty.

Nobby *adj.* (*sl.*) smart; fine.

Nobiliary *adj.* of nobility.

Noble *adj.* of high title or birth, splendid, magnificent, excellent, admirable.

Nobody *n.* a person of no importance; not anyone; no person.

Nocent *adj.* hurtful, mischievous.

Nock *v.t.* to set an arrow on the string of a bow. *n.* the notch of an arrow, the forward upper corner of a sail.

Nocturnal *adj.* happening or active in the night.

Nocturne *n.* a short piece of music in a romantic style, especially for the piano.

Nod *v.t.* & *i.* to bend the head slightly and quickly; to be drowys; to signify by a rod.

Noddy *n.* a noodle; a simpleton; a tropical sea bird.

Node *n.* a knob or knot; a hard turmour.

Nodose *adj.* knotty.

Nodule *n.* a small round lump or swelling, especially on a plant.

Nodus *n.* complication; knotty point; difficulty.

Nog *n.* a block or piece of wood, stump of a tree.

Noggin *n.* a small mug or wooden cup or pot.

Noise *n.* clamour, shouting, loud sound, din of voices.

Noisome *adj.* extremely unpleasant; offensive; offensive to the smell; noxious; disgusting.

Noisy *adj.* full of noise, clamorous, loud, violent.

Nomad *adj.* & *n.* wandering, roaming from place to place.

Nomenclature *n.* a vocabulary of names; system of names terminology of a science.

Nominal *adj.* of a noun, existing in names only.

Nominate *v.t.* to appoint; to call by the name of; to propose for an office or election; to propose by name.

Nominative *n.* & *adj.* the case of the subject of a finite verb, of this case.

Nominee *n.* a person who is nominated for an office, a position, etc.; (Commerce) a person in whose name money is invested in a company, etc.

Nonagon *n.* a nine-angled polygon (*Goem.*)

Nonary *n.* having nine as its base; a group of nine.

Non-collegiate *adj.* (of student) not belonging to a college; (of University) not having colleges.

Non-committal *adj.* not comitting oneself.

Non-conductor *n.* a substance or object that does not conduct electricity or heat.

Non-conformist *n.* one who does not conform to the doctrine of the established church.

Non-content *n.* negative vote(r).

Non-co-operation *n.* the act of not co-operating with the established government.

None *pron.* & *adj.* no amount, not the least portion; no person or persons; not any; no one; not one.

Non-entity *n.* an unimportant person; a person utterly without consequence or importance.

Non-existence *n.* a thing having no existence.

Nonest *adj.* missing; wanted.

Non-feasance *n.* omission of an obligatory act.

Non-juror *n.* one who refused the oath of allegiance to William and Mary.

Non-plus *n.* perplexity; standstill.

Non-possumus *n.* refusal to act or permit action; plea of inability.

Non-resident *adj.* & *n.* not residing where his duties require him to reside.

Nonsense *n.* an absurd, foolish or meaningless word; that which has no sense.

Non-sequitur *n.* a conclusion that does not follow from the premises.

Non-slip *adj.* that does slip or helps to prevent somebody slipping.

Nonsmoker *n.* a person who does not smoke tobacco.

Nonsuit *n.* the stoppage of a law suit. *v.t.* to drop a suit.

Non-union *adj.* (of a business, company, etc.) not having trade union members; not belonging to a trade-union.

Non-violence *n.* the policy of using peaceful methods, not force.

Non-white *n.* (a person) not belonging to any of the races with pale skins.

Noodle *n.* a simpleton. **Noodledom,** *n.* foolishness.

Nook *n.* a sheltered quiet place or corner.

Nor *adv.* neither. *conj.* used after a negative statement to introduce another; (used after neither to indicate a second or further alternative) and not; with the subject following the verb.

Normal *adj.* according to standard; usual; ordinary; natural; exact; well adjusted.

Normative *adj.* describing or setting standards or rules of language or behaviour which should be followed.

North *n.* the direction opposite to the south.

North-east *n.* region halfway between the north and the east.

Northern *adj.* situated in or belonging to or characteristic of the north.

Northing *n.* northward progress of a ship.

North-star *n.* the Pole star.

North-west *n.* the region halfway between north and west.

Norwegian *adj.* of Norway. *n.* N. person or language.

Nose *n.* prominent part of a face, the organ of smell, sense of smell, the projecting part of anything.

Nose-bag *n.* a bag tied to a horse's nose.

Nosegay *n.* a small bunch of sweet-smelling flowers worn on a dress or carried in the hand.

Nosing *n.* edge of step, etc. or shield for it.

Nosology *n.* the classification of diseases.

Nostalgia *n.* home sickness.

Nostril *n.* either of the two openings at the bottom of the nose through which a person or an animal breathes.

Nostrum *n.* a secret remedy or prescription.

Nosy *adj.* (*sl.*) inquisitive; ill-smelling; large-nosed; fragrant (tea).

Not *adv.* a word that expresses negation, denial or refusal.

Notable *adj.* remarkable; worthy of notice; striking; conspicuous; capable.

Notary *n.* an officer authorised to attest documents, deeds, contracts, affidavits, bills of exchange, etc.

Notation *n.* the act of practice of representing numbers by symbols.

Notch *n.* a hollow cut; a narrow pass; an indentation; a level or grade; a narrow mountain pass; incision.

Note *n.* distinctive mark, token or sing, a short letter, a mark of censure, a brief record of facts.

Notebook *n.* a book in which notes or memoranda are written.

Noteworthy *adj.* worthy of observation.

Nothing *n.* not anything, non-existence, a trifle, a cipher.

Notice *n.* intimation, information, remark, warning, announcement, attention, consideration, treatment of respect.

Notify *v.t.* to inform somebody of something or report something to somebody, especially formally or officially.

Notion *n.* idea, conception, view, thought, opinion.

Notoriety *n.* notoriousness.

Notorious *adj.* infamous; known and talked of; well-known for some bad quality or deed.

Notwithstanding *prep., adv.* & *conj.* in spite of.

Nougat *n.* sweet-meat of sugar, nuts, etc.

Nought *n.* cipher; not anything; nothing; the figure 0; no number or quantity.

Noun *n.* (Gram.) a word used as the name of a person, thing or place; substantive.

Nourish *v.t.* to nurture; to support; to sustain with food.

Nous *n.* intellect; talent; the pure intellect; (*sl.*) common sense; practical intelligence.

Novel *adj.* strange, unusual, unknown before.

Novelty *n.* a new or strange thing; a novel thing or occurrence.

November *n.* the eleventh month of the English calender.

Novennial *adj.* performed every ninth year.

Novice *n.* a beginner, an inexperienced person, a probationer, a tiro.

Now *adv.* & *n.* at the present time; the present time.

Nowise *adv.* in no way or manner or degree.

Noxious *adj.* unwholesome; injurious; harmful; pernicious or very unpleasant.

Nozzle *n.* the end piece of a nose, the nose.

Nuance *n.* a slight difference, often difficult to detect in meaning, colour or somebody's feelings.

Nub *n.* the central or essential point of a problem or situation.

Nubbin *n.* small imperfect rear of maize.

Nubile *adj.* marriageable.

Nucleus *n.* the central part of a thing, kernal.

Nude *adj.* naked; bare; wearing no clothes; (Law) void. *n.* a naked human figure, especially in art or photography

Nudge *v.t.* to push gently with the elbow. *n.* the act or an instance of nudging; a gentle push.

Nugatory *adj.* useless, trifling, futile, worthless.

Nugget *n.* a lump of a valuable metal or mineral such as gold found in the earth.

Nuisance *n.* anything offensive or injurious, annoying action, something diagreeable.

Null *adj.* invalid; useless; amounting to nothing; void; having no legal force.

Nullity *n.* the lack of legal force or the state of not being valid, especially of a marriage.

Numb *adj.* deprived of feeling, stupefied, without motion.

Numbly *adv.* in a numb manner.

Number *n.* unit, sum, multitude, aggregate, verse, figure, grammatical inflextion.

Numeral *n.* & *adj.* pertaining to number, expresssing number.

Numerator *n.* a person who numbers, the term in a vulgar fraction showing the parts taken.

Numerous *adj.* comprising of several units.

Nummary, Nummulary *adj.* of, in, coin.

Nummet *n.* (dial.) lunch.

Numskull *n.* a blockhead; a foolish person.

Nun *n.* (*mas,* **Monk**) a woman leading a religios and secluded life.

Nuncio *n.* a representative of the Pope in a foreign country; a messenger.

Nuncupate *v.t.* to declare will, etc.; make will, by word of mouth only.

Nunnery *n.* house of nuns.

Nuptials *n. pl.* wedlock or wedding.

Nurse *n.* a woman who tends a child, that which fosters, a woman who takes care of the sick.

Nursery *n.* a room for children and their nurses; a plot of ground for the rearing of plants.

Nurture *n.* bringing up; fostering care; food. *v.t.* to nourish; to bring up; to educate.

Nut *n.* a fruit consisting of edible kernel with a hard shell, the adjusting screw for a bolt.

Nutation *n.* nodding; oscillation of the earth's axis.

Nutmeg *n.* a spice made from the hard seed of an East Indian tree.

Nutrient *adj.* serving as nourishment; promoting growth.

Nutriment *n.* nourishing food; nourishment.

Nutrition *n.* the process of providing and receiving food necessary for health and growth; nourishment.

Nutritive *adj.* nutritious.

Nutting *n.* the gathering of nuts.

Nutty *adj.* tasting of nuts; (*sl.*) crazy (upon); mad.

Nuxvomica *n.* tree yielding a poisonous fruit.

Nuzzle *v.t.* to poke; to press with the nose; to nestle; to foster; to rub with the nose.

Nylghau *n.* a short-horned Indian antelope.

Nylon *n.* a very strong artificial material, used for making clothes, rope, brushes, etc. a nylon fishing line.

Nymph *n.* a semi-divine being, a lovely young girl.

Nymphalid *adj.* relating to nymphs.

Nymphish *adj.* relating to nymphs.

Nympholepsy *n.* rapt state induced by craving for the unattainable.

Nympholept emotionalist.

Nymphomania *n.* uncontrolled sexual desire in women.

Nymphomaniac *n.* a woman who has sex or wants to have sex very often.

Nystagmus *n.* spasmodic oscillatory movement of the eyes; disease with spasmodic movements of eyeballs.

NZ *abbr.* New Zealand (a country).

O

O the fifteenth letter of the English alphabet; (Chem.) symbol for Oxygen.

Oaf *n.* dolt; an idiot; a lout; awkward lout; misbegotten; deformed, or idiot child; elf's child.

Oafish *adj.* an idiot.

Oak *n.* a forest-tree and its wood.

Oaken *adj.* made of oak.

Oaklet *n.* a small oak.

Oakum *n.* loosened fibers of rope; cankling-fibre got by picking rope to pieces.

Oar *n.* a long shaft or pole with a blade attached at one end used in propeling boats.

Oarage *n.* the number of oars.

Oarless *adj.* without an oar.

Oarsman *n.* a rower; a person who rows a boat, especially as a member of a team.

Oasis *n.* a fertile spot in a sandy or barren desert.

Oast *n.* a kiln for hops.

Oat *n.* (*pl.*) a hardy cereal.

Oaten *adj.* of the oat seed.

Oath *n.* an offensive word or phrase used to express anger, surprise, etc.

Oatmeal *n.* meal made from oats.

Obdurate *adj.* impenitent, hard-hearted, stubborn.

Obdurately *adv.* stubborn.

Obeah *n.* a sorcery of the Negroes.

Obedient *adj.* obeying, dutiful, submissive.

Obeisance *n.* a deep bow of respect or obedience; a bow or curtsy; obedience to or respect for somebody; homage, act of respect.

Obelisk *n.* set up in memory of a person; a tall pointed stone pillar with four sides; an event.

Obese *adj.* corpulent; (of people) very fat.

Obesity *n.* fatness; corpulence.

Obey *v.t.* & *i.* to do what one is told or required to do by somebody.

Obi *n.* witch-craft, charm, a Japanese sash.

Obit *n.* the date of a person's death; an obituary.

Obituary *n.* notice of a person's death; an account of a dead person.

Object *n.* anything presented before sense, a pitiable person or thing, end, purpose.

Objection *n.* act of objecting; dislike; a statement or feeling of dislike.

Objective *adj.* & *n.* external to mind, dealing with outward things, symptoms observed by somebody else, not by the patient.

Objurgate *v.t.* to scold.

Oblate *adj.* (of spheroid) flattened at poles.

Oblate *n.* person dedicated to monastic or religious life or work.

Obligate *v.t.* to bind a person to do something legally.

Obligation *n.* binding power, written bond, legal or moral binding, duty, a benefit done or received.

Oblige *v.t.* agreement or moral pressure to do something; to be binding on.

Obligor *n.* a person legally bound to another.

Oblique *adj.* slanting, diverging from the right line, indirect, not perpendicular. *v.i.* to advance obliquely.

Obliterate *v.t.* to remove all signs of something; to make illegible; to destroy something completely; to efface.

Oblivion *n.* disregard, forgetfulness.

Oblivious *adj.* not aware of or not noticing something; (poet.) forgetful, unmindful (of); inducing oblivion.

Oblong *adj.* & *n.* rectangular but with adjacent sides unequal, greater in length than breadth.

Obmutescence *n.* obstinate silence.

Obnoxious *adj.* objectionable, hateful, despised, disliked.

Oboe *n.* organ reed-stop of penetrating tone; a wooden double-reed wind instrument.

Obscene *adj.* indecent, filthy, ill-omened, loathsome, disgusting, lewd.

Obscurant *n.* opponent of enlightenment.

Obscuration *n.* an act of darkening; (Astron.) occultation, eclipse.

Obscure *adj.* indistinct, dim, hidden, obscene, unknown, to fame, full of doubts.

Obsecrat *v.t.* to entreat; to beseech.

Obsequies *n.* funeral ceremonies.

Obsequious *adj.* obedient, dutiful, servile.

Observance *n.* the act of observing, performance of a religious or ceremonial act, a customary rite.

Observancy *n.* customary rites.

Observant *adj.* attentive; headful; careful to obey laws or to keep customs.

Observation *n.* perception, accurate viewing, remark.

Observe *v.t.* & *i.* to adhere to or follow, to perceive, to remark, to examine, to take notice of; to celebrate.

Obsess *v.t.* to harass, to trouble.

Obsidian *n.* a vitreous lava.

Obsolescent *adj.* going out of use.

Obsolete *adj.* gone out of use; disused; out of date; no longer used.

Obstacle *n.* impediment, hindrance, obstruction.

Obstetric, Obstetrical *adjs.* pertaining to childbirth or midwifery.

Obstinate *adj.* stubborn, refractory, self-willed.

Obstinacy Obstinateness, *ns.* resolution; stubbornness.

Obstreperous *adj.* (of people or their behaviour) very noisy and difficult to control; wild; clamorous; calciferous.

Obstruct *v.t.* & *i.* to block up; to retard; to impede.

Obstruction *n.* act of obstructing; state of being obstructed; the action of obstructing somebody; obstacle.

Obstructive *adj.* tending to obstruct.

Obtain *v.t.* & *i.* to procure by effort; to acquire ; to get; (of rules customs, etc.) to be in use.

Obtest *v.t.* & *i.* to supplicate; to protest.

Obtrude *v.t.* to stick out; to become or make something noticeable, especially in a way that is not welcome.

Obtund *v.t.* to blunt or deaden sense.

Obturate *v.t.* to stop up seal. *n.* obturating appliance.

Obtuse *adj.* of blunt form; not pointed; slow to understand; stupid.

Obverse *adj.* having the base narrower than the top, opposite, inverted.

Obvert *v.t.* to turn towards front side; to infer another proposition with contradictory predicate by changing quality of (proposition).

Obviate *v.t.* to get rid of; to make something unnecessary; to clear away.

Obvious *adj.* clear to the mind, clear, palpable, evident.

Occasion *n.* a particular time when something happens; a special event, ceremony or celebration.

Occasional *adj.* occurring at times.

Occident *n.* the country of the west *i.e.* Europe and America; the west.

Occipital *adj.* pertaining to the back of the head.

Occult *adj.* secret, mysterious, mystic, supernatural. *v.t.* (Astron.) to hide by passing in front of.

Occupant *n.* a person who holds a property in actual possession, occupier.

Occupier *n.* a person who lives in or uses a house, room, piece of land, etc.; an occupant.

Occupy *v.t.* to take possession of; to fill; to reside in; to busy; to hold office.

Occur *v.i.* to be found here and there; to happen; to exist; to be found; to take place; (of an idea or a thought) to come into somebody's mind.

Occurrent *n.* incidental.

Ocean *n.* the biggest body of water surrounding the globe.

Oceanid *n.* ocean nymph of Greek mythology.

Oceanography *n.* the scientific study of the ocean.

Ochre *n.* a yellowish orange colour, a kind of clay.

Octagon *n.* a plane figure with eight angle and eight sides.

Octahedron *n.* a solid figure contained by eight plane faces or sides.

Octant *n.* a half-quadrant.

Octave *n.* a group of eight, stanza of eight lines, a device which connects the keys of musical instrument, the eighth day after a church festival.

Octennial *adj.* lasting, recurring every eight years.

Octet *n.* a piece of music for an octet; a group of eight singers or musicians.

Octillion *n.* the eighth power of a million.

October *n.* the tenth month of the English year; next after September.

Octodecimo *n.* (*abbr.* 18 *mo*), book of which each sheet is folded into 18 leaves or 36 pages.

Octodentate *adj.* having eight teeth.

Octogenarian *adj.* & *n.* a person between 80 and 89 years of age.

Octopus *n.* a sea animal with a soft round body and eight long tentacles.

Octroi *n.* duty on goods which enter a town.

Ocular *adj.* of, for, or with the eyes or sight; visual.

Oculist *n.* an eye-specialist.

Odd *adj.* not even, peculiar, unconnected, incalculable, singular, strange, queer.

Oddity *n.* a queer person; an unusual act, event; strangeness; peculiar trait; quality of being odd.

Oddments *n. pl.* odds and ends.

Odds *n. pl.* inequality, strife, probability.

Ode *n.* a poem intended to be sung; a poem addressed to a person or thing or celebrating some special event.

Odeum *n.* a hall or theatre for a musical performance.

Odious *adj.* hateful; offensive; deserving hatred; very unpleasant.

Odium *n.* hatred, hatefulness, dislike.

Odontology *n.* science dealing with the teeth.

Odoriferous *adj.* diffusing odour; fragrant.

Odour *n.* smell, scent, pleasant or unpleasant fragrance.

Oecology *n.* (Biol.) branch of biology dealing with living organism.

Oecumenical *adj.* of the whole Christian church; universal.

Oedema *n.* swollen state of tissue etc.

Oedipus *n.* one who solves riddles.

Oestrum *n.* vehement impulse; gadfly; stimulus.

Of *prep.* from, by, about, out of.

Offal *n.* waste or rejected parts; refuse; waste stuff; the internal parts of an animal.

Offence *n.* an aggressive action, displeasure, annoyance, injury.

Offend *v.i.* & *t.* to displease; to transgress; to make angry.

Offensive *adj.* causing offence, displeasure or injury; aggressive; insulting; disgusting; ill-smelling.

Offer *n.* a proposal, first advance, bidding of a price.

Offertory *n.* collection of money at religious service.

Offhand *adv.* unpremeditated; extempore; without preparation; (of behaviour, speech, etc.) too casual.

Office *n.* service, employment, attention, post, function, duty, place of business.

Officer *n.* he who is commissioned to perform a public duty.

Officious *n.* too ready or willing to give orders, offer, advice or help, or use one's authority.

Offing *n.* the part of the sea seen between the sea and the horizon from the shore.

Offish *adj.* (colloq.) distant or stiff in manner.

Offset *n.* shoots of plants; an offshoot; compensation; a method of printing.

Offshoot *n.* a side shoot or branch of a tree or plant.

Offspring *n.* a child or children of a particular person or couple.

Often *adv.* frequently; in many instances; commonly; many times; at short intervals.

Ogle *v.t.* & *i.* to cast amorous glances.

Ogre *n.* a very frightening person; (in stories) a cruel and frightening giant who eats people.

Oh *inter.* an exclamation of surprise or anxiety, expressing surprise, fear, joy, etc. used to attract somebody's attention.

Ohm *n.* the unit of electrical resistance.

Oil *n.* an unctuous liquid lighter than water.

Oilman *n.* a man who works in the oil industry.

Ointment *n.* an unctuous preparation used to beautify the skin, an unguent.

O.K., Okay *adv.* & *adj.* all right; satisfactory; approved. *v.t.* to pass (things) as.

Old *adj.* advanced in age, ancient, previous, worn out, long practised, decayed. *n.* old time; old people.

Olden *adj.* old, ancient.

Oleander *n.* a poisonous shrub.

Oleaster *n.* a Mediterranean bush with red, white or pink flowers and tough leaves.

Oleic *adj.* pertaining or relating to oil.

Oleograph *n.* a picture produced or printed in oils.

Olfactory *adj.* of or relating to the sense of smell.

Olid *adj.* of bad smell; foul smelling.

Oligarchy *n.* government by the few.

Olio *n.* mixed dish; hotchpotch; miscellany.

Olivary *adj.* shaped like olives oval.

Olive *n.* a small bitter green or black fruit.

Olympic *adj.* of Olympia; of or connected with the Olympic Games.

Omega *n.* the last letter of Greek alphabet.

Omelet, Omelette *ns.* a dish of eggs beaten together and fried, often with cheese, meat, vegetables, etc.

Omen *n.* the occurrence foreboding good or evil, presage.

Ominous *adj.* portentous, inauspicious.

Omission *n.* a thing that is omitted; neglect of duty; the action of omitting or leaving out somebody.

Omissible *adj.* capable of being omitted.

Omit *v.t.* to fail to do something; to exclude something.

Omnibus *n.* a four wheeled public vehicle. *adj.* comprising several items; serving several objects at once.

Omnific *adj.* all creating.

Omniform *adj.* having every form.

Omnigenous *n.* consisting of all kinds.

Omnipotence *n.* infinite power.

Omniscience *n.* unlimited knowledge.

Omnivorous *adj.* eating all types of food, *esp.* both plants and meat.

Omphalos *n.* central point of a system, etc.; hub; nucleus.

Omplate *n.* the shoulder-blade.

On *prep.* as a result of something, because of something; in or into a large public vehicle; supported by or attached to somebody.

Onager *n.* a wild ass.

Onanism *n.* self-abuse; masturbation.

Once *adv.* for one time only a few times, formerly.

Oncoming *n.* & *adj.* advancing towards or approaching one.

Ondit *n.* piece of hearsay.

One *adj.* single in number, some or any, undivided.

Onerous *adj* burdensome.

Oneself *pron.* of one; self; alone; without help.

One-sided *adj.* partial, limited to one side, turned to one side.

Onfall *n.* assault.

Onflow *n.* onward flow.

Onion *n.* an edible bulb with pungent flavour. *v.t.* to rub (eyes) with onion.

Oniony *adj.* having the smell of onion.

Onlooker *n.* a person who watches something happening without getting involved.

Only *adj.* sole, single, alone.

Onrush *n.* rapid or tumultous advance; a strong forward rush or flow; sport.

Onset *n.* an attack, an assault.

Onslaught *n.* a fierce attack.

Ontology *n.* (Philosophy) a branch of thought concerned with the nature of existence.

Onus *n.* burden, obligation, responsibility.

Onward *adj.* & *adv.* directed or moving forward.

Onymous *adj.* not anonymous.

Onyx *n.* a kind of gem.

Oodle *n.* (in *pl.*) great amount of something; superabundance; lots.

Oof *n.* money.

Oogenesis *n.* development of the ovum.

Oolite *n.* granular limestone; series of fossiliferous rocks of this formation.

Ooze *n.* sluggish flow; exudation; wet mud; slime.

Oozily *adv.* in an oozing manner.

Opacity *n.* opaqueness; want of transparency.

Opal *n.* a precious stone.

Opaque *adj.* not allowing light to pass through; not transparent.

Open *adj.* spread out, no longer folded; not closed or blocked up; ready for business, admitting customers or visitors.

Opener *n.* he who opens.

Opera *n.* a dramatic performance accompanied by music.

Operant *adj.* & *n.* operative, active, an operator.

Operate *v.t.* & *i.* to perform; to produce effect; to act; to perform surgical operations; to buy and sell; to manage.

Operation *n.* action, scope, manipulation, influence, method of working, an active process, discharge of duty, surgical performance, movement of troops.

Operative *adj.* operating; having an effect; of surgical operations.

Operator *n.* a person who operates a machine, apparatus etc.

Operculum *n.* valve closing mouth of shell; fish's gill cover.

Operetta *n.* a short opera.

Operose *adj.* industrious; requiring or taking great pains; laborious.

Ophicleide *n.* a powerful organ reed-pipe; a keyed brass wind instrument.

Ophidian *adj.* pertaining snakes.

Ophiology *n.* the study of snakes.

Opiate *adj.* & *n.* a drug containing opium used for inducing sleep or alleviating pain.

Opine *v.t.* to think; to suppose; to express or hold the opinion.

Opinion *n.* judgement without, proof, belief, probable, view, estimation, sentiment.

Opium *n.* a drug prepared from the juice of poppy.

Opiumize *v.t.* to mix opium.

Opossum *n.* a type of small American or Australian animal that lives in trees and carries its young in a pouch.

Oppilate *v.t.* to block or obstruct.

Opponent *n.* an adversary, an enemy. *adj.* opposite, as in position; opposing; contrary.

Opportune *adj.* (of an action or event) done or coming at the right time; (of a time) suitable or favourable for a purpose.

Opportunism *n.* the practice of looking for and using opportunities to gain an advantage for oneself, without considering if this is fair or right.

Opportunity *n.* a favourable time.

Oppose *v.t.* to antagonize; to resist.

Opposite *adj.* (used after the noun) facing the speaker or a specified person or thing; diametrically different to or from.

Opposition *n.* the act of opposing or of setting opposite; Members of Parliament of the political party or parties opposing the government.

Oppress *v.t.* to weigh down; to govern with tyranny; to keep under subjection.

Opprobrious *adj.* (of words, etc.) showing contempt; rude.

Opprobrium *adj.* disgrace; scurrility; infamy; reproachful language.

Oppugn *v.t.* to oppose or call into question.

Opsonic *adj.* having an effect on the bacteria in the body.

Opsonin *n.* the injection of non-living bacteria for curing a disease.

Opt *v.i.* to decide to do something; to choose to do something.

Optative *adj.* expressing wish or desire.

Optic *adj.* of or concerned with the eye or the sense of sight.

Optical *adj.* pertaining to or relating to the eye or eyesight.

Optician *n.* a person qualified to examine the eye and recommend and issue spectacles; a person who makes and sells spectacles and contact lense.

Optimacy *n.* the nobility.

Optimism *n.* the doctrine that good ultimately prevails evil, a hopeful view of things.

Option *n.* choice, choosing, liberty to choose.

Opulence *n.* wealth, riches.

Opulent *adj.* made or decorated in an expensive style; wealthy, having much wealth; well stored; abundant.

Opus *n.* a work of art, especially on a large scale; each of the musical compositions of a composer, usually numbered in order of publication.

Or *conj.* & *prep.* used for uniting two alternatives, each of the two, before.

Oracle *n.* a divine revelation, prophecy, mysterious advice, prophetic judgement.

Oral *adj.* relating to the mouth, spoken, verbal. *n.* a spoken examination.

Orange *n.* a round juicy edible fruit with a thick skin that is reddish-yellow when ripe.

Orangeade *n.* orange-coloured aerated water.

Orangoutang *n.* a drink made of orange juice.

Orant *n.* worshipper.

Orate *v.t.* to make a speech.

Oration *n.* a formal speech made on a public occasion, especially as part of a ceremony.

Orator *n.* an eloquent speaker, a public speaker.

Orb *n.* a sphere, heavenly body, the eye, the eye-ball.

Orbicular *adj.* circular, in the form of an orb.

Orbit *n.* the path of heavenly bodies; a path followed by a planet or moon round another body.

Orchard *n.* a garden of fruit trees.

Orchestra *n.* a usually large group of people playing various musical instruments together.

Orchestrate *v.t.* to compose for an orchestra.

Orchid *n.* a beautiful herb with showy flowers of various colours.

Ordain *v.t.* to appoint; to destine.

Order *n.* class, arrangement, regularity, mandate, social rank, kind, rule, grade.

Ordinal *adj.* & *n.* a number defining a things's position in a series.

Ordinate *n.* (Geom.) straight line from any point drawn parallel to one coordinate axis and meeting the other.

Ordinee *n.* a newly ordanied clergyman.

Ordnance *n.* department for military supplies and materials; mounted guns.

Ordure *n.* excrement; foul language; obscenity; solid waste from the body of a person or an animal.

Ore *n.* native mineral from which precious metal are extracted.

Oread *n.* mountain nymph.

Orectic *adj.* relating to appetite or desire; appetitive.

Organ *n.* a kind of musical instrument, part of the body adapted for special functions.

Organic *adj.* of or affecting an organ or organs of the body; (of food, farming methods, etc.) produced or practised without artificial chemicals.

Organism *n.* the conception of life; organic structure with organized body.

Organist *n.* player of organ, *esp.* as director or church choir.

Organization *n.* act of organizing, organic structure.

Organize *v.t.* to make into a living being; to furnish with organs.

Orgasm *n.* the most intense moment of sexual excitement, or an instance of this.

Orgastic *adj.* pertaining to orgasm.

Orgy *n.* an excessive amount of a particular activity; a wild party, usually with a lot of drinking and sexual activity.

Oriel *n.* projecting part of upper room containing window; such window.

Orient *n.* the eastern part of the sky. *adj.* lustrous; precious.

Oriental *adj.* of or from the countries of the East, especially eastern Asia. *n.* a native of the East.

Oriflamme *n.* any party symbol; blaze of colour; sacred red banner of old French kings.

Origin *n.* beginning, root, source, cause.

Original *adj.* innate; novel; pertaining to the beginning; first or earliest; not imitative or derived.

Originate *v.t. & i.* to take rise; to bring out existence; to initiate or give origin to or be the origin of.

Oriole *n.* a bird with black and yellow plumes.

Orion *n.* a constellation.

Orison *n.* (arch.) a prayer.

Orleans *n.* a kind of plum.

Orlop *n.* the lowest deck of a ship.

Ormolu *n.* a mixed metal with a gold colour used to decorate furniture, make ornaments.

Ornament *n.* a thing used for decoration, embellishment.

Ornate *adj.* elaborately adorned, beautiful.

Ornithology *n.* the scientific study of the birds.

Orography, Oreography *ns.* branch of physical geography dealing with mountains.

Orotund *adj.* imposing, pompous.

Orphan *adj.* a child whose parents are dead; bereaved of parents.

Orphanize *v.t.* to make a child an orphan; to bereave of parent(s).

Orphanage *n.* an asylum for orphans.

Orphic *adj.* melodious.

Orrery *n.* working model of the planetary system.

Orris *n.* a kind of plant.

Ort *n.* refust, fragment, leavings.

Orthochromatic *adj.* giving correct intensity to colours.

Orthodox *adj.* holding correct opinions on religious beliefs.

Orthodoxy *n.* an orthodox belief, practice or policy.

Orthoepy *n.* the science of correct pronounciation.

Orthoepist *n.* one skilled in orthoepy.

Orthography *n.* the part of grammar which treats of letters and the correct way of spelling.

Orthopaedics *n.* (Medical) the branch of medicine that deals with injuries and diseases of bones or muscles.

Orthoptic *adj.* of correct seeing.

Ortolan *n.* a small garden bird.

Oryx *n.* a straight-horned African antelope.

Oscillate *v.t.* to swing to and fro.

Oscular *adj.* of the mouth, of kissing.

Osculate *v.t.* to solute with kiss; to have points of contact or coincidence.

Osier *n.* a kind of water-willow whose twigs are used in basket-making.

Osmium *n.* a metal of the platinum group.

Osmose, Osmosis *ns.* an intermixture of fluids separated by a porous wall.

Osseous *adj.* composed of bones; bony; having bones; resembling bone.

Ossify *v.t.* & *i.* to turn to bone; to make rigid.

Ossuary *n.* a cave with ancient bones; charnel-house; bone urn.

Ostensible *adj.* showy, manifest, not concealed.

Ostensive *adj.* showy.

Ostentation *n.* knowledge or skill, intended to impress people or fill them with envy.

Ostentatious *adj.* fond of show.

Osteography *n.* scientific description of the bones.

Osteology *n.* science of bones.

Osteopathist *n.* a bone-setter.

Osteopathy *n.* (Medical) the treatment of certain diseases based on the manipulation of the bones and muscles.

Osteotomy *n.* a disection of bones.

Ostler *n.* a man who looks after horses at an inn.

Ostracize *v.t.* to exclûde from society; to banish; to expel.

Ostrich *n.* a large swift-running bird whose tail and feathers are valued as ornaments.

Otalgia *n.* earache.

Other *adj.* & *pron.* additional or different to people or things mentioned or implied; those remaining in a group.

Otherwise *adv.* in other or different respects; apart from that; in another or a different way; in different or opposite conditions or circumstances; if not; or else; differently.

Otiose *adj.* impractical, lazy, futile.

Otology *n.* science the ear.

Otoscope *n.* an instrument for examining the ear.

Otter *n.* a fish-eating mammal.

Ottoman *adj.* pertaining to the Turkish Expire. *n.* Turk of Turky; a low cushioned bench without a back.

Oubliette *n.* secret dungeon with trap-door entrance.

Ouch *n.* a socket for the setting of gems.

Ought *aux.* used in the force of expressing duty; to be morally necessary, should.

Ounce *n.* weight equal to one-twelfth in pound Troy and one-sixteenth in pound avoirdupois; the snow-leopard.

Our *adj.* belonging to us.

Oust *v.t.* to eject; to deprive of possession; to drive out.

Out *adv.* & *prep.* without, away from, not at home, at a distance, not in fashion, in a state of disclosure, no longer in possession, to the end, loudly, in an error.

Outbargain *v.t.* to get better in bargain.

Outbid *v.t.* to offer a higher price.

Outbound *adj.* proceeding to a distant port.

Outbrag *v.t.* to exceed in bragging.

Outbrave *v.t.* to defy.

Outbreak *n.* an eruption, a disturbance of peace.

Outbuilding *n.* a building *e.g.* a shed or stable that is separate from the main building.

Outburst *n.* a sudden violent person, especially of strong emotion.

Outcast *adj.* exiled, rejected. *n.* vagabond, an exile.

Outcome *n.* result; issue.

Outcrop *n.* a large mass of rock that stands above the surface of the ground.

Outcry *n.* a strong public protest; clamour; loud cry.

Outdistance *v.t.* to get ahead of.

Outdo *v.t.* to surpass in daring; to exceed; to perform beyond another.

Outdoor *adj.* done in the open air, outside the house.

Outer *adj.* exterior. *n.* hit on outer circles of target.

Outface *v.t.* to defeat an opponent by remaining firm and confident.

Outfall *n.* the mouth of a river.

Outfield *n.* (in cricket and baseball), the part of the field, farthest from the batsman; the players in this part of the field.

Outfit *n.* things required for a journey, equipment. *v.t.* to equip.

Outflank *v.t.* to extend beyond flank of enemy.

Outflow *v.i.* to flow out. *n.* a flowing out, outlet, efflux, issue.

Outfly *v.t.* to surpass in flying.

Outgeneral *v.t.* to defeat by superior generalship.

Outgive *v.t.* to excel in liberty.

Outgo *v.t.* to surpass; to excel.

Outgrow *v.t.* to stop doing something or lose interest in something as one grows older.

Outhouse *n.* a toilet that is enclosed but separate from the main building; a small building *e.g.* a shed outside the main building.

Outing *n.* an excursion.

Outland *n.* land beyond the limit of cultivation.

Outlast *v.t.* to last longer than.

Outlaw *n.* one deprived of the protection of law; (especially formerly) a person who has broken the law and is hiding to avoid being caught.

Outlay *n.* money spent at the beginning of a project or on an item of equipment.

Outleap *v.t.* to leap beyond.

Outlet *n.* a pipe or hole through which water or steam can come out of something.

Outlie *v.i.* to live in the open air.

Outline *n.* the outer line of any figure, a draft, general sketch.

Outlive *v.t.* to survive; to live longer than or beyond.

Outlook *n.* a vigilant watch, a prospect, view-point.

Outlustre *v.t.* to exceed in brightness.

Outlying *adj.* detached; remote; lying at a distance from the centre.

Outmanoeuvre *v.t.* to do better than an opponent, etc. by acting more skilfully and cleverly.

Outmarch *v.t.* to march faster or farther on.

Outmatch *v.t.* to be more than a match for.

Outnumber *v.t.* to exceed in number.

Outpace *v.t.* to be more than something; to go faster than somebody.

Outpatient *n.* the patient of hospital who lives outside it.

Outplay *v.t.* to beat at a game.

Outpost *n.* a post away from the main body of the army.

Outpouring *n.* a large amount of something produced in a short time.

Outpower *v.t.* to excel in power.

Output *n.* the quantity prepared at a time, production.

Outrage *n.* extreme or shocking violation of other's right etc.

Outrageous *adj.* violent; grossly cruel; abusive; immoderate; exceeding all bounds of moderation.

Outre *adj.* (especially of behaviour, ideas, etc.) very unusual and quite shocking.

Outreach *v.t.* to reach beyond limit, to cheat.

Outrider *n.* a person riding a motor cycle or a horse in front of or beside the vehicle of an important person in order to guard her or him.

Outright *adv.* immediately, completely, at once.

Outrun *v.t.* to develop faster than something; to run faster or farther than; to pass the limit of.

Outside *n.* the outer part, external part, the farthest limit.

Outsit *v.t.* to stay longer than.

Outsize *adj.* (especially of clothes) larger than the standard sizes.

Outskirt *n.* border, suburb.

Outspan *v.t.* to unyoke oxen.

Outspeak *v.t.* to speak boldly; to say aloud; to speak more than.

Outspread *v.t.* to spread out, to extend.

Outstand *v.t.* & *i.* to withstand; to remain unpaid.

Outstay *v.t.* to stay longer than somebody.

Outstretch *v.t.* to reach out or stretch; to spread out; to extend.

Outstrike *v.t.* to overpower by excessive beating.

Outstrip *v.t.* to run faster than somebody in a race so that one passes them; to become larger.

Outswear *v.t.* to excel in swearing.

Out-thrust *n.* outward pressure of some part in architecture.

Outvalue *v.t.* to surpass in value.

Outvote *v.t.* to defeat somebody by gaining a larger number of votes.

Outwards *adv.* away from the centre or from a particular point; towards the outside. *adv.* towards the outside.

Outwatch *v.t.* to watch longer than.

Outwear *v.t.* to last longer than; to spend tediously.

Outweary *v.t.* to wear out completely.

Outweigh *v.t.* to be greater or more important than something.

Outwit *v.t.* to overcome or defeat somebody by doing something clever or cunning.

Outwork *n.* work done out of doors.

Outworn *adj.* no longer useful.

Oval *adj.* shaped like the outline of an egg.

Ovary *n.* female reproductive gland; seen vessel in a plant.

Ovate *n.* oval; egg-shaped.

Ovation *n.* demonstration of popular applause.

Oven *n.* a receptacle for baking bread.

Over *adv.* & *prep.* above, across, outward from brink, beyond, upside, down, throughout, in excess, finished.

Overact *v.t.* & *i.* to do more than necessary or required; to act in an exaggerated manner.

Overall *adj.* including everything.

Over-anxious *adj.* anxious beyond limits.

Overarch *v.t.* to arch over; to hang over like an arch.

Overawe *v.t.* & *i.* to awe into submission.

Overbalance *v.t.* to exceed in value; to weigh down.

Overbear *v.t.* to subdue; to overwhelm.

Overbid *v.t.* to make a higher bid than; to offer more than the value of.

Overblown *adj.* fading or withered.

Overboard *adv.* out of a ship; from within ship into water.

Overbuild *v.t.* to build beyond the demand.

Overburden *v.t.* to load too heavily; to burden with too great a weight.

Overbusy *adj.* too officious.

Overcast *adj.* covered with clouds; cloudy; dark; gloomy; sad.

Overcharge *v.t.* & *i.* to load to excess, to charge a higher price.

Overcloud *v.t.* to cause gloom or sorrow.

Overcoat *n.* a heavy coat; a coat worn over another upper coat.

Overcold *adj.* cold to excess.
Overcome *v.t. & i.* to be victorious; to prevail over; to get the better of.
Overdo *v.t.* to overact; to do much; to carry too far.
Overdone *adj.* cooked to excess, overcooked.
Overdose *n.* an excessive dose.
Overdraft *n.* overdrawing of bank account; amount by which balance is over-drawn.
Overdraw *v.t.* to draw beyond one's credit; to exaggerate.
Overdrive *v.t.* to drive too hard.
Overdue *adj.* not paid at the right time; late; beyond the time fixed for arrival.
Overestimate *v.t.* to estimate too highly.
Overfeed *v.t.* to feed immoderately.
Overfill *v.t.* to fill to excess.
Overflow *v.t. & i.* to flood; to flow over.
Overfreight *v.t.* to load too heavily.
Overglance *v.t.* to look hastily over.
Overgo *v.t* to exceed, to cover.
Overground *adj.* above ground.
Overgrow *v.t.* to rise above; to cover with growth.
Overhand *adj.* with hand raised above the elbow.
Overhang *v.t.* to hang over; to impend over; to project over.
Overhappy *adj.* too happy.
Overhardy *adj.* unduly daring.
Overhasty *adj.* unduly hasty.
Overhaul *v.t.* to examine; to pull to pieces for inspection.
Overhead *adv.* over the head.
Overhear *v.t.* to hear by chance; to hear without the knowledge of speaker.
Overheat *v.t.* to heat to excess.
Overindulge *v.t.* to indulge to excess.
Overissue *v.t.* to issue in excess as bank notes or bills of exchange.
Overjoy *v.t.* to fill with great joy.
Overkind *adj.* kind to excess.
Overlabour *v.t.* to overwork.
Overlade *v.t.* to over-work.
Overladen *adj.* too heavily loaded.
Overland *adv.* by land and not by sea; made upon or across the land.
Overlap *v.t.* to lap over.
Overlavish *adj.* lavish to excess.
Overlay *v.t.* to cover completely.
Overleaf *adv.* on the other side of a leaf of book.
Overlie *v.t.* to lie over or upon; to lie on top of; to kill by lying upon.
Overlong *adj.* too long.
Overlook *v.t.* to look over; to have a prospect of from above.
Overlord *n.* a lord over other lord.
Overmantel *n.* ornamental shelves, etc. above mantel-piece.
Overmaster *v.t.* to govern; to subdue; to overpower.
Overmatch *v.t.* to be more than a match, to subdue; to conquer.
Overmodest *adj.* excessively modest.

Overmuch *adj.* & *adv.* too much.
Overnight *adj.* on the previous night.
Overpass *v.t.* to surpass; to pass over or beyond; to pass unnoticed.
Overpay *v.t.* to pay too much.
Overpeople *v.t.* to fill with too many inhabitants.
Overpersuade *v.t.* to persuade against inclination.
Overpitch *v.t.* to bowl so that ball pitches too near wicket.
Overplus *n.* surplus; an excess over a particular amount.
Overply *v.t.* to exert too much force.
Overpower *v.t.* to reduce to submission; to subdue; to defeat; to overwhelm.
Overpraise *v.t.* to praise too highly. *n.* excessive praise.
Overprint *v.t.* to print additional matter on an already printed surface.
Overprize *v.t.* to surpass in value.
Overproduce *v.t.* to produce more goods than necessary.
Overproof *adj.* containing more than a certain amount of alcohol.
Overrate *v.t.* to value excessively; to estimate too high.
Overreach *v.t.* & *i.* to reach beyond limit; to cheat; to rate at too much.
Overrent *v.t.* to exact excessive rent.
Override *v.t.* to ride over; to trample down.
Overrule *v.t.* to set aside by superior authority; to reject.
Oversee *v.t.* to look after work; to superwise; to superintend.
Overseer *v.t.* one who oversees; a superintendent.
Oversell *v.t.* to sell too dear.
Overshade *v.t.* to throw shade over.
Overshoe *n.* a waterproof shoe worn over another.
Overshoot *v.t.* to shoot beyond the mark.
Oversight *n.* to failure to notice something; an error; a mistake; an omission.
Overskip *v.t.* to leap over.
Oversleep *v.t.* to sleep beyond the intended time of rising; to sleep too long.
Oversow *v.t.* to sow too much.
Overspent *adj.* much fatigued.
Overstate *v.t.* to state too strongly; to exaggerate.
Overstay *v.t.* to stay too long.
Overstep *v.t.* to exceed.
Overstrain *v.t.* to strain too much.
Overstream *v.t.* to flow over.
Oversupply *n.* an excessive supply.
Overt *adj.* open to view; apparent; public.
Overtake *v.t.* to come up; to catch up in pursuit.
Overtask *v.t.* to place a very heavy task upon; to burden too heavily.
Overtax *v.t.* to make excessive demand on; to burden with taxes.

Overthrow *v.t.* to throw down; to upset.

Overtime *n.* time at work beyond the regular hours, work done in such time, pay for such work.

Overtone *v.t.* to give a deep tone to a photographic print.

Overtop *v.t.* to be or become higher than; to surpass.

Overtrade *v.t.* to trade beyond capital.

Overtrain *v.t.* & *i.* to train too much; to practise something excessively.

Overtrump *v.t.* to play higher trump than.

Overture *n.* a proposal; an officer.

Overturn *v.t.* & *i.* to upset; to overthrow; to conquer.

Overvalue *v.t.* to value to highly; to set to high a price.

Overwatch *v.t.* to watch exceedingly.

Overween *v.t.* to think too highly of.

Overweight *n.* to be heavier than; to overbalance.

Overwhelm *v.t.* to overpower; to crush; to bury beneath; to submerge utterly; to overcome.

Overwise *adj.* extremely wise.

Overwork *v.t.* & *i.* to work too hard; to exhaust with work.

Overworn *adj.* worn out.

Overwrought *adj.* too much laboured; suffering from excitement.

Overzeal *n.* more ardour.

Ovicular *adj.* pertaining to an egg.

Oviferous *adj.* bearing eggs.

Oviform *adj.* egg-shaped.

Ovine *adj.* of sheep; like sheep.

Oviparous *adj.* producing young ones from eggs.

Oviposit *v.t.* to lay eggs.

Ovipositor *n.* tube with which insect deposits eggs.

Ovoid *adj.* an egg-shaped solid tapering at one end.

Ovum *n.* female germ of animals; an egg.

Owe *v.t.* & *i.* to be under obligation; to be in debt to; to be obliged to.

Owing *adj.* impudable to.

Owl *n.* a night bird of prey; a wise looking dullard.

Owler *n.* one who conveys contraband goods.

Owlish *adj.* foolish; like an owl.

Owlet *n.* a young owl.

Owl-light *n.* flickering light.

Own *adj.* what is one's own (after possessive) and not another's; for one's unaided self.

Owner *n.* a person who own something; passessor; proprietor.

Ox *n.* the male of bovine quadrupeds.

Oxford *n.* the famous university town in England.

Oxgate *n.* a land measure averaging about 13 acres.

Oxide *n.* compound of oxygen with an element or organic radical.

Oxidize *v.t.* & *i.* to combine with oxygen, rust; cover with oxide, make rusty.

Oxonian *n.* a student of the Oxford University.

Oxygen *n.* a colourless and scentless tasteless gas which is essential for animal and plant life.

(xygenate *v.t.* to oxygenize.

Oxygenous *adj.* pertaining to oxygen.

Oxygon *n.* a triangle having two acute angles.

Oxymel *n.* a syrup of honey and vinegar.

Oxymel *n.* a syrup of honey and vinegar.

Oxymoron *n.* a figure of speech combining ideas of contrary meaning.

Oxyopia *n.* acute vision.

Oxyphonia *n.* harshness of voice.

Oxytone *adj.* with acute accent on last syllable.

Oyster *n.* a kind of shellfish.

Ozena *n.* a kind of ulcer in the nostril.

Oz *n.* Australia.

Ozena *n.* a kind of ulcer in the nostril.

Ozone *n.* condensed form of oxygen with pungent smell artifically produced by the working of a dynamo.

Ozonic *adj.* pertaining to ozone.

Ozonizer *adj.* an appliance for ozonizing.

Ozone layer *n.* a layer in the stratosphere containing a high concentration of ozone that absorbs most of the sun's ultraviolet radiation.

P

P *abbr.* Page, penny or Pence (British).

Pabular *adj.* pertaining to food.

Pabulum *n.* food.

Paca *n.* an American rodent.

Pace *n.* a single step, mode of walking gair.

Pachyderm *n.* a thick-skinned quadruped; thick-skinned person.

Pacifiable *adj.* able to be appeased or reconciled.

Pacific *adj.* peace-making, mild, calm.

Pacify *v.t.* to calm; to quiet; to tranquillize; to reduce to quiet; to conciliate; to appease.

Pack *n.* a bundle, a bale, parcel, party, sep of playing cards, number of bounds kept together.

Package *n.* a closely related set of programmes in computers; a parcel.

Packer *n.* one who packs.

Packet *n.* a small pack or package; mailboat; a little bundle or parcel.

Pack-horse *n.* a horse employed in carrying.

Packman *n.* a pedlar.

Packthread *n.* twine for packing goods.

Pact *n.* a agreement; contract.

Pad *n.* a highwayman, an easy paced horse, cushion, sheets of blotting or writing paper tied together.

Paddle *n.* a short pole with a broad blade at one or both ends, used to move a small boat.

Paddock *n.* a small field or enclosure, where horses are assembled before race; a frog or toad.

Paddy *n.* rice growing or in the husk.

Padlock *n.* a detachable lock with pivoted hoop to pass through the staple or ring. *v.t.* to secure with padlock.

Padre *n.* a clergyman or chapain.

Paean *n.* song of praise or triumph.

Pagan *n.* a heathen, an idolater.

Pageant *n.* a brilliant spectacle; empty show.

Pagehood *n.* the state of being a page.

Paginal *adj.* marking to pages.

Paginate *v.t.* to number pages of book.

Pagoda *n.* a sacred building in pyramidal form.

Pah *interj.* expressing disgust.

Pail *n.* a vessel for carrying liquids a bucket.

Pain *n.* bodily distress, suffering, penalty.

Paint *n.* solid coluring matter.

Pair *n.* set of two; two like things; two of a kind; engaged or married or mated couple.

Pal *n.* a companion; a comrade; a friend; a partner.

Palace *n.* a stately building, the residence of a king.

Palatal *adj.* of the palate; made with the tongue and palate.

Palate *n.* & *adj.* roof of the mouth.

Palatable *adj.* pleasant to the taste or agreeable to the mind; savoury.

Palatal *adj.* & *n.* pertaining to palate, a letter pronounced by the palate.

Palatial *adj.* like a palace; magnificent.

Palatine *adj.* & *n.* of or relating to palate.

Palaver *n.* idle talk; flattery.

Pale *n.* a boundary; a fence.

Paletot *n.* loose outer garment.

Palette *n.* artist's flat tablet for mixing colours on.

Palfrey *n.* a small saddle-horse.

Pali *n.* the language of ancient Buddhist scriptures.

Palindrome *n.* a word or a verse that reads the same backward and forwards.

Paling *n.* an enclosure; a fence.

Palingenesis *n.* new birth; regeneration; revival.

Palisade *n.* a fence of pales or railings.

Pall *n.* cloth spread over a coffin; a cloak.

Palladium *n.* safeguard; a rare metal in colour and ductility resembling platinum.

Pallet *n.* a portable platform for transporting and storing loads.

Palliasse *n.* a hard mattress.

Palliate *v.t.* to alleviate disease; to extenuate; to lessen.

Pallid *adj.* pale; dim; wan; sickly-looking.

Pallor *n.* paleness; pallidness.

Palm *n.* a tropical tree with fan shaped leaves; supreme excellence.

Palmetto *n.* a kind of small palm tree.

Palmiped *n.* a kind of web-footed bird.

Palmist *n.* one versed in palmistry.

Palmistry *n.* fortune-telling from the lines on the palm of the hand.

Palmy *adj.* bearing palm-trees; flourishing.

Palmyra *n.* a kind of Indian palm.

Palpable *adj.* that can be felt or touched, perceived by the mind.

Palpate *v.t.* to examine by touch; to handle.

Palpebral *adj.* relating to eyelids.

Palpitate *v.t.* to pulsate; to tremble.

Palpitation *n.* throbbing.

Palsied *adj.* affected with palsy.

Palsy *n.* paralysis; paralytic trembling.

Palter *v.i.* to shuffle; to shift to trifle.

Paltriness *n.* the state of being paltry.

Paltry *adj.* mean and trivial; contemptible; trifling.

Paly *adj.* pale.

Pam *n.* knave of clubs in card game.

Pamper *v.t.* to spoil with luxury; to gratify to the full; to overindulge.

Pamphlet *n.* a small unbound book treating of current topics.

Pan *n.* a vessel of metal; earthenware; bowl; shallow vessel.

Panacea *n.* a medicine for all diseases; universal remedy.

Panache *n.* plum of feathers wornon a helmet.

Panada *n.* bread boiled and sweetened.

Panama *n.* a straw hat.

Panary *adj.* pertaining to cake.

Pancratic *adj.* athletic.

Pancratium *n.* athletic contest combining wrestling & boxing.

Pancreas *n.* gland near stomach which secretes a fluid.

Panda *n.* a large black and white animal that looks like a beer.

Pandal *n.* a temporarily erected shed, booth, or arbour.

Pandect *n.* body of laws.

Pandemic *adj.* of a disease which permeats the whole world.

Pandemonium *n.* a place of lawlessness; utter confusion.

Pander *n.* one who helps in wicked designs; a procurer.

Pandora *n.* a stringed musical instrument.

Pane *n.* a sheet of glass. *v.t.* to make a garment from strips of different colours.

Panegyric *n.* an eulogy; laudatory discourse; an encomium.

Panegyrize *v.t.* to eulogize; to laud; to praise.

Panel *n.* a kind of saddle, strip of parchment, list of jury or inspectors, compartment of a wainscor.

Pang *n.* agony; a sharp or extreme pain.

Pangolin *n.* a scaly ant-eater.

Panic *n.* excessive terror; sudden alarm, fright without cause.

Panivorous *adj.* subsisting on bread.

Panner *n.* general fault-finder.

Pannier *n.* a basket; a wicker-work basket carried by beasts of burden.

Pannikin *n.* a small drinking vessel.

Panoply *n.* complete suit of armour.

Panorama *n.* a roll of picture; continuous view of a scene.

Panoramic *adj.* pertaining to panorama.

Pan-pipe *n.* a kind of mouth organ.

Pansy *n.* a wild garden plant.

Pant *v.t.* & *i.* to breath quickly and audibly; to throb excessively.

Pantalets *n. pl.* woman's knicker-bockers, etc.

Pantaloon *n. pl.* trousers in general; a kind of trousers; a buffoon.

Panter *n.* one who pants.

Pantheism *n.* the doctrine that the universe is God; heathen worship of all gods.

Pantheist *n.* a believer in pant-heism.

Pantheon *n.* a temple devoted to all the gods or divinites.

Panther *n.* a leopard.

Pantile *n.* curved roof.

Pantisocracy *n.* a community in which all sound have equal power.

Pantograph *n.* an instrument for copying a drawing in any size.

Pantomime *n.* performace in dumb show, a mimic actor.

Pantophagist *n.* he who eats all kinds of food.

Pantry *n.* a room in which provisions are kept.

Pants *n. pl.* pantaloon.

Panurgy *n.* skill in performing all kinds of work.

Pap *n.* nipple of breast, soft food for infants.

Papaw *n.* a tree like palm.

Paper *n.* a material made in thin sheets and used for writing, printing or drawing on, or for wrapping and packing things.

Papilla *n.* nipple-shaped protuberance; small fleshy projection on plants.

Papoose *n.* a Red-Indian child.

Papoosh *n.* covering for the foot.

Pappus *n.* downy turf.

Papula *n.* a small projection on plants.

Papyro *pref.* in sense of paper.

Papyrograph *n.* an apparatus for copying.

Par *n.* equality, equal value.

Parable *n.* an allegory; an enigma; a proverb.

Parabola *n.* figurative.

Parachronism *n.* a mistake in chronological order.

Parachute *n.* an apparatus like an umbrella used for descending from a balloon or airship.

Parachutist *n.* one who descends from a baloon or aeroplane by the help of a parachute.

Paraclete *n.* one called to aid, advocate.

Parade *n.* display, show, muster of military troops for inspection, ground used for military display.

Paradigm *n.* a representative set of the infections of a noun, verb etc.

Paradise *n.* heaven; an ideal or perfect place; region or state of felicity.

Paradox *n.* a statement contrary to received opinion; self contradictory statement.

Paraffin *n.* a fatty substance used for making candles etc. *v.t.* to make use of paraffin.

Paragoge *n.* addition of a letter in a word.

Paragon *n.* a model of excellence; an excellent person or thing; very valuable diamond.

Paragram *n.* a play upon words.

Paragraph *n.* a distinct passage in a book; a distinction; a reference mark.

Parakeet *n.* a small long-tailed parrot.

Parakite *n.* a kind of kite for descending from a balloon.

Parallax *n.* an apparent change in the position of an object caused by the position of the observer; angular amount of this.

Parallel *adj.* equidistant, similar, analogous.

Parallelepiped *n.* a solid figure (body) of which each face is a parallelogram.

Parallelism *n.* resemblance; comparison.

Parallelogram *n.* a rectilineal figure of four sides which has its opposite sides parallel.

Paralogism *n.* an illogical reasoning; false reasoning; violation of logic; a fallacy.

Paralogize *v.t.* to reason illogically.

Paralyse *v.t.* to affect with paralysis; to make helpless or ineffectual; to cripple.

Paralytic *adj.* of or affected with paralysis. *n.* a paralysed person.

Paramagnetic *adj.* able to be attracted by the poles of a magnet.

Paramatta *n.* a fabric of soft wool and cotton or silk.

Parameter *n.* a constant quantity in mathematics.

Paramnesia *n.* false memory.

Paramount *adj.* spreme; possessing the highest title; eminent; superior to all others.

Paramour *n.* an illicit lover.

Parang *n.* large heavy sheath-knife used by Malays as weapon.

Parapet *n.* a wall at the edge of a root or bridge; the wall at the side of trench.

Paraph *n.* flourish after a signature.

Paraphernalia *n. pl.* personal belonging; ornaments.

Paraphrase *n.* an account or expression of the meaning of something written or said, using different words, especially in order to make it easier to understand.

Paraplegia *n.* paralysis of the lower limbs.

Paraquito *n.* a small parrot.

Parasite *n.* an animal or plant which gets its nourishment from another; a hanger on.

Parasitize *v.t.* to act as a parasite.

Parasol *n.* a small umbrella.

Parataxis *n.* a number of clauses put together without connecting words.

Paratyphoid *n.* kinds of fever distinguishable from typhoid only by bacteriological examination.

Parboil *v.t.* to boil partially; to scald the surface of in boiling water.

Parcel *n.* a part, a package, bundle, lot. *v.t.* to divide into portions.

Parcenary *n.* joint-heirship.

Parcener *n.* a co-heir.

Parch *v.t.* & *i.* to roast slightly; to scorch; to become hot and dry.

Pard *n.* a leopard.

Pardon *n.* forgiveness; remission of punishment for a crime.

Pardonable *adj.* excusable; venial.

Pare *v.t.* to cut away the skin or outer covering from something.

Paregoric *n.* & *adj.* soothing; tincture of opium.

Parent *n.* father or mother; origin.

Parentage *n.* descent from parents; lineage.

Parenthood *n.* the state of being a parent.

Parentless *adj.* without parents.

Parer *n.* one who pares.

Paretic *adj.* pertaining to paresis.

Parexcellence *adv.* by virtue of special excellence.

Parget *n.* ornamental plaster work; plaster. *v.t.* to plaster wall & etc.

Parhelion *n.* bright spot in solar halo.

Pariah *n.* a person who is not acceptable to society; any person or animal generally despised.

Parian *n.* kind of fine white porcelain. *adj.* of the island of Paros.

Parietal *adj.* pertaining to the walls of the body.

Pari-mutuel *n.* a betting machine.

Paring *n.* a portion cut-off.

Paripassu *adj.* with simultant progress.

Parity *n.* equality; analogy.

Park *n.* an enclosed area of land, usually with fields and trees, attached to a large country house.

Parlance *n.* mode of speech, conversation.

Parley *n.* talk; a conference for debate.

Parliament *n.* the supreme legislative council of the United Kingdom.

Parlour *n.* an ordinary sitting room in a house; a private room in an inn; a drawing-room.

Parlous *adj.* perilous; surprisingly clever; hard to escape from or deal with.

Parmesan *n.* a person hard to deal with; a kind of cheese.

Parodist *n.* one who makes parodies.

Parody *n.* a writing in which an author's characteristics are ridiculed and imitated.

Parole *n.* the release of a prisoner before the end of a sentenced if he or she promises to behave well, or temporarily for a special purpose.

Paronomasia *n.* a play on words of similar but different sense.

Paronym *n.* words alike in sound but different in spelling and meaning.

Paroquet *n.* a small parrot.

Parotid *adj.* situated near the ear. *n.* a parotid gland.

Paroxysm *n.* violent fit of a disease.

Parpen *n.* a smoth-faced stone passing through a wall.

Parquet *n.* wooden flooring.

Parricide *n.* murderer of a parent or near relation.

Parrot *n.* any of various types of usually tropical bird with curved beaks and bright colourful feathers.

Parry *v.t.* to prevent; to avert; to avoid; to ward off; to evade.

Parse *v.t.* to name the parts of speech of a word and to show its relation in a sentence to other words.

Parsee *n.* one who believes in Zoroastrianism.

Parsimony *n.* carefulness in the use of money or other resources; meanness; stinginess.

Parsimonious *adj.* nigardly.

Parsley *n.* a plant with aromatic leaves.

Parsnip *n.* plant with yellow root cooked for food.

Parson *n.* a rector; any clergyman.

Parsonage *n.* a parson's house.

Part *n.* share, allotted portion; a usually essential piece of a machine or structure; some but not all of a things.

Partake *v.i.* to take a share in; have something of the character of.

Partaker *n.* a sharer.

Parted *adj.* severed; separated.

Parterre *n.* space of flowerbeds in ground; floor of a theatre.

Parti *n.* person regarded eligible or in specified light in the marriage market.

Partial *adj.* biased in favour of one side; liking somebody very much.

Partible *adj.* separate; able to be separated.

Participant *n.* a person who takes part in something.

Participate *v.t.* & *i.* to have a share in; to join; to share in by common action.

Participle *n.* an adjective formed by inflexion from a verb.

Particle *n.* a minute portion; the smallest amount.

Particoloured *adj.* differently coloured; variegated.

Particular *adj.* giving close attention to detail, difficult to please, fussy; relating to one as distinguished from others.

Parting *adj.* & *n.* dividing line of combed hair; leave-taking; division; the action or an instance of dividing into parts.

Partisan (Partizan) *n.* an adherent of a party or side or cause; a kind of spear.

Partition *n.* a structure dividing a space into two parts; a division into parts.

Partitive *adj.* Gram. (of a word or phrase) indicating a part of quantity of something.

Partly *adv.* in part; in some measure or degree.

Partner *n.* one who shares in business an associate; a husband or wife.

Partridge *n.* kinds of well-known game-bird; its flesh.

Parturient *adj.* about to bring forth young.

Parturition *n.* child-birth.

Party *n.* a company of persons joined for a cause, a faction, accessory, body of men travelling together detachment of soldiers, a social gathering, a litigant.

Parvenu *n.* a person who has newly risen from obscurity to eminence or notice.

Parvis *n.* enclosed area or court in front of cathedral.

Pas *n.* a step in dancing; precedence.

Pascuous *adj.* growing in pastures.

Pasquinade *n.* a personal satire; a lampoon.

Pass *v.t.* & *i.* to spend; to circulate; to transfer; to be transported from place to place; to charge; to omit; to enact.

Passable *adj.* barely satisfactory; receivable; that may be travelled over or navigated; tolerable; fairly good.

Passage *n.* the passing of a bill by a parliament so that it becomes law; a corridor; the freedom or right to go through the across something.

Passe *adj.* past his, her or its prime; gone off; out of date.

Passenger *n.* a traveller in a public vehicle; a wayfarer.

Passer *n.* a passenger.

Passer-by *n.* person who is going past somebody, especially by chance.

Passerine *n.* of the sparrow kind.

Passim *n.* every here and there; all over the place.

Passion *n.* a strong emotion; anger; intense sexual love; strong enthusiasm; eager desire.

Passionate *adj.* lacking self-control; caused by or showing strong feelings; prone to passion; caused by or showing intense sexual love.

Passive *adj.* patient; suffering ; inactive; inert; submissive; of or in the passive voice.

Passover *n.* the Jewish religious festival in memory of the freeing of the Jews from being slaves in Egypt.

Passport *n.* an authoritative document to travel in a foreign country.

Password *n.* a secret word; a selected word or phrase; countersign.

Past *adj.* & *n.* just gone by, denoting past action, former, past time.

Paste *n.* flour moistened and kneaded; a paste of flour and water.

Pastel *n.* dry pigment-paste used for crayons; a drawing made by it.

Pastelist *n.* artist drawing in pastel.

Pastern *n.* the part of horse's foot between fetlock and hoof.

Pasteurism *n.* Pasteur's method of inoculation with virus as preventive or cure of hydrophobia, etc.

Pastiche *n.* musical or other medley of borrowings.

Pastil, Pastille *ns.* roll of aromatic past; a lozenge.

Pastime *n.* a thing done regularly for enjoyment rather than work; a game, a play, a sport; diversion, recreation.

Pastor *n.* a minister of a church; a shepherd, a spiritual adviser.

Pastorale *n.* a simple song.

Pastry *n.* a mixture of flour, fat and water which is baked and used as a base or covering for pies, etc.

Pasturage *n.* a grazing land for cattle; pasture.

Pasture *n.* a land covered with grass etc. suitable for grazing animals; herbage for cattle.

Pasty *adj.* of or like paste; pale and looking ill. *n.* a pie of venison.

Pat *v.t.* to tap somebody gently with the open hand or with a flat object.

Patch *n.* a piece of material or metal etc. used to mend a hole or as reinforcement; a pad or shield worn over an eye socket, dressing etc.

Patchouli *n.* a sweet-smelling plant grown in East Asia, the perfume made from this plant.

Patchwork *n.* patching; a work composed of pieces sewn together; a thing made up of odds and ends.

Pate *n.* the top of head, head often as seat of intellect.

Paten *n.* a shallow plate used for bread; thin circular plate of metal.

Patent *adj.* a writ from a sovereign conferring a title or sole right (for a specified term) for an invention.

Patented *adj.* for which a patent has been obtained.

Patentee *n.* the holder of a patent.

Pater *n.* (*sl.*) father.

Patefamilias *n.* the head or father of a family.

Paternal *adj.* of a father, fatherly, hereditary.

Paternoster *n.* the Lord's Prayer.

Path *n.* a road; footway; a track.

Pathetic *adj.* exciting or appealing to compassion; causing one to feel pity or sadness; extremely inadequate.

Pathic *adj.* pertaining to a disease.

Pathogeny *n.* the science of the beginning and development of diseases.

Pathognomonic *adj.* characteristic of a disease.

Pathologist *n.* one who is versed in pathology.

Pathology *n.* the study of diseases; the doctrine of diseases.

Pathos *n.* a quality, especially in literature or drama, that causes a feeling of pity of sadness.

Patience *n.* calm; endurance; weariness; perseverance.

Patient *adj.* not easily provoked having or showing patience, forbearant.

Patina *n.* green colour on old bronze.

Patois *n.* form taken by a language among the uneducated of a district.

Patriarch *n.* the head of a family, a bishop, a respected old man.

Patrician *n.* an aristocrat; nobleman; a person of noble birth.

Particidal *adj.* pertaining to particide.

Patricide *n.* a murder of one's father.

Patrimonial *adj.* pertaining to patrimony.

Patriot *n.* a person who loves her or his country, especially one who is ready to defend it against an enemy.

Patrol *n.* a going round a camp or garrison, a detachment of troops, perambulation by a police or soldiers in uniform, a mounted policeman.

Patron *n.* a protector; one who countenances or protects; an advocate.

Patronage *n.* guardianship.

Patronymic *adj.* & *n.* a name derived form father or ancestor.

Patten *n.* an overshoe with a wooden sole.

Patter *n.* the rapid speech used by a comedian or introduced into a song.

Pattern *n.* a way in which something happens, moves, develops or is arranged.

Patty *n.* a small cake of minced potato etc.
Patulous *adj.* open; spreading.
Paucity *n.* fewness; not enough of somthing, a small amount; smallness of number.
Paunch *n.* the belly; stomach.
Pauper *n.* a person who has no means of livelihood; a beggar.
Pauperize *v.t.* to reduce to pauperism.
Pause *n.* a break made in speech or reading; interval of inaction or silence.
Pave *v.t.* to cover with stone or bricks; to prepare the way for; to make easy.
Pavilion *n.* a covering like a tent; projecting subdivision of a building.
Paving *n.* the upper surface of a road.
Paviour *n.* workman employed in paving.
Pavonine *adj.* of or like a peacock.
Paw *n.* foot of a beast with claws; a person's handwriting. *v.t.* & *i.* to touch with paw; to deposit as security; (*sl.*) handle with dirty or clumsy hands.
Pawky *adj.* sly; arch; quiet; dry.
Pawl *n.* Naut. short bar; a lever with catch for teeth of a wheel or bar.
Pawn *n.* the smallest piece in chess; a person left in another's custody; a pledge.
Pawnbroker *n.* a person who lends money in exchange for articles left with her or him.
Pay *v.t.* & *i.* to give as due; to discharge debt to.
Payee *n.* the person to whom money is to be paid or is paid.
Payment *n.* the sum paid for service done.
Pea *n.* a round green seed that grows with others in a pod and is eaten cooked as a vegetable; that plat of this.
Peace *n.* tranquillity; freedom from war; harmony; mental calm; serenity; quiet; calm.
Peach *n.* a stone-fruit of downy delicately coloured skin; its tree.
Peacock *n.* a large male bird with long blue and green tail feathers which it can spread out like a fan.
Peahen *n.* the female of a peafowl.
Peajacket *n.* a sailor's short overcoat.
Peak *n.* brim of cap, pointed summit of a mountain, point. *v.t.* to waste away.
Peakish *adj.* looking sickly.
Peakload *n.* maximum electric power.
Peaky *adj.* pointed; sickly; sick.
Peal *n.* loud ringing of bell; a loud sound; set of bells rung together.
Pear *n.* a fleshy sweet fruit tapering towards the stalk.
Pearl *n.* a white globular concretion formed within the shell of an oyster.

Pearl-like *adj.* like pearls.

Peasant *n.* a farmer; a countryman; a rustic.

Peasantry *n.* peasants collectively; the body of peasants.

Pease *n. pl.* peas collectively.

Peasecod *n.* pods containing pea seeds.

Peat *n.* decomposed vegetable matter used for fuel.

Pebble *n.* rock-crystal used for spectacles.

Pecan *n.* a pinkish-brown smooth nut with an edible kernel.

Peccable *adj.* liable to sin.

Peccadillo *n.* a venial sin that person is prone to a trifling offence or fault.

Peccancy *n.* a sin; criminal offence; sinfulness.

Peccant *adj.* guilty, sinning, producing disease.

Peccary *n.* American gregarious wild animal of pig kind.

Peck *v.t.* & *i.* a dry measure of two gallons.

Pecker *n.* one who pecks, kind of hoe.

Peckish *adj.* (*sl.*) hungry.

Pecten *n.* a comblike structure.

Pectinated *adj.* of the form of a comb.

Pectination *n.* giving the form of a comb.

Pectoral *adj.* worn on the chest or breast.

Peculate *v.t.* & *i.* to misappropriate or embezzle public money.

Peculator *n.* one who embezzles.

Peculiar *adj.* odd or strange, especially in a rather unpleasant way.

Pecuniary *adj.* relating to money; consisting of money.

Pedagogue *n.* a schoolmaster with technical knowledge of many subjects.

Pedagogy, Pidagogics *n.* science of teaching.

Pedal *n.* the foot-lever of an instrument.

Pedant *n.* one who makes a vain display of his learning; a conceited fellow.

Pedantize *v.t.* to play the part of a pedant.

Pedate *adj.* having the structure like a foot.

Peddle *v.t.* & *i.* to spread or promote something, *e.g.* an idea or a rumour, in an attempt to get it accepted.

Pedestrian *n.* one who journeys or walks on foot. *adj.* dull; prosaic; uninspired.

Pedicel, Pedicle *ns.* a little foot stalk; a stalk-like structure in plant.

Pedigree *n.* ancestral line; lineage; the background, history, etc. of a person or thing, especially when this is impressive; derivation (of word).

Pediment *n.* a triangular ornamental portion over the front part of a building.

Pedlar *n.* a travelling salesman.

Pedometer *n.* an instrument for recording the distance travelled on foot.

Peduncle *n.* a foot-stalk or pedicel; the stem of cluster or flower or fruit.

Peek *v.i.* to peep; to peer.

Peel *n.* the skin or rind of fruit.

Peeler *n.* policeman; one who peels.

Peeling *n.* that which is peeled off.

Peen *n.* the back of a hammerhead.

Peep *v.i.* to chip; to squeak; to look through a narrow hole.

Peeper *n.* one who peeps; a young fowl.

Peep-hole *n.* a hole for peeping in.

Peer *v.i.* to make or be equal; to look keenly or without difficulty; to peep.

Peerage *n.* aristocracy; the nobility; rank of a peer.

Peerless *adj.* superior to all others; unequal.

Peeve *v.t.* to make peevish.

Peevish *adj.* quarrelsome; fretful; irritable, especially by unimportant things.

Peg *n.* a pin of wood or metal, a drink of wine (or sodawater).

Peg-top *n.* a child's spinning top.

Pegamoid *n.* kind of imitation leather used in coach building.

Pekin *n.* kind of silk-stuff.

Pekoe *n.* a sweet smelling black tea.

Pelagian *adj.* of or concerning the monk.

Pelagic *adj.* of the open sea.

Pelargonium *n.* genus of plants with showy flowers and fragrant leaves.

Pelerine *n.* woman's long narrow cape or tippet.

Pelf *n.* money; wealth; riches.

Pelican *n.* a large water bird with a bag of skin under its long beak for storing food.

Pelisse *n.* a child's outer garment; woman's long mantle with sleeves or armholes.

Pellet *n.* a small metal ball that is fired from a gun.

Pellicle *n.* a thin skin or membrane or film on a surface.

Pell-mell *adj & adv.* in disorder or confusion; recklessly; with confused violence.

Pellucid *adj.* transparent; mentally clear; free from obsurity.

Pelmanism *n.* a modern system of training memory.

Pelt *n.* raw skin of sheep.

Pelta *n.* a kind of small shield.

Pelter *n.* a shower of missiles; heavy storm of rain.

Pelvic *adj.* pertaining to the pelvis.

Pemmican *n.* preparation of dried and pounded meat.

Pemphigus *n.* a watery eruption on the skin.

Pen *n.* a small enclosure for cattle. *v.t.* to shut up in a pen.

Pen *n.* an instrument for writing with ink. *v.t.* to write with a pen.

Penal *adj.* that can be punished by law; relating to or used for punishment, especially by law.

Penalize *v.t.* to punish somebody for breaking a rule or law by making them suffer a penalty or disadvantages.

Penalty *n.* punishment for breach of law; disadvantage imposed on previous winner in competition.

Penance *n.* the act of self mortification; repentance.

Penates *n.* household gods.

Penchant *n.* inclination or liking for.

Pencil *n.* a pointed instrument used for drawing or writing, rays meeting at a single point.

Pend *v.t.* & *i.* to hold up; to hang as in a balance.

Pendant *n.* hanging jewel; a hanging ornament; an earring.

Pending *adj.* awaiting decision; in process.

Pendulate *v.i.* to swing like a pendulum; to remain undecided.

Penduline *adj.* suspended.

Pendulum *n.* a rod or wire with weight on end for regulating the movement of a clock.

Penelope *n.* chaste wife.

Penetrable *adj.* what may be penetrated.

Penetrate *v.t* & *i.* to understand or discver something that is difficult to understand or hidden.

Penguin *n.* a black and white sea bird living in the Antarctic, Penguins cannot fly but use their wings for swimming.

Penial *adj.* pertaining to the penis.

Peninsula *n.* a piece of land almost surrounded by water, or projecting far into the sea.

Penis *n.* the male organ of generation.

Penitence *n.* sorrow or regret for having done something wrong, repentance.

Penitent *adj.* repentent for sin; contrite; one who repents.

Penitential *adj.* of or relating to penitence or penance; expressing repentance.

Penitentiary *n.* reformatory prison; a penitent. *adj.* relating to penance.

Penman *n.* one who writes a goodhand.

Pen-name *n.* a pseudonym; a writer's assumed name.

Pennant *n.* a penon, a small tapering flag (especially that at the mast-head of a ship in commission).

Pennate *adj.* having wings.

Penniform *adj.* having the form of a feather.

Penniless *adj.* poor; destitute of money.

Pennon *n.* a long triangular or swallow-tailed tapering flag.

Penny *n.* a former British bronze coin in use until 1971.

Pennyroyal *n.* kind of mint formerly used in medicine.

Penny-weight *n.* a unit weight worth twenty-four grains.

Pennywise *adj.* saving small sums.

Pennyworth *n.* as much as may be bought for a penny.

Penology *n.* study of punishment and prison discipline.

Pensile *adj.* hanging down; pendulous.

Pension *n.* a sum of money paid regularly by a government to people above a certain age and to widowed or disabled people, or by former employers or financial institutions to retired people.

Pensioner *n.* the holder of a pension.

Pensive *adv.* thoughtful; meditative; employed in serious study; melancholy.

Penstock *n.* a sluice; a flood-gate.

Pent *adj.* (often used with *up, in*) closely confined.

Penta *pref.* in the sense of 'five'.

Pentachord *n.* series of five notes; a musical instrument of five strings.

Pentacle *n.* a figure used as a symbol in magic.

Pentad *n.* the number 5; group of five.

Pentagram *n.* a five-pointed star.

Pentahedron *n.* solid figure of five faces.

Pentahedral *adj.* having five equal sides.

Pentameter *n.* a line of verse containing five stressed syllables.

Pentane *n.* a colourless fluid extracted from petroleum.

Pentangular *adj.* having five angles.

Pentarchy *n.* government by five person.

Penthouse *n.* a house or flat at the top of a tall building, often thought to be a desirable place to live.

Pentroof *n.* a roof which slopes on one side only.

Pentstemon *n.* a plant yielding beautiful flowers.

Penult *n.* last syllable but one of a word.

Penultimate *adj.* & *n.* the last but one.

Penumbra *n.* a partly shaded outer region round an opaque body.

Penurious *adj.* poor; destitute; sordid, mean; stingy.

Penury *n.* poverty; scarcity; destitution; want of necessaries of life.

Peon *n.* messenger, an attendant, servant.

Peonage *n.* employment, service.

Peony *n.* garden plant with double red or white flower.

People *n.* persons of a community or race; persons in general.

Pep *n.* liveliness, energy and enthusiasm.

Pepper *n.* hot-flavoured berries of certain plants used as seasoning.

Peppermint *n.* a mint plant; the oil of this plant.

Peppery *adj.* having the qualities of pepper; hot-tempered.

Pepsin *n.* a constituent of gastric juice.

Peptic *adj.* digestive.

Peptone *n.* a protein fragment formed by hydrolysis in the process of digestion.

Peradventure *adv.* by chance.

Perambulate *v.t.* & *i.* to walk up and down; to travel through; to go from place to place.

Perambulator *n.* child's carriage propelled by hand from behind.

Percale *n.* a kind of thick cotton fabric.

Perceivable *n.* perceptible.

Perceive *v.t.* to have knowledge of to apprehend; to understand.

Percentage *n.* a rate of proportion percent; a proportion.

Percept *n.* a mental product.

Perceptible *adj.* such as can be perceived by senses or intellect, perceivable; great enough to be noticed.

Perch *n.* a fresh water fish, a horizontal bar for a bird to rest, a measure of length of 5½ yards.

Perchance *adv.* by chance; perhaps; maybe.

Percipient *adj.* having perception; conscious.

Percolate *v.t.* & *i.* to strain through; to filter.

Percolator *n.* a filtering appliance.

Percuss *n.* to tap lightly with finger or instrument for the sake of diagnosis.

Percussion *n.* the act or an instance of percussing; striking of one body against another.

Percutaneous *adj.* through the skin.

Perdition *n.* entire ruin; utter destruction.

Perdu (e) *adj.* in ambush; hidden.

Peregrinate *v.t.* & *i.* to travel from place to place; to wander through.

Peregrine *n.* a large grey and white bird that can be trained to hunt and catch small birds and animals.

Peremptory *adj.* imperious; admitted; dogmatic; final; urgent; authoritative; determinate.

Perennial *adj.* & *n.* lasting all the year round.

Perfect *adj.* having everything that is necessary; complete and not damaged; exact.

Perfectionist *n.* one who holds that religious or moral perfection may be attained.

Perfectly *adv.* completely, quite, quite well.

Perfidy *n.* action which betray a person or a principle, treachery; breach of faith.

Perfoliate *adj.* having the stalk apparently passing through the leaf.

Perforate *v.t.* & *i.* to penetrate (into, through, etc.); to make an opening into.

Perforce *adv.* by force of necessity.

Perform *v.t.* & *i.* to carry into effect; tó accomplish; to go through; to play on musical instrument; to act in a play.

Perfume *n.* fluid containing essence of flowers; sweet smell; scent; odorous fumes of a burning substance.

Perfunctorily *adv.* carelessly, without zeal.

Perfuse *v.t.* to sprinkle with water; to cover; to pour (water) through or over.

Perfusive *adj.* sprinkling, able to spread.

Pergola *n.* an arbour or garden walk arched with climbing plants.

Perhaps *adv.* possibly; it may be; by chance.

Peri *pref.* in the sense of 'round', 'about'.

Perianth *n.* an outer part of flower; calyx and corolla.

Pericardiac *adj.* relating to the pericardium.

Pericardium *n.* membranous sac enclosing the heart.

Pericarp *n.* the envelope of seed.

Pericranium *n.* the covering of the bones of the skull.

Perigee *n.* that point in planet's (*esp.* moon's) orbit at which it is nearest to earth, opp, to *apogee*.

Perihelion *n.* the point in planet's orbit nearest the sun.

Peril *n.* danger; exposure to loss; risk.

Perilous *adj.* dangerous, hazardous.

Perimeter *n.* external boundary of a figure or the sum of all its sides.

Period *n.* a portion of time in the life of a person, nation or civilization.

Peripatetic *adj.* walking from place to place.

Periphery *n.* a position on the outside of a social, political, etc. group, the fringe; a bounding line, especially of a round surface, circumstance.

Periphrasis (*pl.* **Periphrases**) *n.* round-about speech or phrase; circumlocution.

Periscope *n.* an apparatus with mirrors and lenses arranged in a tube so that the user has a view of the area above, *e.g.* the surface of the sea froma submarine when it is under water.

Perish *v.t* & *i.* to suffer destruction; to lose life; to die; to come to an untimely end.

Perishable *adj.* (especially of food) likely to decay or go bad quickly.

Perispheric *adj.* globular.

Peristaltic *adj.* pertaining to peristalsis; contracting in successive circles.

Peristyle *n.* row of columns round temple; cloister, etc.; space surrounded with these.

Peritoneum *n.* the serous membrane of the intestine.

Periwig *n.* a wig.

Perjure *v.i.* to tell a lie, especially in a lawcourt, after one has sworn to tell the truth.

Periwinkle *n.* an evergreen trailing plant with light blue flower.

Perjur *n.* swearing to a false statement; act of perjuring oneself.

Perk *v.t.* & *i.* to make one's clothes, a room, garden, etc. look better or more exciting.

Perlite *n.* a glittering rock.

Permaculture *n.* the development of agricultural ecosystem intended to be complete and self-sustaining.

Permanence *n.* the state or condition of continuing or remaining for a long time; duration or permanent quality, fixedness.

Permanency *n.* permanent occupation; duration.

Permanent *adj.* durable; lasting indefinitely.

Permeable *adj.* that can be permeated by liquid or gases, porous.

Permeance *n.* the quality of being permanent.

Permeant *n.* pervading; lasting.

Permeate *v.t.* & *i.* to make way throughout; to pervade; to pass through the pores of.

Permissible *adj.* allowable.

Permission *n.* the action of allowing somebody to do something, consent.

Permissive *adj.* licensing but not enjoining something; granting liberty.

Permit *v.t.* & *i.* to make something possible; to admit of; to give permission for something; to allow something.

Permittance *n.* allowance.

Permitter *n.* one who permits.

Permutable *adj.* able to be changed one for another.

Permutation *n.* variation in the order of things.

Pernicious *adj.* injurious, destructive, deadly; noxious.

Pernickety *adj.* (colloq.) fastidious; ticklish.

Pernoctation *n.* passing the night in vigil.

Perorate *v.i.* make a peroration; to sum up a speech; to indulge in rhetoric.

Peroration *n.* the concluding part of a speech; a rhetorical passage at the conclusion of a speech.

Perpend *v.t.* & *i.* to weigh in the mind; to ponder.

Perpendicular *adj.* erect, upright, at right angles to a plane, vertical.

Perpetrate *v.t.* to be guilty of; to commit a crime or blunder.
Perpetrator *n.* one who commits a crime.
Perpetual *adj.* eternal; never ceasing; held or holding for life; repeated.
Perpetually *adv.* continually.
Perpetuate *v.t.* not to allow to go out of use or memory; to cause to endure; to make perpetual.
Perpetuity *n.* endless duration; perpetual annuity.
Perplex *v.t.* to bewilder; to entangle; to puzzle or confuse; to complicate.
Perplexity *n.* a complicated or difficult situation or thing; a puzzled state.
Perquisite *n.* an extra profit or allowance additional to a main income etc.
Perron *n.* a raised platform in front of a large building.
Perry *n.* an alcoholic drink make from pear juice.
Persecute *v.t.* to worry; to pursue with enmity; to harass for heresy.
Persevere *v.i.* to be steadfast; to pursue steadily any course commend.
Persiflage *n.* raillery; light irony.
Persist *v.t.* to continue to exist or do something in spite of obstacles.
Persistent *adj.* persevering.
Person *n.* a human being, character in a story, the living body, characters represented.
Personage *n.* eminent character; a person of rank.
Personal *adj.* one's own belonging to a person; private; directed to an individual.
Personality *n.* a famous person, especially in the world of entertainment or sport.
Personate *v.t.* to play or act the part of; to pretend to be (another); to assume.
Personify *v.t.* to attribute personal nature to; to symbolize (quality) by figure in human form.
Personnel *n.* the body of persons engaged in public service.
Perspective *n.* the art of drawing solid objects on a plane surface.
Perspicacious *adj.* having insight; having or showing great judgement or insight, perceptive; penetrating, discerning.
Perspicuity *n.* freedom from obscurity.
Perspicuous *adj.* clear; plain; expressed with clearness; not obscure; easily understood.
Perspiration *n.* exudation of sweat through pores of skin, sweat.
Perspire *v.i.* to sweat through the pores of the body in form or vapour or moisture.
Persuade *v.t.* to convince; to impel by argument; to induce.
Persuasion *n.* a set of especially religious or political belieifs; act of persuading, conviction.

Pertinacious *adj.* persistent; stubborn; resolute; determined.

Pertinent *adj.* to the point; having a real relation to, apposite.

Perturb *v.t.* to agitate; to disturb mentally; to throw into confusion; to confuse.

Perturber *n.* one who disturbs.

Pertusion *n.* act of piercing.

Perusal *n.* reading through or thoroughly; examining carefully.

Peruse *v.t.* to read something, especially carefully or thoroughly.

Peruvian *adj.* of Peru.

Pervade *v.t.* to spread thoroughly; to permeate; to saturate.

Perverse *adj.* (of verdict) against weight of evidence or judge's direction; petulant, peevish.

Perversity *n.* perverseness.

Pervert *v.t.* to turn from the right course; to misapply; to lead astray.

Pervious *adj.* penetrable; accessible (*to* reason etc.).

Pesky *adj.* troublesome; confounded; annoying.

Pessary *n.* instrument worn in the vagina to prevent uterine displacement.

Pessimism *n.* tendency to look at the worst aspect of things (opp. to optimism).

Pest *n.* troublesome or annoying person; a fatal disease, animal, or thing.

Pester *v.t.* to plague; to trouble; to disturb; to annoy.

Pestiferous *adj.* bearing moral contagion, pernicious; spreading infection, noxious, foul.

Pestilent *adj.* destructive to life; deadly or pestiferous; troublesome.

Pestle *n.* an instrument for pounding and breaking substances in a mortar.

Pet *n.* a thing that is given special attention by somebody; a darling, a favourite child; fit of sulks.

Petard *n.* (hist.) a small bomb for attaching to door, etc. to burst it open; kind of firework.

Petasus *n.* a kind of broad brimmed hat.

Peter *v.i.* to diminish gradually and then disappear or cease.

Peterman *n.* a fisherman.

Petiolar *adj.* pertaining to a leaf-stalk.

Petiole *n.* leaf-stalk.

Petit *adj.* petty.

Petition *n.* a formal application made to a court of law; a request, an enteaty, prayer or supplication (especially written).

Petitioner *n.* one who offers a petiton.

Petrean *adj.* pertaining to stone.

Petrel *n.* a black and white sea bird that can fly far from land.

Petrescence *n.* changing into stone.

Petrify *v.t.* & *i.* to convert into stone; to become stone; to stiffen or deprive of vitality.

Petroglyph *n.* act of writing or carving on stone.

Petroglyphy *n.* act of writing or carving on stone.

Petrograph *n.* an inscription on rock.

Petrol *n.* a liquid obtained by refining petroleum..

Petroleum *n.* mineral oil that forms under the ground or the sea and is extracted through holes bored beneath it, petroleum is refined to produce petrol, paraffin, diesel, oil, etc.

Petrology *n.* study of rocks.

Petticoat *n.* woman's undergarment (*pl.*) the female sex.

Pettifog *v.i.* to quibble, wrangle, about petty points; to practise legal chicanery.

Pettily *adv.* in a petty manner.

Pettiness *n.* the quality of being petty.

Pettish *adj.* (of a remark or an act) said or done in a bad-tempered or unreasonable way.

Pettitoes *n. pl.* pig's feet.

Petty *adj.* unkind or mean; minor, inferior; having little importance; unimportant, trival; little-minded.

Petulant *adj.* irritable; perverse; out of temper; touchy; peevish; fretful.

Petulance *n.* peevishness.

Petunia *n.* a garden plant with white, dark violet, purple or violet flowers of funnel shape.

Pewter *n.* an alloy of tin and lead in various proportions.

Phaeton *n.* a light four-wheeled open carriage.

Phagous *suf.* in the sense of "eating."

Phalange *n.* a bone of a finger-digit.

Phalanger *n.* a kind of Australian bird.

Phalanx *n.* bundle of stamens united by filaments.

Phallic *adj.* pertaining to the worship of phallus.

Phallus *n.* worship of the image of male generative organ.

Phanerogram *n.* plant with pistils and stamens.

Phantascope *n.* an optical instrument through which fixed objects appear as if in motion.

Phantasm *n.* illusion; phantom; vision of an absent person.

Phantasy *n.* whim; faculty of imagination.

Phantom *n.* a dim image; a spectre, an apparition; any imagined thing, an illusion; a ghost; (*attrib*) unreal.

Pharaoh *n.* a title of the ancient Egyptian kings.

Pharmaceutical *adj.* of medicinal drugs; of pharmacy; pertaining to the art of preparing medicines.

Pharmacology *n.* theory of pharmacy; the study of drugs.

Pharmacopoeia *n.* book with list and directions for use of drugs.

Pharmacy *n.* a drug-store; a shop or part of a shop where medicines and drugs are sold; the art of dispensing drugs.

Pharos *n.* a lighthouse to guide sailors or mariners; a beacon.

Pharynx *n.* the cavity forming the upper part of the gullet.

Phase *n.* aspect, appearance, state of change, aspect of mon or planet.

Pheasant *n.* a game-bird of handsome plumage.

Phen, Pheno *pref.* pertaining to substance derived from coaltar.

Phenology *n.* study of the times of recurring natural phenomena especially in relation to climatic conditions.

Phenomenal *adj.* concerned with phenomena; extremely remarkable.

Phenomenon *n.* a remarkable person or thing or event; a wonder, something extraordinary.

Phenyl *n.* a radical found in benzene; phenol.

Phial *n.* a small glass bottle.

Philander *v.i.* to dangle after woman; to amuse oneself with love-making.

Philanthrope *n.* a lover of mankind.

Philanthropic *adj.* loving mankind.

Philanthropize *v.t.* & *i.* to practise philanthropy.

Philanthropy *n.* kindness and good deals inspired by concern for people's welfare.

Philately *n.* stamp-collecting.

Philharmonic *adj.* of person who is very fond of music, musical.

Philippic *n.* a bitter invective.

Philippine *n.* an almond or other nut with double kernel.

Philistine *n.* a person who has no interest in or understanding of the arts, or it hostile to them.

Philo *pref.* in the sense of 'lover'.

Philology *n.* science of the structure and development of a language.

Philomath *n.* a lover of learning.

Philomel *n.* the nightingale.

Philoprogenitive *adj.* prolific; fond of one's offspring.

Philosophy *n.* a set of beliefs or an attitude to life that is a guiding principle for behaviour; a particular set or system of beliefs resulting from this search for knowledge.

Phiz *n.* expression of the face.

Phlebities *n.* inflammation of the walls of a vein.

Phlebotomize *v.t.* to let blood from a vein.

Phlebotomy *n.* opening a vein; blood-letting as medical operation.

Phlegm *n.* a viscid fluid secreted by mucous membrane; cold.

Phlegmatic *adj.* abounding in phlegm, sluggish.

Phlox *n.* a kind of plant.

Phoebus *n.* the Greek sun-god.

Phoenix *n.* mythical bird, paragon.

Phonate *n.* to utter inarticulate sound.

Phonatory *adj.* pertaining to inarticulate sound.

Phonautograph *n.* an instrument for recording vibrations of sound.

Phone *n.* simple vowel or consonant sound; a telephone.

Phonetic *adj.* & *n.* representing vocal sounds.

Phonetics *n.* study of phonetic phenomena; the doctrine of sounds.

Phoney *adj.* (of a person) pretending or claiming to be what one is not; (of a thing) false, bogus, counterfeit.

Phonic *adj.* acoustic; pertaining to sound.

Phono *pref.* meaning 'sound'.

Phonofilm *n.* cinematographic film with accompanying sounds supplied by synchronized gramophone record.

Phonology *n.* the study of voice sounds.

Phonogram *n.* sound-symbol in shorthand; sound-record made by phonograph.

Phonograph *n.* a character for expressing a sound; an instrument automatically recording and reproducing sounds.

Phosgene *n.* a poisonous gas used in the great war.

Phosphate *n.* any salt or compound containing phosphorous, especially one used for helping plants to grow.

Phosphorate *v.t.* to combine with phosphorus.

Phosphoric *adj.* pertaining to phosphorous.

Photo *n.* photograph (colloq.) dramatic representation in moving pictures.

Photocopier *n.* a machine for producing photocopies.

Photogenic *adj.* looking well in a photograph; *Biol.* producing light.

Photograph *n.* a picture or portrait taken by means of chemical action on sensitized plate of film; a picture obtained by photography.

Photographer *n.* a person who takes photographs, especially as a job.

Photology *n.* the science of light.

Photometer *n.* instrument for measuring the intensity of light.

Photophobia *n.* intolerancy of light.

Photophone *n.* an apparatus for reproducing sound by light waves.

Photosynthesis *n.* process by which a green plant uses sunlight to build up carbohydrate reserves.

Phototherapy *n.* treatment of disease by the influence of light.

Phototype *n.* photographic impression of an engraving on a metallic plate from which copies can be printed.

Phrase *n.* a mode of expression, diction; a group of words forming a short expression, especially an idiom.

Phraseogram *n.* a symbol for a phrase.

Phraseology *n.* a manner of expression; a choice of words; diction.

Phraseological, *adj.* pertaining to phraseology.

Phratry *n.* a sub-division of a tribe.

Phrenetic *adj.* frantic; mad.

Phrenitis *n.* an inflammation of the brain, attended with fever and delirium.

Phrenology *n.* study of external cranium as indicative of the affections and mental faculties.

Phrenzy *n.* excited madness.

Phut *n.* the bursting up of a bladder.

Phylactery *n.* a small leather box containing Hebrew texts on vellum, worn by jewl; amulet.

Phyllo *pref.* in sense of 'leaf'.

Phyllophagous *n.* leaf eating.

Phyllopod *adj.* with feet in the form of a leaf.

Physic *n.* the medical art or profession; the art of healing; (colloq.) drugs.

Physical *adj.* material, bodily, belonging to physics.

Physician *n.* one who practises the art of healing.

Physicist *n.* student of physics or of natural science.

Physics *n. pl.* the science which treats of the properties and inter-relations of matter and energy.

Physiology *n.* the science of the properties and functions of living being in normal condition.

Physique *n.* a person's bodily structure and development; constitution.

Photogenesis *n.* evolution of plants.

Phytogeny *n.* the study of the generation of plant.

Phytography *n.* the branch of boany dealing with the description of plants.

Phytoid *adj.* plant-like.

Phytology *n.* study of plants; botany.

Phytophagous *adj.* subsisting on plants.

Phytotomy *n.* dissection of plants.

Pi *n.* Greek letter pi (Math.) as symbol of ratio of circumstance of circle to diameter (3.14159).

Piacular *adj.* needing expiation; expiatory.

Piamater *n.* inner-membrane enveloping brain and spinal chord.

Pianino *n.* a small piano.

Pianist *n.* a performer on piano.

Piano *n.* (passage to be played) softly; a musical instrument with metal strings which are struck by keys.

Pianola *n.* kind of mechanical piano-forte player.

Pibroch *n.* form of bag -pipe mucic.

Pica *n.* a size of type (12-point).

Picador *n.* a mounted man with lance in bull-fight.

Picaroon *n.* a pirate. *v.i.* to act as a pirate.

Picayune *n.* a small coin; trifle.

Piccolo *n.* a small high-pitched flute.

Pice *sing.* & *pl.* an Indian coin out of circulation; a coin of 1/4 anna.

Pick *n.* a tool for breaking up hard ground, selection.

Pick *v.t.* to break the surface of; to make hole in; to probe; to cleanse.

Pickaxe *n.* a kind of curved axe.

Pickerel *n.* a kind of fresh water fish.

Picket *n.* strikes in groups; a small body of men on military police duty, an advanced guard; a peg or pointed stake.

Pickle *n.* brine or other liquor for preserving food & etc.; a solution of salt and water; a mischievous child.

Picklock *n.* an appliance to open locks without a key.

Pick-purse *n.* one who steals the purse of another.

Picksome *adj.* fastidious.

Picnic *n.* a pleasure party out of doors. *v.t.* to take part in a picnic.

Picot *n.* a small loop in the edge of lace.

Picotee *n.* carnation with dark-edged petals.

Picture *n.* a painting or drawing of an objects, especially as work of art.

Picturesque *adj.* & *n.* forming a pretty scene, charming.

Piddle *v.t.* to work in a trifling manner.

Pidgin *n.* words of different languages muddled up.

Pie *n.* fruit crust covered with paste and baked; a magpie. *v.t.* to mix types.

Piebald *adj.* diversified, motley, mongrel, heterogeneous; having patches on it of two colours, usually black and white.

Piece *n.* one of the distinct portions forming part of or broken off from a larger object; a fragment.

Piecemeal *adj.* & *adv.* one part at a time, made of pieces, little by little, piece by piece.

Pied *adj.* of black and white colours, of several colours; variegated.

Pier *n.* a structure in water used as a landing-stage; a break water.

Pierage *n.* toll for using a pier.

Pierce *v.t.* & *i.* to make a hole in or through something, especially with something sharp; to go through like a spear or needle; to penetrate; to bore by a pointed instrument.

Piercingness *n.* piercing quality.

Pietism *n.* pious sentiment; principles of piety.

Piety *n.* strong belief in a religion, shown in one's worship and general behaviour, the state of being pious.

Piezometer *n.* an instrument for measuring pressure.

Piffle *n.* nonsence; idle or silly talk.

Pig *n.* a swine, hog, a young boar or sow, molten metal.

Piggish *adj.* pertaining to pigs.

Pigeon *n.* a bird with many varieties, wild and domesticated. *v.t.* to put into a pigeon-hole; to cheat (in gambling).

Piggery *n.* a place for pig-breeding; a dirty place.

Pigment *n.* a substance that gives colour to dyes, paint, etc.

Pigmy *n.* a very small person or thing; a dwarf.

Pigtail *n.* a thin roll of tobacco; a plait of hair hanging on the back.

Pike *n.* a spike or lance, a spear, a kind of fish. *v.t.* to thrust through.

Pilaster *n.* a rectangular pillar.

Pilch *n.* a small wrapper for infants.

Pilchard *n.* a small marine fish; a kind of a oat.

Pile *n.* a piece of timber driven into ground as foundation for building.

Pileate *adj.* of the form of a cap.

Piles *n. pl.* a disease of the lower rectum; haemorrhoids.

Pilfer *v.t.* & *i.* to steal in small quantities.

Pilgarlic *n.* a bald-headed person.

Pilgrim *n.* a person who travels to a holy place for religious reasons.

Pilgrimage *n.* a pilgrim's journey. *v.t.* to go pilgrimage.

Piliferous *adj.* having hair.

Pill *n.* an unpleasant or painful necessity.

Pillage *n.* & *v.t.* & *i.* the action of stealing or damaging property, especially by soldiers in war.

Pillar *n.* a column; a post; anything used as support.

Pillow *n.* a cushion used as support for the head, especially in bed. *v.t.* to rest (one's head on a pillow).

Pilot *n.* one who steers a ship, one who navigates an aeroplane, a guide.

Pilule *n.* a small pill.

Pimp *n.* a man who controls prostitutes and lives on the money they earn.

Pin *n.* a short piece of wood or metal for various special purposes.

Pincers *n. pl.* a gripping tool like pliers with short jaws.

Pinch *v.t.* & *i.* to take or hold something in a tight grip between the thumb and finger.

Pine *n.* to long for; to be very unhappy, especially because somebody had died or gone away.

Pinery *n.* a place where pine-apples are grown.

Pinfold *n.* a pound for shutting up stray cattle.

Pink *n.* a plant with fragrant flowers; light rosy colour; pale red colour.

Pinna *n.* the upper broad part of the external ear.

Pinnace *n.* a warship's boat.

Pinnacle *n.* the highest point, the peak; a small ornament built on to a roof; a rocky peak, a pointed summit; culmination or climax.
Pinnate *adj.* having leaves on each side of the stalk.
Pinner *n.* one who pins.
Pinnule *n.* a secondary division of a pinnate leaf; an organ like a small wing.
Pinny *adj.* childish.
Pint *n.* a measure of capacity; one-eighth of a gallon.
Pintle *n.* a bold on which a part of a machine revolves.
Piny *adj.* of or like or full of pine trees.
Pioneer *n.* a person who is the first to study and develop a new areas of knowledge, culture; explorer.
Pious *adj.* hypocritically virtuous; devout; religious.
Pip *n.* a seed of certain fruits; each spot on playing-cards. *v.t.* to shoot; to defeat.
Pipe *n.* a narrow tube with a bowl at one end, used for making tobacco; a wind-instrument.
Piper *n.* one who plays on a pipe; a bagpiper.
Pipette *n.* a small pipe; a slender tube.
Piping *adj.* shrill; boiling.
Pipkin *n.* a small earthenware pot; a small earthen boiler.
Piquancy *n.* pungency; sharpness; severeness.
Piquant *adj.* pungent; sharp; agreeable; appetizing; stimulating.
Pique *n.* a feeling of annoyance or resentment, usually because one's pride has been hurt.
Piquet *n.* a card-game played by two persons with 32 cards excluding the low cards from two to six.
Piracy *n.* the crime of robbing on the sea; an infringment of the law of copyright.
Pirate *n.* a publisher who infringes copyright; a person or a company that broadcasts without a licence.
Piratical *adj.* pertaining to a pirate.
Piscary *n.* the right of fishing in anothers water.
Piscator *n.* an angler.
Pisces *n.* the fishes; the twelfth sign of the Zodiac.
Pisciculture *n.* artificial rearing of fish; breeding and rearing of fish.
Piscina *n.* a pond for rearing fishes.
Piscine *adj.* of fish. *n.* a bathing pool.
Pish *inter.* expressing contempt.
Pisiform *adj.* of the shape of a pea.
Pistachio *n.* a tree which yields nut with green kernels; a kind of nut with green kernel.
Pistil *n.* the female organ of flowers; the seed-bearing organ in flowers.
Pistol *n.* a small fire-arm. *v.t.* to shoot with a pistol.

Pistolograph *n.* an apparatus for obtaining instantaneous photograph.

Pit *n.* a hole in the ground, usually with steep sides, from which especially minerals are dug off.

Pit-a-pat *adv.* with light quick steps; with palpitation.

Pitch *n.* a black tenacious substance got from distilling coal-tar, resin from pine trees.

Piteous *adj.* deserving or causing pity; stirring or claiming pity, miserable; deplorable.

Pitfall *n.* unsuspected share or danger; a concealed pit prepared as a trap for men or animals; an trap or danger for the unwary.

Pith *n.* spongy cellular tissue in stems of plants, chief part; vigour, energy, strength, force.

Pitiable *adj.* lamentable, deserving of pity, miserable, wretched.

Pity *n.* sorrow aroused by another's condition; grounds for regret; a feeling of tenderness; compassion.

Pivot *n.* a cardinal point in discussion; the central or most important person or thing; a pin on which something turns. *v.t.* to place on a pivot.

Pizzle *n.* the male copulative organ of animals.

Placard *n.* printed or handwritten poster for advertisement.

Placate *v.t.* to make somebody less angry; to calm or satisfy somebody; to conciliate; to propitiate.

Place *n.* locality, part of space, grade, city or town, dwelling, building, calling, residence, occupation.

Placenta *n.* spongy organ nourishing the foetus in mammals; part of carpel to which seeds are attached.

Placid *adj.* (of a person or an animal) not easily excited or irritated; calm and peaceful.

Placket *n.* a pocket in a woman's shirt.

Placoid *adj.* of the shape of a plate.

Plague *n.* a fatal infectious disease; a divine punishment; pestilence.

Plaid *n.* a long piece of woollen cloth; a rug.

Plain *adj.* & *n.* clear; smooth, level, simple, evident, not intriculate, not coloured, a large tract of level ground.

Plaint *n.* a statement of grievance in court; accusation; charge; lamentation.

Plaintiff *n.* a person who brings charge against another in a law-court.

Plait *n.* a fold or crease in cloth; a tress of hair or band of straw made by interlacing.

Plan *n.* a diagram; a scheme or project; a map; a design.

Planch *n.* a slab used in enamelling. *v.t.* to cover with boards.

Planchette *n.* a small heart-shaped board used in psychological experiment.

Plane *n.* a level surface; a level of thought, existence or development.

Planet *n.* a heavenly body revolving round the sun.

Planetoid *n.* a small planet.

Plangent *adj.* thrilling.

Plani *pref.* in sense of 'level, smooth'.

Planimeter *n.* an instrument for measuring the area of a plane figure.

Planish *v.t.* to flatten (metal) smoothly; to polish with a roller.

Plank *n.* a long flat piece of smoothed timber. *v.t.* to cover with planks.

Planner *n.* one who forms a plan.

Plano *pref.* in sense of 'level on one side'.

Plant *n.* a living thing that grows in the earth and usually has a stem, leaves and roots.

Plantable *adj.* able to be planted.

Plantain *n.* any low-growing plant of the genus.

Planter *n.* a cultivator of soil; the owner of a plantation; a machine for planting.

Plantigrade *adj.* of an animal that walks on the soles of its feet.

Plaque *n.* a flat piece of stone, metal, etc.

Plash *n.* a marshy pool; puddle; a sound of plunging into water.

Plasm *n.* the living matter of a cell; the colourless liquid part of blood etc.

Plasma *n.* the colourless coagulable part of blood.

Plaster *n.* a curative application spread on paper or cloth; a plastic mixture for spreading on walls.

Plastic *adj.* capable of being easily moulded, pliant; moulding; (of goods) made of plastic.

Plat *n.* a dish served; a piece of land.

Plate *n.* shallow circular food vessel.

Plateau *n.* a tract of elevated or high ground.

Platform *n.* level surface raised above the surrounding ground or floor; stage.

Platinoid *n.* a white-alloy.

Platitude *n.* dull or stupid remark; triteness; a truism.

Platitudinize *v.t.* to prattle.

Platonic *adj.* confined to words or theory of Plato of his doctrines; harmless or ineffectual.

Platoon *n.* a subdivision of a company in Military; a group of persons acting together.

Platter *n.* a large shallow dish for serving food.

Plaudit *n.* (*usu. pl.*) round of applause; emphatic approval; commendation.

Plausible *adj.* praiseworthy; pleasing; fair; acceptable; popular.

Play *v.i.* to move quickly and lightly, especially often changing direction.

Playwright *n.* a dramatist.

Plea *n.* defence; defendant's or prisoner's statement; an excue, a pleadnig.

Pleach *v.t.* to entwine; to plait; to plash.

Plead *v.i.* & *t.* to make an earnest appeal to; to address court as an advocate or party.

Please *v.t.* & *i.* to make somebody happy; to want; to like; to be agreeable to.

Pleasure *n.* feeling of satisfaction; enjoyment; sensuous enjoyment; delight; will; desire.

Pleat *n.* band of triple thickness on garment.

Plebeian *adj* & *n.* a working class; the common people; popular; base.

Plectrum *n.* an implement of ivory for plucking strings of lyre.

Pledge *n.* a solemn promise; a toast; a thing deposited as security; a thing pawned; a token, earnest proof.

Pledget *n.* small mass of lint etc. for wound.

Pleiad *n.* cluster of stars; a group of seven beautiful things.

Pleistocene *adj.* & *n.* Geol. (of) the division immediately overlying the plicene formation.

Plenary *adj.* complete; absolute; entire; full.

Plenilunar *adj.* pertaining to full moon.

Plenish *v.t.* to fit out; to furnish.

Plentitude *n.* fullness; plenty; abundance; completeness.

Plenty *n.* & *adv.* a situation in which there is a large supply of food, money etc.

Pleonasm *n.* use of more words than are needed to give the sense.

Plethora *n.* excess of blood; oversupply; superabundance.

Pleura *n.* either of the serous membranes enveloping the lungs.

Plexus *n.* a net-work of fibres in the body.

Pliable, Pliant *adjs.* flexible; easily bent or influenced; supple.

Plica *n.* matted filthy condition of hair due to disease; fold, as of skin or membrane.

Plicate *adj.* folded.

Pliers *n. pl.* pincers with flat grip for bending wire.

Plight *v.t.* to pledge one's promise; give as surety.

Plighter *n.* one who pledges.

Plimsoll *n.* cheap rubber-soled canvas shoes.

Plinth *n.* square block or slab on which a column or statue stands.

Pliocene *adj.* Geol. (of) the newest division of Tertiary formations.

Plod *v.t.* & *i.* to walk or work doggedly; to drudge.

Plonker *n.* a foolish or inept person; the penis.

Plop *n.* sound made by the fall of a smooth object on water.

Plot *n.* a secret plan made by several people to do something, usually something wrong or illegal.

Plough *n.* implement for furrowing and turning up the soil.

Plover *n.* kinds of shore-bird.

Ploy *n.* undertaking; occupation; job.

Pluck *v.t.* & *i.* a twitch, the heart, liver and lungs, failure in examination, courage.

Plug *n.* a piece of favourable publicity in the media for a commercial product, *e.g.* a book or recording; a piece of metal, rubber or plastic that fits tightly into a hole.

Plum *n.* a sweet fleshy fruit with a pointed stone.

Plumassier *n.* one who trades in ornamental plumes; bird's feathers.

Plumb *n.* plummet; a ball of lead attached to a string for testing perpendicularly of walls.

Plumbago *n.* a kind of black lead used in making pencils; the material of pencils.

Plumbeous *adj.* like lead; stupid.

Plumb-line *n.* a string with a pointed heavy ball attached to it, used by masons for determining the vertical position of a wall.

Plume *n.* feathery ornament (in hat, helmet, hair & etc.).

Plummet *n.* a weight of lead attached to a plumb-line for sounding, for obstructive weight.

Plumose *adj.* feathered; feather-like.

Plump *adj.* rounded with sufficient flesh or flat; stout; round.

Plunder *v.t.* & *i.* to rob; to steal; to embezzle; to carry off goods by open force.

Plunderage *n.* embezzling goods on board a ship.

Plunderer *n.* a robber.

Plunge *v.t.* & *i.* to immerse completely; thrust forcefully or abruptly.

Plunger *n.* one who dives; cavalry-man.

Plunket *n.* a kind of blue colour.

Pluperfect *adj.* & *n.* (-tense) expressing action completed before a past point of time.

Plural *adj.* & *n.* expressing more than one (or two); more than one in number.

Pluri *pref.* in sense of 'more than one'.

Plus *n.* the sign of addition (+).

Plush *n.* cloth of silk or cotton etc. with a long soft nop.

Pluto *n.* the outermost planet of the solar system.

Plutocracy *n.* the wealthy class; state in which power belongs to the rich.

Plutocrat *n.* wealthy man.

Plutocratic *adj.* pertaining to wealthy man.

Plutonic *adj.* infernal; dark.

Pluvial *adj.* of or caused by rain.

Pluviometer *n.* rain-guage.

Ply *v.t.* & *i.* (of a ship, vehicel, & etc.) to go to and fro between places.

Plyer *n.* he who or that which pile.

Pneumatic *adj.* of or acting by wind or air; filled with air.

Pneumato *pref.* in the sense of "breath, spirit."

Pneumonia *n.* inflammation of the lungs.

Poa, Poagrass *ns.* meadow-grass.

Poach *v.t.* to cook the contents of an egg by droping it (without shell) in water, in frying pan.

Poachy *adj.* wet and damp.

Pochard *n.* a European diving bird with bright reddish-brown head & neck.

Pock *n.* an eruptive spot (in small pox & etc.), pustule raised on skin.

Pocket *n.* a small bag attached to a garment for carrying purse & etc.

Pocket-book *n.* a small book for the pocket.

Pocky *adj.* infected with small-pox.

Pod *n.* seed-vessel of plants.

Podagra *n.* gout in the feet.

Podge, Podgy *ns.* a short fat person.

Podium *n.* a continuous platform round a building.

Poem *n.* a piece of poetry, a metrical compostion (*esp.* of elevated tone).

Poesy *n.* metrical composition; poems or the art of making them.

Poephagous *adj.* eating grass.

Poet *n.* a writer of poems.

Poetaster *n.* a petty versifiser.

Poetic *adj.* having the good quantities of poetry; of poets or poetry.

Poetics *n.* the art of writing poetry; criticism of poetry.

Poetry *n.* the poet's art of work; expression, *esp.* in metrical form, of elevated thought or feeling, verse; poems.

Pogo *n.* a kind of mechanical toy.

Pogrom riot against Jews or other class in Russia; an organized massacre.

Poignant *adj.* sharp or acute; pungent; stinging; keen; penetrating; very painful.

Point *n.* fielder at cricket near to point of bat; a sharp end, tip; a dot; an exact moment; degree of measurement.

Poise *v.t.* & *i.* to be balanced; to hang suspended; to hold in a balanced or steady position.

Poison *n.* anything which destroys life or injures health; an injurious thing; a venom.

Poke *n.* to cause to stick out; to stir (a fire) with a stick; to meddle, intrude; to search curiously.

Polar *adj.* of the pole; near the pole.

Pole *n.* a flagstaff; measurerod 5½ yards; a native of Polan; the two points in the celestial sphere (*North & South P.*) about which the stars appear to revolve.

Pole-axe *n.* butcher's slaughtering axe; battle axe. *v.t.* to kill or strike with pole-axe.

Pole-star *n.* lodstar (useful as a guide); a star near North Pole of the heavens.

Police *n.* public order; the civil force charged with keeping order.

Policy *n.* prudent conduct; a contract of insurance; statecraft; course of action.

Polish *v.t. & i.* to make smooth and bright by friction; to refine. *n.* smoothness; glossiness.

Polite *adj.* (of literature) refined, elegant, cultivated, well-bred; courteous.

Politic *adj. & n.* sagacious; judicious; expedient; prudent.

Political *adj.* of politics; pertaining, crafty; judicious, expedient.

Politics *n. pl.* affairs of State; questions of policy.

Polity *n.* to form of civil government; an organized State.

Polka *n.* a kind of lively dance; a woman's under-jacket.

Poll *n.* the head or back part of the head; the process of voting at an election.

Pollable *adj.* able to be polled.

Pollack *n.* a sea-fish similar to cod.

Pollard *n.* a hornless animal; a tree made by cutting off the top to produce a close head of young shoots.

Pollen *n.* fertilizing powder discharged from flowers.

Polent *adj.* mighty; strong.

Pollinate *v.t.* to shed pollen upon.

Pollute *v.t.* to taint or infect morally; to make filthy; to destroy the purity of.

Polo *n.* a game of Eastern origin like hockey played on horse-back.

Polonium *n.* a rare radio-active metallic element.

Polt-foot *adj.* club-footed.

Poltroon *n.* a coward; a spiritless person.

Poly *pref.* denoting much or many; in the sense of 'many'.

Polyandry *n.* polygamy in which one woman has more than one husband, plurality of husbands.

Polyanthus *n.* kinds of cultivated primula.

Polyarchy *n.* government by many.

Polycarpic *adj.* fruiting several times.

Polychromatic *adj.* many-coloured.

Polychromy *n.* the art of colouring.

Polycladous *adj.* with many branches.

Polycracy *n.* government by many.

Polydactyl *adj.* having more than five fingers or toes.

Polydemonism *n.* worship of many gods.

Polydipsia *n.* excessive thirst.

Polygamy *n.* state or custom of having more than one wife or more than one husband at once.

Polygastric *adj.* having many stomach.

Polygenous *adj.* consisting of several kinds.

Polyglot *adj.* & *n.* one who speaks or writes in several languages.

Polygon *n.* a figure with many angles or sides.

Polygram *n.* a figure consisting of several lines.

Polygraph *n.* a contrivance for multiplying copies of a writing.

Polygyny *n.* plurality of wives.

Polyhedron *n.* many-sided solid; a body of many sides.

Polyhistor *n.* a very learned man, a great scholar.

Polymathy *n.* the knowledge of several arts.

Polymorphic *adj.* pertaining to many shapes.

Polymorphism *n.* the occurrence of something in different types.

Polynomial *adj.* of many names.

Polyopia *n.* multiple vision.

Polyophagous *adj.* subsisting on several kinds of food.

Polyp *n.* kinds of animal of low organization as sea-anemones.

Polypetalous *adj.* having several petals.

Polyphony *n.* harmonizing of separate simultaneous melodies.

Polypod *n.* an animal with several feet.

Polypody *n.* fern growing on rocks, walls, etc.

Polypus *n.* kinds of tumour, *esp.* on nose.

Polyspermous *adj.* containing several seeds.

Polystome *n.* an animal with many mouths.

Polytechnic *adj.* comprehending many arts, dealing with or devoted to various arts. *n.* a technical school.

Polytheism *n.* belief in more than one god; doctrine of plurality of gods.

Pomace *n.* crushed apples in cider; any pulp; refuse of fish etc. used as fertilizer.

Pomaceous *adj.* pertaining to apple.

Pomade, Pomatum *ns.* scented ointment for the hair.

Pome *n.* succulent fruit with firm fleshy body enclosing carpels forming the core.

Pomegranate *n.* the fruit of a tree with golden ring and many seeds; its tree.

Pomeranian *n.* a breed of small dogs.

Pomfret *n.* a kind of fish.

Pomiculture *n.* fruit-growing.

Pommel *n.* horn of side-saddle; the knob on the hilt of a sword.

Pomology *n.* the art of fruit-growing.

Pomp *n.* a splendid display; splendour.

Pompom *n.* a quick-firing gun, loaded and fired with great rapidity.

Pompon *n.* tuft of ribbon, etc. on hat, shoe, etc.

Pond *n.* a small pool of water; a small body of still water artificially formed.

Ponder *v.t.* & *i.* to weigh in mind; to consider with deliberation; to think over.

Ponderous *adj.* heavy, dull (style); unwidely by weight.

Pondweed *n.* any of various aquatic plants of the genus.

Pone *n.* bread of maize.

Poniard *n.* a small dagger.

Pontiff *n.* the Pope; the chief priest.

Pont-levis *n.* a draw bridge.

Pony *n.* a horse of any small breed.

Poodle *n.* kind of a pet dog with clipped hair. *v.t.* to clip dog's hair.

Pooh *inter.* expressing disgust at a bad smell; expressing impatience and contempt.

Pool *n.* combination of manufacturers; collective stakes in cards or betting.

Poon *n.* a kind of tree.

Poop *n.* the stern of a ship.

Poor *adj.* despicable, insignificant; (of soil) unproductive.

Pop *n.* abrupt explosive sound; a shot with a firearm; champagne, ginger-beer.

Pope *n.* the head of the Roman Catholic Church.

Popery *n.* Romanizing tendencies; the papal system.

Popinjay *n.* a parrot; a conceited person; coxcomb.

Populace *n.* the multitude; the common people; the commonality.

Popular *adj.* liked or admired by many people or by a specified group of the people.

Populate *v.t.* to fill or furnish with inhabitants; to inhabit.

Porch *n.* a covered entrance to a building; a portico.

Porcine *adj.* pertaining to or like swine.

Pore *n.* one of the small openings making skin, wood, brick & etc. permeable to fluids, a minute opening in the skin.

Pork *n.* flesh of swine used as food.

Porous *n.* full of pores.

Porpoise *n.* a mammal with a round snout.

Porridge *n.* a food made by mixing meal or cereal in boiling water.

Porringer *n.* a small basin for porridge; a small basin of metal.

Port *n.* a harbour; a town possessing a harbour; the lefthand side of a ship; external experience.

Portable *adj.* that can be carried about, easily carried; moveable.

Portage *n.* carrying; cost of carrying; an arch over a doorway.

Portal *n.* doorway; gateway.

Portcullis *n.* grating raised and lowered in grooves as defence of gateway.

Portend *v.t.* to foreshadow; to give warning of.

Portent *n.* an omen; something marvellous.

Porter *n.* a dark-brown bitter beer; attendant at door or gate.

Portfire *n.* a device for igniting explosives.

Portfolio *n.* office of minister of state; a case for loose drawings or sheets of paper.

Portico *n.* a roof supported by pillars.

Portiere *n.* a curtain over door.

Portion *n.* a part of the whole; dowry; destiny or lot; a part allotted a share.

Portly *adj.* of stately appearance; bulky, corpulent.

Portmanteau *n.* a leather bag to carry clothes.

Portrait *n.* likeness of a living being made either by photographic process or by drawing.

Portraiture *n.* a portrait.

Portray *v.t.* to describe graphically; to paint or draw likeness of.

Portreeve *n.* the chief magistrate of a port town.

Portress *n.* a female porter.

Pory *adj.* full of pores.

Pose *v.t.* & *i.* to puzzle (a person) with a question or problem; to propound for solution; to set up or give one-self out as.

Posit *v.t.* to put in position; to lay down as basis of argument or inference.

Position *n.* proper place; situation; social rank; an office; strategic point or condition; the way a thing is placed.

Positive *adj.* explicit, certain, convinced, sure, confident, direct, absolute, downright, opposed to negative.

Posse *n.* body (of constables), strong force or company.

Possess *v.t.* to own; to hold as property; to have; to maintain; to accomplish.

Possession *n.* property; a thing possessed; subject territory, foreign dominions; occupancy.

Possessive *adj.* pertaining to possession.

Possibility *n.* the state or condition of being possible; occurrence.

Possible *adj.* that may come to pass; tolerable; practicable.

Post *n.* a strong pole, station, employment, size of paper 26 × 20 inch; a letter-carrier, letters disptached; a kind of writing paper.

Postage *n.* the charge for carriage of letters or other articles by post.

Postal *adj.* of the post office.

Post-date *v.t.* to affix or assign a later date than the real one.

Poster *n.* one who posts; a large advertisement.

Posterior *adj.* later in time or order; hinder. *n.* the state being subsequent.

Postern *n.* a private door; the back or side entrance. *adj.* being behind.

Posthumous *adj.* born after the death of one's father; occurring after death.

Postillion *n.* man riding one of the horses that draw a carriage and guiding the team.

Post-meridiem *adj.* after noon.

Post-mortem *adj.* medical examination after death.

Post-obit *adj.* & *n.* bond given by expectant heir for money to be paid on succession to the property; taking effect after death.

Post-paid *adj.* on which postage has been paid.

Postpone *v.t.* & *i.* to defer; to delay; to put off for a future or later time; to delay.

Postprandial *adj.* of speech, etc.) after-dinner.

Postscript *n.* paragraph added to a letter after the signature.

Postulate *v.t.* to take for granted; to assume without proof.

Posture *n.* attitude of body or mind; condition.

Post-war *adj.* of, pertaining to, or characteristic of a period following a war.

Posy *n.* short motto; a bunch of flowers.

Pot *n.* a vessel of earthenware, metal or glass.

Potable *adj.* drinkable.

Potamic *adj.* pertaining to rivers.

Potash *n.* an alkali in an impure state used in soap.

Potassium *n.* a white metal; a basic element of potash.

Potato *n.* a plant with tubers used as food; the tuber of potato.

Potent *n.* cogent; powerful; influential; strong.

Potential *adj.* capable of existing; latent.

Potentiality *n.* possibility.

Pother *n.* disturbance, din; choking smoke or cloud of dust; display of sorrow.

Potion *n.* a dose, draught of medicine or poison.

Pot-pourri *n.* mixture of rose petals, spices, kept in jar for its perfume; musical or literary medley.

Pottage *n.* meat soup; soup or stew.

Potter *n.* one who makes earthenware vessels.

Pottery *n.* potter's work or workshop; earthware.

Pottle *n.* measure for liquids; a small wickerwork basket.

Potty *adj*. insignificant; crazy.

Pouch *n*. a detachable pocket; a hag-like cavity, protuberant belly; a small bag.

Poult *n*. a young fowl; turkey; young chicken.

Poulterer *n*. a dealer in poultry.

Poultice *n*. soft dressing applied to a sore or inflammed part. *v.t.* to apply poultice to.

Poultry *n*. domestic fowls; barn-door and other fowls reared for food.

Pounce *v.i.* to fall on suddenly; to swoop; to come suddenly down upon.

Pounce *n*. a stencil with the pattern shown by fine holes.

Pound *n*. an enclosure for animals; a place of confinement.

Pound *n*. a measure of weight 16. oz; an English coin.

Pour *v.t.* & *i.* to send forth; to give vent to; to throw in profusion.

Pourparler *n*. (*usu.* in *pl.*) informal discussion preliminary to negotiation between diplomatists.

Poussette *n*. a country dance in pairs.

Pout *n*. a kind of fish; sulkiness.

Pouter *n*. a kind of pigeon.

Poverty *n*. want of means; the state of being poor; need; indigence.

Powder *n*. a mass of fine dry particles; cosmetic or dose of medicine in thin form.

Power *n*. mental of physical strength; mechanical energy applicable to work; state having international influence.

Practical *adj*. of or shown in action rather than theory or words.

Practice *n*. lawyer's or doctor's professional business; an exercise to improve skill; action as opposed to theory; an established method.

Pragmatic *adjs*. meddlesome; positive, dictatorial, (*usu. -ic*) treating facts of history with reference to their practical lessons of State affairs.

Praedial *adj*. pertaining to land or its products; landed.

Prairie *n*. grassland of North America.

Praisable *adj*. deserving praise.

Praise *v.t.* to glorify; to extol the merits of; to applaud.

Praiseful *adj*. glorious.

Praiseworthy *adj*. deserving of praise or applause; meritorious.

Praline *n*. sweetmeat of nuts and sugar.

Pram permbulator a milk man's hand-cart.

Prance *v.i.* to spring on hind legs; to behave in elated or arrogant manner.

Prancing *n*. a springing or bounding movement.

Prandial *adj*. of or at dinner.

Prank *v.t.* & *i.* to decorate; to adorn in a showy manner.

Prase *n*. a green quartz.

Prate *v.i.* to babble; to chatter; to discourse foolishly.

Prating *n.* an idle talk; a chatter.

Prattle *v.t.* to talk in childish manner; to talk idly.

Prawn *n.* crustancean like large shrimp. *v.i.* to fish for prawns.

Praxis *n.* an accepted practice or custom.

Pray *v.t.* & *i.* to offer prayers; to ask earnestly; to beseech earnestly; to beg for.

Prayer *n.* an entreaty; one who prays; petition made to God; praying.

Pre- *pref.* before (in time, place, order, or importance).

Preach *v.t.* & *i.* to deliver a sermon publicly; to proclaim; to give moral advice.

Preamble *n.* preliminary statement; introduction; preface. *v.i.* to make preamble.

Preambulate *v.i.* to walk before.

Preappoint *v.t.* to appoint previously.

Preapprehension *n.* opinion which is formed before examination.

Prearrange *v.t.* & *i.* to arrange before-hand.

Prebend *n.* a part of the revenue of a church or cathedral granted to a clergyman.

Precarious *adj.* dependent on chance; unsettled; uncertain; perilous.

Precative *adj.* expressing entreaty.

Precaution *n.* a thing done beforehand to prevent an apprehended evil.

Precede *v.t.* & *i.* to come or go before in place or time or rank or importance.

Precedence *n.* priority in time or succession; superiority.

Precedent *n.* a previous case taken as an example or justification of a rule to be followed in subsequent cases.

Precentor *n.* one who starts the singing of a choir.

Precept *n.* a rule for action or conduct; maxim, command, divine command; kinds of wirt or warrant; moral instruction.

Precession *n.* the act of going before.

Precinct *n.* (*pl.*) the environs of; boundary; ground pertaining to a sacred or official building or place.

Preciosity *n.* over refinement in art.

Precious *adj.* costly; valuable; highly valued; fine.

Precipitate *v.t.* to cause to go hurriedly or violently; to cause (solid matter in solution) to be deposited.

Precis *n.* summary.

Precise *adj.* definite, exact, particular, strictly worded.

Precision *n.* accuracy; exactness; correctness; definiteness.

Preclude *v.t.* to make impracticable; to shut out; to impede; to prevent.

Preclusion *n.* the act of precluding.

Preclusive *adv.* tending to prevent.

Precocious *adj.* too forward; (of plant) flowering of fruiting early; (of person) remarkable for early development.

Precogitate *v.t.* to consider beforehand; to precontrive.

Preconceive *v.t.* to form an opinion beforehand.

Preconcert *v.t.* previous agreement; to agree upon beforehand.

Precondemn *v.t.* to condemn beforehand.

Preconize *v.t.* to proclaim in a public manner; to call by name.

Precursor *n.* a forerunner, a harbingr; a person or thing serving to herald the coming of another.

Predacious *adj.* naturally praying others.

Predatory *adj.* (of animal) preaying upon others; of or addicted to plunder or robbery, plundering, pillaging.

Predecease *v.t.* to die before another. *n.* death before another's.

Predestinate *v.t.* to appoint or ordain beforehand.

Predestine *v.t.* to appoint or obtain beforehand.

Predetermine *v.t.* to determine beforehand.

Predicable *adj.* that can be predicted. *n.* predicable thing.

Predicament *n.* dangerous state; unpleasant or trying situation.

Predicant *adj.* engaged in religious teaching.

Predicate *v.t.* to assert; to affirm; to state as true of or pertaining to something.

Predict *v.t.* & *i.* to foreshow; to foretell; to prophesy.

Prediction *n.* the act of foretelling; a prophecy.

Predispose *v.t.* to render liable or fit beforehand; inclined beforehand.

Predisposition *n.* previous inclination or tendency; antecedent state favourable to (ailment, purpose, & etc.)

Predominant *adj.* superior; ruling; having chief power or influence.

Pre-eminence *n.* superiority.

Pre-eminent *adj.* eminent above others; excelling or passing others.

Pre-emption *n.* purchase of a thing before it is offered to others; right to first refusal.

Preen *v.t.* to trim feathers with beak; (of person) trim oneself.

Preface *n.* preamble (of speech, & etc.) prelude; introductory remarks prefixed to a book.

Prefatory *adj.* introductory.

Prefect *n.* a person put in authority; senior scholar entrusted with maintaining discipline, civil and military.

Prefer *v.t.* to bring forward (claim, & etc.) to promote to an office.

Preference *n.* liking of one thing more than another; object of choice; favoured position.

Preferment *n.* a superior office or post.

Prefigure *v.t.* to be a type of; foreshadow.

Prefine *v.t.* to limit beforehand.

Prefix *v.t.* to add at the beginning.

Pregnant *adj.* big with consequences; fruitful in results; with child; suggestive.

Prehensile *adj.* capable of grasping.

Prehistoric *adj.* before the days or time recorded by history.

Prejudice *n.* an opinion formed in the mind beforehand; bias.

Prelacy *n.* the dignity of a prelate Church government by prelates.

Prelect *v.i.* to lecture publicly on a subject; to read a discourse.

Preliminary *adj.* preceding and leading up to the main discourse or business; preparatory, introductory.

Prelude *n.* an introductory event or performance.

Prelusive *adj.* introductory.

Premature *n.* hasty; too early; untimely; occurring or done before the right or usual time.

Premeditate *v.t.* to meditate on or think out beforehand.

Premier *adj.* having precedence of all others; foremost; leading.

Premise *v.t.* (*pl.*) any house or building with its belongings.

Premium *n.* reward; bonus; sum paid in addition to interest; amount or instalment payable for insurance policy; a bonus.

Premonition *n.* forewarning of previous information.

Premonitor *n.* one who warns beforehand.

Premorse *adj.* with the end abruptly terminated.

Premotion *n.* previous excitement.

Premunition *n.* objections anticipated beforehand.

Prenasal *adj.* in front of the nostrile. *n.* a bone at the tip of a pig's nose.

Prenotion *n.* a fore knowledge.

Preoccupation *n.* occupying beforehand; mental absorption; prejudice.

Preordain *v.t.* to determine previously; to decree beforehand.

Prepare *v.t.* & *i.* to make ready; to get ready previously; to make preparations for.

Prepay *v.t.* to pay (charge) beforehand.

Prepense *adj.* (placed after *n.*) deliberate; intentional.

Preponderance *adj.* excess of weight; force, power.

Preposition *n.* indeclinable word serving to make relation between the noun or pronoun it governs and another word.

Prepositive *adj.* proper to be prefixed.

Prepossess *v.t.* to take possession of beforehand; to prejudice.

Prepossession *n.* prejudice esp. in favour of a person or things.

Preposterous *adj.* utterly; ridiculous; absurd; contrary to reason; irrational.

Prerequisite *adj.* required previously.

Prerogative *n.* unrestricted right of the sovereign.

Presage *n.* omen; presentiment. *v.t.* to foreshadow; to foretell; to foresee.

Presbyopia *n.* long-sighted-ness incident to old age.

Presbyter *n.* a priest; an elder in church.

Presbyterian *adj.* of the Church which is governed by the elders.

Prescient *adj.* foreknowing; having foreknowledge or foresight.

Prescribe *v.t. & i.* to advise the use of; to lay down authoritatively.

Prescript *n.* an ordinance or decree.

Prescription *n.* a physician's recipe; thing prescribed; a claim or uninterrupted use or possession.

Prescriptive *adj.* according to custom.

Presence *n.* the state of being present; place whare person is.

Present *adj.* & *n.* on the spot; a gift; ready; at hand.

Present *v.t.* to exhibit; to hold out; to make personally known, to introduce.

Presentable *adj.* of decent appearance; fit to be shown.

Presentation *n.* a formal intro-duction; exhibition; representation.

Presentee *n.* one who is presented to a benefice, one who is recommended for an office.

Presentiment *n.* vague expectation; foreboding.

Presently *adv.* forthwith, speedily, immediately.

Presentment *n.* laying of a formal statement before a court.

Preservation *n.* the act of preserving; escape from danger; safety.

Preserve *v.t.* to keep alive; to maintain; to keep safe.

Preside *v.i.* to excercise control over; to have the post of a chairman or president at a meeting.

President *n.* the elected head of a province, territory or state or of a republic.

Presidiary *adj.* serving as a garrison.

Press *v.t.* & *i.* crowd, throng, hurry, instrument for flattering or squeezing, a printing machine, newspaper literature, journalism.

Pressure *n.* the force exerted by one body acting on another.

Prestidigitation *n.* sleight of hand.

Prestige *n.* influence or reputation.

Prestimony *n.* sum reserved for petty payments.

Prest-money *n.* fund for the support of priest.

Presto (used in conjuring) quickly.

Presume *v.t.* & *i.* to take for granted; to take the liberty.

Presupposition *n.* a thing assumed as basis.

Pretence *n.* pretext; claim; pretending; make-belive.

Pretend *v.t.* & *i.* to feign; to venture; to lay claim; to profess falsely.

Pretender *n.* claimant to title.

Pretension *n.* assertion of a claim; pretentiousness.

Pretentious *adj.* ostentatious; lacking in modesty.

Preterite *adj.* of the tense expressing past action.

Pretermit *v.t.* to pass over without mention; to omit.

Pretext *n.* excuse; ostensible reason to cover the real reason.

Pretone *n.* a vowel sound before a stressed syllable.

Pretty *adj.* pleasing; beautiful; fine; attractive; neatly arranged.

Prettyish *adj.* somewhat pretty.

Prevail *v.i.* to gain the mastery; to attain one's object to predominate.

Prevalent *adj.* in general operation; generally experienced at atime or place.

Prevaricate *v.i.* to make evasive or misleading statements; to quibble

Prevenient *adj.* anticipatory; going before; preceding something else.

Prevent *v.t.* to secure the non-occurrence of; to hinder; to stop.

Prevention *n.* precaution; obstruction; the act of preventing.

Preventive *adj.* serving to prevent something.

Previous *adj.* comming before in time or order; prior to; former.

Previse *v.t.* to foresee; to have foreknowledge.

Prevision *n.* foresight, foreknowledge.

Prey *n.* a person's victim; an animal hunted and killed by carnivorous animal for food.

Price *n.* consideration or sacrifice necessary to obtain a thing.

Priceless *adj.* invaluable; too precious to be priced; inestimable.

Prick *v.t.* & *i.* make minute hole in; to feel pain; to pierce slightly with a sharp pointed thing.

Pricker *n.* a pricking instrument.

Prickle *n.* kind of wicker basket or measure; sharp growth such as thorn or hedgehog's spine.

Prickly *adj.* having prickles; prickling.

Pride *n.* feeling of elation and pleasure, object of praise; inordinate self-esteem; arrogant bearing.

Prie-dieu *n.* kneeling-desk; chair with tall sloping back for use in praying.

Priest *n.* a religious minister; a clergyman.

Prig *n. Arch.* coxcomb; a low or mean thief; precision in speech or manners.

Prim *adj.* formal; prudish; precise. *v.t. & i.* to assume a prim air.

Primage *n.* percentage paid in addition to freight.

Primal *adj.* primitive or primeval; original; fundamental.

Primary *adj.* holding or sharing the first place (in time or importance or development), principal; orignal.

Primates *n. pl.* monkeys, lemrus and bats; highest order of mammals including man.

Prime *adj.* of highest quality; chief, most important; primary; fundamental.

Primely *adv.* orignally.

Primer *n.* an elementary school-book for children.

Primitive *adj.* ancient; of an early, original, simple or old-fashioned kind; original.

Primness *n.* nicety.

Primogenial *adj.* first born; original.

Primogeniture *n.* principle by which property descends to the oldest son or child.

Primordial *adj.* existing at or from the beginning; first in order.

Primrose *n.* a pale-yellow spring flower; plant bearing it.

Primula *n.* kinds of flowering plant including primroses.

Primus *adj.* the first; the eldest.

Prince *n.* sovereign; ruler of feudatory State; male member of royal family.

Princely *adj.* royal; befitting a prince; magnificent; splendid; sumptuous.

Princess *n.* prince's wife; a female member of the royal family.

Principal *adj.* chief; leading; first in importance.

Principle *n.* fundamental truth; a rule by which conduct may be guided; primary source or element.

Prink *v.t. & i.* to dress up in a showy manner; to trim; to strut.

Print *n.* engraving; newspaper, photograph or picture produced from negative; impression left on paper by inked type or photography.

Printer *n.* a workman employed as a compositor; a pressman or a machine-minder.

Prior *n.* superior of a religious house; chief magistrate.

Priority *n.* being earlier; precedence; pre-eminence.

Prism *n.* a solid figure whose ends are similar, equal and parallel, rectillineal figure whose sides are parallelograms, a transparent figure of this form.

Prison *n.* a place of captivity for lawbreakers; a place of confinement. *v.t.* to confine in a prison.

Pristine *adj.* ancient; original; first.

Privacy *n.* a place of seclusion; solitude; retreat.

Private *adj.* reserved, secret, confidential; unofficial; not public; secluded.

Privet *n.* a white-flowered every-green used for hedges.

Privilege *n.* monopoly, patent; right, advantage or immunity belonging to a person, class or office.

Privily *adv.* secretly.

Privity *n.* secrecy; private assistance; knowledge shared with another of something kept private.

Privy *adj.* hidden; secret; private; confidential.

Prize *n.* reward in lottery, competition; etc.

Probable *adj.* that may be expected to happen or prove true or correct.

Probably *adv.* most likely.

Probate *n.* an official proving of a will.

Probation *n.* noviciate; the period of trial; testing of a person's conduct or character.

Probe *n.* blunt-ended surgical instrument for exploring wound, & etc.

Probity *n.* moral integrity; incorruptibility; uprightness; high principle.

Problem *n.* a difficult question to be solved; a thing difficult to understand.

Problematic (al) *adj.* disputable; presenting a problem; unsettled, doubtful, questionable, uncertain.

Procedure *n.* manner of conducting business; legal action; a course of action.

Proceed *v.i.* to go on to stay; to make one's way (to place); be carried on.

Process *n.* summons or writ; progress; advance; method of operation in manufacture, etc.

Procession *n.* a train of persons proceeding in orderly succession.

Proclaim *v.t.* to tell openly; to prohibit (a meeting); to announce publicly and officially.

Proclivity *n.* tendency; inclination; propensity.

Proconsul *n.* modern colonial governor; (pro-consul) deputy consul.

Procreant *n.* producing; generating.

Procreate *v.t.* to generate; to produce an offspring; to beget; to engender.

Procuration *n.* service rendered for acting as another's agent.

Procurator *n.* a person's proxy or agent; holder of power of attorney.

Procure *v.t.* to acquire; to obtain with effort; to bring about.

Prod *v.t.* to poke with the end of a stick; to arouse or urge on.

Prodigal *adj.* wasteful; lavish; expending wastefully.

Prodigally *adv.* in an extravagant manner.

Prodigious *adj.* astonishing marvellous; enormous; extraordinary; very great.

Prodigy *n.* a miracle; marvellous thing; wonderful person.

Proditor *n.* a traitor.

Produce *n.* agricultural or natural products; that which is produced, yield.

Product *n.* a thing produced; yield; result.

Production *n.* a thing produced by human activity.

Productive *adj.* fertile; tending to production; producing good crops.

Proem *n.* prefatory discourse; preface; premable to book or speech.

Profanation *n.* the act of profaning.

Profane *adj.* impure; unholy; not sacred.

Profanity *n.* profane swearing; profane conduct; blashphemy.

Profess *v.t.* to pretend to be; to lay clain to; to declare freely.

Professed *adj.* openly declared; acknowledged.

Profession *n.* declaration; vocation; occupation; employment; a religious order.

Professional *adj.* pertaining to a profession.

Professor *n.* one who makes profession (of a religion).

Proffer *v.t.* to offer spontaneously; to offer a gift.

Proficiency *n.* progress or improvement in anything, adeptness.

Proficient *adj.* expert; fully acquainted with a subject; adept.

Profile *n.* outline of the face as seen from the side; any edge outlined against the sky or other background.

Profit *n.* advantage; gain; benefit.

Profiteer *n.* the maker of great profits.

Profligate *adj.* & *n.* dissolute; vicious; licentious; reckless.

Profuse *adj.* lavish extravagant (*in, of,* gifts, promises, expenditure).

Profusion *n.* extravagance; prodigality; lavishness; profuseness.

Prog *n.* food; grub; eatables for journey.

Progenitor *n.* a person or animal in relation to his descendants.

Progeniture *n.* offspring.

Progeny *n.* offspring; descendant.

Prognosis *n.* forecast or course of disease.

Prognostic *n.* a forecast, prediction, omen.

Prognosticate *v.t.* to foretell; to tell beforehand.

Programme *n.* a descriptive outline of a series of events; proceeding.

Progress *n.* forward movement; development; increase.

Progression *n. Math.* series of quantities each in the same relation to preceding one; act of progressing forward.

Prohibit *v.t.* to interdict; to prevent; to inhibit; to forbid the doing, to debar, making, practice or use of.

Project *v.t.* & *i.* represent as plane surface; to produce; to stick out; hurl, send forth into space.

Projectile *adj.* capable of being projected by force; impelling.

Projection *n. Geom.* projecting of a figure; projecting, a part that protrudes.

Projector *n.* one who forms a project.

Prolapsus *n.* forward or downward displacement of an organ of the body.

Prolate *adj.* (of sphere) lengthened in the direction of the polar diameter, extending.

Prolegomenon *n.* preliminary remarks.

Prolepsis *n.* anticipation; anticipatory use of some words.

Proletarian *n.* the proletriate; of; member of.

Proletariate *n.* the poorest labouring class; lowest classes.

Prolicide *n.* the killing of an offspring.

Proliferate *v.t.* & *i.* to reproduce itself; to grow.

Prolific *adj.* producing offspring; abundantly productive; fruitful.

Proligerous *adj.* bearing offspring.

Prolix *adj.* lengthy; tedious, speaking at great length.

Prolixity *n.* great length; tediousness.

Prologue *n.* first of a series (of events, & etc.), preface (*of epilogue*); poem recited befre first part of a play.

Prolong *v.t.* to make longer; to lengthen out; to extend.

Prolongation *n.* extension; a part prolonged; delay.

Proluscry *adj.* pertaining to prolusion.

Promenade *n.* a going up and down in a public place; a place used or specially set apart for a public walk.

Prominence, Prominency *ns.* conspicuousness; distinction; a protuberance.

Prominent *adj.* distinguished; projecting; conspicous, eminent, jutting out.

Promiscuity *n.* promiscuousness.

Promiscuous *adj.* mingled; of mixed and disorderly composition.

Promise *n.* explicit undertaking to do or not to do something; favourable indications.

Promontory *n.* headland; the point of land jutting out into sea.

Promontored *adj.* containing a headland.

Promote *v.t.* to encourage; to move up to a higher office or position.

Promotion *n.* advancement.

Prompter *n.* (*esp.*) a person stationed to prompt actors.

Promptitude *n.* readiness; quickness of decision.

Promulgate *v.t.* to make known; to publish as coming into force or having authority; to proclaim.

Promulge *v.t.* to publish.

Prone *adj.* lying face or front downwards; inclined; disposed; (loosely) steep; headlong.

Prong *n.* a forked instrument; spike of a fork. *v.t.* to pierce.

Pronominal *n.* belonging to a pronoun.

Pronoun *n.* a word used in place of noun.

Pronounce *v.t.* & *i.* to give one's opinion; to affirm; to declare; to utter formally; to pass judgement.

Pronouncer one who pronounces.

Pronouncing *adj.* pertaining to pronunciation.

Pronunciation *n.* the mode of uttering words; the way a word is pronounced.

Proof *n.* a fact, evidence or reasoning that proves the truth of something.

Proofless *adj.* not established as true.

Prop *n.* a strong support; a stay; supporter of cause.

Propagable *adj.* able to be propagated.

Propaganda *n.* means for propagating a doctrine or practice.

Propagandist *n.* one who spreads some system.

Propagate *v.t.* & *i.* to spread abroad; to diffuse; to disseminate; to multiply or reproduce by sowing, grafting, breeding, etc.

Propel *v.t.* to drive or push forward; to give forward motion to.

Propend *v.t.* to incline or lean forward.

Propensity *n.* predisposition to anything; tendency, bent of mind, inclination.

Proper *adj.* one's own; belonging exclusively to.

Property *n.* attribute; things or thing owned; nature; ownership; quality.

Prophecy *n.* inspired prediction or utterance; prophesying.

Prophesy *v.t.* & *i.* to foretel future events; to predict; to foreshadow.

Prophet *n.* an inspired teacher, a person who predicts or foretells future events.

Prophylactic *adj.* & *n.* measure done or used as preventive or warding off a disease.

Propine *v.t.* to offer in kindness.

Propinquate *v.t.* to appraoch.

Propinquity *n.* nearness in time; vicinity; neighbourhood; close kinship.

Propitiate *v.t.* to gain the forgiveness of favour of; to appease.

Propitious *v.t.* well disposed; gracious; favourable; kind of good omen.

Proportionable *adj.* that may be proportioned.

Proportional *adj.* of proportion; aiming or aimed at due proportion. *n.* one of the terms of a proportion.

Proposal *n.* a scheme or design; an offer; an offer of marriage.

Propose *v.t.* & *i.* to put forward for consideration; to nominate as a member.

Proposition *n.* offer of terms of consideration, proposal; statement, assertion.

Propound *v.t.* to offer for consideration; to propose.

Propulsion *n.* a pushing forward.

Prorogue *v.t.* & *i.* to defer; to discontinue meetings of parliament at the end of a session.

Prosaic *adj.* like prose; dull; unpoetical; lacking in beauty.

Proscenium *n.* part of theatre stage in front of curtain.

Proscribe *v.t.* to excile; to ostracize; to publish the name as condemned.

Prose *n.* universified language; plain speech. *v.t.* & *i.* to talk in prose.

Prosector *n.* an anatomical dissector.

Prosecute *v.t.* & *i.* to purse or carry on; to institute legal proceedings.

Prosecution *n.* the prosecuting party in a lawsuit.

Proselyte *n.* a convert to a religion.

Prosenchyma *n.* tissue of elongated cells placed with their ends interpenetrating, *esp.* fibro-vascular tissue.

Prosify *v.t.* to turn into prose.

Prosily *adv.* in a prosy manner.

Prosodial *adj.* pertaining to the rules of prosody.

Prosody *n.* the science of versification and vowel quantity.

Prosopopoeia *n.* personification of abstract things.

Prospect *n.* anticipation, expectation; a view, mental view.

Prospector *n.* a searcher for minerals.

Prospectus *n.* a circular of the chief features of an enterprise, school-books & etc.

Prosper *v.t.* & *i.* to be successful; to thrive; to render prosperous.

Prosperous *adj.* flourishing; successful; auspicious.

Prostate *n.* large gland, each of several small glands, accessory to male generative organs in mammals.

Prostatic *adj.* pertaining to the prostate glands.

Prosthesis *n.* a branch of surgery which makes up the deficiencies of the body.

Prostitue *n.* a harlot.

Prostrate *adj.* lying flat on grond; exhausted, overcome; stretched on the ground.

Prosy *adj.* tedious; dull; like prose.

Protagonist *n.* a champion in a contest.

Protection *n.* the act of protecting; shelter; shield; defence; system of protecting home industries by taxing imports.

Protector *n.* a person who protects; appliance for protecting something.

Protectorate *n.* government by a protector; a State or territory protected or controlled by another State.

Protege *n.* a person who is under the protection of another.

Proteid *n.* essential parts of food.

Protein *n.* kinds of organic compound forming the most essential part of food of animals.

Protempore *adv.* for the time being.

Protend *v.t.* to stretch; to hold out.

Protervity *n.* pertness.

Protest *v.t.* & *i.* to affirm solemnly; to make a protest (*against*).

Protestation *n.* solemn declaration.

Prothalamion *n.* a nuptial song.

Proto *pref.* in gsense of 'original' 'primitive.'

Protocol *pref.* draught of terms agreed upon as the basis of a formal treaty; formal statement of transaction.

Protogenic *adj.* first formed.

Prototype *n.* the original of a copy.

Protract *v.t.* to prolong; to lengthen, to delay.

Protractor *n.* an instrument for measuring angles.

Protrude *v.t.* & *i.* to thrust forward; to project; to stand out prominently.

Protrudent *adj.* protruding.

Protuberance *n.* a swelling or hump; a knob, bulging shape.

Protuberant *adj.* swelling out; prominent.

Proud *adj.* (of things) imposing, splendid.

Prove *adj.* to test the accuracy of; to give proof of; to demonstrate; to verify; to ascertain by experience; to try.

Proven *adj.* proved.

Provenance *n.* what source something comes from.

Provender *n.* fodder for livestock; food in general.

Proverb *n.* notoriety, byword; a short pithy saying in general use.

Proverbial *adj.* accepted generally; notorious or constantly spoken of.

Proviant *n.* supply of food to an army.

Provide *v.t.* & *i.* to furnish; to procure beforehand; to make due preparation; to equip.

Provided *conj.* on the condition or understanding that.

Providence *n.* divine superintendence; thrift; timely care, provision or preparation; beneficent care of God; God.

Provident *adj.* showing foresight; prudent; cautious; economical; thrifty.

Providential *adj.* arranged by providence; affected by divine foresight; lucky.

Province *n.* territory; portion of an empire; sphere of action.

Provincial *adj.* having the speech or manners of the provinces; rustic; narrow; illiberal.

Provision *n.* legal or formal statement providing for something, clause of this; providing.

Provisional *adj.* temporary; subject to revision.

Proviso *n.* a conditional provisions, a stipulation; a limiting clause.

Provisor *n.* the steward of a religious house.

Provoke *v.t.* to excite; to irritate; to offend; to instigate; to allure.

Provost *n.* the head of a college; the chief magistrate of a burgh.

Prow *n.* the part of a ship or boad immediately about its stem.

Prowl *v.t. & i.* to go about in search of plunder or prey.

Proximal *adj.* situated towards the centre.

Proximo *adv.* of next month.

Proxy *n.* a document authorizing one to vote on another's behalf.

Prude *n.* a woman of extremely affected modesty.

Prudish *adj.* affectedly modest.

Prune *n.* dried plum; the colour of its juice.

Prunella *n.* a kind of herb; a stong silk or worsted stuff.

Prurient *adj.* given to or springing from lascivious thoughts.

Prussian *adj.* of or from Prussia. *n.* a native of Prussia.

Prussic *adj.* of, got from, Prussian blue.

Pry *v.i.* to look inquisitively; to inspect impertinentyly.

Psalm *n.* a sacred song; a hymn

Psalter *n.* the book of psalms; volume of psalms.

Psaltery *n.* an obsolete stringed instrument.

Pseudo *pref.* sham.

Pseudoscope *n.* a kind of optical instrument.

Pshaw *inter.* expressing impatience or contempt.

Psilosis *n.* stripping bare, *e.g.*, of hair of flesh.

Psittacine *adj.* like a parrot; pertaining to a parrot.

Psoriasis *n.* a kind of skin disease with red patches.

Psyche *n.* genus of day-flying moths; spirit; soul, mind.

Psychiatry *n.* treatment of diseases of the mind.

Psycho *pref.* in sense of 'soul of mind'.

Psychosis *n.* mental derangement.

Ptarmigan *n.* kind of grouse changing to white in winter.

Ptomaine *n.* poisonous matter produced by the putrefaction of animal tissues.

Puberty *n.* sexual maturity, functional capability of procreation.

Pubescent *adj.* reaching puberty.

Public *adj.* open to or shared by the people in general; of the people as a whole.

Publication *n.* the act of making known to the public; a published book, periodical, & etc.

Publicly *adv.* in public manner openly.

Publish *v.t.* to preapre and issue copies (of a book, & etc.) for sale or publication; to announce publicly, to make generally known; to announce formally.

Publisher, *n.* on who publishes.

Pucker *v.t. & i.* to contract or gather into wrinkles or folds.

Pud *n.* a child's hand.

Pudder *n.* uproar; tumult.

Pudding *n.* a mixture of animal or vegetable ingredients made into food.

Puddle *n.* kind of rough cement of kneaded clay; a small dirty pool.

Pudency *n.* modesty; bashfulness.

Pudendal *adj.* pertaining to pudendum.

Pudendum *n.* private parts.

Pudgy *adj.* stout and short.

Pudibund *adj.* indecent; shameful.

Pudicity *n.* modesty; chastity.

Puerile *adj.* childish; trifling; trivial.

Puerperal *adj.* of childbirth; pertaining to childbirth.

Puff *n.* a small quantity of vapour; a whiff.

Pug *n.* a monkey; a kind of dog; prepared clay for brick-making.

Pug *n.* foot-print of a beast. *v.t.* to track a beast by foot-prints.

Pugfaced *adj.* monkey faced.

Puggish *adj.* like a monkey.

Pugh *inter.* used in contempt.

Pugil *n.* the quantity that can be taken up between the thumb and first two fingers.

Pugilism *n.* boxing.

Pugmill *n.* a mill for grinding clay.

Pugnacious *adj.* quarrelsome.

Pugnacity *n.* inclinatin to quarrel.

Puisne *adj. & n.* later; subsequent to; inferior or junior in rank.

Puissant *adj.* having great influence; potent; mighty; forcibe; strong.

Puke *v.t. & i.* to vomit.

Pull *v.t. & i.* propel boat by pulling (oar); to pluck; to gather; to exert pulling force; to draw forcibly towards one.

Pullet *n.* a young owl.

Pulley *n.* a grooved wheel turning on a pin in a block.

Pullicate *n.* a kind of coloured handkerchief.

Pullover *n.* a kind of jersey which is worn by being pulled over the head.

Pullulate *v.t.* & *i.* to sprout.

Pulmonary *adj.* of the lungs; pertaining to the lungs.

Pulmonate *adj.* having lungs.

Pulp *n.* the flesh of soft fruits; any fleshy or soft part of animal body; soft formless mass.

Pulpify *v.t.* to make pulpy.

Pulpit *n.* a raised platform in a church from which a preacher delivers a sermon.

Pulsate *v.t.* to throb; to vibrate; to quiver; to expand and contract rhythmically.

Pulsative *adj.* throbbing; pertaining to pulsation.

Pulse *n.* throbbing of the arteries as blood is poured through them.

Pultaceous *adj.* pulpy; soft.

Pulverize *v.t.* & *i.* to crumble; to demolish (an argument, an opponent); to reduce to powder or dust.

Pulvil *n.* sweet-scented powder. *v.t.* to sprinkle with perfumed powder.

Pulvinate *adj.* swelling up; cushion-like.

Puma *n.* a large tawny American carnivorous beast.

Pumice *n.* a kind of hard stone used for polishing.

Pump *n.* kind of light shoe; a machine used for raising water from a well or to a higher level.

Pun *n.* humorous use of words having several meanings; a play on words.

Punch *v.t.* to strike with the fist; drive nail with punch; to bore or perforate with a punch.

Punch *n.* the chief character of a puppet show; an English comic journal.

Punchinello *n.* fate person of comical appearance.

Punctate *adj.* marked with dots; spotted.

Punctilio *n.* nice point of ceremony; formality.

Punctilious *adj.* laying stress on punctilios, very exact in behaviour.

Punctual *adj.* observant of appointed time; exact; not late; of a point.

Puncture *n.* prick, *esp.* accidental pricking of pneumatic tire; pricking; a hole made by pricking.

Pungent *n.* sharply affecting the tongue, caustic; stringing, bitting.

Punic *adj.* Carthaginian; faithless.

Punish *v.t.* to inflict penalty; to subject to retributive or disciplinary suffering.

Punishable *adj.* liable to punishment.

Punishment *n.* penalty; pain inflicted by authority on a person for crime.

Punitive *adj.* that punishes or is designed to punish; inflicting punishment.

Punk *n.* prostitute; rotten wood.

Punkie *n.* kind of small biting fly.

Punner *n.* a tool for beating earth.

Punnet *n.* a small basket.

Punster *n.* a maker of puns; a quibbler.

Punt *n.* flat-bottomed boat propelled by a pole.

Punt *n.* a kick in certain sports, such as rugby.

Punty *n.* a glass-blower's iron rod.

Puny *adj.* undersized; feeble, week; tiny; insignificant.

Pup *n.* a puupy; a young dog.

Pupa *n.* a chrysalis.

Pupil *n.* a person, usually, who is learning in a school; the circular opening in the centre of the eye.

Pupilage *n.* the state of time of being a pupil.

Pupilar *adj.* pertainning to a pupil.

Pupilate *adj.* marked with a central point.

Pupil-teacher *n.* a student who is trained to teach.

Puppet *n.* a person controlled by another; the figure of a person worked by wires & etc.

Puppy *n.* a conceited fellow; a vain young man; coxcomb; a young dog.

Purbeck *n.* a kind of hard limestone.

Purblind *adj.* partly blind; dull; dim-sighted; lacking discermment.

Purchasable *adj.* able to be purchased.

Purchase *v.t.* to acquire at a cost; to buy.

Pure *n.* chaste; unadulterated; unmixed; free from sin; innocent.

Purely *adv.* solely; clearly, entirely.

Purfle *n.* the embroidered border of garment. *v.t.* to adorn with purfle.

Purgative *adj.* that tends to purge; cathartic.

Purge *v.t. & i.* to make clean; to wipe out offence; to clean bowels by evacuation; to become pure.

Purger *n.* he who or that which purges.

Purification *n.* act of purifying; ritual cleansing.

Purifier *n.* kinds of apparatus for purifying gas, flour, etc.

Purify *v.t.* to make pure; to clean; to clear of foreign elements.

Purist *n.* one who is particular about the purity of language.

Puritan *n.* person of professed strictness in religion or morals.

Purity *n.* chastity; cleanness; freedom from physical or moral pollution.

Purl *v.i.* to flow with a murmuring sound. *v.t.* to work in gold-thread.

Purler *n.* a headlong fall.

Purlieu *n.* limit; boundary; enclosure. (*pl.*) outskirts.

Purloin *v.t.* to steal; to pilfer.

Purple *n.* the colour between crimson and violet.

Purport *n.* tenor or apparent meaning or substance, import.

Purpose *n.* fact or facility of resolving on something; design of effecting something.

Purposeful *adj.* full of intention; having a purpose.

Purr *n.* vibrating sound with which cat express pleasure.

Purse *n.* a small pouch for carrying money; a sum of money; a treasury.

Purslane *n.* a herb formerly much used in salads.

Pursuance *n.* the act of pursuing; consequence.

Pursue *v.t.* & *i.* to proceed along; to assail persistently.

Pursuer *n.* on who pursues, also (Law) prosecutor.

Pursuit *n.* the act of pursuing; employment; bussiness.

Pursuivant *n.* a follower; attendant; a heraldic officer of the lowest class.

Pursy *adj.* fat; puffy; short-winded.

Purulent *adj.* full of pus.

Purvey *v.t.* & *i.* to procure and supply (provisions).

Purveyor *n.* one whose business is to supply provisions on a large scale.

Purview *n.* enacting clauses of a statute; scope; range; extent.

Pus *n.* the matter produced by festering or inflammation.

Push *v.t.* & *i.* to exert force on a body; to surpass other.

Pusillanimity *n.* faint-heartedness; timidity; cowardice.

Puss *n.* a playful or coquettish girl; a cat; a hare; a tiger.

Pussy *n.* a pet name for a cat; a kitten.

Pustule *n.* pimple.

Put *v.t.* & *i.* to set; to place; to entrust; to lay the blame on.

Putative *adj.* renowned; supposed.

Putrefaction *n.* decomposition.

Prtrefy *v.t.* & *i.* to rot; to go bad; to fester; to become putrid.

Putrid *adj.* decomposed; rotten; corrupt; noxious; tinking.

Putty *adj.* a paste of whiting and linseed oil used by glaziers.

Puzzel *n.* a problem or toy designed to test ingenuity; a perplexing question.

Puzzler *n.* perplexing question; a problem, the solving of which requires great intelligence.

Pyaemia *n.* bloodpoisoning. **Pyaemic,** *adj.*

Pycno *pref.* in the sense of 'thick or dense'.

Pygmean *adj.* dwarfish.

Pygmy, Pigmy *ns.* a very small person of thing.

Pie,-Pyedog *n.* an ownerless dog.

Pylon *n.* a gateway of a temple.

Pylorus *n.* opening from stomach into bowels.

Pyogenic *adj.* pertaining the formation of pus.

Pyoid *adj.* like pus.

Pyorrhoea *n.* disease of the gum.

Pyramid *n.* a solid figure with triangular or square or polygonal base and sloping sides meeting at apex.

Pyramidist *n.* a student of structure and history of Egyptian pyramids.

Pyre *n.* a pile of combustibles for burning a corpse, a funeral pile.

Pyrexia *n.* fever.

Pyridine *n.* a liquid preparation obtained from bone-oil used for asthma.

Pyrites *n.* a combination of sulphur with other metals; sulphite or iron or copper.

Pyro *pref.* in sense of 'fire'.

Pyrolatory *n.* worship of fire.

Pyrologist *n.* one who is versed in the scienceof heat.

Pyrology *n.* the science of heat.

Pyrometer *n.* an instrument for measuring the expansion of bodies by heat.

Pyrophanous *adj.* made transparent by heat.

Pyrotechnic *adj.* art of making or using fire-works.

Pyrotic *n.* a caustic medicine.

Pyroxylin *n.* a kind of explosive.

Pyrrhic *n.* a metrical foot of two short syllables.

Pyrrhonic *adj.* pertaining to scepticism.

Pyrrhonism *n.* doctrine that certainty of knowledge is unattainable.

Pyrus *n.* a king of tree.

Pythagorean *adj.* of Pythagoras or his doctrines, esp. the transmigration of souls. *n.* follower of Pythagorus.

Pythian *adj.* Apllo's oracle.

Python *n.* soothsayer; large snake that crushes its prey.

Pythoness *n. fem.* a priestess; witch.

Pythonist *n.* a magician; a foreteller.

Pyx *n.* a box in which specimen coins are deposited at the mint.

Pyxis *n.* a small box; a casket.

Q

Q seventeenth letter of English alphabet, it always followed by '*u*' in English words,Roman numeral for 500.

Quack *n.* a charlatan; the harsh sound made by ducks.

Quakish *adj.* like a quack.

Quacksalver *n.* a quack doctor; (rare) a quack.

Quad *n.* quadrangle; quadruplet.

Quadra *n.* a square border or frame.

Quadragenarian *n.* forty-year-old person.

Quadrangle *n.* (also quad) a four-sided court, *esp.* in colleges; a four-sided figure (*esp.* square or rectangle).

Quadrant *n.* a quarter of a circle's circumference; an instrument for taking angular measurements.

Quadraphonic *adj.* (of a system of recording or broadcasting sound) coming from four different speakers at the same time-compare mono, stereo.

Quadrate *n.* square or rectangular; a square surface or figure. *adj.* square; rectangular. *v.t.* & *i.* to square.

Quadrature *n.* the process of constructing square; position of heavenly body in relation to another 90º away.

Quadrel *n.* a square stone or tile.

Quadrennial *adj.* occurring every (of lasting) four years.

Quadri *pref.* in the sense of 'four'.

Quadrilateral *adj.* & *n.* having four sides; a foursided figure.

Quadrille *n.* a kind of dance; a square dance, music for it.

Quadripartite *adj.* divided into four parts; shared by or involving four people; consisting of four parts.

Quadrisyllable *adj.* consisting of four syllables.

Quadroon *n.* hybrid of similarly proportioned descent between other human, animal, or vegetable stock.

Quadruple *adj.* fourfold; four times greater than.

Quadruplet *n. pl.* for children at a birth; four things working together.

Quadruplicate *v.t.* to multiply by four.

Quaere *v.t.* to enquire. *n.* a question.

Quaestor *n.* ancient-Roman official with financial and other duties.

Quaff *v.t.* & *i.* to drink deeply or in long draughts; to drain to the bottom.

Quag *n.* a marshy spot; a bog.

Quagmire *n.* also quags, quaking bog, marsh.

Quail *n.* a bird allied to partridge.

Quaint *adj.* old-fashioned; peculiar; odd.

Quake *v.t.* to tremble; to move or be agitated; to quiver.

Quaker *n.* a member of the religious Society of Friends who advocated peace.

Qualification *n.* modification; things that qualifies; suitable quality.

Qualify *v.t.* & *i.* to modify; to limit; to soften or moderate; to mitigate; to attribute a quality to.

Quality *n.* a distinguishing attribute; character; degree of excellence; relative nature; faculty; high rank; accomplishment.

Qualm *n.* momentary feeling of sickness.

Quandary *n.* a state of perplexity; a difficult situation.

Quantify *v.t.* to express as a quantity.

Quntitative *adj.* concerned with quantity.

Quantity *n. Math.* thing having quantity, figure or symbol representing it.

Quarrel *n.* an occasion of complaint, violent contention; rupture of friendly relations.

Quarry *n.* a victim; a prey; an object of pursuit; a place where excavations are made for stone.

Quart *n.* a quarter of a gallon or two pints. *v.t.* to draw back.

Quartan *n.* a paroxysm of fever & etc. occurring every fourth day.

Quarter *n.* a fourth part, one of the four parts into which a thing is divided, region, place, fourth part of a hundred-weight, shelter given to any enemy. (*pl.*) lodgings; abode.

Quarterage *n.* quarterly allowance.

Quarterly *adj.* occurring or due in each quarter of the year. *n.*quarterly magazine.

Quarto *n.* size given by folding sheet of paper twice; book of sheets so folded.

Quartz *n.* a rock crystal; kinds of silicious mineral often containing gold.

Quash *v.t.* to reject as not valid; to put an end to; to subdue; to annul.

Quasi *conj.* that is to say; as if; almost.

Quassation *n.* act of shaking.

Quassia *n.* a kind of tree; its wood or bark or root.

Quaternary *a ndj.* belonging to period subsequent to Teritiary; having four parts. *n.* set of four things.

Quaternion *n.* a set or group four.

Quatrain *n.* a stanza of four lines with alternate lines rhyming.

Quaver *v.t.* to vibrate; to thrill; to shake; to tremble.

Quay *n.* a landing place in the sea; wharf.

Quean *n.* an ill-behaved girl; a prostitute.

Queasy *adj.* (of digestion) easily upset; feeling or liable to qualms or scruples.

Queen *n.* king's wife; perfect female of bee, wasp, ant, etc.; the female sovereign of a kingdom, a pre-eminent female, woman.

Queening *n.* a kind of apple.

Queer *adj.* strange; peculiar eccentric; odd; out of sorts; singular.

Quell *v.t.* to suppress; to crush; to put down or cause to cease; to quiet.

Quench *v.t.* to extinguish; to suppress; to allay, to cool; to silence.

Quenchless *adj.* unextinguishable.

Quenelle *n.* a ball of fish or meat reduced to paste.

Querent *n.* an enquirer.

Querimonious *adj.* querulous.

Querist *n.* a quetioner; a person who asks question.

Quern *n.* a rude stone hand-mill for grinding corn.

Querulous *adj.* expressive of complaint; habitually complaining; peevish.

Query *n.* a mark of interrogation; a question (*esp.* one disputing a fact, & etc.) or an enquiry to be answered.

Quest *n.* a search; a request; an official inquiry; an examination.

Question *n.* doubt about a thing; a sentence put in interrogative form; subject of discussion or voting.

Questor *n.* a treasurer.

Queue *n.* a line of persons or vehicles waiting their turns behind each other; hanging plaited tail of hair, pigtail.

Quibble *n.* an evasion; a play on words; equivocation. *v.i.*to play upon words.

Quick *adj.* living, sprightly, sharp, pregnant with child, vigorous, sensitive, prompt to act.

Quicken *v.t.* & *i.* to vivify; to animate; to inspire; to kindle; to accelerate; to excite; to give life to.

Quick-eyed *adj.* having acute sight.

Quick-firer *n.* a quickfiring gun.

Quick-lime *n.* unslaked lime; lime burned but not slaked with water.

Quicksand *n.* watery land.

Quick-sight *n.* acute vision.

Quick-silver *n.* mercury.

Quisling *n.* he who helps the enemy of his native land and thus a traitor to his own country.

Quick witted *adj.* having a ready wit.

Quid *n.* a sovereign; chewing tobacco.

Quidam *n.* somebody.

Quiddity *n.* essence of a thing; quibble; subtlety.

Quidnunc *n.* person given to gossip; a news-monger.

Quiescent *adj.* silent; calm; motionless; inert.

Quiet *n.* tranquillity; repose; calm; silence; undisturbed state.

Quietism *n.* passive attitude towards life as a form of religious mysticism.

Quietly *adv.* in a quiet manner.

Quill *n.* a large feather or wing of a tail; porcupines spines; a writing pen.

Quilt *n.* bed-covering made of padding.

Quinary *adj.* consistig of five things.

Quinate *adj.* composed of five leaves.

Quince *n.* a kind of pear-shaped fruit used as preserve; tree bearing it.

Quincunx *n.* five object set so that four are at corners of square or rectangle and the other at its centre.

Quindecagon *n.* a figure of fifteen sides.

Quinine *n.* an alkaloid found in the cinchona bark.

Quinquagenarian *adj.* of fifty years of age.

Quinqua *pref.* in the sense of 'five'.

Quinquangular *adj.* having five angles.

Quinquefoliated *adj.* having five leaves.

Quinqueliteral *adj.* consisting of five letters.

Quin-quennium *adj.* a period of five years.

Quinsy *n.* an inflammation of the throat or tonsils or of the part adjacent.

Quintain *n.* mark set up to be tilted at,with sand-bag on pivoted bar.

Quintal *n.* a weight of 100 kilograms.

Quintan *adj.* & *n.* a fever occurring every fifth day; (ague or fever) with paroxysm every fifth day.

Quintessence *n.* extract; purest form or manifestation of some quality; most essential part.

Quintet(te) *n.* (performers of) piece for five voices or instruments; set of five.

Quip *n.* epigram; equivocation; quibble.

Quire *n.* a batch of twenty-four sheets of paper.

Quirinal *n.* the Italian Government of Court.

Quirk *n.* flourish in writing; trick of gesture, etc.

Quit *v.t.* & *i.* to get rid of; to abandon; to leave; to repay.

Quite *adv.* completely; wholly, altogether; perfectly; entirely.

Quiteron *n.* an electronic device.

Quits *n.* on even terms by repayment or retaliation.

Quitter *n.* one who quits; a person lacking in determination or strength of will.

Quiver *n.* a case for holding arrows.

Quivive *v.t.* to be on the alert; watching for something to happen.

Quixotic *adj.* aiming at an impossible ideal or visinory ends.

Quixotary *n.* absurd notion.

Quiz *v.t.* examine or coach by questioning; to make sport of; regard with mocking air.

Quiz-master *n.* question master.

Quoad *adv.* as far as possible.

Quod *n.* (*sl.*) prison.

Quod *n.* neuter of Latin word = which.

Quodibet *n.* genuine logic.

Quoin *n.* corner-stone; an external angle of a building.

Quoit *n.* a heay circular iron ring thrown to encircle an iron peg. *v.t.* to fling like a quoit.

Quondam *adj.* & *adv.* that was; something; having been formerly, former.

Quorum *n.* a fixed number of members required to be present in a meeting to pass a resolution.

Quota *n. pl.* fixed proportion; a share to be contributed to or received from a total by one of the parties concerned; a proportional part.

Quotable *adj.* worth quoting from or quoting.

Quotation *n.* a passage quoted; current price.

Quotative *adj.* pertaining to a quotation.

Quote *v.t.* & *i.* to state of price of; to cite or appeal to (an author, book) in confirmation of some view.

Quotidian *adj.* occurring daily; ordinary. *n.* a quotidian ague or fever.

Quotient *n.* the number resulting from the division of one quantity by another.

Quotiety *n.* number as a category.

Quotum *n.* share; proportion.

Qwerty *adj.* [usually before noun] (of a keyboard on a computer or TYPE WRITER) with the keys arranged in the usual way with Q, W, E, R, T and Y on the left of the top row of letters.

R

R the eighteenth of the English alphabet.

Ra *n.* the Egyption sun-God.

Rabat *v.t.* to take rounds frequently around each other.

Rabbit *n.* a well-known wild and domesticated rodent of hare family; (*sl.*) feeble player or person. *v.t.* to hunt rabbits; to confuse or confound.

Rabid *adj.* (of dog) affected with rabis, mad; furious, unreasoning; headstrong.

Race *n.* rapid current in the sea or river; contest of speed; course of life; career; channel; progress.

Rack *n.* kinds of wooden or metal framework for holding fodder, or for keeping various articles on or in, or for torturing victims by stretching the joints.

Racy *adj.* of distinctive quality or vigour; vernacular.

Radial *adj.* of the rays; having position or direction of a ray. *n.* a radial nerve or artery.

Radiance *n.* the quality of being radiant; splendour.

Radical *adj.* essential, original, fundamental, primary. *n.* a main principle; one desiring radial reforms; a root or primitive word or letter.

Radicle *n.* root-like sub-division of nerve or vein; part of seed that develops into the root.

Radio *pref.* of radium; of rays or radiation.

Radish *n.* plant with fleshy pungent edible roots.

Radium *n.* a metal yielding by pitchblende and named from its radio-active power.

Radius *n.* the straight line from the centre of a circle to its circumference.

Raffia *n.* a kind of palm; fibre from its leaves.

Raffish *adj.* of bad reputation. **Raffishness,** *n.* dissipation; ill-repute.

Raffle *n.* lottery in which article is assigned by drawing lots or throw of dice; rubbish.

Raft *n.* a fleet made of logs or casks.

Rafter *n.* one of the sloping beams of pieces of timber of a roof.

Rag *n.* torn piece of woven material; remnant; fragment; a scrap; roofing stone or tile.

Rag *v.t.* & *i.* (*sl.*) play rough jokes on; to torment tease; to scold.

Rage *n.* violent anger; object of widespread temporary popularity.

Rage *n.* a party; a good time.

Ragman *n.* a man who collects rag; a devil.

Ragout *n.* meat in small pieces stewed with vegetables and highly seasoned.

Raid *n.* sudden incursion; a hostile expedition; a surprise visit by police.

Rail *n.* iron bar making part of the track of a railway or tramway.

Railway *n.* road laid with rails for heavy wagons & etc.

Raiment *n.* clothing; dress; apparel.

Rain *n.* condensed moisture of atmosphere falling visibly in separate drops.

Rainbow *n.* arch of prismatic colours formed in rain or spray by the sun's rays. *adj.* many-coloured.

Rainy *adj.* in or on which rain falls; abounding with rain; showery.

Raise *v.t.* to make stand up; to breed; to set upright; to rouse.

Raisin *n.* a partially dried grape.

Rake *n.* pole with comb like cross bar for drawing hay & etc.

Rakehell *n.* a lewd fellow.

Raking *n.* collection with a rake.

Rakish *adj.* debauched.

Rallicart *n.* a kind of carriage; light two-wheeled driving trap for four.

Rally *v.t.* & *i.* (of prices) recover from depression; to banter, to chaff.

Ram *n.* a male sheep; a sign of the zodiac (Aries); a pile driving machine; an instrument for battering walls of forts & etc.

Ramal *adj.* pertaining to the branch of a tree.

Ramble *v.t.* to walk for pleasure.

Rambler *n.* one who rambles.

Rambling *adj.* moving irregularly; irregularly arranged; wandering.

Ramicorn *adj.* with thorny branches.

Ramify *v.t.* & *i.* to develop into a complicated system; to branch out.

Rammish *adj.* foul smelling.

Rammishness *n.* rankness.

Rammy *adj.* strong-scented.

Ramp *v.t.* & *i.* to stand on hind legs, with forepaws in air; to ascend or descend to different level; to assume or be in threatening posture.

Rampage *v.t.* to ramp, an excited condition. *n.* an exited condition.

Rampant *adj.* violent; aggressive; exuberant; unrestrained; aggressive.

Rampart *n.* defence, protection; defensive mouth of earth.

Rancid *adj.* having a rank smell.

Rancour *n.* bitterness; malice; deep-seated enmity, malignant hate.

Rand *n.* the inner strip of leather in a shoe.

Randan *n.* a boat for one sculler and two oarsmen; spree.

Randiness *n.* boisterousness.

Random *adj.* & *adv.* haphazard, without aim or purpose.

Randy *adj.* having a rude aggressive manner; boisterous; noisy.

Range *v.t.* & *i.* to arrange in a row; to run in a line, to extend, to wander.

Range-finder *n.* a device for ascertaining distance.

Ranger *n.* the keeper of a park. (*pl.*) mounted riflemen trained to fight on foot.

Ranine *adj.* like a frog.

Rank *n.* place in a scale; row queue; distinct social class; station; (*pl.*) common soldiers.

Rankle *v.t.* & *i.* to fester; to give constant pain; to irritate.

Ransack *v.t.* to plunder, to pillage; to make a thorough search, to search the recesses of.

Ransom *n.* release from prison on consideration of some money; the fine paid for pardon.

Rant *v.t.* & *i.* to use bombastic language; to preach noisily.

Ranula *n.* a swelling under the tongue.

Ranunculus *n.* a kind of plant with flowers.

Rap *n.* a knock, *esp.* on door; a smart slight blow. *v.t.* & *i.* to make the sound of a rap; to deal a rap to.

Rap *n.* an atom; the least bit.

Rape *n.* violation of chastity; carrying off by force.

Rapid *adj.* swift, fast, quick, acting in a very short time.

Rapine *n.* act of plundering; robbery.

Rappee *n.* a kind of snuff.

Rapport *n.* relationship, communication, connexion.

Rapscallion *n.* a rascal; a rogue.

Rapt *adj.* enraptured; carried away in spirit; absorbed.

Rapture *n.* extreme delight; ecstasy.

Raraavis *n.* kind of person or thing rarely met with.

Rare *adj.* not dense; unusual; uncommon excellence; seldom occurring; very amusing; remarkably good.

Rarity *n.* uncommon thing; rareness.

Rascal *n.* a mean fellow; a rougue; a dishonest person; a knave.

Rash *n.* skin eruption in spots or patches.

Rasher *n.* thin slice of bacon.

Rasp *n.* a scrapper.

Raspatory *n.* rasp used in surgery.

Raspberry *n.* a plant yielding small juicy berries.

Rasper *n.* a person that rasps; a scraper.

Rasure *n.* act of scraping.

Rat *n.* kinds of rodent resembling but larger than the mouse.

Rata *n.* a kind of large tree.

Ratal *n.* the amount on which a rate is fixed.

Rate *n.* the standard or way of reckoning; assesment levied by local authorities.

Rathe *adj.* coming or blooming early.

Rather *adv.* more truly or readily; to some extent; on the other hand.

Ratify *v.t.* amount of rate fixed by municipality; ranking; angry reprimand.

Rating *n.* amount of rate fixed by a municipality; angry reprimand.

Ratio *n.* the relation between two similar quantites; proportion.

Ratiocinate *v.i.* to argue; to reason formal way.

Ration *n.* fixed daily allowance of food served out.

Rationale *n.* fundamental reason; reasoned exposition.

Ratline *n.* a rope-ladder used in ships.

Ratoon *n.* (send up) new shoot springing from sugar-cane root after cropping.

Rattan *n.* continuous beat of a drum.

Ratten *v.t.* to injure the tools of a workman out of malice.

Rattle *v.t.* & *i.* to give out rapid succession of short sharp sounds; to talk thoughtlessly.

Raucous *adj.* hoarseness of voice; harsh-sounding.

Ravage *v.t.* & *i.* to pluner; to lay waste; to make a havoc. *n.* devastation; waste.

Ravel *v.t.* & *i.* to complicate; to entangle; to perplex; to examine or enquire into a thing.

Ravelin *n.* an outwork outside a fort.

Raven *n.* a large black bird of prey of the crow kind.

Raven *v.t.* & *i.* to eat rapaciously; to obtain by violence.

Ravin *n.* robbery; plunder; seizing and devouring of prey.

Ravine *n.* a deep and narrow gorge; a mountain cleft.

Ravish *v.t.* to commit a rape upon a woman; to enrapture; to fill with delight; to carry off by force.

Raw *adj.* unripe; not analysed; uncooked; crude; unfinished; untrained; crude.

Ray *n.* a single beam of light, a gleam of intellect, a glance, a radiating line, an array, a kind of large sea-fish.

Rayon *n.* artificial silk.

Raze, Rase *v.t.* to erase; to throw out; to destroy completely; to demolish.

Razor *n.* an instrument for shaving hair.

Reach *v.t.* & *i.* to stretch out; to attain; to arrive at; to take without stretching hand.

React *v.i.* to act again; to respond to some stimulus.

Reaction *n.* response to stimulus; *Chem.* action set up by one substance in another; responsive or reciprocal action.

Read *v.t.* & *i.* to express in words; to understand.

Reader *n.* a person employed to read and report, one who corrects proof-sheets of press.

Ready *adj.* willing; promt; quick; within reach; prepared in advance.

Reagent *n.* substance used to detect presence of another by reaction.

Real *adj.* actual; genuine; free; sincere; authentic; consisting of immovable property.

Realism *n.* doctrine that general ideas have objective existence.

Realize *v.t.* to convert (a hope, plan, & etc.) into fact, make realistic.

Realm *n.* kingdom; sphere; domain.

Realty *n.* real estate or property.

Reannex *v.i.* to reunite.

Reap *v.t.* & *i.* to cut the crop; to gather harvest from field; to obtain the fruits of one's labour.

Reapply *v.t.* & *i.* to apply again.

Rear *v.t.* & *i.* to breed, nourish, foster, raise, educate, grow; to bring up, to cultivate, to build; to raise.

Reargue *v.t.* & *i.* to argue a second time.

Rear-arise *n.* to rise again.

Reason *n.* the faculty of distinguishing good from bad; argument; cause.

Reasonable *adj.* inexpensive; sound of judgement, moderate; not extortionate.

Reassume *v.t.* to assume again.

Reassure *v.t.* to dispel apprehensions of; to restore to confidence.

Reattach *v.t.* to attach a second time.

Reave, Reive *v.t.* & *i.* to commit ravages; take by violence.

Reavow *v.i.* to avow again.

Rebate *v.t.* to diminish the force of; to deduct ; to blunt; to subtract.

Rebec *n.* three stringed musical instrument.

Rebel *n.* a person who rises in arms against established government.

Rebeller *n.* one who revolts.

Rebellion *v.t.* revolt.

Rebind *v.t.* to hind again.

Reboil *v.t.* & *i.* to boil again.

Rebound *v.t.* recoil upon agent; to spring back after impact.

Rebuff *n.* a sudden check; repulse; defeat; refusal.

Rebuild *v.t.* to build up again, to renew.

Rebuke *v.t.* to reprimand; to censure; to reprove.

Rebury *v.t.* to inter again.

Rebus *n.* a kind of enigma or riddle.

Rebut *v.t.* to force back; to refute, to disprove (evidence, charge).

Rebutter *n.* one who refutes.

Recalcitrant *adj.* refractory, refusing compliance.

Recalcitrate *v.i.* to refuse; to comply; to be refractory.

Recalesce *v.t.* to regain heat.

Recall *v.t.* to revoke, annual; to summon back.

Recallable *adj.* able to be recalled.

Recant *v.t.* & *i.* to retract; to unsay; to withdraw.

Recaption *n.* the act of retaking.

Recaptor *n.* one who takes again.

Recast *v.t.* to put into new shape; to make a new mould; to throw again; to compute a second time.

Recede *v.i.* to shrink back; to retreat; to withdraw; to decline in value.

Receipt *n.* an amount of money received.

Receive *v.t.* & *i.* to accept; to take into possession.

Recency *n.* a newness, lateness.

Recension *n.* a revised text; revision of a text; review.

Recent *adj.* not long past; modern; fresh.

Reception *n.* act of receiving; welcome to specified kind.

Receptive *adj.* able to receive ideas.

Recess *n.* a niche; retreat; seclusion; temporary suspension of business.

Recession *n.* receding, withdrawl, from a place or point; preceding part of object.

Recharge *v.t.* to charge again; to make a fresh attack.

Rechauffe *n.* warmed up dish; rehash.

Recherche *adj.* far fetched.

Recheat *v.t.* to whistle up. *n.* recalling dogs in hunting.

Rechristen *v.t.* to convert to Christianity again.

Recidivism *n.* the habit of relapsing into crime.

Recipe *n.* statement of ingredients and procedure for a medicine or dish.

Recipient *adj* & *n.* one who receives; the person who accepts something.

Reciprocal *adj.* expressing mutual relation; (Gram.) reflexive.

Recital *n.* a detailed account or narration of facts; the act of reciting.

Recitation *n.* reciting as entertainment; rehearsal.

Recitative *adj.* reciting.

Recite *v.t.* & *i.* to declaim from memory; to enumerate; to repeat aloud.

Reciter *n.* a narrator; person who recites.

Reck *v.t.* & *i.* to reck it; to pay heed to; to care about.

Reckon *v.t.* & *i.* to calculate; to reason with oneself.

Reckoner *n.* one who computes; a calculator.

Reclaim *v.t.* & *i.* & *n.* to win from vice or error; to recover; to reform; to win back.

Reclinate *adj.* bending downwards.

Recline *v.t.* & *i.* to lie or lean on one side; to rest; to rely.

Reclothe *v.t.* to dress up again.

Recluse *adj.* & *n.* living in retirement or isolation; a hermit or anchorite.

Recoal *v.t.* & *i.* to fill a ship with coal.

Recognizance *n.* bond by which person engages before court or magistrate to observe some condition.

Recognize *v.t.* to identify; to know again; to acknowledge validity of.

Recoil *v.i.* to retreat; to start back; to retire; to shrink in horror or disgust or fear; to rebound after impact.

Recolour *v.t.* to colour again.

Recombine *v.t.* to combine again.

Recomfort *v.t.* to pacify again; to give new strength.

Recommend *v.t.* to place in the care of; to suggest as fit for; to advise; to make acceptable.

Recommit *v.t.* to commit again; to refer a second time.

Recompense *v.t.* to make amends to; to requite; to compensate.

Recompose *v.t.* to from in a new way again; to quieten.

Reconcile *v.t.* to make friendly after estrangement; to set a quarrel; to heap up.

Record *n.* recorded state, register, official report of proceedings, remembrance, a public document, facts known, the plate of gramophone.

Recorder *n.* one who records.

Recourse *n.* resorting to some source of help, thing resorted, helper, a flow or running-back, return.

Recover *v.t.* & *i.* to regain possession of; to cure; to reclaim; to secure; to regain health or consciousness; to get over.

Recreate *v.t.* & *i.* to reanimate; to refresh; to amuse; to occupy agreeably; to create again.

Recruit *n.* newly enlisted and not yet trained soldier; a tiro.

Recruiter *n.* one who recruits.

Rectal *adj.* pertaining to the rectum.

Rectangle *n.* a plane rectilinear four-sided figure with four right angles, the opposite sides of which are equal and parallel and all the four angles are right angles.

Rectify *v.t.* to put right; to correc; to adjsut.

Rectitude *n.* moral uprightness; correctness; honesty.

Recumbent *adj.* & *n.* lying down; inactive; leaning; reclining; reposing.

Recuperate *v.t.* & *i.* to recover from illness; to regain pecuniary loss.

Recur *v.t.* to occur again; to go back in thought or speech to; to return to mind.

Recurrence *ns.* return.

Recurrent, Recurring *adjs.* returning again.

Recurvate *v.t.* to curve again.

Recurvature *n.* a curve or bend backward.

Recurve *v.t.* & *i.* to bend backwards.

Recusant *n.* person who refuses submission or compliance.

Recusation *n.* the act of challenging a judge.

Red *adj.* of the colour of blood; burning; violence or revolution.

Redact *v.t.* to arrange for publication; to put into literary form; edit.

Redaction *n.* preparing for publication; new edition.

Redd *v.t.* to arrange; to clear up; to tidy; to put right.

Redden *v.t.* & *i.* to become red; to blush.

Reddition *n.* surrender.

Reddle *n.* red ochre. *v.t.* to colour with red ochre.

Rede *v.t.* to advise; to read (riddle). *n.* advice; counsel.

Redeem *v.t.* to buy back; to recover by expenditure of effort; to ransom; to save.

Redeliverance *n.* a second deliverance.

Redemption *n.* deliverance from sin by atonement.

Redingote *n.* a woman's overcoat.

Redintegrate *v.t.* to restore to perfect state; to renew; to re-establish.

Redirect *v.t.* to re-address; to direct again.

Rediscover *v.t.* to find out again.
Redly *adv.* in a red manner.
Redolent *adj.* fragrant; possessing a sweet smell; emitting odour.
Redouble *v.t.* & *i.* to intensify.
Redoubt *n.* a small temporary fort; an outwork. *v.t.* to fear.
Redound *v.t.* to contribute in the end (to one's advantage & etc.); come as final.
Redress *v.t.* to put right again; to remedy; re-adjust; to set right; to recitify.
Redressive *adj.* affording redress.
Redsear *v.t.* to break a thing when red-hot.
Red-short *adj.* breaking when red hot; brittle.
Reduce *v.t.* to bring back to original position; lower, weaken, impoverish.
Reduction *n.* the act of reducing; diminution.
Redundant *adj.* superfluous; excessive; copious; pleonastic; full; luxuriant.
Reduplicate *v.t.* to make double; to repeat.
Reed *n.* kind of water or marsh plant with tall straight stalk.
Re-edify *v.t.* to build up again.
Reediness *n.* slenderness.
Re-edit *v.t.* to edit again.
Reedy *adj.* abounding in reeds; like a reed; weak; slender.
Reef *n.* one of several strips along the top of bottom of a sail that can be taken in, mass of rock or shingle just above water.
Reefer *n.* a double-breasted coat worn by sailors.
Reel *n.* a frame on which thread, paper & etc. are wound.
Re-elect *v.t.* to elect again.
Re-emerge *v.t.* to emerge again.
Re-enact *v.t.* to enact again.
Re-enforce *v.t.* to strengthen again.
Re-engine *v.t.* to attach an engine again.
Re-enlist *v.t.* to take into service again.
Reeve *n.* the chief magistrate of town or district; a governor; (Canada) president of village or town council.
Re-exist *v.t.* to come into being again.
Refectory *n.* a room where meals are taken.
Refer *v.t.* & *i.* to submit for information or decision; to have relation; to appeal.
Refree *n.* a person chosen to decide between opposing parties; an umpire in a game. *v.i.* act as referee.
Reference *n.* an act of refering; relation; allusion; respect.
Refine *v.t.* & *i.* to free from impurities; to purify; to make elegant or cultured.
Refit *v.t.* & *i.* to renew or repair ship; to repair again.

Reflect *v.t.* & *i.* to throw back the image; to consider seriously; to meditate.

Reflex *n.* an image in mirror, etc. relfected light or colour or glory.

Reflux *n.* backward flow; a running back.

Reform *v.t.* & *i.* to improve; to form again.

Reformation *n.* the act of reforming; the state of being roformed.

Refractor *n.* the refracting lens of a telescope.

Refrain *n.* recurring phrase or line, *esp.* at the end of stanzas.

Refrangible *adj.* refractable; capable of being refracted.

Refresh *v.t.* & *i.* to reanimate; to cool again; to give new strength to.

Refrigerate *v.t.* to cool or become cool; to preserve in cold.

Reft *adj.* robbed.

Refuge *n.* a place of shelter; a person or thing that gives shelter.

Refugee *n.* one who flees for shelter.

Refulgence *n.* a flood of light.

Refulgent *adj.* shining; splendid.

Refund *v.t.* & *i.* to pay back what is received; to reimburse.

Refurnish *v.t.* to furnish again.

Refusal *n.* a denial of something offered.

Refuse *v.t.* & *i.* to decline a request or offer.

Refuse *n.* what is left as worthless or not wanted, dregs, scum, dross.

Refuser *n.* one who refuses.

Refutal *n.* act of refuting, rebuttal.

Refute *v.t.* to prove falsity or error of; to disprove; to rebut by argument.

Regain *v.t.* to reach (a place) again; to recover possession of.

Regal *n.* pertaining to a King; magnificent.

Regale *n.* a feast of dainty food.

Regalia *n. pl.* insignia of royalty; privileges of a King; insignia of an order.

Regalism *n.* undue excercise of royal authority; supremacy of king in religious matters.

Regard *v.t.* & *i.* to gaze upon; to pay attention to; to give heed to.

Regatta *n.* a meeting for boat races.

Regelate *v.t.* to be fused into one mass.

Regency *n.* office of a regent.

Regenerate *v.t.* & *i.* to invest with new and higher spiritual nature.

Regent *n.* person administering kingdom during minority, absence, or incapacity of a monarch.

Regicide *n.* the murder of a king; one who kills a sovereign.

Regime *n.* the method of government; prevailing system of things.

Region *n.* tract of land; a country; a separate part of the world.

Register *n.* a book in which regular accounts are kept or details entered, recorder, list, (print) exact correspondence of printed matter on two sides of leaf.

Registration *n.* act of registering; enrolment.

Registry *n.* registration; place where registers are kept.

Reglet *n.* a slip of wood used for separating lines of printing type.

Regnant *adj.* reigning; ruling; prevalent; predominant.

Regorge *v.t. & i.* to bring up again; to flow back; vomit; disgorge.

Regrate *v.t.* to buy and sell provisions in the same market.

Regress *n.* the power of going back; backward tendency.

Regression *n.* reversion; retrogression; backward movement.

Regret *v.t.* to be sorry; to lament; to repent; to grieve at.

Regular *adj.* following or exhibiting a principle, orderly, systematic, harmonious, consistent, recurring uniformly, having the parts symmetrical, methodical, usual, having the sides and angles equal.

Regulate *v.t.* to adapt to requirements; to control by rule; to subject to restrictions.

Reguline *adj.* pertaining to regulus.

Regurgitate *v.t. & i.* to gush back; to pour or cast up again.

Regulus *n.* purer or metallic part of mineral separated by sinking to bottom in crucible; bright star in Leo (R.).

Rehabilitate *v.t.* to bring back to former position.

Rehear *v.t.* to hear again; to try over again.

Rehearse *v.t & i.* to repeat from beginning to end; to say over; to give list of.

Reif *n.* plunder.

Reify *v.t.* to convert mentally into a material thing.

Reign *n.* sovereignty; rule; period of a king's rule. *v.i.* to rule as a king.

Reimburse *v.t.* to repay; to recompense.

Rein *n.* means of control (oft. *pl.* in the same senses); a long narrow strap used to guide horse.

Reincarnate *v.t.* to embody again.

Reincrease *v.t.* to increase again.

Reindeer *n.* a kind of deer of cold climates used for drawing sledges.

Reinforce *v.t.* to strengthen by additional force; to enforce again.

Reins *n. pl.* the kidneys; loins.

Reinspect *v.t.* to make a second inspection.

Reinstate *v.t.* to re-establish in former position; to replace.

Reinsure *v.t. & i.* to insure against.

Reinvest *v.t.* to invest again; to lay out money again for profit.

Re-issue *v.t.* to issue again.

Reiterate *v.t.* to repeat over again or several times, a reuest, a word or a statement, to walk over a place again, to repeat.

Reject *v.t.* to put aside; to throw away.

Rejection *n.* the act of rejecting; refusal.

Rejoice *v.t.* & *i.* to cheer up; to make glad; to feel joy; to gladden.

Rejoin *v.t.* & *i.* to join (one's companion, etc.) again; reunite; to say in answer.

Rejuvenate *v.t.* & *i.* to make or become young again.

Rejuvenize *v.t.* to make young again.

Relapse *v.i.* to fall back into worse state after improvement.

Relate *v.t.* & *i.* to narrate; to recount; to bring into relation.

Relater *n.* one who narrates.

Relation *n.* narration; a narrative, connexion between persons or things.

Relative *adj.* corresponding in some way, having a relation, related to each other, referring to.

Relativism *v.t.* doctrine that knowledge is of relations only.

Relax *v.t.* & *i.* to cause or allow to become loose or slack; to enfeeble.

Relaxant *n.* a soothing medicine.

Relaxation *n.* the act of relaxing.

Relaxed *adj.* loose, slackened.

Relay *n.* set of fresh horse or gang of men to replace tired ones.

Release *v.t.* to allow a person to come out of a place; to allow something to fly.

Relegate *v.t.* to banish; to exile; to transfer for decision; to consign to an inferior position.

Relent *v.t.* to become less stiff; to yield to compassion; to give up harsh intention.

Re-let *v.t.* to let a house etc. again.

Relevant *adj.* bearing up or pertaining to the purpose in hand; applicable.

Reliable *adj.* that may be relied upon or trusted; of trustworthy quality.

Reliance *n.* trust; confidence; act of relying; thing depended on.

Relict *n.* man's widow; a remaining part; a survivor; a surviving trace.

Relief *n.* alleviation or end of pain, deliverance from pain, redress.

Relier *n.* one who relies.

Relieve *v.t.* to ease; to give relief to; to assist; to alleviate; to redress.

Religion *n.* a prevalent system of faith and worship; recognition of God and duty towards him.

Religious *adj.* imbued with religion; godfearing; teaching religion; devout; belonging to a monastic order; pious.

Relinquent *adj.* relinquishing.

Relinquish *v.t.* to give up; to abandon; to resign; to surrender.

Reliquary *n.* a shrine for holding relics.

Reliquiae *n. pl.* withered remains of leaves decaying on stem.

Relish *n.* distinctive flavour or taste of; attractive quality; enjoyment of food or other things; zest.

Relucent *adj.* bright; transparent; shining.

Reluct *v.t.* to feel reluctance; to show repugnance.

Reluctant *adj.* unwilling to do something; offering resistance; disinclined.

Reluctate *adj.* producing reluctance.

Relume *v.t.* to rekindle; to make bright again.

Rely *v.i.* to have trust in; to rest on; to depend upon.

Remain *v.i.* to be left behind after any event; to abide; to stay in some place or condition.

Remainder *n.* remaining persons or things; residue.

Remains *n. pl.* what remains over; surviving parts or amount.

Remake *v.t.* to make afresh.

Remand *v.t.* to send back (a prisoner) into custody to allow of further evidence being obtained.

Remanent *adj.* remaining; residual.

Remark *v.t.* & *i.* to take notice of; to perceive.

Remarry *v.t.* to marry a second time.

Remedial *adj.* pertaining to healing.

Remedy *n.* cure for a disease; healing medicine; means of relieving an evil.

Remember *v.t.* to retain in the memory; to bear in mind; make present to.

Remiform *adj.* of the shape of an oar.

Remind *v.t.* to put in mind; to cause to remember; to bring to the remembrance of.

Reminiscence *n.* (*pl.*) collection in literary form of incidents that person remembers; recovery of knowledge by mental effort; remembering.

Remint *v.t.* to cast coins again in mint.

Remise *v.t.* to make over or surrender a claim.

Remiss *adj.* negligent; careless of duty; sluggish; weakened; lacking energy.

Remit *v.t.* & *i.* to pardon; to abate; to slacken; to transmit money; to put in the previous condition.

Remittal *n.* remittance.

Remittee *n.* the receiver of a remittance.

Remnant *n.* a small remaining quantity; fragment; remainder.

Remodel *v.t.* to model or fashion again.

Remonstrance *n.* a protest; expostulatory counsel or advice, remonstrating.

Remorse *n.* stings of conscience, bitter repentance, compunction.

Remote *adj.* far away in place or time; distant from; out-of-the way; secluded; least.

Remould *v.i.* to mold or shape anew.

Remount *v.t & i.* to mount again; to ascent again.

Removable *adj.* dismissal from a post; able to be removed.

Remove *v.t. & i.* to take off or away from place occupied; to change one's residence; to dismiss.

Remunerable *adj.* fit for being rewarded.

Renaissance *n.* revival of arts and letters in 14th-16th centuries.

Renal *adj.* of the kidneys.

Renascence *n.* rebirth.

Rend *v.t. & i.* to tear; to split into two; to divide.

Render *v.t.* to give in return; to pay as due; to execute; to translate; to deliver up; to portray; to convert into.

Rendezvous *n.* a meeting-place; a place appointed for the assembling of troops & etc.

Rendition *n.* act of rendering or performing.

Renegade *n.* one who deserts his party or faith; a turncoat.

Renew *v.t. & i.* to bring to original state; to make new.

Renewable *adj.* that may be renewed.

Renewer *n.* one who renews.

Renidify *v.t.* to build a new nest.

Reniform *adj.* kidney shaped.

Rennet *n.* curdled milk from calf's stomach, or artificial preparation, usd in curdling milk for cheese etc.

Renominate *v.t.* to nominate again.

Renounce *v.t.* to repudiate; to forsake; to withdraw from, discontinue.

Renovate *n.* to make new again; to restore to good condition.

Renown *n.* a reputation; high distinction; celebrity.

Rent *n.* periodical payment for use of land, tear, cleft, gorge, a tenant's periodical payment to landlord, payment for hire.

Renter *n.* a tenant; one who holds a lease by paying rent for.

Renunciation *n.* self-denial; renouncing; document expressing it.

Rep *n.* person of loose character; (school sl.) verse etc. learnt by heart.

Repair *v.t.* to resort; to go; to restore; to make amends for; to mend; renovate.

Repand *adj.* with wavy margin.

Reparable *adj.* that may be made good; satisfactory.

Repartee *n.* a witty reply or retort. *v.t.* to make a retort.

Repast *n.* food supplied for being eaten; meal.

Repay *v.t.* & *i.* to return; to retaliate; to pay back; to requite.

Repeal *v.t.* to annul; to abrogate; to revoke. *n.* abrogation; revocation.

Repeat *v.t.* & *i.* to say or do over again.

Repeater *n.* one who repeats.

Repel *v.t.* to refuse acceptane to; to drive back; to ward off.

Repellent *adj.* (of manner etc.) unsociable, uninviting.

Repent *v.t.* & *i.* to feel regret or penitence about something; to be regretful about; to remember with self-reproach.

Repentance *n.* sorrow; grief; penitence.

Reperuse *v.t.* act of thinking or reading over again.

Repetition *n.* the act of doing or uttering a second time.

Repine *v.i.* to be discontented; to complain discontentedly; to fret.

Replace *v.t.* to put back in place; to substitute for; to refund; to fill up a place.

Replenish *v.t.* to fill up again.

Replete *adj.* fully filled; well stocked; thoroughly imbued.

Replica *n.* copy, fascimile; duplicate of work made by the artist.

Replicate *adj.* folded back on itself. *v.t.* to repeat; to fold back.

Replication *n.* echo; (*Law*) plaintiff's reply to defendant's plea; fold.

Reply *v.t.* & *i.* to answer; to respond.

Repopulate *v.t.* to populate a fresh.

Report *v.t.* & *i.* to make official or formal statement; to bring back account of; to relate an ascertained fact; to tell as news; to narrate; to announce.

Reportable *adj.* able to be published.

Repose *v.t.* to give rest; to take rest; to place trust in.

Reposit *v.t.* to lay in safety.

Reposure *n.* peace; rest.

Repousse *adj.* & *n.* (of metal) hammered into relief from reverse side.

Reprehend *v.t.* to rebuke; to censure; to find fault with; to take exception to.

Represent *v.t.* to place likeness of before mind or senses; to call up before the mind; to describe or depict; to play the part of.

Representable *adj.* that may be represented.

Repress *v.t.* to quell; to subdue; to put down; to keep under; to suppress.

Reprieve *v.t.* to suspend the execution of (condemned person).

Reprimand *v.t.* to rebuke for a fault. *n.* a severe reproof.

Reprint *v.t.* to print another edition of.

Reprisal *n.* the act of retaliation.

Reprise *n.* yearly payment of rent; retaliation.

Reproach *v.t.* (of look, etc.) convey reproach to; to upbraid; to scold.

Reprobate *v.t.* to reject; to express disapproval for.

Reproduce *v.t.* & *i.* to produce copy of representation of.

Reproduction *n.* the act of reproducing; propagation.

Reproof *n.* blame; reproach; rebuke.

Reprove *v.t.* to blame; to rebuke; to charge with a fault orally.

Reptant *adj.* creeping.

Reptile *n.* crawling animal of the class including snakes; an animal that crawls or moves on its belly.

Republic *n.* a state in which the government is carried on by elected representatives; a commonwealth.

Repudiate *v.t.* & *i.* to disown; to divorce one's wife; to disavow or to reject.

Repugn *v.t.* & *i.* to offer opposition; to strive against.

Repugnance *n.* inconsistency; aversion; dislike.

Repulse *v.t.* to rebuff; to reject; to drive back (attack, attacking enemy) by force of arms.

Repulsion *n.* the act of repulsing; aversion.

Repulsive *adj.* repellant; loathsome.

Reputable *adj.* of good repute; honourable; held in esteem.

Reputation *n.* what is generally said or belived about a person's or thing's character; good name.

Repute *n.* to consider; to reckon.

Request *n.* asking for something; prayer; petition; a thing asked for; demand; entreaty; suit.

Requiem *n.* mass or musical service for the dead; dirge.

Require *v.t.* to demand as of right; to order; to claim as call for.

Requisite *adj* & *n.* essential, needed.

Requisteness *n.* necessity.

Requisition *n.* order to furnish supplies for army, etc.

Requite *v.t.* to reply; to make return for; to reward.

Reredos *n.* ornamental screen covering wall above back of alter.

Res *n.* thing; property.

Rescind *v.t.* to revoke; to cancel; to abrogate; to render null.

Rescribe *v.t.* to write again.

Rescript *n.* a ruler's edict; what is rewritten.

Rescue *v.t.* to set free from custody; to deliver from an attack, danger.

Research *n.* a careful inquiry; a critical investigation. *v.t.* to search again.

Resect *v.t.* (*Surg.*) to pare down (bone, cartilage, etc.)

Resemble *v.t.* to be like; to have similarity to; to bear similitude of.

Resent *v.t* & *i.* to feel indignation at; to be angry at; to consider as affront.

Reservation *n.* reserve; limitation.

Reserve *v.t.* to hold over; to lay up for future time; to retain possession or control of by stipulation; to postpone use or enjoyment or treatment of.

Reserved *adj.* reticent; not free; protected; cautious.

Reservedly *adv.* without openness; with reserve.

Reservist *n.* member of reserve forces.

Reservoir *n.* a receptacle for fluid, *esp.* one for storing water.

Reship *v.t.* to put again on board a ship.

Reside *v.t.* to dwell permanently; to be inherent in; to sink or settle down as a deposit; to rest.

Residence *n.* a place where one resides; habitation; abode.

Resident *adj.* residing; having quarters in a place; inherent.

Residual *adj.* & *n.* remaining after a part has been separated; left as residuum.

Residue *n.* (*Chem.*) residuum; the remainder; what is left over.

Resign *v.t.* & *i.* to relinquish; to surrender; to hand over; to retire.

Resignation *n.* resigning of an office; submission; document conveying it.

Resigned *adj.* having resigned oneself; submissive.

Resile *v.t.* to rebound; to recoil; to resume former shape.

Resiliency *n.* the act of rebounding.

Resin *n.* a kind of gum secreted by certain trees. *v.t.* to paint with resin.

Resiniferous *adj.* yielding resin.

Resinify *v.t.* to make resinous.

Resist *v.t.* & *i.* to oppose; to repel.

Resoluble *adj.* that can be dissolved.

Resolute *adj.* determined; firm; constant; unshrinking; steadfast.

Resolution *n.* resolute temper or character or conduct.

Resolve *v.t.* & *i.* to analyse; to break up into component parts; to explain.

Resolvent *adj.* having the power of resolving.

Resonant *v.t.* resounding; echoing.

Resonator *n.* appliance for giving resonance to sounds.

Resorb *v.t.* to abrorb again.

Resorbence *n.* absorption.

Resort *v.i.* to have recourse; to turn for help to; to go.

Resort *v.t.* to sort again.

Resound *v.i.* & *t.* to produce an echo; to repeat loudly; to fill with sound.

Resource *n.* means of supplying a want; an expedient; quick intelligence; possibility of help, country's collective means for support and defence.

Respect *n.* deferential esteem; honour; estimation; due attention; partiality.

Respectable *adj.* deserving respect; holding a fair social status.

Resperse *v.t.* to sprinkle.

Respire *v.t.* & *i.* to breathe or inhale air; to recover one's breath.

Respite *n.* dealy permitted in the discharge of an obligation or suffering of a penalty, postponement, interval of rest.

Resplendence *n.* lustre; brilliance.

Respond *v.t.* to reply; to make answer; to correspond; be analogous.

Response *n.* an answer given; a reply or retort; feeling.

Rest *v.i.* & *t.* to lie or relay on; to lie in sleep or death; to be still; to place on support; to depend or rely on something; to give relief or respose to.

Restaurant *n.* a place where refreshments are sold; an eating-house.

Restful *adj.* soothing; free from disturbance; quiet.

Rest-harrow *n.* a toughrooted shrub.

Resting *adj.* relying.

Restitution *n.* resumption of original state by elasticity; reparation, amend, indemnification.

Restive, Restiff *adjs.* refusing to go forward; refractory; obstinate; stubborn.

Restless *adj.* sleepless; uneasy; never still, turbulent; unsettled.

Restock *v.t.* to store up again.

Restoration *n.* act of restoring; recovery; renewal.

Restore *v.t.* to bring back to original condition; to renew; to return; to re-establish.

Restrain *v.t.* to keep in check; to put under control; to press; to confine; to limit.

Restrict *v.t.* to confine; to limit; to restrain within bounds.

Resty *adj.* indolent; restive.

Result *v.t.* to come out; to follow; to end in a specified way.

Resultant *adj.* & *n.* following a result.

Resume *v.t.* & *i.* a summary; a recapitulation.

Resummon *v.t.* to call again.

Resupinate *adj.* (Bot. of leaf etc.), inverted; bottom up.

Resurge *v.t.* to rise again from death.

Resurgence *n.* the act of resurging.

Resurrect *v.t.* to revive practice or memory of; to take out from the grave.

Resurvey *v.t.* to make a survey again.

Resuscitate *v.t.* & *i.* to revive; to restore to life.

Retable *n.* the frame at the back of an altar.

Retail *n.* sale of goods in small quantities.

Retain *v.t.* to keep in possession; to reserve; to keep in mind.

Retake *v.t.* to take back.

Retaliate *v.t. & i.* to repay in kind; to retort; to revenge.

Retard *v.t. & i.* to make slow; to delay progress; to put off.

Retaste *v.t.* to taste again.

Retch *v.t.* to make motion of vomiting.

Retecious *adj.* resembling as network.

Retention *n.* power of retaining; failure to secrete.

Retentive *adj.* having the power of characteristic of retaining things.

Reticence *n.* reserve in speech; uncommunicative.

Reticulate *v.t.* to divide into a network.

Reticule *n.* a lady's netted or other bag for carrying things.

Reticulum *n.* reticulated membrane, net-like structure, etc.

Retiform *adj.* of the form of a net.

Retina *n.* the layer at the back of the eyeball consisting of a fine network of optic nerves.

Retinue *n.* a train of attendants upon someone.

Retire *v.t. & i.* to withdraw from place or company or occupation.

Retirement *n.* state of having retired from office; seclusion; privacy.

Retort *v.t. & i.* to requite in kind; to turn; to throw back; to tell againt.

Retorter *n.* one who retorts.

Retouch *v.t.* to touch again; to improve by fine touches.

Retrace *v.t.* go back over again; to trace back (one's step, way) to source.

Retract *v.t. & i.* to draw back; to shrink back; to withdraw.

Retraverse *v.t.* to traverse again.

Retread *v.t.* to tread again.

Retreat *v.t.* to recede; to go back; to retire.

Retrench *v.t. & i.* to cut off; to deduct; to reduce the amount of; to live at a less expense; to deduct.

Retrial *n.* a fresh trail.

Retribute *v.t.* to pay back.

Retrieve *v.t. & i. & n.* to regain possession of; to gain back; to restore to a good state; to recover by investigation.

Retriever *n.* a dog used for retrieving game.

Retro *pref.* in the sense of 'backwards', 'behind'.

Retrogress *v.t.* to move backwards.

Retroject *v.t.* to cast back.

Retrospect *n.* backward view; review of past time; survey of past events.

Retroversion *n.* a turning back.

Retrude *v.t.* to thrust back.

Rettery *n.* a place for softening hemp of flax.

Return *v.t. & i.* to come or go back; to bring; to send back; to retort; to mention; to say in reply.

Retuse *adj.* (*Bot.*) with broad end and central depression (of leaf or similar part).

Reunite *v.t.* & *i.* to unite again; to join after separation.

Revalue *v.t.* to value again.

Reveal *v.t.* to make known in a supernatural manner; to disclose; to divulge; to show; to let appear.

Reveille *n.* the bugle or drum call for the troops to get up in the morning.

Revel *v.i.* to make merry, to be riotously festive; to carouse; to take keen delight in.

Revelation *n.* disclosing of knowledge by a supernatural legency.

Revelry *n.* noisy festivity.

Revendication *n.* claiming back in a formal way.

Revenge *v.t.* to satisfy oneself by retaliation; to return injury for injury; to avenge.

Revenue *n.* a state's annual income from different sources; department collecting state revenue.

Reverberate *v.t.* & *i.* (rare) rebound, react upon; to echo or throw or reflect (sound, light, heat); to relfect or be reflected.

Revere *v.t.* to regard as sacred; to venerate.

Reverence *n.* feeling of deep respect; veneration.

Reverend *adj.* deserving reverence by age; a title of respect for the clergy.

Reverent *adj.* feeling or showing reverence.

Reverential *adj.* proceeding from reverence.

Reverie *n.* a day-dream; musing; delusion; a fanatic theory.

Reversal *n.* a change or overthrowing; reversing or being reversed.

Reversing *adj.* turning in the opposite direction.

Reversion *n.* passing of an estate back to grantor or his heirs; right of succession to such estate; reverting.

Revert *v.i.* to turn back; to return to the original position; to fall back; to recur in thought or talk.

Revest *v.t.* to clothe again.

Revet *v.i.* to face a wall with a harder material.

Review *n.* survey inspection; periodical in which events, books, etc. are reviewed.

Reviewal *n.* a reviewing.

Revigorate *v.t.* to invigorate; to add new energy to.

Revile *v.t.* to abuse, to vilify, to upbraid, to rail at; to call by ill names.

Revisal *n.* revision.

Revise *v.t.* to look over again; to re-examine; to reconsider and amend faults.

Reviser *n.* one who revises.

Revision *n.* the act of re-examining; revising.

Revisit *v.t.* to visit again.

Revival *n.* reviving or being revived; recovery to life; restoration to bodily or mental vigour or to life or consciousness.

Revive *v.i.* & *t.* to bring to consciousness; to reanimate; to restore to natural form.

Revivify *v.t.* to restore to vigour or life; to animate.

Reviviscence *n.* return to life.

Reviviscent *adj.* restoring life.

Revoke *v.t.* & *i.* to repeal; to withdraw; to cancel; to annul; to declare void.

Revolt *v.t.* & *i.* to rise to rebellion; to rise against a ruler; to cast off allegiance; to affect with disgust.

Revolute *adj.* with edge rolled backwards. *v.i.* (*sl.*)to engage in political revolution.

Revolution *n.* revolving; fundamental change, complete change.

Revolutionary *adj.* & *n.* an instigator of a revolution; pertaining to revolution.

Revolve *v.t.* & *i.* to turn round to rotate; to cause to turn; to ponder over.

Revolver *n.* (*esp.*) a pistol that will fire several shots without reloading; one who or that which revolves.

Revue *n.* loosely constructed play or series of scenes satirizing current events.

Revulsion *n.* a drawing away; sudden change of feeling; counter irritation.

Reward *n.* retribution; a return for services of for merit; recompense.

Rex *n.* a king.

Reynard *n.* proper name for the fox.

Rhapsody *n.* an epic poem; an extravagant composition in high-flown style.

Rhapsodist *n.* one who writes rhapsodies.

Rhea *n.* a kind of American ostrich.

Rhenish *adj.* & *n.* Rhine wine.

Rhetor *n.* ancient Greek or Roman teacher or professor of rhetoric, an orator.

Rhetoric *n.* art of speaking or writing in an impressive style.

Rhetorical *adj.* pertaining to rhetoric.

Rheum *n.* watery secretion from the body.

Rheumatic *adj.* subject to rheumatism.

Rheumaticky *n.* (colloq.) like or having rheumatism.

Rheumatism *n.* a disease marked by inflammation and pain in the joints.

Rheumy *adj.* full of rheum.

Rhinal *adj.* of nostril or nose.

Rhinoceros *n.* large quadruped with thick plated skin and strong horn on the nose.

Rhodanic *adj.* producing a red colour.

Rhodium *n.* a kind of metal; a kind of scented wood.

Rhododendron *n.* evergreen shrub with large flowers like those of rose.

Rhomboid *adj.* & *n.* a figure like a rhomb with only the opposite sides equal.

Rhotacism *n.* erroneous pronunciation of the letter '*r*'.

Rhythm *n.* measured flow of words in verse or prose; movement with regular succession.

Riant *adj.* cheerful; smiling.

Rib *n.* one of the curved bones from sternum of spine.

Ribald *adj.* scurrilous; irreverent; indecent. *n.* a lewd person.

Ribaldry *n.* ribald talk; vulgar, obscene language.

Rhomb *n.* a quadrilateral figure with equal sides but unequal angles.

Rhubarb *n.* kind of garden plant used in cookery.

Rhythm *n.* metre, measured flow of words (regular movements), periodical accent.

Ribbands *n.* strips of wood.

Riant *adj.* cheeful, similing.

Ribald *n.* & *adj.* a jester, one who uses indecent language, obscene.

Riband *n.* a ribbon.

Ribes *n.* the plants of goose-berry.

Ribston *n.* a kind of apple.

Rice *n.* the plant; pearl-white seeds of an oriental plant used as food.

Rich *adj.* wealthy, having riches; (of sounds, smells, colours) deep, not thin; valuable; fertile.

Rick *n.* a stack of hay or corn.

Rickets *n.* a disease of children in which the bones are softened.

Ricochet *n.* skipping on water or ground of a cannon-ball or bullet.

Rictus *n.* expanse or gape of person's or animal's mouth; bird's beak or flower with two-lipped corolla.

Rid *v.t.* to abolish (pest); to relieve of. *adj.* free; clear.

Riddle *n.* an enigma or puzzle; a mysterious question; a coarse sieve.

Riddling *adj.* perplexing.

Ride *v.t.* & *i.* to sit on horse back; to be carried by a horse, cycle or train etc. *n.* a journey in public conveyance.

Ridge *n.* a line of junction in which two sloping surfaces meet; a mountain range.

Rife *adv.* of common occurrence; prevailing; current; numerous.

Rifle *v.t.* to search and rob; to plunder; to injure; to break; to strip off; to make spiral groves in the barrel of a gun.

Rift *n.* fissure, chasm, crack in earth or rock; opening in cloud etc.

Rig *v.t.* to provide a ship with spars, to fit; to clothe.

Riggish *adj.* wanton.

Right *adj.* correct; straight; just; fit; lawful; true; most convenient; well performed; on the right hand; satisfactory; well-advised.

Righteous *adj.* just, holy, equitable, virtuous, upright, honest.

Rightful *adj.* legitimate; just; lawful.

Right-minded *adj.* well dsiposed.

Rightness *n.* conformity to truth.

Rightwards *adj.* towards the right.

Rigid *adj.* harsh, strict; that cannot be bent, inflexible; unyielding.

Rigidity *n.* inflexibiltiy; stiffness; strictness; severity.

Riglet *n.* a piece of wood used for picture frames.

Rigmarole *n.* meaningless talk or string of words.

Rigor *n.* sudden chill with shivering before fever.

Rigour *n.* strictness; harshness; hardship; austerity of life; intense coldness.

Rile *v.t.* to irritate; to make angry.

Rill *n.* a tiny stream.

Rille *n.* a trench or narrow valley on the moon's surface.

Rim *n.* (*Naut.*) surface of the water; the raised edge or border of a thing, the margin; verge.

Rime *n.* hoar-frost. *v.t.*to congeal into frost.

Rimple *n.* a fold or wrinkle.

Rind *n.* skin; bark, external husk; surface; peel.

Rinderpest *n.* disease of ruminants *esp.* oxen; cattle-plague.

Ring *v.t.* & *i.* to sound like a bell.

Ring *n.* a circlet band usually of precious metal worn on the fingers; metallic sound of bell; anything circular.

Ringent *adj.* (*Bot.*) grinning; gaping.

Ringleader *n.* the leader of a ring of people; instigator in riot.

Ringlet *n.* small ring; a hanging curl; lock of hair; ring-shaped mark (rare.)

Ringworm *n.* a contagious skin-disease in circular patches.

Rink *n.* a sheet of ice used for curling or skating. *v.t.* to skate on ring with roller-skates.

Rinker *n.* one who skates on a rink.

Rinse *v.t.* to wash out or cleanse with water; to wash off soap from cloth.

Riot *n.* disturbance of the peace by a crowd; tumult, disorder; unrestrained indulgence or display.

Rip *v.t.* & *i.* to tear up forcibly; to split; to rush along. *n.* act of ripping; a worthless horse; a disolute person; a tear or rent.

Ripe *adj.* mature; ready to be used; eaten or drunk; consummate; developed; ready for action.

Ripen *v.t.* & *i.* to mature; to make ripe; to become ready.

Riposte *n.* quick return thrust in fencing. *v.i.* to deliver riposte.

Ripper *n.* a tool for ripping.

Rise *v.i.* to get out of bed; to get up from !ying; sitting posture; to become erect; to make revolt; to grow up.

Riser *n.* one who rises.

Risible *adj.* inclined to laugh, ludicrous.

Rising *n.* eminence; the act of ascending; insurrection; prominence.

Risk *n.* chance or possibility of hazard; danger; chance of bad consequences; peril.

Risorial *adj.* concerning laughter.

Risque *adj.* of doubtful propriety; suggestive of indecency.

Rissole *n.* fried ball or cake of meat or fish mixed with breadcrumbs etc.

Rite *n.* a religious ceremony; religious deservance.

Ritual *n.* a prescribed order for performing religious ,service; performance of ritual acts.

Rivage *n.* a bank or coast; shore; bank.

Rival *adj.* & *n.* a person or thing that competes with another.

Rive *v.t.* & *i.* to split; to strike or rend asunder.

Rivet *n.* a bolt for fastening together two pieces of metal.

Roach *n.* a small fresh-water fish; upward curve in foot of square sail.

Road *n.* a way prepared to travel on; an open way or public passage; a higher way; route.

Roam *v.t.* & *i.* to wander; to ramble; to walk about in an unsystematic manner; to range.

Roan *adj.* bay or sorrel; with coat of which the prevailing colour is thickly interspersed with another.

Roar *v.t.* & *i.* to make a loud sound; to utter a loud deep sound as of a lion.

Roaring *n.* a loud cry.

Roast *v.t.* & *i.* to cook or heat by exposure to the open fire or sun, to ridicule; heat or calcine ore in furnace.

Roaster *n.* one who roasts.

Rob *v.t.* & *i.* to plunder; to deprive of; to take forcibly; to commit robbery.

Robe *n.* a long loose garment; a lady dress in one piece.

Robin *n.* a small sing ng bird with red breast.

Robot *n.* an apparently human automation; an intelligent and obedient but impersonal machine.

Roburite *n.* a flameless explosive of high power.

Robust *adj.* of strong health and physique; of strong constitution; vigorous.

Robustly *adv.* in a robust manner.

Roc *n.* gigantic bird of Eastern tales.

Rock *v.t.* & *i.* to move gently to and fro; to shake; to oscillate.

Rock *n.* solid part of earth's crust; a mass of this.

Rocker *n.* one of the curved bars on which a cradle etc. rocks.

Rocket *n.* a kind of plant; a cylindrical propelled by ignition.

Rocking *adj.* moving backwards and forwards.

Rococo *adj.* antiquated; (of furniture, architecture, etc.) much conventional. *n.* the rococo style.

Rod *n.* a cane or birch for flogging; a slender straight round stick or metal bar.

Rodent *n.* an animal with strong cutting teeth that gnaws its food.

Roe *n.* a kind of small deer; the female of hart; the eggs of fishes.

Roebuck *n.* the male of roe-deer.

Rogatory *adj.* relating to investigation.

Rogue *n.* elephant living apart from the herd and of savage temper, any large wild animal of similar character.

Roister *v.t.* to revel in a noisy manner; to make an uproar.

Role *n.* an actor's part; a man's appoin- ted duty.

Roll *n.* a cylinder formed by turning paper, cloth etc. over on itself without folding; continuous sound of thunder or drum of shouting.

Roller *n.* a cylinder used alone or as part of a machine.

Rolling *adj.* turning on axis; moving from side to side.

Rollick *v.t.* to enjoy; to be jovial.

Rom *n.* a gipsy.

Romaic *n.* language of modern Greece. *adj.* of or in Romaic.

Roman *adj.* & *n.* citizen of Rome; a kind of type.

Romance *n.* medieval tale of chivalry; a novel; fabulous rale of adventure.

Rood *n.* quarter of an acre; small piece of land; a cross or crucifix.

Roody *adj.* coarse.

Roof *n.* the upper covering of house or building; top of a covered vehicle.

Room *n.* an apartment in a house; opportunity; scope; space occupied; status; capacity.

Roost *n.* a bird's resting place; sleeping accommodation.

Root *n.* the part of the plant below the surface of the earth; imbedded part of a structure; source; origin; basis.

Rope *n.* a stout cordage; a string.

Roquet *n.* & *v.t.* striking of a croquet-ball against another; to make roquet; to hit (ball) thus.

Roral *adj.* pertaining to dew.

Rosaceous *adj.* of the Rosaceae or order of plants including the rose.

Rosaniline *n.* a kind of red dye.

Rosary *n.* a rose garden bed; a string of beads; a chaplet, prayer; a garland of roses.

Rose *n.* prickly bush bearing beautiful fragrant flowers.

Roseate *adj.* rose coloured; rosy.

Rosemary *n.* an evergreen fragrant shrub.

Rosette *n.* imitation of rose made of ribbons.

Rosicrucian *adj.* & *n.* (member) of a society devoted to occult lore.

Rosin *n.* a solid residue or resin left after distilling oil from turpentine. *v.t.* to rub the bow of a violin with rosin.

Rosinels *n.* the state of being rosy.

Roster *n.* a list showing persons who perform the duties in turn.

Rostrate *adj.* having the form a beak.

Rostrum *n.* platform for public speaking; a beak.

Rosulate *adj.* packed like the petals of a rose.

Rosy *n.* coloured like a red rose.

Rot *v.t.* & *i.* to undergo decay by putrefaction or from want to use.

Rota *n.* a list of persons who work in rotation; a round of duties.

Rotary *adj.* acting by rotation; revolving.

Rotate *v.i.* & *t.* to revolve; to move round a centre or axis.

Rotation *n.* the act of turning; established order of succession.

Rotative *adj.* turning on its axis like a wheel.

Rote *n.* mere habituation; a frequent repetition as a means of fixing some fact.

Rotor *n.* the revolving part of a machine.

Rotten *adj.* decayed; putrid; decomposed; worthless.

Rotund *adj.* sonorous grandiloquent; rounded, plump.

Rouble *n.* Russian silver coin worth 2s 1½ d.

Roue *n.* a debauchee; rake.

Rouge *n.* red powder used to colour cheeks and lips; plate-powder of oxide of iron.

Rough *adj.* uneven or irregular surface; deficient in finish; incomplete not smooth or level; violent, disorderly.

Rough-cast *adj.* coated with mixed lime and gravel. *n.* plaster of lime and gravel for walls. *v.t.* to plaster in a rough manner.

Roulette *n.* a kind of gambling game; a device of keeping hair curly; a toothed wheel used by engravers.

Round *adj.* candid; done with or involving circular motion; entire, continuous, all together; spherical or circular or cylindrical.

Round *adv.* circularly; on all sides. *prep.* on every side of; about.

Round *n.* a round object; circumference; series of action; turn of duty; extent; circular motion.

Roundel *n.* a circle; a small round disk.

Roundelay *n.* a country song; birds' song.

Rounder *n.* (*sl.*) a habitual loafer or drunkard; (*pl.*) a ball game.

Roundly *adv.* bluntly; plainly; in a thorough going way.

Roundsman *n.* a tradesman's employee going round for orders.

Roup *v.t.* kinds of poultry disease. *n.* an acution.

Rouse, Roose *v.t.* & *i.* to stir up from sleep or equiescence, to stir up; to become active (*usu.* up), to provoke temper of; to start; draught of liquor.

Roust *v.t.* to drive away.

Rout *n.* disorderly retreat of defeated troops, uproar, a party of revellers or rioters.

Route *n.* a way or road; passage taken to reach a destination.

Routine *n.* a fixed order of doing things; a regular course of action.

Rove *v.i.* to wander aimlessly; to roam; to move from place to place.

Rover *n.* a pirate; a wanderer; a sea-robber.

Row *n.* a rank or file; number of persons or things in a line.

Rowing *n.* the act of moving boats.

Rowdy *adj.* noisy and disorderly. *n.* a rowdy person.

Rowel *n.* spiked revolving disk at end of spur. *v.t.* to insert a rowel in.

Royal *adj.* splendid, princely, majestic, belonging to family of, in service or under patronage of, a king or queen.

Rub *v.t.* & *i.* to subject to friction; to clean or to polish or to smooth by friction; to erase; to grind; to sharpen.

Rubber *n.* a tough elastic substance made from coagulated juice of certain plants.

Rubric *n.* the heading of a chapter or special passages printed in red or in conspicuous types.

Ruby *n.* size of type; glowing red colour, red pimple on nose or face.

Ruche *n.* a plaited frill; frill or quilling of gauze. *v.t.* to trim with ruche.

Ruck *n.* a heap, a ruffle.

Ruckle *v.t.* & *i.* to rattle; to crease; to gurgle.

Rucksack *n.* kind of knapsack slung from shoulders & resting on back.

Ruction *n.* dispute; row.

Rudder *n.* a flat piece hanged to the stern of a ship or boat for steering with; guiding principle.

Ruddle *n.* red ochre; red chalk.

Rude *adj.* primitive; simple; rough; in natural state; coarse; uncivilized.

Rudiment *n.* the first principles of a subject; imperfect beginning of something.

Rue *v.t.* to wish undone or unbefallen; to repent of; to regret.

Rue a bitter-leaved evergreen shrub.

Ruff *n.* a frill of linen worn round the neck; a bird allied to the sandpiper.

Ruffian *n.* a lawless brutal person; a robber; a murderer.

Ruffle *v.t. & i.* to disturb smoothness or tranquility of (feathers, hair, water, temper, brow).

Ruffler *n.* a swaggerer; a beggar posing as a maimed soldier.

Ruffling *n.* mental disturbance; low sound of a drum.

Rug *n.* a coverlet of thick wool.

Rugate *adj.* wrinkled, with ridges.

Rugby *n.* form of foot-ball in which ball may be carried.

Rugged *adj.* harsh, unpolished, austere; of rough uneven surface.

Rugose *adj.* wrinkled; corrugated.

Ruin *n.* destruction; downfall; ruined state; fallen or impaired state.

Ruination *n.* perdition.

Ruinous *adj.* in ruins; bringing to ruin; decayed.

Rule *n.* government, sway, principle to which action conforms or should conform; canon; test; established.

Ruler *n.* a person bearing rule; one who rules or governs; a sovereign.

Ruling *n.* authoritative pronouncement. *adj.* governing; reigning.

Rulley *n.* flat four-wheeled dray; lorry.

Rum *n.* spirit made from sugarcane.

Rumble *v.i.* to make sound as of distant thunder.

Ruminant *n. & adj.* an animal that chews the cud; contemplative.

Ruminate *v.i.* (*fig.*) to meditate upon; to chew the cud; to chew again and again.

Ruminator *n.* one who ruminates.

Rummage *v.t. & i.* to ransack; to make a thorough search.

Rummer *n.* a large drinking-glass.

Rumour *n.* general talk, report, or current statement of doubtful accuracy.

Rump *n.* a person's posterior; the tail-end of a beast or bird; the buttock.

Rumple *v.t.* to crease; to wrinkle.

Rumpus *n.* an uproar; disturbance.

Run *v.t. & i.* smooth motion; to move swiftly; to spread rapidly; to gallop; to flee; to turn as a wheel.

Runabout *n.* a vagabond; roving; a small open wagon or motor-car.

Runagate *n.* a vagabond.

Runaway *n.* a fugitive; horse bolting.

Runcinate *adj.* having saw-like teeth.

Rune *n.* (*usu.* in *pl.*) letter of early Teutonic alphabet; marks of mysterious significance resembling them.

Rung *n.* a short stick fixed as cross-bar *esp.* in ladder.

Runlet *n.* a small stream; a cask for wine.

Runnel *n.* a small brook; gutter.

Runner *n.* a racer; a messenger; a creeping stem that issue for main stem.

Running *adj.* consecutive; successive.

Runt *n.* an ox or cow of a very small breed.

Rupee *n.* the silver coin of India.

Ruption *n.* a bursting out.

Rupture *n.* breach of relation; breaking; fracture; hernia.

Rural *adj.* in or of the country, suiting the country, rustic.

Ruse *n.* a trick; stratagem; wile.

Rush *n.* marsh plant with slender pithy stem; a thing of no value; a swift movement; attack; charge.

Rushy *adj.* full or rushes.

Rusk *n.* a piece of bread cut from loaf and rebaked; a kind of light biscuit.

Russ *n.* the Russian language.

Russian *n.* native and language of Russia. *adj.* pertaining to Russia.

Rust *n.* plant disease with rust-coloured spots; kinds of fungus.

Rustic *adj.* of or like country people or peasants; unpolished; of rude workmanship.

Rusticate *v.t.* & *i.* to retire to the country; to send down from university for a time as punishment.

Rusticity *n.* rustic manner.

Rustle *v.t.* & *i.* sound as of blown leaves or pattering rain.

Rustler *n.* a person who steals farm animals.

Rusty *adj.* affected with rust; impaired; unfit with disuse.

Rut *n.* periodic sexual excitement of male deer, etc.

Rutted *adj.* (of a road or path) with deep tracks that have been made by wheels.

Rutting *adj.* (of male animals, especially deer) in a time of sexual activity.

Ruth *n.* pity, 'compassion' mercy; sorrow for the misery of others.

Rutilant *adj.* shining brilliant.

Rutty *adj.* filled with sexual desires.

Ryot *n.* an Indian peasant.

S

S nineteenth letter of the English alphabet; any object shaped like S. Roman numerial for 70 to 70,000.

Sab *n.* an opponent of blood sports.

Sabre *n.* a cavalry sword with a blade curved backward at the point. *v.t.* to strike with sabre.

Sac *n.* a bag of membrane forming a cavity; a receptacle for liquid.

Sack *n.* a large bag of coarse textile stuff; a kind of loose garment; plunder. *v.t.* to put in sacks; to plumber; to defeat in match or fight.

Sacred *adj.* consecrated to a deity; holy; divine; pertaining to the worship of God.

Sacredly *adv.* in a holy manner.

Sacrifice *n.* the slaughter of an animal for offering to a deity; victim; offering; abandonment; surrender; ruin; the giving up of something.

Sad *adj.* sorrowful; incorrigible, shocking, deplorably bad; showing or causing sorrow; (of colour) dull.

Saddle *n.* a rider's seat on the back of a horse or on a bicycle; the seat of a bicycle; any thing shaped like it.

Safe *adj.* uninjured; out of danger; affording security or not involving danger; secure.

Safety *n.* freedom from danger or risks; preservation from hurt.

Saffian *n.* tanned and dyed leather of goatskin or sheepskin.

Saffron *n.* the stigma of a plant of crocus family used for colouring. *v.t.* to colour with saffron.

Sag *v.i.* to sink unevenly under pressure; decline in price.

Sagittarius *n.* the ninth sign of the Zodiac; the Archer.

Sago *n.* a kind of palm which yields a dry granulated starch.

Sail *n.* a piece of canvas extended on rigging to catch the wind and propel a vessel, voyage or excursion in a sailing-vessel.

Saint *n.* a canonized person; one of the blessed; one of God's chosen people; a saint-like person.

Salable, Saleable *adjs.* fit for sale.

Salacious *adj.* lustful; lecherous.

Salamander *n.* a person who can endure great heat; a lizard-like animal supposed to live in fire.

Sal-ammoniac *n.* ammonium chloride.

Salangane *n.* a kind of swallow.

Salary *n.* periodical payment for service; pay. *v.t.* to pay for service.

Sale *n.* buying and selling transaction.

Salience *n.* the state of being salient.

Saline *adj.* like salt; impregnated with salt; chiefly composed of salt.

Saliva *n.* the liquid of the mouth and the tongue that assists digestion.

Salivate *v.t. & i.* to produce unusal secretion of saliva; discharge saliva in excess.

Sallenders *n. pl.* eruption inside the hock of the hindleg of a horse.

Sallow *n.* low-growing kinds of willow. *adj.* of pale-brown colour.

Sally *n.* a rush of the besieged upon the besiegers; a sudden rush, a leap.

Saloon *n.* a spacious hall; large room; a large cabin; a railway carriage without compartments.

Salt *n.* substance obtained from sea water by evaporation or from the earth by mining used as seasoning, chloride of sodium.

Salter *n.* person who salts fish, etc.; workman at salt works; manufacturer of, dealer in salt.

Saltpan *n.* a hollow near the sea (or a vessel) used in getting salt by evaporation.

Salubrious *adj.* favourable to or promoting health; wholesome.

Salutation *n.* act of saluting; greeting; swords used in saluting.

Salute *n.* gesture of respect; homage; discharge of cannons as a sign of respect.

Saluter *n.* he who salutes.

Salutiferous *adj.* bringing health.

Salvation *n.* fact or state of being saved from sin and its consequences.

Salve *n.* a remedy; healing ointment for wounds or sores; something that soothes.

Salver *n.* a tray on which refreshment are served or anything presented.

Same *adj.* & *adv.* uniform; aforesaid; unvarying; previously referred to.

Sample *n.* specimen or pattern. *v.t.* to take or give samples of; to get an experience.

Sanatory *adj.* healing; pertaining to health.

Sanctify *v.t.* to purify from sin; to consecrate.

Sanction *n.* penalty or reward attached to a law; confirmation of law by supreme authority; influence that causes a rule to be observed.

Sanctitude *n.* saintliness.

Sanctity *n.* holiness; sacredness; purity.

Sanctuary *n.* a place recognized as holy or inviolable; a sacred place; church or holiest part of it; private retreat; a place of refuge; a church or temple; a place of safety.

Sand *n.* minute fragments of stone. *v.t.* to sprinkle or mix with sand; to bury under sand.

Sane *adj.* of sound mind; healthy; sensible; not mad.

Sangaree *n.* a kind of spiced wine.

Sanguification *n.* formation of blood from food.

Sanguinary *adj.* attended by slaughter; bloody; blood-thirsty.

Sanguine *adj.* & *n.* habitually hopeful; the colour of blood; optimistic; ardent; confident; anticipating the blast.

Sanhedrim *n.* supreme council and court of justice in ancient Jerusalem, of 71 members.

Sanicle *n.* a kind of plant.

Sanies *n.* thin matter secreted from a wound.

Sanify *v.t.* to improve health.

Sanitary *adj.* hygienic; free from the influences that deteriorate health; pertaining to health.

Sanitize *v.t.* to free from dirt, germs etc.; to make (a story, news etc.) less disturbing, shocking etc.

Sans *prep.* without.

Sap *n.* the vital juice of plants. *v.t.* to drain of sap; to dig up; to undermine.

Sapful *adj.* full of sap.

Sapid *adj.* not tasteless; (of talk, writing) not uninteresting; having (*esp.* agreeable) flavour, savoury.

Sapling *n.* a young tree.

Sapodilla *n.* a kind of evergreen tropical tree.

Saponaceous *adj.* having the qualities of soap; soapy.

Sponify *v.t.* to convert into soap.

Sapor *n.* sensation of taste; the peculiar taste of an object.

Sapphire *n.* kinds of humming bird; a transparent blue precious-stone.

Sappy *adj.* full of juice.

Sapro *pref.* in the sence of 'rotten', in scientific terms.

Saprogenic *adj.* growing on decaying matter.

Sapwood *n.* the external part of wood.

Saracen *n.* a Arab.

Saratoga *n.* lady's large travelling trunk.

Sarcasm *n.* a taunt, an ironical, bitter of wounding remark.

Sarcoma *n.* tumour of embryonic connective tissue.

Sarcophagus *n.* a stone coffin; a stone chest for receiving a dead body.

Sarcous *adj.* consisting of flesh.

Sard *n.* a variety of cornelian.

Sardine *n.* a kind of small fish of the herring kind; a kind of precious stone.

Sardonic *adj.* grimly jocular; mocking; full of bitter mockery.

Sardonyx *n.* a kind of precious stone.

Sargasso *n.* kinds of floating sea-weed.

Sark *n.* a shirt.

Sarmentose *adj.* having long roots.

Sarsaparilla *n.* kinds of smilax; drug made from their roots.

Sarsenet *n.* soft silk fabric used in lining.

Sartorial *adj.* pertaining to a tailor; tailoring.

Sash *n.* a scarf worn round the waist as part of uniform or as an ornament the frame holding window-glass.

Sassaby *n.* a large antelope of Africa.

Sassafras *n.* kind of scented bark used in medicine.

Sassolite *n.* native boric acid.

Satan *n.* personal name for the Devil.

Satanic, Satanical *adjs.* pertaining to Satan; diabolical.

Satchel *n.* a small bag of leather; a school bag.

Sate *v.t.* to gratify to the full; to surfeit.

Sateen *n.* glossy cotton or woollen fabric.

Satellite *n.* a planet revolving round another; a person's servile follower; a hanger-on.

Satire *n.* composition in which vice or folly is held up to ridicule; irony; this branch of literature; sarcasm.

Satiric *adj.* of or containing satire; sarcastic; bitter.

Satisfaction *n.* gratification of desire; payment of debt.

Satisfy *v.t.* & *i.* to meet the wishes of; to gratify; to make payment; to content.

Satrap ancient Persain provincial governor.

Saturate *v.t.* to impregnate thoroughly with; to fill with moisture; to soak.

Saturday *n.* the seventh day of the week.

Saturnine *adj.* morose, grave; of a sluggish gloomy temperament.

Satyr *n.* a woodland deity, half-man and half-goat; a lustful person.

Sauce *n.* a liquid perparation used with articles of food for improving their relish; a condiment; impudence.

Saucer *n.* a curved plate placed under a cup or flower-pot.

Saucy *adj.* impudent to superiors; insolent; cheeky; smart.

Saunter *v.t.* to walk in a leisurely manner; to wander or stroll about idly.

Saury *n.* a kind of sea-fish.

Sausage *n.* minced meat seasoned and stuffed into cylindrical cases.

Savable *adj.* able to be saved.

Savage *adj.* uncivilized; wild; furious; untamed; fierce; cruel; barbarous; out of temper.

Savant *n.* a man of learning; a distinguished person.

Save *v.t.* & *i.* to rescue or preserve from danger or harm; to make safe; to keep for future use.

Saveloy *n.* a highly seasoned dried sausage.

Saver *n.* one who saves; thrifty.

Savin *n.* a tree that yields a volatile oil.

Savionette *n.* a perfumed soap.

Saviour *n.* one who saves from destruction; a redeemer; deliverer.

Savory *n.* a herb like mind used in cookery.

Savour *n.* charcteristic taste or smell; flavour; suggestion of some quality. *v.t.* to have a particular taste.

Saw *n.* an old saying; a maxim.

Saw *n.* an instrument with toothed edge used for dividing wood, metal or stone. *v.t.* & *i.* to cut or make with saw.

Saxatile *adj.* living; growing on rocks.

Saxon *n.* North-German tribe who conquered England in the fifth century.

Say *v.t.* & *i.* to utter or to recite in speaknig voice; to recite; to promise; to form an opinion; select as example; as near enough.

Scabious *adj.* scabby; affected with mange.

Scaffold *n.* an elevated platform of timber for the execution of criminal.

Scalable *adj.* that may be scaled or climbed.

Scalariform *adj.* like a ladder.

Scald *v.t.* to injure or pain with hot liquid; to scorch; to cleanse with hot water.

Scale *n.* thin horny plate or layer projecting on the skin of animals; flake of skin; thin lamina on the surface of rust; dish of a balance; the sign Libra in the Zodiac.

Scalp *n.* skin and hair of the upper part of the head; top of the head.

Scamble *v.t.* to cut roughly; to mangle.

Scambler *n.* one who makes an interruption.

Scammony *n.* purgative resin.

Scamp *n.* a knave; a rascal; a rougue. *v.i.* to execute a work carelessly.

Scan *v.t.* & *i.* to test meter; to examine the metrical correctness of a line of poetry; to scruntinize; read over with emphasis on rhythm.

Scandal *n.* a shocked feeling; disgrace; defamation; backbiting; malicious talk. *v.t.* to defame; to reproach.

Scant *adj.* barely or not sufficient; deficient; having a scanty supply.

Scanty *adj.* of small amount or extent; barely sufficient; not ample.

Scape *n.* shaft of column; an escape; a slip.

Scapegoat *n.* one who is made to suffer for another.

Scapple *v.t.* to make a stone surface straight.

Scapula *n.* the shoulder-blade.

Scar *n.* mark left by a wound.

Scarab *n.* sacred beetle of ancient Egypt.

Scaramouch *n.* a baffoon; boastful coward.

Scarce *adj.* not plentiful; scanty; rare; uncommon; hard to find.

Scarcely *adv.* hardly; rarely; with difficulty; surely not.

Scare *v.t.* to strike with sudden terror; to terrify; to frighten.

Scaremonger *n.* one who creats panic.

Scarf *n.* a sort of light shawl; a long narrow piece of cloth worn round the neck of shoulders; necktie.

Scarf *v.t.* to join with scarf flench (whale).

Scarify *v.t.* to scratch skin or surface of all over; to make incisions in.

Scarlet *n.* & *adj.* brilliant red colour; scarlet cloth or clothes.

Scarp *n.* a steep slope; the inner slope of a ditch; perpendicular slope.

Scarred *adj.* marked with scars.

Scarus *n.* kinds of bright hued fish with parrot-like beak.

Scathe *n.* harm; injury. *v.t.* to injury; to damage.

Scathing *adj.* withering.

Scatter *v.t.* & *i.* to throw here and there; to disperse; to spread.

Scaup *n.* a kind of duck.

Scauper *n.* engraver's gouge.

Scavenger *n.* a person employed to keep the streets clean by removing refuse.

Scenario *n.* the plot of a play in which the order of scenes, story etc. are laid out.

Scene *n.* a place of actual or fictitious occurrence; stage of a theatre.

Scenery *n.* the natural features of a district; landscape characteristics; stage scenes.

Scenic *adj.* picturesque in grouping; of the stage.

Scent *v.t.* to discern by smell; to perfume; sniff to detect the odour of.

Scepsis *n.* philosophic doubt; sceptical philosophy.

Sceptic *n.* a person who questions the truth of religious doctrines; an atheist.

Sceptre *n.* a rod symbolizing sovereignty; royal power or authority.

Schedule *n.* a table of details or items.

Schema *n.* diagram; outline; essentiality.

Scheme *n.* a systematic arrangement; plan for doing a thing; an outline; project.

Schemer *n.* one who makes a scheme a plotter.

Scheming *n.* the act of planning; intriguing.

Schism *n.* the separation of the church; faction.

Schist *n.* crystalline rock whose components are arranged in layers.

Scholar *n.* a learned or erudite person; a person's discipline; a child at an elementary school.

Scholium *n.* ancient grammarian's marginal note on passage or word in classical author.

School *n.* an educational institution for boys and girls; a place of instruction.

Schooner *n.* a small sailing vessel with two or more masts.

Sciatic *adj.* of the hip.

Sciatica *n.* a neuralgia affecting the hip or thigh.

Science *n.* systematic knowledge; the physical or natural sciences as a whole.

Scientist *n.* one who is versed in science; a person learned in one or moral of the natural sciences.

Sciolism *n.* assumption of knowledge; conceit based on fancied wisdom.

Scion *n.* the shoot of a plant; a descendant.

Scissel *n.* a metal plate from which disks have been cut out; able to be cut.

Scissors *n. pl.* a cutting instrument consisting of two blades mounted on a pin.

Scoff *v.i.* to speak derisively of *esp.* religion or object of respect; to moct at.

Scoffer *n.* one who scoffs.

Scold *v.t.* & *i.* to find fault; to rail; to chide; to rebuke.

Scolex *n.* a tape-worm in its early stage.

Scolopendra *n.* centipede.

Scolytus *n.* a beetle which is destructive to trees.

Scomber *n.* a kind of fish.

Sconce *n.* a fort or earthwork; a candlestick to be attached to a wall.

Scone *n.* soft cake of barley meal or wheat-flour.

Scoop *n.* a short-handled deep shovel; a large dipping vessel for transferring liquids.

Scoot *v.i.* (*sl.*) to run; to dart off; shoot along.

Scooter *n.* a kind of child's toy.

Scope *n.* end aimed at; purpose; intention; sphere of observation or action; extent to which person or thing may or can range.

Scorch *v.t.* & *i.* to burn the surface of so as to discolour or injure or pain; become discoloured etc. with heat.

Score *n.* a notch cut; starting point of a race; a line cut or scratched or drawn; a set of twenty; dead-eye to hole strap; reckoning; number of points made by a player in certain games; piece of good fortune.

Scorer *n.* a keeper of score.

Scoria *n.* cellular lava or fragments of it; slag.

Scorn *n.* an object of contempt; derision; disdain; contempt.

Scornful *adj.* contemptuous; disdainful.

Scorpio *n.* the Scorpion; the eighth sign of zodiac.

Scorpioid *adj.* of the form of a scorpion's sting.

Scorpion *n.* lobster-like reptile with poisoned sting at its tail.

Scot *n.* a native of Scotland; payment of tax.

Scotch *v.t.* to wound without killing; to prevent motion; to support on wheel.

Scotfree *adj.* exempt from the payment of a tax.

Scotia *n.* moulding at the bottom of a column.

Scoto *pref.* in sense of 'darkness'.

Scotograph *n.* a writing instrument for the blind.

Scotoma *n.* obscuration of part of the field of vision.

Scoundrel *n.* a villain; a man without virtue; an unscrupulous person.

Scour *v.t.* to hasten; to cleanse by rubbing.

Scour *v.t.* & *i.* to rove; range; go along hastily, *esp.* in search or pursuit.

Scourge *n.* a lash for chastising something regarded as a means of bringing divine evil.

Scout *n.* a man sent out to reconnoitre; a kind of small fast-going aeroplane; a boy scout.

Scovel *n.* a mop for sweeping ovens.

Scow *n.* flat-bottomed boat.

Scowl *v.i.* to frown; to wear sullen look.

Scrabble *v.t.* & *i.* to scrawl.

Scrag *n.* a lean person; anything thin and lean; inferior part of neck of mutton.

Scramble *v.t.* & *i.* to struggle with competitors to secure a share of something.

Scran *n.* food; eatables.

Scranch *v.t.* to crunch; to grind with teeth.

Scrannel *adj.* (of sound) weak; feeble.

Scrap *n.* a small detached piece; fragment of something; rubbish.

Scrape *v.t.* & *i.* to level the surface of thing for polishing.

Scratch *v.t.* & *i.* to score surface of; wound slightly with claws or nails or something pointed; get scratched.

Scrawl *v.t.* & *i.* to write in hurried untidy way.

Screak *n.* a screech. *v.t.* to utter a sharp sound.

Scream *v.t.* & *i.* to utter a shrill cry; to whistle; to laugh loudly; to hoot.

Screech *v.t.* & *i.* to utter a shrill cry.

Screed *n.* a vehement address.

Screen *n.* a partition; an object of shelter; a curtain; sheet for display of lantern pictures; a large sieve.

Screw *n.* a piece of metal wire with spiral thread all round it used for fastening pieces of wood or metal.

Scribacious *adj.* habituated to writing.

Scribal *adj.* pertaining to a scribe.

Scribe *n.* a clerk or secretary; a writer; a penman.

Scrim *n.* a lining-cloth.

Scrinium *n.* a cylindrical box for rolled manuscripts.

Scrip *n.* a wallet; a small bag; a provisional certificate of money for a bank.

Script *n.* handwriting; a type resembling hand writing.

Scrivener *n.* one who makes a draft of documents; a writer; money-lender.

Scroll *n.* a roll of parchment or paper; a schedule or list; an architectural ornament; a tracery or ribbon in a spiral form.

Scroop *n.* a grating noise. *v.i.* to make a grating sound.

Scrotum *n.* the pouch containing the testicles.

Scrub *v.t.* & *i.* an insignificant person, animal, plant; worn or short bristled brush or moustache.

Scrubber *n.* one who or that which scrubs.

Scruff *n.* of the neck.

Scruple *n.* weight-unit of 20 grains; moral considerations.

Scrutator *n.* investigator; one who scrutinizes; a critic.

Scuddle *v.i.* to run with haste.

Scuffle *v.i.* to struggle confusedly with pushing about etc. *n.* a confused conflict; discoderly fight.

Scug *n.* an unmannerly spiritless person; sociability; sportsmanship.

Scull *v.t.* & *i.* to propel a boat by one oar only; to move boat with short oar.

Scullery *n.* back kitchen in which dishes are washed, etc.

Scullion *n.* one who washes kitchen utensils.

Sculpture *n.* art of forming representations by chiselling; carving; casting or modelling.

Scum *n.* impurities that rise to the surface of liquids; refuse; dregs.

Scupper *n.* a hole in ship's side to carry off water from desk.

Scurf *n.* fine flakes cast off when the underskin develops; any scaly matter.

Scurvy *adj.* paltry; dishonourable; contemptible; low; mischievous. *n.* a disease due to lack of fresh food.

Scutum *n.* a shield-like plate in certain animals; the knee-pan.

Scylla *n.* six-headed monster living on a rock.

Sea *n.* the large expanse of salt water covering the greater part of the earth's surface; the ocean; a large wave of the sea.

Seal *n.* an aquatic flesh-eating mammal; an impression attached to a document; a similar impression made on paper; significant mark.

Seam *n.* the joining line of two pieces of cloth; a scar; line of separation. *v.t.* to sew; to unite; to scar.

Seamy *adj.* containing seams.

Seance *n.* a meeting for exhibition or investigation of spiritualistic phenomenon.

Seaport *n.* a town with harbour.

Seasick *adj.* suffering sickness caused by motion of ship etc.

Sear *n.* to make callous or insensible; to deaden; to wither or blast; to scorch with hot iron.

Search *v.t.* & *i.* to look to find something; to seek out.

Season *n.* one of the four divisions of the year; one of the divisions of the year with distinguishable characteristics of temperature; suitable opportunity; rainfall;

time of plenty; period of indefinite length; period of indefinite or various length.

Seat *n.* a thing made or used for sitting on; chair; throne; stool; bench; occupation of a seat; situation.

Sebacious *adj.* of tallow or fat; fatty; secreting oily matter.

Secant *adj.* cutting. *n.* secant line; the radius of a circle produced to meet a tangent; ratio of this to radius.

Secession *n.* act of seceding.

Seclude *v.t.* to separate; to keep retired or away from company or restort.

Seclusion *n.* retirement; a secluded place or state; privacy; secluding.

Second *adj.* & *n.* next after the first; one who follows another; of subordinate importance or value.

Secondary *adj.* next in importance; subordinate; inferior in rank; supplementary.

Secret *adj.* kept private; concealed; not revealed; unrevealed; confidential.

Secretary *n.* a person employed to deal with correspondence.

Sect *n.* any religious denomination; adherents or a number of people of the same school of thought.

Sectary *n.* a member of a sect.

Sectile *adj.* able to be cut.

Section *n.* severance with a knife; a part cut of; a part of structure.

Sector *n.* a plane figure bounded by two radii of a circle; a mathematical instrument.

Secular *adj.* lasting for ages; coming once in a century; worldly.

Secund *adj.* arranged on one side only.

Secure *adj.* safe; confident; untroubled by danger or fear; impregnable; reliable.

Securiform *adj.* of the shape of an axe.

Securite *n.* an explosive used in mines.

Security *n.* thing that serves as a guard or guarantee or pledge.

Sadate *adj.* tranqil; calm; free from agitation; serious.

Sedative *adj.* & *n.* soothing; soothing medicine.

Sedent *adj.* quiet; inactive.

Sederunt *n.* sitting of ecclesiastical or other court, or of a company in conversation.

Sedge *n.* water-side plants resembling coarse grass.

Sediment *n.* matter which settles to the bottom of a liquid; dregs.

Sedition *n.* conduct or speech inciting to rebellion.

Seduce *v.t.* to lead astray; to lead into crime; to allure; to corrupt.

Seduction *n.* seducing; being seduced; tempting to an evil action.

Sedulous *adj.* diligent; laborious; persevering.

See *v.t.* & *i.* to perceive; descry; look at; to discover; to discern mentally.

Seed *n.* germs of flowering plants; unit of reproduction; single grain of this.

Seek *v.t.* & *i.* to try to make search or inquiry for; to endeavour to do; to get.

Seel *v.t.* to shut or close the eyes; to hoodwink.

Seem *v.i.* to have the air or appearance of being; to appear to be true; have the sensation of.

Seer *n.* one who sees visions; an inspired person; a prophet.

Seesaw *n.* vacillation; game in which two children sit one at each end of a plank and move each other up and down.

Seethe *v.t.* & *i.* to cook by boiling to be agitated.

Segment *n.* a part cut off from something; a part cut off from a figure.

Seigneur, Seignior *ns.* a feudal lord; a title of respect.

Seigniory *n.* lordship.

Seine *n.* a large fishing net.

Seizable *adj.* able to be seized.

Seize *v.t.* & *i.* to take possession of by warrant or legal right; to confiscate.

Seizor *n.* one who takes possession.

Seizure *n.* the act of seizing; sudden attack; taking possession by force.

Select *adj.* (of society etc.) exclusive; choosen for excellence; picked.

Self *n.* a person's identity or individuality; one's own interest; sameness.

Selfish *adj.* deficient in consideration for others; actuated by self-interest.

Sell *v.t.* to make over or dispose of in exchange for money.

Selvage *n.* the edge of a cloth.

Semaciology *n.* branch of philology which treats of the meaning of words.

Semaphore *n.* military signalling by operator's two arms or two flags.

Semantics *n. pl.* science of the origin and evolution of language.

Sematic *adj.* of colour which serves protection from enemy.

Semblance *n.* likeness; outward aspect; superficial appearance.

Semen *n.* male generative fluid of animals.

Semester *n.* a half year course in some institutions.

Semicircle *n.* the half of a circle or a circumference.

Semicolon *n.* the mark used in punctuation.

Semi-final *n.* the match or round preceding the final one.

Seminal *adj.* of seed or semen; propagative; rudimentary.

Seminary *n.* a place of education; academy.

Semi-vowels *n.* letters which are half vowels.

Senate *n.* upper or second chamber in some parliaments; the governing body of universities.

Send *v.t.* & *i.* to have conveyed; to cause to go.

Send *n.* impulse given by the down slope of a wave.

Senescence *n.* the state of growing old; decay.

Seneschal *n.* steward of medieval great house.

Senile *adj.* pertaining to old age.

Senior *adj.* older in age or standing; elder of a higher degree or rank.

Senna *n.* dried leaves of a plant used as a laxative.

Sennet *n.* signal-call or trumpet.

Sennight *n.* seven nights; a week.

Sensation *n.* perception by means of the senses.

Sense *n.* any of the special bodily faculties by which sensation is roused; discernment.

Senseless *adj.* wildly foolish; unreasonable.

Sensible *adj.* having or showing good sense; appreciable; judicious; practical; intelligent.

Sensitize *v.t.* to render sensitive.

Sensory, Sensorial *adjs.* pertaining to sensorium.

Sensorium *n.* (*Biol.*) whole sensory apparatus; the seat of sensation in the brain, and spinal chord.

Sensual *adj.* of the senses; pleasing to the senses; licentious; voluptuous.

Sensualist *n.* a voluptuary.

Sensually *adv.* in a sensual manner.

Sentence *n.* a man's opinion on something; maxim; verdict of a judge; a set of words with a complete meaning.

Sentient *adj.* that feels or is capable of feeling; susceptible of feeling; sensible.

Sentiment *n.* thought which is prompted by emotion; sensibility.

Sentinel *n.* a soldier posted to keep guard on any place; a watch.

Sentry *n.* a soldier on guard.

Separate *adj.* physically disconnected; distinct.

Sepia *n.* a kind of fish; brown pigment made from fluid secreted by cuttle-fish.

Sepoy *n.* an Indian soldier in Brithish-Indian army.

Septal *adj.* of a thing partitioned into many parts.

September *n.* the ninth month of the English year.

Septet *n.* a party of seven.

Septfoil *n.* having seven leaves.

Septic *adj.* & *n.* causing putrefaction.

Septicaemia *n.* blood poisoning.

Septule *adj.* sevenfold.

Septum *n.* partition such as that between the chambers of some fruits.

Sepulchre *n.* a tomb; a burial cave; a grave; a vault. *v.t.* to place in tomb.

Sepulture *n.* burying; laying in sepulchre; putting in the tomb.

Sequacious *adj.* inclined to follow; servile.

Sequel *n.* the succeeding part; a consequence; what follows; aftereffects.

Sequence *n.* succession; coming after or next; unbroken series; consequence; order or series without gaps.

Sequentes, Sequentia *ns.* the following lines; that follows.

Sequential *adj.* pertaining to sequence.

Sequestrum *n.* a piece of dead bone detached from living bone but remaining in place.

Seraglio *n.* the palace of the Sultan of Turkey; the harem.

Seraph *n.* a celestial being; one of the highest of the nine orders of angles.

Serb *n.* native or language of Serbia.

Sere, Sear *ns.* the catch of the hammer of a gun.

Serein *n.* fine shower of rain.

Serenade *n.* music sung or played at night by lover at his lady's window.

Serene *adj.* calm; clear; undisturbed.

Serenity *n.* stillness; sereneness; calmness.

Serf *n.* a slave employed to work in the field; a slave.

Serge *n.* a durable twilled worsted fabric.

Sergeant *n.* a lawyer of high rank; a non-commissioned officer in the army.

Sergette *n.* a thin kind of serge.

Serial *adj.* pertaining to or forming a series.

Seriate, Seriated *adjs.* in the form of a series.

Seriatim *adv.* one after another; in continuous order.

Series *n.* a number of things of which each is similar to the preceding order.

Serif *n.* the short line at the top or bottom of a printing type.

Seringa *n.* a kind of rubber tree.

Serio-comic *adj.* having a mixture of gravity and humour.

Serious *adj.* sincere; demanding thought; thoughful

Sermon *n.* a piece of religious exhortation delivered from the pulpit; a moral reflection.

Serotine *n.* a brown European bat.

Serotinous *adj.* appearing late in season.

Serous *adj.* like serum; of the consistency of whey; watery.

Serpent *n.* a snake *esp.* of large kinds; kind of fire-work.

Serpentine *adj.* like or as of a serpent; spiral; crooked.

Serra *n.* a serrated structure.

Serrate *adj.* notched like a saw.

Serried *adj.* shoulder to shoulder in close order; without gaps.

Serum *n.* whey; thin transparent portion of the blood; watery fluid in animal organism.

Servant *n.* one who is employed to carry out the orders of some one.

Serve *v.t.* & *i.* to be useful to; to be employed; to wait upon at the table; to labour; to obey.

Server *n.* one who serves.

Serviette *n.* a table-napkin.

Servile *adj.* of slaves; cringing; mean-spirited; completely dependent.

Servility *n.* slavishness; flattery.

Servitor *n.* a henchman or servant; an attendant.

Sesame *n.* an annual herbaceous tropical plant with oily seeds.

Sesamoid *adj.* shaped like a seasame-seed.

Session *n.* being assembled for deliberative or judicial which such meetings are held; a school or university term; being seated.

Set *v.t.* & *i.* to put; to lay; cause to stand; to assign; place ready; dispose suitably.

Seton *n.* a skein of thread on a wound to keep it open.

Settee *n.* a seat accommodating two or more; double arm-chair; a kind of ship.

Setter *n.* a kind of hunting dog; one who sets.

Settle *v.t.* & *i.* to establish or become established in an abode.

Settle *n.* a bench with high back and box below seat.

Settlement *n.* terms on which adjustment; jointure.

Sever *v.t.* & *i.* to disjoing; to separate; to divide in two; to cut or break off.

Several *adj.* separate; distinct; various; consisting of a number.

Severe *adj.* austere; strict; harsh; vehement; violent; exacting; terse.

Severity *n.* harshness; severe quality; rigour.

Severy *n.* (*Archit.*) compartment of vaulted ceiling.

Sew *v.t.* & *i.* to fasten or join or enclose by sewing.

Sewage *n.* matter conveyed in sewers; filthy matter which passes through sewers.

Sewel *n.* a scare crow.

Sewer *n.* covered undergrond drain carrying off refuse of houses and towns.

Sewn *adj.* joined by sewing.

Sex *n.* being male or female; males or females collectively.

Shabbily *adj.* in a shabby manner.

Shabby *adj.* worn or threadbare; mean; paltry; dissipated.

Shabrack *n.* a saddle-cloth.

Shackle *n.* a line for connecting chains; fetter enclosing ankle or wrist.

Shad *n.* a kind of fish.
Shade *n.* a place sheltered from the sun; shadow; obscurity; darkness.
Shadeless *adj.* without shade.
Shadoof *n.* a series of buckets used to raise water.
Shadow *n.* a patch of shade; the shade cast by an object; faint representation.
Shady *adj.* giving or situated in shade; disreputable.
Shaft *n.* a slender pole; stem (stalk); a long arrow; the rib of feather.
Shag *n.* a crested cormorant; a rough mass of hair; coarse kinds of fine-cut tobacco.
Shaggy *adj.* rough; coarse; rough-haired; with a wild overgrowth.
Shagreen *n.* untanned leather usually dyed green.
Shake *v.t.* & *i.* to move violently; to agitate; to cause to tremble; to shiver; to disturb; to weaken; to make tremulous; jolt or jar.
Shallow *adj.* having little depth; trivial; superficial; not wise.
Sham *v.t.* & *i.* to feign; to make false pretence; to cheat.
Shamble *v.i.* & *n.* to walk or run in an awkward manner. *n.* a shambling gait.
Shame *n.* feeling of humiliation; disgrace; excited b consciousness of guilt or from some other cause.
Shampoo *v.t.* to treat the head of a person with lather and rubbing; to rub; to wash the hair of the head.
Shanghia *n.* drug and ship as sailor while unconscious.
Shank *n.* vertical part of a bird's foot; the part of leg from knee to ankle; shin-bone.
Shan't *n.* contraction of 'shall not'.
Shanty *n.* a hut; a mean dwelling.
Shape *n.* configuration; external from of a thing; appearance; guise; sort; porper condition.
Share *n.* the part that falls to an individual; portion; one of the equal parts of a company's capital entitling holder to profits.
Shareholder *n.* the owner of a share or shares in a company or joint fund.
Shark *n.* large voracious sea-fish; a swindler; a cheat.
Sharp *adj.* with fine edge of point not blunt; acute; pungent; rugged; shrill; painful; piercing; harsh; severe; clever; painful; sensitive; keen-witted.
Sharp-set *adj.* hungry, eager in appetite.
Shatter *v.t.* & *i.* to break suddenly in pieces; to split; to derange.
Shave *v.t.* & *i.* to pare the surface of (wood etc.) with plane, etc.
Shaving *n.* the act of removing hair with razor, curled pieces of wood planed off.
Shaw *n.* a small thicket; wood.
Shay *n.* chaise.
She *pron.* the female in question.

Sheaf *n.* bundle of arrows, papers or long objects; a bundle of coornstalks tied together after reaping.

Shealing *n.* a small hut or a cottage.

Shear *v.t.* & *i.* to cut with a sword or shears; to clip with scissors.

Sheath *n.* a close-fitting case for the blade of tools or weapons; a covering membrane of body.

Sheathe *v.t.* to encase; to put into a sheath; to cover.

Sheave *n.* the groove in a pulley. *v.t.* to gather into sheaves.

Shed *v.t.* to part with; to throw off; to spread abroad; to give forth; to diffuse.

Sheen *n.* radiance; splendour; brightness.

Sheep *n.* a woolly ruminant; a timid beast kept in flocks for the mutton and wool and leather it yields.

Sheer *adj.* & *adv.* mere; simple; absolute; outright; perpendicular.

Sheet *n.* a broad piece of linen or cotton cloth spread on a bed; a flat piece of any thn material.

Sheldrake *n.* a kind of wild duck; a bright-plumaged wild duck.

Shelf *n.* a slab of stone or board projecting from the wall or hung on it for keeping things; a projecting cliff.

Shell *n.* a hard husk; bomb; an outer crust; inner coffin; outling of a plan; a kind of light boat.

Shellac *n.* lac prepared in thin plates used in making varnish.

Shelter *n.* protection against exposure to harm; refuge; a place of safety.

Shelty *n.* a kind of pony; a rude hut.

Shelve *v.t.* to put (books, etc) ona shelf; to lay aside or defer consideration of.

Shepherd *n.* a man who tends sheep; a pastor. *v.t.* to tend or drive sheep.

Sheriff *n.* the chief officer of the crown in a country or shire who administer justice.

Shield *n.* a piece of defensive armour; a protective part; one who protects.

Shift *v.t.* & *i.* to change from one position to another; to transfer.

Shillelagh *n.* Irish cudgel of black thorn or oak.

Shim *n.* & *v.t.* (to fit or fill up with) thin chip or wedge.

Shin *n.* the fore part of the leg below the knee. *v.t.* & *i.* to climb a tree.

Shinny *n.* a game resembling hockey; stick used in it.

Shiny *adj.* bright; luminous.

Ship *n.* a large vessel of three to five masts; any sea-going big vessel. *v.t.* & *i.* to embark; to put on board a ship.

Shirk *v.t.* & *i.* to avoid; to slink; to get out of duty. *n.* one who lives by tricks; a shirker.

Shirt *n.* a man's undergarment.

Shit *v.i.* to evacuate bowels. *n.* abusive word.

Shiver *v.t.* & *i.* to tremble; to shake; to break into small fragments; to shatter. *n.* a fragment; part.

Shoal *n.* a great number of fish swimming together; shallow water.

Shoaly *adj.* shallow.

Shock *n.* violent emotion; a concussion; violent onset; disturbing influence; sudden attack.

Shocking *adj.* giving or causing shock; scandalous; offensive; very bad or repugnant.

Shoddy *n.* a fibre got by shredding old cloth; cloth partly made of this.

Shoe *n.* the outer covering for the foot; the metal plate nailed to the hoof of a horse; anything of the shape of a shoe.

Shog *n.* a jog; a shock. *v.t.* & *i.* to shake; to move on.

Shook *n.* staves of a barrel.

Shoot *v.t.* & *i.* to come or go swiftyly or suddenly; dart; to drive with force.

Shooter *n.* one who shoots.

Shooting *n.* the act of discharging arrows, shots & etc.

Shop *n.* a building or room for retail sale of goods; one's profession, trade, thins connected with it.

Shore *n.* the border of the sea; beam of a ship; support.

Short *adj.* not long in space or time; scantly; lacking.

Shorthand *n.* kinds of writing enabling reporter to keep pace with speaker.

Shortsighted *adj.* deficient in foresight; having short sight.

Shot *n.* an attempt to hit something by shooting; a single missile for firearms.

Shot *n.* reckoning, one's share of tavern-bill.

Shot gun *n.* a shoulder-held firearm that fires multiple pellets through a small bore.

Shoulder *n.* the point of the body at which the arm or the foreleg at which the arm or the foreleg or wing is attached; support.

Shout *v.t.* a loud cry from a person of company calling attention or expressing joy; defiance.

Shove *v.t.* & *i.* to push with a sudden motion.

Show *v.t.* & *i.* to make known; to present to view; to inform; to prove; to appear.

Showman *n.* a proprietor or manager of menagerie of travelling show.

Showy *adj.* of attractively brilliant appearacne; ostentatious.

Shrag *n.* a lopped off twig. *v.t.* to lop; to prune.

Shrapnel *n.* the entrails of a bomb which scatter on explosion.

Shred *n.* least amount; torn-out fibre; rag; paring; scarp.

Shrew *n.* a peevish woman; a small mammal like a long snouted mouse feeding on insects.

Shriek *v.t.* to scream; to utter a shrill cry; to laugh loudly.

Shrill *n.* importunate; uttering an acute sound; piercing and highpitched in sound.

Shrilly *adv.* in a shrill manner.

Shrimp *n.* a kind of long-tailed saltwater crustacean with ten feet; a diminutive person.

Shrine *n.* sacred or revered place; saint's tomb; hallowed spot.

Shrive *v.t.* to hear the confession of; to absolve.

Shrivel *v.t.* & *i.* to contract into wrinkles or folds; to shrink.

Shroff *v.t.* & *i.* a banker or money changer.

Shrub *n.* a kind of cordial; woody plant of small size.

Shrubbery *n.* plantation of shrubs.

Shrug *v.t.* & *i.* to raise the shoulders to express helplessness.

Shudder *n.* spasm of shivering; shaking; tremor. *v.t.* to tremble; to quake; to feel repugnance.

Shuffle *v.t.* & *i.* to drag one's feet; walk thus; to evade; to change position of playing-cards.

Shun *v.t.* to avoid; to eschew; to try to keep clear.

Shun *n.* *abbr.* of attention.

Shunt *v.t.* & *i.* to divert railway carriages, tram cars & etc.

Shut *v.t.* & *i.* to confine; to become closed; to encircle; to separate; to desist; to imprison.

Shuttle *n.* a small drawer in a shelf; a weaving implement by which weft thread is carried across the warp threads.

Shy *adj.* timed; avoiding observation; reserved in society; bashful.

Siamang *n.* a kind of big ape.

Siamese *adj.* & *n.* (a native, language) of Siam.

Sibilance *n.* a hissing letter.

Sibilant *n.* a hissing, sounded by a hiss; a letter uttered with a hissing sound.

Sibilate *v.t* & *i.* to pronounce with a hissing sound.

Sibyl *n.* an old hag; pagan prophetess, fortune-teller.

Sic *adv.* so; thus.

Siccation *n.* the act of drying.

Sick *adj.* vomiting; affected with a disease; ill; disturbed; disgusted.

Sicken *v.t.* & *i.* to grow ill or show signs of illness.

Side *n.* & *adj.* the part of the body that is right or left; visible surface; either surface of thing regarded and having only two; margin.

Sidesaddle *n.* a saddle for a woman rider.

Sidetrack *n.* a siding or by-path.

Siege *n.* operations of encamped force for gaining possession of a fortified place.

Sienna *n.* earth of brownish-yellow colour used as pigment.

Siesta *n.* a short sleep at mid-day in hot countries.

Sieve *n.* a person who cannot keep secrets.

Sift *v.t.* & *i.* to separate with or pass through a sieve; to examine in detail.

Sigh *v.t.* & *i.* to express grief by sighs; to draw a deep audible breath.

Sight *n.* faculty of vision; a scene or spectacle; the act of seeing.

Sign *n.* short signature; symbol; token; gesture; an omen; gesture used instead of words.

Signal *adj.* remarkable; note-worty; notable. *n.* a sign conveying information or direction.

Signatory *n.* the party who has signed a contract or treaty.

Signature *n.* signed name of initials; indication letter or figure at foot of first page of book-sheet.

Significance *n.* importance; expressiveness; import; meaning; force.

Silence *n.* being silent; stillness; taciturnity; oblivision; secrecy.

Silencer *n.* an appliance for reducing sounds.

Silent *adj.* marked by silence; soundless; mute; not uttering a sound; saying nothing on some subject.

Silica *n.* a mineral forming quartz and the chief part of flint; sand, etc.

Silicon *n.* a non-metallic element found only in combination.

Silk *n.* a fine soft thread produced in the cocoon by a silkworm.

Silly *adj.* innocent; unwise; foolish; week-minded.

Silo *n.* a pit or air-tight chamber for storing green crops for fodder.

Silt *n.* sediment deposited by running water; a deposit of mud or fine earth from running water.

Silurian *n.* a series of rocks forming the lowest sub-division of the Palaeozoic.

Silver *n.* a white soft lustrous precious metal; a coin of silver.

Similar *adj.* having resemblance to; alike.

Simile *n.* a comparison of two things for the purpose of illustration or ornament.

Simmer *v.t.* & *i.* to keep boiling; to be in a state of suppressed anger or indignation.

Simoom *n.* a dust-laden wind of the Arabian desert.

Simp *n.* a fool; simpleton.

Simper *v.t.* & *i.* to smile in a silly or affected manner.

Simplicity *n.* plainness; innocence; silliness.

Simple *adj.* plain; unsophisticated; artless; natural.

Simpleton *n.* a silly or half-witted person; a fool.

Simplify *n.* to make simple or easy to understand; to take plain.

Simulacrum *n.* an image; deceptive likeness; pretence.

Simultaneous *adj.* happening or operating at the same time.

Sin *n.* disobedience of moral laws of the divine command.

Since *prep.* after, in the period between some specified time and the present. *conj.* since the time when, because that. *adv.* before this; ago.

Sine *n.* line drawn from one extremity of arc perpendicularly to radius at other extremity.

Sinew *n.* a fibrous tissue which unites muscles to bone; a framework.

Sing *v.t.* & *i.* to utter words in a tune; to produce melodious sound; to celebrate in verse; to compose poetry.

Singe *v.t.* & *i.* to burn slightly; to scorch; to apply fire to the surface or edge of.

Singing *n.* vocal music.

Single *adj.* one only; separate; not double or multiple; unmarried; solitary.

Singular *adj.* extraordinary; single; individual; unusal; surprising.

Sinister *adj.* on the left side of a shield; unlucky; ill-looking; dishonest.

Sink *v.t.* & *i.* to immerse; to fall slowly down-wards.

Sinner *n.* a sinful person; one who sins.

Sinogram *n.* a Chinese written character.

Sinologist *n.* one who is versed in sinology.

Sinologure *n.* a sinologist.

Sinology *n.* knowledge of the Chinese language, history and customs.

Sinter *n.* incrustration; a mineral.

Sinuate *adj.* of wavy border.

Sinuosity *n.* a bend in a road or river.

Sinuous *n.* meandering; of a winding form; with many curves; crooked.

Sip *v.t.* & *i.* to drink in small quantities.

Siphon *n.* a bent tube with one leg larger than the other used in drawing of liquids.

Sippet *n.* one of the piece of toast or fried bread served with soup; mince.

Sir *n.* word used in addressing a master or superior.

Sircar *n.* the Government of India.

Sirdar *n.* an Indian chief; a leader.

Sire *n.* a word of respect for a king or prince.

Siren *n.* hooting instrument used for sound-signals.

Sirgang *n.* the green jackdaw.

Sister *n.* the daughter of same parents as another person; a hospital-nurse; a woman of a religious community.

Sisyphean *adj.* endless and fruitless, Greek condemned to push a stone up hill and begin again when it rolled down.

Sit *v.t.* & *i.* to take a position in which the body rests on the ground.

Site *n.* a place on which a building & etc. stands; position; locality.

Sitology *n.* the science of regulation of the diet.

Sitter *n.* a person sitting for portrait; (*sl.* with ref. to shooting bird sitting) easy job; easy shot at goal, etc.

Situation *n.* the site and surroudings of a place; post as a servant or a wage-earner.

Sizar *n.* an undergraduate at Cambridge, etc. receiving college assistance on the ground of poverty.

Size *n.* dimension; bulk; magnitude; a gelatinous solution.

Sizy *adj.* glutinous.

Skate *n.* one of a pair of implements attachable to the boots and enabling wearer to glide over ice.

Skein *n.* a bundle of yarn or thread or silk; a flock of wild geese in flight.

Skeleton *n.* the bony framework of the body; a general outline.

Skep *n.* straw or wicker bee-hive; kinds of wooden or wicker basket.

Skerry *n.* a rock.

Sketch *n.* a rough drawing or painting; an outline; a rough draft or general account of something.

Skew *adj.* set askew; oblique; not in straight lines or at right angles.

Skewer *n.* a wooden or metal pin with which meat is held together while cooking.

Ski *n.* & *v.t.* tunners of a wood fastened under the feet for travelling over snow.

Skid *n.* a frame used as support; iron-shoe or other device to check vehicle's pace; slide of wheel on muddy ground.

Skilful *adj.* expert; having skill; ingenious; dexterous.

Skill *n.* practised ability; expertness; dexterity; aptitude.

Skim *v.t.* & *i.* to read superfically; to take or remove the scum or cream off.

Skimmer *n.* a scoop used for skimming.

Skimp *v.t.* to give poor quantify of food; be parsimoniuous with.

Skin *n.* the natural covering of the body; the outer covering of the animal body; complexion; the outer coating of plant.

Skinflint *n.* a great miser.

Skink *n.* a kind of small lizard.

Skinny *adj.* lacking flesh; consisting of skin only.

Skip *v.t.* & *i.* to leap; to jump; to move lightly from one foot to the other; to omit; to disappear.

Skipper *n.* skip-jack; the master of a small trading vessel.

Skippet *n.* a wooden box used to protect seals of documents.

Skipping *n.* leaping.

Skirl *v.i.* & *n.* shrill sound; (make) sound of bagpipes; to make chirping sound.

Skirimish *n.* an irregular fighting; a brief contest; a witty argument.

Skirmisher *n.* one who skirmishes.

Skirret *n.* kind of water parsnip.

Skirt *n.* women's outer garment hanging from the waist; edge; border.

Skittle *n.* the game played with nine pins.

Skiver *n.* a knife for paring leather.

Skua *n.* a large gull found on river-side.

Skulk *v.i.* to move stealthily or lurk; to stay away; to shrink danger or duty.

Skull *n.* a bony case of the brain; cranium.

Skunk *n.* a small American carnivorous animal; a contemptible fellow.

Sky *n.* the firament; the apparent arch or vault of heaven; climate; a regin.

Slab *n.* a flat thin piece of stone or some rigid material outer cut or plant of a log.

Slabber *n.* slaver; excessive saliva.

Slabby *adj.* muddy; watery; viscous; dirty.

Slab-stone *n.* a flagstone.

Slack *adj.* sluggish; not busy; slow; negligent; relaxed; loose.

Slacken *v.t.* & *i.* to make less tight; to relax; to be remiss.

Slag *n.* vitreous smelting refuse; dross separated from a metal; volcanic scoria.

Slake *v.t.* to appease; to extinguish (fire); to cool with water; to diminish one's efforts.

Slam *v.t.* & *i.* to shut with a bang; to hit; to hang; gain easy victory over.

Slander *v.t.* calumny; a false report maliciously uttered to a person's injury. *n.* defamation; calumny.

Slang *n.* expressions in common colloquial use but regarded as vulgar and not standard English.

Slant *v.t.* & *i.* to be or put in an oblique position; to turn obliquely; to slope.

Slap *v.t.* to strike with a palm of the hand; to smack.

Slash *v.t.* & *i.* to make sweeping cut with sword; to cut in long strips; to lash with a whip.

Slat *n.* a thin narrow piece of metal or wood; a roofing slate; a thin stone slab for roofing.

Slate *n.* kinds of rock easily split into thin smooth plates; such a slice used for writing.

Slaughter *n.* killing of animals for food; slaying, *esp.* of many persons or animals at once, massacre, carnage.

Slave *n.* a person in bondagae; a serf; a helpless person; a drudge; contemptible person.

Slaver *n.* fromt the mouth; a ship or person engaged in slave-trade. *v.t.* & *i.* to let slaver flow; to let spittle flow from the mouth.

Slavery *n.* the condition of a slave bondage.

Slavey *n.* maid servant.

Slavish *adj.* servile; mean; base.

Slay *v.t.* to kill by violence; to put to death.

Slayer *n.* one who slays; a murderer.

Sleave *v.t.* to separate into threads.

Sleazy *adj.* flimsy.

Sledge-hammer *n.* blacksmith's heavy hammer.

Sleek *adj.* soft and smooth; sleek haired or skinned; smooth; of well-fed comfortable appearance.

Sleekly *adv.* in a sleek manner.

Sleeky *adv.* smooth.

Sleep *n.* condition in which the eyes are closed and the nervous system inactive; slumber; repose; death.

Sleet *n.* snow or hail falling mixed with rain. *v.t.* to rain with sleet.

Sleeve *n.* that part of garment that is fitted to cover the arm.

Slender *adj.* long and thin; not stout; slim; scanty; feeble.

Sleuth *n.* a detective; bloodhound.

Slew, Slue *v.t.* & *i.* to turn or swing from one direction to another. *n.* a turn; a swing.

Slice *n.* a thin broad piece cut off from meat or bread; an instrument with a broad blade.

Slick *adj.* simple; absolute; mere (*adv.*) directly, excatly, completely.

Slide *v.i.* & *t.* to move along a smooth surface; to slip in; to glide over ice.

Slight *adj.* slender; fair-looking; not thorough; inadequate; weak. *v.t.* to treat with neglect; to disregard.

Slim *adj.* of slender make, shape; not stout or thick-set; crafty.

Slime *n.* muscus; semen; fine ozzy mud or glutinous substance.

Slink *v.i.* to creep away meanly; to go in an ashamed manner; to miscarry.

Slip *n.* a narrow piece of material or paper; the act of slipping; a blunder; a kind of loose garment; a thin piece of wood; one of the fielders stationed for balls glancing off bat to off side behind batsman.

Slit *v.t.* & *i.* to tear lengthwise; to make a long cut in.

Sliver *n.* piece of wood torn from tree or timber; splinter.

Slobber *v.t.* & *i.* to besalver; to run saliva from the mouth; to do a task badly; bungle. *n.* running saliva.

Sloe *n.* a kind of wild plum.

Slog *v.t.* & *i.* to strike a hard blow; to walk doggedly.

Slogan *v.t.* & *i.* party catchword; high-hand war-cry; watch-word; motto.

Sloop *n.* a kind of one-masted fore-and aft rigged ship.

Slop *n.* a policeman.

Slop *n.* (in *pl.* sense only) dirty water of a household; liquid food; ready-made clothing for sailors.

Slope *n.* inclined position; declivity; uneven ground; a piece of rising or falling ground.

Slops *n. pl.* liquid food; dirty or waste water of kitchen, etc; ready-made clothes.

Slot *n.* a groove or slit of a machine; the trap-door of a stage; track of deer known by footsteps.

Sloth *n.* laziness; indolence; sluggishness; a kind of American mammal which moves very slowy.

Slothful *adj.* inactive; indolent.

Slouch *n.* an awakward gait; broad brimmed hat.

Slough *n.* a layer of dead tissue on a wound or sore.

Sloven *n.* dirty; a man careless of his dress.

Slovenly *adv.* careless in person or methods of word.

Slow *adj* & *adv.* not swift; deficient in speed; lingering.

Slub *n.* slightly twisted wool.

Sludge *n.* thick greasy mud; sewage.

Sludgy *adj.* muddy.

Slue *v.t.* & *i.* turn or swing forcibly.

Slug *n.* line of type in lino-type printing.

Slugabed *n.* one who indulges in lying abed.

Sluggard *n.* a man who is habitually lazy and sluggish.

Sluice *n.* sliding gate for adjusting outflow or inflow of water; an artificial water-chennel; flood-gate.

Slum *n.* a low dirty crowded district in a town. *v.i.* to go about dirty streets.

Slumber *n.* sleep.

Slummock *v.t.* & *i.* to swallow greedily; to speak in a awkward way.

Slump *n.* diminution of interest taken in subject or undertaking.

Slung *adj.* suspended.

Slunk *adj.* (of calves) cast prematurely.

Slur *v.t.* & *i.* to pronounce indistinctly; to conceal; to decrease.

Slush *n.* thawing snow; watery mud; a silly sentiment.

Slut *n.* a slovenly woman, girl.

Sluttery *n.* dirtiness; disorder.

Sly *adj.* cunning; witty; artful; done in secret; insinuating; crafty; secretive.

Smack *n.* a sounding blow; slap; flavour; slight sound; a kind of ship; loud kiss.

Small *adj.* of little size or strength; petty; unimportant; trifling; poor.

Smallage *n.* wild celery.

Smalt *n.* glass coloured blue with cobalt; pigment made by pounding it.

Smart *adj.* of some severity; pungent; sharp; clever; quick-witted.

Smash *v.t. & i.* to break into pieces; to shatter; to rout utterly.

Smasher *n.* a smashing blow.

Smatter *v.t.* to talk uselessly.

Smear *v.t. & i.* to blot; to stain with some thing greasy; to stain or obscure.

Smeary *adj.* adhesive.

Smectite *n.* a kind of whitish clay for taking out grease.

Smegma *n.* a soapy secretion from skin under the prepuce.

Smell *n.* the quality perceived by the nose; odour; the sense pecuilar to the nose; bad odour; act of inhaling.

Smilax *n.* kinds of climbing plant yielding sarsaparilla.

Smile *n.* a relaxation of the features expressive of pleasure; amusement; contempt etc.

Smiling *adj.* with a smile; happy.

Smirch *v.t.* to smear; to stain.

Smirk *v.t.* to smile in an affected manner. *n.* a silly smile.

Smite *v.t. & i.* to strike; to defeat; to chastise; to injure; to hit.

Smiter *n.* a hard hitter.

Smith *n.* black-smith; one who works or a worker in iron or other metal.

Smithery *n.* smith's work.

Smithy *n.* the workshop of a black-smith; forge.

Smitten *adj.* beaten; struck; defeated.

Smock *n.* a chemise; child's garment.

Smoke *n.* a spell of tobacco smoking; visible vapour emitted by a burning substance.

Smooth *adj.* of even surface; without undulations; glossy; free from harshness; polite; unruffled.

Smoulder *v.i.* to burn in a suppressed manner without flame; to exist without visible effects.

Smug *adj.* self-complacent; prim.

Smuggle *v.t. & i.* to import or export goods unlawfully.

Smut *n.* a plant-disease with blackening of grain; obscene talk.

Snack *n.* a share; a slight hasty meal.

Snaffle *n.* a simple bridle consisting of a slender bit-mouth without curb.

Snag *n.* jagged projecting stump or point.

Snaggy *adj.* full of snags.

Snail *n.* a slimy slow-creeping insect with spiral shell.

Snake *n.* a kind of scaly limbless repitile; serpent; some poisonous; treacherous person; cold-hearted person.

Snap *v.i & t.* to break with a sharp noise; to bite.

Snaphook *n.* a kind of hook in which cord can be admitted but does not come out.

Snappish *adj.* angry.

Snappy *adj.* cruel.

Snap-shot *n.* a shot fired without time for deliberate aim.

Snare *n.* a trap for catching animals or birds; anything used for tempting.

Snarl *v.t.* & *i.* to growl; to complain to speak roughly; to be entangled.

Snatch *v.t.* & *i.* to seize quickly or unexpectedly; to stretch hands for seizing.

Sneak *v.t.* & *i.* to creep privately; to go furtively; to behave meanly.

Sneer *v.t.* to utter words ironically; to smile derisively; to show contempt by looks.

Sneeze *v.i.* explosive sound made through the nostrils. *n.* the act of sneezing.

Sniff *v.t.* & *i.* to smell (flower, etc.) by sniffing; to draw up air audibly with the nose. *n.* the act of sniffing.

Snigger *v.i.* & *n.* to laugh in a half-suppresed manner.

Snip *v.t.* & *i.* to cut with scissors or shears *esp.* small quick strokes.

Snipe *n.* a kind of game-bird found in marshes.

Snivel *v.i.* to run at the nose; to be lachrymose; to cry like a child.

Snook *n.* a kind of fish; contemptuous gesture with the thumb at the tip of the nose and fingers spread out.

Snoop *v.i.* to pry or sneak about.

Snooze *v.i.* & *n.* a nap; to doze; pass time; *esp.* in day time in lazy indifference.

Snore *v.t.* & *i.* to breathe with a rough rattling hoarse noise during sleep.

Snort *v.t.* & *i.* to force air through the nostrils making an explosive sound.

Snot *n.* mucus of the nose.

Snotty *adj.* foul with mucus.

Snout *n.* beast's nose and mouth, (contempt.) person's nose; nozzle.

Snow *n.* the light white flakes in which frozen vapour falls to the earth.

Snowily *adv.* in a snowy manner.

Snub *v.t.* to rebuff with words or coldness. *n.* rebuff; a snubbing.

Snubber *n.* a device for checking recoil of motor-car springs.

Snuff *n., v.t.* & *i.* black excrescence on the wick of a lighted candle/

Snuffle *v.t.* & *i.* to make sniffing sounds; to speak nasally.

Snug *adj.* sheltered from weather; concealed; comfortable.

Snugly *adv.* in a snug manner.

So *adv.* & *conj.* therefore; in that way; in the same way; in a like manner; to the same extent as.

Soap *n.* a substance used in washing (consisting of far or oil combined with alkali).

Soapy *adj.* smeared with soap; having the qualities of soap.

Soar *v.i.* to mount to a great height; to fly high

Soarer *n.* one who soars.

Sob *n.* convulsive drawing of breath especially in weeping.

Sobbing *n.* the act of sighing in a convulsive manner.

Sober *adv.* temperate; moderate; serious; quiet; not passionate.

Soberly *adv.* in a sober manner.

Soccer *n.* (*sl.*) Association football.

Sociability *n.* the quality of being sociable.

Social *adj.* living in communities, gregarious; relating to society.

Sociality *n.* socialness.

Socially *adv.* in a social manner.

Socialism *n.* the principle that freedom of the individual should be completely subordinate to the interest of the society.

Society *n.* an association of person united by a common airor interest, or principle.

Sociology *n.* study of the history and nature of human society.

Sock *n.* a short stocking; inner sole of shoe; a kind of light shoe.

Socle *n.* rectangular block of pedestal.

Socratic *n.* of, like, following, worthy of Socrates.

Sod *n.* a piece of turf pared off; a turf.

Sod *p.t. of* **Seethe** boiled.

Soda *n.* one of the compounds of sodium in common use.

Soddy *adj.* covered with sod.

Sodic *adj.* pertaining to sodium.

Sodium *n.* a silver white alkaline metal burning with bright yellow flame.

Sodomite *n.* one who is guilty of sodomy.

Sodomy *n.* an unnatural sexual intercourse, *esp.* between males.

Sofa *n.* a kind of long couch with back and arms.

Soffit *n.* lower surface of arch; balcony.

Soft *adj.* delicate; not hard; yielding to pressure; smooth to the touch.

Soften *v.t.* & *i.* to alleviate; to molify; to palliate; to make or grow soft.

Softener *n.* he who or that which softens.

Softening *adj.* the act of making softer.

Softy *adj.* somewhat soft.

Soggy *adj.* sodden; saturated; water-logged; hoggy.

Soil *v.t.* & *i.* to smear or stain with dirt; to feed cattle on green fodder; defile.

Soiree *n.* a social gathering, especially in the evening.

Sojourn *n.* temporary stay at a place.

Sol *n.* the fifth note of the octave.

Solace *n.* comfort in grief or disappointment; alleviation.

Solanum *n.* a large genus of plants including potato; nightshade.

Solar *adj.* relating to or concerned with the sun.

Sold *adj.* disposed of by sale.

Solder *n.* fusible alloy used in joining metals.

Soldier *n.* member of army; a military commander of specified ability; one of the fighting section of ant; a man.

Sole *n.* kind of flat-fish much esteemed as food.

Solecism *n.* blunder in speaking or writing.

Solemn *adj.* accompanied with ceremony; sacred; full of importance; weighty.

Solemnity *n.* a solemn rite; solemness; impressiveness.

Solemnize *v.t.* to make solemn; to celebrate.

Solen *n.* a kind of molluse.

Solenoid *n.* a magnet made coiling a wire round into cylinder and traversed by electric current.

Soleferino *n.* a kind of red colour.

Solicit *v.t.* & *i.* to make request to; to importune; to try to obtain; to entice.

Solicitor *n.* member of branch of legal profession chiefly concerned with advising clients and preparing their cases.

Solicitous *adj.* anxious; desirous; concerned.

Solid *adj.* whole; compact; of stable shape; of the same material throughout; reliable; uninterrupted; firm.

Solifidian *n.* one who holds that faith alone suffices for justification.

Solitaire *n.* a gem set by itself or an ear-ring, stud, etc. adorned with it.

Solitary *adj.* lonely; secluded; single.

Solitude *n.* a solitary place; a lonely life; being solitary.

Solivagant *adj.* wandering alone.

Solmisation *n.* repetition of the notes of the gamut.

Solo *n.* a song sung by one person; a musical performance by one man.

Soloist *n.* the performer of solo.

Solo-flight *n.* flying alone in an aeroplane.

Solomon *n.* kind of Israel reputed wisest of men.

Solon *n.* a wise legislator.

Solstice *n.* time at which the sum is farthest from the equator and appears to pause before returning.

Solstitial *adj.* pertaining to solstice.

Soluble *adj.* dissolvable in liquor.

Solution *n.* the act of dissolving or being dissolved; separation; resolution; removal of doubt; explanation.

Solve *v.t.* to find answer to a problem; to dissovle; to loosen; to explain.

Solvency *n.* the ability to pay all debts.

Somato *pref.* in sense of 'bodily'.

Somatogenic *adj.* producing in the body.

Somatology *n.* the doctrine of material substance.

Sombre *adj.* dark-coloured; gloomy; dark; dismal. *v.t.* & *i.* to make gloomy and dark.

Sombrely *adv.* in a gloomy manner.

Some *adj.* particular but un-known; an unspecified amount or number of; an appreciable or considerable amout of.

Somebody *n.* an unknown person.

Somehow *adv.* no matter how; in some way of for some reason or other not yet known.

Someone *n.* somebody. some one (any particular one).

Somersault *n.* a leap in which a person turns heels over head in the air.

Sometimes *adv.* now and then; at intervals.

Somnambulate *v.t.* to walk in sleep.

Somnambulator *n.* a sleep-walker.

Somnambulism *n.* walking about during sleep.

Somni *pref.* in sense of 'sleep'.

Somniloquist *n.* one who talks in sleep.

Somnioquy *n.* habit of talking in sleep.

Son *n.* one's male child; male descendant; a devotee or slave of.

Sonancy *n.* the quality of being sonant.

Sonant *adj.* & *n.* able to be continuously sounded; a sonant letter.

Song *n.* set of words for singing; singing; musical cry of some birds.

Song-craft *n.* the art of song making.

Sonnet *n.* piece of rhymed verse of fourteen ten-syllable lines.

Sonneteer *n.* the composer of sonnets.

Sonny *n.* a familiar term for a boy.

Sonometer *n.* an instrument for testing the hearing power of a deaf person.

Sonorous *adj.* (of speech, style) high sounding; having a resonant or rich or powerful sound.

Soon *adv.* in a short time; not long after; quickly; easily.

Sop *n.* bride offered to pacify; a piece of bread, etc.; soaked in gravy; milk; etc.

Sophisticate *v.t.* & *i.* to make artificial; to tamper with (text etc.) for argument.

Soporific *adj.* & *n.* (drug or agency) tending to produce sleep.

Soppy *adj.* soaked in liquid; swampy.

Sore *adj.* suffering tender; or mental pain; morbidly; tender; irriatating.

Sorrel *n.* a kind of shrub. *adj.* of a reddish brown colour.

Sorrow *n.* mental pian; grief; sadness; regret; misfortune.

Sorry *adj.* painted at or regretful over something; melancholoy.

Sort *n.* a kind or variety; species; manner.

Sot *n.* a habitual drunkard; man constantly stupid with drink.

Sottish *adj.* given to drinking.

Sottishly *adv.* in a sottish manner.

Souffle *n.* made light and frothy; dish made of beaten white of egg.

Souffle *n.* a low sound heard in some parts of the body.

Sough *n.* a whistling sound made by wind. *v.i.* to sigh as wind.

Soul *n.* the immaterial part of man regarded as immortal; intellectual.

Sound *n.* audible air-vibration; the sensation perceived by the ear; articualte utterance.

Sound *adj.* whole; entire; perfect; healthy; solid; right; stout; not deranged.

Soup *n.* liquid food made by stewing bones; meat, vegetables etc.

Sour *adj.* of acid taste; pungent; peevish; harsh.

Source *n.* place of origin; foundation-head; the place from which a stream issues.

Souse *n.* a pickle prepared with salt; a dip or plunge.

Souvenir *n.* a thing given or kept as a memento; keepsake.

Sovereign *adj.* possessing supreme power; lofty; chief; predominant. *n.* a supreme ruler; a monarch.

Sow *n.* the female of the swine or hog; adult female pig.

Sow *v.t. & i.* to scatter or plant seed for reproduction.

Sowback *n.* low sandy bank.

Spa *n.* a place resorted to for medicinal water.

Space *n.* extension; an interval between things; distance.

Spacial *adj.* pertaining to space.

Spacious *adj.* extended; enclosing a large space.

Spade *n.* a broad-bladed digging tool with long handle.

Spadework *n.* preparatory work of an arduous kind; hard labour.

Spad *n.* a person incapable of procreation.

Spall *v.t. & i. & n.* to clip; chippings.

Span *n.* full extent; short; distance; measure of nine inches.

Spaniard *n.* a native of Spain.

Spaniel *n.* a kind of dog with long hairs and ears.

Spank *v.t. & i.* to slap with the hand; go at a great pace. *n.* a blow.

Spanless *adj.* without extent; beyond measure (poet.).

Spanner *n.* one who spans; an instrument for turning nuts on screws.

Spar *v.i.* to box; to fit with spars; strike out with the spars; to dispute.

Spare *v.t. & i.* to be frugal; to abstain from hurting or destroying; to save.

Spare *adj.* scanty; frugal; lean. *n.* a small part; a slit at the top of a skirt.

Spareness *n.* leanness.

Spark *n.* fiery particle of burning substance; a small bright object or point; a gay yound fellow.

Spark *n.* a gay fellow; a lover; a woman of great beauty.

Sparkle *v.t.* to seem; to emit sparks; to glitter; to be bright with shifting points of light.

Sparrow *n.* a small bird haunting houses.

Sparse *adj.* thin; scattered; not dense; occurring at irregular intervals.

Spartan *adj.* pertaining to Sparta; brave and hardy.

Spasmodical *adj.* relating to spasm; convulsive.

Spasmology *n.* a treatise on convulsions.

Spat *n.* the egg of fish or oyster.

Spatter *v.t. & i.* to splash; to scatter in small drops.

Spatula *n.* an instrument with edgeless blade for working pigments; an instrument for pressing tongue.

Spatular *adj.* of the shape of a spatula.

Spatule *n.* broad spoon shaped formation or part.

Spavin *n.* a disease in horses.

Spawn *n.* eggs of fish; frogs, molluscs, etc; when ejected; (contempt.) progeny; white fibrous matter from which fungi are produced.

Spay *v.t.* to castrate; to remove ovaries.

Speak *v.t. & i.* to utter words; to hold conversion (with a person about something).

Speaker *n.* one who makes discourse; the president of a deliberative assembly.

Spear *n.* a long pointed hurling weapon; a lance.

Spearman *n.* one armed with a spear.

Spec *n.* speculation; enterprise.

Special *adj.* of a peculiar or restricted kind; not general; extra-ordinary; chief in excellence.

Species *n.* a class of things having some common characteristics; a sub-division of a genus; variety; kind.

Specific *adj.* possessing, concerned with, the properties that characterize a species.

Specimen *n.* sample; pattern.

Speciology *n.* science of species.

Speciosity *n.* good appearance.

Specious *adj.* plausible, fair-seeming, colourable; .

Speck *n.* a small spot; stain; a blemish; dot; mark of rottenness; a flaw.

Spectacle *n.* (*pl.*) pair of lenses to correct or assist defective eyesight.

Spectral *adj.* of the spectrum; ghost-like.

Spectre *adj.* a ghost; an apparition.

Spectro *pref.* in sense of 'spectrum'.

Spectrum *n.* the image of something seen continuing when the eyes closed or turned away; the seven coloured band formed by passing a light through a glass prism; the coloured bond into which a beam of light is decomposed.

Specular *adj.* having the qualities of a mirror; of the nature of a speculum.

Speculate *v.i.* to make an inquiry; to meditate; to form an opinion.

Speech *n.* faculty of speaking; anything said; particular language; an oration.

Speed *n.* relative pace of motion or action; dispatch; rapidly of movement.

Spell *v.t.* to write or name the letters that form a word; to take the place of.

Spend *v.t.* & *i.* to pay for a purchase; to expend or use up; to lay out.

Spendthrift *n.* one who spends lavishly.

Sperm *n.* the male generative cell; seminal fluid; supermaceti.

Spermatozoa *n.* sperm-cells.

Spermo *pref.* in sense of 'seed'.

Spew, Spue *v.t.* & *i.* (of gun) to droop at muzzle from too quick firing; (vulg.) to vomit.

Sphagnum *n.* a kind of moss which grows in marshes.

Sphenoid *adj.* of the shape of a wedge.

Sphere *n.* a solid figure having all points of its surface equidistant from a point within it; ball; the heavens.

Spherograph *n.* an instrument for projecting the relative positions of the earth on a disk.

Spheroid *n.* a sphere-like solid; body of approximately spherical shape.

Sphincter *n.* ring-muscle of orifice.

Sphinx *n.* a fabulous monster with a woman's head and a lion's body.

Spice *n.* an aromatic or pungent vegetable substance used as flavouring food; spices collectively.

Spicery *n.* spices in general; a room for keeping spices.

Spicy *adj.* having much spice; aromatic.

Spiel *n.* a talk; speech. *v.t.* to make speeches.

Spider *n.* an eight-legged insect of many varieties which spin webs.

Spigot *n.* vent-peg or part of tap by which flow in controlled.

Spile *n.* a wooden peg. *v.t.* to pierce hole in a barrel.

Spin *v.t.* & *i.* to draw out and twist into threads; to twist; to prolong. *n.* a revolving motion; whirl.

Spinal *adj.* of the spine or back bone.

Spindle *n.* a pin on which something revolves.

Spindrift *n.* the spray of the sea waves.

Spine *n.* the backbone; the series of vertebrae forming the back-bone.

Spined *adj.* having a backbone.

Spinel *n.* a scarlet ruby-like precious stone.

Spinet *n.* a musical instrument.

Spinnaker *n.* a large extra sail of racing yacht.

Spinney *n.* a small thicket.

Spiracular *adj.* pertaining to spiracle.

Spiral *adj.* coiled in a plane or around a cylinder or cone. *n.* spiral curve.

Spirality *n.* the stage of being windy.

Spirant *n.* the pronunciation of a consonant.

Spire *n.* tapering structure, coil; spiral; a steeple.

Spirit *n.* strong liquor; the soul; mental disposition; rational.

Spiritless *adj.* despodent; without spirit.

Spiritual *adj.* not material; divine; religious; relating to the mind; holy; concerned with religious things.

Spirituous *adj.* of the nature of or containing distilled spirit.

Spit *n.* point of land running out into the sea, etc.

Spit *n.* a slender bar on which meat is roasted; a small point of land running into the sea; spitting; spaded depth.

Splash *v.t.* & *i.* to agitate liquid so that drops of it fly about.

Splatter *v.t.* & *i.* to make a continuous sound of splashing.

Spleen *n.* moroseness; irritability; abdominal organ acting on the blood; spite.

Splenalgia *n.* pain in spleen.

Splendid *adj.* brilliant; shining; glorious; excellent.

Splendour *n.* splendidness; great brightness; magnificence; pomp.

Splenius *n.* the muscle on the sides and the back of the neck which holds the head in position.

Splice *v.t.* to join (pieces of rope or wood) into one length.

Spline *n.* rectangular key fitting into grooves in hub and shaft of wheel.

Splint *n.* a strip of wood for holding broken bone when set.

Splinter *n.* a pointed, sharpedged or narrow fragment.

Split *v.t.* & *i.* to divide into parts; to break forcibly; to devide lengthwise; to divide into hostile parties.

Splotch, Splodge *ns.* daub; smear.

Spoil *n.* plunder taken from enemy in war; robbery; things found or acquired; emoluments of office, etc.

Spoilage *n.* paper spoilt in printing.

Spoilation *n.* pillaging; despoiling; plunder; robbery.

Spoiler *n.* plunderer; one who corrupts.

Spoke *n.* a bar preventing a wheel from turning *esp.* down-hill; a rung of a ladder; a round of a ladder.

Spokesman *n.* one who speaks for or represents another person.

Spondee *n.* a metrical dot of two long syllables.

Spondyl (e) *n.* the joint of back bone.

Sponge *n.* an aquatic animal of low order with pores in the bodywall.

Spongy *adj.* soft as sponge.

Sponsor *n.* godfather or godmother; a surety.

Sponsorship *n.* the office of a sponsor.

Spontaneity *n.* the quality of being spontaneous.

Spontaneous *adj.* voluntary; resulting from natural impulse; on one's own freewill; not deliberate or laboured.

Spoof *n.* to cheat; to swindle. *n.* a cheat.

Spook *n.* a ghost.

Spool *n.* a reel for winding yarn of photographic film; bobbin.

Spoon *n.* shallow oval bowl with long handle; a simpleton; a silly fellow.

Spoor *n.* track of animal. *v.t.* & *i.* to follow by track.

Sport *n.* play; fun; amusement; game; pastime; diversion.

Spot *n.* a small mark of stain; a particular locality or space; a pimple on skin; blot; a blemish in character.

Spouse *n.* husband or wife. **Spousal** *adj.* matrimonial; nuptial.

Spout *n.* sloping trough; a jet of liquid.

Sprag *n.* a piece of wood or metal used as a brake on the wheel of a car.

Sprain *n.* the wrench (a joint) so as to cause pain and swelling. *v.t.* to twist the muscles so as to injure.

Sprawl *v.t.* & *i.* to spread oneself irregularly.

Spray *n.* a slender branch of a tree; sprig.

Spread *v.t.* & *i.* to extend the surface of; to unfold; display thus to eye or mind.

Spree *n.* a lively frolic; a noisy merri- ment; bout of drinking.

Spring *n.* a leap; the season of the year in which vegetation begins.

Sprinkle *v.t.* & *i.* to scatter in small drops or particles.

Sprint *v.t.* & *i.* to run a short distance; to run at full speed.

Sprit *n.* a small spar reaching diagonally from mast to upper outer corner of sail.

Sprocket *n.* each of several teeth on wheel on the links of which a chain moves.

Sprout *v.t.* & *i.* to shoot forth; to germinate; to grow; to produce.

Spruce *adj.* of trim smart appearance; neat in dress and appearance.

Sprue *n.* passage through which metal is poured into mould.

Spry *adj.* mimble; lively; active.

Spud *n.* (*sl.*) a potato; a short thick thing; a kind of small spade.

Spuddle *v.i.* to dig slightly.

Spume *n.* froth; foam.

Spumescence *n.* frothiness.

Spunk *n.* courage; spirit.

Spunky *adj.* spirited; brave.

Spur *n.* a pricking goad worn on horseman's heel; stimulus; a projecting mountain.

Spurious *adj.* not genuine; pretended; fictitious, false, counterfeit.

Spurn *v.t.* & *i.* to thrust back with foot; to disdain; to treat contemptuously.

Spurrier *n.* a spur-maker.

Spurt *v.t.* & *i.* to make a sudden violent effort; to drive liquid from a small pipe.

Spy *n.* a person secretly collecting and reporting information; a scout.

Spyism *n.* the business of spying.

Squab *n.* a cushion; couch; a short fat person; an unfledged bird.

Squabble *v.t.* & *i.* to engage in a wrangle; to quarrel.

Squadron *n.* a divisoin of cavalry regiment consisting of 120 to 200 soldiers.

Squail *n.* (*pl.*) a kind of game played with small wooden disks on round table or board.

Squalid *adj.* dirty; foul; mean; nasty.

Squall *n.* a discordant cay; a sudden gust of wind; a thunderstorm.

Squaloid *adj.* like a shark.

Squalor *n.* squalidness.

Squama *n.* a scale like structure.

Squander *v.t.* to scatter lavishly; to spend wastefully; to fling away.

Square *adj.* having four equal sides and four right angles; fair; just.

Squarely *adv.* completely; equally.

Squarish *adj.* nearly square.

Squarrose *adj.* rough with scale-like processes.

Squarson *n.* a squire and parson in one.

Squash *v.t.* & *i.* to press into pulp; to crush; to squeeze.

Squat *v.i.* (of animals) to crouch close to ground; to sit on one's hams or heels; or on ground with knees drawn up.

Squawk *v.i.* (to utter) harsh cry of pair of fear (chiefly of birds).

Squeak *n.* a short shrill cry.

Squeamish *adj.* fastidious; overscrupulous; tending to vomit.

Squeegee *n.* a rubber-edged mop for sweeping deck; a small similar instrument or roller used in photography.

Squeeze *v.t.* & *i.* to exert pressure upon; to compress with hand.

Squelch *v.t.* & *i.* to crush flat; to finish; to silence.

Squib *n.* firework which makes a hissing sound when thrown on ground.

Squiffy *adj.* slightly drunk.

Squint *v.t.* & *i.* look sidelong; to have the eyes turned in different direction.

Squinter *n.* one who sees obliquely.

Squire *n.* a country gentleman; an attendant of a knight.

Squirehood, Squireship *ns.* the rank of a squire.

Squirely *adv.* like a squire.

Squireen *n.* a small land-owner in Ireland.

Squirm *v.t.* & *n.* to show, feel, embarrassment; to writhe like a worm.

Squirt *v.t.* & *i.* to eject fluid in a jet.

Stab *n.* a blow; a thrust.

Stable *adj.* not easily moved; firm; durable; constant; firmly fixed.

Stabilize *v.t.* to make firm.

Stabling *n.* act of putting in a stable.

Stablish *v.t.* to make stable.

Stack *n.* a pile of hay; number of chimneys standing together.

Stadium *n.* an athletic ground; a stage; period of a disease.

Staff *n.* a stick or pole as weapon or support or as symbol of office.

Stag *n.* male of red deer; a castrated bull.

Stage *n.* a raised platform; platform of a theatre; raised place on which anything is exhibited.

Stage-coach *n.* a coach running at regular stages for the conveyance of passengers.

Stagecraft *n.* skill in writing or staging plays.

Stager *n.* a person of experience.

Stage-manager *n.* the manager of a stage.

Stage-player *n.* a player of the stage.

Stagery *n.* exhibition on a stage.

Staggard *n.* a stag of four years old.

Stagger *v.t.* & *i.* to go unsteadily as if about to fall; to totter; to sway helplessly. *n.* a tottering movement.

Staggering *n.* tottering.

Staggers *n. pl.* a disease of the brain.

Stagnant *adj.* unchanging; inert, sluggish; motionless; not flowing in a current, without curret or tide.

Stagnate *v.i.* to cease to flow; to become motionless.

Stagy *adj.* theatrical in a manner, appearance.

Stain *n.* fact that sullies a person's reputatijon, cause of reproach; colouring liquid for standing; a coloured spot.

Stair *n.* set of fixed steps for ascending; one such step.

Staircase *n.* the part of a building which contains flights of stairs.

Staithe *n.* a place for loading and unloading coal.

Stake *n.* a pointed stick used as support or a boundary mark.

Stalactite *n.* a deposit of carbonate of lime hanging from roof of cave etc.

Stale *adj.* lacking freshness insipid; musty; tasteless.

Staleness *n.* the triteness.

Stalk *n.* slender stem of plant of flower support of anything.

Stalked *adj.* having a stem.

Stalkless *adj.* without a stalk.

Stall *n.* space appropriated to one dealer in market or bazaar; compartment for one animal in stable or cow-house.

Stalwart *adj.* courageous; tall and strong; stouthearted.

Stalwartly *adv.* in a resolute manner.

Stamen *n.* the organ of a flower containing polen; the male organ of fructification in plant.

Stammer *v.t.* & *i.* & *n.* to utter (an excuse etc.) with hesitation; to speak haltingly.

Stamp *v.t.* & *i.* to affix postage or other stamp to; to impress on the memory.

Stampede *n.* a rush of horses or cattle or people under sudden common impulse, *esp.* panic.

Stance *n.* position taken for stroke in golf or cricket.

Stanch *v.i.* to stop the flow of blood; to cease to flow blood.

Stand *n.* a stationary condition; a halt; stoppage; a thing on which anything is placed.

Standard *n.* the flage of a regiment; a principle.

Stander *n.* one who stands.

Standing *adj.* permanent established; fixed.

Standpoint *n.* point of view; a fundamental principle.

Standstill *n.* inability to proceed; arrest of progress.

Stannic *adj.* pertaining to tin-mines.

Stanza *n.* a group of lines of a poem.

Stanzaic *adj.* concerning a stanza.

Staple *n.* settled market; principle article of commerce; raw mateial; chief material; fibre of wool or cotton.

Staple *n.* important or principle article of commerce in a district or country.

Stapler *n.* a dealer in staple goods.

Stapler *n.* a type of instrument by which one can join two or more things (paper) by the help of a pin.

Star *n.* any celestial body normally seen as a point of light; the asteris used in printing (*); a prominent person; destiny.

Starboard *n.* the right side of a ship or boat as one looks forward; to turn the ship to the right-hand side.

Starch *n.* a white odourless powder obtained from corn and potatoes.

Starchedly *adv.* in a starched manner.

Starchy *adj.* consisting of starch.

Stare *v.t. & i.* to look with fixed eyes; to gaze intently.

Starfish *n.* a kind of fish.

Stargazer *n.* an astronomer or astrologer.

Staring *adj.* of a fixed look.

Stark *adj.* rigid *esp.* in death; (of folly etc.) sheer or unmitigated; resolute.

Start *v.t. & i.* to set out; to make a sudden movement; to give way; to make a beginning.

Starter *n.* starting in race; a person who gives signal for start in race.

Startle *v.t.* to give shock of surprise to; to alarm suddenly.

Startler *n.* startling fact or statement.

Starvation *n.* the act of starving.

Starve *v.t. & i.* to die or suffer acutely from lack of food or cold.

Stasis *n.* stoppage of circulation of any of the fluids of the body.

State *n.* a body politic; rank; dignity; mode of existence; nation; pomp.

Stateliness *n.* dignity.

Stately *adj.* marked by great dignity; majestic.

State-monger *n.* one who is versed in politics.

State-servant *n.* a servent of the state.

Statesmanlike *adj.* having the qualities of a statesman.

Station *n.* a stopping place for railway trains; standing; the place where a thing rests or stands for a particular purpose.

Stationer *n.* a merchant who sells writting materials.

Stationery *n.* writing materials and connected goods writing articles sold by stationers.

Statistics *n.* (*pl.*) the collection of facts and figures regarding the condition of a people.

Statoscope *n.* a barometer for showing the minute variations of pressure.

Statuary *adj.* pertaining to statues.

Statue *n.* a life like sculptured of an animal or a person.

Status *n.* one's standing or rank; position held by a person or community; state of affairs.

Statutory *adj.* enacted by statute; of the nature of a statute.

Staunch *adj.* constant to obligations or purpose; untiring in service or loyalty; air-tight; water-tight.

Stave *n.* one of the curved wooden strips forming sides of cask etc.; a rung o a ladder.

Stay *n.* a sojourn or its duration; a prop or support; suspension of judicial proceedings.

Stayorder *n.* suspension of judgment for a time.

Stead *n.* room; place.

Steady *adj.* firm in position; constant; not changing.

Steak *n.* a slice of meat cut for broiling.

Steal *v.t. & i.* to take away secretly without permission.

Steam *n.* the vapour of boiling water; energy; vigour.

Steamer *n.* a steam-ship or boat; a vessel moved by steam.

Stearin *n.* the chief ingredient of tallow used in the manufacture of candles.

Stearinery *n.* a factory in which candles are made.

Steatite *n.* kind of talc; soapstone.

Steel *n.* kinds of alloy of iron with carbon or other elements; extreme hardness.

Steep *adj.* precipitous; exaggerated; not reasonable.

Steeple *n.* high church tower running into a spire; a tower with a spire.

Steer *n.* a young male ox *esp.* a castrated one.

Steer *v.t. & i.* to guide a vessel, motor car, airship, bicycle & etc.

Steersman *n.* the helmsman of a ship.

Stellar *adj.* full of stars.

Stellate *adj.* resembling a star.

Stellular *adj.* shaped like small stars.

Stem *n.* the main body of a tree or plant; the branch of a family; stem-shaped part.

Stench *n.* an offensive smell.

Stencil *n.* a thin plate (of metal etc.) with a pattern cut through it.

Steno *pref.* in the sense of 'narrow'.

Stentor *n.* a person with a loud and powerful voice.

Step *n.* a mark left by foot on the ground; pace; manner of walking.

Step *v.t. & i.* to set as the foot; to move with alternate feet; go by stepping.

Stepney *n.* a substitue wheel for a motor-car.

Steppe *n.* a level uncultivated grassland.

Stereo *pref.* in sense of 'solid'.

Stereobate *n.* the solid platform on which a building is constructed.

Sterile *adj.* unproductive; barren; unfruitful; not bearing seed.

Sterility *n.* barrenness; unfruitfulness.

Sterling *adj.* sound; genunine; of solid worth; undoubted; of excellent quality.

Stern *adj.* enforcing obedience; rigid; severe; harsh; cruel.

Sternum *n.* the bone running from neck to stomach; breastbone.

Stet *n.* proof-correcting direction.

Stethoscope *n.* an instrument making patient's heart-action and other internal sounds audible to the user.

Stevedore *n.* a man employed in ship-loading.

Stew *n.* a house of ill-fame; meat or fruit stewed; mental agitation; worry; pond of keeping fish.

Steward *n.* an official managing an entertainment, meeting or show.

Sthenic *adj.* (of disease, etc.) with morbid increase of vital action *esp.* of heart and arteries.

Stibium *n.* antimony.

Sticcado *n.* a kind of musical instrument.

Stick *n.* the shoot of a tree; a walking cane; a staff; twig.

Stick *v.t.* & *i.* to keep position as if rooted or embedded; to pierce a pointed thing into.

Sticklac *n.* lac in its natural state.

Stickleback *n.* a small fish with sharp spines on back.

Sticker *n.* an insisting contender.

Sticky *adj.* tending to stick; glutinous; tenacious.

Stiff *adj.* hard to bend or mould; difficult to achieve or perform; rigid.

Stiff-market *n.* when prices remain firm.

Stiff-neck *n.* a rheumatic affection of the neck.

Stifle *v.t.* & *i.* to suppress; to suffocate; to choke; to smother.

Stigma *n.* a moral spot or stain or brand, a mark of infamy, disgrace; *Bio.* part of ovary surface that receives pollen in impregnation.

Stigmatize *v.t.* to use abusive language; to mark with a stigma.

Stigmatization *n.* use of abusive ferms.

Stile *n.* upright timber of door or window.

Stiletto *n.* a small dagger; an instrument for making eyelets.

Still *n.* a distilling apparatus. *v.t.* to distil.

Still *adj.* silent; motionless; without sound; silent; peaceful.

Stilt *n.* one of a pair of poles with brackets raising walker's feet above ground; a long-legged bird.

Stilton *n.* a kind of cheese.

Stiltpetrel *n.* a bird with long legs.

Stimulant *adj.* producing transient increase of vital energy.

Stimulate *v.t.* to apply stimulus to; to excite; to animate.

Stimulation *n.* the act of exciting.

Stimulating *adj.* exciting.

Stimulus *n.* a thing that evokes activity in tissues etc.

Sting *n.* a sharp-pointed weapon in insects and some animals & etc.

Stinger *n.* sharp frost; painful bow.

Stink *v.i.* to emit an offensive smell. *n.* a disagreeable smell.

Stint *v.t.* to supply on a niggardly scale; limitation of supply or effort; restriction as to quantity.

Stipe *n.* a stalk; the stem of a plant.

Stipel *n.* secondary stipule at base of leaflets.

Stipellate *adj.* having secondary leaves.

Stipend *n.* a salary; a fixed pay for service.

Stipple *v.t.* & *i.* to engrave in dots instead of lines. *n.* dotted engraving.

Stipulate *v.t.* & *i.* to state to be part of one's terms; to make a demand; to make a contract.

Stipulation *n.* a contract.

Stipule *n.* a small leaf at the base of the stem of a plant.

Stir *v.t.* & *i.* to set in motion.

Stirpiculture *n.* the breeding of a special stock.

Stirps *n.* a generation or race; progenitor.

Stirrup *n.* rider's foot-rest.

Stitch *n.* acute pain in side; a single pass of needle in sewing.

Stoat *n.* an animal of the weasel tribe. *v.t.* to sew.

Stock *n.* money contributed by way of loan to form the Capital of a company; the main trunk or stem of a plant or tree; stump or butt or trunk.

Stocking *n.* a close-fitting, knitted covering for the legs or feet.

Stocky *adj.* short and strongly built; thickset.

Stodge *n.* full meal; a greedy eater. *v.t.* & *i.* to eat greedily; to stuff.

Stodgy *adj.* indigestible; bulging out.

Stogie *n.* a long slender cigar; (U.S.) kind of heavy boot.

Stoic *n.* a person of great fortitude or austerity.

Stoical *adj.* pertaining to the doctrine of stoics.

Stoicism *n.* indifference to pleasure or pain.

Stoke *v.t.* & *i.* to feed the fire of an engine.

Stole *n.* a hanging garment.

Stolid *adj.* not easily moved; dull.

Stomach *n.* the cavity into which food passes for digestion; belly; abdomen.

Stone *n.* a piece of rock; of any shape and of no great size; a gem.

Stony *n.* abounding in stones.

Stook *n.* a stock of bundles of stalks; group of cornsheaves.

Stool *n.* evacuation of bowels; a window sill; root of plant from which shoots spring; movable seat without a back.

Stoop *n.* unroofed platform or porch.

Stoop *v.t.* & *i.* to bend down so as to bring the head near the ground; to submit.

Stop *n.* cessation of motion; check; punctuation mark.

Stop *v.t.* & *i.* to close; to stuff up; to put a stop to; to prevent passage through; stifle; to obstruct.

Stopple *n.* the stopper of a bottle; a plug. *v.t.* to close with a stopper.

Storage *n.* the safe storing of goods; charges paid for this.

Storax *n.* a resinous balsam used in medicine.

Store *n.* a place where things ae kept; a great quantity or number; abundance; plenty; warehouse.

Storge *adj.* love for one's progeny; parental affection.

Stork *n.* a tall steady (*usu.* white) wadig bird that fed on fishes, etc.

Storm *n.* a tempest; violent disturbance of the atmosphere, great excitement; tumult.

Stormy *adj.* boisterous; associated with or threatening storms.

Story *n.* legends or tradition; a place between two floors; an account given of an incident.

Stoup *n.* drinking vessel; flagon, beaker.

Stout *adj.* strong; resolute; brave; sturdy; strongly built; vigorous.

Stoutish *adj.* some-what stout.

Stoutly *adv.* boldly.

Stove *n.* kinds of closed apparatus in which heat is produced.

Stover *n.* fodder for cattle.

Stow *v.t.* to pack goods in a compact form; to fill things in a well-arranged manner.

Straddle *v.t.* & *i.* to take or be in attitude with legs apart; to part one's legs.

Strafe *v.t.* to thrash; to abuse; to attack; to punish. *n.* abusive language.

Straggle *v.i.* to be scattered; to get dispersed.

Straggler *n.* one who straggles; a rover or wanderer; a vagabond.

Straight *adj.* not curved or crooked; without bend; correctly placed or in proper order.

Straightarm *n.* a straight-forward thrust.

Straightaway *n.* straight forward.

Straightway *adv.* immediately.

Strain *v.t.* & *i.* to exert one's self; to wrest or distort from true meaning; to injure by over-exertion.

Strainer *n.* an appliance through which liquid is poured to be cleared of matter suspended in it.

Strait *adj.* strict; limited, narrow.

Strake *n.* the iron band of a wheel.

Stramonium *n.* a plant whose seeds are used in medicine.

Strand *n.* one of the strings or wires by twisting which a rope is made; the margin of sea or lake.

Strange *adj.* wonderful; foreign; unfamiliar.

Stranger *n.* a person strange to some one or to something.

Strangely *adv.* in a peculiar manner.

Strangle *v.t.* to kill by pressing the neck; to suppress; to suffocate.

Strangulation *n.* constriction of the throat.

Strangury *n.* disease in which urine is passed painfully and in drops.

Strap *n.* (*Bot.*) tongue-shaped part in ligulate floret; a strip of leather or other material.

Strappado *n.* a kind of torture.

Strapper *n.* one who strikes with a strap.

Strapping *adj.* stalwart; tall and strong.

Stratagem *n.* a device for deceiving the enemy; a clever plan, a trick to obtain, advantage.

Strategy *n.* the art of war; the science of military tactics.

Strategic *adj.* pertaining to a stratagem.

Strategist *n.* an expert in strategy.

Strath *n.* a broad mountain valley; a stretch of flat land by the river side.

Straticulate *adj.* (*Geol.*) arranged in thin layers.

Stratum *n.* a layer of deposited matter forming part of earth's crust; social grade.

Stratus *n.* a continuous expanse of cloud; low horizontal sheet of cloud.

Straw *n.* single stalk of straw; the dry stalks or stems of certain kinds of grain.

Strawberry *n.* a kind of perennial plant.

Strawboard *n.* a thick paper made of straw.

Strawcutter *n.* an instrument for cutting fodder.

Strawy *adj.* full of straw.

Stray *v.t.* to ramble; to wander without aim; to lose one's ways.

Streak *n.* a long narrow irregular line or band. *v.t.* to make with streaks.

Streakily *adv.* by way of streaks.

Stream *n.* a body of running water; a current; direction of flow.

Street *n.* a town or village road lined with houses, the roadway.

Strength *n.* vigour; power; force; that which is encouraged by argument; robustness.

Stress *n.* emphasis; accent; stretch or pressure or tension or compulsion.

Stretch *n.* to straighten; to lengthen; to spread; to tighten; to extend; to exert to the utmost; to spread.

Strew *v.t.* to scatter on surface; to cover with small objects.

Stria *n.* the mark of lines on a surface; a slight furrow.

Striate *adj.* striated.

Striately *adv.* in a striated manner.

Stricken *adj.* wounded in the chase; struck with a blow.

Strickle *n.* a rod used in strike-measure.

Strict *adj.* accurate; tense; severe; rigid; requiring exact performance.
Strictured *adj.* censured; obstructed.
Stride *v.t.* & *i.* to walk with long steps; to bestride.
Stridulate *v.t.* to make a shrill cry by rubbing the parts of the body.
Strife *n.* struggle, contention; quarrels.
Strifeful *adj.* contentious.
Strigil *n.* an appliance for scraping the skin at the bath.
Strike *n.* a refusal of employes to work unless their grievances are remedied.
Strike *v.t.* & *i.* to hit; to deliver a blow; to dash against; to punish; to bring into specified condition by striking.
Striker *n.* one who strikes.
String *n.* twine or fine cord; a slender rope used for typing; length of this material; stretched piece of wire.
Stringed *adj.* provided with strings.
Stringency *n.* severe pressure.
Strip *v.t.* & *i.* to remove clothes or covering from; (of screw) lose thread.
Stripe *n.* a long narrow band generally of equal breath attached to a surface of a different colour.
Stripling *n.* a lad; a youth.
Strive *v.i.* to endeavour; to try hard; to try earnestly; to contend.
Strobile *n.* cone of pine etc.
Strobiliform *adj.* cone-shaped.
Strocal *n.* a shovel used by glass-makers.
Stroke *v.t.* to pass the hand gently in one direction. *n.* the act of stroking.
Stroke *n.* shock given by a blow; sudden attack; favourable turn of luck.
Stroker *n.* one who strokes.
Stroll *v.i.* to walk leisurely along; to ramble; to saunter; to rove from place to place.
Stroma *n.* connective tissue of organ or cell.
Stromatic *adj.* miscellaneous.
Strong *adj.* having power or resistance; powerful by size or number or resources or quality.
Stronghold *n.* a fortress.
Strong-room *n.* a strong room in which valuables are kept.
Strong-set *adj.* firmly fixed.
Strontia *n.* an ingredient of fire-works.
Strop *n.* a strip of leather on which razors & etc. are sharpened.
Strophe *n.* a stanza.
Strophiolate *adj.* furnished with a garland.
Strophulus *n.* tooth-rash.
Structural *adj.* pertaining to structure.
Structure *n.* manner in which a building or organism holds together; supporting framework of something.

Struggle *v.t.* to make a violent effort; to contend with; to make great efforts under difficulties; to strive hard.

Strum *v.t. & i.* to twang the strings of a musical instrument.

Struma *n.* (*Bot.*) cushion-like dilatation of an organ; scrofula.

Strumpet *n.* a prostitue.

Strut *v.i.* to walk with affected dignity; to walk in stiff pompous way.

Struthious *adj.* pertaining to or like an ostrich.

Struttingly *adv.* in a strutting manner.

Stub *n.* remnant of pencil, cigar, etc.

Stubble *n.* stumps of grain left sticking up after harvest; cropped hair.

Stubbly *adj.* stubbled; short and stiff.

Stubborn *adj.* not yielding; obstinate.

Stucco *n.* a fine plaster or cement for walls *v.t.* to face with stucco.

Stud *n.* projecting knob on a surface; a two-headed button; a small post.

Stud-farm *n.* a place where horses are bred.

Stud-horse *n.* a stallion.

Student *n.* a person who studies for some occupation; one who studies some branch of learning; a scholar.

Studied *adj.* carefully examined; deliberate or intentional.

Studio *n.* the working room of an artist or photographer.

Studious *adj.* given to study; delligent; anxious; deliberate; attentive to.

Study *n.* meditation; devotion of time and mind to books; pursuit of knowledge; investigation; sketch of a picture; a room used for study or for transacting any business.

Stuff *n.* material; substance or things of inferior quality; woollen fabric; nonsense.

Stuffer *n.* he who or that which stuff.

Stuffy *adj.* packed up; lacking ventilation; difficult to breathe.

Stultify *v.t.* to reduce to absurdity.

Stultifier *n.* one who befools another person.

Stultiloquy *n.* a silly or foolish talk.

Stum *n.* unfermented juice of grapes.

Stumble *v.i. & t.* to feel scruples or doubt about; to be checked in speech.

Stumer *n.* a counterfeit coin or cheque.

Stump *n.* a stub, when the rest has been cut or has fallen away; any of the three uprights of a cricket wicket.

Stun *v.t.* to knock senseless; to overwhelm; to stupefy by a shock; to make senseless temporarily; to bewilder.

Stunner *n.* one who stuns.

Stunt *v.t.* to check the growht of. *n.* a special effort or display.

Stupe *n.* flannel wrung out of hot water and applied as fomentation.

Stupefacient *adj.* having stupefying power.

Stupendous *adj.* amazing; wonderful; prodigious.

Stupeous *adj.* with long loose scales.

Stupid *adj.* uninteresting; foolish.

Stupidity *n.* foolishness; lack of intelligence.

Stupidly *adv.* in a foolish manner.

Stupor *n.* utter amazement; dazed or torpid state; insensibility.

Stupose *adj.* with tufts of long hair.

Stuprate *v.t.* to ravish.

Stupration *n.* violation of woman's chastity.

Sturdy *adj.* not easily knocked down or pushed aside; strongly built; robust; hardy.

Sturdily *adv.* in a sturdy manner.

Sturgeon *n.* large fish like shark with mailed body and head.

Stutter *v.t.* & *i.* to speak in a stammering way; to stammer. *n.* hesitation in speech.

Sty *n.* filthy room or dwelling; place of debauchery; inflamed swelling on the edge of the eyelid.

Stygin *adj.* infernal; gloomy.

Style *n.* manner of writing or speaking; a small pointed rod used for scratching on a waxed plate.

Stylo *n. prefix* meaning 'pillar'.

Suable *adj.* that can be sued.

Suasible *adj.* easily persuaded.

Suasion *n.* persuasion; reasoning or advice as incentive.

Suave *adj.* bland; polite.

Suavely *adv.* in a polite manner.

Sub *pref.* in the sense of 'under', 'subordinate'.

Subject *adj.* under government; subjacent; obedient, submissive, owing obedience to; politically dependent; liable or exposed or prone to.

Subjectivism *n.* the theory that knowledge is subjective only and incapable of objective test of truth.

Subjoin *v.t.* to append; to add at the end.

Subjudice *adj.* under judicial consideration.

Subjugable *adj.* able to be subdued.

Subjugate *adj.* to conquer and force to submit; to bring into subection.

Subjunctive *adj.* subordinate; subjoined. *n.* a mood of a verb.

Sub-kingdom *n.* main division of animal or vegetable kingdom.

Sub-lease *n.* & *v.t.* to sublet, letting to another person of what the lessor himself holds on lease.

Sublesee *n.* one to whom a holding is sublet.

Sublimate *v.t.* to refine; to convert from a solid state to vapour and again allow to solidify.

Sublime *adj.* so impressive as to inspire awe or wonder; lying near the surface; elevated aloft, exalted; surpassing.

Sublingual *adj.* situated under the tongue.

Sublunar *adj.* beneath the moon.

Sublunary *adj.* pertaining to this world.

Submarine *adj.* growing or acting under sea water. *n.* submersible boat.

Submerge *v.t.* & *i.* to sink; to contain below the surface.

Submission *n.* submitting; obedience to authority; humble or suppliant behaviour, meekness.

Submit *v.t.* & *i.* to yield or to surrender oneself to power or authority.

Submuscular *adj.* under the muscle.

Suboctuple *adj.* containing one part in eight.

Subocular *adj.* under the eye.

Suboctuple *adj.* containing one part in eight.

Suborbicular *adj.* almost circular.

Subordinate *adj.* of inferior importance or rank.

Suborn *v.t.* to cause to take a false oath; to induce to commit perjury or other crime.

Suborner *n.* one who commits perjury.

Subovate *adj.* nearly in the form of an egg.

Subpoena *n.* & *v.t.* a writ commanding the presence of a person in a court as a witness under a penalty.

Subpolar *adj.* near the pole.

Subquadrate *adj.* nearly square.

Subquintuple *adj.* containing one part in five.

Subramous *adj.* having a few banches.

Subrigid *adj.* moderately rigid or stiff.

Subreption *n.* the act of obtaining favour by surprise.

Subrotund *adj.* almost round.

Subsaline *adj.* moderately salt.

Subscribable *adj.* able to be subscribed.

Subscribe *v.t.* & *i.* to express adhesion to; to give consent to; to sign (one's name or a document etc.); to contribute to a fund or an object.

Subscriber *n.* one who subscribes.

Subscript *n.* something written below.

Subscription *n.* the act of subscribing; share or sum subscribed.

Subsection *n.* division of a section.

Subsequence *n.* the state of succeeding.

Subserve *v.t.* & *i.* to promote; to serve; to answer the purpose.

Subservience *n.* operation that promotes some end.

Subserviency *n.* subservience.

Subside *v.i.* to fall into a state of quiet; to abate; to disappear.

Subsidence *adj.* the act of subsiding.

Subsidiary *adj.* serving to help; supplementary to; auxiliary. *n.* an accessory.

Subsidy *n.* money grant from state to private concerns of public utility; money grant to sovereign; or to another state in return for support.

Subsist *v.t.* & *i.* to find sustenance; to inhere; to remain alive; to exist; to contrive; to contrive; to feed.

Subsoil *adj.* the soil which lies just beneath the surface soil.

Substance *n.* the essential part; gist; being; purport; matter; real meaning.

Substitute *n.* a person or thing put in place of another. *v.t.* to put a person or thing in place of another.

Subsultus *n.* convulsive motion.

Subsume *v.t.* to include under a rule.

Subterfuge *n.* evasion (*esp.* in argument of excuse), a dishonest shift.

Subterranean *adj.* lying under the surface of the earth; underground.

Subtil *adj.* thin; nice; subtle; delicate.

Subtle *adj.* crafty, cunning; ingeniously minute, capable of nice distinctions.

Subtrahend *n.* what is to be subtracted in a subtraction sum.

Subulate *adjs.* awl-shaped.

Suburb *n.* outskirts of a city outlying district of a city.

Suburban *adj.* pertaining to suburbs.

Suburbs *n. pl.* the environs.

Subursine *adj.* almost like a bear.

Subvert *n.* to effect destruction or throw of (religion etc.).

Subvertible *adj.* able to be subverted.

Subway *n.* an underground footway.

Succade *n.* a sweetmeat.

Succedaneum *n.* a substitute.

Succeed *v.t.* & *i.* to attain one's purpose, be successful; to inhert.

Success *n.* the prosperous termination of anything; favourable issue; attainment of one's object; good fortune; prosperity.

Successfully *adv.* in a successful manner.

Succession *n.* a following in order; order of descendants.

Successor *n.* one who succeed; a person or thing succceeding to another.

Succour *n.* aid given at the time of need. *v.t.* to come to the assistance of.

Succourer *n.* a helper; one who gives relief.

Succourless *adj.* without help.

Such *adj.* of the kind or degree indicated.

Suck *v.t.* & *i.* to draw a liquid into the mouth; to imbibe; to draw milk.

Sucker *n.* a person or thing that sucks; organ or pipe through which liquid is drawn by suction; pump-piston.

Sucrose *n.* cane-sugar.

Suction *n.* production of partial vacuum by removal of air etc.

Sudation *n.* excessive sweeting.

Sudatory *adj.* stimulating perspiration.

Sudd *n.* floating mass of plants.

Sudden *adj.* occurring unexpectedly; abrupt; hurried.

Sudorific *adj.* & *n.* a sweat-producing medicine.

Sue *v.t.* & *i.* to prosecute in court; to apply in a court for redress.

Suede *n.* undressed kid-skin as used for gloves.

Suet *n.* the hard fat of an animal; fat enclosing kidneys and loins of ox.

Suffer *v.t.* & *i.* to undergo pain or damage or punishment; to allow; to bear what is inconvenient.

Suffice *v.t.* & *i.* to be enough or sufficient; to meet the needs of.

Sufficiency *n.* self-confidence; adequate power; ability.

Suffix *n.* letter or syllable appended in word-formation.

Suffrage *n.* a vote for deciding a question; right of vote.

Suffragette *n.* a woman who agitated for woman suffrage.

Suffuse *v.t.* to overspread with a fluid or colour.

Sugar *n.* kinds of sweet crystalline substance, *esp*. the sugarcane.

Sugary *adj.* sweetened with sugar.

Suggest *v.t.* propose for acceptance; to give a hint or inkling of.

Suggestion *n.* the act of suggesting presentation of an idea to the mind

Suicide *n.* self-murder, intentional slaughter of oneself; action destructive to one's own interest.

Suit *n.* prosecution of a claim in law-court; set of clothes; any of the four sets into which a pack of cards is divided.

Suitable *adj.* appropriate to; fitted for the purpose; competent.

Suitcase *n.* a travelling bag.

Suite *n.* set of rooms, furniture, etc; a retinue company of followers.

Sum *n.* total resulting from addition of items; magnitude; arithmetical calculation; summary; quantity of money; particular amount of money.

Summary *adj.* done with dispatch; effected by a short way. *n.* an abridged account; an abstract.

Summit *n.* highest point, top, utmost elevation; highest degree.

Summon *v.t.* to invite to give notice to a person to appear in court; to call upon; to demand the presence of; to excite into action; to call upon to surrender fort.

Sump *n.* cesspool; pit or well for receiving superfluous water etc.

Sumpter *n.* a pack-horse.

Sumption *n.* major premiss in syllogism.

Sumptuary *adj.* regulating expenditure.

Sun *n.* the heavenly body that the earth travels round and receives light and warmth from; any fixed star with satellite (s); sun's light or warmth.

Sunday *n.* first day of the week observed as the day of worship and rest from work.

Sunken *adj.* lying at the bottom of a river.

Sunless *adj.* without the sun; shaded.

Sunnily *n.* brightly.

Sun-picture *n.* picture drawn by the help of the sun's ray.

Sunset *n.* the setting of the sun.

Sunward *adv.* towards the sun.

Sup *v.t.* & *i.* to sip; to take the evening meal. *n.* a sip; mouthful of a liquid.

Super *n.* a super-numeary actor; extra or unwanted person.

Superb *adj.* pompous; grand; magnificent; rich.

Superbly *adv.* in a superb manner.

Superficial *adj.* of or on the surface only without depth; shallow.

Superficies *n.* the exterior part of a thing; the suface.

Superfine *adj.* overfine; extremely fine; of extra quality.

Superfluity *n.* something beyond what is wanted; superabundance.

Superfluous *n.* more than enough; not needed.

Superior *adj.* higher or more elevated in place; dignity or excellence surpassing others; better in some respect, much more than average.

Supernatural *adj.* heavenly; lofty, divine.

Supernumerary *adj.* in excess of the normal number.

Supersaturation *n.* the state of being suprsaturated.

Superscribe *v.t.* to engrave or write at top or outside a surface.

Superscription *n.* the address on a letter; inscription over something.

Superstitious *adj.* addicted to superstition; full of idle religious notions.

Superstruct *v.t.* to erect; to build upon.

Superstructure *n.* a building in relation to, or what rests on a foundation.

Supertax *n.* an additional income-tax on large incomes.

Superterrestrial *adj.* being above the earth.

Supertragical *adj.* ecessively tragical.

Supervene *v.i.* to come extraneously; to follow closely.

Supervise *v.t.* to oversee; to manage; to inspect.

Supervisor *n.* one who supervises.

Supine *adj.* sloping or leaning backward; headless; thoughtless.

Supplant *v.t.* to displace; to undermine; to oust in favour of one's self; to displace and take possession.

Supple *adj.* flattering; submissive; easily bent, flexible. *v.t.* & *i.* to make or grow supple.

Supplicate *v.t.* & *i.* to seek by prayer; to entreat for; to implore; to beseech.

Supplication *n.* entreaty; petition; an earnest request; solicitation.

Supply *v.t.* fill (place) as substitute; to provide; to furnish.

Support *v.t.* to uphold; to sustain; to nourish; to endure.

Suppose *v.t.* to take for granted; to assume as true; to think to be the case; to conceive; to imagine. suppose so.

Suppress *v.t.* to put down; quell (rebellion, sedition etc.); put an end to the existence or activity of; to overpower and crush.

Supreme *adj.* highest in power or authority; most excellent; of the utmost importance or merit.

Surcharge *n.* extra load or charge; an excessive load or burden; overcharge; a mark printed on postage-stamp changing its value.

Surcingle *n.* the band or girdle over a saddle to fasten it.

Surculose *adj.* producing suckers.

Surd *adj.* & *n.* an irrational quantity; uttered with the breath.

Surdimute *n.* one who is both dumb and deaf.

Sure *adj.* faithful; having adequate reason for belief.

Surely *adv.* certainly.

Surety *n.* thing pledged as surely; person who goes bail for another's appearance in court or payment of sum; certainly.

Surf *n.* the wave between the rocks and the shore; foam and commotion of the sea breaking on shore or reefs.

Surface *n.* the external part of anything; outward aspect; a plane that has length and breadth but no thickness.

Surfeit *n.* disgust caused by excess, *esp.* in food; satiety.

Surge *n.* a large wave; a swelling undulation. *v.t.* to rise high and roll.

Surgeon *n.* a medical practitioner having a diploma qualifying him to practise surgery.

Surgery *n.* the act of healing diseases by manual operations.

Suricate *n.* a kind of mongoose.

Surly *adj.* rough; sour in manner; gloomy; rudely unsociable.

Surmise *n.* supposition; conjecture; suspicion of the existence or nature of something; a guess.

Surmount *v.t.* to get over by effort; to overcome.

Surmullet *n.* the red mullet; a kind of sea-fish.

Surname *n.* the name common to all members of a family; family name.

Surplice *n.* loose white-linen garment worn by clergy.

Surplus *n.* what remains over; excess; beyond what is wanted.

Surprise *n.* the act of surprising; astonishment; wonder; emotion excited by something.

Surrender *n.* to give oneself over to (habit, emotion, etc.).

Surrogacy *n.* the practice in which a woman carries and bears a child for another woman.

Surrogate *n.* a deputy of bishop.

Surround *v.t.* to come or be all round.

Surrounding *n.* an encompassing.

Surveillance *n.* superintendence; watch kept on a suspected person.

Survey *v.t.* to take a general view of; to examine; to view with attention; to ascertain particularly; to inspect.

Surveyor *n.* one who measures land; one who inspects progress of work.

Survival *n.* relic of the past; a living beyond another's life.

Susceptible *adj.* accessible or sensitive to.

Suspect *v.t.* to be inclined to think that; to doubt; to imagine guilty; distrust; mistrust; to be inclined to think.

Suspected *adj.* mistrusted.

Suspend *v.t.* to hang up, delay, put off; to adjourn; to deprive of office for a time.

Suspense *n.* undetermined state; indetermination; indecision.

Suspension *n.* the act of suspending; delay; interruption.

Suspensive *adj.* doubtful.

Suspicious *adj.* inclined to suspect; entertaining suspicion; mistrustful.

Suspiral *n.* a breathing hole.

Suspire *v.t.* to sigh.

Sustain *v.t.* to enable to last out; to undergo.

Sustenance *n.* support; maintenance; nourishing; subsistence.

Sutler *n.* a camp-follower selling provisions.

Sutural *adj.* relating to suture.

Suture *n.* (*Surg.*) stitching of wound; a thread or wire used for this.

Sutured *adj.* knit together.

Suzerain *n.* feudal lord; a paramount ruler.

Svelte *adj.* slender.

Swab *n.* a mop for cleaning floors or decks; an absorbent pad used in surgery.

Swad *n.* a short fat person.

Swaddle *v.t.* to wrap up tight and warm; to swathe in bandage.

Swag *n.* a bundle containing cloth and provisions; burglar's booty.

Swage *v.t.* to soften; to mitigate.

Swagger *v.t.* to walk in a gaudy manner; to brag; to behave arrogantly; to boast.

Swain *n.* a lover; a suitor; a yound rustic; hind.

Swale *n.* a tract of land; a valley.

Swallow *n.* the throat; engult; the act of swallowsing; a kind of migratory bird.

Swamp *n.* a wet spongy land; a bog or marsh; low ground filled with water.

Swampy *adj.* like a swamp; boggy.

Swan *n.* a large long-necked webfooted water bird.

Swannery *n.* a place where swans are kept.

Swan-skin *n.* a kind of soft flannel.

Swap *n.* a blow; a stroke.

Swarm *n.* a cluster of honey bees; a large number (of insects, birds, small animals); large number of people.

Swash *v.t.* & *i.* to make the sound (of water etc.) of washing or rising of falling; to strike violently (*Arch.*).

Swat *n.* an elastic bat for killing flies.

Swath *n.* a line of grass, corn & etc. lying after being cut; ridge of mowed grass.

Sway *v.t.* & *i.* to oscillate in an irregular manner; have influence over; to lean.

Sweal *v.i.* to melt and run down; to blaze away.

Swear *v.t.* & *i.* to utter something on oath; to affirm on solemn declaration.

Sweat *n.* labour, toil, drudgery; state of anxiety; sweating state; drops exuding from any any surface.

Sweep *v.t.* & *i.* to glide swiftly; to brush with a broom; clear everything from; to carry with a long swinging motion.

Sweet *adj.* tasting like sugar or honey; agreeable to the taste; smelling like perfumes.

Swell *v.t.* & *i.* to grow bigger or larger; to expand; to increase in volume; to be inflated; to bulge out; to strut.

Swelling *n.* & *adj.* timid; bombastic; prominence; tumour; inflammation.

Sweltry *adj.* oppressive with heat, sultry.

Swift *adj.* rapid; fleet; prompt; speedy; moving with velocity.

Swig *v.t.* & *i.* to drink in large draughts. *n.* a large draught.

Swill *v.t.* & *i.* to drink in excessive quantities; to rinse; to wash. *n.* rinsing.

Swim *v.i.* to float on or at surface of liquid; to go with gliding motion.

Swindle *v.t.* & *i.* to cheat; to defraud.

Swing *v.t.* & *i.* to move with to and fro motion; to sway like a pendulum or door; oscillate, revolve, rock.

Swinge *v.t.* to beat soundly; to chastise.

Swinger *n.* a great liar.

Swingle *n.* a flax-beating instrument; swinging bar of flail.

Swink *v.t. & i.* to labour; to drudge.

Swirl *v.t. & i.* to move in a whirling motion.

Swish *v.t. & i.* to flog with whip so quickly as to make a whistling, audibly cut (air, flower) with a cane.

Switch *n.* kinds of mechanism for making and breaking connexion of electric circuit, flexible shoot cut from a tree.

Swivel *n.* ring and pivot connecting two parts of something and enabling one of them to revolve without the other.

Swoon *v.i.* a fainting fit; to faint; to sink into a fainting fit.

Swoop *n.* carrying off many things at once; falling on and seizing.

Sword *n.* a weapon with long blade, boyonet; a keen-edged cutting or thrusting weapon, emblem of power or justice.

Sworn *adj.* having taken an oath; bound by an oath; promised by an oath.

Sybarite *n.* one devoted to luxury and pleasure.

Sycamine *n.* the black mulberry tree.

Sycamore *n.* a kind of fig tree of Egypt.

Syce *n.* an Indian groom.

Sycoma *n.* a figshaped tumour.

Sycophancy *n.* obsequious flattery.

Sycosis *n.* a disease on the scalp of the face.

Syenite *n.* kind of grey crystalline rock.

Syllable *n.* word or part of word containing one vowel-sound.

Syllabus *n.* a compendium; an abstract containing the heads of a discourse; course of teaching & etc.

Sylph *n.* spirit of the air; a slender graceful girl.

Sylvan *n.* one who lives in a forest; a forest god.

Symbol *n.* sign; an emblem or representation of something.

Symmetry *n.* right proportion of the several parts of a body to each other.

Sympathetic *adj.* expressing or feeling sympathy; inducing sympathy.

Sympathy *n.* fellow-feeling compassion; the qualtiy of being affected by the affection of another.

Sympodium *n.* a stem whose successive sections are strictly branches each springing from the preceding.

Syn *pref.* in the sense 'with', 'together'.

Synagogical *adj.* pertainting to the Jewish assembly for worship.

Synarchy *n.* joint sovereignty.

Synarthrosis *n.* immovable articulation.

Synchronal *adj.* happening at the same time; simultaneous.

Synchysis *n.* confusion of words in a sentence.

Synclastic *adv.* concave or convex all over.

Syncopate *v.t.* to contract or shorten by omiting the letters or syllables of a word.

Syncopation *n.* the act of syncopating.

Syncope *n.* the cutting short of one or more letters from a word.

Syncretic *adj.* combining different religious systems into one.

Syndic *n.* a municipal officer, a chief magistrate.

Syndicate *n.* a body of syndics; the office of syndics; a council.

Synochus *n.* continuous fever.

Synomosy *n.* sworn brotherhood.

Synonym *n.* a work identical in sense and usage with another.

Synonymic *adj.* pertaining to similar meaning.

Synonymite *n.* the state of being synonymous.

Synopsis *n.* summary; a general view; abstract.

Synoptic *adj.* & *n.* general survey.

Synoptically *adv.* in a synoptical manner.

Syntax *n.* sentence construction; the grammatical and due arrangement of words in a sentence.

Synteretic *adj.* preserving health.

Synthesis *n.* putting several things together.

Syntonic *adj.* sharp; intense.

Syntonin *n.* muscle fibrin.

Syntony *n.* the tuning of a wireless set.

Sypher *v.t.* to join (planks) with overlapping edges into flush surface.

Syphon *n.* a bent pipe or tube with unequal legs for conveying liquids from a higher to a lower level.

Syrian *adj.* pertaining to the native of Syria.

Syringa *n.* a shrub with white scented flowers.

Syringe *n.* a pipe furnished with piston by which liquids are sucked and then ejected in a fine stream.

Syrinx *n.* a pan-pipe; narrow rock-cut gallery.

Syrtis *n.* name of two large quicksands off the northern coast of Africa.

Syrup *n.* a saturated solution of sugar; vegetable juice saturated with sugar.

Systasis *n.* political union.

System *n.* an arraged scheme; classification.

Systole *n.* the contraction of heart and arteries; the shortening of a long syllable.

Systolic *adj.* pertaining to systole.

Systyle *adj.* & *n.* placing of columns near each other.

T T the twentieth letter of the English alphabet.

Tab *n.* the metallic binding at the end of a shoe-lace; a small flap.

Tabby *n.* a cat of mottled colour.

Tabernacle *n.* a movable building; a place of worship; the human body; receptacle of pyx; a tent; a temporary habitation.

Tabernacular *adj.* latticed.

Tabes *n.* emaciation; wasting disease of the spinal cord.

Tabetic *adj.* affected with tabes.

Tabic *adj.* pertaining to tabes.

Tabinet *n.* watered fabric of silk and wool.

Tablature *n.* mental picture; a painting on a wall; graphic description;

Table *n.* a flat surface; a slab; an article of furniture consisting of a flat surface of wood, marble etc.

Tablet *n.* a small flat cake of medicine; a small slab; a thin sheet of anything on which to write.

Taboo, Tabu *ns.* a ban; setting apart of a person or thing as accursed or sacred.

Tabor *n.* a small drum.

Taborer *n.* one who plays on a tabor.

Tabula *n.* hard flat surface (or bone etc.)

Tabular *adj.* in the form of a table.

Tabulate *adj.* shaped like a table.

Tach (e) *n.* a loop or button; a clasp; link.

Tachometer *n.* an instrument for measuring velocity of currents.

Tacit *adj.* implied; unspoken; understood; not expressed.

Tacitly *adj.* by implication.

Taciturn *adj.* reserved; silent; not talkative.

Taciturnity *n.* reserve in speaking.

Taciturnly *adj.* in a reserved manner.

Tack *n.* a rope for fastening sails; a term of a lease; small nail with a broad head.

Tacket *n.* a small nail with large head.

Tackle *n.* a mechanism for lifting or lowering heavy weights.

Tact *n.* adroitness in dealing with others; delicate perception of the right thing to do or say.

Tactician *n.* one clever in tactics.

Tactics *n.* (*sing.* & *pl.*) (*pl.*) art of disposing military or naval forces in actual contact with enemy; skilful device.

Tactile *adj.* tangible; having the sense of touch.

Taction *n.* the act of touching.

Tactual *adj.* pertaining to touch.

Tadpole *n.* larva of frog; the frog in its first stage after leaving the eggs.

Taenia *n.* tape-worm; (*Anat.*) ribbon-like part *esp.* of brain.

Taffeta *n.* a fine smooth stuff of silk & etc.

Taffrail *n.* the rail round the stern of a ship.

Tag *n.* a flap of garment; a loose or ragged end; a small thread with pointed metal pieces for binding.

Taglia *n.* a combination of pulleys for hoisting.

Taigle *v.t.* & *i.* to entangle; to hinder; to delay; to loiter; to trudge.

Tail *n.* lower or inferior or later part of somehting; the hindmost part of an animal; slender prolongation or appendage.

Tailing *n.* the part of a projecting stone inserted in a wall.

Tailless *adj.* without a tail.

Tailor *n.* one whose occupation is to make outer garments *esp.* for men.

Tailpiece *n.* an ornamental engraving or block printed at the end of a book or chapter.

Tailrope *n.* a rope which is attached behind.

Tain *n.* the thin plate of tin, tinfoil.

Taint *n.* stain; blemish on reputation; corruption.

Take *n.* amount of fish caught; money received at theatre.

Take *v.t.* & *i.* to get hold of; to lay hold of; to receive.

Taker *n.* one who takes.

Taking *adj.* attracting; captivating; alluring; infectious.

Talbot *n.* a kind of bound.

Talc *n.* a very soft, pliable, silvery white transparent mineral; magnesium silicate.

Talcose *adj.* abounding in talc.

Tale *n.* report; reckoning; a fictitious story or legend; narrative or story.

Talent *n.* high mental ability; a disposition; a standard weight; faculty or aptitude for something; superior.

Tales *n. pl.* a writ for summoning jurors.

Taliped *adj.* club-footed.

Talipes *n.* club-footedness; tailped formation.

Talisman *n.* an object endowed with magical powers; an amulet.

Talk *v.i.* to converse; to prate; to speak; to discuss in words.

Tall *adj.* long in height; of more than average height; boastful.

Tallow *n.* harder kinds of fat. *v.t.* to grease with tallow; to fatten.

Tally *n.* a notched stick of number with; accound of goods entered in seller's and in purchaser's book.

Talon *n.* the heel of a sword blade; claw of a bird of prey.

Talpa *n.* the genus which includes the mole.

Tamable *adj.* that may be tamed or subdued.

Tamarin *n.* a kind of South African squirrel-monkey.

Tamarind *n.* a tropical leguminous tree.

Tamboc *n.* an alloy of copper and zinc.

Tambour *n.* circular frame for stretching embroidery work on.

Tambourine *n.* a small shallow drum with loose jingling metal disks.

Tame *adj.* (of animals) domesticated, tractable; lacking spirit.

Tamely *adv.* in a tame manner.

Tamer *n.* some who tames.

Tamkin *n.* a cannon stopper.

Tampan *n.* a kind of venomous snake.

Tamper *v.t.* & *i.* to meddle; to make unauthorized changes in a document.

Tampon *n.* plug used to stop the flow of blood.

Tan *n.* bark of oak tree crushed in use for tanning hide.

Tan-bed *n.* a bed made of tan-bark.

Tandem *adj.* & *n.* with two horses one behind the other.

Tangent *n.* a straight line which touches a circle but being produced does not cut it.

Tangential *adj.* pertaining to tangent.

Tangible *adj.* clearly intelligible; actual, palpable; corporal; perceptible by touch; that may be realised.

Tangle *n.* confused mass or state; a knot of things united confusedly.

Tangram *n.* a square cut into seven pieces which may be combined to form various shapes.

Tank *n.* a pond; a locomotive boiler; an armoured car; a large wooden or metal basin; a reservoir; a large receptacle for storing liquid.

Tannable *adj.* able to be tanned.

Tanner *n.* one whose occupations is to tan hides.

Tannery *n.* a tanning manufactory.

Tannic *adj.* pertaining to tannin.

Tanning *n.* the art of converting raw hide into leather.

Tansy *n.* an aromatic herb used in medicine and cookery; a kind of bitter aromatic plant.

Tantalum *n.* a rare metal used for electric lamp filaments.

Tantalus *n.* son of Zeus condemned to stand up to chin in water which he could never drink and so died of starvation.

Tantrum *n.* a fit of ill-temper.

Tanyard *n.* an enclosure where hides are tanned.

Tap *n.* a tool for cutting screws; a tap-room; a short pipe; a gentle or slight blow with a thing.

Tap-borer *n.* a gimlet.

Tape *n.* a narrow strip of linen, etc.

Tape measure *n.* a tape used in measuring.

Taper *n.* a thin wax candle; a small light.

Tape-worm *n.* a parasite worm of the form of a tape.

Tapir *n.* a hoofed mammal like a rhinoceros; an American swine-like mammal.

Tapis *n.* a carpet; tapestry; a cover for a table.

Tappet *n.* collar, used in machinery to impart intermittent motion.

Tap-room *n.* a room in which liquor is sold or drunk.

Tapster *n.* an attendant serving liquor at an inn; one whose business is to draw ale.

Tar *n.* a sailor; dark thick liquid distilled from wood or coal.

Tarantism *n.* a dancing mania.

Tarantula *n.* a kind of large poisonous spider.

Taraxacum *n.* a kind of flowering plant from the roots of which a tonic laxative drug is prepared.

Tarboosh *n.* the inner part of a turban; a cap like fez.

Tardy *adj.* slow-moving; sluggish; reluctant.

Tardigrade *adj.* moving slowly.

Tardily *adv.* in a tardy manner.

Tare *n.* an allowance made from the gross weight of goods; a weed that grows amongst corn.

Target *n.* a mark to fire at; a small round shield.

Tariff *n.* duty on goods; a list of table of duties or customs to be paid on exportation and importation; a schedule of customs duties; a list of charges.

Tarlatan *n.* a kind of very thin muslin.

Tarn *n.* a small mountain lake.

Tarnation *n.* damnation.

Tarnish *v.t.* & *i.* to sully or dim (reputation etc.); to lose the lustre or colour.

Tarpan *n.* the wild horse of Central Asia.

Tarpaulin *n.* tar-covered water-proof canvas; a sailor.

Tarpon *n.* a jew-fish.

Tarrace *n.* a volcanic earth used as cement.

Tarragon *n.* a savoury herb.

Tarry *v.t.* to wait for; to delay; to stay.

Tarsal *adj.* pertaining to tarsus.

Tarsia *n.* a beautiful kind of mosaic wood-work.

Tarsus *n.* the part of the root to which the leg is articulated.

Tart *adj.* bitter or acrimonious; of acid taste.

Tartan *n.* a checkered or striped woollen fabric of various patterns.

Tartar *n.* incrustation that forms on the teeth; a native of Tartary.

Tartaric *adj.* obtained from tartar.

Tartarin *n.* potash.

Tasimeter *n.* an electrical instrument for determining variation in temperature.

Task *n.* a piece of work to be done; a work voluntarily undertaken; a business imposed by another.

Tasker *n.* one who imposes a task.

Taskmaster *n.* a man who assigns work to be done.

Taskwork *n.* a piece of work given as a task; forced labour; oppressive work.

Tass *n.* a drinking-cup.

Tassel *n.* a ribbon sewn in a book serving as a bookmark.

Taste *n.* the sense peculiar by which we taste; relish; personal preference; judgement.

Tasteful *adj.* savoury; having good taste.

Tasty *adj.* of good taste; savoury.

Tatting *n.* trimming for woven work.

Tattle *n.* trifling talk; idle talk.

Tattoo *n.* a mark of figure made on the body by punctures and stains; a beat of drum for recalling soldiers to the headquarters.

Taube *n.* type of German aeroplane.

Taunt *n.* sarcastic reproach; upbraid; insulting words; a thing said to anger or wound a person.

Taunter *n.* one who taunts.

Taurian *adj.* of a bull.

Tautology *n.* a repetition of the same meaning in different words.

Tautologist *n.* one who uses tautology.

Tautologous *adj.* repeating the same thing.

Tautophony *n.* repeating the same thing.

Tavern *n.* an inn or restaurant; a public house where liquors are sold.

Taverner *n.* one who keeps a tavern.

Taverning *n.* a feasting at taverns.

Taw *n.* a large playing marbles. *v.t.* to make (hide) into leather, *esp.* by soaking in solution of alum and salt.

Tawdry *adj.* gaudy; pretentious but common; cheap and showy.

Tawny *adj.* brownish; yellow.

Tawse *n.* a thick leather strap.

Tax *n.* a rate or sum of money levied on persons or property for the benefit of the state.

Taxi *v.t.* & *i.* to manoeuvre an aeroplane on the ground or on water.

Taxidermal *adj.* pertaining to taxidermy.

Taxidermist *n.* one who is skilled in taxidermy.

Taxidermy *n.* the art of preparing and mounting skins of animals in life-like manner.

Taxonomy *n.* the principle of classifying plants and animals.

Tea *n.* decoction of dried tea leaves; the dry leaves of a plant of the camellia family. *v.i.* to drink tea.

Teach *v.t.* to give lessons at school; to instruct; to impart knowledge or skill; to inform; to explain; to admonish; to make familiar; to counsel.

Teacher *n.* one who teaches; an instructor; a preceptor.

Teague *n.* a Irishman (in contempt.)
Teak *n.* a tropical tree producing hard wood; timber of this tree producing hard wood.
Teal *n.* small fresh water duck.
Team *n.* two or more horses, oxen & etc. harnessed together; a set of players on one side of a game; a company.
Teamster *n.* one who drives team.
Tea-pot *n.* a vessel in which tea is prepared.
Teapoy *n.* small three or four-legged table for a tea tray.
Tear *n.* a drop of liquid secreted by the lachrymal glands; tear-like thing.
Tear *v.t.* & *i.* to separate by violence or pulling; to rend; to make hole.
Tear-gas *n.* a poisonous gas which causes excessive flow of tears from the eyes.
Tearing *adj.* violent.
Tearless *adj.* shedding no tears; without tears.
Tease *v.t.* to importune or banter; to annoy, vex, torment; pick into separate fibres, comb or card; dress (cloth etc.) with teasels.
Teasel *n.* kinds of plant with dried prickly flower-head, used for raising nap on cloth.
Teaser *n.* teasing person, problem of thing.
Technical *adj.* of or peculiar to a particular art or science or craft; pertaining to the mechanical arts.
Technique *n.* the manner of artistic execution; mechanical skill in art.
Technology *n.* science of the industrial arts; explanation of terms of art.
Techy *adj.* peevish; irritable.
Ted *v.t.* to turn over and spread out (grass) to dry.
Tedder *n.* one who teds; a machine for spreading grass.
Teddybear *n.* child's toy-bear.
Tedious *adj.* tiresome; wearisome; tiresomely long; prolix; irksome; slow.
Tedium *n.* irksomeness; wearisomeness.
Teem *v.t.* & *i.* to bear offspring; to bring forth yound; to be pragnant; to abound; to pour out; to empty.
Teeming *adj.* producing young one fruitful.
Teen *n.* suffix of numbers from 13 to 19.
Teeth *pl.* of Tooth.
Teethe *v.i.* to grow or cut teeth.
Teetotal *adj.* pertaining to abstinence from all intoxicating drinks.
Teetotalism *n.* total abstinence from intoxicating drinks.
Teetotum *n.* a top with four sides lettered to decide spinner's luck. a kind of children's small toy with numbered sides.
Teg *n.* a young sheep in the second year.

Tegular *adj*. pertaining to or resembling a tile.

Tegument *n*. the skin as the covering of the body; a natural covering.

Teinoscope *n*. an instrument consisting of two prisms combined to correct chromatic aberration and increase or decrease dimensions of objects.

Telaesthesia *n*. direct perception of distant object or occurrences not effected by the recognized senses.

Telautograph *n*. telegraph that reproduces writing.

Tele in comb. (far).

Telegony *n*. influence of previous sire seen in subsequent sire's progeny by the same mother.

Telegram *n*. a message by telegraph; a telegraphic message.

Telegrammic *adj*. pertaining to telegrams.

Telegraph *n*. instantaneous conveyance of messages by means of electricity or by signals.

Telekinesis *n*. movement at a distance from the motive cause without material connexion.

Telemechanics *n*. *pl* art of transmitting power by radio and so controlling machinery from a distance.

Telemeter *n*. an instrument for determining distance.

Telemetry *n*. range-finding.

Teleological *adj*. pertaining to teleology.

Teleology *n*. the doctrine of final causes.

Telepathy *n*. thought transference.

Telephone *n*. apparatus for transmitting speech or sound to distant hearer by means of electricity.

Telephonic *adj*. relating to the telephone.

Telergy *n*. force conceived as effecting brain in telepathy.

Telescope *n*. tube with lenses or mirrors for magnifying the image of a distant object.

Telescopic *adj*. pertaining to or like a telescope.

Teleseme *n*.. a kind of electric signal.

Telesia *n*. sapphire.

Telesm *n*. a talisman; a kind of magical charm.

Telestich *n*. a poem in which the final letters of the lines make a name or a word.

Television *n*. electrical transmission of images, by aid of Hertzian waves or otherwise.

Telic *adj*. denoting a purpose.

Tell *v.t. & i.* to relate in words; utter or express in words; to make known.

Teller *n*. one who counts or communicates.

Telling *adj*. having great effect.

Tell-tale *n*. one who informs about the private affairs of men.

Tellural *adj*. pertaining to the earth.

Tellurium *n.* a rare element resembling sulphure.
Telotype *n.* printing electric telegraph.
Temper *v.t.* to mitigate severity of; to bring to proper consistence of hardness; to tune; modulate.
Tempera *n.* distemperpainting.
Temperament *n.* constitution; disposition; the whole of a person's natural tendencies as determined by his physical constitution.
Temperance *n.* self-restraint; moderation; sobriety; calmness; abstinence.
Temperate *adj.* remote from extremes; moderate; avoiding excess; of mild temperature.
Temperature *n.* (*Med.*) a thing's degree of hear indicated by the thermometer; internal heat of the body.
Templar *n.* a student of law
Temple *n.* building treated as the dwelling place or devoted to the worship of a god.
Temporal *adj.* pertaining to time; pertaining to the time in this life or this world, secular, pertaining to the temples of the head.
Temporary *adj.* lasting or meant to last only a short time, transient.
Temporize *v.i.* to postpone; to discuss terms or to negotiate.
Tempt *v.t.* to rouse or try to rouse appetite or impulse in; to draw or allure into.
Temptable *adj.* liable to be tempted.
Temptation *n.* enticement; a thing that attract; impulse.
Tempter *n.* one who entices to evil.
Temulence *n.* intoxication.
Temulent *adj.* intoxicated.
Ten *n.* two times five; one more than nine; 10.
Tenable *adj.* (of office etc.) that can be held for a period; that can be maintained against attack or objection.
Tenace *n.* the opponent's highest of the suit, two cards, one next above, the other next below.
Tenacious *adj.* holding fast or keeping firm hold of; adhesive; retentive; clinging tightly; slow to relinquish anything; apt to retain long.
Tenacity *n.* relativeness; adhesiveness; stickness.
Tenaille *n.* a rampart raised in the main ditch.
Tenancy *n.* tenant's position.
Tenant *n.* a person who rents land or house from a landlord; an occupant of a place.
Tend *v.i.* to have a certain tendency; to be inclined; to watch; to guard.
Tendency *n.* inclination; drift; aptness to move or act in a particular direction or way.
Tender *n.* an estimate for a piece of work; one who takes care of; a truck attached to a locomotive; an officer to execute work at a fixed price.

Tender-foot *n.* a person new to his surroundings.

Tendon *n.* a bundle of fibres by which a muscle is attached to a bone.

Tenebrific *adj.* causing darkness.

Tenebrose *adj.* dark and gloomy.

Tenebrous *adj.* dark; gloomy.

Tenessmus *n.* straining effort in relieving the bowels.

Tenet *n.* dogma; doctrine (held by a part, sect. etc.); opinion; principle.

Tennis *n.* a game played by striking a rubber ball with a racket over a net.

Tenon *n.* the end piece of wood which is inserted in a mortise.

Tenonsaw *n.* a steel or brass-backed saw for cutting tenons.

Tenor *n.* prevailing course; stamp; purport or drift; true intention.

Tenotomy *n.* operation of dividing a tendon.

Tense *n.* a modification in verbs, to distinguish time of action.

Tensely *adv.* in a tense manner.

Tensile *adj.* capable of being drawn out; of tension.

Tension *n.* the act of straining; intense effort; tenseness.

Tensor *n.* the muscle that tightens a part.

Tent *n.* a portable shelter or dwelling of canvas; a roll of linen cloth & etc. inserted in wound.

Tentacle *n.* the organ of feeling in insects; a long slender flexible appendage of animal used for exploration or locomotion.

Tentation *n.* temptation; trial.

Tenth *adj.* ordinal of ten.

Tentorium *n.* the membrane which separates the two portions of the brain.

Tenuity *n.* slenderness; thinness; simplicity.

Tenuous *adj.* not dense; thin; slender.

Tenure *n.* the holding of property or office; the manner of holding a tenancy; right of holding an estate.

Tepor *n.* a moderate warmth.

Tephromancy *n.* divination from the ashes of burnt offerings.

Teraphim *n.* small images as domestic oracle of ancient Hebrews.

Teratology *n.* the study of animal and vegetable monstro cities; dealing in the marvellous.

Terce *n.* a weight of about forty two gallons.

Tercel *n.* a male falcon.

Terebene *n.* oil of turpentine.

Terebinth *n.* a turpentine-yielding tree.

Terebrate *v.t.* to bore.

Tergerminate *adj.* (of leaf) having at base a pair of leaflets and forking with a pair on each branch.

Tergiferous *adj.* carriying on the back.

Term *n.* a limit; boundary; a limited period; an expression with determinate meaning; stipulations made.

Terms *n. pl.* relation; condition.

Termagancy *n.* tumultuousness.

Termagant *n.* & *adj.* brawling woman; boisterous; quarrelsome.

Terminable *adj.* that may be terminated; limitable; coming to an end after a certain time.

Terminal *adj.* relating to the end; of a term; occurring in each term.

Terminate *v.t & i.* to put an end; to complete; to limit to bound.

Termination *n.* the act of ending; issue ending; conclusion; limit.

Terminative *adj.* serving to end.

Terminus *n.* the station at the end of a railway line; a boundary mark.

Termite *n.* the white ant.

Termitary *n.* the mound of white ants.

Tern *n.* a fork-tailed sea-bird.

Ternary *adj.* composed of three.

Ternate *adj.* arranged in three; having three leaflets.

Terpsichorean *adj.* of dancing of the muse Tersichore.

Terra *n.* earth.

Terra-alba *n.* pipe-clay.

Terrace *n.* row of natural shelf or one made for vine-growing in hill side.

Terra-cotta *n.* a model or cast of baked earth.

Terra-firma *n.* dry soil.

Terrain *n.* a tract of land.

Terramare *n.* kinds of earthly deposit containing bones.

Terranean *n.* pertaining to land.

Terraneous *adj.* (*Biol.*) growing on land; comprising of land and water.

Terrapin *n.* kinds of fresh-water turtle and tortoise.

Terraqueous *adj.* of land and water.

Terrene *adj.* consisting of earth; terrestrial; of the earth.

Terrible *adj.* grievous; frightful, horrible.

Terrific *adj.* causing great terror; dreadful.

Terrify *v.t.* to alarm; to frighten severly.

Territorial *adj.* or territory or land; limited to a district.

Territory *n.* large tract of land; dominion; land or region under the dominion of a ruler of State.

Terror *n.* that which excites dread; extreme fear; person or thing that causes this.

Terrorism *n.* govern by terror; state of fear.

Terrorist *n.* one who uses terror inspiring methods in governing.

Terse *adj.* brief and forcible in style; concise; free from superfluity.

Tertiary *adj.* of the third order, formation, degree.

Tertius *adj.* (in schools) third of the name.

Tesseler *adj.* formed in squares.
Tessellated *adj.* formed in little squares; of or resembling mosaic.
Test *n.* critical trail or examination of person's or thing's qualities.
Testacea *n. pl.* animals like shells.
Testacel *n.* a little shell.
Testaceous *adj.* of shells; having a shell or hard covering.
Testament *n.* a will.
Testate *adj.* & *n.* having made a will.
Testator *n.* one who makes and leaves a will at death.
Tester *n.* one who tests; a device for testing; a canopy over a bed.
Testicle *n.* one of the glands which secretes male seminal fluid.
Testiculate *adj.* shaped like testicles.
Testify *v.t.* & *i.* to affirm; to bear witness to; to give testimony.
Testimony *n.* solemn declaration; affirmation; a certificate of character.
Testy *adj.* short-tempered; peevish; fretful.
Testiness *n.* peevishness.
Testudo *n.* a genus of tortoise.
Tetanus *n.* a disease marked by painful contraction of voluntary muscles.
Tetchily *adj.* fretfully
Tetchy *adj.* testy; easily put out.
Tether *n.* a rope by which a grazing animal is restricted to a radius; scope of one's knowledge. *v.t.* to tie with such a rope.
Tetrahedral *adj.* bounded by four equal and equilateral triangles.
Tetrameter *n.* a verse of four feet.
Tetrapod *n.* an insect having only four perfect feet.
Tetrapetran *adj.* having four wings.
Tetraspermous *adj.* having four seeds.
Tetrastich *n.* a stanza of four verses.
Tetrastyle *n.* a building with four columns in front.
Tetter *n.* kinds of skin-disease.
Teuton *n.* a member of any of the Teutonic nations.
Text *n.* subject of discourse; any selected passage of scripture; the original words of an author; authentic form of a document or passage or book.
Textbook *n.* a book set for study; a manual instruction.
Textile *adj.* of weaving; woven.
Textual *n.* of or in the text.
Texture *n.* a web; arrangement of threads in textile fabric.
Thalmus (*n.* an inner room; women's apartment.
Thalassic *adj.* pertaining to sea.
Thalassography *n.* the science of the sea.
Thalia *n.* Greek muse of comedy and pastoral poetry.
Thallium *n.* rare soft white metallic element used in alloys and glass-making.

Thallus *n.* vegetation in which there is no difference in leaf, stem or roots.

Than *conj.* & *prep.* (introducing a second ember of comparison).

Thanatoid *adj.* like death.

Thanatology *n.* the study of death.

Thane *n.* an old English title of dignity; a gentleman below rank of Earl.

Thank *v.t.* gift or service; to make acknowledgments for kindness; to express gratitude for a thing.

Thatch *n.* roofing of straw or rushes.

Thatcher *n.* one who covers with straw.

Thaumaturge *n.* a worker of miracles.

Thaw *v.t.* & *i.* to pass into a liquid state; to melt or dissolve.

The *definit article or demonstrative pronoun,* denoting a certain person or thing. *adv.* in whatever degree; on that account; by so much; in that much.

Theandric *adj.* combining the divine and human nature.

Theanthropic *adj.* both divine and human.

Thearchy *n.* the rule of gods.

Theatre *n.* room or building for lectures, surgery etc.

Theatrical *adj.* suitable for the stage, the theatre or acting; sensational; pertaining to the theatre.

Theism *n.* belief in a divine creation and conduct of the universe.

Theist *n.* one who believes in the existence of God.

Theistical *adj.* pertaining to theism.

Them *pron.* objective case of 'They'.

Theme *n.* an essay or composition; a subject or topic on which one writes, speaks or thinks.

Themselves *pron.* emphatic and reciprocal form of *they* and *them*.

Then *adv.* (*conj.*) under those circumstances; accordingly; at that time.

Thenar *n.* palm of hand.

Thence *adv.* for that reason; from that place or time.

Theo *pref.* having the meaning of God.

Theocracy *n.* the union of soul with God.

Theodolite *n.* an instrument for measuring horizontal and vertical angles.

Theogony *n.* the genesis of gods.

Theogonic *adj.* pertaining to theogony.

Theogonist *n.* one who is versed in the mythology of gods.

Theologian *n.* a divine; one who is versed in theology.

Theological *adj.* pertaining to theology.

Theologist *n.* a theologian.

Theology *n.* the science treating of God and His relation to man.

Theophany *n.* a visible manifestation of a god to man.

Theorem *n.* speculative truth; a proposition which is to be proved by reasoning.

Theorematic *adj* pertaining to theorem.

Theoretical *adj.* depending on theory or speculation.

Theorist *n.* holder of a theory; a person given to theories.

Theorize *v.t.* to form or state a theory; to speculate.

Theorization *n.* the act of speculating.

Theory *n.* t[illegible]here of speculation as distinguished from that of practice; an exposition of the general principles.

Theosophy *n.* a system of philosophy professing to attain intimate knowledge of God by spiritual ecstasy.

Theosophic *adj.* pertaining to theosophy.

Therapeutic *adj.* of the healing art; curative.

There *adv.* in or at that place, thither, at that point. *n.* that place or point. used merely as introductory. *There was a king.*

Therm *n.* unit of coal-gas supplied; the unit of heat necessary to raise one pound of water to one degree Fahrenheit.

Thermantidote *n.* an apparatus for driving current of cooled air into a room.

Thermatology *n.* medical treatment by means of hot springs.

Thermionic *adj.* giving electric current by means of heat.

Thermodynamics *n.* science of the relation between heat and mechanical energy.

Thermometer *n.* an instrument for measuring temperature.

Thermomotive *adj.* of motion produced by heat.

Thermopile *n.* an electrical measure of heat.

Thermos *n.* a kind of vacuum flask.

Theroid *adj.* beast like.

Therology *n.* the science of mammals.

Thesaurus *n.* a treasury; a lexicon or cyclopaedia

Thesis *n.* an independent essay on a definite subject presented for a doctorate degree; a proposition which is to be maintained; a theme.

Thesmothete *n.* a law giver.

Thespian *adj.* pertaining to dramatic acting.

Theurgy *n.* miraculously effective art; the art of magic.

Thewless *adj.* lacking vigour.

They *pron.* (*pl.* of He, She, or It) persons or things.

Thick *adj.* dense; compact; broad; crowded together; cloudy.

Thicket *n.* a tangle of shrubs of trees closely set together.

Thick-headed *adj*. dull; stupid.

Thieve *v.t.* & *i.* to practise theft; one who takes away by stealth what belongs to another.

Thig *v.i.* to beg; to live on alms.

Thigger *n.* one who obtains alms by means of threats.

Thigh *n.* the muscular portion of the leg between the hip and the knee.

Thigmotropic *adj*. pertaining to response to stimulus of touch.

Thill *n.* shaft of cart or carraige.

Thiller *n.* a horse which goes between thills.

Thimble *n.* a metal cap worn on a finger for protection in sewing.

Thimble-case *n.* a very little amount.

Thimble-rig *n.* a swindling game played with three thimbles & a pea.

Thin *adj*. meagre; weak; easily seen through; not dense or crowded; of little thickness; slender; shallow.

Thine *pron*. belonging to thee.

Thing *n.* a material object; a person or animal regarded in pity; a substance; any possible object of thought.

Think *v.t.* & *i.* to consider; to fancy; to intend; to have one's mind at work.

Thinly *adv*. in a thin manner.

Thinner *n.* one who makes thin.

Thio *n.* a prefix meaning 'sulphur'.

Third *adj*. next after second.

Thirst *n.* sensation or state of requiring drink; dryness; a desire for drink; intense desire.

Thirsty adj. feeling thirst; craving for some satisfaction; having an ardent desire; causing thirst.

Thirteen *adj*. & *n.* one more than twelve.

This *adj*. & *pron*. the person or thing close at hand or drawn attention to.

Thistle *n.* kinds of prickly plant common as weeds.

Thole *n.* a pin in the gun-wale of a boat serving as fulcrum for the oar.

Thong *n.* a narrow strip of leather for fastening anything.

Thorn *n.* prickly shrub; the skin of plant; impediment.

Thorny *adj*. abounding in thorns; troublesome; sharp; difficult to tackle.

Thorough *adj*. out-and-out; radical; passing to the end; complete; perfect; not superficial. *adv*. & *prep*. through.

Thorp *n.* a village; a hamlet.

Those *pron. pl.* of That.

Thou *pron*. second person singular. *v.t.* to address a person as 'thou.'

Though *conj*. admitting; even if; granting; notwithstanding.

Thought *n.* the act of thinking; a conception or mental image.

Thoughtful *adj*. considerable; contemplative; engaged thought.

Thousand *n.* the number of ten hundred, 1000.

Thrall *v.t.* to enslave.

Thraldom *n.* slavery; bondage.

Thrash *v.t.* & *i.* to beat soundly with a stick.

Thrasher *n* one who thrashes; that threshes.

Thrashing *n.* the operation of beating out grain from husk; a whipping.

Thrasonical *adj*. bragging; boasting.

Thread *n.* something contrived in a long course; theme of argument.

Threader *n.* contrivance for threading.

Thready *adj*. like thread.

Threat *n.* indication of coming evil; menace; intimidation; denunciation.

Thremmatology *n.* the science of breeding animals and plants.

Threnetic *adj*. pertaining to threnode.

Threnody *n.* a song of lamentation.

Thresh *v.t* & *i.* to separate the grain or seeds from corn by beating.

Threshing *n.* act of beating out grain; process of threshing corn.

Threshold *n.* the plank or stone forming the bottom of a doorway.

Thrice *adv*. three times.

Third *v.t.* to slip through.

Thrift *n.* money saving; a kind of plant; frugality; economical management.

Thrill *n.* a wave of sensation; a nervous tremor due to intense emotion; a tremulous sound.

Thrive *v.i.* to grow rich; to flourish; to prosper.

Throat *n.* gullet, wind-pipe; passage or entrance; front part of the neck.

Throb *n.* (of heart) to pulsate with abnormal force.

Throe *n.* birth pangs; extreme pain; agony; anguish.

Thrombosis *n.* complete or partial coagulation of blood in the blood vessels.

Throne *n.* a chair of state; a royal seat; sovereign power or dignity.

Throng *n.* a crowd; a great multitude.

Throstle *n.* the song-thrush; a machine for spinning wool, cotton & etc.

Throttle *n.* throat; gullet; windpipe.

Through *prep.* by agency, means or fault of; by reason of; from end to end or side to side of; between the sides of.

Throw *v.t* & *i.* to send forth by violence; to toss; to fling; to propel; to put on; to overturn.

Throwster *n.* one who throws silk; a gambler.

Thrum *n.* unwoven end of a warp thread left when the finished web is cut away; the end of a weaver's thread.

Thrush *n.* a disease of the throat; a small singing bird.

Thrust *n.* a violent push; an assault.

Thumb *n.* the short thick finger of the human palm.

Thumbless *n.* without a thumb.

Thump *v.t.* & *i.* to hit with a fist; to beat heavily with something thick.

Thunder *n.* thunderbolt; any loud noise; the sound made by lightning.

Thunderbolt *n.* a flash of lightning with crash of thunder.

Thunderer *n.* that which thunders.

Thurible *n.* a censer of metal.

Thursday *n.* the fifth day of the week.

Thus *adj.* accordingly; in this way; to this extent.

Thwart *adv.* across something.

Thy *adj.* & *pron.* of or belonging to thee.

Thylacine *n.* a kind of wolf; a zebra-wolf.

Thymol *n.* a powerful disinfectant; oil of thyme.

Thyroid *adj.* shaped like a shield.

Thyself *pron.* reflexive or emphatic form of thou.

Tiara *n.* kind of turban; a conical cop; jewelled band worn in the front of the hair by ladies.

Tibia *n.* the shin-bone.

Tic *n.* a contraction of the muscle of the face.

Tick *n.* a small mark; credit; the beat of a watch; a kind of parasitic insect; the cover of bed.

Ticket *n.* a marked piece of paper or card entitling its holder to admission.

Ticking *n.* a sift cloth used for bedding; strong material for bed ticks.

Tickle *v.t.* & *i.* to amuse; to excite in an agreeable manner; apply light touches so as to create a thrilling sensation.

Tickly *adj.* ticklish. **Tidal** *adj.* pertaining to tides.

Tide *n.* the rise and fall of the sea occurring twice in a lunar day; a season; a period of time; a trend of opinion or feeling.

Tidy *adj.* methodically arranged; pretty large; neat, orderly, dressed with neatness; acceptable.

Tier *n.* a row or rank, especially when two or more rows are placed one above the other.

Tiff *n.* a fit of peevishness; a petty quarrel; a small draught of liquor.

Tiffany *n.* kind of gauzy silk.

Tiffin *n.* & *v.t.* slight repast after dinner; light meal.

Tig *n.* a touch; a game of children.

Tige *n.* shaft of column; stem; stalk.

Tiger *n.* smart small boy as groom; a fierce carnivorous beast; final burst of applause.

Tight *adj.* fitting close to the body; well-knit; impenetrable; close; compact.

Tilbury *n.* a kind of two-wheeled carriage.

Tile *n.* silk-hat; a thing slab of baked clay used for covering the roofs of a house. *v.t.* to cover with tiles.

Tilery *n.* a place where tiles are made.

Till *n.* a kind of stiff clay; money-drawer in a shop-counter. *v.t.* to cultivate soil.

Till *prep.* up to; up to the time; when.

Tilt *n.* a covering for cart; unlevel; sloping position; act of tilting with lance.

Tilt-boat *n.* a boat covered with a canvas roof.

Tilth *n.* preparation of ground for crop; tillage.

Timber *n.* a piece of wood; wood as material suitable for building purposes or carpentry; trees suitable for this.

Timbre *n.* the characteristic quality of vocal or instrumental sound.

Timbrel *n.* a tambourine.

Timbrology *n.* the study of postage stamps.

Time *n.* a period with its events etc.; a season or distinguishable part of the year or day.

Time-keeper *n.* a clock or watch, one who keeps the time of workmen.

Timely *adj.* opportune; seasonable; occurring in good time. *adv.* soon; early.

Timepiece *n.* a clock or watch.

Timid *adj.* wanting in courage; faint-hearted; easily frightened.

Timocracy *n.* government by men of position.

Timorous *adj.* one who is easily alarmed; timid; fearful of danger.

Tin *n.* a vessel of tin or tin-plate; a canister; money; a silvery-white malleable metal. *v.t.* to coat with tin.

Tinctorial *adj.* pertaining to colours

Tincture *n.* a slight taste; a tinge of colour; an alcoholic extract of some medicine.

Tinder *n.* a dry substance readily taking fire from spark.

Tine *n.* the point or spike of a fork or harrow.

Ting *v.t.* & *i.* to make a tinkling sound; to tinkle. *n.* such a sound.

Tinge *n.* flavour; slight degree of some colour (tint).

Tingle *v.i.* to feel a thrilling sensation; to feel sharp pain.

Tinker *n.* a botcher; rough and ready worker; one who mends household utensils.

Tinkle *n.* a clinking sound; quick sharp ringing noise.

Tinsel *n.* tawdry brilliance; decorations of bright metal threads.

Tin-smith *n.* a worker in tin.

Tint *n.* a faint colour spread over a surface; a variety of colour.

Tiny *adj.* very small; little.

Tip *n.* a hint; a small present; extremity; end; a gentle hit; secret information.

Tippet *n.* a muffler.

Tipple *v.t.* & *i.* to drink strong liquor habitually. *n.* a strong drink.

Tipstaff *n.* a stuff which is tipped with metal.

Tipster *n.* a man who gives secret information in racing.

Tipsy *n.* intoxicated; unsteady in gait or speech with drink.

Tipsily *adv.* in a tipsy manner.

Tipsiness *n.* the state of being tipsy.

Tiptoe *n.* the point of the toe; on the tips of toes.

Tiptop *n.* & *adj.* the highest degree.

Tirade *n.* a declamatory speech of censure; long passage of declamation.

Tire *n.* a hoop of iron attached round a wheel; a head-dress; attire; furniture.

Tired *adj.* weary.

Tiredness *n.* weariness.

Tireless *adj.* of inexhaustible energy; never getting fatigued.

Tiresome *adj.* fatiguing; tedious; exhausting.

Tirl *v.t.* & *i.* to make a quivering sound; to twist; to strip; to unroof; to quiver.

Tiro *n.* a beginner.

Tissue *n.* set; interwoven series; a fabric formed of cells; a fine woven cloth. *v.t.* to variegate; to interweave.

Titan *n.* & *adj.* a person of superhuman strength and intellect; relating to giants.

Tithe *n.* a small part; the tenth part of anything. *v.t.* to pay the tenth part.

Titian *n.* & *adj.* reddish yellow; a red-yellow colour.

Title *n.* an appellation of honour; right to ownership; a name; the distinguishing inscription put over anything.

Titled *adj.* having a title.

Titmouse *n.* a small perching bird.

Titration *n.* a chemical analysis; action of titrating.

Tittle *n.* a whit; a small particle.

Tittup *v.i.* to go mincingly; to move along.

Titubation *n.* uneasiness caused by nervous irritation; act of stumbling.

Titular *adj.* existing in name only; nominal.

Tivy *adv.* with great speed.

To *adv.* to or in the required position; to a stand-still; in closed state.

Toad *n.* a frog-like reptile breeding in water but living chiefly on land.

Toady *n.* sycophant.

Toadstool *n.* kinds of umbrella shaped fungus.

Toadyism *n.* a sycophancy.

Toast *n.* a person in honour of whome others raise their glasses in salutation and then drink; bread baked and browned on open fire. *v.t.* & *i.* to cook before fire; to drink to the health or honour of.

Tobacco *n.* a plant with narcotic leaves used for smoking or chewing.

Tobine *n.* twilled silk used in dress.

Toboggan *n.* hand-sledge for sliding down snow-covered place; a sledge used on snow.

Toby *n.* a jug or mug in the shape of old man with three-cornered hat.

Tobyman *n.* a highwayman.

Tocher *n.* dowry; property received by a bride on her marriage.

Toco *n.* punishment.

Tocsin *n.* alarm-signal on a bell.

Tod *n.* bush; a fox; a weight of wool of about 28 lbs.

Today *n.* & *adv.* on this day; this day.

Toddle *v.t.* & *i.* to walk leisurely; to walk with tottering steps.

Toe *n.* the fore-part of the hoof; a digit of the foot. *v.t.* to furnish with toes; to kick.

Toffee *n.* sweet-stuff of boiled butter and sugar; a kind of sweetmeat.

Toga *n.* a plain piece of woollen stuff; a loose outer garment.

Togated *adj.* wearing a toga.

Together *adv.* simultaneously; in union with; in company with; in the same time or place.

Toggle *n.* a pin inserted through the eye of a rope for keeping it in place.

Toil *n.* hard labour; drudgery. (*pl.*) a net or snare. *v.i.* to labour.

Toiler *n.* one who toils.

Toils *n. pl.* a net or snare.

Toilet *n.* a room for dressing; the mode of dressing or arranging the hair & etc.

Toilsome *adj.* laborious; involving toil; fatiguing.

Tolerably *adv.* in a tolerable manner.

Tolerance *n.* the power of tolerating; sufferance; endurance.

Tolerant *adj.* favouring toleration; broad-minded; disposed to tolerate others of their opinions.

Tolerantly *adv.* with toleration.

Tolerate *v.t.* to endure; to suffer; to allow by not preventing.

Toleration *n.* forbearance; recognition of personal rights in matters of religion.

Toll *n.* a tax or duty levied for some privilege; the solemn sound of a bell; charge payable for permission to pass a barrier.

Tolu *n.* a kind of resin.

Tom *n.* (*abbr*) of Thomas; a male animal. *v.t.* to act in a foolish manner.

Tomahawk *n.* war-axe.

Tomato *n.* a plant with edible fruit.

Tomb *n.* sepulchral monument; a grave.

Tomboy *n.* a girl who acts or dresses in a boyish way; a ramping girl.

Tombstone *n.* a monumental stone placed over a grave.

Tomecat *n.* a full grown male cat.

Tome *n.* a large volume of a book.

Tomelet *n.* a little volume.

Tommy *n.* a kind of wrench; a private soldier in the British army.

Tom-nody *n.* a dolt.

Tomorrow *n.* & *adv.* on the following day; the day after the present day.

Tomtom *n.* a native Indian drum.

Ton *n.* a unit of weight equal to 2240 pounds.

Tonal *adj.* of tone or tones; of tonality.

Tone *n.* effect of light and shade in a picture; a musical sound; note; accent; modulation of voice.

Tonga *n.* a two-wheeled Indian carriage.

Tongue *n.* faculty or manner of speech or speaking; muscular organ in the mouth which serves the purpose of taste, swallowing & etc.

Tonic *n.* & *adj.* a medicine that gives vigour to the system; invigorating; increasing strength.

Tonicity *n.* elasticity of muscles.

Tonight *n.* & *adv.* the coming or present night; the night of today.

Tonite *n.* a powerful explosive.

Tonk *v.t.* to hit hard.

Tonnage *n.* import duty on ships; the nominal capacity of a ship; ship's cubic content or carrying capacity.

Tonneau *n.* part of some motor-cars that contains the back seats.

Tonometer *n.* an instrument for measuring pitch of tones.

Tonsil *n.* one of the two glandular organs in the throat.

Tonsile *adj.* that may be clipped.

Tonsorial *adj.* pertaining to a barber.

Tonsure *n.* the rite of shaving the head.

Tony *n.* a simpleton; a fool.

Too *adv.* in an excessive degree; moreover; likewise; more than enough; in addition; over and above; as well.

Tool *n.* an instrument; an implement for mechanical operations.

Tooler *n.* a stone-mason's chisel.

Tooling *n.* workmanship perfomed with a tool.

Toon *n.* a kind of Indian cedar tree.

Toot *v.t.* to produce a harsh sound. *n.* the sound of a horn.

Tooter *n.* one who plays on a toot.

Tooth *n.* a pointed thing; the hard substance growing in jaws of animals used for chewing food.

Tooth-powder *n.* a powder for cleaning teeth.

Top *n.* the highest rank; the upper part; the children's toy for spinning; upper side; the hightest point; the summit or the upper part or the surface of something.

Topaz *n.* a precious stone of various colours; a kind of gem.

Tope *n.* a kind of shark; Buddhist mound or monument. *v.i.* to drink to excess.

Toper *n.* one who drinks to excess.

Topful *adj.* full to the brim.

Tophet *n.* hell.

Topiary *adj.* pertaining to the art of clipping or cutting shrubs in fanciful shapes.

Topic *n.* theme; subject of popular interest; a subject of conversation.

Topical *adj.* pertaining to a discourse; having reference to current event; local.

Topographical *adj.* descriptive of the physical features of a place.

Topography *n.* the detailed description on a map; local geography.

Toponymy *n.* study of the place, names of a region.

Topping *n.* the cutting off of the top.

Topple *v.t.* & *i.* to totter and fall down; to be unsteady or hang as if about to fall.

Topside *n.* the upper part.

Top-stone *n.* a stone which forms the top.

Topsyturvy *adj.* & *adv.* in a state of confusion; upside down; in inverted position or way. *v.t.* to turn upside down.

Torch *n.* a light carried in the hand; an inflammable stick or rope that can be carried as a light.

Torchon *n.* coarse loose kind of lace; a duster or dish-clot.

Torment *n.* severe bodily or mental suffering.

Tormenting *adj.* causing annoyance.

Torementor *n.* one who or that which torments.

Tormentress *n.* a female tormentor.

Tormina *n.* colic; griping pain in bowels.

Torminous *adj.* of colic pain.

Tornado *n.* tempest; a very violent storm; a hurricane.

Torpedo *n.* a submarine weapon in the form of a cigar designed for blowing up a ship.

Torpent *adj.* having no activity; benumbed.

Torpescence *n.* insensibility; torpidness.

Torpid *adj.* stupefied; inactive; benumbed; sluggish; dull.

Torpidity *n.* stupidity; inactivity.

Torpify *v.t.* to make torpid.

Torpor *n.* inactivity; laziness; dullness.

Torps *n.* ship's torpedo officer.

Torrefy *v.t.* to parch; to dry by fire.

Torrefaction *n.* a process of drying.

Torrents *n.* a heavy pouring of rain.

Torrid *n.* intensely hot; parched by the heat of the sun.

Torsel *n.* anything twisted.

Torsion *n.* act of twisting.

Torsive *adj.* twisted in a spiral manner.

Torso *n.* trunk of statue; unfinished work.

Tort *n.* breach of duty imposed by law; a wrong done to a person or private property.

Tortile *adj.* twisted; coiled.

Tortious *adj.* injurious.

Tortoise *n.* a four-legged reptile enclosed in a horny shell; a kind of turtle.

Torture *n.* mental or bodily anguish; extreme bodily pain; torment.

Torus *n.* the base of a floral receptalce.

Tory *n.* one of the conservative party.

Toss *v.t.* & *i.* to agitate; to cause to rise and fall.

Tot *n.* anything very small; a small child.

Total *adj.* comprising the whole; complete.

Tote *n.* the handle of a carpenter's plane. *v.t.* to carry.

Totem *v.t.* a figure used as a relationship.

Totter *v.i.* to stagger; to stand or walk unsteadily; to shake; to reel.

Tottery *adj.* unsteady.

Touch *v.t.* & *i.* to treat lightly; to move; to strike; to interfere; to come into or be in contact with.

Touchstone *n.* a black jasper used for testing, criterion.

Tough *adj.* hard to masticate; hard to break; strong; firm; stiff; flexible; unyielding. *n.* a street ruffian.

Toupee *n.* a false lock of hair.

Tour *n.* a short journey for pleasure; a roving journey including stops at various places; a rambling excursion.

Tourelle *n.* a slender tower.

Tourist *n.* one who makes a tour; an excursionist.

Tournament *n.* a contest in any game of skill between a number of competitors; a contest of skill.

Touse *v.t.* to pull; to haul.

Tousle *v.t.* to put into disorder; to pull about.

Tousy *adv.* rough, tousled.

Tout *v.t.* to inspect movement of horses while trainings; to solicit customers.

Touter *n.* one who touts.

Tow *v.t.* to drag over the surface of water; to pull a boat by a rope along the coast.

Towage *n.* the price paid for towing.

Toward *adj.* near; favourable; docile; apt; approaching.

Towards *prep.* as regards; in relation to; in the direction of.

Towel *n.* a cloth for drying the hands and face with after washing.

Tower *n.* citadel; elevation; a lofty tall structure; a place of defence.

Towline *n.* a rope for dragging boat in water.

Town *n.* a collection of houses larger than a village.

Townfolk *n.* the inhabitants of a town.

Townwards *adv.* towards the town.

Toxic *adj.* pertaining to poison; poisonous.

Toxical *adj.* like poison.

Toxin *n.* an organic poisonous substance.

Toxophilite *n.* a lover of archery.

Toy *n.* a trifling object; a trifle; a plaything; a thing for amusement.

Toyer *n.* one who toys.

Toyful full of trifles.

Toyman *n.* one who deals in toys.

Toyshop *n.* a shop where toys are sold.

T-plate *n.* a plate in the form of T.

Trabeation *n.* use of beams in construction.

Trabecula *n.* a little beam.

Trace *n.* footprint; indication; track; remains; a strap or chain by which a horse pulls; a vestige.

Tracer *n.* a trace-horse; a boy attending a trace-horse; one who traces; an instrument for tracing.

Tracheal *adj.* relating to the trachea. -

Tracheitis *n.* inflammation of the windpipe.

Trachoma *n.* a disease of the eye with hard pustules on the inner surface of the eyelids.

Tracing *n.* a reproduction of the lines of a drawing etc.

Track *n.* a continuous line showing where something has passed; a footstep.

Tract *n.* a short treatise on a religious subject; a region or expanse of indefinite extent and shape.

Tractable *adj.* pliant; that may be easily managed; governable; docile.

Tractile *adj.* capable of being drawn into wires.

Tractate *n.* a treatise.

Traction *n.* the drawing of something along a surface; contraction.

Tractor *n.* a powerful motor vehicle for pulling ploughs, drill, etc.

Tractrix *n.* a curve whose tangent is always equal to a given line.

Trade *n.* dealing in commodities for profit; the business of buying and selling; occupation; person engaged in a trade.

Tradewind *n.* the wind blowing continually from the tropics towards the equator.

Trading *n.* carrying on bushness.

Tradition *n.* oral transmission of knowledge or belief from one generation to another.

Traditionist *n.* one who adheres to tradition.

Traduce *v.t.* to calumniate; to misrepresent; to slender; to defame.

Traffic *n.* transportation of goods from one place to another; commerce; trade.

Tragacanth *n.* a kind of gum used as medicine.

Tragedy *n.* serious accident; sad event; a drama of elevated theme and diction with an unhappy ending.

Tragedian *n.* a writer or actor of tragedy.

Tragic *adj.* relating to tragedy; fatal; mournful; in the style of a tragedy.

Tragical *adj.* calamitous; of a terrible nature.

Tragus *n.* the projected part of the entrance of external ear.

Trail *v.t. & i.* to hunt by the track; to carry in a horizontal position; to draw along the ground; to draw along as an appendage.

Trailer *n.* a wheeled vehicle drawn by another; a trailling plant.

Train *v.t. & i.* to go by train; to cause to grow in a required form; to bring to a certain discipline by teaching and practice; to make physically fit for contest; to allure or entice.

Trained *adj.* instructed.

Training *n.* the act of educating.

Trait *n.* touch; an item in a portrait; a stroke.

Traject *n.* a ferry. *v.t.* to throw or cast through.

Tramp *v.t. & i.* to walk with firm heavy tread; to roll; to walk on foot.

Trample *v.t. & i.* to tread under foot with rapidity and force; to tread in contempt. *n.* the act of treading.

Trance *n.* extreme exaltation;state of insensibility; morbid sleep; catalepsy.

Tranced *adj.* lying in trance.

Tranquil *adj.* undisturbed; calm; peaceful; serene.

Tranquility *n.* freedom from agitation; calmness; quietness; peace of mind.

Trans *pref.* signifying 'across, beyond', 'through'.

Transact *v.t.* to carry out; to conduct matters; to perform; to do.

Transaction *n.* performance of a business; commercial business; an affair.

Transalpine *adj. & n.* beyond the Alps; extra-Italian.

Transcend *v.t.* to be beyond the range of; to surpass; to excell.

Transcendental *adj.* supernatural; vague; obscure; surpassing others.

Transcontinental *adj.* traversing a contiment.

Transcribe *v.t.* to reproduce in ordinary writing; to copy out.

Transcript *n.* a written copy; product of transcription.

Transcurrent *adj.* running cross-wise.

Transfer *v.t.* to convey drawings & etc. from one surface to another; to remove from one place to another; to make over possession to property.

Transferee *n.* the person to whom a transfer is made.

Transference *n.* a passage from one place to another; transferring.

Transfigure *v.t.* to invest with a more spiritual or elevated character.

Transfiguration *n.* a change of form.

Transfix *v.t.* to pierce through with a pointed weapon.

Transfixion *n.* piercing through.

Transfluent *adj.* flowing through.

Transflux *n.* a flowing through.

Transform *v.t.* to change the form or character of; to make change in outward appearance.

Transformer *n.* an electrical instrument which changes one form of current into another.

Transfuse *v.t.* to transfer blood of one animal to another.

Transfusion *n.* the act of transferring.

Transgress *v.t.* to violate; to pass beyond limit; to infringe.

Transgressor *n.* a sinner.

Tranship *v.t.* to transfer from one ship to another.

Transhipment *n.* transhipping.

Transhuman *adj.* more than human; super-human.

Transient *adj.* not lasting; of short duration; not permanent.

Transilience *n.* leaping from one thing to another.

Transit *n.* conveyance; apparent motion of heavenly bodies.

Transition *n.* change from one place to another; passage from one state or subject or set of circumstances to another.

Transitive *adj.* requiring a direct object expressed or understood.

Transitorily *adv.* for a short time.

Transitory *adj.* of short duration; continuing only a short time.

Translate *v.t.* to convey to heaven without death; to express into another language; to transform.

Translation *n.* art or act or product of translating; interpretation.

Translator *n.* one who translate.

Translocate *v.t.* to substitute one thing for another.

Translocation *n.* substitution.

Translucence *n.* semi-transparency.

Translucent *adj.* clear; allowing light to pass through.

Translucid *adj.* translucent.

Translunary *adj.* lying beyond the moon.

Transmarine *adj.* beyond the sea.

Transmigrate *v.t.* to pass in a different body; to pass from one country to another.

Transmissible *adj.* that may be transmitted.

Transmission *n.* sending from one place to another.

Transmit *v.t.* to transfer; to pass through; to send from one person to another; to effect conveyance of.

Transmitter *n.* an apparatus for transmitting wireless signals.

Transmogrify *v.t.* to transform in a surprising manner.

Transmontane *adj.* lying across the mountains.

Transmutability *n.* susceptibility of being transmuted.

Transmutably *adv.* with capacity of being transmuted.

Transmutation *n.* an act of transmuting; a change into another form.

Transmute *v.t.* to change from one form or nature to another.

Transnormal *adj.* beyond what is normal.

Transom *n.* horizontal bar of wood or stone across window or top of door.

Transparence (-y) *n.* the quality of being transparent.

Transparent *adj.* that can be clearly seen through; transmitting rays of light so as not to hide the view of anything which is at the back; frank; clear.

Transpire *v.t.* & *i.* to exhale; to ooze out; to come to be known.

Transplant *v.t.* to remove and plant in another place.

Transplantation *n.* an act of transplanting.

Transport *v.t.* to convey by land or sea; to ravish with pleasure; to carry from one place to another.

Transposal *n.* the act of changing places.

Transpose *v.t.* to change the natural order of things; to change the order or place of things.

Transposition *n.* change of order; being transposed.

Trans-ship *v.t.* to transfer from one ship to another.

Transubstantiate *v.t.* to change into a different substance.

Transubstantiation *n.* a change of substance.

Transude *v.t.* to pass through pores.

Transudation *n.* the act of passing through pores.

Transversal *adj.* running across.

Transverse *adj.* lying or situated in a cross direction; set crosswise.

Tranter *n.* a pedlar.

Trap *n.* a scheme for enticing or detecting; a contrivance to catch animals; an ambush.

Trapanner *n.* one who ensnares.

Trapes *v.i.* to tramp noisily.

Trapeze *n.* a swinging horizontal bar used for gymnastic exercises.

Trapezoid *n.* a quadrilateral of which no two sides are parallel.

Trapflower *n.* a flower in which insects are shift up.

Trapper *n.* one who ensnares animals.

Trappous *n. pl.* ornamental harness for horses.

Trappy *adj.* resembling a trap; treacherous.

Traps *n. pl.* luggage.

Trash *n.* loppings of trees; nonsense talk; waste or worthless matter; rubbish.

Trashily *adv.* in a trashy manner.

Trashy *adj.* worthless.

Trass *n.* volcanic earth used as cement.

Trauma *n.* morbid condition of body; an injury of body produced by wound or violence.

Traumatic *adj.* pertaining to wounds.

Travail *n.* labour with pain; pangs of childbirth; severe toil.

Travel *v.t.* & *i.* to move from one place to another place; to make a journey; to wander.

Travelogue *n.* an illustrated narrative of travels.

Traverse *v.t.* & *i.* to wonder over; to discuss; to thwart; to obstruct; to travel across.

Traverser *n.* an appliance for turning a railway engine.

Travertin(e) *n.* a porous light yellow rock.

Travesty *n.* ridiculous dress; literary composition of imitation or description that misrepresents the original.

Trawl *n.* a large wide-mouthed net dragged by boat along bottom of fishing bank.

Tray *n.* a flat domestic vessel of wood or metal.

Treachery *n.* a breach of trust; violation of faith; deception; faithlessness.

Treacle *n.* uncrystallized syrup got in refining sugar; molasses.

Tread *v.t.* & *i.* to follow the example; to walk on; to set one's foot on.

Treadler *n.* one who treadles.

Treadmill *n.* a cylinder turned by treading on movable steps projecting from it, *esp.* the kind used in prisons as punishment; monotonous work.

Treason *n.* violation by a subject of his allegiance to sovereign or State; treachery; disloyalty.

Treasure *n.* great abundance; a valued thing or person; accumulated wealth; valued object.

Treasurer *n.* the person in charge of treasury or funds; officer authorised to receive and disburse public revenues.

Treasury *n.* a book containing much valuable information; a place where treasure is kept.

Treat *v.t.* & *i.* to entertain with food or drink; to act or behave towards in a specified way; to give medical care; to manage; to discourse on; to negotiate.

Treater *n.* one who discourses on a subject.

Treatise *n.* a literary composition on a definite subject.

Treaty *n.* a formal agreement between nations.

Treble *adj.* three times; threefold; multiplied by three.

Trebly *adv.* in a three fold manner.

Tree *n.* anything like tree; a perennial plant with a trunk and branches.

Treen *adj.* pertaining to trees.

Treenail *n.* a wooden nail.

Trefoil *n.* a plant with three leaflets; an ornament of three cups in a circle.

Trek *v.t.* to travel by bullockcart.

Trellis *n.* summer-house or screen of such work; a lattice work of wood.

Tremble *v.i.* to quake; to shiver; to shake with fear, excitement or weakness.

Tremendous *adj.* dreadful; considerable; causing terror; terrific; awful.

Tremolo *n.* a vibration in voice or instrumental music.

Tremor *n.* trembling; a thrill of fear or other emotion; shaking.

Tremulant *adj.* quivering; trembling.

Tremulous *adj.* trembling; affected with tremor; quivering; shivering.

Trench *v.t.* & *i.* to fortify by cutting a ditch; to dig into pits or ditches; to cut a groove.

Trenchant *adj.* vigorous; sharp; keen; severe.

Trencher *n.* a flat round wooden block or piece for cutting meat.

Trencherman *n.* an eater, glutton.

Trenching *n.* act of digging the earth very deep.

Trench-mortar *n.* a light gun used in trenches for throwing a heavy charge of explosives at short distances.

Trend *n.* tendency in a particular direction. *v.i.* to tend in a particular direction; to incline.

Trepan *n.* surgeon's cylindrical saw for making or opening in the skull.

Trephine *n.* improved form of trepan with centre-pin.

Trepid *adj.* shaking; trembling.

Trepidation *n.* involuntary trembling of limbs.

Trespass *v.t.* to go beyond; to intrude; of offend; to make unlawful encroachment upon the rights of others.

Tress *n.* (*pl.*) a woman's or child's flowing hair; a lock or curl or braid of hair.

Trestle *n.* a movable frame for supporting anything; the supporting frame of a table.

Tret *n.* an allowance of extra weight given to purchaser for waste or refuse matter.

Trevet *n.* a stool with three legs.

Trews *n. pl.* trousers.

Tri *pref.* signifying 'three'.

Triad *n.* trinity; a chord of three notes; a union of three.

Triable *adj.* subjected to trial.

Triacontahedral *adj.* having thirty sides.

Trial *n.* test; judicial examination; experience; essay competition.

Trialism *n.* doctrine of the existence of body, soul and spirit.

Trialogue *n.* a conversation between three persons.

Triangle *n.* a rod of polished steel bent in the form of a triangle.

Triangular *adj.* three cornered; having three angles; in the form of a triangle.

Triangulation *n.* use of triangles in trigonometrical survey.

Triarchy *n.* government by three persons.

Triatomic *adj.* consisting of three atoms.

Tribe *n.* distinct class of people; race; clan.

Tribesman *n.* the member of a tribe.

Triblet *n.* a goldsmith's tool for making ring.

Tribulation *n.* vexation; severe suffering.

Tribunal *n.* a court of justice.

Tribune *n.* platform from which speeches are delivered.

Tribunal *n.* a court of justice.

Tributarily *adv.* in a subordinate manner.

Tributary *adj.* subordinate; auxiliary; of the nature of or paying tribute.

Tribute *n.* periodical payment expected by one prince or State from another; contribution.

Tricar *n.* a three wheeled motor car.

Trice *n.* a very short time; moment; an instant.

Tricennial *adj.* occurring every thirty years.

Tricephalous *adj.* having three heads.

Triceps *n.* a muscle with three heads.

Trichiasis *n.* urinary disease in which hair-like filaments appear in urine.

Trichina *n.* a hair-like worm which infests man's body.

Trichology *n.* the study of hair.

Trichord *n.* lyre having three strings.

Trichosis *n.* disease due to presence of hair-like worms parasitic in the body (of man, swine etc.).

Trichotomy *n.* classification into three parts.

Trick *n.* feat of dexterity; prank; piece of guile; piece of skill; cards played in.

Trickery *n.* artifice; deceitful conduct; cheating; imposture.

Tricksome *adj.* artful; deceptive.

Trickle *v.t. & i.* to flow in drops; to flow in a small gentle stream.

Tricksy *adj.* artful; play-ful; full of tricks.

Tricky *adj.* crafty; skilful; prone to deceit.

Triclinic *adj.* having three unequal angles.

Tricorn *adj.* with three horns or corners.

Tricornute *adj.* having three horns.

Tricorporal *adj.* pertaining to three bodies.

Tricuspid *adj.* having three points.

Tricycle *n.* a three-wheeled cycle.

Trident *adj.* having three prongs.

Tridentate *adj.* having three teeth.

Tridigitate *adj.* having three fingers or toes.

Triduan *adj.* lasting for three days.

Triennial *adj.* continuing three years; happening or done every three years.

Trifle *n.* small amount of money; a dish of sweetmeats; a thing of slight value or importance.

Trifler *n.* one who trifles.

Trifoliate *adj.* having three leaves.

Triform *adj.* having or appearing in three forms.

Trifurcate *v.t.* to divide into three parts.

Trig *adj.* neat; trim; smart.

Trigamous *adj.* having three wives or husbands at once; thrice-married.

Trigamy *n.* the condition of having three husbands or three wives at the same time.

Trigger *n.* a lever or catch for firing a gun.

Triglot *adj.* in three languages.

Trigon *n.* a triangle.

Trigonic *adj.* pertaining to a trigon.

Trigonometry *n.* the science of measuring the sides and angles of a triangle by means of certain data.

Trigram *n.* three letters sounded as one.

Trigrammic *adj.* containing three sets of letters.

Trigraph *n.* a triphthong.

Trihedron *n.* a figure having three equal sides.

Trilabe *adj.* a surgical instrument with three prongs.

Trilateral *adj.* having three sides.

Trilemma *n.* a choice between three alternatives.

Trilinear *adj.* having three lines.

Triliteral *adj.* consisting of three letters.

Trill *n.* quevering or vibrating sound.

Trilling *n.* each of three children born at a time; a crystal with three faces.

Trillion *n.* the power of a million multiplied by itself three times.

Trilobite *n.* kind of fossil crustacean.

Trilogy *n.* set of three tragedies to be acted in immediate succession, each complete in itself.

Trim *adj.* in good order; neat; right; nice; compact.

Trimerous *adj.* having three pieces.

Trimly *adv*. neatly; nicely.
Trimmer *n*. a time server; a kind of instrument for clipping; one who trims; one who stands neutral.
Trimness *n*. cleanliness; neatness.
Tritmorphic *adj*. existing in three forms.
Trinal, Trinary *adjs*. three- fold.
Trine *n*. the third part of a circle.
Tringle *n*. a curtain rod of a bedstead; small squary moulding.
Trinitarian *n*. one who believes in the Trinity.
Trinitarianism *n*. the doctrine of the Trinity.
Trinity *n*. a group of three; a union of three God heads.
Trinket *n*. a small fancy article; a trifling ornament; a thing of little value.
Trinketer *n*. a secret petty dealer.
Trinketry *n*. ornaments of dress.
Trinomial *adj*. employing three terms.
Trio *n*. a set of three performers or three persons.
Triode *n*. a kind of valve for wireless.
Triolet *n*. a poem of eight lines; an eight line poem with strict rhyme-scheme.
Trional *n*. an anaesthetic medicine.
Trip *v.t.* & *i*. to stumble and fall; to skip; to go lightly and quickly along.
Tripartite *adj*. divided into three parts.
Tripartition *n*. a division in three parts.
Tripe *n*. the stomach of ox & etc. used as food; entrails.
Tripedal *adj*. having three feet.
Trip-hammer *n*. tilt hammer.
Tripetalius *adj*. having three petals.
Triphthong *n*. a group three vowels forming one sound.
Triplane *n*. an aeroplane with three planes.
Triple *adj*. consisting of three parts; threefold.
Triple alliance *n*. an alliance between three kingdoms.
Triple headed *adj*. with three heads.
Triplet *n*. three lines rhyming together; a set of three things.
Triplex *n*. a composition in three parts.
Triplicate *adj*. & *n*. each of a set of three copies; made three at a time.
Tripod *n*. a stool; a three-legged or threefooted stand.
Tripoli *n*. rotten stone.
Trippant *adj*. trotting.
Tripper *n*. one who walks gently.
Tripsis *n*. reducing something to powder.
Triptych *n*. picture or carving on three panels, side by side.
Tripudiate *v.t*. to dance in joy.
Triquatrous *adj*. three-cornered.
Triradiated *adj*. having three rays.
Trisect *v.t*. to divide into three equal parts.

Trisection *n.* a division into three equal parts.

Trismus *n.* lockjaw.

Trisoctahedron *n.* a solid of twenty-four equal faces.

Trist *adj.* sad; unhappy.

Trisulcate *adj.* having three forks.

Trisyllable *n.* a word of three syllables.

Trite *adj.* commonplace; state.

Tritely *adv.* in a trite manner.

Tritheism the doctrine of the Trinity.

Tritheist *n.* one who believes in the Trinity.

Triton *n.* kind of lizard-like animal; a sea-god.

Triturate *v.t.* to masticate thoroughly; to grind or rub to a fine powder.

Triturium *n.* a vessel used for separating liquors of different densities.

Triumph *n.* joy for success; joys; the state of being victorious. *v.t.* to rejoice at victory; to attain victory.

Triumphal *adj.* pertaining to triumph.

Trimphant *adj.* victorious; successful.

Triumvir *n.* a member of board of three; one of the three men united in power.

Triune *n.* three in one.

Trivalent *adj.* having combining power of three.

Trivet *n.* an iron tripod or stool for holding cooking pots.

Trivial *adj.* trifling; of little importance; ordinary; insignificant.

Trivium *n.* a place where three roads meet.

Trocar *n.* a surgical instrument for withdrawing fluid from body.

Trochal *adj.* shaped like a wheel.

Trochanter *n.* second joint of insect's leg.

Trochee *n.* a foot of two syllables in which the first is long and the second short.

Trochilic *adj.* having the power to turn round.

Tochlea *n.* a pully-like cartilage.

Trochoid *n.* & *adj.* wheellike; the curve traced by a fixed point in the plane of a rolling circle.

Troglodyte *n.* a cave-dweller of pre-historic times.

Trojan *adj.* & *n.* a warrior of Troy; inhabitant of Troy.

Troll *v.t.* & *i.* to roll; to turn about; to fish; to move circularly; to turn; to sing in succession.

Trolley, Trolly *ns.* kinds of low truck; a power-pulley running overhead; a small truck from which wheels can be easily removed.

Trollop *n.* a slattern; prostitute; a disreputable girl or woman.

Trollopy *adj.* slatternly.

Trombone *n.* a large trumpet-like musical instrument.

Tromometer *n.* an instrument for measuring slight shocks of earthquake.

Troop *n.* a company of person; body of soldiers; multitude; set of congregated persons or animals.

Trope *n.* the figurative use of a word or expression.

Trophesy *n.* deranged nutrition.

Trophic *adj.* pertaining to nutrition.

Trophy *n.* prize; pile of the enemy's spoil set up by ancient army after victory.

Tropic *n.* the line drawn parallel to the equator 23º-28' north and south.

Tropical *adj.* pertaining to the tropics.

Tropology *n.* a moral interpretation of the Bible; figurative language.

Tropological *adj.* figurative.

Trot *v.t.* & *i.* to walk so as to excite admiration; to walk in a steady manner.

Trotter *n.* a trotting horse.

Troth *n.* truth; belief; faith.

Trouble *n.* affliction; disturbance of mind; disturbed state; perplexity; vaxation.

Through *n.* a long narrow vessel of wood or metal for holding water & etc.

Trounce *v.t.* to harass; to trouble; to beat severely; to punish.

Trouncing *n.* severe beating.

Troupe *n.* a company of performers or actors.

Trousered *adj.* wearing trouser.

Trousering *n.* cloth for trousers.

Trousers *n.* (*pl.*) a garment extending from waist to ankles.

Trousseau *n.* the oufit of a bride.

Trout *n.* a kind of fresh-water fish. *v.i.* to fish trout.

Trover *n.* gaining possession of a man's personal property.

Trow *v.t.* to suppose; to think; to believe.

Trowel *n.* gardener's scoop for lifting small plants; a mason's tool for spreading mortar & etc.

Troy (-weight) *ns.* the weight used for gold, silver and precious stones.

Trogan *n.* a computer programme which is designed to sabotage a computer system.

Truant *n.* a child who absents himself from school without leave.

Truce *n.* a temporary cessation of hostilities by agreement for a time.

Trucidation *n.* act of killing.

Truck *n.* a strong car for carrying heavy goods; exchange; barter; nonsense; open railway wagon.

Truckage *n.* the practice of bartering goods.

Trucker *n.* one who maker an exchange of goods.

Truckle *n.* a small wheel; truckle-bed.

Truculence *n.* savageness; merciless nature; ferociousness.

Truculent *adj.* savage; merciless; fierce; of or showing bellicose;

Trudge *v.t.* & *i.* to walk or move along laboriously. *n.* such a walk.

Trudgen *n.* swimming with alternate stroks of right and left arm.

True *adj.* accurate; faithful; honest; sincere; real; conformable to fact; not false; in accordance with reason; genuine.

Truism *n.* a self-evident truth; statement too obviously true or too hackneyed to be worth making.

Trull *n.* a prostitute; a woman of loose habits; a harlot.

Truly *adv.* in reality, sincerely; accurately; honestly.

Trump *n.* a trumpet; a card of the winning suit; a good fellow.

Trumpery *n.* worthless; useless matter; rubbish; things of no real value.

Trumpet *n.* a wind instrument with long bent tube.

Truncal *adj.* of the trunk of a body or tree.

Truncate *v.t.* to lop off the top of a tree; to maim.

Truncated *adj.* cut short.

Truncation *n.* the state of being lopped of.

Truncheon *n.* a short staff as symbol of authority.

Truncheoneer *n.* a person who is armed with a truncheon.

Trundle *v.t.* & *i.* to bowl at cricket; to roll or bowl along.

Trunk *n.* a box for clothes & etc.; the main body of a tree; telegraph or telephone.

Trunnion *n.* the lateral support of a gun; hollow grudgeon supporting cylinder in steam engine.

Truss *n.* a bandage used in rupture; a bundle of hay or straw.

Trussed *adj.* supported by a truss.

Trust *n.* credit combination of several firms for business purposes.

Trustee *n.* one who holds the management of property in trust.

Truster *n.* one who trusts.

Trustful *adjs.* confiding; full of trust; not given to suspicion.

Trustier confident.

Trusty *adj.* faithful; loyal.

Truth *n.* honesty; sincerity; constancy; a true statement.

Try *v.t.* & *i.* to examine judicially; to refine; to purify; to test by experiment; to make an attempt at.

Trying *adj.* putting to severe test; wearisome; exhausting; difficult to bear.

Trying-plane *n.* a carpenter's small smoothing instrument.

Trypanosome *n.* kinds of blood parasite causing diseases.

Tryst *n.* a secret assembly; an appointed meeting.

Tsar *n.* the title of the Emperor of Russia.

Tsetse *n.* an African fly whose bite is fatal to horses, cattle.

Tub *n.* a small cask; an open wooden vessel used for washing and other purpose.

Tubful *adj.* as much as tub can hold.

Tuba *n.* a kind of trumpet; a large low-toned trumpet.

Tube *n.* a hollow long cylinder; a hollow tube-shaped organ.

Tubewell *n.* a perforated iron pointed at the end sunk deep in the earth for getting water from underground.

Tuber *n.* a morbid swelling of gland.

Tubercle *n.* a small tumour; pimple or knob; consumption.

Tubercled *adj.* having tubercles.

Tuberculate *adj.* having small knots.

Tuberculous *adj.* pertaining to phthisis.

Tuberculize *v.t.* to be affected with tuberculosis.

Tuberculosis *n.* consumptive state; consumption of the lungs.

Tuberose *adj.* covered with tubers, knotty.

Tuberous *adj.* covered with tubers; knotty; of the nature of a tuber.

Tubiform *adj.* of the shape of a tube.

Tubing *n.* an indefinite length of tube or quantity of tubes; materials for tubes.

Tubular *adj.* tube-shaped; resembling a pipe.

Tubule *n.* a small tube.

Tubulous *adj.* containing tubules.

Tuck *n.* flourish of trumpet; beat of a drum; a tap; eatables; a flat fold; the part of a ship's hull; a pull; a kind of narrow sword.

Tucker *n.* a piece of lace for the neck.

Tuckshop *n.* a pastry shop at school.

Tuesday *n.* third day of the week.

Tufa *n.* kinds of porous rock.

Tufaceous *adj.* pertaining to tufa.

Tuft *n.* the head of a flower; a bunch or cluster of soft objects; a clump.

Tufted *adj.* growing in clusters.

Tufty *adj.* abounding with tufts.

Tuft-hunter *n.* one who seeks the society of great men.

Tug *v.t.* & *i.* to drag; to pull with force; to make a vigorous pull at; to labour.

Tug-of-war *n.* a contest in which half of the players take hold of one end of a rope and the other half the other end and try to pull up the rope across a marked line.

Tuition *n.* instruction; fee for teaching; the act of teaching; tutorship.

Tuitionary *adj.* pertaining to instruction.

Tulchan *n.* calf-skin stuffed with straw to induce the cow to give milk.

Tulip *n.* kinds of plants with bell-shaped flowers.

Tulle *n.* a kind of fine silk.

Tumble *v.t. & i.* to disturb; to toss the body about; to fall suddenly; to turn over.

Tumble-down *adj.* in ruinous state.

Tumbler *n.* a kind of pigeon; an acrobat; one who tumbles.

Tumbly *adj.* uneven.

Tumbrel *n.* a dung-cart; a two-wheeled cart for carrying tools.

Tumefy *v.t. & i.* to cause to swell; to rise in a tumour; to inflate.

Tumefaction *n.* a process of swelling.

Tumescence *n.* swelling.

Tumid *adj.* protuberant; inflated; swollen.

Tumidly *adv.* in a tumid manner.

Tumour *n.* a morbid growth or swelling; a local permanent swelling.

Tumoured *adj.* swollen.

Tumourous *adj.* protuberant.

Tump *n.* a little hillock.

Tumular *adj.* formed in a heap.

Tumulose *adj.* full of hills.

Tun *n.* a large cask for wine; a measure of 252 gallons. *v.t.* to store in tun.

Tunable *adj.* harmonious; musical.

Tunableness *n.* the state of being tunable.

Tundun *n.* a toy which produces a roaring sound when whirled in the air.

Tundra *n.* a mossy and often marshy plain in N. Russia.

Tune *n.* melody; suitable mood; fit temper; a series of the musical notes; a melody or air; agreement; harmonious relation; right disposition.

Tuneful *adj.* melodious; musical.

Tuner *n.* one who tunes musical instruments.

Tungsten *n.* a heavy metallic element of grey colour.

Tunic *n.* a woman's blouse; a soldier's coat.

Tunicle *n.* a short vestment; fine or delicate tunic.

Tuning *n.* the act of putting a musical instrument in tune.

Tunnel *n.* opening of a chimney; a tubular opening; a subterranean artificial passage through a hill or under a river.

Tup *n.* a ram; a male sheep.

Turbinate *adj.* shaped like a top spinning; conical; like a turbine.

Tubine *n.* kinds of rotary motor driven by water or air or steam.

Turbit *n.* a kind of domestic pigeon.

Turbot *n.* a kind of flat fish esteemed as food.

Turbulence *n.* the state of being turbulent.

Turcophil *n.* a lover and admirer of the Turks.

Tureen *n.* a deep dish for holding soup.

Turf *n.* a sod; a racecourse.

Turgescence *n.* inflation; pomp; the state of being swollen.

Turgid *adj.* swollen; inflated, rhetorical.

Turion *n.* young scaly shoot rising from the ground; an underground shoot of a plant.

Turk *n.* a member of the Ottoman race; a native of Turkey.

Turmeric *n.* a tropical plant of ginger family, powdered root used as dye-stuff.

Turmoil *n.* trouble; commotion; disturbance; agitation.

Turn *v.t.* & *i.* to be inclined in one position; to cause to move on an axis; to transform; to change.

Turn-bench *n.* a watchmaker's portable lathe.

Turn-cap *n.* revolving chimney-top.

Turner *n.* one who works on a lathe.

Turning *n.* the art of shaping; a place where roads meet.

Turning-point *n.* that which decides a matter.

Turnip *n.* a plant of the mustard family whose roots are used as vegetable.

Turtle *n.* a kind of dove; a marine tortoise.

Tush *inter.* pshaw! *n.* a long pointed tooth.

Tusk *n.* tusk-like part in harrow; a long pointed tooth *esp.* a protruding one. *v.t.* to tear up with tusk; to thrust.

Tusker *n.* an elephant with long tusks.

Tussis *n.* cough.

Tussive *adj.* pertaining to cough.

Tussle *n.* a struggle; a scuffle. *v.t.* to struggle.

Tussock *n.* a tuft of grass or twigs.

Tutelage *n.* protection; guardianship.

Tutening *n.* a kind of white metal like German silver.

Tutor *n.* a private teacher; a guardian of a minor. *v.i.* to treat with authority or sternness; to instruct.

Tutoress, Tutrix *ns.* female teacher; a female guardian.

Tutorial *adj.* belonging to a tutor; pertaining to teaching.

Tutty *n.* impure oxide of zinc.

Tuwhit, tu-whoo *v.i.* cry of owl.

Twaddle *n.* a silly talk; senseless talker.

Twain *n.* two; a pair. *adj.* twice.

Twaite *n.* woodland covered with arable land.

Twang *v.t.* & *i.* to make a ringing metallic sound. *n.* a sharp quick sound.

Tweed *n.* a kind of woollen fabric.

Tween *adv.* & *prep.* between.

Tweeny *n.* small cigar; between-maid.
Tweezer *n.* a pair of tongs for plucking up small objects.
Twelvefold twelve times.
Twi or Twy *pref.* in sense of 'two'.
Twice *adv.* two times.
Twicer *n.* a compositor who also works as a pressman.
Twiddle *n.* a light twist.
Twig *n.* minor shoot of a tree or shrub; a small branch of a tee or plant.
Twiggy *adj.* abounding in twigs or shoots.
Twill *contr.* of 'it will'.
Twill *n.* a fabric with small raised ribs; a kind of cloth.
Twin *n.* & *adj.* one of the two children born at a birth.
Twin-born *adj.* born at the same birth.
Twinned *adj.* like twins.
Twine *n.* cord twisted to the thickness used for tying small parcels.
Twiner *n.* climbing plant.
Twinge *n.* a sharp pain; a transitory sharp local pain; a tweak.
Twinkle *v.t.* & *i.* to shine with quick gleams; to sparkle; to blink one's eyes.
Twinkling *n.* an instant; a moment.
Twin likeness *n.* near resemblance.
Twinling *n.* a twin lamb.
Twirl *n.* a rapid circular movement; a whirl.
Twist *n.* made by winding two or more strands together; the act of twisting a roll of paper, tobacco & etc.
Twister *n.* he who or that which twists.
Twit *v.t.* to reproach; to upbraid; to taunt.
Twitch *v.t.* & *i.* to give a momentary sharp pull at; to pull with sudden jerk; to snatch.
Twitten *n.* a narrow lane connecting two roads.
Twitter *v.i.* to chirp; to make a succession of light tremulous noise. *n.* such a series of sounds.
Twixt *prep.* betwixt.
Two *adj.* & *n.* one and one.
Two-pence *n.* silver coin worth two pence.
Two-penny *n.* a kind of beer; (*sl.*) one's head. *adj.* (*colloq.*) cheap; worthless.
Two-ply *adj.* consisting of two thicknesses.
Two-tongued *adj.* deceitful.
Tyke *n.* a dog.
Tyler *n.* the door-keeper of a lodge.
Tylopod *adj.* & *n.* having padded hoof.
Tylosis *n.* an inflammation of eyelids.
Tympan *n.* stretched sheet of membrane or thin material; frame of equalizing pressure in some printing presses.

Tympanites *n.* the swelling of abdomen.

Tympanitis *n.* the inflammation of the membrane of the middle year.

Tympanum *n.* a drumwheel for raising water; the middle ear; the panel of a door.

Type *n.* class of things having common characteristics; symbol.

Typewriter *n.* a machine for writing by means of types; a keyed machine enabling user to produce printed characters instead of writing.

Typhlitis *n.* inflammation of the caecum and vermiform appendix.

Typhoid *adj.* & *n.* a kind of fever resembling typhus.

Typhomania *n.* the muttering delirium in typhus.

Typic *adj.* one that is regular in its attacks or follows a particular type.

Typical *adj.* true to type; symbolical; fit to serve as a type; representative.

Typicalness *n.* the state of being typical.

Typify *v.t.* to foreshadow; to prefigure; to show by image; to represent by a type.

Typist *n.* one who uses a typewriter.

Tyrannical *adj.* cruel; given to or characteristic of tyranny; acting like a tyrant; despotic.

Tyrannize *v.i.* & *t.* to rule despotically and cruelly; to act as a tyrant.

Tyrannous *adj.* tyrannical; unjustly; severel; impervious; despotic.

Tyrant *n.* one who exercises unlawful authority; an oppressive ruler.

Tyre *n.* a rind or band of rubber, either solid or hollow and inflated, or of metal, placed over the rim of a wheel to provide traction, resistance to wear, or other desirable properties.

Tzar *n.* an emperor or king.

U

U the fifth vowel and the twenty-first letter of the English alphabet.

Uberous *adj.* yielding abundance; fruitful.

Uberty *n.* fruitfulness; abundance.

Ubiety *n.* local relation.

Ubiquitary *adj.* existing everywhere.

Ubiquity *n.* being everywhere or in an indefinite number of places at once.

Udder *n.* teats of cattle; one of the mammary glands of a mammal.

Ugh *inter.* exclamation of disgust.

Ugly *adj.* hateful; given to quarrelling; unpleasing to sight; deformed.

Ulcer *n.* a moral blemish; a discharging sore.

Ulcuscle *n.* a small ulcer.

Uliginose *adj*. growing in a muddy place.
Uliginous *adj*. muddy; slimy.
Ulmic *adj*. produced by decaying vegetable matter.
Ulmin *adj*. a gymmy substance obtained from vegetables.
Ulna *n*. inner of two bones of the fore-arm.
Ulnar *adj*. pertaining to the ulna.
Ulster *n*. a long loose overcoat originally made of frieze cloth.
Ult *adj*. a contraction of ultimo; last.
Ulterior *adj*. situated beyond; remote; on the farther side of.
Ultimate *adj*. most remote, last; final; primary.
Ultimatum *n*. ultimate conclusion; fundamental principle; the final proposal or statement of terms.
Ultimo *adv*. in last month; in the month preceding the present one.
Ultra *pref.* in sense of 'beyond, on the other side of.' *adj*. advocate of extreme views or measures.
Ultramontane *adj*. situated beyond the mountains (*esp.* the Alps).
Ultramundane *adj*. beyond the world system; of another life.
Ultra-violet *adj*. (of invisible rays of the spectrum) beyond the violet rays.
Ultroneous *adj*. spontaneous; voluntary.
Ululate *v.t*. to howl as a dog or wolf.
Umbellar *adj*. of the form of an umbel.
Umber *n*. a dark brown mineral pigment.
Umbilical *adj*. pertaining to the navel, connected through the female line.
Umbilicular *adj*. of the navel.
Umbo *n*. the boss of shield.
Umbonal *adj*. protuberant.
Umbra *n*. the dark central of sun-spot; a shadow; the cone of shadow projecting from a planet.
Umbrageousness *n*. the state of being shady.
Umbrel *adj*. shady.
Umbrella *n*. a portable circular canopy for sheltering a person from the sun or rain.
Umbril *n*. a visor of a helmet.
Umbrose *adj*. shady.
Umpire *n*. a person chosen to decide a question when arbitrators disagree.
Umpirage *n*. the decision of an umpire; an arbiter's judgement.
Un *pref.* used before nouns, pronouns and adjectives signifying a negative meaning.
Unable *adj*. weak; impotent; not having sufficient strength.
Unabridged *adj*. not curtailed or abridged.
Unabsolved *adj*. not forgiven.
Unacclimated *adj*. not accustomed to the climate.

Unaccompanied *adj.* without companions; not attended.

Unaccordant *adj.* not harmonious.

Unaccredited *adj.* not authorized.

Unaccustomed *adj.* not usual.

Unaching *adj.* not giving pain.

Unacknowledged *adj.* not recognized.

Unacquirable *adj.* not acquirable.

Unacquitted *adj.* not declared innocent.

Unactuated *adj.* not moved.

Unadapted *adj.* not suited.

Unadmired *adj.* not regarded with respect; not praised.

Unafflicted *adj.* free from trouble.

Unafraid *adj.* without fear.

Unagitated *adj.* calm; not agitated.

Unaided *adj.* not helped or assisted.

Unalarmed *adj.* not disturbed with fear.

Unalloyed *adj.* unmixed; pure; not alloyed.

Unalluring *adj.* not tempting.

Unamazed *adj.* free from amazement.

Unambiguous *adj.* not of doubtful meaning.

Unambitious *adj.* free from ambition.

Unamenable *adj.* unlovely; ill-natured.

Unanalysable *adj.* not capable of being analysed.

Unanimity *n.* agreement in opinion of several men.

Unanimous *adj.* agreeing in opinion of several men given with one accord.

Unannexed *adj.* not joined.

Unanointed *adj.* not anointed.

Unanxious *adj.* not anxious.

Unapparent *adj.* obscure; invisible; not clear.

Unappeasable *adj.* that cannot be pacified.

Unappeased *adj.* not pacified.

Unapplauded *adj.* not praised.

Unapplicable *adj.* not applicable.

Unappreciated *adj.* not properly estimated.

Unapprehended *adj.* without fear; not understood.

Unapprised *adj.* not informed beforehand.

Unapproved *adj.* not approved.

Unapt *adj.* not qualified; unfit.

Unaptly *adv.* improperly.

Unarmed *adj.* not equipped or furnished with arms.

Unarrayed *adj.* not put in order; not dressed.

Unartificial *adj.* not artificial.

Unascertainable *adj.* that cannot be certainly known.

Unashamed *adj.* not ashamed.

Uuasked *adj.* unsolicited; not asked.

Unaspiring *adj.* not ambitious.

Unassayed *adj.* not tested.

Unassailable *adj.* that cannot be assailed.

Unassigned *adj.* not transferred.

Unassuming *adj.* making little of ones's own merits or status; not assuming.

Unattached *adj.* not attached.

Unattackable *adj.* not attackable.

Unattested *adj.* without attestation.

Unauthorized *adj.* not warranted by proper authority.

Unavailing *adj.* not availing useless.

Unavoidable *adj.* inevitable; certain; that cannot be made void.

Unaware *adj.* inattentive; without thought.

Unawares *adv.* unexpectedly; suddenly; unintentionally.

Unbacked *adj.* not supported.

Unbaffled *adj.* not confounded.

Unbalanced *adj.* unsteady.

Unbank *v.t.* to cause (fire) to burn by removing ashes from top.

Unbar *v.t.* to open; to unfasten.

Unbarbed *adj.* without barbs.

Unbay *v.t.* to free from restraint.

Unbeaten *n.* unsurpassed; not beaten.

Unbecoming *adj.* not suited to; improper; not befitting.

Unbeknown *adv.* not known.

Unbelief *n.* incredulity; scepticism.

Unbelieved *adj.* not believed.

Unbeliever *n.* an atheist; agnostic.

Unbend *v.t.* & *i.* rid oneself of constraint; to make straight.

Unbenign *adj.* malignant; not favourable.

Unbequeathed *adj.* not given by legacy.

Unbent *adj.* no subdued.

Unbestowed *adj.* not given.

Unbewailed *adj.* not lamented.

Unbiased *adj.* impartial; free from prejudice.

Unbiasedly *adv.* without bias.

Unbid, Unbidden *adjs.* spontaneous; not commanded.

Unblamable *adj.* faultless.

Unbleached *adj.* not bleached.

Unblended *adj.* not mingled.

Unblest *adj.* not happy; accursed.

Unblock *v.t.* to remove an obstacle.

Unblossoming *adj.* not producing blossoms.

Unblushing *adj.* impudent; shameless. **Unblushingly** *adj.* impudently.

Unboastful *adj.* not boastful; modest.

Unboiled *adj.* not boiled.

Unbolt *v.t.* to unfasten or open a door; to remove the bolt.

Unbookish *adj.* practical; not depending too much on books.

Unborn *adj.* nonexistent; not brought into life.

Unbosom *v.t.* to revel in confidence; to disclose freely one's secret opinions or feelings.

Unbound *adj.* not bound; loose; wanting a cover.

Unboyish *adj.* not like a boy.

Unbraid *v.t.* to separate the strand of a braid.

Unbred *adj*. not educated; unpolished; not well-bred.

Unbrewed *adj*. pure; unmixed.

Unbriddle *v.t.* to remove the briddle; to set free.

Unbridged *adj*. not crossed by a bridge.

Unbroken *adj*. not interrupted; not trained; not broken; not subdued.

Unbruised *adj*. not hurt.

Unbuckle *v.t.* to unfasten by loosening the buckles.

Unbuilt *adj*. not erected.

Unburden *v.t.* to remove a burden from.

Unbusied *adj*. idle; not employed.

Unbutton *v.t.* to loose by unfastening buttons.

Uncage *v.t.* to loose from confinement; to set free.

Uncalled *adj*. not invited; not necessary.

Uncandid *adj*. not frank or candid.

Uncanny *adj*. weird; mysterious; unearthy.

Uncap *v.t.* to remove a cap or cover from.

Uncaressed *adj*. not caressed.

Uncarted *adj*. unloaded from a cart.

Uncase *v.t.* to disengage from covering; to flay; to take out of a case.

Uncaught *adj*. not caught.

Unceasing *adj*. continual; uninterrupted; not intermitting.

Uncelestial *adj*. not heavenly.

Uncertain *adj*. doubtful; not certainly knowing or known; changeable; capricious.

Uncharged *adj*. not charged; not loaded.

Uncharm *v.t.* to release from charm.

Unchaste *adj*. lewd; not chaste; not pure.

Unchecked *adj*. unrestrained; not hindered.

Uncheerful *adj*. not cheerful.

Unchewed *adj*. not masticated.

Unchided *adj*. not rebuked.

Unchronicled *adj*. not recorded in a chronicle.

Unciform *adj*. having the form of a hook.

Uncircumspect *adj*. not cautious.

Uncivil *adj*. ill-mannered; unpolished; rude.

Unclad *adj*. not dressed.

Unclaimed *adj*. not claimed or demanded.

Unclasp *v.i.* to loosen the clasp.

Unclassical *adj*. not according to high ideals.

Uncle *n*. the brother of a father or mother.

Unclean *adj*. unchaste; ceremonially impure; dirty; not clean.

Unclinch *v.t.* to open the closed fist.

Unclog *v.t.* to remove impediments.

Unclose *v.t.* to break the seal of; to lay open.

Uncloud *v.t.* to clear from cloud or obscurity.

Unco *adv.* exceptionally; very.

Uncock *v.t.* to let down hammer of (gun) gently.

Uncoil *v.t.* to unwind.

Uncometable *adv.* not accessible or attainable.

Uncomely *adj.* wanting grace or beauty; not becoming.

Uncomfortable *adj.* not giving comfort; uneasy.

Uncommon *adj.* unusual; remarkable; strange.

Unconceivable *adj.* that cannot be conceived.

Unconcern *n.* indifference; absence of concern or anxiety.

Uncondensed *adj.* not condensed.

Unconditional *adj.* not subject to conditions; absolute.

Unconducted *adj.* not guided.

Unconfined *adj.* free from restraint.

Unconformable *adj.* not consistent.

Uncongealed *adj.* not frozen.

Unconscious *adj.* devoid of consciousness; not aware of.

Unconsecrated *adj.* not set apart for sacred purposes.

Unconsenting *adj.* not consenting.

Unconsidered *adj.* disregarded; not attended to.

Unconstitutional *adj.* contrary to the constitution.

Unconstraint *adj.* freedom from constraint.

Uncontented *adj.* not satisfied.

Unconventional *adj.* not bound by convention or custom; free in character or treatment.

Unconversant *adj.* not familiar with.

Uncoop *adj.* to set free.

Uncork *v.t.* to remove the cork from.

Uncounselled *adj.* not having advice.

Uncouple *v.t.* to set loose; to disconnect; to disjoin.

Uncourteous *adj.* impolite; uncivil.

Uncouth *adj.* odd; awkward; strange.

Uncovenanted *adj.* not based on or subject to a covenant.

Uncover *v.t.* & *i.* to deprive of clothes; to remove covering from.

Uncramped *adj.* not confined.

Uncredited *adj.* not believed.

Uncropped *adj.* not gathered.

Uncritical *adj.* not according to the principles of criticism; disinclined or incompetent to criticize.

Uncrown *v.t.* to dethrone.

Uncrowned *adj.* of a person having power but not the office of a king.

Unction *adj.* gusto; the act of consecration; a thing used in anointing; affected enthusiasm.

Unctuous *adj.* resembling oil; full of unction; greasy.

Unculled *adj.* not gathered.

Uncumbered *adj*. not burdened.

Uncustomary *adj*. not usual.

Uncut *adj*. with full untrimmed margins.

Undamped *adj*. not damped.

Undated *adj*. having no date.

Undaunted *adj*. fearless; bold.

Undazzled *adj*. not confused by splendour.

Undebauched *adj*. not corrupted; pure.

Undecayed *adj*. not impaired by age or accident; not decayed.

Undeceive *v.t*. to free from deception.

Undecenary *adj*. eleventh; occurring once in eleven years.

Undeclared *adj*. not declared.

Undefaced *adj*. not disfigured.

Undefended *adj*. not protected; open to attack.

Undefiled *adj*. not polluted; spotless; innocent.

Undelighted *adj*. not delighted.

Undemonstrative *adj*. not given to showing strong feelings.

Undeniable *adj*. true; indisputable.

Undenominational *adj*. of no particular sect.

Undepraved *adj*. not corrupted.

Undepressed *adj*. not depressed.

Under *prep*. inferior to; liable to; during the time of; bound by; beneath; in or to a position lower than; below; less than.

Underact *v.t*. to act inadequately; to perform feebly.

Unerdraction *n*. suborninate action.

Underbear *v.t*. to endure; to support.

Underbid *v.t*. to offer less than another in an auction.

Underbred *v.t*. vulgar; ill-bred.

Underbrush *n*. small trees in a forest.

Undercharge *n*. a charge that is too little; insufficient charge. *v.t*. to charge too little.

Underclothes *adj*. clothes worn beneath outside garments.

Undercroft *n*. crypt.

Undercurrent *n*. a hidden influence; the current under the surface of water.

Undercut *v.t*. to reduce (prices) in competition.

Underdo *v.t*. to act below one's abilities.

Underdress *v.t* & *i*. to dress too plainly or lightly.

Under-estimate *v.t*. to form too low an estimate of.

Underfoot *adj*. low. *adv*. beneath.

Undergo *v.t*. to pass through; to sustain; to endure.

Undergraduate *n*. a member of a university who has not taken a degree.

Underground *n*. a space below the surface of the ground.

Undergrowth *n*. shrubs growing under trees.

Underhand *adv.* by secret means. *adj.* secret; fraudulent; clandestine.

Underhung *adj.* protruding from beneath.

Underlaid *adj.* laid beneath.

Underlay *v.t.* to lay beneath.

Underlet *v.t.* to sublet; to let under a lease.

Underlie *v.t.* to lie under or beneath.

Underline *v.t.* to mark with a line below words & etc.

Underlinen *n.* an underwear.

Underling *n.* a mean fellow; an inferior person.

Underman *v.t.* to provide with insufficient men.

Undermeal *n.* a light repast taken before dinner.

Undermine *v.t.* to injure; to excavate.

Undermost *adj.* lowest in place.

Underneath *adv.* under; beneath.

Underpart *n.* a subordinate part.

Underpay *v.t.* to pay inadequately.

Underpin *v.t.* to support form beneath.

Underprize *v.t.* to undervalue.

Underproof *adj.* having less than standard strength.

Underprop *v.t.* to put prop under; to support from beneath.

Underquote *v.t.* to announce lower price than.

Underrate *n.* price less than the acknowledged value.

Underrun *v.t.* to run along under.

Undersell *v.t.* to sell at a cheaper price than another.

Underset *v.t.* to support; to prop.

Undershot *adj.* moved by water passing under a wheel.

Undersign *v.t.* to write one's name at the end.

Undrsoil *n.* a soil beneath the surface.

Understand *v.t.* & *i.* to interpret; to be informed; to know; to comprehend; to apprehend.

Understate *v.t.* to represent less strictly.

Understrapper *n.* a subordinate.

Understudy *v.t.* to prepare oneself to act for another in a theatre.

Undertake *v.t.* & *i.* to make an attempt; to venture; to promise; to begin; to perform.

Undertenant *n.* a subtenant.

Undertone *n.* subdued colour; a low tone.

Undervalue *v.t.* to esteem lightly; to despise. *n.* a price less than the real one.

Underwear *n.* wearing under the outer clothing.

Underwood *n.* brushwood; undergrowth.

Underwork *n.* a subordinate work.

Underworld *n.* the world of dead; and inferior world.

Underwrite *v.t.* & *i.* to write under something; to guarantee.

Undescribable *adj*. that cannot be described.

Undesignated *adj*. not designated.

Undesigning *adj*. sincere; upright.

Undesired *adj*. not desired or solicited.

Undespairing *adj*. not despairing.

Undestined *adj*. not destined.

Undetermined *adj*. unsettled; not determined.

Undeveloped *adj*. not developed.

Undevout *adj*. without devotion.

Undextrous *adj*. clumsy.

Undid *v.t*. ruined; brought to nought.

Undigested *adj*. not digested; crude.

Undignified *adj*. lacking dignity; not dignified.

Undiminishable *adj*. not capable of diminution.

Undine *n*. a water nymph.

Undiscerning *adj*. wanting discernment.

Undischarged *adj*. not carried out; not discharged.

Undisclosed *adj*. not revealed.

Undisgraced *adj*. not dishonoured.

Undisguised *adj*. artless; frank; plain.

Undismayed *adj*. not disheartened; unafraid.

Undisputable *adj*. not disputable.

Undissipated *adj*. not dissolute in character; not scattered.

Undistended *adj*. not enlarged.

Undistilled *adj*. not distilled.

Undisturbed *adj*. not disturbed; free from interruption; calm; serene.

Undivided *adj*. not limited; unbroken.

Undivine *adj*. not divine.

Undivorced *adj*. not divorced.

Undo *v.t*. to bring to poverty; to ruin; to annul; to open; to unfasten; to loose.

Undomesticated *adj*. not tamed.

Undoubted *adj*. not called in question.

Undowered *adj*. without a dowery.

Undramatic *adj*. contrary to the rules of the drama.

Undrape *v.t*. to uncover; to strip off clothing.

Undress *v.t*. to take off the dressing from a wound; to strip off clothes; to disrobe.

Undrossy *adj*. free from impurity.

Undue *adj*. excessive; not yet demandable by right; not right or agreeable; not due.

Undulate *v.t*. & *i*. to vibrate; to have wavy motion or look; to move like waves. *adj*. vibratory.

Unduly *adv*. excessively; in an undue manner; wrongly.

Unearth *v.t*. to uncover; to draw out the earth.

Uneasily *adv*. with uneasiness.

Uneconomic *adj*. not economic.

Uneducated *adj*. not educated.

Uneffectual *adj*. not effectual.

Unembarrassed *adj.* not confused.
Unembodied *adj.* free from corporal body.
Unemphatic *adj.* not emphasised.
Unemployable *adj.* unfit for employment.
Unemulating *adj.* not emulating.
Unencumbered *adj.* not burdened.
Unending *n.* eternal; everlasting.
Unengaging *adj.* unable to attach attention; not inviting.
Unentangle *v.t.* to disentangle.
Unequal *adj.* inadequate; inferior; of varying quality; not regular; not equal to.
Unequipped *adj.* not equipped.
Unequivocal *adj.* evident; plain; clear; not ambiguous.
Unerring *adj.* committing no error; not erring or failing or missing the mark; certain.
Unespied *adj.* not seen.
Unessayed *adj.* not attempted.
Unessential *adj.* not constituting the essence; not necessary.
Uneven *adj.* not smooth or level; not uniform or equal; not straight.
Unexacted *adj.* not extorted.
Unexampled *adj.* having no similar case; having no precedent.
Unexceptionable *adj.* with which no fault can be found; not liable to exception.
Unexcised *adj.* not charged with excise duty.
Unexempt *adj.* not free from duty.
Unexhausted *adj.* not tired.
Unexpected *adj.* coming without warning; sudden; not expected.
Unexpired *adj.* not ended; still running.
Unexposed *adj.* sheltered; not exposed to view.
Unexpounded *adj.* not explained.
Unextirpated *adj.* not rooted out.
Unfaded *adj.* not faded.
Unfailing *adj.* certain; not liable to fail; that does not fail.
Unfair *adj.* dishonest; not equitable or honest, or impartial.
Unfaltering *adj.* unhesitating.
Unfamiliar *adj.* not familiar.
Unfashioned *adj.* not modified by art; not brought into shape.
Unfasten *v.t.* to unfix; to unloose.
Unfathomable *adj.* the depth of which cannot be ascertained.
Unfavourable *adj.* not favourable; not propitious; discouraging.
Unfeatured *adj.* deformed.
Unfeeling *adj.* devoid of sympathy with others; insensible; cruel.
Unfeigned *adj.* not counterfeit; sincere.
Unfeignedly *adv.* sincerely.
Unfeminine *adj.* not beseeming a woman.
Unfence *v.t.* to remove a fence from.
Unfetter *v.t.* to set free; to free from restraint.
Unfilial *adj.* not befitting a son or daughter.
Unfinished *adj.* wanting the last hand or touch; not complete.

Unfirm *adj*. weak; feeble.
Unfirmness *n*. the quality of being feeble.
Unfit *adj*. unsuitable; incompetent. *v.t.* to disable or disqualify; to make unsuitable for.
Unfix *v.t.* to loosen; to detach; to dissolve.
Unflagging *adj*. maintaining strength or spirit; not drooping.
Unfledged *adj*. not fledged; not furnished with feathers.
Unflinching *adj*. resolute; not shrinking.
Unfoild *adj*. not baffled.
Unfold *v.t.* & *i.* to spread out; to reveal; to open out.
Unforbidden *adj*. not allowed.
Unforced *adj*. not urged.
Unforeknown *adj*. not previously foreseen.
Unforeseen *adj*. not expected.
Unforgiving *adj*. implacable; not pardoned.
Unformed *adj*. not moulded into regular shape.
Unforsaken *adj*. not deserted.
Unfortunate *adj*. not prosperous; having ill fortune; unlucky.
Unfound *adj*. not met with.
Unfragrant *adj*. not fragrant.
Unfraternal *adj*. not brotherly.
Unfrequent *adj*. not common.
Unfrugal *adj*. not economical.
Unfumed *adj*. not fumed.
Unfurl *v.t.* to loosen; to become spread out; to unfold.
Unfurnished *adj*. empty; not supplied with.
Unfused *adj*. not melted.
Ungainful *adj*. not profitable.
Ungainfulness *n*. ungainful state.
Ungainly *adj*. clumsy; ill-made; uncouth.
Ungallant *adj*. not attentive to women; not brave.
Ungarnished *adj*. not adorned.
Ungenerous *adj*. not liberal; not kind; dishonourable.
Ungenial *adj*. not favourable to nature.
Ungenteel *adj*. rough; rude.
Ungird *v.t.* to loosen from a band.
Unglue *v.t.* to separate a thing that is glued.
Ungodliness *n*. the quality of being impious.
Ungodly *adj*. not godly; impious; wicked.
Ungovernable *adj*. unruly; that cannot be governed; licentious; wild.
Ungraced *adj*. not graced.
Ungracious *adj*. hateful; not kindly; wicked.
Ungrammatical *adj*. contrary to rules of grammar; not in conformity with the rules of grammar.
Ungrateful *adj*. making ill returns for kindness; not grateful; not feeling gratitude.
Ungreen *n*. a person who is not concerned about the environment.

Ungrounded *adj*. without a foundation or support.

Ungrudging *adj*. heartily; giving freely; done or given with goodwill.

Ungual *adj*. having nails, claws or hoofs.

Unguent *n*. any soft substance used as ointment; an ointment.

Unguical *adj*. pertaining to a claw.

Unguiform *adj*. shaped like a claw.

Unguinous *adj*. consisting of fat or oil.

Ungulate *n*. a hoofed mammal. *adj*. shaped like a hoof.

Unhair *v.t.* to remove hair from hide.

Unhallow *v.t.* to profane.

Unhand *v.t.* to let go from the hands.

Unhandily *adv*. clumsily.

Unhandsome *adj*. not trained; ugly; unbecoming.

Unhandy *adv*. awkward; clumsy; not dexterous.

Unharbour *v.t.* to drive from shelter.

Unharmonious *adj*. not consistent with harmony.

Unhappy *adv*. unlucky; miserable; unfortunate.

Unhealthy *adv*. sickly; morbid; wanting in health.

Unheard *adj*. unknown; not heard; obscure.

Unhedged *adj*. not surrounded by a hedge.

Unhewn *adj*. not hewn; rough.

Unhindered *adj*. not obstructed.

Unhinge *v.t.* to displace; to take from the hinges.

Unhive *v.t.* to deprive of habitation.

Unhoard *v.t.* to scatter.

Unhonoured *adj*. not honoured.

Unholy *adj*. wicked; impious.

Unhook *v.t.* to loose from a hook.

Unhorse *v.t.* to throw from a horse.

Unhouse *v.t.* to dislodge; to drive from house.

Unhumbled *adj*. not humbled.

Unhurt *adj*. not harmed; free from injury.

Unhusbanded *adj*. not managed frugally; without a husband.

Unhusked *adj*. not deprived of husk.

Unicellular *adj*. one-celled.

Unicorn *n*. a fabulous animal like horse with one horn in the middle of is bead.

Unicycle *n*. a cycle with one wheel.

Unideal *adj*. not perfect; not ideal.

Unidentate *adj*. having but one tooth.

Unification *n*. the act of uniting.

Uniflorous *adj*. bearing only one flower.

Uniform *adj*. not different; conforming to the same rule; having always the same form; constant; regular.

Unify *v.t.* form into one; to make one or uniform.

Unigeniture *n*. state of being the only one begotten.

Unigenous *adj.* of the same genus; of one kind.

Unilateral *adj.* binding one side only.

Unimaginable *adj.* not to be imagined.

Unimitated *adj.* not imitated.

Unimpassioned *adj.* free from passion; calm.

Unimpeachable *adj.* giving no opening to censure; blameless; free from passion.

Unimpeded *adj.* not hindered; not obstructed.

Unimprisoned *adj.* not imprisoned.

Uningenious *adj.* not ingenious; dull.

Uninitiated *adj.* not initiated.

Uninspired *adj.* not having received supernatural instructions or illuminations; not inspired.

Unintelligent *adj.* not intelligent; dull.

Unintermitted *adj.* not interrupted; continuous.

Uninterpreted *adj.* not explained.

Unintroduced *adj.* not introduced; not discovered.

Uninvited *adj.* not invited; not requested.

Uninviting *adj.* unattractive; not attractive.

Uninvoked *adj.* not invoked.

Union *adj.* harmony; agreement; combination; confederacy; a junction; combination; concord; coalition.

Uniparous *adj.* producing one at a birth.

Unipartite *adj.* not divided into parts.

Uniped *adj.* one footed.

Unique *adj.* being the only one of its kind; without an equal; unmatched; unequalled.

Unirrigated *adj.* not supplied with water by irrigation.

Unisexual *adj.* having pistil or stamens but not both.

Unison *n.* unity of pitch; concord; agreement or harmony.

Unit *n.* an individual thing; quantity chosen as standard; a single person or thing; the number one.

Unitarian *adj.* one who believes in the unity of divine nature; a monotheist; an advocate of unity or centralization.

Unitary *adj.* marked by uniformity; relating to unit.

Unite *v.t.* & *i.* to make or become one; to put together; to join.

Univalent *adj.* having a combing power of one.

Univalve *n.* a mollusc of one valve; having one valve only.

Universal *adj.* belonging to all; applicable to all cases; general; of the world; whole; all round.

Universe *n.* mankind; all existing things; all creation.

University *n.* the institution where the higher branches of art and sciences are taught and degrees conferred.

Unjust *adj.* not equitable; dishonest; not just; faithless.

Unkempt *adj.* of rough or uncared for appearance; unpolished; uncombed.

Unkenned *adj.* unknown.

Unkept *adj.* not preserved.

Unkind *adj.* harsh; cruel.

Unking *v.t.* to deprive or regal authority.

Unknit *v.t.* to separate threads; to open.

Unknot *v.t.* to free from knots.

Unknown *adj.* not known; not found out or ascertained.

Unlaboured *adj.* spontaneous; natural; not cultivated; easy.

Unlade *adj.* to unload cargo from a ship.

Unlaid *adj.* not fixed.

Unlamented *adj.* not lamented.

Unlawful *adj.* illegal; contrary to law.

Unlearn *v.t.* to forget what is learnt; to expel from one's memory.

Unleash *v.t.* to remove leash of dog.

Unlent *adj.* not lent.

Unless *conj.* if not; except; if it be not that.

Unlessoned *adj.* not instructed.

Unlettered *adj.* illiterate; unlearned.

Unlevelled *adj.* not levelled.

Unlicked *adj.* shapeless; not licked into shape; undefeated.

Unlike *adj.* not like; not similar.

Unlimber *v.t.* to detach (gun, gun-carriage) from limber.

Unlimited *adj.* very numerous; boundless; not limited.

Unline *v.t.* to remove lining from; to empty.

Unlineal *adj.* not in succession.

Unlink *v.t.* to remove links from.

Unliquidated *adj.* not paid; not settled.

Unlively *adj.* not lively; dull.

Unload *v.t.* to discharge; to disburden.

Unlocated *adj.* not fixed in place.

Unlock *v.t.* to unfasten; to remove lock from.

Unlovely *adj.* not attractive.

Unlucky *adj.* unfortunate; hapless; ill-contrived.

Unmailable *adj.* that cannot be sent by post.

Unmake *v.t.* to annul; to destroy the form of.

Unmalleable *adj.* not malleable.

Unman *v.t.* to deject; to emasculate; do dishearten.

Unmanageable *adj.* not manageable; not controllable.

Unmanliness *n.* want of manliness.

Unmanned *adj.* not supplied with men.

Unmannerly *adj.* rude; ill-bred; wanting in good manner.

Unmarked *adj.* not marked; undistinguished.

Unmarred *adj.* not spoiled.

Unmarried *adj.* not married.

Unmasculine *adj.* effeminate.

Unmask *adj.* to take off one's mask; to expose; to deprive or put off mask.

Unmatched *adj.* without an equal; unrivalled.

Unmeasurable *adj.* that cannot be measured.

Unmechanical *adj.* not mechanical.

Unmeditated *adj.* not previously thought.

Unmeet *adj.* not worthy; unfit.

Unmelted *adj.* not dissolved.

Unmercantile *adj.* not according to the rules of commerce.

Unmerciful *adj.* cruel-hearted; not merciful.

Unmerited *adj.* unjust.

Unminded *adj.* forgotten; not heeded.

Unmitigated *adj.* absolute; unqualified.

Unmixed *adj.* not mixed; pure.

Unmoaned *adj.* not lamented.

Unmodifiable *adj.* that cannot be altered.

Unmoist *adj.* dry.

Unmoor *v.t.* to loose the form of.

Unmortified *adj.* not ashamed.

Unmould *v.t.* to change the form of.

Unmoved *adj.* firm; not changed in purpose; not moved.

Unmusical *adj.* not melodious; harsh.

Unmuzzle *v.t.* to loose from a muzzle; relieve of obligation; to remain silent.

Unnamable *adj.* too bad to be named.

Unnatural *adj.* lacking natural feelings; artificial; not natural; contrary to nature.

Unnerve *v.t.* deprive of composure of the mind; to weaken; to deprive of strength.

Unnoticed *adj.* not observed; sudden; not taken notice of.

Unnumbered *adj.* not numbered; countless.

Unnutritious *adj.* not giving nourishment.

Unobvious *adj.* not readily understood.

Unoffended *adj.* not taking offence.

Unofficial *adj.* not pertaining to office.

Unoperative *adj.* producing no effect.

Unopposed *adj.* without opposition; not resisted.

Unorderly *adj.* irregular.

Unorthodox *adj.* not orthodox.

Unowned *adj.* not acknowledged or admitted; without an owner.

Unpacific *adj.* not disposed to peace.

Unpack *v.t.* to open and remove; to disburden; to open a bundle.

Unpaid *adj.* remaining due; not paid; not discharged as a debt.

Unpalatable *adj.* disgusting to the taste; not agreeable.

Unparagoned *adj.* having no equal; unmatched.

Unpardonable *adj.* that cannot be forgiven.

Unpardoned *adj.* not forgiven.

Unpawned *adj.* not pledged.

Unpeaceful *adj.* not peaceful.

Unpeg *v.t.* to loose from a peg.

Unpenal *adj.* not subject to penalty.

Unpenetrable *adj.* not entered.

Unpeople *v.t.* to depopulate.

Unperceived *adj.* not observed.

Unperformed *adj.* not done.

Unperplexed *adj.* not perplexed.

Unpersecuted *adj.* free from persecution.

Unperused *adj.* not read.

Unpick *v.t.* to remove stitches.

Unpierced *adj.* not penetrated.

Unpiteous *adj.* cruel; pitiless.

Unplaced *adj.* not placed, *esp.* in a race or list.

Unplagued *adj.* not harassed.

Unplayable *adj.* incapable of being played.

Unpleasant *adj.* not giving pleasure; disagreeable.

Unpoetic *adj.* unpoetical.

Unpointed *adj.* without a point.

Unpolished *adj.* uncivilized; rude; uncultured; not made bright.

Unpopular *adj.* not pleasing to be people; disliked.

Unposted *adj.* not posted.

Unpractised *adj.* raw; unskillful; not skilled; not put into practice.

Unprecise *adj.* not exact.

Unprejudiced *adj.* free from bias; impartial.

Unprepared *adj.* not ready; not fitted by previous measures.

Unprepossessed *adj.* unprejudiced.

Unpresentable *adj.* not fit to be presented to company; not presentable; not fit to be seen.

Unpresuming *adj.* not pretentious.

Unpresumtuous *adj.* modest; submissive.

Unpretending *adj.* not pretending to any distinction; making little show.

Unprevailing *adj.* unavailing.

Unprevalent *adj.* not prevalent.

Unpriestly *adj.* not fit for priest.

Unprivileged *adj.* not enjoying a privilege.

Unproclaimed *adj.* not publicly declared.

Unproductive *adj.* not producing large crops; not productive; not efficient.

Unprofaned *adj.* not violated.

Unprofessional *adj.* not belonging to a profession.

Unprofitable *adj.* without profit; of no avail.

Unprogressive *adj.* not progressive.

Unpromising *adj.* not affording success.

Unpropitious *adj.* inauspicious.

Unproposed *adj.* not proposed.

Unprovided *adj.* not prepared; not furnished.

Unprovoked *adj.* without provocation or just cause; not incited.

Unpruned *adj.* not lopped.

Unpurchased *adj.* not purchased or brought.

Unpurged *adj.* not purified.

Unpurified *adj.* unsanctified.

Unquaffed *adj.* not drunk.

Unqualified *adj.* not legally qualified; not modified; not qualified.

Unquenchable *adj.* that cannot be quenched; inextinguishable.

Unquestionable *adj.* that cannot be questioned or doubted; certain.

Unquietly *adv.* in a restless manner.

Unraised *adj.* not elevated.

Unransomed *adj.* not freed from captivity.

Unravel *v.t.* to separate the threads of; to unfold; to explain.

Unread *adj.* not learned in books.

Unready *adj.* not ready; not fit; not prompt in action.

Unreal *adj.* not substantial; illusive; visionary; having appearance only.

Unreality *n.* want of reality; an unreal thing.

Unreason *adj.* absence of reason; folly; nonsense.

Unrebukable *adj.* not to be rebuked.

Unreckoned *adj.* not reckoned.

Unreclaimed *adj.* not reformed; not claimed again; not claimed back from waste state.

Unrecognized *adj.* not known.

Unreconcilable *adj.* irreconcilable.

Unrecorded *adj.* not kept in remembrance; not registered.

Unredeemed *adj.* not redeemed or fulfilled.

Unredressed *adj.* not reformed.

Unreduced *adj.* not reduced.

Unreel *v.t. & i.* to become unwound from reel; to unwind.

Unrefined *adj.* unpolished; not refined; not purified.

Unreflecting *adj.* not reflecting.

Unreformed *adj.* not amended.

Unregistered *adj.* not registered.

Unregretful *adj.* without regret.

Unrehearsed *adj.* not prepared beforehand; without rehearsal.

Unrejoicing *adj.* not joyous.

Unrelated *adj.* not connected with.

Unrelenting *adj.* having no pity, rigid; cruel; not relenting.

Unreliable *adj.* not trustworthy.

Unrelieved *adj.* not succoured; not released from pain.

Unremembered *adj.* not remembered.

Unremitted *adj.* not forgiven.

Unremorseful *adj.* remorseless.

Unremovable *adj.* fixed; that cannot be removed.

Unremunerative *adj.* not profitable.

Unrenewed *adj.* not made new.

Unrepaired *adj.* not mended.

Unrepentant *adj.* not penitent.

Unreported *adj.* not reported.

Unreproached *adj.* not upbraided.
Unreproved *adj.* not censured.
Unrepugnant *adj.* not contradictory.
Unrequested *adj.* not requested.
Unrescued *adj.* not delivered.
Unreserved *adj.* frank; free; not reserved. **Unrest** *n.* disquiet.
Unrestrainable *adj.* not controlled.
Unretentive *adj.* not retentive.
Unretentive *adj.* not retentive.
Unreturnable *adj.* that cannot be returned.
Unrevered *adj.* not respected.
Unrevived *adj.* not brought into life.
Unrhythmical *adj.* without rhythm.
Unriddle *v.t.* to explain; to solve a riddle.
Unrighteous *adj.* wicked; sinful; unjust; evil.
Unrip *v.t.* to rip open or apart; to disclose.
Unrivalled *adj.* peerless; having no equal.
Unrobe *v.t.* & *i.* to undress.
Unroll *v.t.* & *i.* to unfold; to open what is rolled.
Unroof *v.t.* to remove the roof of a house.
Unroot *v.t.* to tear up by the roots.
Unsaddle *v.t.* to take the saddle from; to throw from the saddle.
Unsafe *adj.* hazardous; not safe from danger.
Unsaleable *adj.* not meeting a ready sale; not saleable.
Unsancified *adj.* unholy.
Unsanitary *adj.* lacking sanitation; not hygienic.
Unsatiable *adj.* that cannot be satisfied.
Unsatisfactorily *adj.* with dissatisfaction.
Unsaturated *adj.* not saturated.
Unsavouriness *adj.* want of relish.
Unsavoury *adj.* unpleasing; disgusting; tasteless; uninviting.
Unsay *v.t.* to retract what has been said.
Unscalable *adj.* that cannot be scaled.
Unscared *adj.* not frightened.
Unscathed *adj.* uninjured; without suffering injury.
Unscholarly *adj.* not like a scholar.
Unschooled *adj.* not educated.
Unscorched *adj.* not burnt by fire.
Unscoured *adj.* not cleaned by rubbing.
Unscrew *v.t.* to unfasten by removing screws; to pull out the screw from.
Unscriptural *adj.* not in accordance with scripture; not agreeing with the scriptures.
Unscrupulous *adj.* unprincipled; without a doubt; having no scruples.
Unseal *v.t.* to remove the seal of.
Unsealed *adj.* having no seal.
Unseam *v.t.* to undo seams.
Unseat *v.t.* to remove from a seat; to throw from horse-back.

Unseaworthy *adj.* unfit to go to sea.

Unsectarian *adj.* free from sectarian limitations.

Unsedendary *adj.* not accustomed to sit much.

Unseduced *adj.* not seduced.

Unseemliness *adj.* indecency.

Unseemly *adj.* indecent; not fit; improper.

Unseen *adj.* invisible; not discovered.

Unselfish *adj.* regardful of others rather than oneself; not selfish.

Unsent *adj.* dispatched.

Unserved *adj.* not served.

Unset *adj.* not sunk below the horizon.

Unsettle *v.t.* to disturb; to unhinge.

Unsevered *adj.* not parted.

Unsex *v.t.* to make unfeminine.

Unshackle *adj.* to remove the fetters; to set free.

Unshaded *adj.* not over-spread with darkness.

Unshamed *adj.* not ashamed.

Unshapen *adj.* ugly; deformed.

Unshared *adj.* not shared.

Unsheathe *v.t.* to draw from the sheath or scabbard.

Unshifting *adj.* not changing place.

Unship *v.t.* to remove from a ship.

Unshod *adj.* having no shoes; wearing no shoes.

Unshot *v.t.* to take shot out of a gun.

Unshowered *adj.* not watered by showers.

Unshrinking *adj.* fearless; firm; not shrinking.

Unshunned *adj.* not avoided.

Unsightly *adj.* repulsive to look at; not pleasing to the eye.

Unsinewed *adj.* weak; deprived of strength.

Unskilled *adj.* without special skill or training.

Unslacked *adj.* not saturated with water.

Unsoaped *adj.* not washed with soap.

Unsociable *adj.* reserved; unsocial.

Unsold *adj.* not sold.

Unsolicited *adj.* not requested; unasked.

Unsought *adj.* not searched.

Unsound *adj.* diseased; rotten; unreliable; questionable; not sound.

Unsown *adj.* not sown.

Unsparing *adj.* profuse; not forgiving; not sparing; not liberal.

Unspeakable *adj.* good or bad beyond description; unutterable.

Unspecified *adj.* not mentioned in detail.

Unspeculative *adj.* not theoretical.

Unspent *adj.* not wasted.

Unspoiled, Unspoilt *adjs.* not corrupted.

Unspotted *adj.* free from stain; not contaminated.

Unstable *adj.* not steady; irresolute; inconstant; not fixed.
Unsteady *adj.* not steady; inconsistent; shaking; fluctuating.
Unstimulated *adj.* not excited.
Unstitch *v.t.* to open the stitches.
Unstooping *adj.* not stooping.
Unstop *v.t.* to remove stopper from; to free from obstruction.
Unstored *adj.* not laid in store.
Unstrained *adj.* not forced; easy; not strained.
Unstring *v.t.* to deprive of string; to relax the strings of; to loosen.
Unstressed *adj.* not emphasized; not pronounced with a stress.
Unstudied *adj.* natural; unskilled; not laboured; not premeditated.
Unstudious *adj.* not diligent in a study.
Unstuffed *adj.* not stuffed.
Unsubmissive *adj.* disobedient.
Unsubstantial *adj.* not real; having little or no solidity or reality.
Unsuccessful *adj.* not successful.
Unsugared *adj.* not sweetened with sugar.
Unsuitable *adj.* unfit, not suitable.
Unsuited *adj.* not suited; unfit; not adapted to.
Unsullied *adj.* not tarnished.
Unsung *adj.* not sung.
Unsupplied *adj.* not supplied.
Unsuppressed *adj.* not suppressed.
Unsurmountable *adj.* insuperable.
Unsurpassed *adj.* not surpassed.
Unsuspected *adj.* unforeseen; not suspected.
Unsuspended *adj.* not hung up.
Unswathe *v.t.* to relieve from slavery.
Unswayed *adj.* not influenced.
Unswept *adj.* not swept.
Unsworn *adj.* not bound by oath; not having taken an oath.
Unsymmetrical *adj.* not characterized by symmetry.
Unsystematic *adj.* wanting system; disorderly.
Untack *v.t.* to separate; to remove tacks from; to disjoin.
Untained *v.t.* unblemished.
Untamable *adj.* uncontrollable; that cannot be tamed.
Untarnished *adj.* not blemished; not soiled or stained.
Untasted *adj.* not enjoyed or tasted.
Untaught *adj.* illiterate; not educated.
Untempted *adj.* not enticed.
Untenable *adj.* not defensible; that cannot be held in possession.
Untended *adj.* not watched or looked after.
Untender *adj.* not affectionate; not tender.
Unterminated *adj.* not terminated.
Unthinkable *adj.* not thinkable; that cannot be thought.
Unthread *v.t.* to loosen; to draw out threads from.
Untidy *adj.* not neatly dressed; not seasonable.

Untie *v.t.* to unbind; to undo a knot or cords of.

Until *prep.* till the point or degree that; till; to the time that.

Untilled *adj.* not cultivated.

Untinged *adj.* not stained.

Untiring *adj.* not becoming tired.

Untitled *adj.* without a title.

Unto *prep.* to.

Untold *adj.* not told; not related.

Untoward *adj.* perverse; awkward; troublesome.

Untraced *adj.* not traced.

Untracked *adj.* not marked by footsteps.

Untractable *adj.* unworkable; rough; unmanageable.

Untrading *adj.* not trading.

Untrained *adj.* not instructed; not disciplined.

Untrembling *adj.* not trembling; steady.

Untried *adj.* not tried; not attempted.

Untrod, Untrodden *adjs.* not trodden or pressed.

Untrue *adj.* contrary to the fact; not loyal; inconstant; false.

Untrustworthy *adj.* not deserving confidence.

Untruth *adj.* falsehood; lie.

Untutored *adj.* uninstructed; not taught.

Untwine *v.t.* to separate; to untwist

Unused *adj.* not used; unaccustomed.

Unuseful *adj.* useless.

Unutterable *adj.* above or beyond expression; not expressible.

Unvalued *adj.* not valued; not prized; neglected.

Unvaried *adj.* not altered.

Unvarnished *adj.* plain; not varnished.

Unvarying *adj.* constant; uniform.

Unveil *v.t.* to uncover; to remove a veil from; to disclose.

Unversed *adj.* not put in verse; not experienced.

Unvindicated *adj.* not established.

Unviolated *adj.* not broken.

Unvisited *adj.* not visited.

Unvoiced *adj.* not spoken.

Unwarily *adj.* incautiously; heedlessly.

Unwarmed *adj.* not warmed.

Unwarped *adj.* untwisted; unperverted; impartial.

Unwarranted *adj.* not authorized; not ascertained.

Unwary *adj.* not vigilant or cautious; careless.

Unwasted *adj.* not dissipated.

Unwatched *adj.* not guarded.

Unwearying *adj.* persistent; continual; indefatigable.

Unwed *adj.* unmarried.

Unweighed *adj.* not weighed.

Unwelcome *adj.* not pleasing; not well received.

Unwell *adj.* not in good health; not well; ailing.

Unwept *adj.* not wept for; not lamented.

Unwholesome *adj.* not favourable to health, harmful.

Unwilled *adj.* not produced by will.

Unwind *v.t.* & *i.* to become unwound; to wind off; to draw out at length.

Unwise *adj.* injudicious; imprudent.

Unwished *adj.* not wished or desired.

Unwitting *adj.* unconscious; unaware of the state of the case.

Unwomanly *adj.* not becoming a woman.

Unwonted *adj.* unused; unaccustomed; infrequent.

Unwooed *adj.* not courted.

Unworthily *adv.* in an unworthy manner.

Unworthy *adj.* not worthy; vile; devoid of merit; worthless.

Unwreathe *v.t.* to untwist.

Unwritten *adj.* not reduced to writing; not written; traditional.

Unyielding *adj.* not yielding; unbending; stiff; obstinate.

Unyoke *v.t.* & *i.* to free from yoke; to disjoin.

Up *adv.* ready to act; out of bed.; aloft; on high; to high place, amount etc. in question. *prep.* at or in higher part of.

Upas *n.* a kind of poisonous tree.

Upbear *adj.* to bear up; to elevate.

Upbind *v.t.* to bind up.

Upbraid *v.t.* to chide; to reproach.

Upbringing *n.* bringing up; early education.

Upcast *n.* an upward current of air. *adj.* thrown upward; casting up.

Upcountry *adj.* inland; towards the interior.

Upcurl *adj.* to curl upwards.

Upheaval *n.* the uplifting of the soil from beneath; heaving up; vast social or other change.

Upheld sustained; kept up.

Uphold *v.t.* to give support; to sustain; to elevate; to raise on high.

Upholster *v.t.* to supply furniture.

Upkeep *n.* means of maintenance.

Upland *adj.* higher in situation. *n.* an elevated ground or high land.

Uplift *v.t.* to exalt; to raise aloft intellectual or moral improvement of community.

Upmost *adj.* highest.

Upon *prep.* relating to; not under; resting on.

Upper *adj.* situated above; superior in dignity; higher in place; superior in ranks. *n.* the upper part of shoe.

Uppish *adj.* proud; arrogant; self-assertive.

Upraise *v.t.* to raise up; to ascend.

Upright *adj.* just; strictly honourable; perpendicular; erect; vertical; honest.

Uprise *v.i.* to ascent; to rise up.

Uproar *n.* tumult; a great disturbance and noise.

Upshot *n.* final issue; end or conclusion; general effect.
Upside *n.* the upper side.
Upstairs *n.* the upper part of a house.
Upstanding *adj.* well set up; erect.
Upstart *v.i.* to start or spring up suddenly. *n.* one who suddenly rises in wealth.
Upstream *adv.* towards the source of a stream.
Upstroke *n.* upwards line in writing.
Uptake *n.* apprehension; lifting.
Upthrow *n.* an upward displacement of rock on one side of fault.
Upthrust *n.* upheaval.
Upturn *v.t.* to overturn; to turn up.
Upward *adj.* towards a higher place; ascending up.
Uraemia *n.* morbid condition of blood due to retention of urinary matter normally passed out by kidneys.
Uranic *adj.* pertaining to the heavens.
Uranium *n.* a heavy white metallic element found in pitchblende; a radioactive metallic element.
Uranus *n.* a primary planet, son of earth and father of Saturn.
Uranus *n.* a primary planet.
Urban *adj.* a city or town; refined; of polished.
Urceolate *adj.* with large body and small mouth; pitcher-shaped.
Urea *n.* a soluble colourless crystalline compound.
Uretar *n.* the duct which conveys urine from kidney to bladder.
Uretic *adj.* pertaining to medicine which promotes flow of urine.
Urge *v.t.* to press earnestly; to drive forcibly; to provoke; to apply force to;
Urgent *adj.* requiring immediate attention; pressing with necessity;
Urging *adj.* importunate.
Uric *adj.* of urine.
Urinal *n.* a place for discharging urine; a vessel for urine.
Urinary *adj.* pertaining to urine.
Urinate *v.t.* to discharge urine.
Urine *n.* the fluid secreted by the kidney.
Urn *n.* a ballotbox; a vase-shaped vessel with a tap for tea.
Uroscopy *n.* estimating diseases by inspection of urine.
Ursa *n.* one of the northern constellations.
Ursiform *adj.* of the shape of a bear.
Ursine *adj.* resembling a bear.
Urson *n.* a kind of porcupine.
Urticaria *n.* nettlerash.
Us *pron.* plural of 'we'; objective case.
Usage *n.* customary practice; practice long continued; treatment.
Usance *n.* proper treatment; interest paid on money.
Use *n.* application; a customary act; practice; employment.

Useful *adj.* efficient; highly creditable; advantageous; serviceable; beneficial.

Useless *adj.* serving no useful purpose; fruitless.

Usher *v.t.* to introduce. *n.* one who introduces strangers; an under-teacher.

Ustion *n.* the state of being burnt; the act of burning.

Ustorious *adj.* having the quality of burning.

Ustulate *adj.* burnt and blackened.

Usual *adj.* common, such as commonly occurs; habitual; customary.

Usually *adv.* ordinarily.

Usualness *n.* the state of being usual.

Usufruct *n.* the right of enjoying the use of another's property without power to alienate.

Usurer *n.* one who lend money at high interest.

Usurious *adj.* taking high interest.

Usurp *v.t. & i.* to seize crown, sovereignty etc. without right or title.

Usury *n.* lending of money at exorbitant interest; the practice of taking an exorbitant interest.

Ut *conj.* as shown or stated above.

Utensil *n.* a vessel used for domestic work.

Uterine *adj.* born of the same mother; pertaining to the womb.

Uterus *n.* the womb.

Utilitarian *adj.* pertaining to utility.

Utility *n.* usefulness; profitableness to some valuable end.

Utilize *v.t.* to turn to account; to make use of; to put to use.

Utmost *adv.* extremely; being in the greatest degree.

Utopia *n.* the social state of the highest perfection.

Utopian *adj.* imaginary; fanciful.

Utricle *n.* a cell; small cavity in the body.

Utricular *adj.* like a utricle.

Utter *adj.* absolute; final, perfect; total; complete.

U-turn turning a vehicle in opposite direction.

Uveous *adj.* resembling a grape.

Uvula *n.* the fleshy soft plate over the root of the tongue.

Uvular *adj.* pertaining to the uvula.

Uxorious *adj.* excessively fond of one's wife.

V

V the twenty-second letter of the English alphabet.

Vacancy *n.* empty space; an unoccupied post; available place.

Vacate *v.t.* to make vacant; to leave unoccupied; to annul.

Vacation *n.* holidays; the act of vacating.

Vaccinate *v.t.* to inoculate with vaccine as protection against small-pox.
Vaccine *n.* & *adj.* pertaining of cows, cowpox or vaccination.
Vaccinia *n.* an eruptive disease in cattle.
Vacher *n.* a kettle keeper.
Vachery *n.* an enclosure for cows.
Vacillate *v.i.* to fluctuate in mind; to oscillate; to waver.
Vacuity *n.* space unfilled or unoccupied; emptiness.
Vacuole *n.* a minute empty cavity in organic body.
Vacuous *adj.* empty; unfilled.
Vacuum *n.* the space empty of all matter; space exhausted of air.
Vagabond *adj.* an idle scamp; a rogue; a vagrant, having no fixed habitation.
Vagabondage *n.* the state of being a vagabond.
Vagary *n.* a whim; a wild freak; unaccountable proceeding.
Vagina *n.* passage to womb; a sheath-like part; the canal which leads from the external orifice to the uterus.
Vagrant *n.* a vagabond; a begger.
Vague *adj.* not precise; unsettled.
Vaguely *adv.* in a vague manner.
Vails *n.* gratuity given to a servant; tip.
Vain *adj.* conceited; showy and valueless; false; empty.
Vain-glory *n.* empty pride.
Valance *n.* a short curtain round frame or canopy of bed-stead.
Vale *inter.* & *n.* sayings of farewell; good-bye.
Valedictory *adj.* & *n.* binding farewell.
Vale *n.* a small trough or channel carrying off water from pump.
Velediction *n.* a farewell.
Valency *n.* combing or replacing power of an atom as compared with standard hydrogen atom.
Valentine *n.* sweet-heart chosen on Feb. 14; a love-letter.
Valerian *n.* kinds of flowering herb.
Valet *n.* a personal attendant; a gentleman's servant; iron pointer stick for training horse.
Valetudinarian *adj.* compelled to live the life of an invalid.
Valetudinarianism *n.* weak health.
Valiance *n.* bravery; valour.
Valiancy *n.* valiantness.
Valiant *adj.* heroic; brave; intrepid.
Valiantly *adv.* bravely.
Valid *adj.* having sufficient strength; legal.
Validity, Validness *ns.* soundness; justness.
Validly *adv.* in a valid manner.
Vallidate *v.t.* to give validity to.
Valinch *n.* tube for drawing liquors from a cask.
Valise *n.* soldier's knapsack; a bag for clothes.
Vallar *adj.* pertaining to a rampart.

Vallation *n.* a rampart; an entrenchment.
Vallecula *n.* a groove or furrow.
Valley *n.* a vale; the interior angle formed by intersecting planes of roof.
Vallum *n.* a defensive earth wall.
Valorous *adj.* courageous; brave.
Valour *n.* bravery; great courage.
Valuable *adj.* costly; having worth; worthy; estimable; of great value or use.
Value *n.* importance; precise significance; price; worth; price equal to the worth of the thing bought.
Valueless *adj.* worthless.
Valuer *n.* one who holds in esteem.
Valve *n.* a lid or contrivance which opens on one side only.
Valvet *n.* a small valve.
Valvular *adj.* containing small valves; of an anatomical value.
Vambrace *n.* an armour for the forearm.
Vamose *v.t.* & *i.* to decamp.
Vamp *n.* an adventuress; a flirt.
Vamp *n.* the upper leather of a shoe. *v.t.* to patch; to repair.
Vampire *n.* blood sucker; a blood-sucking ghost.
Vamps *n. pl.* a kind of hose.
Van *n.* a railway wagon for luggage and the guard; the front part of an army.
Vanadium *n.* a silvery metallic element.
Vandal *n.* one who destroys the work of art.
Vandalic *n.* barbarous.
Vandyke *n.* a deep-cut point on the border of a dress; a covering for the neck.
Vane *n.* an appliance for showing the direction in which the wind blows.
Vanguard *n.* the front part of army.
Vanilla *n.* a kind of plant; extract of this.
Vanish *v.i.* to disappear; to pass away.
Vanishing *adj.* passing from sight.
Vanity *n.* an unsubstantial or unreal thing; emptiness; ostentation.
Vanquish *v.t.* to defeat; to refute; to conquer; to overcome.
Vantage *n.* advantage.
Vapid *adj.* spiritless; dead; insipid; unanimated; lacking interest.
Vapour *n.* moisture in the air or atmosphere; water in the atmosphere; vain imagination.
Vapulation *n.* flogging.
Varanus *n.* a kind of lizard.
Variable *adj.* fickle; changeable; alterable.
Variance *n.* discord; disagreement; dissention.
Variation *n.* alternation; change; inflexion.
Varicella *n.* chicken-pox.
Varicocele *n.* tumour composed of varicose veins of spermatic cord.
Varicoloured *adj.* of different colours; variegated.

Varicose *adj.* enlarged or dialted as a vain; affected with.

Varied *adj.* diverse; altered.

Variedly *adv.* diversely.

Variegate *v.t.* to make change in external appearance

Variegated *adj.* showing patches of different colours; diversely coloured.

Variegation *n.* diversity of colour.

Variety *n.* a different sort; collection of different things; difference.

Variform *adj.* having different forms.

Variola *n.* small-pox.

Variolation *n.* inoculation with small-pox virus.

Variole *n.* a shallow pit like small pox mark.

Varioloid *n.* smallpox modified by vaccination.

Variolous *adj.* pertaining to small pox.

Variometer *n.* an instrument for tuning aerial of wireless.

Various *adj.* of several kinds; multiform; different; uncertain; diversified.

Varix *n.* the dilation of a vein.

Varlet *n.* a servant; a low fellow; a scoundrel.

Varletry *n.* the crowd.

Varnish *v.t.* to cover with a transparent resinous liquid; to apply varnish to.

Varvel *n.* a metal ring attached to a hawk's leg to connect it with the leash.

Vary *v.t.* & *i.* to differ; to disagree; to alter in appearance; to diversiy.

Vascular *adj.* pertaining to conducting vessel.

Vasculose *n.* chief substance of vessels of plants.

Vasculum *n.* botanist's collecting-case; pouch.

Vassal *n.* a political slave; dependent; a tenant.

Vast *adj.* huge amount or size; very spacious; mighty; great.

Vastitude *n.* immensity.

Vastly *adv.* to a great extent.

Vat *n.* a square vessel or tank for holding liquids; a large tub.

Vault *n.* a cave; an arched roof; a rooflike covering; a leap; a cellar.

Vaunt *n.* boast; ostentation. *v.t.* & *i.* to talk with ostentation; to boast; to brag.

Vegetable *n.* a plant or part of a plant used in a cookery or for feeding cattle.

Vehement *adj.* with great force; ardent; forcible; fervent; very eager or urgent.

Vehicle *n.* a conveyance moving on wheels.

Veil *n.* a piece of transparent material to hide or protect the face.

Vein *n.* a rib of insect's wing or of a leaf.

Velamen *n.* enveloping membrane, *esp.* of brain.

Velar *adj.* of soft palate; or a veil or velum.

Velarium *n.* a sheet stretched under a roof.

Veliferous *adj.* bearing sails.

Velocity *n.* speed; rate of motion; swiftness; rapidity.

Velours *n.* kinds of plush used for hats.

Velum *n.* a portion; a veil.

Velvet *n.* a rich silk stuff with soft small fine nap. *adj.* made of velvet.

Velveteen *n.* cotton fabric with pile like velvet; kind of velvet made of silk and cotton.

Velvety *adj.* soft and smooth like velvet.

Vena *n.* a vein.

Venal *adj.* that may be had for money; pertaining to veins; mercenary.

Venatic *adj.* employed in hunting.

Venation *n.* the occupation of hunting.

Vend *v.t.* to offer for sale; to sell.

Vendance *n.* a small and delicate fish found in European lakes.

Vendee *n.* a person to whom a thing is sold.

Vendetta *n.* blood-feud.

Vendible *n.* saleable.

Vendition *n.* the act of selling.

Vendor *n.* one who vends; seller.

Vendue *n.* a public sale by an auctioneer.

Veneer *n.* a thin layer of superior kind of wood over an inferior one.

Venerable *adj.* worthy of reverence; entitled to veneration.

Venerate *v.i.* to regard with deep respect; to feel veneration for.

Venereal *adj.* pertaining to sexual intercourse.

Venesect *v.t.* & *i.* to cut vein.

Venesection *n.* bloodletting by opening a vein.

Vengeance *n.* infliction for an injury or offence.

Vent *n.* an exit; a hole; a slit in cloth or coat; an opening.

Ventage *n.* a small hole.

Venter *n.* mother; the womb; the abdomen.

Ventiduct *n.* airpassage.

Ventil *n.* a valve in musical instrument; a shutter for regulating air in organ.

Ventose *adj.* windy.

Ventosity *n.* empty pride; windiness.

Ventral *adj.* pertaining to the belly; of or pertaining to the side towards the belly.

Ventriloquist *n.* one who practises ventriloquism.

Ventriloquise *v.t.* to practise ventriloquism.

Ventripotence *n.* the ability to eat a great quantity.

Ventripotent *adj.* able to eat enormously.

Venture *v.t.* & *i.* to hazard; to summon up courage to do; to risk.
Venturesome *adj.* disposed to take risk; daring; hazardous.
Venue *n.* country or district in which a case must be tried and jury must be gathered.
Venus *n.* goddess of love; a beautiful woman; a planet.
Veracious *adj.* true; truthful; one who observes truth.
Veracity *n.* truthfulness.
Verandah *n.* a covered balcony; an open portico.
Verb *n.* a word which asserts something; the part of speech which serves to express action.
Verbal *adj.* spoken; oral; literal; derived from a verb.
Verbose *adj.* exuberant in the use of words.
Verdancy *n.* greenness; rawness.
Verdict *n.* opinion arrived at; judgement; the decision of the jury.
Verdigris *n.* the green rust of copper.
Verdure *n.* freshness; greenness of vegetation.
Verdurous *adj.* covered with greenery.
Verge *n.* range; border; a rod; border-line or brink.
Veridical *adj.* truthtelling.
Verifiable *adj.* what may be confirmed.
Verifier *n.* one who verifies.
Verify *v.t.* to fulfil; to support by proof.
Verily *adv.* in truth; certainly.
Verisimilar *adj.* having the appearance of truth.
Verisimilitude *n.* likelihood; probability.
Veritable *n.* agreeable to fact; real; actual.
Verity *n.* a really existent thing.
Verjuice *n.* an acid liquor got from sour grapes.
Vermian *adj.* worm-like; of worms.
Vermeil, Vermil *n.* & *adj.* vermilion; of the colour of vermilion.
Vermicelli *n.* paste made in slender threads; little worms.
Vermiceous *adj.* pertaining to worms.
Vermicide *n.* a worm-killer.
Vermicular *adj.* pertaining to or like a worm.
Vermiculate *v.t.* to inlay work in the form of tracts made by worms.
Vermicule *n.* a small worm.
Vermilion *n.* beautiful red colouring matter; real sulphide of mercury.
Vermin *n.* noxious people; a noxious insect, destructive to crops & etc.
Vernal *adj.* belonging to the spring.
Vernant *adj.* flourishing as in spring.

Vernicose *adj*. looking as if varnished.

Verricule *n*. a thick tuft of upright hairs.

Verrucose *adj*. having little knobs on the surface.

Versant *adj*. familiar.

Versatile *adj*. turning readily from one occupation to another.

Verse *n*. a line of poetry; stanza; metrical composition.

Versify *v.t. & i*. to make verses; to relate in verse.

Version *n*. translation; a statement of account.

Versionist *n*. one versed in translating.

Verso *n*. any left hand page of a book (*cf*. Recto); reverse of a coin.

Versus *prep*. against.

Versute *adj*. cunning; crafty.

Vert *n*. all that bears green leaves in forest; the tincture green.

Vertebra *n*. single segment of the back-bone.

Vertex *n*. thing's topmost point; top; tip; the zenith of heavens.

Vertical *adj*. straight up and down; of the crown of the head.

Verticil *n*. a whorl; set of parts; radiating from axis.

Vertiginous *adj*. turning round; whirling.

Vertigo *n*. dizziness in the head; giddiness.

Verve *n*. energy; vigour; spirit; enthusiasm.

Very *adv*. in great degree; in the fullest sense; greatly; exceedingly.

Vesical *n*. pertaining to the bladder.

Vesicant *n*. a blistering application.

Vesicate *v.t*. to raise blisters on.

Vesicle *n*. a small bladder or blister or bubble on the skin.

Vespa *n*. a wasplike insect.

Vesper *n*. the evening star; evening.

Vespiary *n*. a wasp's nest.

Vessel *n*. a ship or boat of any kind; a tube in which the blood is circulated.

Vest *n*. a waistcoat; body-garment worn next the skin.

Vestment *n*. a covering or garment.

Vestal *adj*. pure; chaste.

Vestiary *n*. wardrobe.

Vestibule *n*. the cavity of the ear; an entrance into a house.

Vestige *n*. a footprint left on the ground; a trace of something.

Vestigial *adj*. of the nature of a footprint.

Vestment *n*. garrn ent worn officially.

Vestuary *n*. a ward-robe.

Vestural *n*. pertaining to clothes.

Vesture *n*. clothing; dress; a garment.

Vesuvian *n*. a smoker's slow burning match.

Vesuvianite *n*. a mineral containing aluminium, silicon & magnesium given out by vesuvius.

Veteran *adj*. one grown old in service.

Veto *n.* constitutional right to reject a legislative enactment.

Vex *v.t.* to afflict; to torment; to disturb; to provoke; to irritate.

Vexil *n.* a standard.

Vexillation *n.* a company of soldiers under one standard.

Vexillum *n.* processional banner or cross; military standard.

Via *n.* a way; going by way of. *adv.* by way of.

Viable *adj.* capable to living.

Viaduct *n.* a long overbridge.

Viage *n.* a sea-journey.

Vial *n.* a small vessel, phial, for holding liquid medicine.

Vialled *adj.* filled in a vial.

Viand *n. pl.* food; articles of food necessary for life.

Viander *n.* an entertainer; a host; one who supplied viands.

Viarian *adj.* pertaining to roads.

Viatic *adj.* pertaining to a journey.

Viaticals *adj.* baggage.

Viaticum *n.* provisions for a journey.

Viator *n.* a traveller; a way farer.

Vibex *n.* a streak on the skin due to subcutaneous flow of blood.

Vibrate *v.t.* & *i.* to oscillate; to move rapidly to and fro.

Vicar *n.* a deputy; the priest of a parish; a substitute in office.

Vicarious *adj.* substituted; deputed.

Vice *n.* a screwed tool for firmly grasping; defect; habitual indulgence in evil; blemish. *pref.* signifying 'second in rank.' *prep.* in place of.

Vicinity *n.* nearness in place.

Vicious *adj.* ill-tempered; addicted to vice; corrupt; wicked; depraved; defective.

Victim *n.* a living animal sacrificed to a deity.

Victor *n.* a vanquisher; conqueror; one who conquers in war; a winner.

Victory *n.* the winning of a battle or contest; conquest; triumph.

View *n.* display; show; appearance; purpose; design; prospect; scene.

Vigesimal *adv.* twentieth.

Vigia *n.* a warning of hidden danger.

Vigil *n.* eve of a festival watching; the evening before any fast day.

Vigilant *adj.* on the outlook; watchful.

Vigilante *n.* the member of a Vigilance Committee.

Vigneron *n.* a vine-grower.

Vignette *n.* a picture in which the edges fade up; a small ornament engraving on the title page of a book.

Vigour *n.* activity and strength of body or mind; physical force.

Vigorous *adj.* full of physical strength; strong; energetic.

Viking *n.* the chief of pirates; Northern sea-robber of 8th & 10th centuries.

Vile *adj.* depraved; base; despicable; worthless; mean; wicked.

Vilification *n.* a defaming.

Vilify *v.t.* to make vile; to defame; to debase.

Villa *n.* a country residence.

Villadom *n.* a collection of villas.

Village *n.* assemblage of dwellings in the country.

Villatic *adj.* pertaining to village.

Villain *n.* one who holds a tenure in service; a wicked person.

Villarsia *n.* an acquatic plant.

Villi *n. pl.* fine fibres.

Villous *adj.* shaggy; covered with long fine hair.

Villus *n.* each of the short hair-like processes on some membranes.

Vim *n.* vigour; energy.

Vinaceous *adj.* wine-red; of the red-colour of grapewine.

Vinaigrette *n.* a smelling-bottle.

Vinicible *adj.* that may be conquered; able to the brought under submission.

Vindicable *adj.* able to be supported.

Vindicate *v.t.* to defend; to justify; to maintain; to avenge.

Vine *n.* the creeper which bears grapes.

Vineyard *n.* vine-plantation.

Vinous *adj.* addicted to wine; having the qualities of wine.

Viny *adj.* producing grapes; belonging to vine.

Violence *n.* injury; impetuousness; force; outrage.

Violet *adj.* of dark blue. *n.* the colour produced by a mixture of red and blue; purple; a kinds of plant.

Violin *n.* a fiddle; a musical instrument with four strings.

Viper *n.* the adder; a malignant person; a poisonous snake.

Virago *n.* a termagant; a masculine woman; a man-like woman.

Virent *adj.* green; fresh.

Virescent *adj.* slight green.

Virgate *adj.* slim; of the shape of a rod.

Virgin *n.* a female having no carnal knowledge of man; a maiden; a girl or woman who has not known sexual intercourse. *adj.* pure; chaste.

Virgo *n.* sixth zodiacal.

Virgule *n.* a small rod; a comma.

Virid *adj.* green.

Viridescent *adj.* turning green.

Virile *adj.* pertaining to the male sex; having masculine vigour or strength.

Virose *adj.* poisonous.

Virtu *n.* love of fine-arts; objects of art.

Virtual *adj.* potential, such in practice though not in name; being in effect.

Virtue *n.* efficacy; good quality; inherent power.

Virtuous *adj.* chaste; morally good; practising virtue.

Virulence *n.* extreme malignity; acrimony of temper.

Virus *n.* poisonous matter; poison of contagious disease.

Visage *n.* face; countenance.

Visaged *adj.* having a visage.

Vis-a-vis *adv.* & *n.* opposite to; face to face; in a position.

Viscera *n. pl.* the contents of the abdomen; the internal organs of the body.

Viscerate *v.t.* to deprive of the viscera.

Viscid *adj.* sticky; adhesive; semifluid.

Viscosity *n.* stickiness.

Viscous, Viscid *adjs.* glutinous; of a semifluid clinging consistence.

Visible *adj.* perceptible by the eye; apparent; open; clear; conspicuous.

Vision *n.* phantom; thing seen in a dream; the act of seeing; sight; object seen in imagination only.

Visional *adj.* pertaining to a vision.

Visit *n.* the act of going to see another person.

Visitation *n.* official visits; the act of visiting.

Vista *n.* a long narrow view as between rows of trees.

Visual *adj.* pertaining to sight.

Vital *adj.* most important; essential to success; pertaining to life.

Vitamin *n.* a factor regarded as necessary to health; the essential constituent of food plants.

Vitiate *v.t.* to corrupt or spoil; to destroy; to make defective.

Viticulture *n.* the culture of the vine.

Vitiosity *n.* corrupted state.

Vitreous *adj.* consisting of or pertaining to glass.

Vitrifiable *adj.* capable of being turned into glass.

Vitriol *n.* sulphuric acid.

Vitriolic *adj.* pertaining to sulphuric acid.

Vitta *n.* strips of colour; a garland; oil-tube in fruit.

Vituline *adj.* belonging to a calf.

Vituperable *adj.* blameworthy.

Viva *inter.* & *n.* long live; long life to.

Vivacious *adj.* sportive; active; lively; animated; having strong vital powers.

Vivacity *n.* liveliness; animation.

Viva-voce *adv.* by word or mouth; orally.

Vivarium *n.* a zoological garden; place in which live wild creatures are kept.

Vivency *n.* the manner of supporting life.

Vivers *n. pl.* food; victuals.

Vivid *adj.* intense; life-like; striking; vigorous; bright.

Vivificate *v.t.* to animate; to give life to.

Vivify *v.t.* to animate; to put life into; to quicken.

Vivisect *v.t.* to dissect living animal for scientific purposes.

Vivisection *n.* the dissection of living animals.

Vixen *n.* a quarrelsome woman; a female fox. **Vixenish** *adj.* like a vixen.

Viz (Contraction of Videlicet) that is; namely.

Vizard *n.* a mask.

Vocabulary *n.* a collection of words arranged in an alphabetical order and explained.

Vocal *adj.* uttered by the voice; pertaining to voice or speech.

Vocation *n.* employment; trade; occupation; designation of a profession.

Vociference *n.* clamour.

Vociferate *v.t.* & *i.* to speak loudly and insistently.

Vociferation *n.* exclamation; clamour.

Vociferous *adj.* clamorous; turbulent; noisy.

Vocule *n.* a feeble vocal sound.

Vogle *n.* a cavity in a mineral vein.

Voe *n.* creek; a small bay.

Vogue *n.* a custom or practice; the fashion of a particular time.

Voice *n.* sound; language; the expressed opinion; command.

Void *adj.* having no binding force; not valid; ineffectual.

Voile *n.* thin dress-material.

Volant *adj.* nimble; rapid; flying; active.

Volapuk *n.* an artificial international language.

Volar *adj.* of the palm or sole.

Volcano *n.* a burning mountain; a conical hill which emits fire and lava.

Vole *n.* kinds of mouse like rodent.

Volley *n.* shouting of words in rapid succession.

Volplane *v.t.* & *i.* to descend by gliding without using its engine.

Voltage *n.* measurement in volts.

Volte-face *n.* turning round; complete change of front.

Voluble *adj.* having fluency of speech; overfluent; apt to roll.

Volucrine *adj.* pertaining to birds.

Volume *n.* bulk; dimensions.

Voluntary *adj.* spontaneous; unrestrained; free; done without design.

Volunteer *n.* a person who comes forward with offer of service at need.

Volute *n.* a kind of spiral scroll used in capitals.

Vomit *n.* matter ejected from the stomach.

Vortex *n.* a whirl in water; a circular motion in water; a whirlpool.

Votarist *n.* a votary.

Votary *n.* a person vowed to the service of a god.

Vote *n.* an expression of majority; the right to take part in such vote.

Votive *adj.* devoted; given as a result of some vow.

Votively *adv.* by way of a vow.
Vouch *v.t.* & *i.* to support; to call upon solemnly to witness.
Vouchsafe *v.t.* to grant or to do something; to guarantee.
Voussoir *n.* each of the wedge-shaped stones forming an arch.
Vow *v.t.* to consecrate to god by a solemn promise; to devote.
Vowel *n.* a letter which can be sounded by itself.
Vower *n.* one who makes a vow.
Voyage *n.* a passage by water from one place to another.
Vulcan *n.* the god of fire.
Vulcanic *adj.* pertaining to volcanoes.
Vulgar *n.* the common people; the common language of a country.
Vulgate *n.* Latin translation of the Scriptures.
Vulnerable *n.* the state of being vulnerable.
Vulnerate *v.t.* to hurt; to wound.
Vulnerose *adj.* full of wounds.
Vulpicide *n.* the killing of a fox.
Vulpine *adj.* crafty; cunning; pertaining to foxes.
Vulpinism *n.* cunningness.
Vulture *n.* a rapacious person; a carrion-eating bird of prey.
Vulturous *adj.* rapacious.
Vulva *n.* (*Anat.*) orifice; opening.
Vulviform *adj.* of the form of a cleft.
Vulvitis *n.* in a fissure.
Vying *adj.* competing.

W

W the twenty-third letter of the English alphabet.
Wabble *v.i.* to move to and fro.
Wabbly *adj.* in wabbling manner.
Wadding *n.* a soft material for padding garments; material from which gun-wads are made.
Waddle *v.i.* to walk with short steps; to walk like a duck; to walk with slow rocking gait, rock from one side to the other.
Wade *v.t.* & *i.* & *n.* to go with difficulty or labour; to walk through water.
Wafer *n.* a thin paste used in sealing letters; a small thin sweet cake.
Waft *v.t.* & *i.* to beckon.
Waftage *n.* conveyance through air or water.
Wafter *n.* a passage boat.
Wag *v.t.* & *i.* to vibrate; to move quickly one way and the other.
Wage *v.t.* to stake; to bet.
Wager *n.* a stake; a bet.
Waggle *v.t.* & *i.* to waddle; to sway about; to move from side to side.
Waggonage *n.* money paid for carrying on a wagon.
Wagonette *n.* an open four-wheeled carriage with seats facing each other.
Wagtail *n.* a small bird which frequently shakes its tail.
Waif *n.* a neglected child; anything found without the owner.

Wail *n.* lamentation; loud weeping; a prolonged plaintive cry; wail-like sound.

Wailer *n.* one who wails.

Wain *n.* a wagon; a carriage for the transport of goods.

Waist *n.* the widest part of a ship; the part of the human body below ribs and above hips.

Wait *v.t.* & *i.* to remain stationary; to stay in expectation.

Waitress *n.* a female waiter in a hotel.

Waiter *n.* an attendant (at the table).

Waive *v.t.* to put off; to forgo; to relinquish.

Waiver *n.* the act of relinquishing.

Wake *n.* to put in motion; to cease to sleep; to awake; to revive.

Walk *n.* place of wandering; excursion on foot.

Wall *n.* upright structure serving as defence of a town; a structure of brick or stone.

Wallet *n.* a bag for carrying necessities; a knapsack.

Wallop *v.t.* & *i.* to boil with a bubbling noise; to beat soundly.

Wallow *v.i.* to tumble and roll; to roll one's body. *n.* a rolling walk.

Walnut *n.* a handsome and valuable tree; a tree with edible fruits.

Walrus *n.* a large tusked carnivorous sea-animal; sea-horse.

Walt *adj.* tottering.

Wamble *n.* uneasiness or feeling of nausea in the stomach.

Wan *adj.* pale; to depart; pallid; pale as with illness; to roam.

Wand *n.* a small stick or rod; a long slender rod.

Wander *v.i.* to roam; to depart; to migrate; to travel aimlessly.

Wander-lust *n.* craving for travel.

Wandy *adj.* like a wand.

Wane *v.t.* to decrease; to diminish.

Wangle *v.t.* to secure favour astutely.

Want *n.* defect; deficiency; need; poverty; indigence.

Wantage *n.* deficiency.

Wanting *adj.* absent; deficient.

Wanton *v.t.* to sport; to revel; to live amorously; to ramble without restraint.

Wapper *v.i.* to move quickly; to totter.

War *n.* fighting; hostility; enmity; a contest between nations.

Warfare *n.* contest (hostility).

War-field *n.* a field of battle.

Warhorse *n.* a charger.

Warsong *n.* a song inciting war.

Warble *n.* a hard lump on horse's back from galling of saddle.

Warble *v.t.* & *i.* to quaver the voice.

Ward a suffix denoting direction.

Ward *n.* minor under care of guardian; watch; a ridge in lock or key.

Ware *n.* an article of merchandise.

Warehouse *n.* & *v.t.* a store house for goods; to deposit in a warehouse.

Warely *adv.* cautiously.

Wares *n. pl.* goods; commodities.

Warm *adj.* vigorous; enthusiastic; having a moderate degree of heat; ardent; zealous; sympathetic; animated; keen.

Warming *adj.* making moderately hot.

Warmth *n.* warmness; earnestness; gentle heat; zeal; ardour.

Warn *v.t.* to inform of probable danger; to make aware of.

Warning *n.* previous notice; what is said or done to warn a person; caution.

Warp *v.t. & i.* to twist; to turn from the true direction; to pervert; to deviate.

Warrant *n.* authority; power that authorizes an act; right; security.

Warren *n.* a place or ground for the breeding of rabbits.

Warrior *n.* a distinguished or veteran soldier; a brave man; a fighting man.

Wart *n.* a hard, firm, small excrescence on the skin.

Wary *adj.* circumspect; cautious of danger.

Wase *n.* a pad of straw or cloth placed on the head to relieve pressure of burden.

Wash *n.* a bog; lotion or liquid cosmetic; the act of washing; the blade of an oar; break of waves on the shore; thin coat of paint on metal.

Washer *n.* a flat ring or perforated piece used to give tightness.

Washy *adj.* faded looking; feeble; too watery; insipid; weak.

Wasn't *v.t.* short form of was not.

Wasp *n.* a stinging insect; a winged insect with venomous sting.

Waspish *adj.* having a very slender waist; peevish; petulant.

Wast second person singular of 'Be'.

Wastage *n.* loss by waste.

Waste *n.* extravagance; an uncultivated country; destruction; spoil; refuse.

Waster *n.* a person whose existence is regrettable; an article spoilt in making.

Wastrel *n.* a stray child; a wasteful person; a thing spoilt in making; good-for-nothing fellow.

Watch *n.* the act of watching; the place where a guard is kept; a small timepiece for the pocket.

Water *n.* liquid compound of oxygen and hydrogen; a transparent liquid; urine; luster of a precious stone.

Waterfall *n.* stream falling over precipice; cascade.

Water-melon *n.* elliptical smooth kind of melon with watery juice; a kind of sweet fruit.

Waterrot *v.t.* to rot in water.

Waterside *n.* land by the edge of water.

Watertight *adj.* so tightly closed as to prevent ingress of water.

Waterway *n.* a canal; a navigable river.

Water-wings *n.* walls erected on the banks of a river to minimize the current.

Watt *n.* the electrical unit of power.

Waul *v.i.* to cry like a cat.

Wave *v.t. & i.* to waft; to brandish; to beckon; to reject; to move like a wave.

Wavelet *n.* a small wave; a ripple.

Wavelike *adj.* like a wave.

Waver *v.i.* to hesitate; to oscillate unsteadily; to move to and fro; to fluctuate; to totter.

Wax *v.t. & i.* to grow; to increase in size; to become large; to smear or join with wax; to stop a hole with wax.

Way *n.* passage; travelling distance; scope; sphere; range; branch of business; state; assumption.

Wayfarer *n.* one who travels on foot.

Waygone *adj.* tired by travelling.

Waylay *v.t.* to lie in ambush; to watch with the aim of stealing.

Wayside *n.* side of road (*esp.* attrib.)

Wayward *adj.* perverse; wilful; full of troublesome whims; childishly self-willed.

Way-worn *adj.* tired with travel.

We *pron.* first person plural of 'I'; men in general.

Weak *adj.* spiritless; slight; irresolute; feeble; frail; not strong; soft.

Weal *n.* public interest.

Wealth *n.* affluence; abundance; prosperity; riches; material possessions.

Wean *v.t.* to cure of or rescue from habit.

Weanling *n.* a child newly weaned.

Weapon *n.* an instrument of offence or defece; (*pl.*) stings.

Wear *n.* the act of wearing; thing worn; diminution by friction; capacity for resisting wear and tear.

Wearable *adj.* able to be worn.

Weariness *n.* the state of being wearied; fatigue; impatience.

Wearish *adj.* weak; somewhat weary.

Wearisome *adj.* tiresome; causing weariness; monotonous.

Weary *adj.* tedious; tiresome; fatigued; tired; impatient of.

Weasand *n.* the tube through air passes in the lungs; the wind pipe.

Weasel *n.* a small nimble carnivorous beast.

Weather *n.* change in the state of the wind.

Weave *v.t. & i.* to practise weaving; to form fabric by interlacing threads.

Weaver *n.* a loom-worker; a weaver bird.

Web *n.* a texture of threads; the plexus of spider

Webbing *n.* fabric of hemp for stuffing.

Wed *v.t.* & *i.* to expouse; to marry; to take for husband or wife.

Wedding *n.* pertaining to marriage; a marriage ceremony.

Wedlock *n.* marriage; the married state.

Wedge *n.* a piece of wood or metal sharp at one end and gradually growing thicker; a solid of five sides.

Weed *v.t.* to free from weeds.

Weeding *n.* the operation of removing weeds.

Week *n.* the six days between Sundays; the space of seven days.

Weel *n.* a snare for fish.

Weem *n.* an underground dwelling.

Ween *v.t.* to be of opinion; to think; to imagine.

Weep *v.t.* & *i.* to express sorrow; to shed tears; to lament; to complain.

Weeper *n.* one who sheds tears.

Weeping *n.* lamentation.

Weetless *adj.* not knowing.

Weevil *n.* destructive granary-beetle; a plant-eating beetle.

Weigh *v.t.* & *i.* to consider; to regard; to ascertain the weight of; to raise or lift.

Weigher *n.* one who weighs.

Weight *n.* pressure; burden; power; influence.

Weir, Wear *ns.* a dam in a river.

Weird *adj.* acquainted with fate; unearthly; supernatural.

Weirdness *n.* the state of being weird.

Welcome *n.* kind of glad reception; the reception of a guest.

Weld *n.* a kind of plant from which yellow dye is made.

Weld *v.t.* & *i.* to join metal by hammering or pressure after heating to redness.

Welk *v.i.* to fade; to wither.

Welkin *n.* the sky.

Well *n.* source of knowledge or happiness; a water-spring; a foundation; a pit in the earth for water supply.

Welsh *adj.* pertaining to the inhabitant or language of Wales.

Welt *v.t.* to furnish with a border. *n.* a border; a strip of leather between the upper and the sole.

Wen *n.* abnormally large or congested city; a moveable fleshy tumour.

Wench *n.* a yound woman; a maid servant; a woman of bad character.

Wencher *n.* a lewd man.

Wend *v.t.* to wander; to go.

Wentletrap *n.* a shell-fish.

Were *n.* 1*st*, 2*nd*, & 3*rd person pl.* of the verb 'Be'.

Werewolf, Werwolf *ns.* a human being turned into wolf.

Wert *v.* 2*nd pers. sing.* of the verb.

West *n.* the point of horizon where the sun goes down.

Westminster *n.* city forming part of London; the Houses of Parliament.

Westward *adv.* towards the west.

West-wardly *adv.* towards the west.

Wet *n.* moist state; moisture; standing water; storm; downpour of rain.

Wettish *adj.* somewhat wet.

Whack *v.t.* to strike heavily; to thwack; to give a smart blow.

Whale *n.* the largest of marine animals.

Whall *n.* a disease of the eyes.

Whang *n.* a leather thong. *v.t.* to flog.

Whap *n.* a blow.

Wharf *n.* a landing place; platform to which ships or barges may be moored to load and unload.

What *inter.* & *pron.* that which; which part.

Whatever *pron.* being one thing or another; whole that.

Whaup *n.* a kind of bird.

Wheat *n.* a plant with edible seeds; the grain or kinds of corn.

Wheatear *n.* an ear of wheat; a small bird.

Wheedle *v.t.* & *i.* to coax; to flatter; to fool by flattery.

Wheel *v.t.* & *i.* to convey on wheels; to cause to turn round; to turn on an axis; to push or pull along.

Wheelman *n.* a cyclist.

Wheelwork *n.* a combination of wheels.

Wheelbin *n.* a large refuge bin on wheels.

Wheen *n.* a small quantity.

Wheeze *v.t.* to breathe hard with audible sound.

Whelm *v.t.* to engulf; to swallow up; to cover with water; to immerse.

Whelp *v.t.* & *i.* to bring forth young.

When *adv.* while; at what time?

Whence *adv.* from what place or source? how, by what means from what things? wherefore.

Where *adv.* in what respect; at what part.

Whereabout *adv.* near what or which place.

Whereas *adv.* taking into consideration the fact that; considering that.

Whereat *adv.* at which; at what matter.

Whereby *adv.* by which.

Wherein *adv.* in which.

Whereupon *adv.* after which; and thereupon.

Wherewith *adv.* with which.

Wherewithal *adv.* where with.

Wherret *v.t.* & *n.* to give a sharp blow; a blow.

Wherry *n.* a shallow boat; a light boat.

Whet *n.* the act of sharpening; something that increases appetite.

Whet-stone *n.* a stone for tool sharpening; thing that sharpens the wits.

Whether *pron.* & *conj.* which of the two; which of the two alternatives.

Whettle *n.* a woodpecker.

Whey *n.* the liquid left when milk forms curds; the watery part of milk.

Which *pron.* relative or interrogative; asking for selection from limited or known alternatives.

Whichever *adv.* whether one or the other.

Whichsoever *adv.* which ever.

Whiff *v.t.* to throw in puffs. *n.* a sudden expulsion of air from the mouth.

Whiffle *v.t.* & *i.* to fickle; to blow lightly; to evade; to scatter by puffing.

Whiffling *n.* a shuffling.

Whig *n.* a liberal in English politics.

While *adv.* during the time that. *n.* the timer or expense needed.

Whilst *adv.* while.

Whim *adv.* caprice; a sudden state of mind; freak.

Whimbrel *n.* kind of curlew.

Whimper *v.t.* & *i.* feeble sound; cry with a low whining voice.

Whimsey *n.* freak; a whim; fad.

Whim-wham *n.* a plaything.

Whimchat *n.* a small singing bird.

Whin *n.* hard sandstone.

Whine *n.* a plaintive tone.

Whinger *n.* a short sword, dirk or long knife.

Whinny *v.i.* to neigh in a joyful way.

Whinyard *n.* a sword.

Whip *n.* the member of Parliament who summons the members of his party to be present while there is a division; a lash attached to a rod.

Whiphand *n.* an upper hand; advantage over.

Whiplash *n.* the lash of a whip.

Whippet *n.* a kind of grey hound; a small armoured car.

Whipsaw *n.* a saw worked by two persons.

Whipster *n.* a small child; a trifling frivolous person; a nimble little fellow.

Whir *n.* velocity; the sound made by rapid whirling of something.

Whirl *n.* a turning with high velocity; whirling movement.

Whirblast *n.* a whirling blast of wind.

Whirligig *n.* a kind of top which turns on its axis like a wheel.

Whirlpool *n.* an eddy of water; a vortex.

Whirlwind *n.* a violent whirling wind; an eddy of the wind.

Whirr *n.* & *v.i.* continuous buzzing or clincking sound.

Whisk *n.* a brush or small broom; sweeping motion of tall, beating-up instrument; bunch of grass, hair & etc.

Whisket *n.* a basket.
Whisky *n.* a spirit distilled from barley; a liquor prepared from malted barley.
Whisper *n.* a low soft voice; buzzing sound. *v.t.* & *i.* to prompt secretly.
Whist *n.* a game of cards played by four players with 13 cards each & with a declared trump.
Whist *inter.* silent.
Whistle *n.* sound made by pressing lips and ejecting air forcibly through mouth.
Whit *n.* a point; a jot; a particle; the smallest part.
White *n.* the white colour; a white thing.
Whiten *v.t.* & *i.* to make white; to bleach; to blanch.
Whitethorn *n.* a kind of prickly plant.
Whitewash *n., v.t.* & *i.* to cover with a white composition.
Whither *adv.* to what or which place? in what direction?
Whitish *adj.* somewhat white.
Whitlow *n.* inflamed tumour on a finger.
Whittle *n.* a small pocket-knife; butcher's knife. *v.t.* to cut small strips with a knife.
Whiz, Whizz *ns.* hissing sound. *v.t.* to make a hissing sound.
Whizzbang *n.* a high velocity shell.
Whizzing *n.* humming sound.
Who *pron.* what person?, *interrogative pron.* which person.
Whosoever *pron.* any person whatsoever.
Whole *n.* the entire thing; a system; an aggregate.
Wholesale *n.* selling of things in large quantities.
Whom *pron.* objective case of 'Who'.
Whoop *n.* shout of war; hoop.
Whop *n.* a sudden fall.
Whopper *n.* extraordinary thing.
Whore *n.* an unchaste woman; a prostitute; a harlot.
Whoredom *n.* acts of sexual immorality.
Whoremaster *n.* a pimp; a pander.
Whorish *adj.* lewd; unchaste.
Whorl *n.* one turn of spiral; a ring of leaves or flowers; a raised ridge.
Whose *pron. poss. case* of Who or Which.
Why *adv.* for what reason or purpose?, for which.
Wick *n.* web of a lamp; number of threads twisted into a string used in candle.
Wicket *n.* a set of three upright stumps used in the game of cricket.
Wide *n.* expanse; a wide ball.
Widen *v.t.* & *i.* to extend; to make or grow wider.
Widespread *adj.* spread to great distance.

Widow *n.* a woman whose husband is dead.

Width *n.* breadth; distance or measurement from side to side; wideness.

Wield *n.* to use with power; to control.

Wife *n.* a married woman; the lawful consort of a man.

Wig *n.* artificial covering for the head.

Wiggle *v.t.* to twist the body to and fro.

Wight *n.* a person; a supernatural being; a creature.

Wild *n.* a forest; a desert.

Wilding *n.* a plant sown by natural agency; a wild apple.

Wile *n.* a trick; a stratagem.

Wilful *adj.* refractory; obstinate; wayward; self-willed; refractory.

Will an auxiliary verb, sign of future.

Will *n.* command; a written document disposing of property after death.

Willow *n.* a plant with pliant branches.

Willy-nilly *adv.* willingly or unwillingly.

Wilsome *adj.* obstinate.

Wily *adj.* sly; crafty; using stratagem.

Wimble *n.* a gimlet. *v.t.* to bore holes.

Wimp *n.* a cowardly person.

Win *v.t.* & *i.* to gain by success; to gain by victory; to allure by kindness.

Winner *n.* one who wins; a victor.

Winning *adj.* charming; adapted to win or gain favour.

Wince *v.i.* to flinch; to show uneasiness; to start in pain.

Wincer *n.* a horse which kicks.

Winch *n.* a reel; an instrument for straining.

Wind *v.t.* to turn; to change; to entwist; to unfold.

Wind *n.* the current of air; air in motion; breath; flatulence.

Windbag *n.* a man who uses empty words.

Windiness *n.* flatulence; a tendency to generate wind.

Winding *adj.* bending; twisting.

Windless *adj.* wanting in wind.

Windmill *n.* a mill turned by the wind.

Window *n.* an opening in a wall for admitting light and air.

Windpipe *n.* the air passage from throat to lungs; the trachea.

Windy *adj.* windward; generating flatulence; verbose; wind-swept.

Wine *n.* the fermented juice of grapes; intoxicating liquor.

Wing *n.* flight; side extension of something; sides of stage.

Wink *n.* the act of closing and opening the eyelids; a hint given by the eyes.

Winnow *v.t.* to separate chaff from grain by the help of wind.

Winsome *adj.* attractive; charming; winning merry.

Winter *n.* the cold season of the year; the last and coldest of the four seasons.

Wintry *adj.* pertaining to winter; cold.

Wipe *v.t.* & *i.* to clean by rubbing; to rub with soft thing; to cheat.

Wire *n.* a thread of metal; a telegram.

Wiredraw *n.* a plate of steel with holes for drawing in wire.

Wire-gauze *n.* a fine texture resembling gauge.

Wireless *n.* the communication through electromagnetic waves without wires.

Wireness *n.* the state of being wiry; state of being strong or endurable.

Wiring *n.* an arrangement of wires.

Wisdom *n.* natural instinct; the quality of being wise.

Wise *adj.* learned; skilful; discerning; sagacious.

Wiseacre *n.* a dunce; one who pretends to be wise; a simpleton.

Wise-hearted *adj.* skilful.

Wish *n.* an eager desire; desire expressed.

Wisher *n.* one who desires.

Wish-wash *n.* a kind of watery drink.

Wisp *n.* a small bundle of straw.

Wist *v.t.* to wit (know).

Wistly *adv.* thoughtfully; attentively.

Wit *n.* imaginative and inventive faculty; intellect.

Witch *n.* a sorceress; a woman using magic; an ugly old woman; a hag.

Witchcraft *n.* sorcery; enchantment.

Wite *n.* blame.

With *prep.* on the side of; among; beside.

Withal *adv.* besides; with the rest; at the same time; moreover; as well.

Withdraw *v.t.* & *i.* to pull aside or back.

Withdrawal *n.* the act of withdrawing.

Withe *n.* a band of twisted twigs.

Wither *v.t.* & *i.* to fade; to pine away (to lose moisture); to cause to dry.

Withered *adj.* dried; faded.

Withhold *v.t.* to refuse to give or put in operation; to hold back.

Within *prep.* & *adv.* the inner part; inside; not beyond; not exceeding.

Without *prep.*, *adv.* & *conj.* not within; beyond.

Withstand *v.t.* to hold out against; to oppose; to resist.

Withstood *adj.* hindered; opposed.

Witling *n.* a man of little understanding.

Witness *n.* one who gives testimony in a court; attestation of an event; testimony.

Witticism *n.* phrase or remark; a witty remark; facetious or witty sentence.

Witty *adj.* amusing; judicious; full of verbal wit; possessing wit or humour.

Wive *v.t.* & *i.* to wed; to marry.

Wivern, Wyfern *ns.* two-legged dragon; winged.

Wizard *n.* a person of extraordinary powers; genius; conjurer; a magician.

Wizen *v.t.* to dry; to wither.

Wo, Whoa *inter.* stop.

Woad *n.* a kind of plant like indigo.

Wobble *v.t.* & *i.* to sway from side to side; to vacillate; to move to and fro.

Woe *n.* grief; curse; sorrow; misery; affliction; heavy calamities.

Woe-begone *adj.* overwhelmed with grief; melancholy.

Woeful *adj.* bringing calamity; sorrowful; mournful; distressed.

Wold *n.* a forest; a wood; piece of open uncultivated country.

Wolf *n.* a rapacious person; fierce carnivorous animal.

Woman *n.* the female sex; female of man; lady in waiting; a female servant.

Womb *n.* the part of the body where the young of an animal is conceived.

Wonder *n.* amazement; that which excites surprise; strange or remarkable thing; astonishment.

Wonderful *adj.* exciting surprise; strange; very remarkable.

Wonderstruck *adj.* struck with wonder.

Wonderworker *n.* worker of wonders.

Wondrous *adj.* wonderful; remarkable; admirable; marvellous; strange.

Wondrously *adv.* in a strange manner.

Wont *adj.* habituated; accustomed to do. *n.* habit; a custom.

Wonted *adj.* made familiar; habitual; usual.

Woo *v.t.* to make love of; to solicit in love; to ask in marriage.

Wooer *n.* one who wooes; a lover.

Woobut, Woubit *ns.* woolly-bear.

Wood *n.* a small forest; the solid part under the bark of a tree.

Woodbine *n.* the wild honeysuckle.

Woodcarving *n.* engraving in wood.

Woodcock *n.* a bird similar to snipe; a kind of apple; a simpleton.

Woodcraft *n.* forestry; act of woodwork.

Wooden-head *n.* a block-head.

Woody *adj.* of the nature abounding in woods; consisting of wood.

Woodland *n.* wooded country.

Wood-monger *n.* timber merchant.

Woodnote *n.* the note of a forest bird.

Woodpecker *n.* kinds of bird clining to tree-stem in search of insects.

Woof *n.* the weft; cloth; texture.

Wool *n.* woolen clothes; the fleecy coat of sheep; short hair.

Woolgrower *n.* one who raises sheep for production of wool.

Woolen *adj.* pertaining to wool; covered with wool as a mark of penance.

Woor *n.* a lover.

Word *n.* motto; a short sentence; statement or remark or saying.

Wordily *adv.* in a wordy manner.

Work *n.* occupation; duty; undertaking; performance; exertion or effort; labour; employment.

Working *adj.* & *n.* operation; movement; engaged in activity.

Workman *n.* a hired labourer.

Workshop *n.* a room or building in which manufacture is carried on.

World *n.* the earth; public life or society; the globe; the state of human existence; a very great quantity.

Worldly *adj.* temporal or secular.

Worldwide *adj.* wide as the world; spread over or known to all the world.

Worm *n.* a small creeping animal; a spiral tube; anything that destroys; that which torments; ligament under dog's tongue; a snake.

Worn *adj.* enfeebled; (of time) past or spent; impaired by use or exposure; exhausted by toil.

Worried *adj.* harassed.

Worriment *n.* anxiety.

Worry *v.t.* & *i.* to fatigue; to vex; to trouble; to tease; to harass or importune.

Worse *adj.* bad or evil in greater degree; more unwell; more bad; in or into worse health.

Worship *n.* homage or service paid to idols; adoration felt for a person or principle; worthiness; adoration.

Worst *n.* most severe state. *adj.* most bad; most evil; pernicious.

Worsted *adj.* made of worsted yarn. *n.* wool combed straight.

Wort *n.* a kind of herb; plant.

Worth *n.* value; price; virtue; merit; importance.

Worthless *adj.* of no value or merit; not deserving.

Worthy *adj.* suitable; having suitable value; estimable or deserving.

Would *v.i.* used as an auxiliary, wish or prayer.

Wouldst *v.i. second pers. sing.* of will.

Wound *p.t.* & *p.p.* of wind.

Wound *n.* a cut; bruise; bodily hurt or injury; damage.

Wove-paper *n.* a writing paper of smooth surface.

Wow *inter.* an exclamation of wonder.

Wrack *n.* wreckage; a flying cloud.

Wrackful *adj.* destructive.

Wraith *n.* an apparition of a person about to die or just after death.

Wrangle *n.* a noisy quarrel. *v.i.* to engage in wrangle; to quarrel noisily.

Wrangler *n.* one who disputes.

Wrap *v.t. & i.* to envelop in folded material; to fold together.

Wrappage *n.* the act of wrapping; wrapping material.

Wrathily *adj.* with anger.

Wrawl *v.t.* to cry like a cat.

Wreak *v.t.* to punish out of revenge.

Wreakless *adj.* unrevengeful; unpunished.

Wreath *n.* drift of smoke; a garland.

Wreathy *adj.* adorned with a wreath.

Wreathe *v.t. & i.* to encircle with or as with a wreath; to twist; to entwine.

Wreck *n.* the destruction of a vessel dashing against a rock or by foundering.

Wreckmaster *n.* one who takes charge of a wreckage.

Wren *n.* kinds of small bird.

Wrench *n.* a tool for gripping and turning nuts; a violent twist.

Wrest *n.* a violent twist; distortion.

Wrestle *v.t.* to strive by grappling.

Wrestler *n.* one who is skilled in wrestling.

Wrestling *n.* the act of contending; struggle.

Wretch *n.* an ill-fated or pitiable person; a miserable person; one sunk in voice; a base person.

Wretched *adj.* very miserable; unhappy; calamitous; in misery.

Wriggle *v.t. & i.* to squirm; to put into a wriggling motion.

Wright *n.* a worker in wood; an artificer; a maker or builder.

Wring *v.t. & i.* to twist; to squeeze tightly; to distort.

Wrinkle *n.* a fold; a small ridge; a crease or furrow of the skin or face.

Wrist *n.* the joint by which the hand is united to the arm.

Write *v.t. & i.* to transcribe; to work as an author.

Writer *n.* one who writes; a clerk in certain offices; an author.

Writing *n.* anything written; a manuscript; a book

Writhe *v.t. & i.* to twist the body in pain.

Wrong *n.* injury; injustice; error.

Wrung *p.t. & p.t.* of Wring.

Wry *adj.* twisted; distorted; turned to one side.

Wych *pref.* in the names of trees etc. with pliant branches.

Wych-hazel-North American Shrub, astringent extract of its bark.

Wyvern *n.* an imaginary winged & two-legged monster.

X the twenty-fourth letter of the English alphabet.

X-film adult film.

Xangti *n.* the Supreme Being of the Chinese mythology.

Xanthein *n.* the yellow colouring matter of flower which is soluble in water.

Xanthian *adj.* pertaining to Xanthus, the capital of Lycia in Asia.

Xanthium *n.* a flowering plant like aster.

Xanthochroia *n.* the act in which colour of skin become yellowish.

Xanthochronic *adj.* pertaining to men with smooth light coloured hair and pale complexion.

Xanthoma *n.* a type of disease in which yellow patches appear on skin.

Xanthomatous *adj.* pertaining to xanthoma.

Xanthomelanous *adj.* applied to a type of man having black hair and yellow skin.

Xanthophyll *n.* certain yellow pigments found in autumn leaves.

Xanthosia *n.* a type of plant which is covered with yellow down.

Xanthosis *n.* formation of yellow pigment.

Xantippe *n.* a quarrelsome woman; a shrew.

Xebec *n.* a pirate ship; a small three-masted square-rigged vessel.

Xema *n.* a genus of forktailed bird.

Xenarthral *adj.* joined like a vertebrae.

Xenial *adj.* pertaining to hospitality.

Xenium *n.* a picture of still life.

Xenodochium *n.* a room for guests.

Xenodochy *n.* reception of guests.

Xenogamy *n.* (*Bot.*) cross fertilization.

Xenogenesis *n.* production of heterogeneous generation.

Xenomania *n.* undue attachment to foreign things.

Xenomorphic *adj.* of irregular and abnormal shape.

Xenon *n.* a chemical element.

Xenops *n.* a kind of American creeper.

Xerasia *n.* a disease of the hair in which it does not grow and become dry.

Xerochastic *adj.* opening when dried.

Xerocollyrium *n.* dry collyrium.

Xeroderma *n.* morbid dryness of skin.

Xerophagy *n.* the habit of living on meagre and dry dies.

Xerophilous *adj.* adapted to hot and dry climate; loving dryness.

Xerophyte *n.* a plant suitable for dry soil.

Xerosis *n.* dryness of skin.

Xerotes *n.* the dry disposition of body.

Xerotribia *n.* dry friction.

Xiphiolid *adj*. pertaining to the sword fish.

X-rays *n*. (*pl.*) the invisible rays emitted by an electric current by which the interior of solids can be photographed, these rays are discovered by the German scientist Rontgen Wurzburg in 1895.

Xylanthrax *n*. coal obtained from wood.

Xylem *n*. woody tissue.

Xylocarp *n*. a woody and hard fruit.

Xylograph *n*. wood-engraving.

Xylography *n*. the art of engraving on wood.

Xyloid *adj*. like wood.

Xyloidine *n*. an explosive similar to gun cotton.

Xylol *n*. oil obtained from wood.

Xylophagan *n*. a wood-eating insect of th e xylophaga family.

Xylophone *n*. a musical instrument like harmonica in which glass slips are replaced by graduated hard bars of wood.

Xylopyrography *n*. poker painting; the act of engraving on wood.

Xyst *n*. an covered or open court for athletic exercises.

Xyster *n*. a surgical instrument for scraping bones.

Xystos, Xystus *ns*. a garden walk; a covered court for athletic exercises.

Y

Y the twenty-fifth letter of the English alphabet; a Roman numeral for 150.

Yabber *n*. to talk meaninglessly.

Yacca *n*. a kind of tree which always remain green.

Yacht *n*. a light sailing vessel for racing or pleasure.

Yaffle *n*. green wood-pecker.

Yager *n*. a German light infantryman.

Yah *inter*. of derision.

Yahoo *n*. a bestial person; a rude brutish fellow.

Yak *n*. a kind of Tibetan ox covered with long silky hair.

Y'all *pron*. you all.

Yam *n*. the root of tropical plant.

Yama *n*. the God of death in Hindu mythology.

Yammer *v.t.* to lament; to whine.

Yamun *n*. a Chinese government office.

Yang *n*. (in chinese philsophy) the bright active male principle of the universe—compare **yin.**

Yank *v.t.* to pull with a jerk.

Yankee *n*. an inhabitant of the U.S. American.

Yanoloite *n*. axinite; a kind of crystalline mineral.

Yap *v.i.* to yelp; to bark like a dog.

Yapon *n*. a kind of tea.

Yapp *n*. a kind of binding in which the eges of books are overlaps by cover of book.

Yappie *n*. young aspiring professional.

Yard *n.* a spar for spreading a sail; an enclosure; a measuring rod of thirty-six inches.

Yardage *n.* size measured in yards or square yards.

Yardarm *n.* the end of a ship's yard.

Yard sale *n.* a sale of things from sb's house, held in their yard.

Yardwand *n.* a yard stick.

Yare *adj.* dexterous; quick; eager.

Yarn *n.* one of the threads of which a rope is made; spun thread; a story.

Yarr *v.i.* to snarl; to growl.

Yarrish *adj.* having a try taste.

Yataghan *n.* a short curved sword.

Yate *n.* a gate.

Yaup *v.i.* to cry like a child.

Yaw *v.i.* to rise in blisters.

Yawl *n.* a fishing boat; a warships boat.

Yawn *n.* a gape; opening of the mouth; a crack.

Yawning *adj.* dull; opening wide.

Yaws *n.* cutaneous tumour.

Ye *pron.* nominative plural of 'Thou'.

Yea *adv.* yes; certainly; verily.

Yeanling *n.* the young of a sheep lamb.

Yean *v.t.* & *i.* to bring forth young; to yeen.

Year *n.* any period of twelve calender months; twelve months; (*pl.*) old age.

Yearbook *n.* a book of up to date information published annually.

Yearling *adj.* & *n.* a young beast one year old; a year old.

Yearlong *adj.* lasting a year.

Yearly *adj.* & *adv.* every year; once a year; occurring yearly.

Yearn *v.t.* & *i.* to long; to be distressed; to have an earnest desire; to grieve.

Yearnful *adj.* distressing.

Yearning *n.* longing desire; strong emotion.

Yeast *n.* a preparation used for raising dough.

Yeasty *adj.* frothy; foamy.

Yeldrin *n.* yellow bunting.

Yell *n.* a sharp outcry; a shrill cry.

Yellow *n.* a bright golden colour.

Yellowish *adj.* somewhat yellow.

Yelp *n.* a dog's cry of excitement or pain.

Yen *n.* Japanese monetary unit.

Yeoman *n.* a middle class farmer or countryman; a free holder.

Yerk *v.t.* to strike suddenly.

Yer-nut *n.* the earth-nut.

Yes *adv.* a particle serving as a substitute for affirmative answer.

Yesterday *n.* the day preceding today or the day in questionpast.

Yesternight *n.* last night.

Yet *adv.* besides; still; at this time; at least; after all; by this or that time.

Yew *n.* a dark-leaved green tree; an evergreen tree.

Yewn *adj.* made of yew.

Yex *n.* hiccup, a sole.

Yield *v.t.* & *i.* to admit; to grant; to submit; to give consent; to concede; to produce; to give in return for.

Yieldance *n.* the act of yielding.

Yielder *n.* one who yields.

Yielding *adj.* & *n.* inclined to comply.

Yoicks *inter.* a fox hunting cry urging on the hounds.

Yoke *n.* a mark of servitude; bond of connection; slavery; a pair or couple.

Yokemate *n.* a mate.

Yokel *n.* a country-fellow; an ignorant rustic fellow.

Yolk *n.* wool-oil; the yellow part of an egg.

Yon *adv.* yonder.

Yond *adj.* furious; mad.

Yonder *adv.* within view; being at a distance.

Yonker *n.* a young fellow.

Yore *n.* the past; old time.

Yorker *n.* a ball that pitches just under the bat.

You *pron.* second person, plural, nominative as well as objective.

Young *n.* the offspring of animals.

Your *pron.* (*pl.*) belonging to you.

Youth *n.* young person collectively; the state of being young; a young man.

Youthsome *adj.* youthful.

Yowl *v.t.* to bark; to cry like a dog.

Youcca *n.* a plant of the lily family.

Yuck *v.t.* to itch.

Yucker woodpecker of America.

Yuga *n.* one of the Hindu ages of the world.

Yulan *n.* a beautiful flowering tree.

Yule *n.* the Christmas festival.

Yuletide the time of Christmas.

Yummy *adj.* very good to eat delicious a yummy cake.

Yunx *n.* a kind of bird.

Yurt *n.* a tent of the people of the Arctic region.

Ywis *adj.* certainly.

Z

Z the last and twenty-sixth letter of English alphabet.

Zabaglione Italian sweet of whipped and heated egg yolks and sugar.

Zabra *n.* a small vessel of the Spanish coast.

Zabrus *n.* a kind of large beetle.

Zaccho *n.* the lowest part of a column.

Zaffre *n.* impure oxide of cobalt.

Zambo *n.* the child of a Negro and an American Indian.

Zambomba *n.* a kind of Spanish musical instrument.

Zamouse *n.* a short-horned bush cow.

Zampogna *n.* an Italian bagpipe.

Zanella *n.* a fabric for covering umbrellas.

Zany *n.* a baffoon; a fool; a merry-andrew.

Zanyism *n.* the character of buffoonery.

Zap *v.* to destroy, kill of hit someone/something suddenly and with force.

Zaphara *n.* a mineral used by potters.

Zapper *n.* Remote control.

Zarathustra *n.* a pleader of persian religion.

Zariba *n.* In Sudan an elclosure of thorn-bushes against wild beasts.

Zarf *n.* an ornamental coffee-cup.

Zax *n.* a slate-cutter's tool.

Zea *n.* maize; Indian corn.

Zeal *n.* passionate ardour for a anything; fervour in a cause; earnestness.

Zealotical *adj.* ardently zealous.

Zealous *adj.* ardent; enthusiastic.

Zebra *n.* a striped South African mammal like horse.

Zebra crossing *n.* an area of road marked with broad black and white lines where vehicles must stop for people to walk across.

Zebrine *adj.* pertaining to zebra.

Zebu *n.* a humped domestic ox.

Zed *n.* a bar of metal in the form of the letter 'Z'.

Zedoary *n.* kinds of aromatic substance.

Zein *n.* the protein of maize.

Zeitgeist *n.* spirit of the times.

Zemstvo *n.* the Russian provincial assembly for purposes of local government.

Zeitgeist *n.* spirit of the times.

Zenith *n.* acme or culmination; the point in the heavens which is immediately overhead (opposite of nadir).

Zeolite a kind of mineral.

Zephyr *n.* soft breeze; an athlete's thin jersey; the west wind personified.

Zeppelin *n.* a cigar-shaped airship; German military airship.

Zero *n.* figure 0; cypher; nothing; nil.

Zest *n.* something that gives taste.

Zeta *n.* a small parlour.

Zetetic *n.* a seeker.

Zeticula *n.* a small retiring room.

Zeugma *n.* a figure in which an objective or verb agreeing with a nearer word also refers to a remote one.

Zeus *n.* king of the Olympian gods; the greatest divinity of Greece.

Zigzag *adj.* having short sharp turns. *n.* something that has a sharp turn.

Zinc *n.* white meal much used in the arts.

Zinciferous *adj.* containing zinc.

Zincite *n.* the positive anode of a galvanic battery.

Zincode *n.* the positive pyle of a galvanic battery.

Zincous *n.* having the characteristics of zinc.

Zinke *n.* a wind instrument like corner.

Zip *n.* the sound made by a bullet as it strikes or passes anything.

Zither *n.* a stringed musical instrument.

Zizania *n.* a kind of aquatic grass.

Zizel *n.* a squirrel related to Europe.

Zoanthropy *n.* a sort of delusion in which a man believes himself to be a beast.

Zobo *n.* an ox-like beast of burden.

Zodiac *n.* an imaginary broad circle in the heavens containing the twelve constellations called the signs of Zodiac.

Zoetrope *n.* wheel of life; a scientific toy in which pictures are seen moving.

Zoiatria *n.* veterinary surgery.

Zoic *adj.* containing fossils; pertaining to animals.

Zoilism *n.* unjust criticism.

Zonal *adj.* pertaining to zones.

Zongaro *n.* a gipsy.

Zone *n.* a belt; any of the five bands into which the arctic and antarctic circles and the two tropics divide the earth; a girdle.

Zoned *adv.* having zones.

Zonula *n.* a small girdle.

Zonure *n.* a spiked lizard.

Zoo *n.* public garden or park with a collection of animals kept for exhibition; a zoological garden.

Zoochemy *n.* animal chemistry.

Zoodynamics *n.* the science in which one treats of the vital powers of animals.

Zoograft *n.* a piece of animal tissue grafted in human body.

Zoography *n.* the description of animal forms.

Zoolatry *n.* the worship of animals.

Zoolite *n.* fossil animal.

Zoological *adj.* pertaining to zoology.

Zoologist *n.* a student of zoology.

Zoology *n.* the science which treats of the natural history of animals.

Zoom *v.i.* to force aeroplane to mount at high speed and steep angle.

Zoomorphic *adj.* after an animal form representing animals in art.

Zoomorphism *n.* representation of a god or man in animal form.

Zoon *n.* the total product of a fertilized ovum.

Zoonite *n.* one of the segments of an articulated animal.

Zoonosis *n.* a disease which is cummunicated to man from lower animals.

Zoophagan *n.* an animal that feeds on others.

Zoophagous *adj.* feeding on animals.

Zoophilist *n.* a lover of animals.

Zoophoric *adj.* pertaining to a column supported on the figure of animal or man.

Zoophysics *n.* study of physics in relation to animal anatomy.

Zoophyte *n.* organisation which partakes of the nature of plant and animal life.

Zoophytic *adj.* pertaining to Zoophytes.

Zooscopy *n.* mental delusion in which peculiar animals are seen.

Zoosperm *n.* the male seed cell.

Zootaxy *n.* scientific classification of animals.

Zootomy *n.* the dissection of animals.

Zootrophic *adj.* pertaining to the nourishment of animals.

Zoozoo *n.* a wood pigeon.

Zoroastrain *n.* a follower of Parsee religion.

Zoaster *n.* a kind of skin disease.

Zotheca *n.* an alcove

Zounds *inter.* contracted form of 'God's wounds; an exclamation of anger.

Zulu *n.* a South African tribe.

Zuna *n.* a kind of sheep.

Zygal *adj.* formed like the letter 'H'.

Zygodont *adj.* pertaining to molar teeth.

Zygoma *n.* bony arch of cheek; yoke-bone.

Zygomatic *adj.* pertaining to the cheek bone.

Zygon *n.* a connecting bar.

Zygophyllum *n.* a kind of plant.

Zygote *n.* product of the fusion of two gametes.

Zylonite *n.* celluloid.

Zymic *adj.* relating to fermentation.

Zymogen *n.* that which causes fermentation.

Zymoid *adj.* of the nature of a ferment.

Zymome *n.* the protein of wheat which is not soluble in alcohol.

Zymometer *n.* an instrument for ascertaining the degree of fermentation.

Zymosis *n.* zymotic disease; an epidemic due to living germs; fermentation.

Zymotic *adj.* pertaining to fermentation.

Zymurgy *n.* chemistry of fermentation.

Zythepsary *n.* a brewery.

❑❑